SUBARU

ff-1/1300/1400/1600/1800/BRAT
1970-84 REPAIR MANUAL

CHILTON'S

Senior Vice President	Ronald A. Hoxter
Publisher & Editor-In-Chief	Kerry A. Freeman, S.A.E.
Executive Editors	Dean F. Morgantini, S.A.E., W. Calvin Settle, Jr., S.A.E.
Managing Editor	Nick D'Andrea
Special Products Manager	Ken Grabowski, A.S.E., S.A.E.
Senior Editors	Jacques Gordon, Michael L. Grady, Debra McCall, Kevin M. G. Maher, Richard J. Rivele, S.A.E., Richard T. Smith, Jim Taylor, Ron Webb
Project Managers	Martin J. Gunther, Will Kessler, A.S.E., Richard Schwartz
Production Manager	Andrea Steiger
Product Systems Manager	Robert Maxey
Director of Manufacturing	Mike D'Imperio
Editor	Thomas A. Mellon

CHILTON BOOK COMPANY

ONE OF THE **DIVERSIFIED PUBLISHING COMPANIES,**
A PART OF **CAPITAL CITIES/ABC,INC.**

Manufactured in USA
© 1996 Chilton Book Company
Chilton Way, Radnor, PA 19089
ISBN 0-8019-8790-3
Library of Congress Catalog Card No. 96-83138
1234567890 5432109876

Contents

961020

Contents

SAFETY NOTICE

Proper service and repair procedures are vital to the safe, reliable operation of all motor vehicles, as well as the personal safety of those performing repairs. This manual outlines procedures for servicing and repairing vehicles using safe, effective methods. The procedures contain many NOTES, CAUTIONS, and WARNINGS which should be followed along with standard procedures to eliminate the possibility of personal injury or improper service which could damage the vehicle or compromise its safety.

It is important to note that the repair procedures and techniques, tools and parts for servicing motor vehicles, as well as the skill and experience of the individual performing the work vary widely. It is not possible to anticipate all of the conceivable ways or conditions under which vehicles may be serviced, or to provide cautions as to all of the possible hazards that may result. Standard and accepted safety precautions and equipment should be used when handling toxic or flammable fluids, and safety goggles or other protection should be used during cutting, grinding, chiseling, prying, or any other process that can cause material removal or projectiles.

Some procedures require the use of tools specially designed for a specific purpose. Before substituting another tool or procedure, you must be completely satisfied that neither your personal safety, nor the performance of the vehicle will be endangered.

Although information in this manual is based on industry sources and is complete as possible at the time of publication, the possibility exists that some car manufacturers made later changes which could not be included here. While striving for total accuracy, Chilton Book Company cannot assume responsibility for any errors, changes or omissions that may occur in the compilation of this data.

PART NUMBERS

Part numbers listed in this reference are not recommendation by Chilton for any product by brand name. They are references that can be used with interchange manuals and aftermarket supplier catalogs to locate each brand supplier's discrete part number.

SPECIAL TOOLS

Special tools are recommended by the vehicle manufacturer to perform their specific job. Use has been kept to a minimum, but where absolutely necessary, they are referred to in the text by the part number of the tool manufacturer. These tools can be purchased, under the appropriate part number, from your local dealer or regional distributor, or an equivalent tool can be purchased locally from a tool supplier or parts outlet. Before substituting any tool for the one recommended, read the SAFETY NOTICE at the top of this page.

ACKNOWLEDGMENTS

The Chilton Book Company expresses appreciation to Subaru of America, Inc. for their generous assistance.

1

GENERAL INFORMATION AND MAINTENANCE

HOW TO USE THIS BOOK

Chilton's Total Car Care Manual for the Subaru is intended to teach you more about the inner working of your vehicle and save you money on its upkeep. The first two sections will be used the most, since they contain maintenance and tune-up information and procedures. The following sections concern themselves with the more complex systems of your vehicle. Operating systems from engine through brakes are covered to the extent that we feel the average do-it-yourselfer should get involved. This book will not explain such things as rebuilding the differential for the simple reason that the expertise required and the investment in special tools make this task uneconomical. We will tell you how to do many jobs that will save you money, give you personal satisfaction, and help you avoid problems.

A secondary purpose of this book is as a reference for owners who want to understand their vehicle and/or their mechanics better. In this case, no tools at all are required.

Before moving any parts, read through the entire procedure. This will give you the overall view of what tools and supplies will be required.

The section begins with a brief discussion of the system and what it involves, followed by adjustments, maintenance, removal and installation procedures, and repair or overhaul procedures. When repair is not considered feasible, we tell you how to install the new or rebuilt replacement. In this way, you at least save the labor costs. Backyard repair of such components as the alternator is just not practical.

Two basic mechanic's rules should be mentioned here. One, whenever the left side of the vehicle or engine is referred to, it is meant to specify the driver's side of the vehicle. Conversely, the right side of the vehicle means the passenger's side. Secondly, most screws and bolts are removed by turning counterclockwise, and tightening by turning clockwise. Safety is always the most important rule. Constantly be aware of the dangers involved in working on an automobile and take the proper precautions. Use jackstands when working under a raised vehicle. Don't smoke or allow an exposed flame to come near the battery or any part of the fuel system. Always use the proper tool and use it correctly. Bruised knuckles and skinned fingers aren't a mechanic's standard equipment. Always take your time and have patience. Once you have some experience, working on your vehicle will become an enjoyable hobby.

TOOLS AND EQUIPMENT

▶ **See Figures 1, 2, 3, 4, 5, 6, 7, 8, 9 and 10**

➡**Special tools are occasionally necessary to perform a specific job or are recommended to make a job easier. Their use has been kept to a minimum. When a special tool is indicated, it will be referred to by manufacturer's part number, and, where possible, an illustration of the tool will be provided so that an equivalent tool may be used. Subaru manufacturers its' own line of special tools. For information as to where to purchase these tools, contact your local dealer.**

It would be impossible to catalog each and every tool that you may need to perform all the operations included in this book. It would also not be wise for the amateur to rush out and buy an expensive set of tools on the theory that he/she may need one of them at some time. The best approach is to proceed slowly, gathering together a good quality set of those tools that are used most frequently. Don't be misled by the low cost of bargain tools. It is far better to spend a little more for quality, name brand tools. Forged wrenches, 10 or 12 point sockets and fine-tooth ratchets are by far preferred to their less expensive counterparts. As any good mechanic can tell you, there are few worse experiences than trying to work on a vehicle or truck with bad tools. Your monetary savings will be far outweighed by frustration and mangled knuckles.

Begin accumulating those tools that are used most frequently; those associated with routine maintenance and tune-up. In addition to the normal assortment of screwdrivers and pliers, you should have the following tools for routine maintenance jobs:
- Metric wrenches, sockets and combination open end/box wrenches
- Jackstands for support
- Oil filter wrenches
- Oil filler spout for funnel
- Grease gun for chassis lubrication
- Hydrometer for checking the battery
- A low flat pan for draining oil
- Lots of rags for wiping up the inevitable mess

In addition to the above items, there are several others that are not absolutely necessary, but are handy to have around. These include oil drying compound, a transmission funnel, and the usual supply of lubricants, antifreeze and fluids, although these can be purchased as needed. This is a basic list for routine maintenance, but only your personal needs can accurately determine your list of tools.

The second list of tools is for tune-ups. While the tools involved here are slightly more sophisticated, they need not be outrageously expensive. There are several inexpensive tach/dwell meters on the market that are every bit as god for the average mechanic as a professional model. Just be sure that it goes to at least 1200-1500 rpm on the tach scale, and that it works on 4, 6, and 8 cylinder engines. A basic list of tune-up equipment could include:
1. Tach/dwell meter;
2. Spark plug wrench;
3. Timing light (preferably a DC light that works from the vehicle's battery);
4. A set of flat feeler gauges;
5. A set of round wire spark plug gauges.

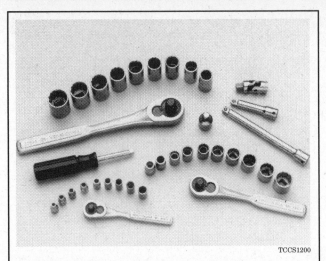

TCCS1200

Fig. 1 All but the most basic procedures will require an assortment of rachets and sockets

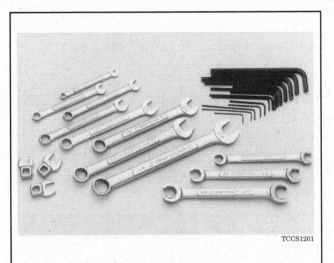

TCCS1201

Fig. 2 In addition to rachets, a good set of wrenches and hex keys will be necessary

TCCS1202

Fig. 3 A hydraulic floor jack and a set of jackstands are essential for lifting and supporting the vehicle

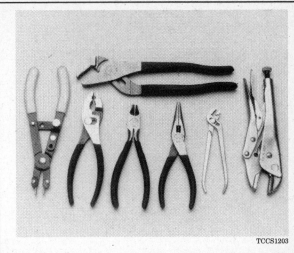

TCCS1203

Fig. 4 An assortment of pliers will be handy, especially for old rusted parts and stripped bolt heads

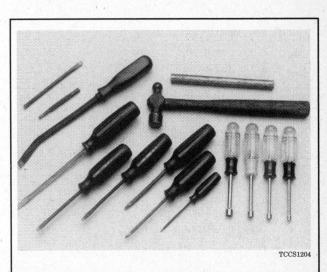

TCCS1204

Fig. 5 Various screwdrivers, a hammer, chisels and prybars are necessary to have in your toolbox

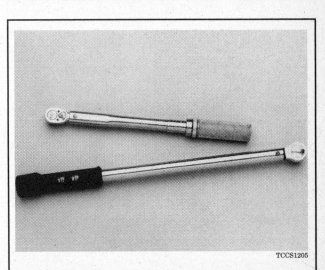

TCCS1205

Fig. 6 Many repairs will require the use of a torque wrench to assure the components are properly fastened

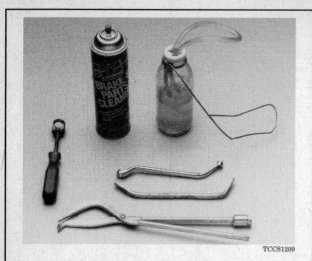

Fig. 7 Although not always necessary, using specialized brake tools will save time

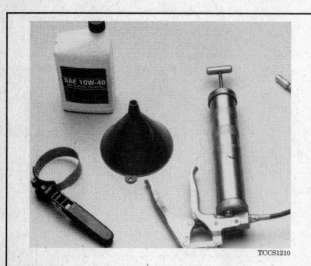

Fig. 8 A few inexpensive lubrication tools will make regular service easier

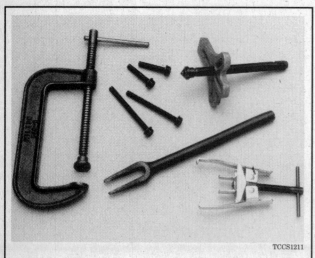

Fig. 9 Various pullers, clamps and separator tools are needed for the repair of many components

Fig. 10 A variety of tools and gauges are needed for spark plug service

In addition to these basic tools, there are several other tools and gauges you may find useful. These include:

6. Compression gauge. The screw-in type is slower to use, but eliminates the possibility of a faulty reading due to escaping pressure;

7. A manifold vacuum gauge;

8. A test light;

9. An induction meter. This is used for determining whether or not there is current in a wire.

These are handy for use if a wire is broken somewhere in a wiring harness. As a final note, you will probably find a torque wrench necessary for all but the most basic work. The beam type models are perfectly adequate, although the newer click type are more precise.

Special Tools

Normally, the use of special factory tools is avoided for repair procedures, since these are not readily available for the do-it-yourself mechanic. When it is possible to perform the job with more commonly available tools, it will be pointed out, but occasionally, a special tool was designed to perform a specific function and should be used. Before substituting another tool, you should be convinced that neither your safety nor the performance of the vehicle will be compromised.

SERVICING YOUR VEHICLE SAFELY

It is virtually impossible to anticipate all of the hazards involved with automotive maintenance and service but common sense will prevent most accidents.

The rules of safety for mechanics range from "don't' smoke around gasoline, to use the proper tool for the job. The trick to avoid injuries is to develop safe work habits and take every possible precaution.

Do's

• Do keep a fire extinguisher and first aid kit within easy reach.

• Do wear safety glasses or goggles when cutting, drilling, grinding or prying. If you wear glasses for the sake of vision, then they should be made of hardened glass that can serve also as safety glasses, or wear safety goggles over your regular glasses.

• Do shield your eyes whenever you work around the battery. Batteries contain sulfuric acid. In case of contact with the eyes or skin, flush the area with water or a mixture of water and baking soda and get medical attention immediately.

• Do use safety stands for any under-vehicle service. Jacks are for raising vehicles. Safety stands are for making sure the vehicle stays raised until you want it to come down. Whenever the vehicle is raised, block the wheels remaining on the ground and set the parking brake.

• Do use adequate ventilation when working with any chemicals, the asbestos dust resulting from brake lining wear can cause cancer.

• Do disconnect the negative battery cable when working on the electrical system. The primary ignition system contains an extremely high voltage.

• Do follow manufacturer's directions whenever working with potentially hazardous materials. Both brake fluid and antifreeze are poisonous if taken internally.

• Do properly maintain your tools. Loose hammerheads, mushroomed punches and chisels, frayed or poorly grounded electrical cords, excessively worn screwdrivers, spread wrenches (open end), cracked sockets, slipping ratchets, or faulty droplight sockets can cause accidents.

• Do use the proper size and type of tool for the job being done.

• Do when possible, pull a wrench handle rather than push on it, and adjust your stance to prevent a fall.

• Do be sure that adjustable wrenches are tightly adjusted on the nut or bolt and pulled so that the face is on the side of the fixed jaw.

• Do select a wrench or socket that fits the nut or bolt. The wrench or socket should sit straight, not cocked.

• Do strike squarely with a hammer. Avoid glancing blows.

• Do set the parking brake and block the drive wheels if the work requires that the engine be running.

Don'ts

• Don't run an engine in a garage or anywhere else without proper ventilation-**EVER!** Carbon monoxide is poisonous. It is absorbed by the body 400 times faster than oxygen. It takes a long time to leave the human body and can build up a deadly supply of it in your own system to simply breathing in a little every day. You may not realize you are slowly poisoning yourself. Always use power vents, windows, fans or open the garage doors.

• Don't work around moving parts while wearing a necktie or other loose clothing. Short sleeves are much safer than long, loose sleeves. Hard-toed shoes with neoprene soles protect your toes and give a better grip on slippery surfaces. Jewelry such as watches, fancy belt buckles, beads or body adornment of any kind is not safe when working around a vehicle. Long hair should be kept under a hat or cap.

• Don't use pockets for toolboxes. A fall or bump can drive a screwdriver deep into your body. Even a wiping cloth hanging from the back pocket can wrap around a spinning shaft or fan.

• Don't smoke when working around the battery. When the battery is being charged, it gives off explosive hydrogen gas.

• Don't use gasoline to wash your hands. There are excellent soaps available. Gasoline may contain additives, which can enter the body through a cut, accumulating in the body until you are very ill. Gasoline also removed all the natural oils from the skin so hot bone dry hands will suck up oil and grease.

• Don't service the air conditioning system unless you are equipped with the necessary tools and training. The refrigerant, R-12, is extremely cold and when exposed to the air, will instantly freeze any surface it comes in contact with, including your eyes. Although the refrigerant is normally non-toxic, R-12 becomes a deadly poisonous gas in the presence of an open flame. One good whiff of the vapors from burning refrigerant can be fatal.

• Don't use screwdrivers for anything other than driving screws! A screwdriver used as a prying tool can snap when you least expect it, causing injuries.

• Don't use a bumper jack (that little rachet, scissors, or pantograph jack supplied with the vehicle) for anything other than changing a flat These jacks are only intended for emergency use out on the road: they are **NOT** designed as a maintenance tool. If you are serious about maintaining your vehicle yourself, invest in a hydraulic floor jack of at least 1½ ton capacity, and at least two jackstands.

HISTORY

Subaru vehicles are built by Fuji Heavy Industries of Japan. The first Subaru automobile, a minicar, was introduced in 1958. The little vehicle was highly successful in Japan because of its low price and operating cost.

In 1968 the Subaru 360 was introduced into the United States, but the vehicle proved to be too small and was replaced by the larger ff-1 series.

The ff-1, or Star as it was known, was a 1.1 liter engine vehicle. Models included a two door and four door sedan, and a station wagon. All models, as they do today, featured a horizontally opposed (flat) water cooled engine, and independent suspension at all four wheels.

Engine size has increased over the years, from 1100 cc to 1800 cc. A four wheel drive unit, a five speed manual transaxle, and an automatic transaxle were all introduced in 1975. The four wheel drive, which engages the rear wheels when required, first appeared in station wagon models.

From the one model of the late sixties, to the restyled models of the 80's, Subaru (which is the Japanese name for the six star constellation we call Pleiades) has increased its sales in the U.S. market until it is now ranked in the upper Top Ten of all imported vehicles.

SERIAL NUMBER IDENTIFICATION

Vehicle

▶ See Figures 11, 12 and 13

The Vehicle Identification Number (VIN) is stamped on a tab located on top of the dashboard, on the driver's side, where it is visible through the windshield. There is also a vehicle identification plate in the engine compartment on the bulkhead.

The serial number consists of a series of model identification numbers followed by a six digit production number.

Engine

▶ See Figure 14

The engine number is stamped on a plate attached to the front, right hand side of the crankcase, behind the distributor (except 1200 engines) or at the rear-side of the engine below the cylinder head (1200 engines).

The serial number consists of an engine code number which is followed by a six digit production number.

Chassis

▶ See Figure 15

The chassis number is stamped on a plate attached to the firewall underneath the hood.

Transaxle

The transaxle number label is attached to the upper surface on the main case on manual transaxles and on the converter housing on automatic transaxle.

Drive Axle

The drive axle identification number is stamped on a padding, located between the bell joint and the double offset joint, just behind the bell joint.

Transfer Case

The transfer case identification number is stamped on the main shaft rear plate.

87901200

Fig. 11 Close-up view of the VIN plate

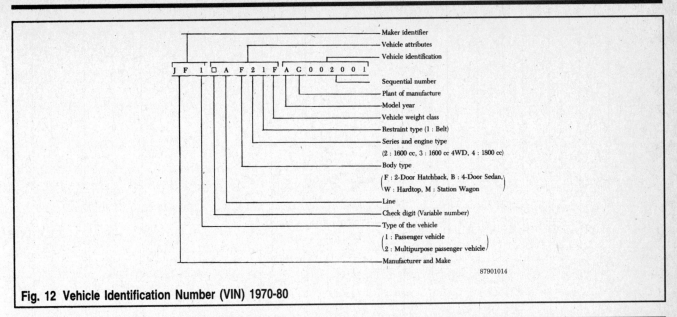

Fig. 12 Vehicle Identification Number (VIN) 1970-80

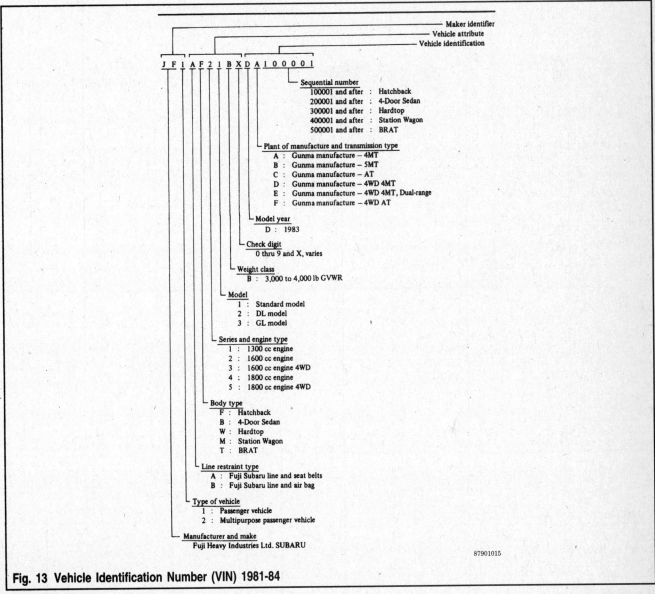

Fig. 13 Vehicle Identification Number (VIN) 1981-84

Fig. 14 Engine number location

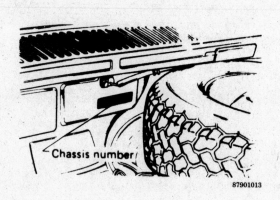

Fig. 15 Chassis number location

Vehicle Identification

Year	Model	Body Type	Transmission Type		Serial Number
1970	FF-1	2-dr sedan	4-speed	A14L	700001 to 703999
		4-dr sedan	4-speed	A14L	200001 to 203999
		4-dr wagon	4-speed	A43L	200001 to 203999
1971	FF-1	2-dr sedan	4-speed	A14L	704000 and after
		4-dr sedan	4-speed	A14L	204000 and after
		4-dr wagon	4-speed	A43L	204000 and after
	1300G	2-dr sedan	4-speed	A15L	700001 to 702121
		4-dr sedan	4-speed	A15L	200001 to 200986
		4-dr wagon	4-speed	A44L	200001 to 202201
1972	1300G	2-dr sedan	4-speed	A15L	702122 and after
		4-dr sedan	4-speed	A15L	200987 and after
		4-dr wagon	4-speed	A44L	202202 and after
	1300 GL	2-dr coupe	4-speed	A23L	700001 and after
	1300 DL	2-dr sedan	4-speed	A23L	900001 and after
		4-dr sedan	4-speed	A23L	800001 and after
		4-dr wagon	4-speed	A63L	700001 and after
1973	1400 GL	2-dr coupe	4-speed	A22L	700001 to 711000
	1400 DL	2-dr sedan	4-speed	A22L	900001 to 908000
		4-dr sedan	4-speed	A22L	800001 to 807000
		4-dr wagon	4-speed	A62L	700001 to 708000
1974	1400 GL	2-dr coupe	4-speed	A22L	711001 and after
	1400 DL	2-dr sedan	4-speed	A22L	908001 and after
		4-dr sedan	4-speed	A22L	807001 and after
		4-dr wagon	4-speed	A62L	708001 and after
1975	1400 DL	2-dr sedan	4-speed	A22L	923001 to 924000
			automatic	A22L	102001 and after
		4-dr sedan	4-speed	A22L	819001 to 819500
			automatic	A22L	602001 and after
		2-dr coupe	4-speed	A22L	726001 and after
			5-speed	A22L	402001 to 404000
			automatic	A22L	202001 and after
		station wagon	4-speed	A62L	725001 to 735500
			automatic	A62L	602001 and after
	1400 GF	hardtop	4-speed	A22L	020001 and after
			5-speed	A22L	002001 and after
			automatic	A22L	302001 and after
	1400 4WD	station wagon	4-wheel drive	A64L	802001 and after
1976	1400 STD	2-dr sedan	4-speed	A22L	924001 and after
	1400 DL	2-dr sedan	4-speed	A22L	924001 and after
		4-dr sedan	4-speed	A22L	819501 and after
		2-dr coupe	5-speed	A22L	404001 and after
		station wagon	4-speed	A62L	735501 and after
	1400 GF	hardtop	5-speed	A22L	005001 and after
	1400 4WD	station wagon	4-wheel drive	A64L	806001 and after
	1600 DL	2-dr sedan	automatic	A26L	106001 to 730000
		4-dr sedan	automatic	A26L	605001 to 610000
		station wagon	automatic	A66L	604001 to 609000
	1600 GF	hardtop	automatic	A26L	305001 to 309000
1977	1600 STD	2-dr sedan	4-speed	A26L	205001 to 209000
	1600 DL	2-dr sedan	4-speed	A26L	405001 to 409000
			automatic	A26L	730001 to 732000
		4-dr sedan	4-speed	A26L	505001 to 507000
			automatic	A26L	610001 to 612000

Vehicle Identification (cont.)

Year	Model	Body Type	Transmission Type		Serial Number
1977		2-dr coupe	5-speed	A26L	905001 to 909000
		station wagon	4-speed	A66L	705001 to 710000
			automatic	A66L	609001 to 612000
	1600 GF	hardtop	5-speed	A26L	805001 to 808000
			automatic	A26L	309001 to 310000
	1600 4WD	station wagon	4-wheel drive	A67L	002001 to 010000
1978	1600 STD	2-dr sedan	4-speed	A26L	209001 to 215000
	1600 DL	2-dr sedan	4-speed	A26L	409001 to 419000
			automatic	A26L	732001 to 739000
		4-dr sedan	4-speed	A26L	507001 to 511000
			5-speed	A26L	662001 to 670000
			automatic	A26L	612001 to 618500
		2-dr coupe	5-speed	A26L	909001 to 915500
		station wagon	4-speed	A66L	710001 to 716500
			5-speed	A66L	302001 to 313000
			automatic	A66L	612001 to 619000
	1600 GF	hardtop	5-speed	A26L	808001 to 816500
			automatic	A26L	310001 to 314500
	1600 4WD	station wagon	4-wheel drive	A67L	010001 to 047000
1979	1600 STD	2-dr sedan	4-speed	A26L	215001 and after
	1600 DL	2-dr sedan	4-speed	A26L	419001 and after
			automatic	A26L	739001 and after
		4-dr sedan	4-speed	A26L	511001 and after
			5-speed	A26L	670001 and after
			automatic	A26L	618501 and after
		2-dr coupe	5-speed	A26L	915501 and after
		station wagon	4-speed	A66L	716501 and after
			5-speed	A66L	313001 and after
			automatic	A66L	619001 and after
			4-wheel drive	A67L A69L	047001 and after
		BRAT (M.P.V.)	4-wheel drive	A69L	026001 and after
	1600 FE	2-dr coupe	5-speed	A26L	670001 and after
	1600 GF	hardtop	5-speed	A26L	816501 and after
			automatic	A26L	314501 and after
	1600 GL	station wagon	4-wheel drive	A67L	502001 and after
		BRAT (M.P.V.)	4-wheel drive	A69L	505001 and after
1980	1600 STD	2 door	4-speed	AF21FAG	002001 and after
		2 door with converter	4-speed	AF21FAG	802001 and after
		2 door	4-wheel drive	AF31FAG	702001 and after
	1600 DL	hardtop	5-speed	AW21FAG	502001 and after
		hardtop with converter	5-speed	AW21FAG	402001 and after
		2 door	5-speed	AF21FAG	202001 and after
		2 door with converter	5-speed	AF21FAG	AF21FAG 402001 and after
		2 door	4-wheel drive	AF31FAG	AF31FAG 702001 and after
		4 door	4-speed	AB21FAG	AB21FAG 002001 and after
		4 door with converter	4-speed	AB21FAG	
		station wagon	4-speed	AM21AG	802001 and after
		station wagon	4-wheel drive	AM31FAG	002001 and after
		BRAT (M.P.V.)	4-wheel drive	A69L	702001 and after
					041001 and after

87901C03

Vehicle Identification (cont.)

Year	Model	Body Type	Transmission Type	Serial Number	
1980	1600 GL	4 door	4-wheel drive	AB21FAG	202001 and after
		station wagon	5-speed	AM21FAG	202001 and after
		station wagon	4-wheel drive	AM31FAG	702001 and after
		BRAT (M.P.V.)	4-wheel drive	A69L	515001 and after
	1600 GLF	hardtop	5-speed	AW21FAG	202001 and after
	1800 DL	2 door	automatic	AF41FAG	502001 and after
	1800 GL	4 door	automatic	AB41FAG	502001 and after
		station wagon	automatic	AM41FAG	502001 and after
	1800 GLF	hardtop	automatic	AW41FAG	502001 and after
1981	1600 STD	2 door	4-speed	AF21BBA	100001 and after
	1600 DL	2 door	5-speed	AF22BBB	100001 and after
		4 door	4-speed	AB22BBA	200001 and after
		4 door	5-speed	AB22BBB	200001 and after
		hardtop	4-speed	AW22BBA	300001 and after
		hardtop	5-speed	AW22BBB	300001 and after
	1800 STD	2 door	4-wheel drive	AF51BBD	100001 and after
	1800 DL	2 door	4-wheel drive	AF52BBD	100001 and after
		station wagon	4-speed	AM42BBA	400001 and after
		station wagon	5-speed	AM42BBB	400001 and after
		station wagon	4-wheel drive	AM52BBD	400001 and after
		BRAT (M.P.V.)	4-wheel drive	AR52BBD	500001 and after
	1800 GL	2 door	5-speed	AF43BBB	100001 and after
		2 door	automatic	AF43BBC	100001 and after
		2 door	4-wheel drive dual range	AF53BBE	100001 and after
		4 door	5-speed	AB43BBB	200001 and after
		4 door	automatic	AB43BBC	200001 and after
		station wagon	5-speed	AM43BBB	400001 and after
		station wagon	automatic	AM43BBC	400001 and after
		station wagon	4-wheel drive dual range	AM53BBE	400001 and after
		BRAT (M.P.V.)	4-wheel drive dual range	AR53BBE	500001 and after
	1800 GLF	hardtop	5-speed	AW44BBB	300001 and after
		hardtop	automatic	AW44BBC	300001 and after
1982	1600 STD	hatchback	4-speed	AF21BXA	100001 and after
	1600 DL	hatchback	5-speed	AF22BXB	100001 and after
		4 door	4-speed	AB22BXA	200001 and after
		4 door	5-speed	AB22BXB	200001 and after
		hardtop	4-speed	AW22BXA	300001 and after
		hardtop	5-speed	AW22BXB	300001 and after
	1800 STD	hatchback	4-wheel drive	AF51BXD	100001 and after
	1800 DL	hatchback	4-wheel drive	AF52BXD	100001 and after
		station wagon	4-speed	AM42BXA	400001 and after
		station wagon	5-speed	AM42BXB	400001 and after
		station wagon	4-wheel drive	AM52BXD	400001 and after
		BRAT (M.P.V.)	4-wheel drive dual range	AT53BXE	500001 and after
	1800 GL	hatchback	5-speed	AF43BXB	100001 and after
		hatchback	automatic	AF43BXC	100001 and after
		hatchback	4-wheel drive dual range	AF53BX	100001 and after
		4 door	5-speed	AB43BXB	200001 and after
		4 door	automatic	AB43BXC	200001 and after
		station wagon	5-speed	AM43BXB	400001 and after
		station wagon	automatic	AM43BXC	400001 and after

87901C04

Vehicle Identification (cont.)

Year	Model	Body Type	Transmission Type	Serial Number	
1982	1800 GL	station wagon	4-wheel drive dual range	AM53BXE	400001 and after
		BRAT (M.P.V)	4-wheel drive dual range	AT53BXE	500001 and after
	1800 GLF	hardtop	5-speed	AW44BXB	300001 and after
		hardtop	automatic	AW44BXC	300001 and after
1983–86	1600 STD	hatchback	4-speed	AF21BXDA	100001 and after
	1600 DL	hatchback	5-speed	AF22BXDB	100001 and after
	1600 DL	4 door	5-speed	AB22BXDB	200001 and after
	1600 DL	hardtop	5-speed	AW22BXDB	300001 and after
	1800 GL	hatchback	5-speed	AF43BXDB	100001 and after
	1800 GL	hatchback	automatic	AF43BXDC	200001 and after
	1800 STD	hatchback	4-wheel drive	AF51BXDD	100001 and after
	1800 GL	hatchback	4-wheel drive dual range	AF53BXDE	100001 and after
	1800 GL	4 door	5-speed	AB43BXDB	200001 and after
	1800 GL	4 door	automatic	AB43BXDC	200001 and after
	1800 GL	hardtop	5-speed	AW43BXDB	300001 and after
	1800 GL	hardtop	automatic	AW43BXDC	300001 and after
	1800 DL	station wagon	5-speed	AM42BXDB	400001 and after
	1800 GL	station wagon	5-speed	AM43BXDB	400001 and after
	1800 GL	station wagon	automatic	AM43BXDC	400001 and after
	1800 DL	station wagon	4-wheel drive	AM52BXDD	400001 and after
	1800 GL	station wagon	4-wheel drive dual range	AM53BXDE	400001 and after
	1800 GL	station wagon	4-wheel drive	AM53BXDF	400001 and after
	1800 BRAT DL	pickup	4-wheel drive	AT52BXDD	500001 and after
	1800 BRAT GL	pickup	4-wheel drive dual range	AT53BXDE	500001 and after
	1800 BRAT GL	pickup	automatic	AT53BXDF	500001 and after
	1800 GL Turbo	station wagon	automatic	AM55BXDF	404768
	1800 BRAT GL Turbo	pickup	automatic	AT55BXDF	500376

87901C05

ROUTINE MAINTENANCE

Air Cleaner

▶ See Figures 16, 17, 18 and 19

REMOVAL & INSTALLATION

The air cleaner element used on all Subaru models covered in this book is of the oil-impregnated, disposable type, and no attempt should be made to clean, wash, or re-oil it.

Replace the element at the following intervals, months or miles whichever comes first:

- 1970-73: 24 months/24000 miles (40,000 km)
- 1974: 18 months/18000 miles (30,000 km)
- 1975-79: 12 months/12000 miles (20,000 km)
- 1980-84: 30 months/30000 miles (50,000 km)
- 1985-86: 35 months/30000 miles (50,000 km)
- 1987: 30 months/30000 miles (50,000 km)

To remove the air cleaner element;

1. Remove the wing nut(s) from the top of the air cleaner housing and lift off the top section.

2. Set it aside carefully, as on some models the emission control system hoses are fastened to it.

3. Lift out the old element and clean the inside of the air cleaner housing with a paper towel or clean rag.

To install:

4. Install a new air cleaner element.

5. Install the top on the air cleaner and secure it with the wing nut(s).

✳✳WARNING

If there is an arrow on the top of the air cleaner, it should be positioned toward the front of the vehicle.

Fig. 16 Check for any labels on the air cleaner and read their instructions carefully

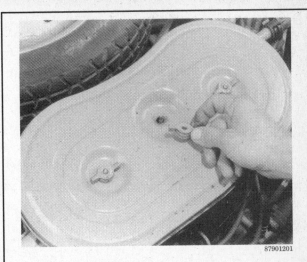

Fig. 17 Remove the wing nut(s) from the top of the air cleaner housing and lift off the top section

Fig. 18 Remove the old element

Fuel Filter

All Subarus use a cartridge fuel filter, located in the fuel line. The filter is the disposable type which cannot be cleaned. It should be replaced every 12 months/12000 miles (20,000 km) on pre-1980 vehicles and 15 months/15000 miles (25,000 km) whichever occurs first, on 1980 and later vehicles.

REMOVAL & INSTALLATION

➡Before removing the fuel lines, use two small pairs of locking pliers to pinch off the fuel lines on both sides of the fuel filter. Place a small piece of rubber between the jaws of the pliers to prevent damage to the fuel lines.

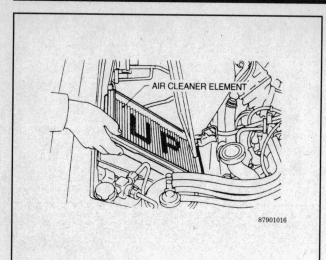

Fig. 19 Disposable air cleaner element — fuel injected models

Carbureted Models

▶ **See Figure 20**

On the carbureted models, the fuel filter is located in the engine compartment.

1. Disconnect the negative battery cable. Loosen, but **DO NOT** remove, the two hose clamp retainers, located at either end of the filter.
2. Work the hoses from the filter necks.
3. Snap the filter out of it's mounting bracket.
4. Discard the old filter.

✳✳WARNING

When removing the old filter, be careful not to allow any fuel to drop onto hot engine components.

To install:

5. Install the new filter in it's mounting bracket.
6. Check the hoses for cracks and wear.
7. Install the hoses on the filter necks and tighten the hose clamps securely.

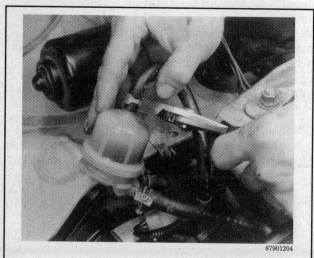

Fig. 20 Use pliers to loosen the two hose clamp retainers

8. Connect the negative battery cable.
9. Start the vehicle and check for leaks.

Fuel Injected Models

▶ **See Figure 21**

The fuel filter is located on a bracket in the engine compartment on the front-left fender.

1. Reduce the fuel pressure by performing the following procedures:

   a. Disconnect the electrical wiring connector from the fuel pump.

   b. Crank the engine for more than five seconds. If the engine starts, let the engine run until it stops.

   c. Turn the ignition switch **OFF** and reconnect the electrical wiring connector of the fuel pump.

2. Disconnect the negative battery cable. Loosen the hose clamp screws and pull the filter from the bracket.

To install:

3. Install the filter in the bracket.
4. Install the hoses on the filter and tighten the hose clamps securely.
5. Start the engine and check for leaks.

Positive Crankcase Ventilation (PCV) Valve

▶ **See Figures 22 and 23**

The small filter element (on models so equipped) located on the inner back right side of the air cleaner base should be changed at the same interval as the air cleaner element.

If equipped, check the PCV valve to see if it is free and not gummed up. The PCV valve is located in the intake manifold beside the Exhaust Gas Recirculation (EGR) valve, and connected by a hose from the #2 and #4 cylinder rocker cover. To check the valve, remove it from the engine and work the valve by sticking a screwdriver in the crankcase side of the valve. It should move. It is possible to clean the PCV valve by soaking it in a solvent and blowing it out with compressed air. This can restore the valve to some level of operating order. This should be used only as an emergency measure. Other-

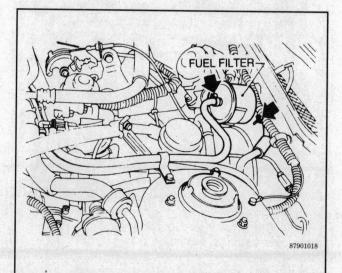

Fig. 21 Fuel filter location on fuel injected models

wise the valve should be replaced. Under normal conditions the PCV valve should be replaced every 30 months or 30,000 miles (50,000 km), whichever occurs first. The PCV hose filter and secondary air cleaner (if equipped) should be serviced at the same times as the PCV valve. Refer to Section 4 for details.

REMOVAL & INSTALLATION

1. Grasp the valve and pull it from the base of the air cleaner.

2. Holding the valve in one hand and the hose in the other, carefully pull the valve from the hose and remove it from the vehicle.

➡**Some PCV valve hoses will be retained to the valve using a clamp. If so, use a pair of pliers to slide the clamp back on the hose until it is clear of the bulged area on the end of the PCV valve nipple. With the clamp in this position, the hose should be free to slip from the valve.**

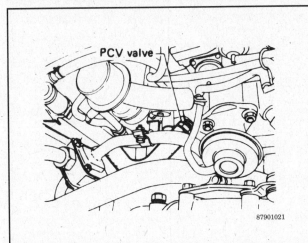

Fig. 22 Common PCV valve location on models covered by this manual

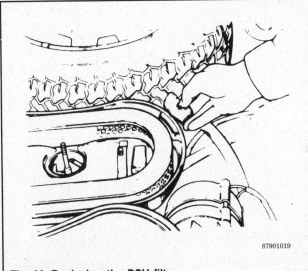

Fig. 23 Replacing the PCV filter

3. Check the PCV valve for deposits or clogging.

To install:

4. Install the PCV valve back in the base of the air cleaner and connect the PCV hose and clamp (if equipped).

Crankcase Ventilation System

Some late model Subarus and all earlier models have a Crankcase Ventilation System which does not use a PCV valve.

For a description of the system, as well as procedures for component removal and servicing, see Section 4.

The only regular check necessary is an inspection of the PCV hose(s), which run from the crankcase to the air cleaner. These should be checked every 12 months/12000 miles (20,000 km) on 1970-73 models, or every 24 months/24000 miles (39,000 km) on later models. Be sure that all of the connections are tight and that none of the hoses are pinched, clogged, or cracked: replace as required.

On ff-1 models, the oil separator should be cleaned every 12 months/12000 miles (20,000 km), whichever occurs first.

Evaporative Emission Canister

The evaporative emission canister (sometimes referred to as the charcoal canister) is part of a system that prevents fumes from the gas tank from being discharged into the air. The canister is located in the engine compartment. The gas fumes are absorbed by activated charcoal located in the canister.

SERVICING

1. Inspect the hoses to the canister for holes, cracks or other damage.

2. Check the purge lines from the canister for proper installation.

3. Replace the canister and/or hoses if damaged.

4. On 1977-79 models a canister filter located in the bottom should be replaced every 25,000 miles (40,000 km).

For a detailed description and service procedures of the evaporative emission control system refer to Section 4.

Battery

GENERAL MAINTENANCE

All batteries, regardless of type, should be kept clean on the outside and should be kept tightly secured by a battery hold-down device. If this is not done, battery acid can leak out, shortening the life of the battery, make it discharge more quickly and the corrosive acid can eat away components under the hood. A battery that is not a maintenance-free type must be checked periodically for water level. A maintenance-free type battery cannot have water added to it, but it must also be checked for electrolyte level. This can be done by looking at the color of the "eye". If this battery is too low on electrolyte, it must be replaced.

FLUID LEVEL

Except Maintenance-Free Batteries

✳✳CAUTION

Batteries give off hydrogen gas which is explosive. Keep any spark or flame source away and DO NOT SMOKE around the battery! The battery electrolyte contains sulfuric acid; if you should splash any into your eyes or skin, flush with plenty of clear water and get immediate medical help.

Fill each cell to about ³⁄₈ in. (9.5mm) above the tops of the plates. Always use distilled water (available in supermarkets or auto parts stores). Most tap water contains chemicals and minerals that may slowly damage the plates of your battery.

Maintenance-Free Batteries

Some later model cars are equipped with sealed maintenance-free batteries which do not require normal attention as far as fluid level checks are concerned. However, the terminals require periodic cleaning which should be performed at least once a year.

CABLES AND CLAMPS

▶ **See Figures 24, 25, 26 and 27**

Once a year, the battery terminals and the cable clamps should be cleaned. Loosen the clamps and remove the cables, negative cable first. On batteries with posts on top, the use of a puller specially made for the purpose is recommended. These are inexpensive, and available in most auto parts stores. Side terminal battery cables are secured with a bolt.

Clean the cable clamps and the battery terminal with a wire brush, until all corrosion, grease, etc. is removed and the metal is shiny. It is especially important to clean the inside of the clamp thoroughly, since a small deposit of foreign material or oxidation there will prevent a sound electrical connection

and inhibit either starting or charging. Special tools are available for cleaning these parts, one type for conventional batteries and another type for side terminal batteries.

Before installing the cables, loosen the battery hold-down clamp or strap, remove the battery and check the battery tray. Clear it of any debris, and check it for soundness. Rust should be wire brushed away, and the metal given a coat of anti-rust paint. Replace the battery and tighten the hold-down clamp or strap securely, but be careful not to overtighten, which will crack the battery case.

After the clamps and terminals are clean, reinstall the cables, negative cable last. Do not hammer on the clamps to install. Tighten the clamps securely, but do not distort them. Give the clamps and terminals a thin external coat of grease after installation, to retard corrosion.

Check the cables at the same time that the terminals are cleaned. If the cable insulation is cracked or broken, or if the ends are frayed, the cable should be replaced with a new cable of the same length and gauge.

✳✳WARNING

Keep flame or sparks away from the battery. It gives off explosive hydrogen gas. Battery electrolyte contains sulfuric acid. If you should splash any on your skin or in your eyes, flush the affected area with plenty of clear water. If it lands in your eyes, get medical help immediately.

TESTING

▶ **See Figure 28**

Specific Gravity

Check the specific gravity of the battery at every tune-up. It should be between 1.20 and 1.30 at room temperature. The specific gravity is checked with a hydrometer, an inexpensive instrument available in most auto parts stores, auto departments and many hardware stores. The hydrometer looks like a turkey baster, having a rubber squeeze bulb on one end and a nozzle at the other. Insert the nozzle end into each battery cell

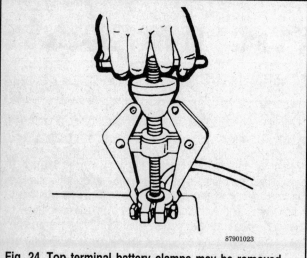

Fig. 24 Top terminal battery clamps may be removed with this inexpensive tool

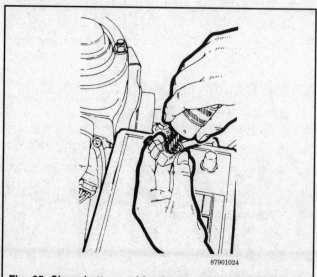

Fig. 25 Clean battery cable clamps with a wire brush

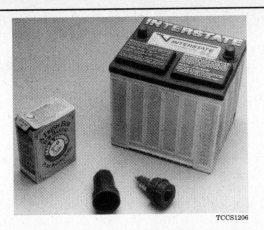

Fig. 26 Battery maintenance may be accomplished with household items (such as baking soda to neutralize spilled acid) or with special tools such as this post and terminal cleaner

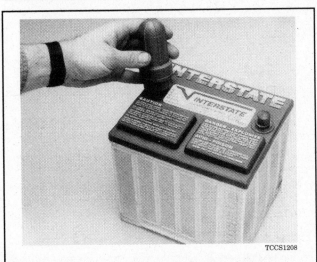

Fig. 27 Place the tool over the terminals and twist to clean the post

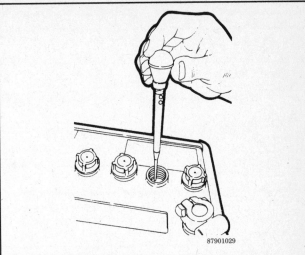

Fig. 28 An inexpensive hydrometer will check the battery state of charge

and suck enough electrolyte (battery water) into the hydrometer to just lift the float. The specific gravity is then read by the graduations on the float. Some hydrometers are color coded, with each color signifying a certain range of specific gravity.

All cells of your battery should produce nearly equal specific gravity readings. Do not be extremely alarmed if all of your battery's cells are equally low (but check to see if your alternator belt is tight); however, a big difference between two or more cells should be a concern. Generally, if after charging, the specific gravity between any two cells varies more than 50 points (0.050), the battery is bad and should be replaced.

Batteries should be checked for proper electrolyte level at least once a month or more frequently. Keep a close eye on any cell or cells that are unusually low or seem to constantly need water. This may indicate a battery on its last legs, a leak, or a problem with the charging system.

The maintenance-free battery cannot be checked for charge by checking the specific gravity using a hand-held hydrometer. Instead, the built-in hydrometer must be used in order to deter-

mine the current state of charge. Check your owners manual or with your local car dealer for the proper color of the "eye' on your battery. Most (not all) built in hydrometers are a green color when the battery is charging properly. If you are unable to see the hydrometer color make sure that the "eye' is clean by wiping it with a paper towel or clean rag. If you are still unable to read the hydrometer **gently** shake the battery. If the eye on top of the battery is green, the battery electrolyte level is all right. If the eye is dark, the electrolyte level is too low and the battery must be replaced.

Load Testing

1. Connect a battery load tester and a voltmeter across the battery terminals (the battery cables should be disconnected from the battery). Apply a 300 amp load to the battery for 15 seconds to remove the surface charge. Remove the load.

2. Wait 15 seconds to allow the battery to recover.

3. Apply the appropriate test load for 15 seconds, while reading the voltage. Disconnect the load.

4. Check the results against the appropriate chart. If the battery voltage was at or above the specified voltage for the temperature listed, the battery is good. If the voltage falls below what's listed, the battery should be replaced.

CHARGING

❊❊CAUTION

Always connect the battery charger according to manufacturers instructions.

Generally, a battery should be charged at a slow rate to keep the plates inside from getting too hot. However, if some batteries are allowed to discharge until they are almost "dead', they may have to be charged at a high rate to bring them back to life. On maintenance-free batteries it may be necessary to tip the battery from side to side to get the built in hydrometer "eye' to register it's green color after charging.

Charge the battery at the proper charging rate (amps) and time span.

- 75 amps - 40 min.
- 50 amps - 1hr.
- 25 amps - 2hr.
- 10 amps - 5hr.

❊❊CAUTION

Batteries naturally give off a certain amount of explosive hydrogen gas, more so when they are being charged. Keep any flame or spark source away from batteries at all times. Do not charge the battery for more than 50 amp/hours (to figure this, multiply the amps of the charging rate by the number of hours). If the green dot appears, or if electrolyte squirts out of the vent hole, stop the charge.

REPLACEMENT

When it becomes necessary to replace the battery, select a battery with a rating equal to or greater than the battery originally installed. Deterioration, embrittlement and just plain aging of the battery cables, starter motor, and associated wires makes the battery's job harder in successive years. The slow increase in electrical resistance over time makes it prudent to install a new battery with a greater capacity than the old. Details on battery removal and installation are covered in Section 3.

1. Carefully disconnect the negative cable from the battery terminal.

❊❊CAUTION

Always use caution when working on or near the battery. Never allow a tool to bridge the gap between the negative and positive battery terminals. Also, do not wear metal watches or jewelry and be careful not to allow a tool to provide a ground between the positive cable and any metal component on the vehicle. Either of these conditions will cause a short leading to sparks and possibly, personal injury.

2. With the negative battery cable disconnected and out of the way, carefully disconnect the positive cable from the battery terminal.

3. Loosen the nut and/or bolt retaining the battery strap or clamp. Remove the battery retainer.

4. Wearing an old pair of work gloves or using a battery lifting tool, carefully lift the battery out of the vehicle and place it in a safe location. Be sure to keep the battery away from an open flame.

To install:

5. Inspect the battery tray and cables for damage and corrosion. As necessary, clean or repair the tray and cables.

6. Carefully lower the battery and position it in the tray, making sure not to allow the terminals to short on any bare metal during installation.

7. Position and secure the battery retainer strap or clamp.

8. Connect the positive cable to the positive battery terminal.

9. Connect the negative cable to the negative battery terminal.

Belts

INSPECTION

The condition and proper adjustment of the drive belt should be checked every 15 months or every 15,000 miles (24,000 km), whichever occurs first. Inspect belts for signs of glazing or cracking. A glazed belt will be perfectly smooth from slippage, while a good belt will have a slight texture of fabric visible. Cracks usually start at the inner edge of the belt and run outward. Replace the belt at first sign of cracking or if glazing is severe.

Proper drive belt tension adjustment is important, inadequate tension will result in slippage and wear, while excessive tension will damage the water pump and alternator bearings and cause the belt to fray and crack.

Refer to the illustrations for the proper recommended tensions.

ADJUSTING

▶ **See Figures 29 and 30**

Alternator Belt

1. Apply penetrating oil to the alternator mounting and adjusting bolts. Loosen the bolts.

2. Pull or pry on the alternator until the belt seems tight.

3. Temporarily snug the adjusting bolt and check belt deflection.

➡**Replace the belt if cracked or defective in any way.**

4. If belt tension is OK, tighten the alternator mounting and adjusting bolts.

Power Steering Belt

1. Remove the idler cover cap by turning and pulling. Adjustable jawed pliers with a piece of rag between the jaws can be used.

2. Turn the adjusting bolt until the correct belt tension is obtained. If removing the belt, loosen the adjusting bolt until the drive belt can be removed.

3. After a new belt is installed and the correct tension obtained, install the idler cap cover by pushing in and turning.

REMOVAL & INSTALLATION

1. Clean all mounting and adjustment bolts and apply penetrating oil.

2. Loosen the components adjusting and mounting bolts.

3. Move the component toward or away from the engine until there is enough slack in the belt to slip it over the pulley.

To install:

4. Replace the worn or broken belt.

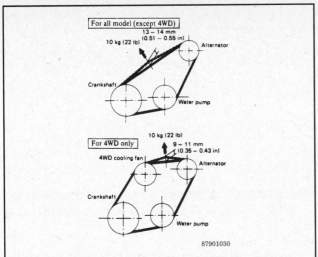

Fig. 29 Belt tension for models without power steering and air conditioning

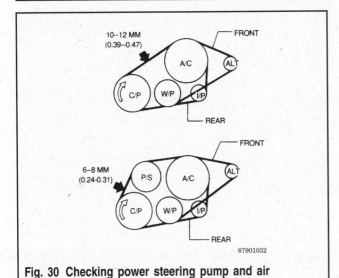

Fig. 30 Checking power steering pump and air conditioning belt tension

5. Temporarily snug the adjusting bolt and check belt deflection.

➡ **Replace the belt if cracked or defective in any way.**

6. If belt tension is OK, tighten the alternator mounting and adjusting bolts.

Hoses

Hoses are frequently overlooked in normal maintenance. Both upper and lower radiator hoses and all heater hoses should be checked for deterioration, leaks and loose hose clamps at every tune-up. Check the hoses by feel; they should be pliable. Any hose that feels hard or brittle should be replaced as soon as possible; in any case, replace radiator hoses as necessary every two years or 30,000 miles (48.000 km).

REMOVAL & INSTALLATION

◆ **See Figures 31, 32 and 33**

❋❋CAUTION

Never remove the pressure cap while the engine is running or personal injury from scalding hot coolant or steam may result. If possible, wait until the engine has cooled to remove the pressure cap. If this is not possible, wrap a thick cloth around the pressure cap and turn it slowly to the stop. Step back while the pressure is released from the cooling system. When you are sure all the pressure has been released, (still using the cloth) turn and remove the cap.

1. Remove the radiator pressure cap.
2. Position a clean container under the radiator petcock, then open the drain and allow the cooling system to drain to an appropriate level. For some upper hoses only a little coolant may need to be drained, to remove lower hoses the entire cooling system must be drained.

❋❋CAUTION

When draining the coolant, keep in mind that cats and other animals are attracted by ethylene glycol antifreeze, and are likely to drink any that is left on the ground or in an open container. This can prove to be fatal in sufficient quantity. Always drain coolant into a suitable container. Coolant may be reused unless it is contaminated or several years old.

3. Loosen the hose clamps at each end of the hose requiring replacement. Pull clamps back on the hose away from the connection.

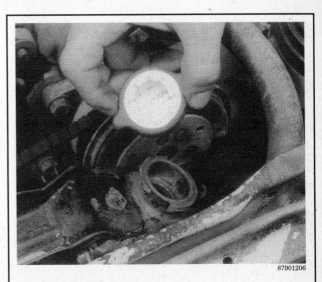

Fig. 31 Remove the radiator cap

4. Twist, pull, and slide the hose off the fitting taking care not to damage the neck of the component.

➡If the hose is stuck at the connection, do not try to insert a screwdriver or other sharp tool under the hose end to release it, as the connection may become damaged. If the hose is to be replaced, use a single-edged razor blade to make a cut perpendicular to the end of the hose. The hose can then be peeled off the connection and discarded.

5. Clean both hose mounting connections. Inspect the condition of the hose clamps and replace them if necessary.

To install:

6. Dip the ends of the hose in coolant for ease of installation.

7. Slide the hose clamps over the hose and slide the hose ends onto the connections.

8. Position and secure the clamps at least $\frac{1}{4}$ in. from the end of the hose. Make sure they are located inside the raised bead of the connector.

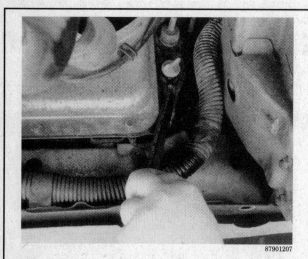

Fig. 32 Loosen the radiator petcock to drain the cooling system

Fig. 33 Loosen the hose clamps at each end of the hose to be replaced

9. Close the radiator petcock and properly refill the cooling system with the drained engine coolant or a suitable $\frac{50}{50}$ mix of ethylene glycol and water.

10. If available, install a pressure tester and check for leaks.

11. Leave the radiator cap off, then start and run the engine until it reaches normal operating temperature. When the engine is at operating temperature and the thermostat has opened, continue to fill the radiator until the level stabilizes just below the filler neck.

12. Install the pressure cap and check the system for leaks.

13. Shut the engine off and allow to cool. After the engine has cooled, recheck the coolant level and add as necessary.

Air Conditioning

SAFETY PRECAUTIONS

➡R-12 refrigerant is a chlorofluorocarbon which when released in the atmosphere can contribute to the depletion of the ozone layer in the upper atmosphere. Ozone filters out harmful radiation from the sun. Be sure to consult the laws in your area before servicing the air conditioning system. In some states it is illegal to preform repairs involving refrigerant unless the work is done by a certified technician.

Because of the the inherent dangers involved with working on air conditioning systems and R-12 refrigerant, the following safety precautions must be strictly adhered to in order to service the system safely.

1. Avoid contact with a charged refrigeration system, even when working on another part of the air conditioning system or vehicle. If a heavy tool comes into contact with a section of tubing, or a heat exchanger, it can cause the relatively soft material to rupture.

2. When it is necessary to apply force to a fitting which contains refrigerant, as when checking that all system couplings are securely tightened, use a wrench on both parts of the fitting involved, if possible. This will avoid putting torque on the refrigerant tubing. (It is advisable, when possible, to use line wrenches when tightening these flare nut fittings.)

3. Do not attempt to discharge the system by merely loosening a filter, or removing the service valve caps and opening these valves. Precise control is possible only when using a proper A/C refrigerant recovery station. Wear protective gloves when connecting or disconnecting service gauge hoses.

4. Never start a system without first verifying that both service valves are properly installed, and that all fittings throughout the system are snugly connected.

5. Avoid applying heat to any refrigerant line or storage vessel. Never allow a refrigerant storage container to sit out in the sun, or any other sources of heat, such as a radiator.

6. Always wear goggles to protect your eyes when working on a system. If refrigerant contacts the eyes, it is advisable in all cases to see a physician as soon as possible.

7. Frostbite from liquid refrigerant should be treated by first gradually warming the area with cool water, and then gently applying petroleum jelly. A physician should be consulted.

8. Always keep refrigerant drum fittings capped when not in use. If the container is equipped with a safety cap to protect

the valve, make sure the cap is in place when the can is not being used. Avoid sudden shock to the drum, which might occur from dropping it, or from banging a heavy tool against it. Never carry a drum in the passenger compartment of a car.

9. Always completely discharge the system into a suitable recovery unit before painting the vehicle (if the paint is to be baked on), or before welding anywhere near refrigerant lines.

10. When servicing the system, minimize the time that any refrigerant line is open to the air, in order to prevent dirt and moisture entering the system. Always replace O-rings on lines or fittings which are disconnected. Prior to installation coat, but do not soak, replacement O-rings with suitable compressor oil.

SYSTEM INSPECTION

The air conditioning system should be checked periodically for worn hoses, loose connections, low refrigerant, leaks, dirt and bugs in the condenser. If any of these conditions exist, they must be corrected or they will reduce the efficiency of your air conditioning system.

Checking the System for Leaks

Refrigerant leaks show up as oily areas on the various components because the compressor oil is transported around the entire system along with the refrigerant. Look for oily spots on all the hoses and lines, and especially on the hose and tubing connections. If there are oily deposits, the system may have a leak, and you should have it checked by a qualified technician.

➡**A small area of oil on the front of the compressor is normal and no cause for alarm.**

Keeping the Condenser Clear

Periodically inspect the front of the condenser for bent fins or foreign material (dirt, bugs, leaves, etc.) If any cooling fins are bent, straighten them carefully with needle-nosed pliers. You can remove any debris with a stiff bristle brush or hose.

Periodic System Operation

A lot of A/C problems can be avoided by simply running the air conditioner at least once a week, regardless of the season. Let the system run for at least 5 minutes a week (even in the winter), and you'll keep the internal parts lubricated as well as preventing the hoses from hardening.

➡**R-12 refrigerant is a chlorofluorocarbon which when released in the atmosphere can contribute to the depletion of the ozone layer in the upper atmosphere. Ozone filters out harmful radiation from the sun.Be sure to consult the laws in your area before servicing the air conditioning system. In some states it is illegal to preform repairs involving refrigerant unless the work is done by a certified technician.**

Refrigerant Level Check

The first order of business is to find the sight glass. It will either be in the head of the receiver/drier, or in one of the metal lines leading from the top of the receiver/drier. Once you've found it, wipe it clean and proceed as follows:

1. With the engine and the air conditioning system running, look for the flow of refrigerant through the sight glass. If the air conditioner is working properly, you'll be able to see a continuous flow of clear refrigerant through the sight glass, with perhaps an occasional bubble at very high temperatures.

2. Cycle the air conditioner **ON** and **OFF** to make sure what you are seeing is clear refrigerant. Since the refrigerant is clear, it is possible to mistake a completely discharged system for one that is fully charged. Turn the system off and watch the sight glass. If there is refrigerant in the system, you'll see bubbles during the off cycle. If you observe no bubbles when the system is running, and the air flow from the unit in the vehicle is delivering cold air, everything is OK.

3. If you observe bubbles in the sight glass while the system is operating, the system is low on refrigerant. Have it checked by a certified technician.

4. Oil streaks in the sight glass are an indication of trouble. Most of the time, if you see oil in the sight glass, it will appear as a series of streaks, although occasionally it may be a solid stream of oil. In either case, it means that part of the charge has been lost.

GAUGE SETS

Most of the service work performed in air conditioning requires the use of a set of two gauges, one for the high (discharge) pressure side of the system, the other for the low (suction) side.

The low side gauge records both pressure and vacuum. Vacuum readings are calibrated from 0 to no less than 30 in. Hg (0-206 kPa) and the pressure graduations read from 0 to no less than 60 in. Hg (413 kPa).

The high side gauge measures pressure from 0 to at least 600 in. Hg (0-4137 kPa). Both gauges are threaded into a manifold that contains two hand shut off valves. Proper manipulation of these valves and the use of the attached test hoses allow the user to perform the following services:
- Test high and low side pressures.
- Remove air, moisture, and contaminated refrigerant.

The manifold valves are designed so they have no direct effect on gauge readings, but serve only to provide for, or cut off, flow of refrigerant through the manifold. During all testing and hook-up operations, the valves are kept in a closed position to avoid disturbing the refrigeration system.

DISCHARGING THE SYSTEM

➡**R-12 refrigerant is a chlorofluorocarbon which when released in the atmosphere can contribute to the depletion of the ozone layer in the upper atmosphere. Ozone filters out harmful radiation from the sun. Consult laws in your area before servicing the air conditioning system. In some states it is illegal to perform repairs involving refrigerant unless the work is done by a certified technician**

The use of refrigerant recovery systems and recycling stations makes possible the recovery and reuse of refrigerant after contaminants and moisture have been removed. If a recovery and recycling station is available, the following general procedures should be observed, in addition to the operating instructions provided by the equipment manufacturer.

1. Check the system for pressure using the manifold gauge set. Take note, if a recovery system is used to draw refrigerant from the system that is already ruptured and open to the atmosphere, only air may be pulled into the tank.

2. Connect the recycling station hoses to the vehicle's air conditioning service ports and the recovery stations inlet fitting.

➡**Hoses should have shut-off devices or check valves within 12 in. (305mm) of the hose end to minimize the introduction of air into the recycling station and the amount of refrigerant released when the hoses are disconnected.**

3. Turn the power to the recycling station **ON** to start the recovery process. Allow the station to pump the refrigerant from the system until the station pressure goes into a vacuum. On some stations, the pump will be shut off automatically by a low pressure switch in it's electrical system. On other units it may be necessary to turn off the pump manually.

4. Once the recycling station has evacuated the system, close the station inlet valve. Then switch **OFF** the electrical power.

5. Allow the vehicle air conditioning system to remain closed for about 2 minutes. Observe the system vacuum level as shown on the gauge. If the pressure does not rise, disconnect the station's hoses.

6. If the system pressure rises, repeat Steps 3, 4 and 5 until the vacuum level remains stable for 2 minutes.

7. If A/C oil is expelled during the discharge procedure, measure the amount discharged so the proper quantity of oil can be replaced when charging.

EVACUATING/CHARGING THE SYSTEM

Evacuating and charging the air conditioning system is a combined procedure in which the lines are purged, then refrigerant is added to the system in proper quantity. Charging is always conducted through the low pressure fitting. **NEVER** attempt to charge the air conditioner through the high pressure side of the system.

If a charging station and pump is available, the following general procedures should be observed, in addition to the operating instructions provided by the manufacturer.

1. The proper amount of fresh compressor oil must be added to the system before charging. This can be accomplished by disconnecting the suction hose and pouring the fresh oil into the hose or pipe and then reconnecting the system.

2. Properly connect a manifold gauge set to the vehicle, then connect the center manifold gauge hose to a vacuum pump.

3. Turn the vacuum pump **ON** and slowly open the high and the low side valves to the pump. Allow the system to evacuate for 25-30 minutes, then note the gauge readings. If the system is unable to reach 28-29 in. Hg (193-199 kPa), of vacuum, the system and vacuum pump must be checked for leaks and repaired before proceeding further.

4. After the system has been evacuated for at least 25 minutes, close the gauge high and low side valves then shut the pump **OFF**.

5. Watch the low side gauge for vacuum loss. If vacuum loss is in excess of 1 in. Hg (3 kPa), then leak test the system, repair the leaks and return to Step 1. Before leak testing, remember to disconnect the gauge high side connector from the service port.

6. If after 1-3 minutes, the loss is less than 1 in. Hg (3 kPa), then proceed with the system charging.

7. Disconnect the gauge high side connection from the service port and the hose from the vacuum pump.

8. Engage the center manifold connection to an R-12 source. If you are using a refrigerant drum instead of a charging station, place the drum on a scale to determine the amount of refrigerant being used.

9. Open the source and the low side gauge valve, then monitor the weight of the drum or the rate at which the charging system is introducing the R-12 into the system.

10. When 1 lb. (0.454 Kg) of R-12 has been added to the system, start the engine and turn the air conditioning system **ON**. Set the temperature level to full cold, the blower speed on high and the selector lever to the dash outlets. Under this condition, slowly draw in the remainder of the R-12 charge. The proper amount can be found on a label either on the compressor or on the evaporator case on the firewall.

11. When the system is charged, turn the source valve **OFF** and continue to run the engine for 30 seconds in order to clear the gauges and the lines

12. With the engine still running, carefully remove the gauge low side hose from the suction service fitting. Unscrew the connection rapidly to avoid excess refrigerant loss.

❄❄CAUTION

If the hoses of the manifold gauge set can be disconnected from the gauge, NEVER remove a hose from the gauge while the other end of the hose is still connected to the service port. Since the service valve fitting check valve is depressed by the hose connection, this would cause a complete and uncontrolled discharge of the system. Serious personal injury could be caused by the escaping R-12.

13. Install the protective service fitting caps and hand-tighten.

14. Turn the engine and air conditioning **OFF**.

15. If an electronic or halide leak tester is available, test the system for leaks.

16. If there are no leaks, perform the refrigerant level test to verify proper system charging.

LEAK TESTING

Whenever a refrigerant leak is suspected, begin by checking for leaks at the fitting or valves. There are several methods of detecting leaks in the air conditioning system; among them the two most popular are (1) halide leak detection or the "open flame method", and (2) electronic leak-detection. Use of an electronic leak detector, if available, is preferable for ease and safety of operation.

The halide leak detector is a torch-like device which produces a yellow-green color when refrigerant is introduced into the flame at the burner. A purple or violet color indicates large amounts of refrigerant at the burner.

An electronic leak detector is a small portable electronic device with an extended probe. With the unit activated the probe is passed along those components of the system which contain refrigerant. If a leak is detected, the unit will sound an alarm signal or activate a display signal depending on the manufacturer's design. Follow the manufacturer's instructions carefully. Move the probe at approximately 1 in. (25mm) per second around the suspected leak area. When escaping refrigerant gas is located, the ticking or beeping signal from the detector will increase in beeps per second. If the gas is relatively concentrated, the signal will be a constant shrill.

✳CAUTION

Care should be taken to operate either type of detector in well ventilated areas, so as to reduce the chance of personal injury, which may result from coming in contact with the poisonous gases produced when R-12 is exposed to flame or electric spark.

If a tester is not available, perform a visual inspection and apply a soap and water solution to the questionable area or fitting. Bubbles will form to indicate a leak. Make sure to rinse the solution from the area before making repairs.

Windshield Wipers

For maximum effectiveness and longest element life, the windshield and wiper blades should be kept clean. Dirt, tree sap, road tar and so on will cause streaking, smearing and blade deterioration if left on the glass. It is advisable to wash the windshield carefully with a commercial glass cleaner at least once a month. Wipe off the rubber blades with the wet rag afterwards. Do not attempt to move the wipers by hand. Damage to the motor and drive mechanism will result.

If the blades are found to be cracked, broken or torn, they should be replaced immediately. Replacement intervals will vary with usage, although ozone deterioration usually limits blade life to about one year. If the wiper pattern is smeared or streaked, or if the blade chatters across the glass, the elements should be replaced. It is easiest and most sensible to replace the elements in pairs.

There are basically three different types of refills, which differ in their method of replacement. One type has two release buttons, approximately ⅓ of the way up from the ends of the blade frame. Pushing the buttons down releases a lock and allows the rubber filler to be removed from the frame. The new filler slides back into the frame and locks in place.

The second type of refill has two metal tabs which are unlocked by squeezing them together. The rubber filler can then be withdrawn from the frame jaws. A new refill is installed by inserting the refill into the front frame jaws and sliding it rearward to engage the remaining frame jaws. There are usually four jaws. Be certain when installing that the refill is engaged in all of them. At the end of its travel, the tabs will lock into place on the front jaws of the wiper blade frame.

The third type is a refill made from polycarbonate. The refill has a simple locking device at one end which flexes downward

out of the groove into which the jaws of the holder fit, allowing easy release. By sliding the new refill through all the jaws and pushing through the slight resistance when it reaches the end of its travel, the refill will lock into position.

Regardless of the type of refill used, make sure that all of the frame jaws are engaged as the refill is pushed into place and locked. The metal blade holder and frame will scratch the glass if allowed to touch it.

Tires and Wheels

TIRE ROTATION

▶ **See Figure 34**

Tire wear can be equalized by switching the position of the tires about every 6000 miles, (9700 km). Including a conventional spare in the rotation pattern can give up to 20% more tire life.

Due to their design, radial tires tend to wear faster in the shoulder area, particularly in the front positions. Radial tires in non-drive locations, may develop an irregular wear pattern that can generate tire noise. It was originally thought the radial tires should not be cross-switched (from one side of the vehicle to the other); because of their wear patterns and because they would last longer if their direction of rotation is not changed. The manufacturer's tire rotation recommendations for most late model vehicles covered by this manual now allows for, and even suggests, cross-switching radial tires to allow for more uniform tire wear.

➡**Some specialty tires may be directional (certain snow or performance tires), meaning they may only be mounted to rotate in one direction. Some special performance tires/wheels will fall into this category and will be marked with directional rotation arrows on the tire sidewalls. NEVER switch the direction of rotation on tires so marked or poor performance/tire damage could occur. This should be taken into consideration in choosing a rotation pattern for directional tires.**

If you have any doubt as to the correct rotation pattern for the tires which are currently mounted on your vehicle, consult the tire manufacturer or one of their facilities for recommendations

➡**When radials or studded snows are taken off the car, mark them, so you can maintain the same direction of rotation.**

TIRE DESIGN

When buying new tires, give some thought to the following points about tire design, especially if you are considering a switch to larger tires or a different profile series:

1. All four tires must be of the same construction type. This rule cannot be violated. Radial, bias, and bias belted tires must not be mixed.

2. The wheels should be the correct width for the tire. Tire dealers have charts of tire and rim compatibility. A mismatch will cause sloppy handling and rapid tire wear. The tread width

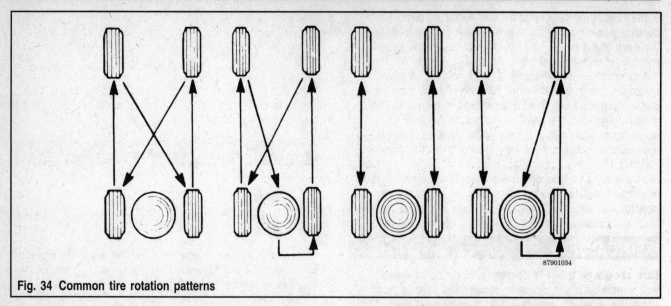

Fig. 34 Common tire rotation patterns

should match the rim width (inside bead to inside bead) within an inch. For radial tires, the rim width should be 80% or less of the tire (not tread) width.

3. The height (mounted diameter) of the new tires can change speedometer accuracy, engine speed at a given road speed, fuel mileage, acceleration, and ground clearance. Tire manufacturers furnish full measurement specifications.

4. The spare tire should be usable, at least for short distance and low speed operation, with the new tires.

5. There should not be any body interference when loaded, on bumps or in turns.

TIRE STORAGE

Store the tires at the proper inflation pressure if they are mounted on wheels. Keep them in a cool dry place, laid on their sides. If the tires are stored in the garage or basement, do not let them stand on a concrete floor. Set them on strips of wood.

TIRE INFLATION

Tire inflation is the most ignored item of auto maintenance. Gasoline mileage can drop as much as 0.8% for every 1 pound per square inch (psi) of under inflation.

Two items should be a permanent fixture in every glove compartment: a tire pressure gauge and a tread depth gauge. Check the tire air pressure (including the spare) regularly with a pocket type gauge. Kicking the tires won't tell you a thing, and the gauge on the service station air hose is notoriously inaccurate.

The tire pressures recommended for your vehicle are usually found in the owner's manual. Ideally, inflation pressure should be checked when the tires are cool. When the air becomes heated it expands and the pressure increases. Every 10° rise (or drop) in temperature means a difference of 1 psi, which also explains why the tire appears to lose air on a very cold night. When it is impossible to check the tires cold, allow for pressure build-up due to heat. If the hot pressure exceeds the

cold pressure by more than 15 psi, reduce your speed, load or both. Otherwise internal heat is created in the tire. When the heat approaches the temperature at which the tire was cured, during manufacture, the tread can separate from the body.

✳✳CAUTION

Never counteract excessive pressure build-up by bleeding off air pressure (letting some air out). This will only further raise the tire operating temperature.

Before starting a long trip with lots of luggage, you can add about 2-4 psi to the tires to make them run cooler, but never exceed the maximum inflation pressure on the side of the tire.

TREAD DEPTH

▶ **See Figures 35, 36 and 37**

All tires made since 1968, have 7 built-in tread wear indicator bars that show up as ½ in. (6mm) smooth bands across

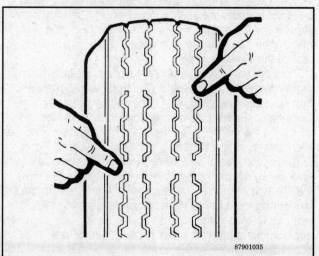

Fig. 35 Tread wear indicators are built into the tire tread and appear as bands when the tire is worn.

the tire when 1/16 in. (1.5mm) of tread remains. The appearance of tread wear indicators means that the tires should be replaced. In fact, many states have laws prohibiting the use of tires with less than 1/16 in. (1.5mm) tread.

You can check your own tread depth with an inexpensive gauge or by using a Lincoln head penny. Slip the Lincoln penny into several tread grooves. If you can see the top of Lincoln's head in 2 adjacent grooves, the tires have less than 1/16 in. tread left and should be replaced. You can measure snow tires in the same manner by using the tails side of the Lincoln penny. If you can see the top of the Lincoln memorial, it's time to replace the snow tires.

CARE OF SPECIAL WHEELS

If you have invested money in mag, aluminum alloy or sport wheels, special precautions should be taken to make sure your investment is not wasted, and that your special wheels look good for the lifetime of the vehicle.

Special wheels are easily scratched and/or damaged. Occasionally check the rim for cracks, damage or air leaks. If any of these conditions are found, replace the wheel. In order to

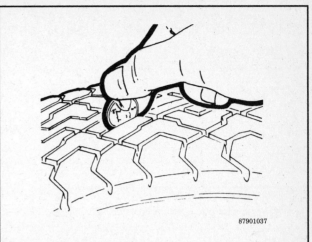

Fig. 37 A penny can also be used to approximate tread depth. If the top of Lincolns head is visible in two adjacent grooves, replace the tire.

prevent this type of damage, and the costly replacement of a special wheel, observe the following precautions:

Take special care not to damage the wheels during removal, installation, balancing etc. After removal of the wheels from the vehicle, place them on a rubber mat or other protective surface.

While the vehicle is being driven, be careful not to drive over sharp obstacles or allow the wheels to contact the shoulder of the road.

When washing, use a mild detergent and water. Avoid using cleansers with abrasives, or hard brushes. And a little polish after washing will help your wheels keep that new look.

If possible, remove your special wheels from the vehicle during the winter months, and replace them with regular steel rims. Salt and sand that is applied to the roadways for snow removal during these months can do severe damage to special wheels. Make sure that the recommended lug nut torque is never exceeded, or you may crack your wheels. Never use snow chains with special wheels.

If you intend to store the wheels, lay them flat on a protective surface and cover them. Do not stack them on top of each other and do not place anything else, except a protective cover, on them.

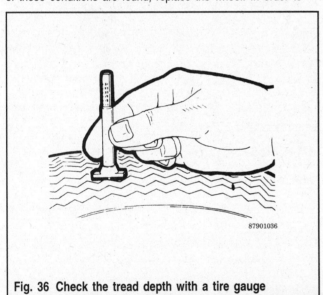

Fig. 36 Check the tread depth with a tire gauge

FLUIDS AND LUBRICANTS

Fluid Disposal

Used fluids such as engine oil, transaxle fluid, antifreeze and brake fluid are hazardous wastes and must be disposed of properly. Before draining any fluids, check local laws concerning the disposal of hazardous wastes. In many areas, waste oils, etc. are being accepted as a part of recycling programs. A number of service stations and auto parts stores are also accepting waste fluids for recycling.

Be sure of the recycling center's policies before draining any fluids, as many will not accept different fluids that have been mixed together, such as oil and antifreeze.

Fuel and Engine Oil Recommendations

When adding oil to the crankcase or changing the oil and filter, it is important that oil of an equal quality to original equipment be used in your vehicle. The use of inferior oils may void the warranty, damage the engine, or both.

The Society of Automotive Engineers (SAE) grade number indicates the viscosity of the engine oil, and thus its ability to lubricate at a given temperature. The lower the SAE grade number, the lighter the oil. The lower the viscosity, the easier it is to crank the engine in cold weather but the less the oil will lubricate and protect the engine at high temperature. This number is marked on every oil container.

Oil Viscosity Chart

Model	Ambient Temperature	Oil Viscosity (SAE)
'70–'80	20°F or below	5W-30 ①
	20°F to 90°F	10W-30, 10W-40
	40°F to 90°F	#30
	90°F or above	20W-40, 20W-50, #40
'81–'87	−10°F or below	5W-30 ①
	−10°F to 90°F	10W-30, 10W-40, 10W-50
	30°F to 90°F	30, 20W-40, 20W-50
	90°F or above	40
1800 Turbo	−30°F to 90°F ②	10W-30, 10W-40, 10W-50
	30°F to 90°F	30, 20W-40, 20W-50
	90°F or above	40

① 5W-30 is not recommended for sustained high speed driving regardless of outside temperature.
② Turbo engines require more of the oil. Subaru does not recommend 5W-30 oil unless temperatures are so severe (below −13°F) that there's no other way to get the car started. If you must use 5W-30, avoid continuous high speeds and change to a heavier grade as soon as temperatures moderate.

87901090

Oil viscosities should be chosen from those oils recommended for the lowest anticipated temperatures during the oil change interval.

Multi-viscosity oils (10W-30, 20W-50, etc.) offer the important advantage of being adaptable to temperature extremes. They allow easy starting at low temperatures, yet give good protection at high speeds and engine temperatures. This is a decided advantage in changeable climates or in long distance touring.

The American Petroleum Institute (API) designation indicates the classification of engine oil for use under given operating conditions. Only oils designated for use Service **SE** or **SF** or greater should be used. Oils of this type perform a variety of functions inside the engine in addition to the basic function as a lubricant. Through a balanced system of metallic detergents and polymeric dispersants, the oil prevents the formation of high and low temperature deposits, and also keeps sludge and dirt particles in suspension. Acids, particularly sulfuric acid, as well as other by-products of combustion, are neutralized. Both the SAE grade number and the API designation can be found on the oil container.

❊❊WARNING

Non-detergent or straight mineral oils must never be used.

Fuel

Your Subaru is designed to operate on unleaded fuel. The minimum octane rating of the fuels used must be at least 91 RON. All unleaded fuels sold in the U.S. are required to meet this minimum rating.

Use of a fuel too low in octane (a measurement of anti-knock quality) will result in spark knock. Since many factors affect operating efficiency, such as altitude, terrain, air temperature and humidity, knocking may result even though the recommended fuel is being used. If persistent knocking occurs, it may be necessary to switch to a slightly higher grade of gaso-line. Continuous or heavy knocking may result in engine damage.

➡**Your engine's fuel requirement can change with time, mainly due to carbon buildup, which changes the compression ratio. If your engine pings, knocks, or runs on, switch to a higher grade of fuel, if possible, and check the ignition timing. Sometimes changing brands will cure the problem. If it is necessary to retard timing from specifications, don't change it more than a few degrees. Retarded timing will reduce power output and fuel mileage, and will increase engine temperature.**

Engine

OIL LEVEL CHECK

▶ See Figures 38 and 39

The engine oil level should be checked at regular intervals. For example, whenever the vehicle is refueled.

❊❊WARNING

If the low oil pressure warning light comes on while the engine is running, stop the engine immediately and check the oil level.

1. The vehicle should be parked on a level surface.
2. Wait a few minutes after the engine is stopped before checking the oil level or an inaccurate reading will result.
3. Remove the dipstick, which is located on the right (passenger) side of the crankcase. Wipe it with a clean cloth, then reinsert it.
4. Pull the dipstick out again and, holding the dipstick horizontally read the oil level. The oil level should be between the upper mark and lower mark on the dipstick.
5. Add oil of the proper viscosity through the capped opening in the top of the valve cover. See the Oil and Fuel Recommendations chart in this section for the proper viscosity and rating of oil to use.

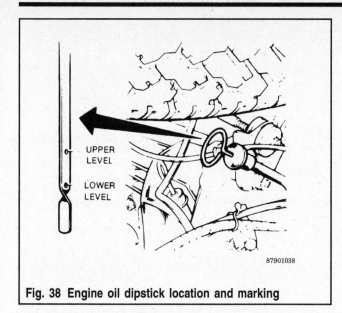

Fig. 38 Engine oil dipstick location and marking

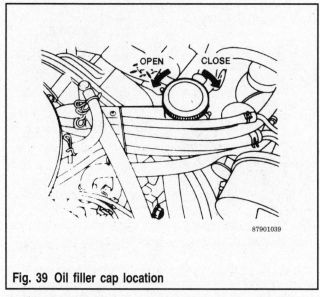

Fig. 39 Oil filler cap location

6. Insert the dipstick and check the oil level again after adding any oil. Be careful not to overfill the crankcase.

OIL AND FILTER CHANGE

▶ See Figures 40, 41, 42, 43, 44, 45, 46 and 47

The oil in the engine of your Subaru should be changed every six months 7500 miles (12,000 km), whichever comes first. If you live in an extremely dusty or smoggy area, or drive for moderately short distances in cold weather (less than four miles with the temperature below freezing), change your vehicle's oil more frequently. The oil should be changed every four months 3000 miles (4800 km), under these conditions. A new filter should be installed with every oil change. The used oil should be placed into a suitable container and taken to a collection or reclamation point for recycling (many garages and gas stations have storage tanks for this purpose).

➡Subaru recommends that the filter be changed every other oil change, unless the vehicle is driven under those conditions requiring more frequent changes or those in which the time limit expires before the mileage limit. Our recommendation is that, regardless of the interval, the filter should be changed at every oil change. This offers excellent protection against a situation in which the filter becomes clogged, bypassing dirty oil directly to the engine's wearing parts. It also permits a more complete removal of dirty oil from the engine's filter and oil galleries, which hold a quart or more of contaminated fluid.

The oil should always be changed while hot, so the dirt and particles will still be suspended in the oil when it drains out of the engine. To change the oil and filter:

1. Run the engine for a short period of time. This will make the oil flow more freely and it will carry off more contaminants.

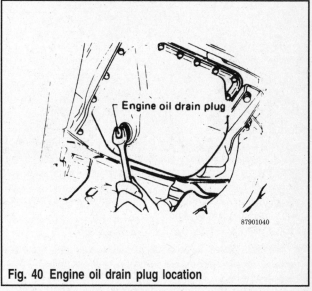

Fig. 40 Engine oil drain plug location

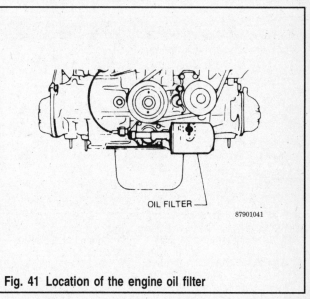

Fig. 41 Location of the engine oil filter

2. Park the vehicle on a level surface and apply the parking brake. Turn the engine **OFF**. Remove the oil filler cap from the oil filler tube which is located on the driver's side of the engine.

3. Raise the vehicle and support it with jackstands.

4. Place a drain pan of adequate capacity below the drain plug which is located either at the rear of the oil pan (ff-1, 1300G models), or on the driver's side of the oil pan (all other models). A large, flat pan makes a good container to catch oil.

5. Use a metric wrench of the proper size (not locking pliers) to loosen the oil pan drain plug. Put on a pair of heavy gloves and turn the drain plug out by hand while maintaining a slight upward force on it, to keep the oil from running out around it.

❊❊CAUTION

When you are ready to release the plug, pull it away from the drain hole quickly, to avoid being burned by the hot oil.

6. Allow the oil to drain completely and then install the drain plug. **DO NOT OVERTIGHTEN** the plug, or you will strip the threads in the drain hole and you'll have to buy a new pan or an over-sized replacement plug.

7. Using an oil filter strap wrench, remove the oil filter. Keep in mind that it's holding about a quart of dirty, hot oil.

8. As soon as you remove the oil filter, hold it upright until you can empty it into the drain pan. Dispose of the filter.

❊❊CAUTION

The EPA warns that prolonged contact with used engine oil may cause a number of skin disorders, including cancer! You should take every effort to minimize your exposure to used engine oil. Protective gloves should be worn when changing the oil. Wash your hands and any other exposed skin areas as soon as possible after exposure to used engine oil. Soap and water, or waterless hand cleaner should be used.

9. Using a clean rag, wipe off the filter mounting adaptor on the engine block. Be sure that the rag does not leave any lint which could clog an oil passage.

10. Wipe a coating of clean engine oil on the rubber gasket of the new filter. Spin it onto the engine by hand. **DO NOT** use the strap wrench. When the gasket starts to snug up against the adaptor surface, give it another ½ to ¾ turn by hand (check the instructions provided by the filter manufacturer). Don't turn it any more, or you'll squash the gasket and the filter will leak.

11. Add clean, fresh oil of the proper amount, grade and viscosity through the oil filler tube on the top of the engine.

12. Lower the vehicle and check the oil level on the oil dipstick.

13. Be sure that the oil level is near the upper mark on the dipstick.

14. Start the engine and allow it to idle. Make sure the oil light goes out.

Fig. 43 Remove the oil filter using a strap wrench

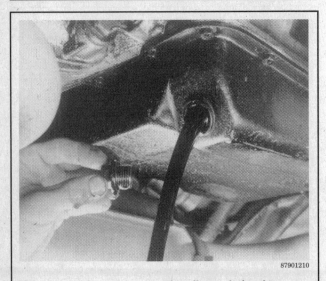

Fig. 42 Loosen and remove the oil pan drain plug

Fig. 44 Before installing a new oil filter, coat the rubber gasket with clean oil.

Fig. 45 Remove the oil filler cap . . .

Fig. 46 . . . then add clean, fresh oil of the proper amount, grade and viscosity

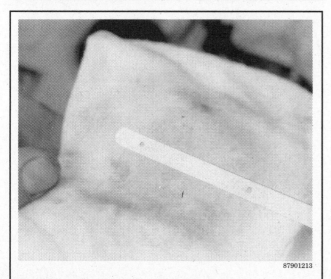

Fig. 47 Check the level on the oil dipstick

15. Stop the engine and allow the oil to drain back down for a few minutes, and check the oil level again. Add oil as necessary, but do not overfill.

16. Remember to install the oil filler cap. Check for leaks around the oil filter and drain plug.

Manual Transaxle

FLUID RECOMMENDATIONS

▶ **See Figure 48**

In all 4-speed, 5-speed and 4-wheel drive models the transaxle and drive axle share a common supply of lubricant. On 1970-73 vehicles the lubricant level should be checked at least every 3 months/3000 miles (5000 km), whichever comes first. For 1974-80 models check the level every 6 months/6000 miles (9700 km). On 1981-84 models, check every 6 months/7500 miles (12,000 km).

Refer to the Capacities chart for the correct amount of lubricant the transaxle and drive axle in your vehicle needs. Use API GL-5 hypoid gear oil of one of the following viscosities:
- SAE 90 — above 30°F (-1°C)
- SAE 85W — below 30°F (-1°C)
- SAE 80W — below 0°F (-18°C)

LEVEL CHECK

▶ **See Figure 49**

The level is checked with a dipstick in much the same manner as the engine oil level. The dipstick is located on the right rear (passenger) side of the transaxle housing.

➡**Be careful not to confuse it with the engine oil dipstick, which is located on the same side of the engine. It may be necessary on some models to remove the spare tire in order to gain access to it.**

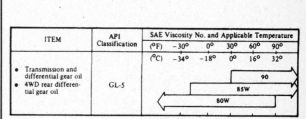

ITEM	API Classification	SAE Viscosity No. and Applicable Temperature				
		(°F) −30°	0°	30°	60°	90°
		(°C) −34°	−18°	0°	16°	32°
• Transmission and differential gear oil • 4WD rear differential gear oil	GL-5				90	
				85W		
		80W				

NOTE:
Each oil manufacturer has its base oil and additives. Thus, do not mix two or more brands.

Fig. 48 Recommended lubricant grades for the manual transaxle

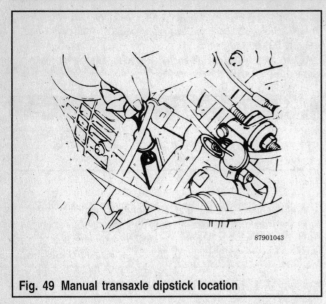

Fig. 49 Manual transaxle dipstick location

1. Check the transaxle oil level with the vehicle parked on a level surface and the engine **OFF**.

➡**The engine should be shut off for at least three minutes before the transaxle oil level is checked.**

2. Remove the spare tire if necessary. Pull the dipstick out and wipe it with a clean cloth. Insert the dipstick again and then remove it.

3. Hold the dipstick horizontally and check the oil level.

4. The oil level should be between the upper and lower marks. If it is below this, replenish it through the dipstick opening with GL-5 hypoid 80 or 90 weight gear oil.

➡**Add a little oil at a time. The distance between the marks on the dipstick is less than a pint. Do not overfill.**

5. Install the dipstick and install the spare tire if removed.

DRAIN AND REFILL

1. Park the vehicle on a level surface. Turn engine **OFF** and apply the parking brake.

2. Raise and support the vehicle with jackstands.

3. Place a container of adequate capacity beneath the drain plug which is located underneath the vehicle, on the bottom of the transaxle housing.

4. Use the proper size metric wrench to loosen the drain plug slowly, while maintaining a slight upward pressure, to keep the oil from leaking out around the plug.

5. Allow all of the lubricant to drain from the transaxle, then install the drain plug and gasket (if so equipped) **DO NOT OVERTIGHTEN**.

6. Remove the transaxle dipstick and fill the transaxle to the capacity shown in the Capacities chart. Do not overfill.

7. Use the dipstick to check the oil level. It should come up to the full mark.

8. Insert the dipstick and lower the vehicle.

9. Check for leaks around the drain plug and check for proper transaxle/transaxle operation.

Automatic Transaxle

It is extremely important that the proper lubricant level be maintained at all times in the automatic transaxle. A level which is either too high or too low will result in poor shifting operation and internal damage.

➡**Unlike the standard transaxle, the lubricant supply in the automatic transaxle is separate from that in the drive axle. To check the level in the drive axle refer to the appropriate procedure in this section.**

FLUID RECOMMENDATION

Dexron II® Automatic Transmission Fluid (ATF) is recommended by Subaru for use in their automatic transaxle.

Unlike the standard transaxle, the lubricant supply in the automatic transaxle is separate from that in the drive axle. The fluid should be changed according to the schedule in the Maintenance Intervals chart. If the vehicle is normally used in severe service the interval should be more frequent. The fluid should be hot before it is drained. A short drive should accomplish this.

LEVEL CHECK

▶ **See Figures 50 and 51**

To check the automatic transaxle fluid, drive the vehicle several miles to bring the transmission up to normal operating temperature.

1. Park the vehicle on a level surface, place the gear selector in **Park** position and leave the engine idling.

2. Open the hood and locate the automatic transaxle dipstick on the left (driver) side of the engine, near the fire wall. Remove the dipstick, wipe it with a clean rag and reinsert it firmly.

3. Remove the dipstick, hold it horizontally and note the reading.

Fig. 50 Remove the transaxle dipstick to check the fluid level

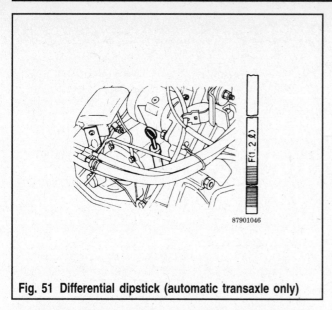

Fig. 51 Differential dipstick (automatic transaxle only)

4. As long as the reading is between the upper level and lower level marks the fluid level is correct. If the level is at or below the lower mark, additional fluid is necessary. Add automatic transmission fluid with the Dexron II ® designation only.

5. Fluid should be added through the neck of the dipstick hole using a funnel. With the engine still idling, add fluid in small quantities at a time and recheck the level after each addition. Stop when the fluid level is close to the upper level mark. Avoid overfilling, do not fill above the upper mark.

6. Replace the dipstick and test drive the vehicle to insure proper Transaxle operation.

❊❊WARNING

The capacity difference between the upper and lower marks is approximately 12 oz. If the drained fluid is discolored, thick, or smells burnt, serious transaxle problems due to overheating should be suspected. Your vehicle's transaxle should be inspected by a transmission specialist to determine the cause.

DRAIN AND REFILL

▶ **See Figure 52**

1. Park the vehicle on a level surface, turn the engine **OFF** and apply parking brake.

2. Raise the vehicle and support it with jackstands.

3. Place a container of adequate capacity beneath the drain plug located at the bottom, center of the transaxle case.

4. Remove the drain plug and allow the fluid to drain.

5. After draining, replace the drain plug and gasket. **do not overtighten**.

6. Lower the vehicle.

7. Remove the transaxle dipstick and using a funnel fill the transaxle through the dipstick hole with the proper amount of automatic transmission fluid (see the Capacities chart).

8. Check the fluid level and road test the vehicle to insure proper transaxle operation.

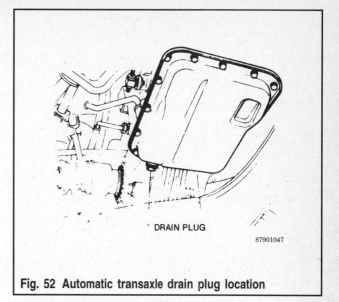

Fig. 52 Automatic transaxle drain plug location

PAN AND FILTER SERVICE

▶ **See Figures 53, 54, 55, 56, 57 and 58**

Normal maintenance does not require removal of the transaxle oil pan, or changing or cleaning of the oil strainer. However, if a leak is detected at the transaxle oil pan, the gasket it must be replaced.

1. Park the vehicle on a level surface. Turn the engine **OFF**

2. Raise the vehicle and support it with jackstands.

3. Remove the drain plug and drain the transaxle fluid into a suitable container.

4. Remove all the front and side pan bolts. Loosen the rear bolts about four turns.

5. Pry the pan loose and let it drain.

6. Remove the pan and gasket. Clean the pan thoroughly with solvent and dry it with clean rags. Be careful not to get any lint from the rags in the pan.

Fig. 53 Raise the vehicle and support it with jackstands

Fig. 54 Remove all the pan bolts

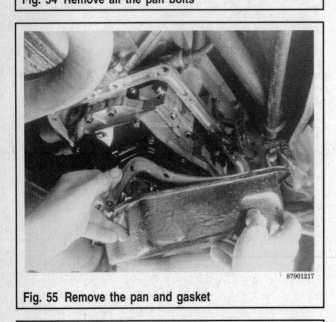

Fig. 55 Remove the pan and gasket

Fig. 56 Clean the gasket mating surfaces

7. To remove the oil strainer, unbolt it from the valve body. It can be cleaned in a nonflammable solvent and dried with compressed air or allowed to air dry.

➡**It is normal to find a SMALL amount of metal shavings in the pan. An excessive amount of metal shavings indicates transaxle damage which must be handled by a professional automatic transmission mechanic.**

To install:

8. Install the oil strainer, new gasket and the pan. Tighten the pan bolts to 2.5-3.3 ft. lbs. (3-4 Nm).

9. Install the drain plug with a new gasket and tighten the plug to 18 ft. lbs. (24 Nm) .

10. Lower the vehicle and using a funnel fill the transaxle with the proper amount of automatic transmission fluid (see the capacities chart).

11. Add fluid in small quantities at a time and recheck the level after each addition. Stop when the fluid level is close to the upper level mark. Avoid overfilling, do not fill above the upper mark.

12. Insert the dipstick and test drive the vehicle to insure proper transaxle operation.

Transfer Case

Lubricant to the transfer case is supplied through the transaxle. If the level of fluid in the transaxle is full, so is the transfer case.

Front Drive Axle

The lubricant should be changed according to the schedule in the Maintenance Intervals chart.

➡**This pertains to vehicles with automatic transaxle only.**

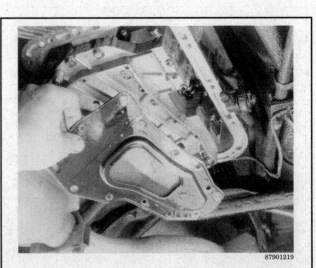

Fig. 57 Unbolt the oil strainer and remove it from the valve body

Fig. 58 Fill the transaxle with the proper amount of automatic transmission fluid

Fig. 59 Remove the dipstick and check the fluid level of the drive axle

FLUID RECOMMENDATIONS

Use gear oil with API classification GL-5. Viscosity should be:
- SAE 90 — 30°F (-1°C)
- SAE 85W — 30°F (-1°C)
- SAE 80W — 0°F (-18°C)

LEVEL CHECK

▶ See Figure 59

The lubricant level in the drive axle is checked in a similar manner as the engine oil.

1. With the engine **OFF** and the vehicle parked on a level surface, open the hood and remove the dipstick. The dipstick is located to the rear of the engine oil dipstick and near the starter motor.

2. If the lubricant level is not at the upper mark on the dipstick additional gear oil is necessary and should be added through the dipstick filler tube. Use the proper weight oil with API classification of GL-5. Do not overfill.

DRAIN AND REFILL

▶ See Figure 60

1. Park the vehicle on a level surface, turn the engine **OFF** and apply the parking brake.

2. Raise and support the vehicle with jackstands.

3. Place a container of adequate capacity beneath the drain plug, located on the lower left side of the differential case, near the left axle shaft.

4. Remove the drain plug and allow the fluid to drain.

5. After draining, replace the drain plug and gasket. Do not overtighten.

Fig. 60 Remove the drive axle drain plug and allow the fluid to drain

6. Remove the differential dipstick and fill the differential to the upper mark on the dipstick.

Rear Drive Axle

The lubricant should be checked at regular intervals and changed at 60,000 mile (96,000km) intervals. When the vehicle is frequently operated under severe conditions, the lubricant should be changed at 30,000 mile (48,000km) intervals.

FLUID RECOMMENDATIONS

Use gear oil with API classification GL-5 for open differentials and GLS for limited slip differential. Viscosity should be:
- SAE 90-above 30°F (1°C)
- SAE 85W-above 30°F (1°C)
- SAE 80W-below 0°F (18°C)

LEVEL CHECK

▶ **See Figure 61**

Unlike the procedures outlined above, the lubricant level in the rear differential must be checked from underneath the vehicle. this procedure applies to four wheel drive models.

1. Park the vehicle on a level surface. Block the wheels, place in gear, turn the engine **OFF** and engage the parking brake.
2. Crawl under the vehicle from the rear until the differential housing can be reached easily.
3. Remove the filler hole (upper) plug from the back of the differential case.
4. If no lubricant trickles out carefully insert your finger (watch out for sharp threads) into the hole and check that the oil is up to the bottom edge of the filler hole.
5. If not add the oil through the hole until the level is at the edge of the hole.
6. Install the filler hole plug.

Cooling System

FLUID RECOMMENDATION

A quality ethylene glycol coolant, containing corrosion inhibitors should be used. A 50/50 mixture of water and coolant is recommended. Antifreeze concentration should be high enough to maintain freezing protection down to -34°F (-37°C).

✳✳CAUTION

When draining the coolant, keep in mind that cats and other animals are attracted by ethylene glycol antifreeze, and are likely to drink any that is left on the ground or in an open container. This can prove to be fatal in sufficient quantity. Always drain coolant into a suitable container. Coolant may be reused unless it is contaminated or several years old.

LEVEL CHECK

✳✳CAUTION

Never add coolant to a hot engine. Stop the engine and allow it to cool. Then, start it to circulate coolant uniformly through the block and add coolant slowly as the engine idles. Otherwise you risk cracking the block. Coolant can be added to the radiator. NEVER REMOVE THE RADIATOR CAP UNTIL THE ENGINE HAS HAD AMPLE TIME TO COOL TO BELOW OPERATING TEMPERATURE.

ff-1 and 1300G Models

▶ **See Figure 62**

These models have a sealed cooling system with two radiators and separate thermal expansion tank.

On 1300G models, it is not necessary to remove the cap to check the coolant level, because the expansion tank is translucent plastic. The coolant should be replenished if its level falls ⅜ in. (9.5mm) below the line molded in the side of the tank.

On ff-1 models, the cap must be removed from the expansion tank in order to check the coolant level which should be flush with the top of the pipe inside of the tank.

If, on either model, the level in the expansion tank is lower than it should be, check the coolant level in the main radiator, as well.

✳✳CAUTION

The cap on the main radiator is not a pressure/vacuum safety cap. Never remove it when the engine is hot. Always remove the cap on the expansion tank first, after depressing the black button on it to release the pressure in the cooling system.

On both models, fill the main radiator to the bottom of the filler port. On the ff-1 models, fill the expansion tank so that the water just covers the pipe inside it. On 1300G models, fill the expansion tank up to the mark on its side. Add a good

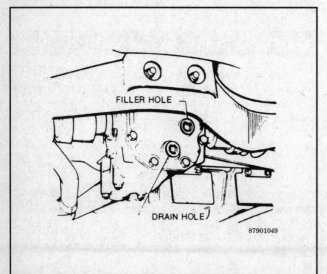

Fig. 61 Rear drive axle drain and filler holes

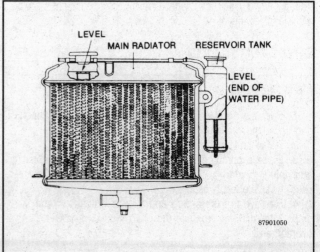

Fig. 62 Checking the coolant level — ff-1 and 1300G models

brand of an anti-corrosive ethylene glycol coolant, and water, in a 50/50 mixture.

✳✳WARNING

Never add cold coolant to an engine which has overheated because of a low coolant level. First allow the engine to cool, and then idle it while adding the fresh coolant slowly.

Except ff-1 and 1300G Models

▶ See Figure 63

These models use a conventional crossflow radiator. Check the coolant level with the engine cold. To check the coolant level:

1. Depress the black button on the top of the radiator cap to allow the pressure to escape from the cooling system.
2. The coolant level should not fall more than ½ in. (12.7mm) below the plate welded inside the tank. Add a good brand of an anti-corrosive, ethylene glycol coolant and water (preferably distilled) in a 50/50 mixture.
3. Install the radiator cap.

DRAINING, FLUSHING AND CLEANING THE SYSTEM

▶ See Figures 64 and 65

1. Remove the radiator and recovery tank caps. Run the engine till the upper radiator hose gets hot. This means that the thermostat is open and the coolant is flowing through the system.
2. Turn the engine **OFF** and place a large container under the radiator. Open the drain valve at the bottom of the radiator. Open the block drain plugs (If equipped) to speed up the draining process.
3. Close the drain valves and the block drain plugs and add water until the system is nearly full.
4. Add a can of quality radiator flush to the radiator, following any special instructions on the can.

5. Turn the engine **ON** and idle the engine as long as is specified on the can of flush, or until the upper radiator hose is hot.
6. Turn the vehicle **OFF** and drain the system again. There should be quite a bit of scale and rust in the drained water.
7. Repeat the draining and filling process several times, until the liquid is nearly colorless.
8. After the last draining, fill the system with a 50/50 mixture of ethylene glycol and water.
9. Run the engine until the system is hot and add coolant, if necessary. Install the caps and check for leaks.

Brake Master Cylinder

FLUID RECOMMENDATIONS

When making additions of brake fluid, use only fresh, uncontaminated brake fluid which meets or exceeds DOT 3 standards (as stated on the container).

LEVEL CHECK

▶ See Figures 66 and 67

The brake master cylinder reservoir(s) are made of translucent plastic so that the fluid level may be checked without removing the caps. Check the brake fluid level frequently. For example, every time that oil level is checked.

✳✳CAUTION

If the brake system warning light comes on, stop the vehicle and immediately check the brake fluid level.

Drain the brake fluid and replace it every 24 months/24000 miles (39,000 km) on drum brake equipped models or every 15 months/15000 miles (24,000 km) on disc brake equipped models (whichever occurs first).

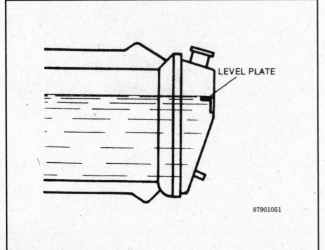

Fig. 63 Checking the coolant level — except ff-1 and 1300G models

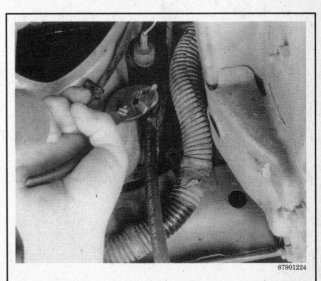

Fig. 64 Loosen the petcock to drain the cooling system

Fig. 65 After the last draining, fill the system with a 50/50 mixture of ethylene glycol and water

If the fluid level in either of the master cylinder reservoir(s) falls below the bottom **(MIN)** line molded on the side of the reservoir, add brake fluid to bring the level up to the top **(MAX)** line.

1. Clean the top of the reservoir off before removing the cap to prevent dirt from entering the master cylinder.

2. Pour the fluid slowly to prevent air bubbles from forming. Brake fluid is a good paint remover, so don't spill any on the vehicle's paint.

❋❋WARNING

Do not use a lower grade of brake fluid than specified. Never mix different types of brake fluid. Doing either of the above could cause a brake system failure.

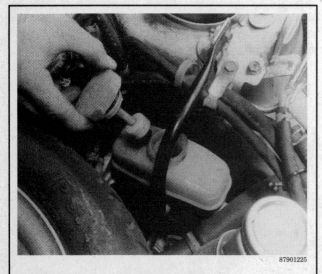

Fig. 66 Remove the master cylinder cap

Fig. 67 Use the proper type and grade of brake fluid to fill the master cylinder

Power Steering Pump

FLUID RECOMMENDATION

Dexron II® Automatic Transmission Fluid (ATF) or its superceding fluid is recommended for the power steering pump.

LEVEL CHECK

1. Drive the vehicle several miles to raise the power steering system up to normal operating temperature.

2. Park the vehicle on a level surface and stop the engine.

3. Remove the level gauge, wipe it clean, then reinsert it fully.

4. Remove it again and read the level at the **HOT** side of the gauge. If the fluid reading is at the lower level or below, add the recommended power steering fluid until it reaches the upper mark.

➡**When the fluid level has to be checked without warming up the power steering system, read the level at the cold side of the gauge and add fluid accordingly.**

Steering Gear

FLUID RECOMMENDATION

Subaru recommends only genuine Subaru Valiant Grease M2, Part No. 003608001.

LEVEL CHECK

The steering box does not require greasing unless it has been disassembled.

Windshield Washer

FLUID RECOMMENDATION

The reservoir should be filled to the top of the container using a wiper fluid solution which can be found in most automotive stores. Do not further dilute the mixture (unless manufacturers instructions tell you to do so) as this will affect it's ability to keep from freezing in low temperatures. Never place other fluids in the reservoir, such as a water/antifreeze mix, as other fluids could damage the pump seals.

LEVEL CHECK

Check the level of the windshield washer solution in the translucent reservoir tank at the same time the oil is being checked. Add the windshield water solution as needed.

❄❄WARNING

Do not operate the windshield washer when the fluid reservoir is empty. This can cause the pump motor to burn out.

Chassis Greasing

LUBRICATION

Steering and Suspension

Under normal conditions regular chassis greasing is unnecessary, because there are no chassis grease fittings used on Subarus. The only time greasing is required is as part of chassis component repair or replacement, or if component dust boots and seals have become damaged. If its boot or seal is damaged or leaking, the component will have to be removed, repacked with grease, and a new boot or seal installed.

Because there are no recommended chassis greasing intervals, the chassis suspension and drivetrain components should be inspected regularly.

If a visual inspection turns up a damaged component, dust boot, or seal, consult the appropriate section for the correct repair or replacement procedure.

Pedals and Linkages

The clutch, brake, and accelerator linkages should be lubricated at the recommended intervals found in the owners manual, with multi-purpose chassis grease.

1. Working inside the vehicle, apply a small amount of grease to the pedal pivots and linkage.

❄❄WARNING

Be careful not to get grease on the pedal pads or floor covering.

2. Working under the hood, grease all pivoting and sliding parts of the accelerator and brake linkages.

➡**In some cases it may be easier to gain access to the linkages from underneath the vehicle.**

Body Lubrication and Maintenance

Body lubrication should be performed every 6 months/6000 miles (10,000 km) on the ff-1 and at recommended intervals on all other models.

Apply multi-purpose chassis grease to the following areas:
- Hood hinges, lock, and striker
- Door hinges, latch, and striker
- Trunk hinges and striker

➡**Use grease sparingly on the door and trunk strikers, as they may come into contact with clothing.**

Use powdered graphite to lubricate the following items:
- Door key lock cylinders
- Trunk key lock cylinders

➡**Do not use oil or grease to lubricate the insides of lock cylinders.**

Use silicone lubricant to preserve the rubber weather stripping around the doors and trunk.

Wheel Bearings

Refer to Section 8 for front axle and 4-wheel drive wheel bearing repacking, adjustment, or replacement.

REMOVAL & INSTALLATION

▶ **See Figures 68, 69, 70, 71, 72, 73 and 74**

1. Apply the parking brake and loosen (but do not remove) the rear wheel nuts.
2. Raise the vehicle, support it with jackstands. Release the parking brake and remove the wheel and tire.
3. Remove the brake drum cap from the drum.
4. Flatten the lockwasher and loosen the axle nut, then remove the nut, washer and the outer bearing. Remove the brake drum.
5. Pry up the spacer with a prybar and remove the spacer and inner bearing inner race. Use a puller if necessary.
6. Remove the outer race of inner bearing from drum. Remove the oil seal at this time.
7. Remove the outer race of outer bearing from drum.
   Clean the removed parts and check them for wear, damage and corrosion. If faulty, repair or replace
   To install:
8. Press the outer race of inner bearing into drum using a Taper Roller Bearing Installer (925220000), or its equivalent, and a press.
9. Apply sufficient grease to the oil seal lip. Install the oil seal into drum until its outer end is flush with the drum surface.
10. Press the outer race of outer bearing into drum using Taper Roller Bearing Installer (921130000), or its equivalent, and a press.

Fig. 68 Use a small prytool to remove the drum cap

11. Apply approximately 14 oz (4g) of grease to the inner bearing and 11 oz (3g) to the outer bearing. Fill the boss of drum with approximately 1.06 oz (30g) of grease.

12. Install the spacer and inner race of inner bearing onto the spindle of trailing arm.

❋❋WARNING

Stepped surface of the spacer must be faced toward the bearing.

13. Install the drum, inner race of outer bearing, washer, lockwasher and the axle nut in this order onto the spindle.

➡**Make sure the old lockwasher is replaced with a new one.**

14. Install the wheel and lower the vehicle and tighten the lock nuts.

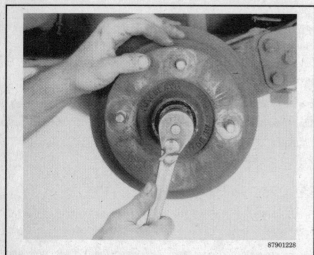

Fig. 69 Flatten the lockwasher, then remove the axle nut

Fig. 71 . . . then the outer bearing

Fig. 70 Remove the washer . . .

Fig. 72 Remove the brake drum

Fig. 73 Remove the bearing from the spindle

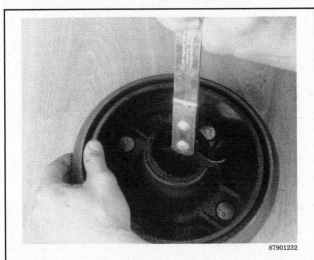

Fig. 74 Use a seal puller to remove the oil seal from the drum

ADJUSTMENT

1. Temporarily tighten the axle nut to 36 ft. lbs. (48 Nm), then turn the drum back and forth alternately several times to properly seat the bearing and ascertain bearing stability.

2. Turn back nut ⅛ to ¼ turn in order to obtain correct starting torque. Measure the starting force as shown.

✳✳WARNING

Starting force when measured at the hub bolt should be 1.87-3.20 lbs. (2.5-4 Nm) Make sure there is no free-play in the bearing.

3. Bend lockwasher.

4. After installing O-ring to drum cap, install cap to brake drum by lightly tapping with plastic hammer.

✳✳WARNING

Do not use a steel hammer on the drum cap and be sure to replace the old O-ring with a new one.

TRAILER TOWING

Subaru's are not recommended as trailer towing vehicles. Factory trailer towing packages are not available, and aftermarket towing hitches should not be installed on your Subaru.

TOWING

▶ **See Figures 75 and 76**

Whenever you are being towed, make sure that the chain or rope is sufficiently long and strong. Attach the chain securely at a point on the frame or tow hook, never on a steering or suspension part. On the Subaru ff-1 and the 1300G use the front crossmember to secure the tow chain. On all other models a towing hook is provided, both in front and back. Never try to start the vehicle while towing, it might run into the back of the towing vehicle. Do not allow too much slack to collect in the tow line, the towed vehicle could run over it and cause damage to one or both vehicles. If the distance to be traveled is less than six miles (9 km), your Subaru may be towed with the front wheels on the ground. If longer than six miles (9 km), are to be traveled, or if the transaxle or running gear is damaged the front wheels must be raised or dollied.

The following precautions should be observed when towing the vehicle:

1. Always place the transaxle in neutral and release the parking brake.

2. Always unlock the steering wheel. The steering column lock is not designed to hold the front wheels straight while the

vehicle is being towed, and damage to the lock or steering could occur.

3. If towing with a rope or chain, go slowly and keep as little slack in the line as possible. Remember safety first.

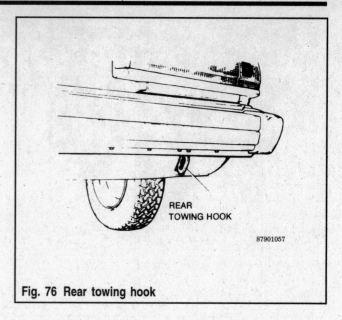

Fig. 76 Rear towing hook

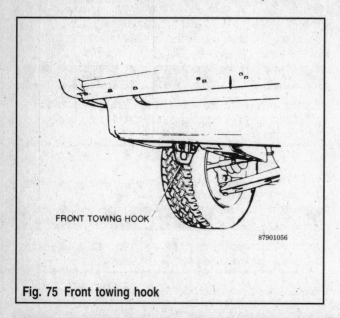

Fig. 75 Front towing hook

JACKING

▶ **See Figures 77, 78, 79, 80 and 81**

All Subaru models come with a scissors type jack for tire changing. The jack on all models is stored in the engine compartment, rather than in the trunk.

Jacking points are located on both sides of the vehicle, just behind the front wheel well and just forward of the rear wheel well. Do not place the jack underneath the floor pan sheet metal or bumpers.

There are certain safety precautions which should be observed when jacking the vehicle:

• Always jack the vehicle on a level surface.

• Set the parking brake if the rear wheels are to be raised (parking brake works on the front wheels). This will keep the vehicle from rolling off the jack.

• If the front wheels are to be raised, block the rear wheels.

• Block the wheel diagonally opposite the one which is being raised.

• If the vehicle is being raised in order to work underneath it, support it with jackstands. Do not place the jackstands against the sheet metal panels beneath the vehicle. The panels will become distorted.

✳✳CAUTION

Do not work beneath a vehicle supported only by a tire changing jack.

• Do not use a bumper jack to raise the vehicle. The bumpers are not designed for this purpose.

• When using a frame contact hoist, place wooden blocks that are at least 2 in. x 2 in. (12 x 12mm), between the hoist contact pads and the four lifting points of the vehicle.

✳✳CAUTION

Never place the contact hoist pads directly under the sheet metal panels beneath the vehicle or the panels will become distorted.

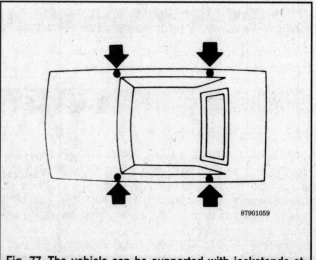

Fig. 77 The vehicle can be supported with jackstands at these points

When raising the front of the vehicle using a hydraulic jack always use the front crossmember as the contact point, never a suspension or steering part and never the engine oil pan. Always block the rear of the back wheels, and always use a block of wood between the saddle of the jack and the crossmember. When raising the rear of the vehicle using a hydraulic jack, place blocks in front of the front wheels and always place the jack in contact with the center of the rear crossmember. On four wheel drive models contact the bottom of the rear differential carrier. Always jack slowly until the vehicle is high enough to place the jackstands in their proper positions. The safety stands should be placed in the same location points as shown on the jacking point diagram. Make sure the stands are set on the flange of the side sill.

❊❊WARNING

Never work under a vehicle that is supported by a jack alone, always use jackstands. Never use cinder blocks or stacks of wood, even if you are only going to be under it for a few minutes.

Drive-on trestles or ramps are also handy and a safe way to both raise and support the vehicle.

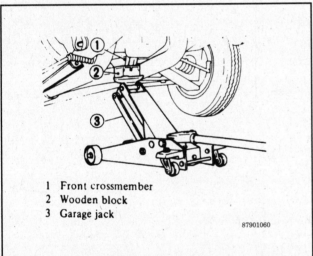

1 Front crossmember
2 Wooden block
3 Garage jack

87901060

Fig. 78 Jacking the front of the vehicle with a hydraulic jack — 1970-82 models

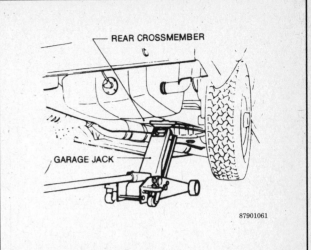

87901061

Fig. 79 Jacking up the rear of the vehicle with a hydraulic jack — 1970-82 models

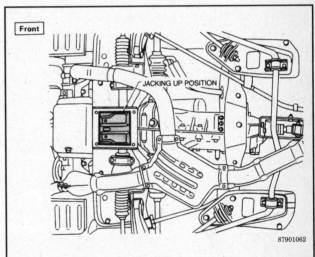

87901062

Fig. 80 Jacking up the front of the vehicle with a hydraulic jack — 1983-84 models

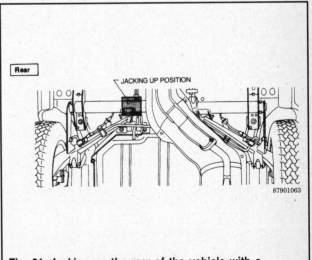

87901063

Fig. 81 Jacking up the rear of the vehicle with a hydraulic jack — 1983-84 models

JUMP STARTING

JUMP STARTING A DEAD BATTERY

▶ **See Figure 82**

The chemical reaction in a battery produces explosive hydrogen gas. This is the safe way to jump start a dead battery, reducing the chances of an accidental spark that could cause an explosion.

Jump Starting Precautions

- Be sure both batteries are of the same voltage.
- Be sure both batteries are of the same polarity (have the same grounded terminal, in most cases negative).
- Be sure the vehicles are not touching.
- Be sure that the vent cap holes are not obstructed.
- Do not smoke or allow sparks around the battery.
- In cold weather, check for frozen electrolyte in the battery.
- Do not allow electrolyte on your skin or clothing.
- Be sure the electrolyte is not frozen.

✳✳WARNING

Make sure that the ignition key, in the vehicle with the dead battery, is in the OFF position. Connecting cables to vehicles with on-board computers may result in computer destruction if the key is not in the OFF position.

Jump Starting Procedure

1. Determine voltage ratings of the two batteries; they must be the same.
2. Bring the starting vehicle close (they must not touch) so that the batteries can be reached easily.
3. Turn **OFF** all accessories and both engines. Put both cars in **NEUTRAL** or **PARK** and set the parking brake.
4. Cover the cell caps with a rag — do not cover terminals.
5. If the terminals on the run-down battery are heavily corroded, clean them.
6. Identify the positive and negative posts on both batteries and connect the cables in the order shown.
7. Start the engine of the starting vehicle and run it at fast idle. Try to start the car with the dead battery. Crank it for no more than 10 seconds at a time and let it cool off for 20 seconds in between tries.
8. If it doesn't start in 3 tries, it is likely that something else is wrong.
9. Disconnect the cables in the reverse order.
10. Install the cell covers and dispose of the rags.

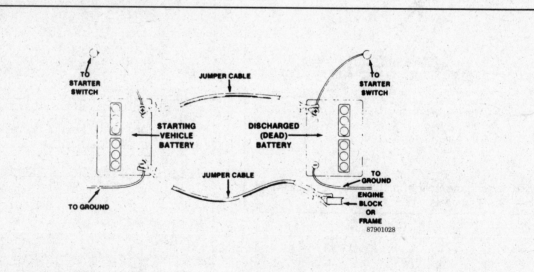

Fig. 82 Connect the battery cables as shown

HOW TO BUY A USED VEHICLE

▶ **See Figure 83**

Many people believe that a two or three year old used vehicle is a better buy than a new vehicle. This may be true. The new vehicle suffers the heaviest depreciation in the first two years, but is not old enough to present a lot of costly repair problems. Whatever the age of the used vehicle you might want to buy, this section and a little patience will help you select one that should be safe and dependable.

Tips

1. First decide what model you want, and how much you want to spend.

2. Check the used car lots and your local newspaper ads. Privately owned vehicles are usually less expensive, however you will not get a warranty that, in most cases, comes with a used vehicle purchased from a lot.

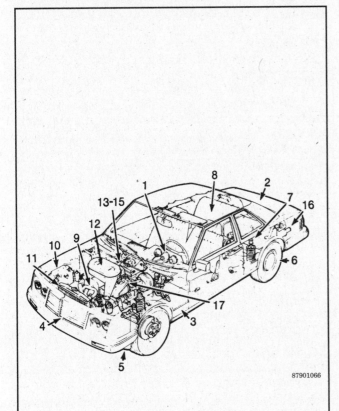

Fig. 83 You should check these points when buying a used car. The "Used Car Checklist" gives an explanation of the numbered items

87901066

3. Never shop at night. The glare of the lights make it easy to miss faults on the body caused by accident or rust repair.

4. Try to get the name and phone number of the previous owner. Contact him/her and ask about the vehicle. If the owner of the lot refuses this information, look for a vehicle somewhere else.

A private seller can tell you about the vehicle and maintenance. Remember, however, there's no law requiring honesty from private citizens selling used cars. There is a law that forbids the tampering with, or turning back of, the odometer mileage. This includes both the private citizen and the lot owner. The law also requires that the seller or anyone transferring ownership of the car must provide the buyer with a signed statement indicating the mileage on the odometer at the time of transfer.

5. Write down the year, model and serial number before you buy any used vehicle. Then dial 1-800-424-9393, the toll free number of the National Highway Traffic Safety Administration, and ask if the vehicle has ever been included on any manufacturer's recall list. If so, make sure the needed repairs were made.

6. Use the Used Car Checklist in this section and check all the items on the used car you are considering. Some items are more important than others. You know how much money you can afford for repairs, and, depending on the price of the vehicle, may consider doing any needed work yourself. Beware, however, of trouble in areas that will affect operation, safety or emission. Problems in the Used Car Checklist break down as follows:

1-9: Two or more problems in these areas indicate a lack of maintenance. You should beware.

9-13: Indicates a lack of proper care, however, these can usually be corrected with a tune-up or relatively simple parts replacement.

14-17: Problems in the engine or transaxle can be very expensive. Walk away from any vehicle with problems in both of these areas.

7. If you are satisfied with the apparent condition of the vehicle, take it to an independent diagnostic center or mechanic for a complete check. If you have a state inspection program, have it inspected immediately before purchase, or specify on the bill of sale that the sale is conditional on passing state inspection.

8. Road test the vehicle. Refer to the Road Test Checklist in this section. If your original evaluation and the road test agree, the rest is up to you.

Used Car Checklist

➡ **The numbers on the illustrations refer to the numbers on this checklist.**

1. Mileage: Average mileage is about 15,000 miles (24,000 km) per year. More than average mileage may indicate hard usage. 1975 and later catalytic converter equipped models may need converter service at 50,000 miles (80,000 km).

2. Paint: Check around the tailpipe, molding and windows for overspray indicating that the vehicle has been repainted.

3. Rust: Check fenders, doors, rocker panels, window moldings, wheelwells, floorboards, under floormats, and in the trunk for signs of rust. Any rust at all will be a problem. There is no way to check the spread of rust, except to replace the part or panel.

4. Body appearance: Check the moldings, bumpers, grille, vinyl roof, glass, doors, trunk lid and body panels for general overall condition. Check for misalignment, loose hold-down clips, ripples, scratches in glass, rips or patches in the top. Mismatched paint, welding in the trunk, severe misalignment of body panels or ripples may indicate crash work.

5. Leaks: Get down and look under the vehicle. There are no normal leaks, other than water from the air conditioning condenser.

6. Tires: Check the tire air pressure. A common trick is to pump the tire pressure up to make the vehicle roll easier. Check the tread wear, open the trunk and check the spare too. Uneven wear is a clue that the front end needs alignment. See the troubleshooting section for clues to the causes of tire wear.

7. Shock absorbers: Check the shock absorbers by forcing downward sharply on each corner of the vehicle. Good shocks will not allow the vehicle to bounce more than twice after you let go.

8. Interior: Check the entire interior. You're looking for an interior condition that agrees with the overall condition of the vehicle. Reasonable wear is expected, but be suspicious of new seatcovers on sagging seats, new pedal pads, and worn armrests. These indicate an attempt to cover up hard use. Pull back the carpets and look for evidence of water leaks or flooding. Look for missing hardware, door handles, control knobs, etc. Check lights and signal operations. Make sure all accessories (air conditioner, heater, radio, etc.) work. Check windshield wiper operation.

9. Belts and Hoses: Open the hood and check all belts and hoses for wear, cracks or weak spots.

10. Battery: Low electrolyte level, corroded terminals and/or cracked case indicate a lack of maintenance.

11. Radiator: Look for corrosion or rust in the coolant indicating a lack of maintenance.

12. Air filter: A dirty air filter usually means a lack of maintenance.

13. Ignition Wires: Check the ignition wires for cracks, burned spots, or wear. Worn wires will have to be replaced.

14. Oil level: If the oil level is low, chances are the engine uses oil or leaks. Beware of water in the oil (cracked block), excessively thick oil (used to quiet a noisy engine), or thin, dirty oil with a distinct gasoline smell (internal engine problems).

15. Automatic Transaxle: Pull the transaxle dipstick out when the engine is running. The level should read Full, and the fluid should be clear or bright red. Dark brown or black fluid that has distinct burnt odor, signals a transaxle in need of repair or overhaul.

16. Exhaust: Check the color of the exhaust smoke. Blue smoke indicates, among other problems, worn rings. Black smoke can indicate burnt valves or carburetor problems. Check the exhaust system for leaks. It can be expensive to replace.

17. Spark Plugs: Remove one of the spark plugs (the most accessible will do). An engine in good condition will show plugs with a light tan or gray deposit on the firing tip.

Road Test Check List

1. Engine Performance: The vehicle should be peppy whether cold or warm, with adequate power and good pickup. It should respond smoothly through the gears.

2. Brakes: They should provide quick, firm stops with no noise, pulling or brake fade.

3. Steering: Sure control with no binding, harshness, or looseness and no shimmy in the wheel should be expected. Noise or vibration from the steering wheel when turning the vehicle means trouble.

4. Clutch (Manual Transaxle): Clutch action should give quick, smooth response with easy shifting. The clutch pedal should have about 1-1½ in. (26mm), of free-play before it disengages the clutch. Start the engine, set the parking brake, put the transaxle in first gear and slowly release the clutch pedal. The engine should begin to stall when the pedal is ½ to ¾ of the way up.

5. Automatic Transaxle: The transaxle should shift rapidly and smoothly, with no noise, hesitation, or slipping

6. Differential: No noise or thumps should be present. Differentials have no normal leaks.

7. Driveshaft, Universal Joints: Vibration and noise could mean driveshaft problems. Clicking at low speed or coast conditions means worn U-joints.

8. Suspension: Try hitting bumps at different speeds. A vehicle that bounces has weak shock absorbers. Clunks mean worn bushings or ball joints.

9. Frame: Wet the tires and drive in a straight line. Tracks should show two straight lines, not four. Four tire tracks indicate a frame bent by collision damage. If the tires can't be wet for this purpose, have a friend drive along behind you and see if the vehicle appears to be traveling in a straight line.

Maintenance Interval Chart

Intervals are for number of months or thousands of miles, whichever comes first.

NOTE: *Heavy-duty operation (trailer towing, prolonged idling, severe stop and start driving, winter operation on salted roads or off-road use) should be accompanied by a 50% increase in maintenance. Cut the interval in half for these conditions. Operation in extremely dusty conditions may require immediate changes of engine oil and all filters.*

Maintenance	1970–71	1972–73	1974	1975–78	1979	1980–84
Air cleaner (Replace)	24	24	18	12	12	30 ①

PCV Valve
  Check
  Replace
	—
	
		—
		
			—
			
				12
				24
					12
					24
						12
						30

Carbon cannister filter	—	—	—	24	24	②
Belt tension (Adjust)	12	12	12	12	15	15
Engine oil (Change)	3	3	3	3	3	7.5
Engine oil filter (Change)	6	6	6	6	6	7.5
Fuel filter (Replace)	12	12	12	12	12	15
Manual transmission (Change)	24	24	24	24	24	30
Automatic transmission (Change)	—	—	—	24	24	30
Transaxle auto trans (Change)	—	—	—	24	24	30
Differential—4WD (Change)	—	—	—	24	24	30
Front and rear wheel bearing (Check and Repack)	24	24	24	24	24	30 ②
Engine coolant (Change)	12	12	24	24	24	30
Chassis lube linkage etc.	6	6	12	12	12	15
Rotate tires	3	3	3	3	3	③
Valve lash (Adjust)	6	6	12	12	12	15
Brake fluid (Change)	12	12	12	12	12	15

① Includes PCV filter and secondary air cleaner
② Inspect
③ As needed

87901C01

Capacities

Year	Model	Engine Displacement (cc)	Engine Crankcase (qts)		Transmission (pts)				Gasoline Tank (gals)	Cooling System (qts)
			With Filter	Without Filter	4-spd	5-spd	Auto	4WD		
1970–71	FF-1	1100	2.8	—	5.3	—	—	—	9.5	6.0
1971–72	1300G	1300	3.4	—	5.3	—	—	—	11.9 ①	6.0
1972	1300GL, DL	1300	3.4	—	5.4	—	—	—	13.2 ①	6.2
1973	1400 series	1400	3.5	—	5.4	—	—	—	13.2 ①	6.2
1974	1400 series	1400	3.5	3.2	5.4	—	—	—	13.2 ②	6.2
1975	1400 series	1400	3.8	3.5	5.2	5.8	12.5 ⑥	6.34 ③	13.2 ④	6.2
1976	1400 series	1400	3.8	3.5	5.2	5.8	—	6.34 ③	13.2 ④	6.3
	1600 series	1595	3.8	3.5	—	—	12.5 ⑥	—	13.2 ④	6.3
1977–79	1600 series	1595	3.8	3.5	5.2	5.8	12.5 ⑥	6.34 ③	13.2 ④	6.3
1980–82	1600 series	1595	3.8	3.5	5.8	5.8	12.5 ⑥	6.34 ③	13.2 ⑤	5.6
	1800 series	1781	3.8	3.5	5.8	5.8	12.5 ⑥	6.34 ③	13.2 ⑤	5.8
1982–84	1600 series	1595	4.2	—	5.8	5.8	10.8–12.6 ⑦	⑧	15.9 ⑨	5.6
	1800 series	1781	4.2	—	5.8	5.8	10.8–12.6 ⑦	⑧	15.9 ⑨	5.8
	1200 series	1200	3.0	1.9	—	2.1	—	—	9.2	4.5

① Station wagon; 9.5 gal
② Station wagon; 11.8 gal
③ 4WD rear differential; 1.7 pts
④ Station wagon and 4WD; 11.9 gal
⑤ 4WD vehicles; 11.9 gal
⑥ Refill is 6.4 pts—level with top mark on dipstick when warm, Automatic transmission differential; 2.5 pts
⑦ 4WD Automatic; 12.6–13.6

Automatic Differential; 2.6
4WD Rear Differential; 1.6
⑧ 4WD Manual 4 + 5 sp.; 6.4
4WD Rear Differential; 1.6
⑨ 4WD; 14.5
Regular Hatchback; 13.2
4WD Hatchback; 11.9

87901C06

2

ENGINE PERFORMANCE AND TUNE UP

TUNE-UP PROCEDURES

In order to extract the full measure of performance, economy and pleasure from your Subaru it is essential that it be properly tuned or inspected and checked at regular intervals. A regular tune-up will keep your car's engine running smoothly and will prevent the minor annoying breakdowns and poor performance associated with an untuned engine.

A complete tune-up should be performed on 1970-72 models every 6 months/6000 miles (10,000 km), whichever occurs first. On 1973-79 models, with the exception of some electronic ignition models, a tune-up should be performed every 12 months/12,000 miles (19,000 km). On 1980 and later models, and on some of the earlier electronic ignition models the time and mileage intervals between tune-ups has increased to 15 months/15,000 miles (24,000 km) for inspection of components and 30 months/30,000 miles (48,000 km) for spark plug replacement.

If the specifications on the tune-up sticker in the engine compartment of your Subaru disagree with the tune-up specifications in this section, the figures on the sticker must be used. The sticker often reflects changes made during the production run.

A complete tune-up consists of more than just checking spark plugs, ignition points, and condenser. A list of items to inspect and service, if necessary, while performing the tune-up follows. All of the listed services, adjustments and repairs are covered in various sections of this book. Check and service if required:

- Spark Plugs
- Spark Plug Wires
- Distributor Breaker Points
- Distributor Cap, Rotor and Condenser
- Operating Parts of the Distributor
- Distributor Vacuum Control
- Ignition Control System (Electronic)
- Ignition Timing
- Battery
- Belts
- Cooling System
- Engine Oil and Oil Filter
- Air Cleaner and PCV Valve
- Emission Control Devices
- Fuel Filter
- Carb Choke
- Carb Idle Speed and Mixture
- Vacuum Fittings, Hoses and Connections
- Hot Air System
- Engine Compression
- Intake Manifold Vacuum
- Cylinder Head and Intake Manifold Bolts
- Valve Clearances

Spark Plugs

Spark plugs ignite the air and fuel mixture in the cylinder as the piston reaches the top of the compression stroke. The controlled explosion that results forces the piston down, turning the crankshaft and the rest of the drive train.

The average life of a spark plug is 12,000 miles (19,000 km); 26,000-30,000 miles (42,000-48,000 km) in models with electronic ignition. This is, however, dependent on a number of factors:

- The mechanical condition of the engine
- The type of fuel
- The driving conditions
- The driver.

When you remove the spark plugs, check their condition. They are a good indicator of the condition of the engine. It is a good idea to remove the spark plugs every 6000 miles (10,000 km) to keep an eye on the mechanical state of the engine.

A small deposit of light tan, gray or rust red material on a spark plug that has been used for any period of time is to be considered normal. Any other color, or abnormal amounts of deposit, indicates that there is something amiss in the engine.

The gap between the center electrode and the side or ground electrode can be expected to increase not more than 0.001 in. (0.025mm) every 1000 miles (1100 km) under normal conditions.

When a spark plug is functioning normally or, more accurately, when the plug is installed in an engine that is functioning properly, the plugs can be taken out, cleaned, regapped, and reinstalled in the engine without doing the engine any harm.

When, and if, a plug fouls and begins to misfire, you will have to investigate, correct the cause of the fouling, and either clean or replace the plug.

There are several reasons why a spark plug will foul and you can learn which is at fault by just looking at the plug.

Spark plugs suitable for use in your Subaru's engine are offered in different heat ranges. The amount of heat which the plug absorbs is determined by the length of the lower insulator. The longer the insulator, the hotter the plug will operate. The shorter the insulator, the cooler it will operate. A spark plug that absorbs (or retains) little heat and remains to cool will accumulate deposits of oil and carbon, because it is not hot enough to burn them off. This leads to fouling and consequent misfiring. A spark plug that absorbs too much heat will have no deposits, but the electrodes will burn away quickly and, in some cases, preignition may result. Preignition occurs when the spark plug tips get so hot that they ignite the fuel/air mixture before the actual spark fires. This premature ignition will usually cause a pinging sound under conditions of low speed and heavy load. In severe cases, the heat may become high enough to start the fuel/air mixture burning throughout the combustion chamber rather than just to the front of the plug. In this case, the resultant explosion will be strong enough to damage pistons, rings, and valves.

In most cases the factory recommended heat range is correct. It is chosen to perform well under a wide range of operating conditions. However, if most of your driving is long distance, high speed travel, you may want to install a spark plug one step colder than standard. If most of your driving is of the short trip variety, when the engine may not always reach operating temperature, a hotter plug may help burn off the deposits normally accumulated under those conditions.

REMOVAL & INSTALLATION

▶ **See Figure 1**

1. Number the wires so that you won't cross them when you reinstall them.

2. Remove the wire from the end of the spark plug by grasping the wire by the rubber boot. If the boot sticks to the plug, remove it by twisting and pulling at the same time. Do not pull the wire itself or you will damage the core.

3. Use a $^{13}/_{16}$ in. spark plug socket to loosen all of the plugs about two turns.

✳✳WARNING

The cylinder head is cast from aluminum. Remove the spark plugs when the engine is cold, if possible, to prevent damage to the threads.

If removal of the plugs is difficult, apply a few drops of penetrating oil or silicone spray to the area around the base of the plug, and allow it a few minutes to work.

4. If compressed air is available, apply it to the area around the spark plug holes. Otherwise, use a rag or a brush to clean the area. Be careful not to allow any foreign material to drop into the spark plug holes.

5. Remove the plugs by unscrewing them the rest of the way from the engine.

To install:

6. Lubricate the threads of the spark plugs with a drop of oil. Install the plugs and hand-tighten them. Take care not to cross-thread them.

7. Tighten the spark plugs with the socket. Do not apply the same amount of force you would use for a bolt. Just snug them in. If a torque wrench is available, tighten to 11-15 ft. lbs. (14-20 Nm)

8. Install the wires on their respective plugs. Make sure the wires are firmly connected. You will be able to feel them click into place.

INSPECTION

▶ **See Figures 2 and 3**

Check the plugs for deposits and wear. If they are not going to be replaced, clean the plugs thoroughly. Remember that any kind of deposit will decrease the efficiency of the plug. Plugs can be cleaned on a spark plug cleaning machine, which can sometimes be found in service stations, or you can do an acceptable job of cleaning with a stiff brush. If the plugs are cleaned, the electrodes must be filed flat. Use an ignition points file, not an emery board or the like, which will leave deposits. The electrodes must be filed perfectly flat with sharp edges. Rounded edges reduced the spark plug voltage by as much as 50%.

Check spark plug gap before installation. The ground electrode must be parallel to the center electrode and the specified size wire gauge should pass through the gap with a slight drag. Always check the gap on new plugs, too. They are not always correctly set at the factory. Do not use a flat feeler gauge when measuring the gap, because the reading will be inaccurate. Wire gapping tools usually have a bending tool attached. Use that to adjust the side electrode until the proper distance is obtained. Absolutely never bend the center electrode. Also, be careful not to bend the side electrode too far or too often. It may weaken and break off within the engine, requiring removal of the cylinder head to retrieve it.

Spark Plug Wires

At every tune-up, visually inspect the spark plug cables for burns, cuts, or breaks in the insulation. Check the boots and the nipples on the distributor cap and coil. Replace any damaged wiring.

Every 36,000 miles (58,000 km) or so, the resistance of the wires should be checked with an ohmmeter. Wires with excessive resistance will cause misfiring, and may make the engine difficult to start in damp weather. Generally, the useful life of the cables is 36,000-50,000 miles (57,000-80,000 km).

TCCS1212

Fig. 1 A variety of tools and gauges are needed for spark plug service

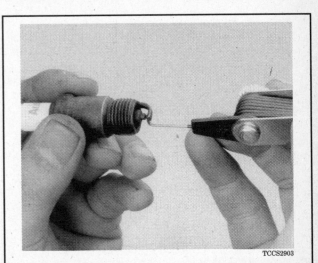

TCCS2903

Fig. 2 Always use a wire gauge to check the electrode gap

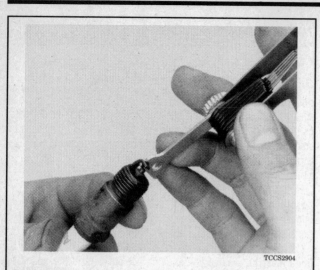

Fig. 3 Adjust the electrode gap by bending the side electrode

To check resistance, remove the distributor cap, leaving the wires attached. Connect one lead of an ohmmeter to an electrode within the cap. Connect the other lead to the corresponding spark plug terminal (remove it from the plug for this test). Replace any wire which shows a resistance over 50,000Ω. Generally speaking, however, resistance should not be over 30,000Ω, and 50,000Ω must be considered the outer limit of acceptability. Test the high tension lead from the coil by connecting the ohmmeter between the center contact in the distributor cap and either of the primary terminals of the coil. If resistance is more than 25,000Ω, remove the cable from the coil and check the resistance of the cable alone. Anything over 15,000Ω is cause for replacement. It should be remembered that resistance is also a function of length; the longer the cable, the greater the resistance. Thus, if the cables on your car are longer than the factory originals, resistance will be higher, quite possibly outside these limits.

REMOVAL & INSTALLATION

▶ **See Figure 4**

➡**To avoid confusion, tag and replace the spark plug wires one at a time.**

To remove the wires, twist and pull the boot off of the spark plug and distributor terminal.

Start by replacing the longest one first. Install the boot firmly over the spark plug. Route the wire over the same path as the original. Insert the nipple firmly into the tower on the cap or the coil.

Fig. 4 Tag and replace the wires one at a time

FIRING ORDER

▶ **See Figure 5**

To avoid confusion, remove and tag the wires one at a time, for replacement.

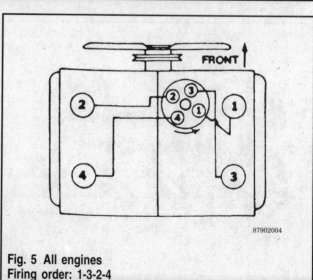

Fig. 5 All engines
Firing order: 1-3-2-4
Distributor rotation: Counterclockwise

POINT TYPE IGNITION

▶ **See Figure 6**

➡Point type ignition systems were used from 1970-77 on California models and 1970-79 on all other models. Electronic ignition systems were introduced to the California models in 1977 and all other models in 1980.

The points function as a circuit breaker for the primary circuit of the ignition system. The ignition coil must boost the 12 volts of electrical pressure supplied by the battery to as much as 25,000 volts in order to fire the plugs. To do this, the coil depends on the points and the condenser to make a clean break in the primary circuit.

The coil has both primary and secondary circuits. When the ignition is turned on, the battery supplies voltage through the coil and onto the points. The points are connected to ground, completing the primary circuit. As the current passes through the coil, a magnetic field is created in the iron center core of the coil. When the cam in the distributor turns, the points open, breaking the primary circuit. The magnetic field in the primary circuit of the coil then collapses and cuts through the secondary circuit windings around the iron core. Because of the physical principle called electromagnetic induction, the battery voltage is increased to a level sufficient to fire the spark plugs.

When the points open, the electrical charge in the primary circuit tries to jump the gap created between the two open contacts of the points. If this electrical charge were not transferred elsewhere, the metal contacts of the points when they open and thus prevent the points from becoming pitted or burned.

Breaker Points and Condenser

INSPECTION

1. Disconnect the high tension wire from the top of the distributor and the coil.

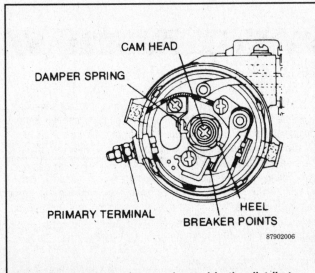

CAM HEAD

DAMPER SPRING

PRIMARY TERMINAL

HEEL
BREAKER POINTS

87902006

Fig. 6 The breaker points are located in the distributor

2. The distributor cap is retained by two spring clips. Insert a screwdriver under their ends and release them. Lift off the cap with the spark plug wires attached. Inspect the inside of the cap. Wipe it clean with a rag and check for burned contacts, cracks and carbon tracks. A carbon track shows as a dark line running from one terminal to another. It cannot be successfully removed, so replace the cap if it has one of these. Generally, a cap and rotor will last 36,000 miles (58,000 km).

3. Remove the rotor from the distributor shaft by pulling it straight up. Examine the condition of the rotor. If it is cracked or the metal tip is excessively worn or burned, it should be replaced. Clean the metal tip with a clean cloth, but don't file it.

4. Pry open the contacts of the points with a screwdriver and check the condition of the contacts. If they are excessively worn, burned or pitted, they should be replaced.

5. If the points are in good condition, adjust them and reinstall the rotor and the distributor cap. If the points need to be replaced, follow the replacement procedure given next.

REMOVAL & INSTALLATION

1. Remove the cap and rotor. Clean the cap and rotor with alcohol, or wipe them clean with a rag.

2. Remove the two Phillips screws that secure the points to the breaker plate.

3. Remove the condenser terminal lead and the ground lead from the points.

4. Remove the screw which secures the condenser to the outside of the distributor body. Remove the condenser lead from the terminal.

➡**Always replace the condenser when replacing the points.**

To install:

5. Install a new condenser and connect the ground lead from the points and the the condenser terminal lead.

6. Install new points, but do not fully tighten the securing screws.

7. To adjust the point gap, rotate the crankshaft until the contact heel of the points rests on a high point of the distributor cam.

➡**If doing a complete tune-up, it is easier to turn the crankshaft with the spark plugs removed.**

8. Place a flat head screwdriver between the outer wall of the distributor and the bottom plate of the points so that the contacts can be opened by turning the screwdriver.

9. Place a feeler gauge of the proper thickness between the breaker points and adjust the points so that a slight drag is felt when the feeler gauge is removed. Tighten the Phillips head screws, being careful not to lose the proper point gap.

10. Recheck the gap after tightening.

11. Lubricate the cam surface, rubbing block, arm pivot, and distributor shaft with distributor grease, which is available from auto supply stores.

12. Reinstall the rotor and distributor cap, making sure that the spark plug wires are installed tightly on the top of the cap.

DWELL ADJUSTMENT

▶ **See Figure 7**

The dwell angle is the number of degrees of distributor cam rotation through which the points remain closed (conducting electricity). Increasing the point gap decreases dwell, while decreasing the gap increases dwell.

The dwell angle may be checked with the distributor cap and rotor installed and the engine running, or with the cap and rotor removed and the engine cranking at starter speed. The meter gives a constant reading with the engine running. With the engine cranking, the meter will fluctuate between zero degrees dwell and the maximum figure for that setting. Never attempt to adjust the points when the ignition is on, or you may receive a shock.

1. Connect a meter as per the manufacturer's instructions (usually one lead to the distributor's terminal of the coil and the other lead to a ground). Zero the meter, if necessary.

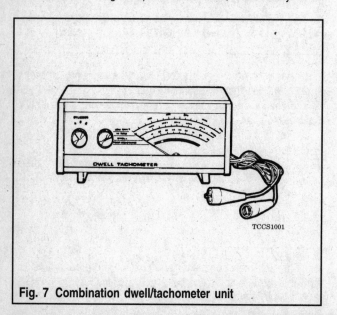

TCCS1001

Fig. 7 Combination dwell/tachometer unit

2. Check the dwell by either the cranking method, or with the engine running. If the setting is incorrect, the points must be adjusted.

❊❊CAUTION

Keep your hands, hair and clothing clear of the engine fan and pulleys. Be sure the wires from the dwell meter are routed out of the way. If the engine is running, block the front wheels, put the transmission in Neutral, and set the parking brake.

3. To change the dwell angle, turn the ignition off, loosen the points hold-down screw and adjust the point gap; increase the gap to decrease dwell, and vice-versa. Tighten the hold-down screw and check the dwell angle with the engine cranking. If it seems to be correct, replace the cap and rotor and check dwell with the engine running. Readjust as necessary.

4. Run the engine speed up to about 2000 rpm, and then let the speed drop abruptly. The dwell reading should not change. If it does, a worn distributor shaft, bushing or cam, or a worn breaker plate is indicated. The parts must be inspected and replaced, if necessary.

5. Ignition timing must be checked after adjusting the point gap, as a 1° increase in dwell results in an ignition timing retard of 2°.

ELECTRONIC IGNITION

Description & Operation

▶ **See Figures 8 and 9**

The breakerless ignition system was introduced on the California models in 1977, and all other models in 1980.

The electronic ignition differs from its conventional counterpart only in the distributor component area. The secondary side of the ignition system is the same as a conventional breaker points system.

Located in the distributor, in addition to the normal ignition rotor, is a four spoke rotor (reluctor) which rests on the distributor shaft where the breaker points cam is found on earlier systems. A pick-up coil, consisting of a magnet, coil, and wiring, rests on the breaker plate next to the reluctor. The system also uses a transistor ignition unit mounted above the ignition coil on the fender well.

When a reluctor spoke is not aligned with the pick-up coil, it generates large lines of flux between itself, the magnet, and the pick-up coil. This large flux variation results in a high generated voltage in the pick-up coil. When a reluctor spoke lines up with the pick-up coil, the flux variation is low. Thus, zero voltage is generated, allowing current to flow to the pick-up coil. Ignition primary current is then cut off by the electronic unit, allowing the field in the ignition coil to collapse, inducing high secondary voltage in the conventional manner. The high voltage then flows through the distributor to the spark plug, as usual.

Because no points or condenser are used, and because dwell is determined by the electronic unit, no adjustments are

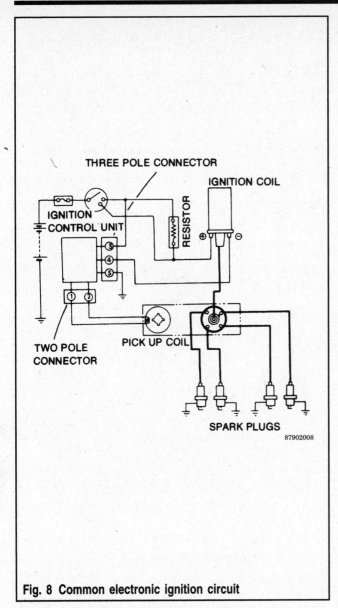

Fig. 8 Common electronic ignition circuit

necessary. Ignition timing is checked in the usual way, but unless the distributor is disturbed it is not likely to ever change very much.

Service consists of inspection of the distributor cap, rotor, and ignition wires, replacing when necessary. These parts can be expected to last for at least 30,000 miles (48,000 km). In addition, the reluctor air gap should be checked periodically.

Diagnosis and Testing

BALLAST RESISTOR

The ballast resistor is mounted on the coil bracket above the ignition coil.

1. With the ignition switch **OFF**, connect an ohmmeter between the terminals of the resistor.

2. Obtain a reading from the ohmmeter and compare it with the specs on the Troubleshooting Electronic Ignition chart in this section.

3. If the reading on the ohmmeter is zero or not within specs, replace the resistor.

PICKUP COIL

1. Unplug the primary ignition wire connector. Connect an ohmmeter between the two prongs of the connector on the distributor side. If the connector has three prongs, connect the ohmmeter to the top single prong and the left double prong (with the connector facing you and the single prong on top).

2. Compare the resistance reading with the values shown in the troubleshooting charts.

AIR GAP

1. The distributor cap is held on by two clips. Release them with a screwdriver and lift the cap straight up and off, with the wires attached. Inspect the cap for cracking, carbon tracks or a worn center contact. Replace it (if necessary) by transferring the wires one at a time from the old cap to the new one.

2. To remove the rotor, pull it straight. Replace it if its contacts are worn, burned or pitted. **DO NOT** file the contacts.

3. Check the reluctor air gap. Using a non-magnetic feeler gauge, rotate the engine until a reluctor spoke is aligned with the pick-up coil (either bump the engine around with the starter or turn it with a wrench on the crankshaft pulley bolt).

4. Adjustment, if necessary, is made by loosening the pickup coil mounting screws (1600 and 1800-2WD) or the stator screw (1600 and 1800-4WD; 1200) and shifting its position, on the "breaker plate", either closer or farther from the reluctor. Tighten the screws and recheck the gap. The air gap specifications are: 0.008-0.016 in. (0.20-0.40mm) on 1600 and 1800 w/2WD; carbureted, 0.012-0.020 in. (0.30-0.50mm) on 1600 and 1800 w/4WD; EFI models or 0.012-0.016 in. (0.30-0.40mm) on 1200 models.

5. Inspect the ignition wires for cracks or brittleness. Replace them one at a time to prevent cross-wiring, carefully press the replacement wires into place. The cores of wires used with electronic ignition are more susceptible to breakage than those of standard wires, so treat them gently.

Parts Replacement

PICKUP COIL

1977-81 Models

1. Remove the distributor cap by releasing the two spring clips. Remove the rotor by pulling straight up and off of the shaft.

2. Disengage the distributor wiring harness connector. Remove the screws fastening the harness to the distributor.

3. Unfasten the two pickup coil mounting screws and remove the pickup coil.

4. Install the new pickup coil in the reverse order.

5. Do not tighten the pickup coil mounting screws until you have adjusted the air gap.

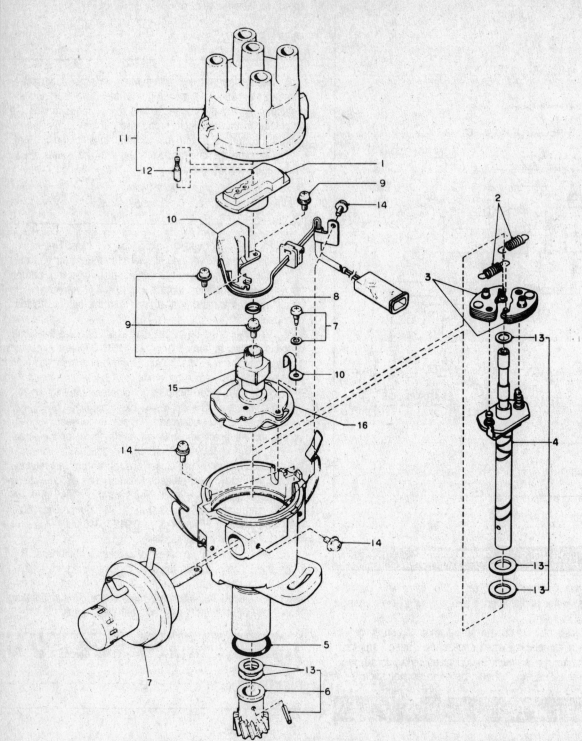

1. Rotor
2. Governor spring set
3. Weight
4. Shaft & governor assembly
5. O-ring
6. Pinion set
7. Vacuum controller assembly
8. Dust proof packing
9. Contact breaker plate assembly
10. Pick-up coil set
11. Cap
12. Carbon point
13. Thrust washer
14. Screw & washer
15. Reluctor
16. Pick-up coil base

87903004

Fig. 9 Common electronic ignition distributor used on models covered by this manual

1982-84 2WD Models

1. Remove the distributor cap, rotor and dust seal.

2. Dismount the vacuum control by first removing the retaining clip from the breaker plate and then the mounting screw to the distributor.

3. Remove the two dust covers protecting the pickup coil and control unit.

4. Remove the two screws retaining the pickup coil assembly to the breaker plate.

5. Remove the two screws mounting the ignition control unit to the distributor. Slide the wiring grommet out of the side of the distributor and disconnect the wiring at the connector.

To install:

6. Mount the ignition control unit and then the pickup coil (with mounting screws loose).

7. Adjust the air gap to 0.008-0.016 in. (0.20-0.40mm) with a non-metallic feeler gauge. Then, tighten screws.

8. Install the two dust covers.

9. Install the vacuum control unit by first engaging the retaining clip and fastening the mounting screw.

10. Install the dust seal, rotor and distributor cap.

4WD Models

NON-TURBOCHARGED

▶ **See Figure 10**

1. Remove the distributor cap, rotor and dust shield.

2. Unmount the vacuum control by removing the mounting screws.

3. Unplug the wire connectors from the control unit. Remove the wires and mounting grommet from the groove in the side of the distributor. Remove the dust seal.

4. Use a small gear puller and lift the reluctor up off the rotor shaft. Be careful to retain the roll pin that retains the reluctor.

5. Loosen and remove the screws that mount the pickup coil and control unit. Remove the control unit and pick-up coil.

To install:

6. Install the control unit and pick-up coil (with mounting screws loose).

7. Install the reluctor on the rotor shaft and install the roll pin.

8. Loosen stator mounting screws, adjust the air gap to 0.012-0.020 in. (0.30-0.50mm), and tighten the mounting screws.

9. Install the dust seal, mounting grommet and the wires. Engage the wire connectors to the control unit.

10. Mount the vacuum control and fasten the screws.

11. Install the dust shield, rotor and distributor cap.

TURBOCHARGED

▶ **See Figure 10**

1. Disconnect the negative battery cable and remove the cap and rotor. Then, unfasten and remove the screw connecting the vacuum controller rod to the breaker plate.

2. Unfasten and remove the screw attaching the vacuum controller to the distributor housing, and remove the controller.

3. Disconnect the wiring connectors at the igniter unit. Remove the screw which attaches the grommet to the distributor, and then slide the wiring grommet up and out of the distributor.

4. Using a flat bladed screwdriver under either side of the reluctor resting against the edge of the distributor body, gently force the reluctor off the top of the distributor shaft. Make sure you don't drop the roll pin that keeps the reluctor from turning on the shaft as you do this! Remove the reluctor and pin from the distributor.

5. Remove the two retaining screws from the igniter unit, and then remove the igniter unit and the two spacers underneath from the distributor.

To install:

6. Install the two spacers and the igniter unit, fasten the two retaining screws.

7. Install the reluctor on the distributor shaft and install the roll pin. When installing the reluctor and roll pin, make sure to position the pin with the cutout portion of the pin parallel to the cutout portion of the top of the rotor shaft.

8. Install the wiring grommet and fasten the retaining screw. Engage the wiring connectors at the igniter unit.

9. Measure the air gap between the stator and one of the reluctor prongs with a nonmetallic feeler gauge. You'll have to turn the engine over so one of the prongs on the reluctor lines

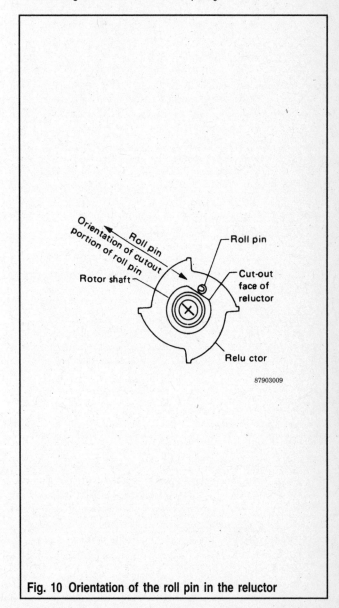

87903009

Fig. 10 Orientation of the roll pin in the reluctor

up with one of the vertical prongs on the stator. The clearance must be 0.012-0.020 in. (0.30-0.50mm) If not, loosen the stator mounting screws, shift the position of the stator, and retighten. Repeat this operation until the clearance is within the specified range.

IGNITION TIMING

General Information

Ignition timing is the measurement, in degrees of crankshaft rotation, of the point at which the spark plugs fire in each of the cylinders. It is measured in degrees before or after Top Dead Center (TDC) of the compression stroke.

Because it takes a fraction of a second for the spark plug to ignite the mixture in the cylinder, the spark plug must fire a little before the piston reaches TDC. Otherwise, the mixture will not be completely ignited as the piston passes TDC and the full power of the explosion will not be used by the engine.

The timing measurement is given in degrees of crankshaft rotation before the piston reaches TDC (BTDC). If the setting for the ignition timing is 8° BTDC, the spark plug must fire 8° before each piston reaches TDC. This only holds true, however, when the engine is at idle speed.

As the engine speed increases, the pistons go faster. The spark plugs have to ignite the fuel even sooner if it is to be completely ignited when the piston reaches TDC. To do this, the distributor has two means to advance the timing of the spark as the engine speed increases: a set of centrifugal weights within the distributor, and a vacuum diaphragm, mounted on the side of the distributor.

If the ignition is set too far advanced (BTDC), the ignition and expansion of the fuel in the cylinder will occur too soon and tend to force the piston down while it is still traveling up. This causes engine ping. If the ignition spark is set too far retarded, after TDC (ATDC), the piston will have already passed TDC and started on its way down when the fuel is ignited. This will cause the piston to be forced down for only a portion of its travel. This will result in poor engine performance and lack of power.

On the carbureted and the MPFI 1600 and 1800 engines, the ignition timing marks are located on the edge of the flywheel, at the rear of the engine. The marks mounted on the flywheel are visible through a port in the flywheel housing located just behind the dipstick. A plastic cover protects the port through which the flywheel-mounted marks are visible.

The ignition timing marks, on the turbocharged (1800) engine, are located on the front right-side near the crankshaft pulley.

The ignition timing marks, on the carbureted 1200 engine, are located on the crankshaft pulley at the front of the engine.

Timing marks consist of a scale of degrees on the flywheel and a pointer on the flywheel cover hole. The scale corresponds to the position of the flywheel and a pointer on the flywheel cover hole. The scale corresponds to the position of the piston in the number 1 cylinder. A stroboscopic (dynamic) timing light is used, which is hooked into the circuit of the No.

10. Install the vacuum controller to the distributor shaft and fasten the retaining screw.

11. Fasten the screw attaching the vacuum control to the breaker plate and install install the rotor and distributor cap.

12. Connect the negative battery cable.

1 cylinder spark plug. Every time the spark plug fires, the timing light flashes. By aiming the timing light at the timing marks, the exact position of the piston within the cylinder can be read, since the stroboscopic flash makes the mark appear to be standing still. Proper timing is indicated when the pointer is aligned with the correct number on the scale.

There are three basic types of timing light available. The first is a simple neon bulb with two wire connections (one for the spark plug and one for the plug wire, connecting the light in series). This type of light is quite dim, and must be held closely to the marks to be seen, but it is inexpensive. The second type of light operates from the car battery. Two alligator clips connect to the battery terminals, while a third wire connects to the spark plug with an adapter. This type of light is more expensive, but the xenon bulb provides a nice bright flash which can even be seen in sunlight. The third type replaces the battery source with 110 volt house current. Some timing lights have other functions built into them, such as dwell meters, tachometers, or remote starting switches. These are convenient, in that they reduce the tangle of wires under the hood, but may duplicate the functions of tools you already have.

If your Subaru has electronic ignition, you should use a timing light with an inductive pickup. This pickup simply clamps onto the No. 1 plug wire, eliminating the adapter. It is not susceptible to crossfiring or false triggering, which may occur with a conventional light, due to the greater voltages produced by electronic ignition.

INSPECTION & ADJUSTMENT

◆ See Figures 11, 12, 13, 14 and 15

➡An inductive timing light is recommended because it is not susceptible to cross-firing or false triggering.

1. After cleaning the timing marks, connect a timing light to the ignition system following the manufacturer's instruction.

2. If equipped with a carburetor, disconnect and plug the distributor vacuum advance line. If equipped with a turbocharger, disconnect the black (8-pole) electrical connector between the distributor and the knock control unit. On turbocharged engines, disconnect the pressure-vacuum line running from the throttle body to the distributor and plug it. If the engine has an octane selector, make sure it's set midway between A and R.

3. Start the engine, allow it to reach normal operating temperature and aim the timing light at the timing marks on the flywheel or the crankshaft pulley. The correct timing mark should align with the timing mark indicator.

Fig. 11 Connect the inductive clamp over the spark plug wire

Fig. 12 Some models use flywheel mounted timing marks . . .

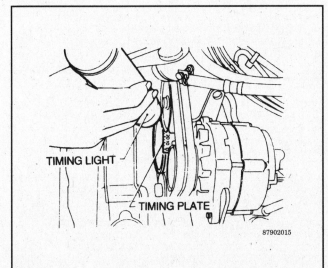

Fig. 13 . . . while others are on the crankshaft pulley

4. If necessary to adjust the ignition timing, loosen the distributor hold-down bolt, then rotate the distributor clockwise to advance or counterclockwise to retard the timing.

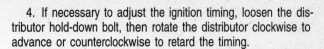

※※WARNING

Do not fully remove the hold-down bolt when adjusting the timing.

5. After adjustment, tighten the distributor bolt and recheck the ignition timing.

➡If equipped with a carburetor, reconnect the distributor vacuum advance line. If equipped with a turbocharger, reconnect the black (8-pole) electrical connector between the distributor and the knock control unit.

6. Connect any removed vacuum or pressure lines.
7. Recheck the engine idle speed and adjust if necessary.

Fig. 14 Aim a timing light at the timing marks on the crankshaft or pulley

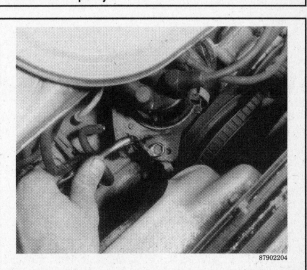

Fig. 15 If necessary, loosen the distributor hold-down bolt and adjust the timing

Octane Selector

The octane selector is used as a fine adjustment to match the vehicle's timing to the grade of fuel being used. The octane selector is located on the distributor retaining plate. It consists of a scale on the plate, a bolt and a pointer.

ADJUSTMENT

➡**There is no octane selector on 1974 and later models.**

1. Center the pointer in the scale, so that it is midway between A (Advance) and R (Retard). Tighten the pointer bolt.

2. Drive the car at about 14 mph (22 kph) in Fourth gear on a level road.

3. Depress the accelerator pedal to the floor. A slight knocking sound should be heard. As the speed increases, the noise should rapidly go away.

4. If the knocking sound is loud or if it fails to disappear as speed increases, retard the timing by loosening the pointer bolt and turning the distributor so that the R (Retard) moves toward the pointer.

5. If there is no knocking sound at all, loosen the pointer bolt and turn the distributor so that the A (Advance) moves toward the pointer.

6. After completing the adjustment, retighten the pointer bolt and recheck the car.

VALVE LASH

General Information

Valve adjustment determines how far the valves enter the cylinder and how long they stay open and closed.

If the valve clearance is too large, part of the lift of the camshaft will be used in removing the excessive clearance. Consequently, the valve will not be opening for as long as it should. This condition has two effects: the valve train components will emit a tapping sound as they take up the excessive clearance and the engine will perform poorly because the valves don't open fully and allow the proper amount of gases to flow into and out of the engine. The carburetion may also be too rich.

If the valve clearance is too small, the intake valves and the exhaust valves will open too far and they will not fully seat on the cylinder head when they close. When a valve seats itself on the cylinder head, it does two things: it seals the combustion chamber so that none of the gases in the cylinder escape and it cools itself by transferring some of the heat it absorbs from the combustion in the cylinder to the cylinder head and to the engine's cooling system. If the valve clearance is too small, the engine will run poorly because of the gases escaping from the combustion chamber. It may also run too lean. The valves will also become overheated and will warp, since they cannot transfer heat unless they are touching the valve seat in the cylinder head.

❊❊WARNING

While all valve adjustments must be made as accurately as possible, it is better to have the valve adjustment slightly loose than slightly tight, as a burned valve may result from overly tight adjustments.

ADJUSTMENTS

▶ **See Figures 16, 17 and 18**

➡**The 1983-84 (OHV) 1800 engine with automatic transmission use hydraulic lash adjusters; no periodic adjustment is necessary.**

The valve lash should be checked and adjusted, if necessary, after the first 1000 miles (1100 km) of operation and then every 6 months/6000 miles (10,000 km) on 1970-73 models; every 12 months/12,000 miles (19,000 km) on 1974-79 models and every 15 months/15,000 miles (24,000 km) on 1980 and later models.

Before adjusting the valves, make sure the cylinder head nuts/bolts are tightened to the proper specifications. Refer to Section 3

1. Rotate the engine so that the No. 1 piston is at Top Dead Center (TDC) of its compression stroke. To determine TDC, remove the distributor cap and the plastic flywheel housing dust cover (normally aspirated engines only). The No. 1 piston is at top dead center when the distributor rotor is pointing to the No. 1 spark plug lead terminal (as though the distributor cap were in place) and the 0 mark on the flywheel or front pulley is opposite the pointer on the housing or front cover.

2. Check the clearance of both the intake and exhaust valves of the No. 1 cylinder by inserting a feeler gauge between each valve stem and rocker arm. See the Tune-Up Specifications chart for the proper stem-to-rocker arm clearance.

3. If the clearance is not within specifications, loosen the locknut with the proper size metric box wrench and turn the adjusting stud either in or out until the valve clearance is correct. The stud should just touch the gauge. Don't clamp the gauge tightly between the stud and head of the valve.

4. Tighten the locknut and recheck the valve stem-to-rocker clearance.

5. The rest of the valves are adjusted in the same way. Bring each piston to TDC of its compression stroke, then check and adjust the valves for that cylinder. The proper valve adjustment sequence is 1-3-2-4, which is the firing order.

6. To bring the No. 3 piston to TDC of its compression stroke, rotate the crankshaft 180° and make sure that the distributor rotor is pointing to the No. 3 spark plug terminal. Rotate the crankshaft 180° after each valve adjustment before going on to the next adjustment.

7. When the valve adjustment is complete, install the distributor cap, the valve covers with new gaskets and the dust cover on the flywheel housing port.

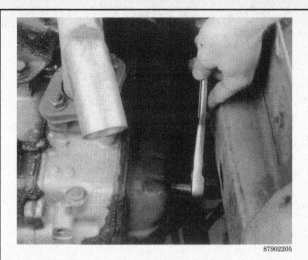

Fig. 16 Remove the valve covers from both sides of the engine

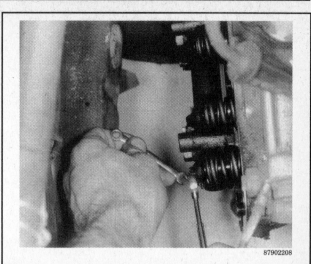

Fig. 18 If the clearance is not within specifications, loosen the locknut and turn the adjusting stud

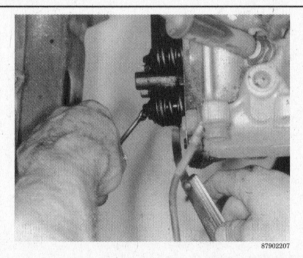

Fig. 17 Check the clearance of the valves by inserting a feeler gauge between each valve stem and rocker arm

IDLE SPEED AND MIXTURE ADJUSTMENTS

Carbureted Engines

▶ See Figures 19 and 20

This section contains only tune-up adjustment procedures for carburetors. Descriptions, adjustments, and overhaul procedures for carburetors can be found in the Fuel System section.

When the engine in your Subaru is running, the air-fuel mixture from the carburetor is being drawn into the engine by a partial vacuum which is created by the movement of the pistons downward on the intake stroke. The amount of air-fuel mixture that enters into the engine is controlled by the throttle plates in the bottom of the carburetor. The throttle plates are connected by the throttle linkage to the accelerator pedal in the passenger compartment of the Subaru. When you depress the pedal, you open the throttle plates in the carburetor to admit more air-fuel mixture to the engine.

When the engine is idling, it is necessary to have the throttle plates open slightly. To prevent having to hold your foot on the pedal when the engine is idling, an idle speed adjusting screw is added to the carburetor linkage.

The idle adjusting screw contacts a lever (throttle lever) on the outside of the carburetor. When the screw is turned, it either opens or closes the throttle plates of the carburetor, raising or lowering the idle speed of the engine. This screw is called the curb idle adjusting screw.

A special mixture circuit is incorporated into the carburetor to enable the engine to run smoothly at idle. This circuit is controlled by the mixture screw, which determines the amount of fuel admitted at idle.

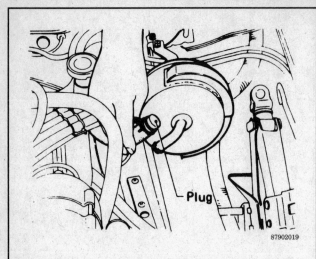

Fig. 19 Plug secondary air cleaner hose and/or purge hose

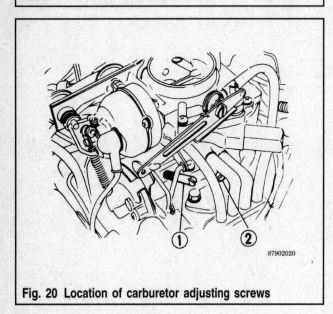

Fig. 20 Location of carburetor adjusting screws

IDLE SPEED & MIXTURE

1. Run the engine and allow it to reach normal operating temperature.

2. Stop the engine and connect a tachometer in accordance with the manufacturer's instructions.

3. Then, do one of the following:

   a. On ff-1 and 1300G models which have air injection (air pump), disconnect the air hoses from the air distribution manifolds. Plug the hoses and the manifold openings.

   b. On other models, disconnect and plug the hose that runs to the distributor vacuum retard unit, if equipped.

   c. Models that have a secondary air cleaner, or purge valve and hose: Remove and plug the hose that connects to the engine.

4. Remove the air cleaner by disconnecting the emission control system hoses from it, unfastening the wing nut(s), and removing the screws which secure it to its mounting brackets.

5. Check proper idle speed in Tune-Up Specifications chart and adjust to that setting by turning the throttle adjusting screw.

➡**On late model California cars the mixture screws may be capped. If this is the case there is no adjustment necessary.**

6. Continue adjusting the idle, this time by means of the throttle adjusting screw and the idle mixture adjusting screw, until a reading of 50 rpm above the proper idle setting is attained.

➡**The idle mixture adjusting screw should have a plastic limiter cap on it. All adjustments must be made within the range of this cap or exhaust emissions will be increased. Do not remove the cap.**

7. Then, turn the idle mixture adjusting screw clockwise until the idle speed drops to the figure given in the Tune-Up Specifications chart.

➡**Following this procedure should keep the carbon monoxide (CO) emission level within pollution law standards. However, it is a good idea to have the CO level checked by a qualified technician with an exhaust analyzer whenever a tune-up is performed.**

8. Disconnect the tachometer. Reconnect any hoses that were removed. Install the air cleaner.

Fuel Injected Models

There are no routine mixture or idle speed adjustments necessary on fuel injected models.

Tune-Up Specifications

When analyzing compression test results, look for uniformity among cylinders, rather than specific pressures.

Year	Engine Displacement (cc)	Spark Plugs Type	Gap (in.)	Point Dwell (deg)	Point Gap (in.)	Ignition Timing (deg)	Intake Valve Opens (deg)	Fuel Pump Pressure (psi)	Idle Speed (rpm)	In	Ex
1970	EA61 (1100)	B6E	.030	49–55	.020	TDC @ 850	20B	—	850	.009	.011
1971	EA61 (1100)	BP6ES	.030	49–55	.020	TDC @ 850	20B	—	850	.009	.011
	EA62 (1300)	BP6ES	.030	49–55	.020	TDC @ 750	24B	—	750	.013	.013
1972	EA62 (1300)	BP6ES	.032	49–55	.020	6B @ 800	24B	—	800	.013	.013
1973–74	EA63 (1400)	BP6ES	.032	49–55	.020	6B @ 800	24B	1.8–2.6	800	.013	.013
1975	EA63 (1400)	BP6ES	.030	49–55	.020	8B @ 800(M) 8B @ 900(A)	24B	1.8–2.6	800M 900A	.012	.014
1976	EA63 (1400)	BP6ES	.032	49–55	.018	8B @ 900	24B	1.8–2.6	900	.011	.015
	EA71 (1600)	BP6ES	.032	49–55	.018	8B @ 900	24B	1.8–2.6	900	.011	.015
1977–79	EA71 (1600)	BP6ES	.032	49–55 ②	.018 ②	8B @ 850	24B	2.6	850 ①	.010	.014
1980	(1600)	BP6ES	.032	Electronic		8B @ 850	24B	2.6	850 ①	.009	.013
	(1800)	BP6ES	.032	Electronic		8B @ 850	24B	2.6	850 ①	.009	.013
1981–82	(1600)	BPES-11	.040	Electronic		8B @ 700	20B	1.3–2.0	700	.010	.014
	(1800)	BPES-11	.040	Electronic		8B @ 700 ③	20B	1.3–2.0	700 ④	.010	.014
1983–84	(1600)	BPR6ES-11	.041	—	.008–.016 ⑤	8B @ 700 ⑦ ⑩	20B	1.3–2.0	700 ④	.010	.014
	(1800)	BPR6ES-11	.041	—	.008–.016 ⑤	8B @ 700 ⑦	20B	1.3–2.0	700 ④	.010	.014
	(1800 Turbo)	BPR6ES-11	.041	—	.012–.020 ⑥	15B @ 800 ⑨	16B	43	800	0 ⑧	0 ⑧

*OEM spark plugs or NGR.
TDC—Top Dead Center
B—Before top dead center
M—Manual transmission
A—Automatic transmission
① California 900
② California—Electronic ignition
③ Automatic transmission 8B @ 800
④ 800 with Automatic transmission
⑤ Air Gap 4WD air gap—.012–.020
⑥ Air Gap
⑦ Automatic trans timing set at 800 rpm.
⑧ Non-adjustable hydraulic lifters
⑨ Disconnect and plug pressure line from throttle body
⑩ 1984 1600 engines—650
⑪ Single Point Fuel Injection 10° BTDC
⑫ 20B @ 700 RPM, SPFI models with automatic transmission.
⑬ 28–43, SPFI models.
NOTE: *The underhood specification sticker often reflects tune-up specification changes made in production. Sticker figures must be used if they disagree with those in this chart.*

87902C06

TROUBLESHOOTING BASIC POINT-TYPE IGNITION SYSTEM PROBLEMS

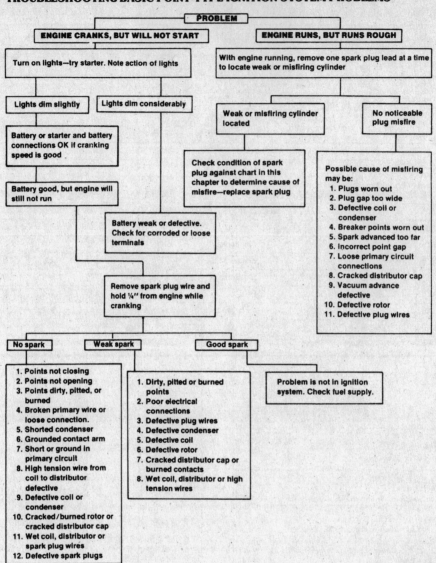

87902042

Troubleshooting Electronic Ignition—1977–82

Condition	Possible Cause	Correction
Engine will not start (Fuel and carburetion known to be OK)	a) External Resistor	Check Resistance; Resistance: 1977–79 　Exc. Calif. 1.6 ohms 　Calif. w/MT 1.4 ohms 　Calif. w/AT. 0.9 ohms 　Exc. 4-WD. 1980 1.1–1.3 ohms 　　　　　　　　1981 1.4–1.6 ohms
	b) Faulty Ignition Coil	Check for carbonized tower. Check primary and secondary resistances. Primary: 1977–79 　Exc. Calif. 1.36–1.65 ohms 　Calif. w/MT. 1.33–1.63 ohms 　Calif. w/AT. 0.81–0.99 ohms 　1980 　Exc. 4-WD 1.33–1.63 ohms 　4-WD 1.17–1.43 ohms 　1981 　Exc. 4-WD 1.06–1.30 ohms 　4-WD 1.04–1.27 ohms 　1981 　Exc. 4-WD 1.13–1.30 ohms 　4-WD 1.04–1.27 ohms Secondary: 1977–79 　Exc. Calif. 6,800–10,200 ohms 　Calif. w/MT. 11,100–13,700 ohms 　Calif. w/AT. 8,500–12,900 ohms 　1980 　Exc. 4-WD 12.600–15,400 ohms 　4-WD 7,800–11,600 ohms 　1981 　Exc. 4-WD 12,150–14,850 ohms 　4-WD 7,360–11,040 ohms 　1981 　Exc. 4-WD 10,795–14,605 ohms 　4-WD 7,360–11,040 ohms Check in coil tester.
	c) Faulty Pickup or Improper Air Gap	Check pick-up coil resistance. Resistance: 1977–80 　Exc. 1980 4-WD 130–190 ohms 　1980 4-WD 600–850 ohms 　1981–82 　Exc. 4-WD 160 ohms 　4-WD 720 ohms Check air gap with a nonmagnetic feeler gauge. Adjust if necessary. Air Gap 　1977–79 　Calif; Manual Transmission .008–.016 　Calif; Auto Transmission .012–.016 　1980 　Exc. 4-WD .008–.016 　4-WD .012–.016 　1981–82 　Exc. 4-WD .008–.016 　4-WD .012–.020
	d) Faulty Wiring	Visually inspect wiring for brittle insulation. Inspect connectors. Molded connectors should be inspected for rubber inside female terminals.
	e) Faulty Control Unit	Replace if all of the above checks are negative. Whenever the control unit or external resistor is replaced make sure the wires are correctly replaced and tight.

87902C01

Troubleshooting Electronic Ignition—1977–82 (cont.)

Condition	Possible Cause	Correction
Engine surges severely (Not lean Carburetor)	a) Wiring	Inspect for loose connections and/or broken conductors in harness.
	b) Faulty Pickup Leads	Disconnect vacuum advance. If surging stops, replace pickup.
	c) Ignition Coil	Check for intermittent primary.
Engine misses (Carburetion OK)	a) Spark Plugs	Check plugs. Gap and replace if necessary.
	b) Secondary Cable	Check cables with ohmmeter.
	c) Ignition Coil	Check for carbonized tower. Check in coil tester.
	d) Wiring	Check for loose or dirty connections.
	e) Faulty Pickup Lead	Disconnect vacuum advance. If miss stops, replace pickup.
	f) Control Unit	Replace if the above checks are negative.

87902C02

Troubleshooting 1983-84 Ignition System

1) Secondary Circuit

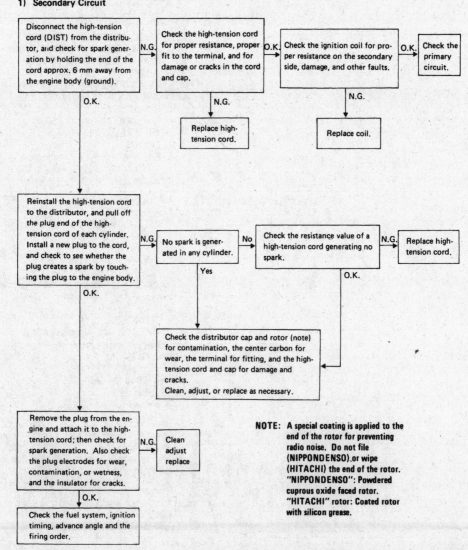

NOTE: A special coating is applied to the end of the rotor for preventing radio noise. Do not file (NIPPONDENSO) or wipe (HITACHI) the end of the rotor. "NIPPONDENSO": Powdered cuprous oxide faced rotor. "HITACHI" rotor: Coated rotor with silicon grease.

87902039

Troubleshooting 1983-84 Ignition System

2) Primary Circuit

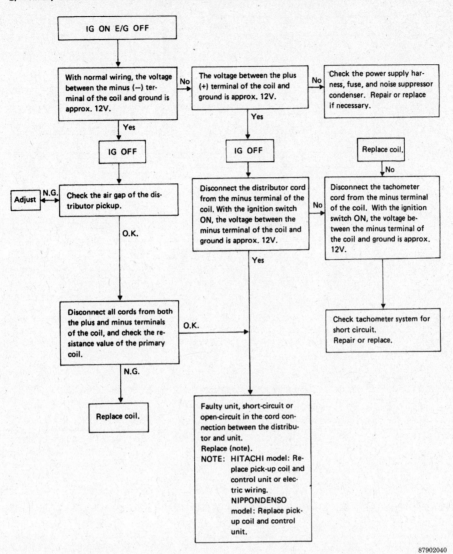

87902040

Troubleshooting Engine Performance

Problem	Cause	Solution
Hard starting (engine cranks normally)	• Binding linkage, choke valve or choke piston	• Repair as necessary
	• Restricted choke vacuum diaphragm	• Clean passages
	• Improper fuel level	• Adjust float level
	• Dirty, worn or faulty needle valve and seat	• Repair as necessary
	• Float sticking	• Repair as necessary
	• Faulty fuel pump	• Replace fuel pump
	• Incorrect choke cover adjustment	• Adjust choke cover
	• Inadequate choke unloader adjustment	• Adjust choke unloader
	• Faulty ignition coil	• Test and replace as necessary
	• Improper spark plug gap	• Adjust gap
	• Incorrect ignition timing	• Adjust timing
	• Incorrect valve timing	• Check valve timing; repair as necessary
Rough idle or stalling	• Incorrect curb or fast idle speed	• Adjust curb or fast idle speed
	• Incorrect ignition timing	• Adjust timing to specification
	• Improper feedback system operation	• Refer to Chapter 4
	• Improper fast idle cam adjustment	• Adjust fast idle cam
	• Faulty EGR valve operation	• Test EGR system and replace as necessary
	• Faulty PCV valve air flow	• Test PCV valve and replace as necessary
	• Choke binding	• Locate and eliminate binding condition
	• Faulty TAC vacuum motor or valve	• Repair as necessary
	• Air leak into manifold vacuum	• Inspect manifold vacuum connections and repair as necessary
	• Improper fuel level	• Adjust fuel level
	• Faulty distributor rotor or cap	• Replace rotor or cap
	• Improperly seated valves	• Test cylinder compression, repair as necessary
	• Incorrect ignition wiring	• Inspect wiring and correct as necessary
	• Faulty ignition coil	• Test coil and replace as necessary
	• Restricted air vent or idle passages	• Clean passages
	• Restricted air cleaner	• Clean or replace air cleaner filler element
	• Faulty choke vacuum diaphragm	• Repair as necessary
Faulty low-speed operation	• Restricted idle transfer slots	• Clean transfer slots
	• Restricted idle air vents and passages	• Clean air vents and passages
	• Restricted air cleaner	• Clean or replace air cleaner filter element
	• Improper fuel level	• Adjust fuel level
	• Faulty spark plugs	• Clean or replace spark plugs
	• Dirty, corroded, or loose ignition secondary circuit wire connections	• Clean or tighten secondary circuit wire connections
	• Improper feedback system operation	• Refer to Chapter 4
	• Faulty ignition coil high voltage wire	• Replace ignition coil high voltage wire
	• Faulty distributor cap	• Replace cap
Faulty acceleration	• Improper accelerator pump stroke	• Adjust accelerator pump stroke
	• Incorrect ignition timing	• Adjust timing
	• Inoperative pump discharge check ball or needle	• Clean or replace as necessary
	• Worn or damaged pump diaphragm or piston	• Replace diaphragm or piston

87902C03

Troubleshooting Engine Performance (cont.)

Problem	Cause	Solution
Faulty acceleration (cont.)	· Leaking carburetor main body cover gasket	· Replace gasket
	· Engine cold and choke set too lean	· Adjust choke cover
	· Improper metering rod adjustment (BBD Model carburetor)	· Adjust metering rod
	· Faulty spark plug(s)	· Clean or replace spark plug(s)
	· Improperly seated valves	· Test cylinder compression, repair as necessary
	· Faulty ignition coil	· Test coil and replace as necessary
	· Improper feedback system operation	· Refer to Chapter 4
Faulty high speed operation	· Incorrect ignition timing	· Adjust timing
	· Faulty distributor centrifugal advance mechanism	· Check centrifugal advance mechanism and repair as necessary
	· Faulty distributor vacuum advance mechanism	· Check vacuum advance mechanism and repair as necessary
	· Low fuel pump volume	· Replace fuel pump
	· Wrong spark plug air gap or wrong plug	· Adjust air gap or install correct plug
	· Faulty choke operation	· Adjust choke cover
	· Partially restricted exhaust manifold, exhaust pipe, catalytic converter, muffler, or tailpipe	· Eliminate restriction
	· Restricted vacuum passages	· Clean passages
	· Improper size or restricted main jet	· Clean or replace as necessary
	· Restricted air cleaner	· Clean or replace filter element as necessary
	· Faulty distributor rotor or cap	· Replace rotor or cap
	· Faulty ignition coil	· Test coil and replace as necessary
	· Improperly seated valve(s)	· Test cylinder compression, repair as necessary
	· Faulty valve spring(s)	· Inspect and test valve spring tension, replace as necessary
	· Incorrect valve timing	· Check valve timing and repair as necessary
	· Intake manifold restricted	· Remove restriction or replace manifold
	· Worn distributor shaft	· Replace shaft
	· Improper feedback system operation	· Refer to Chapter 4
Misfire at all speeds	· Faulty spark plug(s)	· Clean or replace spark plug(s)
	· Faulty spark plug wire(s)	· Replace as necessary
	· Faulty distributor cap or rotor	· Replace cap or rotor
	· Faulty ignition coil	· Test coil and replace as necessary
	· Primary ignition circuit shorted or open intermittently	· Troubleshoot primary circuit and repair as necessary
	· Improperly seated valve(s)	· Test cylinder compression, repair as necessary
	· Faulty hydraulic tappet(s)	· Clean or replace tappet(s)
	· Improper feedback system operation	· Refer to Chapter 4
	· Faulty valve spring(s)	· Inspect and test valve spring tension, repair as necessary
	· Worn camshaft lobes	· Replace camshaft
	· Air leak into manifold	· Check manifold vacuum and repair as necessary
	· Improper carburetor adjustment	· Adjust carburetor
	· Fuel pump volume or pressure low	· Replace fuel pump
	· Blown cylinder head gasket	· Replace gasket
	· Intake or exhaust manifold passage(s) restricted	· Pass chain through passage(s) and repair as necessary
	· Incorrect trigger wheel installed in distributor	· Install correct trigger wheel

87902C04

Troubleshooting Engine Performance (cont.)

Problem	Cause	Solution
Power not up to normal	· Incorrect ignition timing	· Adjust timing
	· Faulty distributor rotor	· Replace rotor
	· Trigger wheel loose on shaft	· Reposition or replace trigger wheel
	· Incorrect spark plug gap	· Adjust gap
	· Faulty fuel pump	· Replace fuel pump
	· Incorrect valve timing	· Check valve timing and repair as necessary
	· Faulty ignition coil	· Test coil and replace as necessary
	· Faulty ignition wires	· Test wires and replace as necessary
	· Improperly seated valves	· Test cylinder compression and repair as necessary
	· Blown cylinder head gasket	· Replace gasket
	· Leaking piston rings	· Test compression and repair as necessary
	· Worn distributor shaft	· Replace shaft
	· Improper feedback system operation	· Refer to Chapter 4
Intake backfire	· Improper ignition timing	· Adjust timing
	· Faulty accelerator pump discharge	· Repair as necessary
	· Defective EGR CTO valve	· Replace EGR CTO valve
	· Defective TAC vacuum motor or valve	· Repair as necessary
	· Lean air/fuel mixture	· Check float level or manifold vacuum for air leak. Remove sediment from bowl
Exhaust backfire	· Air leak into manifold vacuum	· Check manifold vacuum and repair as necessary
	· Faulty air injection diverter valve	· Test diverter valve and replace as necessary
	· Exhaust leak	· Locate and eliminate leak
Ping or spark knock	· Incorrect ignition timing	· Adjust timing
	· Distributor centrifugal or vacuum advance malfunction	· Inspect advance mechanism and repair as necessary
	· Excessive combustion chamber deposits	· Remove with combustion chamber cleaner
	· Air leak into manifold vacuum	· Check manifold vacuum and repair as necessary
	· Excessively high compression	· Test compression and repair as necessary
	· Fuel octane rating excessively low	· Try alternate fuel source
	· Sharp edges in combustion chamber	· Grind smooth
	· EGR valve not functioning properly	· Test EGR system and replace as necessary
Surging (at cruising to top speeds)	· Low carburetor fuel level	· Adjust fuel level
	· Low fuel pump pressure or volume	· Replace fuel pump
	· Metering rod(s) not adjusted properly (BBD Model Carburetor)	· Adjust metering rod
	· Improper PCV valve air flow	· Test PCV valve and replace as necessary
	· Air leak into manifold vacuum	· Check manifold vacuum and repair as necessary
	· Incorrect spark advance	· Test and replace as necessary
	· Restricted main jet(s)	· Clean main jet(s)
	· Undersize main jet(s)	· Replace main jet(s)
	· Restricted air vents	· Clean air vents
	· Restricted fuel filter	· Replace fuel filter
	· Restricted air cleaner	· Clean or replace air cleaner filter element
	· EGR valve not functioning properly	· Test EGR system and replace as necessary
	· Improper feedback system operation	· Refer to Chapter 4

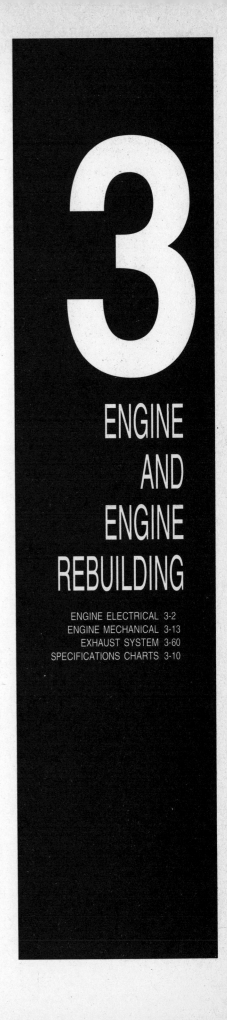

3

ENGINE
AND
ENGINE
REBUILDING

ENGINE ELECTRICAL

Ignition System

Two types of ignition systems are used on your Subaru. A conventional system using breaker points and condenser was used from 1970 through 1976. In 1977 a breakerless ignition was introduced on the California models, the others continued to use the conventional ignition. All models from 1980 use the breakerless ignition.

Both systems employ a distributor which is driven by the crankshaft, a high voltage rotor, a distributor cap, spark plug wiring, and an oil-filled conventional type coil.

The two systems differ in the manner in which they convert electrical primary voltage (12 volt) from the battery into secondary voltage (20,000 volts or greater) to fire the spark plugs.

In the conventional system, the breaker points open and close as the movable breaker arm rides the rotating cam eccentric, thereby opening and closing the current to the ignition coil. When the points open, they interrupt the flow of primary current to the coil, causing a collapse of the magnetic field in the coil and creating a high tension spark which is used to fire the spark plugs. In the breakerless system, a distributor shaft mounted reluctor rotates past a magnetic pick-up coil assembly causing fluctuations in the magnetic field generated by the pick-up coil. These fluctuations in turn, cause the ignition control unit to turn the ignition coil current on and off, creating the high tension spark to fire the spark plugs. The ignition control unit electronically controls the dwell, which is controlled mechanically in a conventional system by the duration which the points remained closed.

Both the conventional and breakerless ignition systems are equipped with dual advance distributors. The vacuum advance unit governs ignition timing according to engine load, while the centrifugal advance unit governs ignition timing according to engine rpm. Centrifugal advance is controlled by spring mounted weights contained in the distributor, located under the breaker point mounting plate on conventional systems and under the fixed base plate on breakerless systems. As the engine speed increases, centrifugal force moves the weights outward from the distributor shaft, advancing the position of the distributor cam (conventional) or reluctor shaft (breakerless), thereby advancing the ignition timing. Vacuum advance is controlled by a vacuum diaphragm which is mounted on the side of the distributor and attached to the breaker point mounting plate (conventional) or the magnetic pick-up coil assembly (breakerless) via the vacuum advance link. Under light acceleration, the engine is operating under a low load condition, causing the carburetor vacuum to act on the distributor vacuum diaphragm, moving the breaker point mounting plate (conventional) or the pick-up coil assembly (breakerless) opposite the direction of distributor shaft rotation, thereby advancing the ignition timing.

The turbocharged engine employs a vacuum advance/pressure retard type of diaphragm. It functions in the normal way until the driver applies enough throttle so that the turbocharger supplies air/fuel at more than atmospheric pressure. At this point, ignition timing is retarded past the normal timing progressively as manifold pressure rises. In addition to the knock prevention function of the pressure retard, an electronic pickup senses engine knock type vibration in one cylinder head and retards the timing electronically still further, should knock occur.

Some earlier models use vacuum advance at normal running throttle openings, but combine it with manifold vacuum retard at idle. The retard mechanism is contained in the rear part of the vacuum diaphragm chamber. When the engine is operating under high vacuum conditions (deceleration or idle), intake manifold vacuum is applied to the retard mechanism. The retard mechanism moves the breaker point mounting plate (conventional) or pickup coil assembly (breakerless) in the direction of distributor rotation, thereby retarding the ignition timing. Ignition retard, under these conditions, reduces exhaust emissions of hydrocarbons, although it does reduce engine efficiency somewhat.

Ignition Coil

TESTING

1. Run the engine until it reaches operating temperature (coil must be hot) and then turn **OFF** the vehicle. Pull the high tension lead out of the coil tower.
2. Measure the primary resistance with an ohmmeter by connecting coil plus and minus terminals. Refer to the Troubleshooting Electronic Ignition — 1977-82 chart for resistance figures if your car was built in those years. For newer models, resistance should be:
   - Except 4WD and turbocharged models, 1.13-1.38Ω
   - 4WD, 1.04-1.27Ω
   - Turbocharged models, 0.837-1.023.Ω
3. Measure secondary resistance, connecting the ohmmeter between the coil tower and the plus primary terminal. Refer to the Troubleshooting Electronic Ignition — 1977-82 chart for resistance figures if your car was built in those years. For newer models, resistance should be:
   - Except 4WD and turbocharged models, 10,795-14,605Ω
   - 4WD, 7,360-11,040Ω
   - Turbocharged models, 8,000-12,000Ω
4. Replace the coil if resistances are incorrect.

REMOVAL & INSTALLATION

▶ See Figures 1, 2 and 3

1. Disengage the electrical connections.
2. Loosen the coil bracket retaining fasteners.
3. Remove the coil.
4. Installation is the reverse of removal

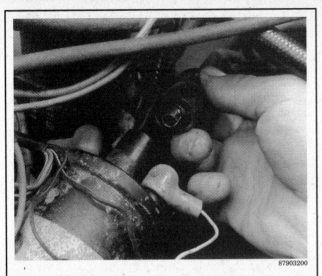

Fig. 1 Remove the wire from the secondary terminal

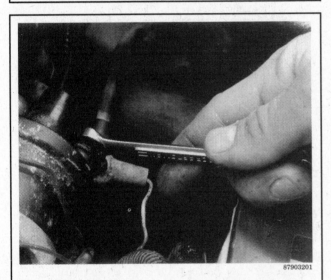

Fig. 2 Disengage the primary coil electrical connections

Fig. 3 Remove the coil from the vehicle

Distributor

REMOVAL & INSTALLATION

▶ See Figures 4, 5 and 6

1. Disconnect the negative battery cable and remove the air cleaner assembly.

2. Tag and disconnect the hoses.

3. On models equipped with conventional ignition system, disconnect the primary wire at the coil.

4. On models equipped with breakerless ignition, disconnect the distributor wiring connector from the vehicle wiring harness.

5. Note the positions of the vacuum line(s) on the distributor diaphragm, tag and disconnect the lines at the diaphragm. Unsnap the two distributor cap retaining clamps and remove the cap. Position the cap and ignition wires to one side.

➡ If it is necessary to remove the ignition wires from the cap to get enough room to remove the distributor, make sure to label each wire and the cap for easy and accurate reinstallation.

6. Use chalk or paint to carefully mark the position of the distributor rotor in relationship to the distributor housing and mark the position of the distributor housing in relationship to the engine block. When this is done, you should have a line on the distributor housing directly in line with the tip of the rotor and another line on the engine block directly in line with the mark on the distributor housing. This is very important because the distributor must be reinstalled in the exact same position from which it was removed, if correct ignition timing is to be maintained.

7. Remove the distributor hold-down bolt. On 1970-73 models with an octane selector, note the position of the selector and remove the bolt. Don't lose the pointer.

8. Remove the distributor from the engine taking care not to damage or lose the O-ring.

Fig. 4 Remove the distributor cap

Fig. 5 Use chalk or paint to carefully mark the position of the distributor

Fig. 6 Unfasten the distributor hold-down bolt and remove the distributor

To install:

➡Do not disturb the engine while the distributor is removed. If you crank or rotate the engine while the distributor is removed you will have to re-time the engine. See Engine Disturbed.

Engine Not Disturbed

1. If the engine was not disturbed while the distributor was removed, position the distributor in the block (make sure the O-ring is in place). Have the rotor aligned with the mark previously scribed on the distributor body and the marks on the distributor body and engine in alignment.

2. Install the octane selector, if so equipped, and tighten the hold-down bolt finger-tight.

3. Install the distributor rotor, cap and wires, if removed. Engage the primary wire to the coil or reconnect the wiring harness.

4. Connect the negative battery cable.

5. Plug the vacuum line(s) to the distributor and recheck the timing using a timing light.

6. Set the ignition timing to the proper specifications. See Section 2 for the proper procedure.

7. Fasten the hold-down bolt and connect the vacuum lines(s) and install the air cleaner.

Engine Disturbed

▶ **See Figure 7**

If the engine has been cranked, disassembled, or the timing otherwise lost, proceed as follows:

1. Disconnect the negative battery cable and remove the air cleaner. Tag and remove the hoses.

2. Remove the plastic dust cover from the timing port on the flywheel housing.

3. Remove the No. 1 spark plug. (No. 1 spark plug is the front plug on the right side of the engine). Use a wrench on the crankshaft pulley bolt (on manual transaxle cars place transaxle in neutral) and slowly rotate the engine until the TDC 0 mark on the flywheel aligns with the pointer.

4. While turning the engine place your finger over the No. 1 spark plug hole, when you feel air escaping past your finger the piston is on the compression stroke and when the marks align with the flywheel pointer, the piston is at Top Dead Center (TDC).

5. The following method can be used to get No. 1 piston on TDC.

   a. Remove the two bolts that hold the right (passenger's) side valve cover and remove the cover to expose the valves on No. 1 cylinder.

   b. Rotate the engine so that the valves in No. 1 cylinder are closed and the TDC 0 mark on the flywheel lines up with the pointer.

6. Align the small depression on the distributor drive pinion with the mark on the distributor body. This will align the rotor with the No. 1 spark plug terminal on the distributor cap. (See illustration for correct pinion alignment). On models with the octane selector, set the pointer midway between the A and R. Make sure the O-ring is located in the proper position.

7. Align the matchmarks you have made on the distributor body with those on the engine block and install the distributor

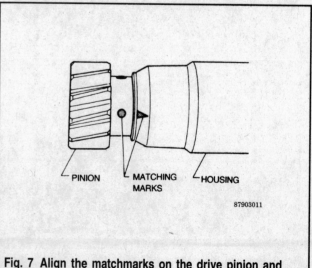

Fig. 7 Align the matchmarks on the drive pinion and housing

in the engine. Make sure the drive is engaged. Install the hold-down bolt finger-tight.

8. Connect the negative battery cable.

9. Plug the vacuum line(s) to the distributor and recheck the timing using a timing light.

10. Set the ignition timing to the proper specifications. See Section 2 for the proper procedure.

11. Fasten the hold-down bolt and connect the vacuum lines(s) and install the air cleaner.

Alternator

▶ See Figure 8

When the ignition switch is turned **ON** current from the battery passes through the ignition switch to the voltage regulator. The current then passes through a series of resistors, points and coils and sends a small amount of current to the alternator post which is connected to the brushes. The brushes contact slip rings on the rotor and pass a small amount of current into the windings of the rotor. The current passing through the rotor coils creates a magnetic field within the alternator.

When the engine is started the rotor is turned by the fan belt. As the rotor turns a magnetic current is induced in the stationary windings, or stator, located in the alternator housing.

The current induced is alternating current (AC) and must be changed to direct current (DC): diodes are used for this purpose. The technical explanation of how a diode works is not important. The diode is a form of electrical check valve, allowing the current to flow one way but not the other. A negative diode will pass current in a negative direction, and a positive in a positive direction. The positive diodes make up the positive rectifier and the negative diodes make up the negative rectifier.

The stationary windings, or stator, are wound into three sets of windings or phases. Each phase winding is connected to a positive and a negative diode. When the phase winding is passing positive current, the current will flow through the positive diode to the output terminal of the alternator. When the phase winding is passing negative current, the negative diode allows the returning current from the grounded circuit, to pass into the windings to complete the circuit.

The direct current flowing from the alternator output terminal to the battery is used to provide current for the electrical system and to recharge the battery. As electrical demand increases the voltage regulator senses the need and directs more current to pass through the rotor, increasing the magnetic field. This produces greater induction voltage which increases the output of the alternator. When the requirements of the electrical system decrease the voltage regulator reduces the current flowing through the rotor, lowering the magnetic field and decreasing the output of the alternator.

ALTERNATOR PRECAUTIONS

• Pay particular attention to the polarity connections of the battery when connecting the battery cables. Make sure that you connect the correct cable to the corresponding terminal.

• If a jumper battery is used to start the vehicle, refer to the correct method of jump starting in Section 1.

• When testing or adjusting the alternator, install a condenser between the alternator output terminal and the ground. This is to prevent the diode from becoming damaged by a spark which occurs due to testing equipment with a defective connection.

• Do not operate the alternator with the output terminals disconnected. The diode would be damaged by the high voltage generated.

• When recharging the battery by a quick charger or any other charging apparatus, disconnect the alternator output terminal before hooking up the charging leads.

• When installing a battery, always connect the positive terminal first.

• Never disconnect the battery while the engine is running.

• Never electric weld around the car without disconnecting the alternator.

• Never apply any voltage in excess of the battery voltage during testing.

• Never jump a battery for starting purposes with more than the battery voltage.

TESTING

If you suspect a defect in your charging system, first perform these general checks before going on to more specific tests.

1. Check the condition of the alternator belt and tighten if necessary.

2. Clean the battery cable connections at the battery. Make sure the connections between the battery wires and the battery clamps are good. Reconnect the negative terminal only and proceed to the next step.

3. With the key **OFF**, insert a test light between the positive terminal on the battery terminal clamp. If the test light comes on, there is a short in the electrical system of the vehicle. The short must be repaired before proceeding. If the light does not come on, then proceed to the next step.

➡**If the vehicle is equipped with an electric clock, the clock must be disconnected.**

4. Check the charging system wiring for any obvious breaks or shorts.

5. Check the battery to make sure it is fully charged and in good condition.

REMOVAL & INSTALLATION

▶ See Figures 9, 10 and 11

1. Disconnect the negative battery cable. Failure to do this could result in damage to the electrical system.

2. Disconnect the plug connecting the alternator to the wiring harness. Disconnect the lead wire. Tag wires for identification.

3. Remove the alternator adjusting bolt, move the alternator toward the engine and remove the drive belt.

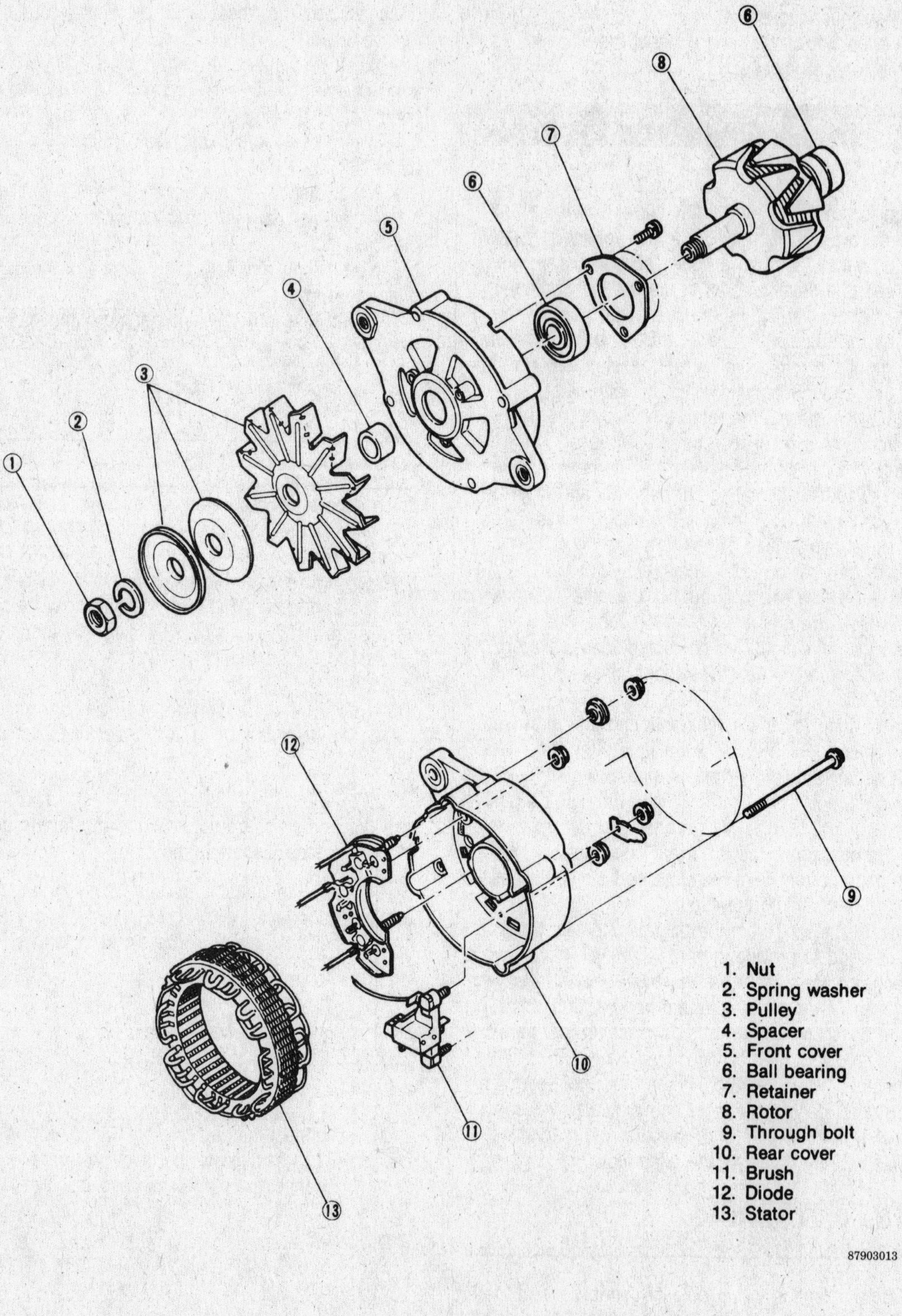

1. Nut
2. Spring washer
3. Pulley
4. Spacer
5. Front cover
6. Ball bearing
7. Retainer
8. Rotor
9. Through bolt
10. Rear cover
11. Brush
12. Diode
13. Stator

87903013

Fig. 8 Exploded view of the alternator

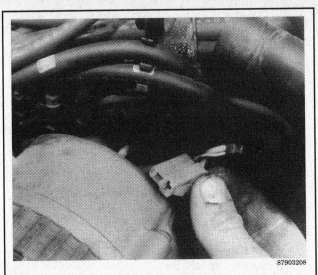

Fig. 9 Tag and disconnect the alternator connections

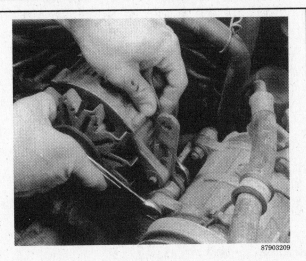

Fig. 10 Loosen and remove the alternator mounting bolts . . .

Fig. 11 . . . then remove the alternator from the vehicle

4. Remove the remaining mounting nuts and bolts while carefully supporting the alternator. Remove the alternator from the engine compartment.

➡**Now is a good time to inspect the drive belt for wear, replace if necessary.**

To install:

5. Position the alternator into the mounting brackets and hand-tighten the mounting bolts. Alternator belt tension is quite critical. A belt that is too tight may cause alternator bearing failure; one that is too loose will cause a gradual battery discharge as well as belt wear. For details on correct belt adjustment, see Belts in Section 1.

6. Install the alternator adjusting bolt and move the alternator away from the engine checking belt tension as you go.

7. When proper tension is achieved tighten all alternator retaining bolts.

Voltage Regulator

The voltage regulator is a device which controls the output of the alternator. Without this voltage limiting function of the regulator, the excessive output of the alternator could burn out components of the electrical system. In addition, the regulator compensates for seasonal changes in temperature as it affects voltage output.

➡**Late models have a solid state regulator built into the alternator. The regulator is non-adjustable and is serviced, when necessary, by replacement.**

REMOVAL & INSTALLATION

External Regulator

1. Disconnect the negative battery cable.
2. Disengage the multi-wire connector and automatic choke lead (1974 and later models) from the regulator.
3. Remove the two regulator mounting screws and remove the regulator from the fender panel.

To install:

4. Install the new regulator and tighten the mounting screws.
5. Engage the multi-wire connector and choke lead.
6. Connect the negative battery cable.

Internal Regulator

1. Remove the alternator as outlined in this section.
2. Matchmark the alternator case and remove the case fasteners.
3. Separate the two case halves.
4. Loosen the voltage regulator retainers and remove the voltage regulator.

To install:

5. Install the voltage regulator and tighten the fasteners.
6. Engage the two halves of the alternator case together making sure to line up the matchmarks. Tighten the case fasteners.
7. Install the alternator in the vehicle.

ADJUSTMENTS

➡Adjustments can be made on external regulators only, internal regulators cannot be adjusted.

Voltage Adjustments

▶ See Figure 12

This test should be made after the engine compartment and the regulator have had a chance to cool down. The test should never be performed on a hot engine.

1. Make sure all electrical equipment on the car is turned **OFF** or disconnected.

2. Using an ammeter, a voltmeter, and a resistor rated at 0.25Ω, connect a test circuit as shown in the illustration.

3. **BEFORE STARTING THE ENGINE:** Connect a jumper wire from the far terminal of the 0.25Ω resistor to the negative (-) terminal of the ammeter. See illustration. After the engine is started, disconnect the jumper, but be sure to reconnect it each time the engine is restarted.

4. Turn the engine **ON** and gradually increase the speed from idle to about 2000 rpm. 2000 engine rpm is equal to about 1200 alternator rpm.

5. The voltage reading shown should compare with that on the alternator and regulator specifications chart, allowing for the temperature around the regulator.

➡The ammeter reading should be below 5 amps. Recharge or substitute the battery with a charged one if the reading is not below 5 amps.

If the voltage is not within the specified range, adjust as follows:

6. Remove the screws and take off the regulator cover.

7. On ff-1 and 1300G models, bend the adjuster tab on the regulator up if the voltage is below specifications or down if the voltage is above specifications.

8. On other models, loosen the locknut and turn the adjusting screw until the voltage falls within specifications.

9. If the voltage cannot be brought within specs, proceed with a mechanical adjustment.

10. If the voltage is now within the required specs: shut off the engine, remove the test equipment, replace the regulator cover and reconnect any electrical system components or accessories you disconnected at the beginning of the test.

Charge Relay Adjustment

▶ See Figure 13

➡The opening voltage of the charge relay is 8-10 volts at alternator terminal (A). However, the coil on the charge relay operates at half of this voltage (i.e., 4-5 volts).

1. Remove the regulator from the car.

2. Hook up the test circuit illustrated with a car battery, 0-150Ω rheostat, voltmeter, heavy duty switch, and a test light.

3. Close the switch with the rheostat set at 150Ω (maximum).

4. Gradually decrease the resistance.

5. When the test light goes out, the voltmeter should read 4-5 volts.

6. If the light doesn't go out at the specified setting, remove the regulator cover and make one of the following adjustments:

7. On ff-1 and 1300G models, bend the charge relay, and turn the adjusting screw until the voltage is within specifications. Tighten the locknut.

8. If the charge relay voltage cannot be brought within specifications, perform the Mechanical Adjustments outlined next.

9. If the charge relay is working properly, put the cover on the regulator and install it in the car.

Mechanical Adjustments

▶ See Figures 14, 15 and 16

> **✳✳WARNING**
>
> All mechanical adjustments must be performed with the regulator removed from the car to prevent battery and charging system damage.

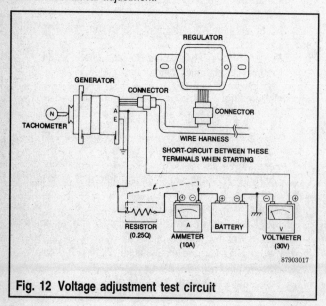

Fig. 12 Voltage adjustment test circuit

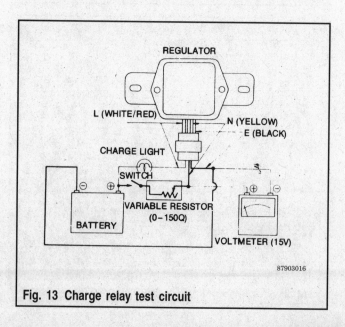

Fig. 13 Charge relay test circuit

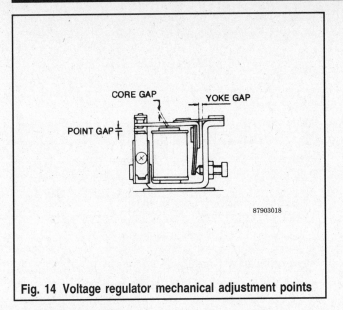

Fig. 14 Voltage regulator mechanical adjustment points

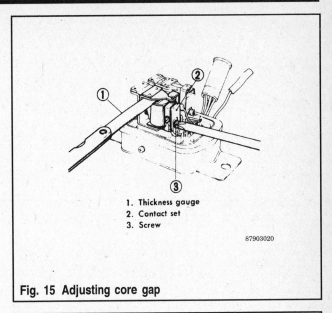

1. Thickness gauge
2. Contact set
3. Screw

Fig. 15 Adjusting core gap

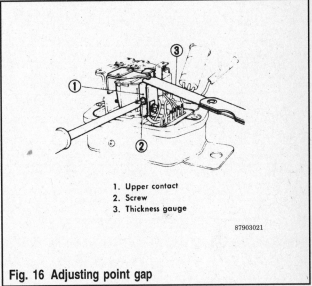

1. Upper contact
2. Screw
3. Thickness gauge

Fig. 16 Adjusting point gap

ff-1 AND 1300G MODELS

1. Remove the regulator from the car, unfasten the cover securing screws, and remove the cover.

2. Inspect both sets of points. If they are rough or dirty, polish them lightly with #500 or #600 emery paper.

➡**If the points are so badly damaged that polishing them doesn't help, replace the regulator.**

3. Measure the gaps of the voltage regulator, with a feeler gauge, in the following sequence:

a. Yoke gap: measure the clearance between the armature and the yoke. Adjust, as necessary, by loosening its securing screws and moving the armature. Tighten the screws.

b. Core gap: measure the clearance between the armature and the core of the voltage coil. Adjust the gap by bending the lower contact, as necessary.

c. Point gap: measure the distance between the points. Adjust by bending the upper contact, as necessary.

4. Measure the gaps of the charge relay, with a feeler gauge, in the following sequence:

a. Yoke gap: measure the clearance between the armature and the end of the yoke. Adjust, as necessary, by loosening the armature securing screws and moving the armature if necessary. Tighten the screws.

b. Core gap: measure the clearance between the armature and the center of the core. Adjust by loosening the contact set securing screw and moving the set up or down, by inserting a screwdriver in the hole.

c. Point gap: measure the distance between the points. Adjust by loosening the point securing screw, inserting a screwdriver, and raising or lowering the screwdriver.

➡**For proper gap specifications, consult the Alternator and Regulator Specifications chart.**

5. After completing the adjustments, replace the cover on the regulator, and install it in the car. Test its operation again, as outlined above. If the voltage still cannot be brought within specifications, replace the regulator. If the voltage is still incorrect, the fault probably lies in the alternator.

EXCEPT ff-1 AND 1300G MODELS

1. Remove the voltage regulator from the car and remove the regulator cover.

2. Inspect both sets of points. If they are rough or dirty, polish them with #500 or #600 emery paper.

➡**If the points are so badly damaged that polishing them doesn't help, replace the regulator.**

3. Measure and adjust the gaps of both the voltage regulator and the charge relay in the same manner. Use the specifications given in the Alternator and Regulator Specifications chart. Adjust both sets of gaps in the following sequence:

a. Core gap: measure the clearances for both the regulator and charge relay between their armatures and coil cores. Adjust each, as necessary, by loosening the 4mm screw which secures the contact set to the yoke and moving the set up or down. Tighten the screw.

b. Point gap: measure the distances between the points for both the voltage regulator and charge relay. Adjust each, as necessary, by loosening the 3mm screw which secures the upper contact and moving the contact up or down. Tighten the screw.

➡ **It is not necessary to adjust the yoke gap.**

4. Reinstall the regulator in the car and test its operation as outlined above. If the voltage still cannot be brought within specifications, replace the regulator. If the voltage is still incorrect, the fault probably lies in the alternator.

Battery

REMOVAL & INSTALLATION

▶ **See Figure 17**

※※CAUTION

When working on the battery, be careful at all times to keep metal wrenches from connecting across the battery terminal posts. DO NOT wear any type of metal jewelry, this includes watches!

1. Unfasten the negative battery terminal, first.
2. Next, unfasten the positive cable at the starter and then the positive battery terminal.
3. Loosen the hold-down clamps and carefully remove the battery using a battery lifting strap or equivalent.

Alternator and Regular Specifications

			Regulator							
			Charge Relay				Voltage Regulator			
Year	Model	Alternator Output (amps) @ 12 Volts	Yoke Gap (in.)	Core Gap (in.)	Point Gap (in.)	Volts to Open	Yoke Gap (in.)	Core Gap (in.)	Point Gap (in.)	Volts @ 1200 & 75°
1970–71	FF-1	30	.035	.032–.039	.016–.020	8–10	.035	.024–.039	.012–.016	13.7
1971–72	1300G	30	.035	.032–.039	.016–.020	8–10	.035	.024–.039	.012–.016	13.7
1972–74	DL & GL	35	.035	.032–.039	.016–.020	8–10	.035	.024–.039	.012–.016	14.0
1975–76	all models	50	.035	.032–.039	.016–.024	8–10	.035	.024–.039	.012–.016	14.0
1977–79	all models	50	.035	.032–.039	.016–.024	8–10	.035	.024–.039	.014–.018	14.0
1980	all models	50 ①	.035	.032–.039	.016–.024	8–10	.035	.024–.039	.014–.018	14.0
1981	Except Hatch-back 4WD, GL & Station Wagon 4WD GL	42	.035	.032–.039	.016–.024	8–10	.035	.024–.039	.014–.018	14.0
	Hatchback 4WD GL & Station Wagon 4WD GL	50	.035	.032–.039	.016–.024	8–10	.035	.024–.039	.014–.018	14.0
1982	all models	50 ②	—	—	—	—	—	—	—	14.5
1983–84	all models	55 ②	—	—	—	—	—	—	—	14.2–14.8 ③
1985–87	All Models Except XT & Justy	60	—	—	—	—	—	—	—	14.1–14.8 ③
	XT	65	—	—	—	—	—	—	—	14.1–14.8 ③
	Justy	45	—	—	—	—	—	—	—	14.2–14.8

① 1980 station wagon 4WD GL: 55A
② Integral regulator
③ at 68°F.

87903C01

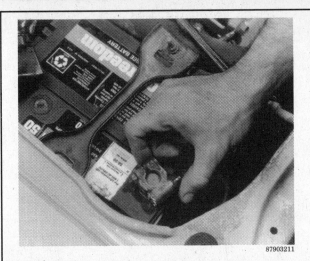

Fig. 17 Always disconnect the negative battery cable first

4. Thoroughly clean the entire battery box area. Use a mild solution of baking soda and water to cut through the corrosion. This is done because the battery retains its charge better in a clean environment.

5. Replace the battery with one having an equal or higher rating in amp/hours. Note that the older a vehicle is, the more likely it is to benefit from an increase in battery capacity due to increased resistance in the wiring.

6. Install the battery in exact reverse order, making sure it is securely mounted before starting to connect the wiring. Make sure the battery terminals are clean, using a special brush designed for that purpose, if necessary.

7. Connect the positive terminal first, and then the negative, tightening them securely. Coat the terminals with petroleum jelly to protect them from corrosion.

✳✳CAUTION

Use care in handling the battery, remember, it is filled with a highly corrosive acid. Don't smoke; the vapors are explosive.

Starter

▶ See Figures 18 and 19

Two types of starter motors are used by Subaru. They are, the direct drive motor and the gear reduction motor.

The gear reduction starter may drive the over-running clutch shaft through its own pinion or an idler gear and pinion, depending on the required reduction. The purpose of this system is to increase the torque produced by the starter for its weight. The armature drive/overrunning clutch (through a single pinion) design is used on 1800cc manual transaxle cars, and the pinion and idler gear system is used on 1800cc cars with automatic transaxle.

The direct drive starter, on the 1200cc and 1600cc engine, uses a permanent magnetic field system instead of field coils inside the yoke. A spring steel retaining ring is used to retain the magnet, and keep it from springing out when an unexpectedly strong shock is applied to the yoke circumference. When the starter is engaged, current flows through the pull-in and

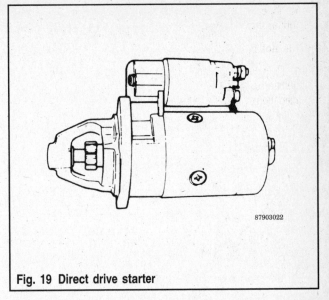

Fig. 19 Direct drive starter

holding coils. This causes the plunger to be pulled in, applying pressure to the shifter lever, which pushes the pinion out. Current flows through the armature and starts it to turn the pinion at a moderate speed, meshing it with the ring gear. When the main switch contacts are closed, full current flows through the armature, fully meshing the pinion with the ring gear, starting the vehicle.

REMOVAL & INSTALLATION

▶ See Figures 20, 21, 22 and 23

1. Remove the spare tire from the engine compartment.
2. Disconnect the cable from the negative battery terminal.
3. Disconnect the wiring harness at the starter, which is located on top of the transaxle at the rear of the engine.
4. Remove the two bolts which secure the starter to the transaxle and pull the starter out.

To install:

5. Install the starter and fasten the retaining bolts.
6. Connect the wiring harness at the starter.

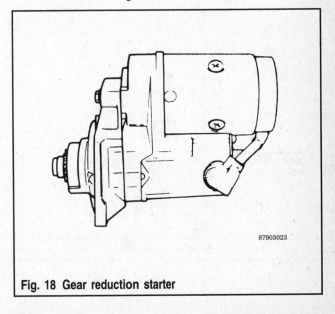

Fig. 18 Gear reduction starter

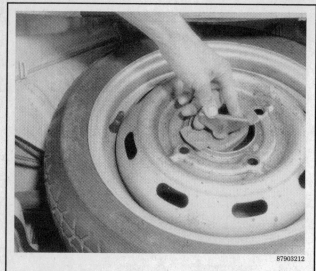

Fig. 20 Remove the spare tire from the vehicle

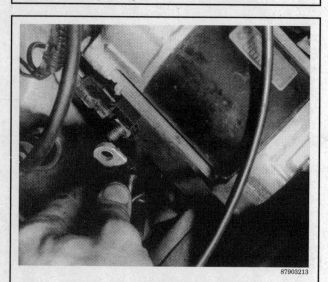

Fig. 21 Disengage the electrical connections

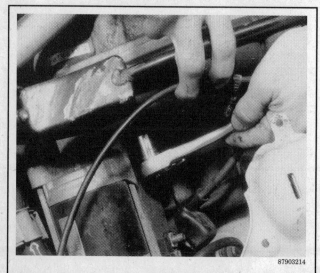

Fig. 22 Loosen and remove the starter fasteners . . .

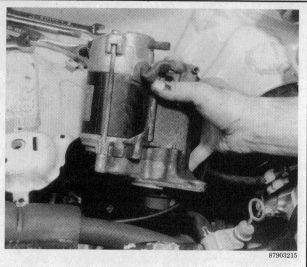

Fig. 23 . . . then remove the starter from the vehicle

7. Connect the negative battery terminal and install the spare tire in the engine compartment.

SOLENOID REPLACEMENT

▶ See Figure 24

➡This procedure is only applicable to the direct drive starter.

1. With the starter removed from the car as outlined earlier, remove the nut underneath the solenoid terminal and disconnect the wires from the starter.

2. Remove the two screws which hold the solenoid to the starter on models up to 1982. On later models, remove the two nuts.

➡It may be necessary to use an impact driver to remove the two screws.

3. Lift the rear of the solenoid up and then pull it toward the rear in order to separate it from the starter.

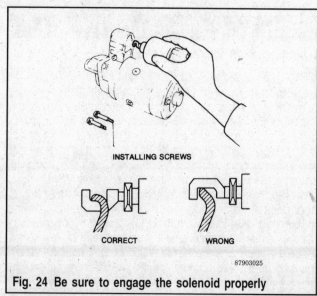

INSTALLING SCREWS

CORRECT   WRONG

Fig. 24 Be sure to engage the solenoid properly

To install:

4. Be sure to engage the hook on the end of the solenoid with the starter drive lever.

5. Install the solenoid securing fasteners.

Battery and Starter Specifications

Year	Model	Battery Amp-Hour Capacity	Volts	Terminal Grounded	Lock Test Amps	Volts	Torque (ft. lbs.)	No Load Test Amps	Volts	rpm	Brush Spring Tension (oz)
1970–71	FF-1	32	12	Neg	430	8.5	7.9	55	11	3,500	35–54
1971–72	1300G	35	12	Neg	470	7.7	9.4	50	11	5,000	35–54
1972–75	all except 1300G	50	12	Neg	470	7.7	9.4	50	11	5,000	35–54
1976	all models	50	12	Neg	470 ①	7.7 ②	9.4 ③	50	11	5,000	35–54
1977–79	all models	50	12	Neg	600	7.7 ②	9.4 ③	50 ④	11	5,000	37–47.6
1980–82	all models	60 ⑤	12	Neg	600 ⑥	7.7 ⑦	9–13 ⑧	50 ⑨	11	5,000 ⑩	37–47.6
1983–84	1600	55	12	Neg	600 ⑬	7.7	9	50	11	5,000	37–47
	1800	65	12	Neg	300 ⑭	2.5	5.1	90	11.5	3,000	—
	1800 AT ⑪	75 ⑫	12	Neg	400 ⑮	2.4	8.0	90	11.5	4,100	—

① Automatic transmission vehicles except California—600
② Automatic transmission vehicles except California—7.0
③ Automatic transmission vehicles except California—13.0
④ Automatic transmission vehicles except California—60
⑤ Optional—65A
⑥ Gear reduction—400A
⑦ Gear reduction—2.4V
⑧ Gear reduction—8 ft. lbs. (5 ft. lbs. if Manual Transmission)
⑨ Gear reduction—90A
⑩ Gear reduction—4100 rpm (3000 rpm if Manual Transmission)
⑪ Automatic transmission
⑫ This model had 85A capacity in 1983
⑬ at 1,200 rpm
⑭ at 1,180 rpm
⑮ at 1,000 rpm

87903C02

ENGINE MECHANICAL

Description

The Subaru Quadrozontal four cylinder engine is a unique design. The cylinders are horizontally opposed (flat) which gives the engine very compact dimensions, as well as make it run smoother than an inline four. Unlike other well known flat fours, the Subaru engine is water cooled. There are two advantages to this: one, the engine is quieter because the water acts as sound insulation and second, water cooling makes it easier to provide heat for the passenger compartment.

The crankcase is a split, aluminum alloy design. Subaru models through 1976 used wet, cast iron cylinder liners. Models since 1976 have dry liners cast into the block.

The one piece cylinder head is also aluminum alloy, with good cooling efficiency which, when combined with the bathtub shaped combustion chambers mean that the engine will run on a regular grade of gasoline, (regular unleaded for late models) despite its rather high compression ratio.

The pistons are made of aluminum, have a tapered elliptical shape and use two compression rings and one oil ring.

Overhead valves are operated by pushrods and solid lifters except on 1984 automatic transaxle models, which use hydraulic lifters. They are driven by a short camshaft which is located beneath the crankshaft. The camshaft journals are supported by the crankcase, thus eliminating bearings.

The forged crankshaft rides in two main bearings at either end and a single, combined main and thrust bearing in the middle.

There have been five different engine sizes imported into the United States, having 1,088cc, 1,267cc, 1,361cc, 1,595cc and 1,781cc displacements respectively.

Starting in 1983, Subaru offers an 1800 4WD Turbo (turbocharged) engine. The turbocharger is essentially a tiny, ultra high speed air pump. Its compressor is a tiny pinwheel whose finely machined vanes grab air and accelerate it, and then collect the air in a housing to force it into the engine under as much as 7.0 psi (48 kPa) of pressure. The engine, instead of gasping for air (actually drawing it in) as is usually the case, is pressure fed air and fuel in much greater quantities than is normally supplied.

At the other end of a metal shaft lies the turbine which drives the turbocharger. Utilizing expansion of the hot exhaust coming out of the engine, the turbine actually converts some of what would usually be wasted heat into the power which spins the turbocharger and helps the engine to breathe.

A precision, full floating sleeve type bearing supports the shaft in the middle. Engine oil is supplied to this bearing by the engine's oil pump through a special supply tube. This oil not only lubricates the bearing, but carries heat from the turbocharger shaft. Because of this extra heat, and that generated by the increased power, this is the only Subaru engine to have an external oil cooler.

Pressure charging can raise the temperature of compressed fuel/air mixture to the point where detonation can occur in the cylinders. Several modifications keep detonation from occurring. One is the use of a reduced (7.7 vs 8.7) compression ratio. Another is the addition of a double acting diaphragm on the distributor. When there is positive pressure in the intake manifold, this diaphragm actually retards distributor timing beyond its normal setting. An electronic knock sensor mounted on the cylinder head detects the particular frequency of detonation and may still further retard spark electronically to compensate for unanticipated variations in fuel quality, engine temperature, etc.

In order to protect the engine from excessive stress, which can occur at high rpm where the turbocharger begins to do its maximum work, a waste gate bypasses exhaust gas that would otherwise drive the turbocharger's turbine. Should this device fail, a pressure relief valve in the intake would protect the engine. The waste gate, by forcing more exhaust through the turbine at lower rpms, also helps guarantee good turbocharger performance, and engine torque, over a wide range of rpms.

Engine Overhaul Tips

Most engine overhaul procedures are fairly standard. In addition to specific parts replacement procedures and complete specifications for your individual engine, this section also is a guide to accepted rebuilding procedures. Examples of standard rebuilding practice are shown and should be used along with specific details concerning your particular engine.

In most instances it is more profitable for the do-it-yourself mechanic to remove, clean and inspect the component, buy the necessary parts and deliver these to a shop for actual machine work. Competent and accurate machine shop services will ensure maximum performance, reliability and engine life.

On the other hand much of the rebuilding work (crankshaft, block, bearings, pistons, rods and other components) is well within the scope of the do-it-yourself mechanic.

TOOLS

The tools required for an engine overhaul or parts replacement will depend on the depth of your involvement. With a few exceptions, they will be the tools found in a mechanics tool kit see Section 1). More in depth work will require any or all of the following:

- a dial indicator (reading in thousandths) mounted on a universal base.
- micrometers and telescope gauges.
- jaw and screw type pullers.
- scraper
- valve spring compressor.
- ring groove cleaner.
- piston ring expander and compressor.
- ridge reamer.
- cylinder hone or glaze breaker.
- Plastigage®.
- engine stand.

Use of most of these tools is illustrated in this section. Many can be rented for a one time use from a local parts jobber or tool supply house specializing in automotive work.

Occasionally, the use of special tools is called for. See the information on Special Tools and the Safety Notice in the front of this book before substituting another tool.

INSPECTION

Procedures and specifications are given in this section for inspecting, cleaning and assessing the wear limits of most components. Other procedures such as Magnaflux® and Zyglo® can be used to locate materials flaws and stress cracks. Magnaflux is a magnetic process applicable only to ferrous materials. The Zyglo® process coats the coats the material with a fluorescent dye penetrant and can be used on any material. Checks for suspected surface cracks can be more readily made using spot check dye. The dye is sprayed onto the suspected area, wiped off and the area sprayed with a developer. Cracks will show up brightly.

PRECAUTIONS

Aluminum has become extremely popular for use in engines, due to its low weight. Observe the following precautions when handling aluminum parts.

1. Never hot tank aluminum parts (the caustic hot tank solution will eat the aluminum).

2. Remove all aluminum parts (identification tag, etc.) from engine parts prior to hot tanking.

3. Always coat threads lightly with engine oil or anti-seize to compounds before installation, to prevent seizure.

4. Never over torque bolts or spark plugs, especially in aluminum threads.

Stripped threads in any component can be repaired using any of several commercial repair kits Heli-Coil®, Microdot®, Keenserts®, etc.).

When assembling the engine, any parts that will be in friction contact must be prelubed to provide lubrication at initial start up. Any product specifically formulated for this purpose can be used, but engine oil is not recommended as a prelube.

When semi-permanent (locked, but removable) installation of bolts or nuts is desired, threads should be cleaned or coated with Loctite® or other similar, commercial non-hardening sealant.

REPAIRING DAMAGED THREADS

▶ **See Figures 25, 26, 27, 28 and 29**

Several methods of repairing damaged threads are available. Heli-Coil® (shown here), Keenserts® and Microdot® are among the most widely used. All involve basically the same principle, drilling out stripped threads, tapping the hole and installing a pre-wound insert, making welding, plugging and oversize fasteners unnecessary.

Two types of thread repair inserts are usually supplied, a standard type for most Inch Course, Inch Fine, Metric Coarse and Metric Fine thread sizes and a spark plug type for to fit most spark plug port sizes. Consult the individual manufacturer's catalog to determine exact applications. Typical thread repair kits will contain a selection of pre-wound threaded inserts, a tap (corresponding to the outside diameter threads of the insert) and an installation tool. Spark plug inserts usually differ because they require a tap equipped with pilot threads and a combined reamer/tap section. Most manufacturers also supply blister-packed thread repair inserts separately in addition to a master kit containing a variety of taps and inserts plus installation tools.

Before effecting a repair to a threaded hole, remove any snapped, broken or damaged bolts or studs. Penetrating oil can be used to free frozen threads. The offending item can be removed with locking pliers or with a screw or stud extractor. After the hole has been cleared, the thread can be repaired as follows:

Checking Engine Compression

▶ **See Figure 30**

A noticeable lack of engine power, excessive oil consumption and/or poor fuel mileage measured over an extended period are all indicators of internal wear. Worn piston rings, scored or worn cylinder bores, blown head gaskets, sticking or burnt valves and worn valve seats are all possible culprits here. A check of each cylinder's compression will help you locate the problems.

As mentioned in the Tools and Equipment in Section 1, a screw in type compression gauge is more accurate than the type that you simply hold against the spark plug hole, although it takes slightly longer to use. It's worth it to obtain a more accurate reading. Engine compression is checked in the following manner:

1. Warm up the engine to normal operating temperature.

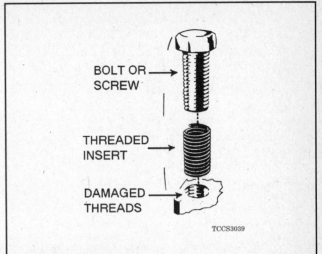

Fig. 25 Damaged bolt hole threads can be replaced with thread repair inserts

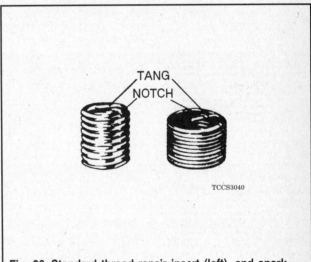

Fig. 26 Standard thread repair insert (left), and spark plug thread insert

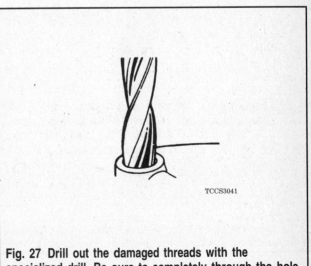

Fig. 27 Drill out the damaged threads with the specialized drill. Be sure to completely through the hole or to the bottom of a blind hole

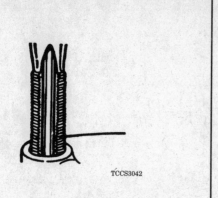

Fig. 28 Using the kit, tap the hole in order to receive the thread insert. Keep the tap well oiled and back it out frequently to avoid clogging the threads.

2. Tag the plug wires and remove all spark plugs.

3. Disconnect the high tension lead from the ignition coil.

4. On carbureted cars, fully open the throttle either by operating the carburetor throttle linkage by hand or by having an assistant floor the accelerator pedal. On fuel injected cars, disconnect the cold start valve and all injector connections.

5. Screw the compression gauge into the No.1 spark plug hole until the fitting is snug.

✳✳WARNING

Be careful not to crossthread the plug hole. On aluminum cylinder heads use extra care, as the threads in these heads are easily ruined.

6. Ask an assistant to depress the accelerator pedal fully on both carbureted and fuel injected cars. Then while you read the compression gauge, ask the assistant to crank the engine two or three times in short bursts using the ignition switch.

7. Read the compression gauge at the end of each series of cranks, and record the highest of these readings. Repeat this procedure for each of the engines cylinders. Compare the highest reading of each cylinder to the compression pressure specifications in the Tune-Up Specifications chart in Section 2. A cylinders compression pressure is usually acceptable if it is not less than 80% of the maximum. The difference between each cylinder should not be more than 12-14 pounds.

8. If a cylinder is unusually low, pour a tablespoon of clean engine oil into the cylinder through the spark plug hole and repeat the compression test. If the compression comes up after adding the oil, it appears that the cylinder's piston rings or bore are damaged or worn. If the compression remains low, the valves may not be seating properly, (a valve job is needed), or the head gasket may be blown near that cylinder. If the compression in any two adjacent cylinders is low, and if the addition of oil doesn't help the compression, there is leakage past the head gasket. Oil and coolant water in the combustion chamber can result from this problem. There may be evidence of water droplets on the engine dipstick when a head gasket has blown.

Fig. 29 Screw the threaded insert onto the installer tool until the tang engages the slot. Thread the insert into the hole until it is ¼-½ turn below the top surface, then remove the tool and break off the tang using a hammer and punch

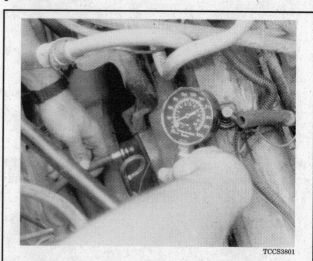

Fig. 30 A screw-in type compression gauge is more accurate and easier to use without an assistant

General Engine Specifications

Year	Engine Type	Engine Displacement (cc/cu in.)	Carburetor Type	Horsepower @ rpm ▲	Torque @ rpm ▲	Bore x Stroke (in.)	Compression Ratio	Normal Oil Pressure (psi)
1970-71	1100	1088/66.4	2-bbl	62 @ 6,000	63 @ 3,200	2.99 x 2.36	9:1	36-57
1971	1300	1267/77.3	2-bbl	80 @ 6,400	73 @ 4,000	3.23 x 2.36	9:1	36-57
1972	1300	1267/77.3	2-bbl	61 @ 5,600	65 @ 4,000	3.23 x 2.36	9:1	36-57
1973-74	1400	1361/83.2	2-bbl	61 @ 5,600	69 @ 3,600	3.35 x 2.36	9:1	36-57
1975	1400	1361/83.2	2-bbl	58 @ 5,200 ①	68 @ 2,400 ②	3.23 x 2.36	9:1	36-57
1976	1400	1361/83.2	2-bbl	58 @ 5,200 ①	68 @ 2,400 ②	3.23 x 2.36	8.5:1	36-57
1976-79	1600	1590/97	2-bbl	67 @ 5,200 ③	81 @ 2,400 ④	3.62 x 2.36	8.5:1	36-57
1980-82	1600	1595/97	2-bbl	68 @ 4,800	84 @ 2,800	3.62 x 2.36	8.5:1	36-57
	1800	1781/109	2-bbl	72 @ 4,800 ⑤	92 @ 2,400	3.62 x 2.64	8.7:1	36-57
1983-84	1600	1595/97	2-bbl	69 @ 4,800	86 @ 2,800	3.62 x 2.36	9.0:1	57
1983-84	1800	1781/109	2-bbl	73 @ 4,800	94 @ 2,400	3.62 x 2.64	8.7:1	57
	1800 Turbo	1781/109	Port Inj.	95 @ 4,800	123 @ 2,000	3.62 x 2.64	7.7:1	57
1985-87	1800	1781/108.68	2-bbl	82 @ 4,866	103 @ 2,800	3.62 x 2.64	9.5:1	57
	1800	1781/108.68	MPFI	94 @ 5,200	103 @ 2,800	3.62 x 2.64	9.0:1	57
	1800 Turbo	1781/108.68	MPFI	111 @ 4,800	136 @ 2,800	3.62 x 2.64	7.7:1	57
	1800	1781/108.68	SPFI	90 @ 5,600	101 @ 2,800	3.62 x 2.64	9.5:1	57
	1200	1200/73	2 bbl	66 @ 5,200	70 @ 3,200	3.07 x 3.27	9.0:1	35-40

▲Beginning 1972, horsepower and torque are given in SAE net figures
① 56 @ 5,200 for 4WD model
② 67 @ 2,400 for 4WD model
③ 65 @ 5,200 for 4WD model
④ 80 @ 2,400 for 4WD model
⑤ 4WD: 71 @ 4,200

87903C04

Valve Specifications

Year	Engine Type	Seat Angle (deg)	Face Angle (deg)	Spring Test Pressure (lbs.)		Spring Compressed Height (in.)		Stem-to-Guide Clearance (in.) ▲		Stem Diameter (in.)	
				Inner	Outer	Inner	Outer	Intake	Exhaust	Intake	Exhaust
1970–71	1100	45	45	42–49	96–111	0.96	1.02	.0010–.0022	.0016–.0030	.3134–.3140	.3125–.3134
1971–72	1300 ①	45	45	40–47	101–116	1.85	1.91	.0010–.0022	.0016–.0028	.3134–.3140	.3128–.3134
1972	1300 ②	45	45	40–47	91–105	1.01	1.16	.0010–.0022	.0020–.0032	.3130–.3136	.3124–0.3130
1973–76	1400	45	45	40–47	91–105	1.01	1.16	.0014–.0026	.0020–.0032	.3130–.3136	.3134–.3130
1976	1600	45	45	39–45	88–101	—	1.16	.0014–.0026	.0020–.0032	.3130–.3136	.3124–.3130
1977–79	1600	45	45	43–50	91–105	—	1.16	.0015–.0026	.0016–.0028	.3130–.3136	.3128–.3134
1980–82	1600	45	45	42–48	112–127	—	1.20	.0014–.0026	.0016–.0028	.3130–.3136	.3128–.3134
	1800	45	45	42–48	112–127	—	1.20	.0014–.0026	.0016–.0028	.3130–.3136	.3128–.3134
1983–84	1600, 1800 Man.	45	45–45.5	19–22.1	32.9–38.1	1.476	1.555	.0014–.0026	.0016–.0028	.3130–.3136	.3128–.3134
	1800 Auto ③	45	45–45.5	26–30	51.4–58.9	1.476	1.555	.0014–.0026	.0016–.0028	.3130–.3136	.3128–.3134
	1200	45	45	112.8–129.8 (@ 1.248	112.8–129.8 @ 1.248	1.25	1.25	0.0008–0.0020	0.0016–0.0028	0.2742–0.2748	0.2734–0.2740

① 1300 used in 1300G models
② 1300 used in 1300 GL and DL models
③ These engines equipped with hydraulic lifters
▲ Valve guides are removable

87903C05

Crankshaft and Connecting Rod Specifications

(All measurements given in in.)

Year	Engine Type	Crankshaft				Connecting Rod		
		Main Brg Journal Diameter	Main Brg Oil Clearance	Shaft End-Play	Thrust on No.	Journal Diameter	Oil Clearance	Side Clearance
1970–71	1100	1.9665–1.9669	.0008–.0024	.0016–.0054	2	1.8900–1.8960	.0012–.0026	.004–.007
1971–72	1300 ①	1.9665–1.9669	.0008–.0024	.0016–.0054	2	1.8900–1.8960	.0012–.0026	.004–.007
1972	1300 ②	1.9688–1.9692	.0004–.0023	.0016–.0054	2	1.8912–1.8918	.0012–.0029	.0028–.0118
1973	1400	1.9688–1.9692	.0004–.0022	.0016–.0054	2	1.8912–1.8918	.0012–.0026	.0028–.0118
1974	1400	1.9688–1.9692	.0004–.0020	.0016–.0053	2	1.7715–1.7720	.0012–.0032	.0028–.0118
1975	1400	1.9667–1.9673 ③	.0004–.0020 ④	.0019–.0054	2	1.7715–1.7720	.0012–.0031	.0028–.0118
1976	1400, 1600	1.9667–1.9673 ③	.0004–.0020 ④	.0016–.0054	2	1.7715–1.7720	.0012–.0029	.0028–.0130
1977–79	1600	1.9667–1.9673 ③	.0004–.0016 ⑤	.0016–.0054	2	1.7715–1.7720	.0008–.0025	.0028–.0130
1980–82	1600	1.9667–1.9673 ③	.0004–.0014 ⑥	.0016–.0054	2	1.7715–1.7720	.0008–.0028	.0028–.0130
	1800	2.1636–2.1642	.0004–.0012 ⑦	.0016–.0054 ⑧	2	1.7715–1.7720	.0008–.0028	.0028–.0130
1983–84	1600	2.1636–2.1642	.0004–.0014 ⑥	.0004–.0037	2	1.7715–1.7720	.0008–.0028	.0028–.0130
	1800	1.9668–1.9673	.0004–.0012 ⑦	.0004–.0037	2	1.7715–1.7720	.0008–.0028	.0028–.0130

① 1300 used in 1300G
② 1300 used in 1300 GL and DL
③ Center bearing: 1.9673–1.9677
④ Center bearing: 0–0.0014
⑤ Center bearing: 0–0.008
⑥ Center bearing: .0004–.0012
⑦ Center bearing: .0004–.0010
⑧ 1982: .0004–.0037

87903C06

Piston and Ring Specifications

Year	Engine	Piston Clearance	Ring Gap			Ring Side Clearance		
			Top Compression	Bottom Compression	Oil Control	Top Compression	Bottom Compression	Oil Control
1970–72	1100 and 1300 (in 1300G)	.001–.002	.008–.020	.008–.020	.012–.035	.001–.003	.001–.003	None
1972	1300 (in GL, DL)	.001–.003	.008–.020	.008–.020	.012–.035	.001–.003	.001–.003	None
1973	1400	.001–.002	.008–.020	.008–.020	.012–.035	.001–.003	.001–.003	None
1974–79	1400, 1600	.001–.002	.012–.020	.012–.020	.012–.035	.001–.003	.001–.003	None
1980–82	1600	.001–.002	.008–.013	.008–.013	.008–.035	.001–.003	.001–.003	None
1980–82	1800	.001–.002	.008–.013	.008–.013	.008–.035	.001–.003	.001–.003	None
1983–84	1600, 1800	.0004–.0016	.0079–.0138	.0079–.0138	.0079–.0354	.0016–.0031	.0012–.0028	None
	1200	.0015–.0024	.0079–.0138	.0079–.0138	.0120–.0350	.0014–.0030	.0010–.0026	None

87903C07

Torque Specifications
(All readings given in ft. lbs.)

Year	Engine Type	Cylinder Head Bolts	Rod Bearing Bolts	Crankcase Halves	Crankshaft Pulley Bolt	Flywheel-to-Crankshaft Bolt	Manifolds	
							Intake	Exhaust
1970–71	1100	30–35	35–38	10 mm nuts 27–31 8 mm nuts 3–4	39–42	30–33	13–16	7–8
1971–72	1300	43 ①	35–38	11 mm bolts 15–29 10 mm nuts 27–31 8 mm nuts 3–4 6 mm nuts 3–4	39–42	30–33	13–16	7–9
1973	1400	47 ① ④	29–31 ②	11 mm bolts 15–29 10 mm nuts 27–31 8 mm nuts 17–19 6 mm nuts 3–4	39–42	30–33	13–16	12–14
1974–79	1400, 1600	47 ① ④	29–31 ② ③	10 mm bolts 29–35 8 mm bolts 17–19 6 mm bolts 3–4	39–42	30–33	13–16	12–15
1980–84	1600	47 ① ⑥	29–31 ⑤	10 mm bolts 29–35 8 mm bolts 17–20 6 mm bolts 3.3–4	39–42	30–33	13–16	19–22 ⑦
	1800	47 ①	29–31 ⑤	10 mm bolts 29–35 8 mm bolts 17–20 6 mm bolts 3.3–4	39–42	30–33 ⑧	13–16	19–22 ⑦
	1200	48–54	29–35	30–35 ⑨	47–57	65–71	18–22	14–22

① These engines use nuts and studs rather than bolts
② 1400 uses nuts and studs
③ 1976–78: 36
④ Cylinder heads should be torqued in 4 stages (in the proper sequence). First, tighten to 22 ft. lbs. Loosen and retighten to 45 ft. lbs. Loosen and tighten again to 45 ft. lbs. Finally, loosen and torque to 47 ft. lbs.
⑤ Oil on threads
⑥ Tighten in sequence to: 22, then to 43, and then to final torque
⑦ 1984 engines (except Turbo)—18–25
⑧ 51–55: 1985 and later

87903C08

Engine

REMOVAL & INSTALLATION

Constantly be aware of the dangers involved when working on an automobile and take the proper precautions. Use a safe chain hoist or floor crane of the proper capacity. Work on level ground. Make sure the engine sling is secured properly before lifting the engine. When working underneath a raised car always support it on jackstands. Be careful not to spill brake fluid or engine coolant on painted surfaces of the car body. Cover the front fenders if possible. Remember safety is always the most important rule.

ff-1 and 1300G

▶ See Figures 31, 32, 33 and 34

➡On ff-1 and 1300G models, the engine and transaxle must be removed as an assembly.

1. Disconnect the battery cables, negative first.
2. Remove the spare tire from the engine compartment.
3. Remove the hood:
   a. Remove the horn multi-connector.
   b. Remove the nut securing the hood stay to the firewall.
   c. Make matchmarks on the hinges and body, and remove the hood hinge bolts from the body, but leave the hinges fastened to the hood.
   d. Lift the hood clear of the body.
4. Remove the two bolts which secure the front bumper to the bumper brackets.
5. Remove the four screws (two on each side) which secure the grille and remove it toward the front of the car.
6. Remove the five bolts securing the hook lock assembly to the radiator support and set it aside.

➡Do not remove the cable from the hook lock.

7. Remove the ten bolts securing the front roll pan and remove it in a downward direction.

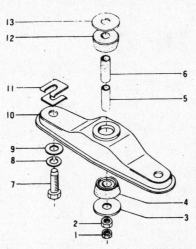

1. Nut
2. Nut
3. Washer
4. Cushion
5. Pipe
6. Tube
7. Bolt
8. Lockwasher
9. Washer
10. Bracket
11. Washer (for adjustment of height)
12. Cushion
13. Washer

87903036

Fig. 31 Common engine mount assembly

8. Remove the hoses from the air cleaner and unfasten it from its brackets.

a. Place a suitable container under the fuel line union to catch the gas, and disconnect the hose at the union by removing the clip and pulling the line off.

b. Drain the engine and transaxle lubricant.

✳✳CAUTION

When draining the coolant, keep in mind that cats and dogs are attracted by ethylene glycol antifreeze, and are quite likely to drink any that is left in an uncovered container or in puddles on the ground. This will prove fatal in sufficient quantity. Always drain the coolant into a sealable container. Coolant should be reused unless it is contaminated or several years old.

9. Drain the coolant in the following manner:

a. Remove the cap from the main radiator, after first pushing the button on the expansion tank cap to allow any pressure to escape from the system.

b. Place a clean container of a suitable size underneath the radiator drain plug to save the coolant. Remove the drain plug.

c. Move the container underneath and loosen, but do not remove, the left and right drain plugs on the cylinder head.

d. Remove all 3 radiator hoses from the engine.

10. Disconnect the following wiring:

a. Alternator multi-connector

b. Starter wiring harness

c. Thermostat harness

d. Oil pressure switch connector

e. High tension line at the coil

f. Three blower motor connectors

g. Distributor primary lead harness

h. Two thermoswitch lines (at the sub-radiator)

11. Remove the starter. Disconnect the heater duct from the blower housing.

12. Remove the circlip which secures the inner and outer control cables, and then detach the cables from the blower housing.

13. Remove the front radiator support with the main radiator, sub-radiator, shroud, blower motor and expansion tank as an assembly, in the following order:

➡**Do not separate the blower motor, itself, from the radiator support because its assembly is quite difficult.**

   a. Remove the two 8mm bolts which secure the blower housing.
   b. Remove the four screws and two bolts which secure the radiator support to the headlamp bracket.

✳✳WARNING

Do not remove the center bolt.

   c. Slowly remove the assembly from the front of the car.

14. Remove the hoses and leads from the windshield washer reservoir, and then lift the reservoir out of its bracket.

15. Disconnect both Double Offset Joints (DOJ) in the following manner:
   a. Apply the parking brake so that the drums can't turn.
   b. Remove the brake drum-to-double offset joint retaining bolts.
   c. Gently lower the joint and the axle shaft.
   d. Repeat for the other side.

16. Disconnect the brake lines from both sides. Use a container to catch the brake fluid, but do not reuse the fluid.

17. Disconnect the following cables and linkages:
   a. Loosen, but don't remove, the screw on the carburetor throttle lever. Detach the end of the cable, and pull the cable out.
   b. Remove the nut which secures the choke cable from its lever and loosen the bracket retaining nut (6mm).
   c. Disconnect the speedometer cable from the speedometer head (from behind the instrument cluster) and pull it out, working from the engine compartment.
   d. Disconnect the gear selector rod from inside the car.
   e. Disconnect the left and right parking brake cables from the turnbuckles inside the car.
   f. Remove the clutch torque rod (ball stud) bolts on the side of the crossmember.

18. Remove the bolts from the manifold pipe flanges and separate the downpipes from the left and right manifolds. Be careful not to lose the insulators and gaskets.

19. Unfasten the brackets which secure the exhaust pipe to the floor pan and remove the bolts which secure the exhaust pipe to the muffler hanger. Remove the exhaust pipe.

20. Disconnect the engine mount in the following order:
   a. Remove the securing nut from the shaft while holding the adjustment nut.
   b. Remove the washer, cushion, pipe and tube.
   c. Unscrew the two retaining bolts and remove the bracket.

21. Remove the left and right bolts from the rear support cushion which is located on the transaxle housing. Leave the cushion attached to the transaxle case. Be careful not to lose the washer.

22. Remove the nut, spring washer, and washer from the front support cushion. Leave the cushion attached to the engine.

23. On station wagons, remove the horizontal damper by removing the front nut and pulling the shaft rearward. Be careful not to lose any components.

24. Check to be sure that everything which was supposed to have been removed was, before going on to the next step.

25. Attach a chain hoist to the front and rear engine lifting hooks (hangers).

26. Hoist the engine/transaxle assembly straight up, high enough so that the brake drums clear the crossmember. Then carefully move the engine forward so that the exhaust manifolds clear the crossmember and torsion bars.

27. Support the engine and transaxle in a suitable workstand.

To install:

28. Using a hoist lower the engine and transaxle into the vehicle

29. On station wagons, when installing the horizontal damper, be sure that the larger of the two rubber cushions is compressed to 0.55 in. (13mm)

30. Install the front support cushion washer, spring washer and nut.

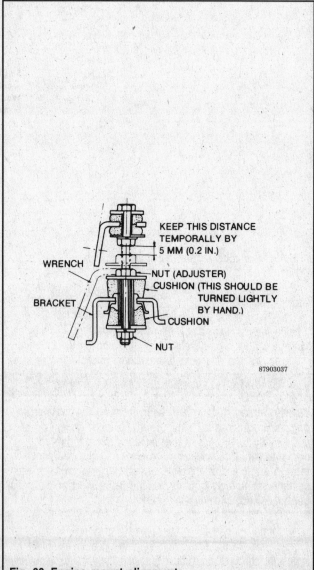

Fig. 32 Engine mount alignment

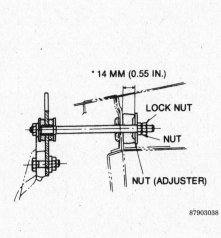

Fig. 33 Aligning the horizontal dampener

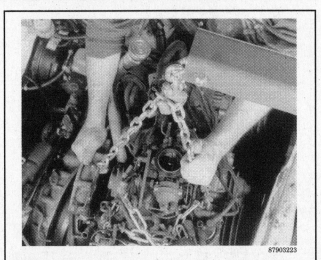

Fig. 34 Use a chain and hoist to remove the engine from the vehicle

31. Install the support cushion washer(s) and the left and right bolts.

32. When installing the engine mount, temporarily raise the adjusting nut so that it is positioned about ¼ in. (6mm) below the nut above it. After installing the body bracket, lower the adjusting nut until the middle cushion can be turned, while tightening the bottom nut.

33. Install the engine mount in the following order:
    a. Install the bracket and two retaining bolts
    b. Install the tube, pipe, cushion and the washer.
    c. Hold the adjustment nut and fasten the securing nut to the shaft.

Be sure to observe the following points during engine/transaxle installation:

34. Tighten the engine mounts to the following specifications:
- Engine mount bolts: 18-20 ft. lbs. (24-27 Nm)
- Front cushion bolts: 18-25 ft. lbs. (24-33 Nm)
- Rear cushion bolts (3): 18-25 ft. lbs. (24-33 Nm)
- Rear cushion side bolt: 22-29 ft. lbs. (29-39 Nm)

35. Install the exhaust pipe and fasten the bolts which secure the exhaust pipe to the muffler hanger. Fasten the brackets which secure the exhaust pipe to the floor pan. Install the insulators and gaskets, engage the downpipes to the left and right manifolds and fasten the manifold flange bolts.

36. Install the clutch torque rod (ball stud) on the side of the crossmember.

37. Connect the left and right parking brake cables from inside the car and apply the brake.

38. Connect the gear selector rod.

39. Connect the speedometer cable.

40. Install the throttle cable and fasten the screw on the carburetor throttle lever.

41. Connect the brake lines.

42. Install the axle shaft, Double Offset Joints and fasten the drum-to-double offset joint bolts.

43. Install the windshield washer reservoir and connect the reservoir hoses and leads.

44. Install the front radiator support with the main radiator, sub-radiator, shroud, blower motor and expansion tank as an assembly, fasten the four screws and two bolts which secure the radiator support to the headlamp bracket. Tighten the two 8mm bolts which secure the blower housing.

45. Install the inner and outer control cables to the blower motor and engage the circlip.

46. Connect the heater duct to the blower housing and install the starter.

47. Connect the following wiring:
    a. Two thermoswitch lines (at the sub-radiator
    b. Distributor primary lead harness
    c. Three blower motor connectors
    d. High tension line at the coil
    e. Oil pressure switch connector
    f. Thermostat harness
    g. Starter wiring harness
    h. Alternator multi-connector

48. Install the radiator hoses.

49. Install the air cleaner and hoses.

50. Install the front roll pan and fasten the ten attaching bolts

51. Fasten the five bolts attaching the hook lock assembly to the radiator support.

52. Install the grill and fasten the four screws.

53. Install and fasten the two bolts which secure the front bumper to the bumper brackets.

54. Install the horn multi-connector.

55. Install the hood and fasten the hood hinge attaching bolts.

56. Top up the engine coolant, transaxle lubricant, engine oil, and windshield washer levels, as detailed in Section 1.

57. Connect the battery cables.

58. Start the vehicle and check for vacuum, coolant, oil, fuel and refrigerant leaks. Adjust timing and idle speed to specification.

1970-82 1400, 1600 and 1979-84 1800

▶ See Figures 35, 36, 37, 38, 34 and 39

➡**On these models, the engine is removed separately from the transaxle.**

1. Open the hood as far as possible and secure it with the stay.

2. Disconnect the ground cable from the negative (-) battery terminal.

3. Remove the bolt which secures the ground cable at the intake manifold and disconnect the cable. It is unnecessary to connect the cable fully. Leave it routed along the side of the body.

4. Remove the spare tire from the engine compartment.

5. Remove the emission control system hoses from the air cleaner.

6. Remove the air cleaner brackets, the wing nut, and lift the air cleaner assembly off the carburetor. Plug the carburetor opening. Place a suitable container under the fuel line union to catch the gasoline and disconnect the hoses at the union, by removing the clip and pulling the hose off.

7. Drain engine oil.

✳✳CAUTION

When draining the coolant, keep in mind that cats and dogs are attracted by ethylene glycol antifreeze, and are quite likely to drink any that is left in an uncovered container or in puddles on the ground. This will prove fatal in sufficient quantity. Always drain the coolant into a sealable container. Coolant should be reused unless it is contaminated or several years old.

8. Drain the coolant and disconnect the radiator hoses:

    a. Place a clean container, large enough to hold the contents of the cooling system, beneath the radiator drain plug so that the coolant may be reused.

    b. Loosen the drain plug on the radiator and turn it so that its slot faces downward.

    c. Disconnect both of the hoses at the radiator, leaving them connected to the engine.

    d. Disconnect the heater hoses from the pipe at the side of the engine.

    e. On automatic transaxle models, disconnect the oil cooler inlet and outlet hoses at the radiator.

9. Disconnect the following electrical wiring:

    a. Alternator multi-connector

    b. Oil pressure sender connection

    c. Three engine cooling fan connectors

    d. Temperature sender connection

    e. Primary distributor lead

    f. Secondary ignition leads (ignition side)

    g. Starter wiring harness

    h. Anti-dieseling solenoid lead

    i. Automatic choke lead

    j. EGR vacuum solenoid

    k. EGR coolant temperature switch

    l. On automatic transaxle models, disconnect the neutral safety switch harness and downshift solenoid harness.

10. Loosen the two radiator securing bolts, remove the ground lead from the upper side of the radiator, and lift the radiator out.

➡**On 4WD models, remove the engine fan from the pulley.**

11. Remove the horizontal damper in the following order:

    a. Remove the front nut from the damper.

    b. Remove the nut on the body bracket and remove the damper.

    c. Pull the damper rearward away from the engine lifting hook. Be careful not to lose any of the damper parts.

12. Remove the starter assembly, as outlined above under Engine Electrical.

13. Disconnect the following cables, hoses and linkages:

    a. Unfasten, but don't remove, the screw in the carburetor throttle lever. Loosen the outer end of the accelerator cable and remove it.

    b. On 1972-73 models, loosen the nut which secures the cable to the manual choke lever, loosen the retaining bracket nut, and detach the choke cable from the carburetor.

    c. Remove vacuum hose and purge hose from vapor canister (1977 and later models).

    d. On standard transaxle models, remove the clutch turn spring from the release lever and intake manifold, and remove the clutch cable from the lever.

    e. On automatic transaxle models, disconnect the vacuum hose attached to the transaxle.

    f. Disconnect the vacuum hose from the power brake unit (if so equipped).

14. Remove the power steering pump on cars so equipped, as follows:

    a. Using a pair of pliers (and protecting it with a rag), remove the cap from the nut on the pump drive idler pulley.

    b. Loosen attaching bolts and adjusting bolts of the idler and then pull off the power steering belt.

    c. Remove remaining mounting bolts and nut and, being careful not to permit oil to leak out of the filler pipe, rest the pump on top of the firewall.

    d. Remove the power steering pump mounting bracket from the front of the engine.

15. On 4WD models up to 1982, remove the under guard by unscrewing the attaching bolts.

16. Raise the front end of the vehicle with a floor jack and install axle stands to support it securely.

17. On 1970-81 models, remove the Y-shaped exhaust pipe and converter (if equipped). Be careful not to lose insulators and gaskets.

➡**This applies primarily to 1975-81 models. On earlier models, see the Exhaust Manifolds procedure later in this section.**

    a. Loosen the clamp fastening the air intake hose to the air stove on the exhaust pipe, and remove the hose.

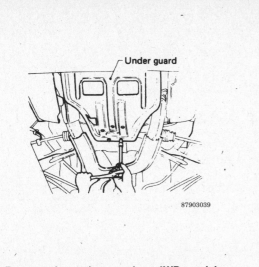

Fig. 35 Remove the under guard on 4WD models

b. Remove the air stove and remove the four nuts attaching the exhaust pipe to the cylinder heads.

c. Remove the two bolts and nuts connecting the exhaust pipe to the resonator (pre-muffler).

18. On 1982 models:

a. Remove hot air intake stove from the exhaust pipe.

b. Disconnect oxygen sensor harness, located right above the catalytic converter.

c. While supporting the exhaust pipe by hand, remove the two bolts attaching the exhaust pipe to the transaxle bracket. Lower the exhaust pipe.

❋❋CAUTION

The exhaust pipe is heavy, it is a good idea to have help supporting and lowering it.

d. Remove the nuts which secure the front exhaust manifold assembly to the engine's exhaust ports.

Fig. 36 Remove the timing hole cover

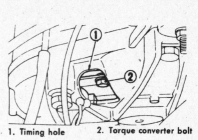

Fig. 37 Remove the torque converter bolts through the timing hole

e. On cars with automatic transaxle loosen the two bolts securing the manifold bracket to the rear engine mounting bracket about 0.4 in. (10mm)

f. On cars with a manual transaxle, remove the bolt securing the manifold bracket to the exhaust manifold assembly and wire the exhaust manifold assembly to the crossmember to prevent it from falling down.

19. 1983-84 Models:

a. Disconnect the oxygen sensor.

b. Remove the nuts securing the front exhaust pipe to the engine exhaust ports.

c. Loosen the bolt connecting the front exhaust pipe to the bracket on the body.

20. On automatic transaxle models, remove the torque converter bolts:

a. Remove the timing hole cover from the torque converter housing.

b. Remove the four bolts connecting the torque converter to the drive plate through the timing hole.

❋❋WARNING

Be careful that the bolts do not fall into the torque converter housing.

21. Set up a chain hoist on the engine, with hooks at the front and rear engine hangers. Adjust the hoist so that the weight of the engine is supported, but do not raise the engine.

❋❋CAUTION

The purpose of supporting the engine at this point is to prevent the unstable movement of the engine and protect the people working underneath the vehicle.

22. Position a suitable jack under the transaxle to support its weight when the engine is removed.

23. Remove the nuts (four each on top and bottom) connecting the engine and transaxle.

24. Remove the nuts holding the front engine mounts (rubber) to the crossmember.

87903221

Fig. 38 Position a suitable jack under the transaxle to support its weight when the engine is removed.

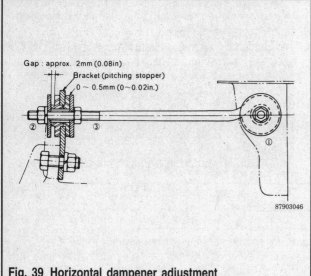

Gap : approx. 2mm (0.08in)
Bracket (pitching stopper)
0 ~ 0.5mm (0~0.02in.)

87903046

Fig. 39 Horizontal dampener adjustment

25. Before going onto the next step, be sure that all of the above steps have been completed.

26. Using the hoist, raise the engine slightly, about 1 in. (25mm). Keeping it level, move the engine forward, off the transaxle input shaft.

❉❉CAUTION

Do not raise the engine more than one inch prior to removing it from the input shaft or damage may occur to the driveshaft double offset joints. On standard transaxle models, be sure that the input shaft does not interfere with the input shaft does not interfere with the clutch spring assembly. On automatic transaxle models, leave the torque converter on the transaxle input shaft.

27. Hoist the engine carefully until it is completely out of the car, and place it on a suitable stand or workbench.

28. Be sure to observe the following during engine installation:

a. Use the following torque specifications when installing the engine:
- Transaxle-to-engine: 34-40 ft. lbs. (46-54 Nm)
- Torque converter: 17-20 ft. lbs. (23-27 Nm)
- Engine mounts: 14-24 ft. lbs. (18-32 Nm)
- Horizontal damper nut: 7-10 ft. lbs. (9-13 Nm)
- Exhaust pipe-to-engine: 12-14 ft. lbs. (16-18 Nm) on 1970-76 models and 19-22 ft. lbs. (25-29 Nm) on 1977-84 models
- Pre-muffler: 31-38 ft. lbs. (42-51 Nm)
- Radiator mounting bolt: 6-10 ft. lbs. (8-13 Nm)

b. Use care not to damage the input shaft splines or the clutch spring while lowering the engine in place. Grease the splines first.

c. When installing the exhaust pipe, always use new gaskets.

d. Perform the following adjustment to the horizontal damper:

29. 1970-81 models:

a. Tighten the body bracket nut.

b. Turn the front nut, until the clearance between the front washer and rubber cushion is zero.

c. Insert the bushing and tighten the front nut to specifications.

30. 1982 models:

a. Insert the damper rod into the bracket on the side of the engine. Tighten it at the side of the car body.

b. Tighten the nut at the rear of the damper so clearance between the rubber bushing and washer meets specifications:
- Manual transaxle: 0.031-0.047 in. (0.7874-1.1938mm)
- Automatic transaxle: 0.071-0.087 in. (1.8-2.2mm)

c. Finally, tighten the front nut using a wrench on the rear nut as a backup. Tighten to 7-13 ft. lbs. (9-17 Nm)

Make all of the clutch and accelerator linkage adjustments as detailed elsewhere in the book. Replenish the engine oil and coolant supplies, as detailed in Section 1.

1983-84 1800 Turbo

▶ **See Figures 40, 41, 38 and 34**

1. Open the hood and prop it securely. Remove the spare tire. Remove the spare tire bracket.

2. Decrease fuel pressure in the injection system by disconnecting the fuel pump connector and then cranking the engine for at least 5 seconds. If the engine starts, allow it to run until it stalls. Then, reconnect the fuel pump connector.

3. Remove the battery ground cable entirely.

4. Disconnect the air temperature sensor plug in the engine compartment.

5. Remove the fuel system hoses and evaporative emissions system hoses.

6. Disconnect the vacuum hoses from the cruise control, Master-Vac®, air intake shutter, and heater air intake door.

7. Disconnect the wiring and remove the harness from the alternator, EGI, thermoswitch, electric fan, A/C condenser, ignition coil, and the main engine harness.

8. Disconnect the ignition high tension wires, and engine ground wire.

9. Disconnect the fusible link assembly.

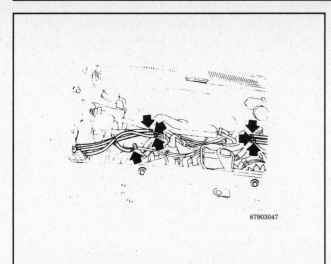

Fig. 40 Disconnect the vacuum hoses shown to remove the 1800 Turbo engine

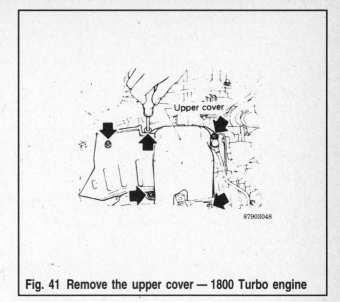

Fig. 41 Remove the upper cover — 1800 Turbo engine

10. Disconnect the accelerator linkage. Remove the washer fluid tank and store it behind the right side strut tower.

11. Remove the power steering pump as follows:

a. Loosen the alternator adjusting and lockbolts, shift the alternator to loosen the belt and then remove the belt.

b. Remove the pump pulley.

c. Remove the pump mounting bolts and clamp.

d. Remove the engine oil filler pipe brace.

e. Then, remove the power steering pump and place it on the bulkhead without disturbing lines.

12. Loosen hose clamps and remove the air intake duct. Seal openings to keep dirt out of air intake passages.

13. Remove the air intake line running to the flowmeter. Cover the openings.

14. Remove the horizontal damper and clip.

15. Remove the center section of the exhaust pipe as follows:

a. Disconnect the temperature sensor connector.

b. Disconnect the exhaust pipe at the turbocharger body.

c. Remove the rear cover.

d. Remove the bolt attaching the center exhaust section to the transaxle.

e. Remove the bolts from the hangers, and carefully remove the pipe (clearance is tight) so as to avoid damage.

16. Slightly loosen the attaching bolts and remove the converter cover.

17. Disconnect the turbocharger oil supply and drain lines. Then, remove the three bolts attaching the turbocharger to the exhaust system, and remove the turbocharger assembly, lower cover, and gasket.

18. Disconnect the O$_2$ sensor connector. Remove the bolts connecting the torque converter to the drive plate.

19. Hook a chain hoist to the horizontal damper bracket and support the engine. Then, remove the upper engine-to-transaxle bolts. Leave the starter in place.

20. Drain the engine coolant, using a hose to lead coolant to a clean container. Then, disconnect upper and lower radiator coolant hoses and oil cooler lines, and ground wire, and remove the radiator.

❊❊CAUTION

When draining the coolant, keep in mind that cats and dogs are attracted by ethylene glycol antifreeze, and are quite likely to drink any that is left in an uncovered container or in puddles on the ground. This will prove fatal in sufficient quantity. Always drain the coolant into a sealable container. Coolant should be reused unless it is contaminated or several years old.

21. Disconnect oil cooler lines at the engine. Drain oil into a clean container. Disconnect the heater hoses from the side of the engine.

22. Remove the front engine mount. Then, remove the lower nuts joining the engine to the transaxle.

23. Locate a jack under the transaxle. Raise both engine and transaxle slightly. Then, pull the engine forward until the transaxle shaft clears the clutch. Carefully raise the engine out of the engine compartment.

To install:

24. Reverse the removal procedure, keeping the following points in mind:

a. After installing all major mounting nuts and bolts finger-tight, tighten upper transaxle-to-engine bolts just snug. Then, remove support from the engine and transaxle. Then, tighten lower transaxle-to-engine bolts. Next, tighten engine mount nuts. Finally, fully tighten upper transaxle-to-engine bolts. Tighten all to 14-17 ft. lbs. (18-23 Nm).

b. when tightening turbocharger mounting and exhaust system mounting bolts, be sure to go back and forth and tighten bolts evenly. Use new gaskets throughout.

c. Observe the following torque figures:

- Torque converter drive plate: 17-20 ft. lbs. (23-27 Nm)

- Turbocharger-to-exhaust system: 31-38 ft. lbs. (42-51 Nm)

- Exhaust system-to-transaxle bolt: 18-25 ft. lbs. (24-33 Nm)

- Exhaust system hanger bolts: 7-13 ft. lbs. (9-17 Nm)

- Rear exhaust pipe joint: 7-13 ft. lbs. (9-17 Nm)
- Power steering pump pulley: 25-30 ft. lbs. (33-40 Nm)
- Power steering pump mounting bolts: 18-25 ft. lbs. (24-35 Nm)

d. Adjust the horizontal damper. Tighten the locknut to 6.5-9.4 lb. ft. (8-12 Nm).

e. Adjust the accelerator pedal so there is 0.04-1.2 in. (1-30mm) between the pin and stop. Adjust the cable for an end-play of 0-0.08 in. (0-2mm) on the actuator side.

f. Install radiator hoses onto radiator connections before installing it.

g. Replenish all fluids. Warm the engine and then run at 4000 rpm to check for leaks in oil cooler and lines.

1983-84 1600 Carbureted Engines

▶ See Figures 42, 43, 44 and 45

➡On all models, the engine is removed separately from the transaxle.

1. Open the hood as far as possible and secure it with the stay. Disconnect the negative battery cable.

2. Remove the ground cable-to-intake manifold bolt and disconnect the cable. It is unnecessary to remove the cable fully; leave it routed along the side of the body.

3. Remove the spare tire from the engine compartment.

4. Disengage the emission control system hoses from the air cleaner. Remove the air cleaner brackets and the wing nut, then lift the air cleaner assembly off the carburetor.

5. Position a drain pan (to catch the gasoline) under the fuel line union. At the union, remove the hose clamp, then pull the hose(s) to disconnect them.

6. Position a drain pan under the engine, remove the drain plug and drain the oil from the crankcase.

7. To drain the engine coolant, perform the following procedures:

a. Position a clean container, large enough to hold the contents of the cooling system, under the radiator drain plug.

b. Open the drain plug on the radiator; turn it so that it's slot faces downward.

c. Disconnect both the hoses from the radiator.

d. Disconnect the heater hoses from the pipe on the side of the engine.

e. If equipped with an automatic transaxle, disconnect the oil cooler lines from the radiator.

8. Disengage the following electrical wiring connectors:

a. Alternator multi-connector

b. Oil pressure sender connector

c. Engine cooling fan connectors

d. Temperature sender connector

e. Primary distributor lead

f. Secondary ignition leads (ignition side)

g. Starter wiring harness

h. Anti-dieseling solenoid lead

i. Automatic choke lead

j. EGR vacuum solenoid

k. EGR coolant temperature switch

l. If equipped with an automatic transaxle, disconnect the neutral safety switch harness and downshift solenoid harness.

9. Loosen the radiator-to-chassis bolts, remove the ground lead from the upper side of the radiator and the radiator.

➡On 4WD models, remove the engine fan from the pulley.

10. To remove the crankshaft damper, perform the following procedures:

a. Remove the front nut from the damper.

b. Remove the nut on the body bracket and withdraw the damper.

c. Pull the damper rearward, away from the engine lifting hook; be careful not to lose any of the damper parts.

11. Remove the starter-to-engine bolts and the starter from the vehicle.

12. Disconnect the following cables, hoses and linkages, by performing the following procedure:

a. Loosen the screw on the carburetor throttle lever. Remove the outer end of the accelerator cable and withdraw it.

b. Remove the vacuum hose and the purge hose from the vapor canister.

c. If equipped with a manual transaxle, remove the clutch return spring from the release lever/intake manifold and the clutch cable from the lever.

Fig. 42 Use an extension to help reach the exhaust pipe bolts

Fig. 43 Remove the timing hole cover from the torque converter housing

d. If equipped with an automatic transaxle, disconnect the vacuum hose from the transaxle.

e. Disconnect the vacuum hose from the power brake unit (if equipped).

13. On 4WD models, remove the skid plate-to-chassis bolts and the plate.

14. To remove the Y-shaped exhaust pipe, perform the following procedures:

a. Remove the exhaust pipe-to-cylinder head nuts.

b. Remove the exhaust pipe-to-pre-muffler nuts/bolts.

c. While supporting the exhaust pipe by hand, remove the exhaust pipe-to-transaxle bracket bolts, then lower the exhaust pipe.

Fig. 44 Using a floor jack, position it under the transaxle to support its weight when the engine is removed

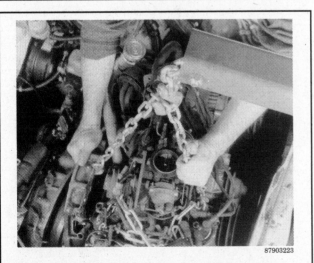

Fig. 45 Use a chain and hoist to remove the engine from the vehicle

15. If equipped with an automatic transaxle, remove the torque converter bolts by performing the following procedures:

a. Remove the timing hole cover from the torque converter housing.

b. Through the timing hole, remove the torque converter-to-drive plate bolts.

✳✳WARNING

Be careful that the bolts DO NOT fall into the torque converter housing.

16. Connect a chain hoist and a cable to the engine, with hooks at the front and rear engine hangers. Adjust the hoist so that the weight of the engine is supported but **DO NOT** raise the engine.

17. Using a floor jack, position it under the transaxle to support it's weight when the engine is removed.

18. Remove the engine-to-transaxle nuts (four each on top and bottom).

19. Remove the front engine mount-to-crossmember nuts.

20. Using the hoist, raise the engine slightly, about 1 in. (25mm). Keeping it level, move the engine forward, off the transaxle input shaft.

✳✳WARNING

DO NOT raise the engine more than 1 in. (25mm) prior to removing it from the input shaft or damage may occur to the driveshaft double offset joints. If equipped with a manual transaxle, be sure that the input shaft does not interfere with the clutch spring assembly; if equipped with an automatic transaxle, leave the torque converter on the transaxle input shaft.

21. Hoist the engine carefully until it is completely out of the vehicle, then secure it onto a workstand.

To install:

22. When installing the engine, use new gaskets and observe the following torque specifications:

- Transaxle-to-engine bolts: 34-40 ft. lbs. (46-54 Nm)
- Torque converter bolts: 17-20 ft. lbs. (23-27 Nm)
- Crossmember bolts: 14-24 ft. lbs. (18-32 Nm)
- Crankshaft damper nut: 7-10 ft. lbs. (9-13 Nm)
- Exhaust pipe-to-engine bolt: 19-22 ft. lbs. (25-29 Nm)
- Premuffler nuts: 31-38 ft. lbs. (42-51 Nm)
- Radiator bolts: 6-10 ft. lbs. (8-13 Nm)

23. Adjust of the clutch and accelerator linkage. Refill the crankcase and cooling system.

➡**Use care not to damage the input shaft splines or the clutch spring when lowering the engine in place.**

24. When installing the crankshaft damper, perform the following adjustments:

a. Tighten the body bracket nut.

b. Turn the front nut until the clearance between the front washer and rubber cushion is zero.

c. Insert the bushing and tighten the front nut.

Rocker Arm (Valve) Cover

REMOVAL & INSTALLATION

▶ See Figures 46 and 47

1. Remove the bolts from the rocker covers.
2. Using a rubber hammer, tap the rocker covers to break the seal between the gasket and the valve cover.
3. Remove the rocker cover from the head.
4. Remove the old gasket from the rocker cover and clean the surface of the cylinder head and the rocker cover.

To install:

5. Spread Permatex® #2 on the mating surface of the rocker cover (to hold the gasket in place during installation), and install a new gasket.
6. Place the rocker cover on the head, install the bolts and torque to 4 ft. lbs. (5 Nm)

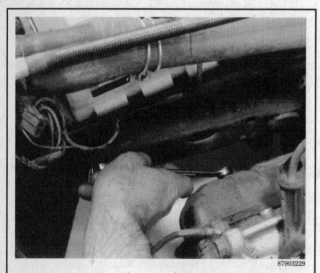

Fig. 46 Remove the bolts from the rocker covers

Fig. 47 Carefully remove the old gasket material using a gasket scraper

Rocker Shafts

REMOVAL & INSTALLATION

▶ See Figures 48, 49, 50 and 51

1. Remove the engine from the vehicle and mount it in a workstand.
2. Remove the valve covers and their gaskets from the heads.
3. Remove the nuts which secure the rocker assemblies to the cylinder heads.
4. Remove the rocker assemblies.
5. Remove the pushrods from their bores, being sure to keep them in the same sequence in which they were removed.

➡ It is a good idea to tag each pushrod as it is removed from its bore, to aid in correct installation.

To install:

6. Install the pushrods in their proper bores.
7. Install the valve rocker assemblies and tighten the assembly mounting bolts to 30-35 ft. lbs. (40-47 Nm) on ff-1 models, 37-43 ft. lbs. (50-58 Nm) on 1970-79 models and 47 ft. lbs. (63 Nm) on 1980-84 models.

INSPECTION

▶ See Figure 52

Inspect rocker arms for pitting or wear on the valve contact point, or excessive bushing wear. Bushings need only be replaced if wear is excessive, because the rocker arm normally contacts the shaft at one point only. Grind the valve contact point of rocker arm smooth if necessary, removing as little material as possible. If excessive material must be removed to smooth and square the arm, it should be replaced. Clean out all oil holes and passages in rocker shaft. If shaft is grooved or worn, replace it. Lubricate and assemble the rocker shaft.

Fig. 48 Remove the valve covers from the heads

Fig. 49 Remove the fasteners which secure the rocker assemblies to the cylinder heads . . .

Fig. 50 . . . then remove the rocker assemblies

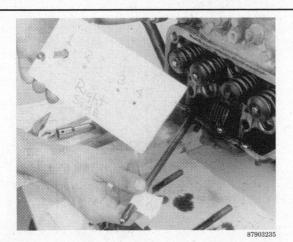

Fig. 51 Remove the pushrods from their bores, being sure to keep them in the same sequence in which they were removed

Thermostat

REMOVAL & INSTALLATION

▶ See Figures 53, 54 and 55

> **✻✻CAUTION**
>
> DO NOT perform this operation on a hot engine. Depress the button on the radiator cap to relieve the pressure in the cooling system.

The thermostat is located on the top of the intake manifold, at the right side of the engine.

1. If necessary, remove the spare tire to gain working clearance.
2. Position a clean drain pan under the radiator, remove the drain plug and the radiator cap, then drain the cooling system to a level below the thermostat.
3. If necessary, remove the air cleaner assembly, with it's hoses, brackets and wing nut.
4. Remove the thermostat housing-to-intake manifold bolts, lift the cover and discard the gasket.
5. Remove the thermostat; be sure to note it's mounting position.
6. Using a putty knife, clean the gasket mounting surfaces. Check and/or replace the thermostat (if necessary).

To install:

7. Install a new gasket, using sealant (if necessary) and the thermostat.

➡ **Be sure that the thermostat is installed with the spring/wax pellet facing downward; MAKE SURE that the jiggle valve is facing upwards.**

8. Install the housing and fasten the housing-to-intake manifold bolts.
9. If removed install the air cleaner assembly, hoses, brackets, and wing nut.
10. Refill the cooling system and check for leaks.

Intake Manifold

REMOVAL & INSTALLATION

▶ See Figures 56, 57, 58, 59, 60 and 61

> **✻✻WARNING**
>
> Do not perform this operation on a warm engine. Wait until the engine is cold.

1. Remove the spare tire from the engine compartment.
2. Tag and disconnect the emission control system hoses.
3. Remove the mounting bracket screws and the air cleaner assembly. On 1800 Turbo models, remove the air intake duct.

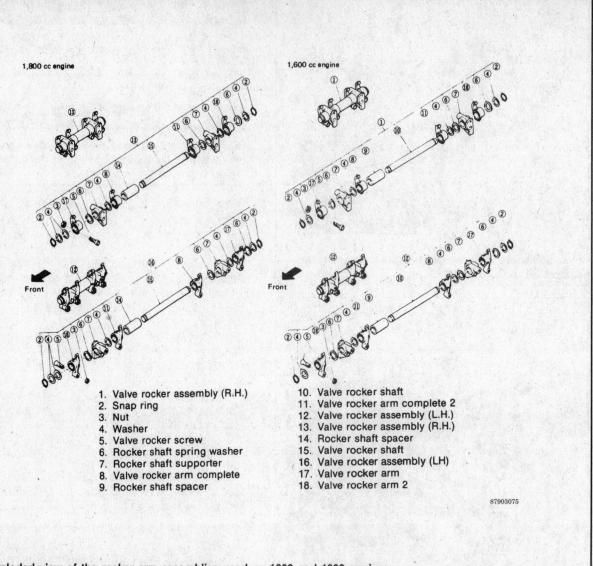

1,800 cc engine

1,600 cc engine

Front

Front

1. Valve rocker assembly (R.H.)
2. Snap ring
3. Nut
4. Washer
5. Valve rocker screw
6. Rocker shaft spring washer
7. Rocker shaft supporter
8. Valve rocker arm complete
9. Rocker shaft spacer
10. Valve rocker shaft
11. Valve rocker arm complete 2
12. Valve rocker assembly (L.H.)
13. Valve rocker assembly (R.H.)
14. Rocker shaft spacer
15. Valve rocker shaft
16. Valve rocker assembly (LH)
17. Valve rocker arm
18. Valve rocker arm 2

87903075

Fig. 52 Exploded view of the rocker arm assemblies used on 1600 and 1800 engines

87903236

Fig. 53 After the bolts are removed, pull the housing from the intake manifold

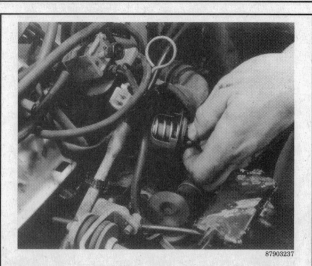

87903237

Fig. 54 When removing the thermostat, note which direction it was installed

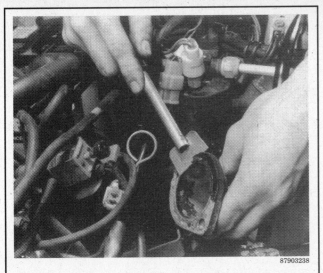

Fig. 55 Clean the gasket mounting surfaces thoroughly

1. Screw
2. Spring washer
3. Accelerator cable clamp
4. Bolt
5. Spring washer
6. Accelerator cable bracket
7. Washer
8. Thermostat cover
9. Thermostat cover gasket
10. Thermostat
11. Hose clamp
12. Water by-pass hose
13. Water by-pass connector
14. Gasket
15. Water by-pass connector
16. Bolt
17. Bolt
18. Intake manifold gasket
19. Intake manifold
20. Stud
21. Plug
22. Temperature sending unit
23. Carburetor gasket
24. Spring washer
25. Nut

87903051

Fig. 56 A common carbureted intake manifold assembly found on models covered by this manual

4. Drain the cooling system and detach all of the water hoses from the thermostat housing.

⁂CAUTION

When draining the coolant, keep in mind that cats and dogs are attracted by ethylene glycol antifreeze, and are quite likely to drink any that is left in an uncovered container or in puddles on the ground. This will prove fatal in sufficient quantity. Always drain the coolant into a sealable container. Coolant should be reused unless it is contaminated or several years old.

5. Disconnect the thermoswitch connector.

6. On models having a distributor vacuum control valve, disconnect the hoses and leads from it. Disconnect the anti-dieseling solenoid leads, as well.

7. On ff-1 and 1300G models, which have an air injection system, perform the following:

   a. Disconnect the lines from the anti-afterburn valve.

   b. Unbolt the air injection manifold mounting brackets from the intake manifold.

   c. Remove the bypass valve (if so equipped).

8. On 1974 and later models, disconnect the following:

   a. Automatic choke-to-voltage regulator wire at the connector.

   b. EGR solenoid wiring (if so equipped).

   c. The EGR pipe by removing the nuts which secure it to the intake manifold and the cylinder head (if so equipped).

9. Disconnect the throttle cable and manual choke cable (if so equipped) from their brackets.

10. Disconnect the fuel line from the carburetor. On 1800 Turbo models, disengage the hose clamps, pull off hoses, and remove the fuel pressure regulator assembly. Also, unbolt and remove the vacuum pipe assembly.

11. Unbolt the intake manifold from the cylinder heads and remove the manifold assembly. On 1982-84 models, air cleaner brackets will come off as the unit is unbolted. Make sure to note locations of these brackets and remove them. Be careful not to lose any of the gaskets.

➡Cover the intake ports in the cylinder head while the manifold is removed to prevent anything from being dropped in them.

12. The manifold may be disassembled further by removing the carburetor or throttle body and the applicable emission control system components from it. See Section 4.

13. On ff-1 models, the intake manifold halves may be separated from the thermostat housing.

14. Be sure to use new gaskets when installing the intake manifold. Tighten the bolts evenly, in stages, to the specifications given in the Torque Specifications chart. Adjust the choke and throttle linkages, as detailed in Section 5.

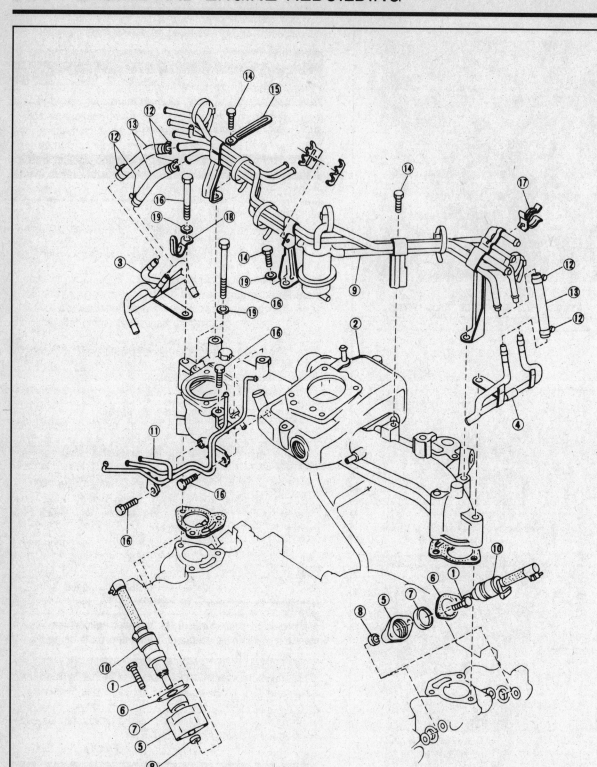

1. Bolt & washer ASSY
2. Intake manifold
3. Fuel pipe (RH)
4. Fuel pipe (LH)
5. Fuel injector holder
6. Fuel injector plate
7. Fuel injector insulator
8. Fuel injector seal
9. Fuel pressure regulator ASSY
10. Fuel injector ASSY
11. Vacuum pipe
12. Hose clamp
13. Hose
14. Bolt & washer ASSY
15. Clip
16. Bolt & washer ASSY
17. Clip
18. Clip
19. Washer

87903053

Fig. 57 Intake manifold used on the turbocharged engine

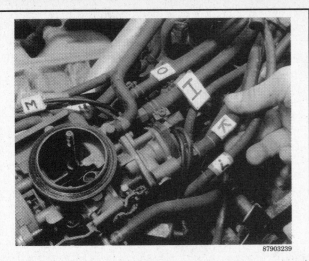

Fig. 58 Tag and disconnect the emission control system hoses

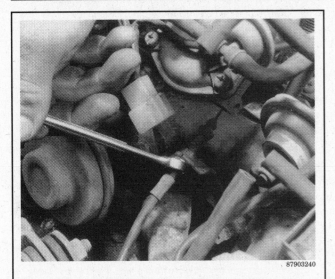

Fig. 59 Disconnect the throttle cable

Fig. 60 Use a flare nut wrench to disconnect the fuel line on carbureted engines

Fig. 61 Unbolt the intake manifold and remove it from the heads

Exhaust Manifolds

REMOVAL & INSTALLATION

▶ See Figures 62 and 63

ff-1 and 1300G

1. Loosen, but do not remove, the brass exhaust manifold-to-cylinder head retaining nuts.
2. Remove the exhaust pipe from the manifold flange.
3. Remove the band which secures the exhaust pipe to the left side of the transaxle.
4. Move the manifold around until the mounting slots permit its removal.

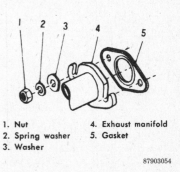

1. Nut
2. Spring washer
3. Washer
4. Exhaust manifold
5. Gasket

Fig. 62 Manifold-to-cylinder head flange assembly found on ff-1 and 1300G models

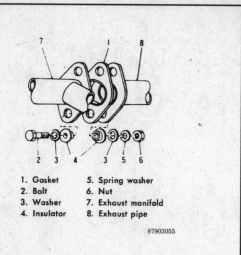

1. Gasket
2. Bolt
3. Washer
4. Insulator
5. Spring washer
6. Nut
7. Exhaust manifold
8. Exhaust pipe

87903055

Fig. 63 Manifold-to-exhaust pipe flange components found on ff-1 and 1300G models

5. Pull the manifold downward, in order to remove it.

✳✳CAUTION

If the car must be raised to remove the manifolds, be sure that it is securely supported on jackstands.

6. Repeat for the other side.
To install:
7. Install the exhaust manifold onto the engine block and tighten the nuts evenly and in stages, to the figure given in the Torque Specifications chart. Use a new insulator in the exhaust pipe-to-transaxle securing band. Replace any damaged gaskets.

1972-74 DL and GL Models

1. Separate the exhaust pipe from the exhaust manifold by unfastening the flange nuts.
2. Loosen, but do not remove, the nuts which secure the exhaust manifold to the cylinder head.
3. Then do one of the following, whichever is most convenient. Loosen the front engine mounting bolt and raise the engine slightly or remove the valve cover.
4. Remove the exhaust manifold by lifting it upward, after working it off the mounting studs.
5. Repeat the procedure for the other side.
To install:
6. Install the exhaust manifold onto the engine block. Tighten the cylinder head-to-exhaust manifold nuts, evenly and in stages, to the figure given in the Torque Specifications chart, above, Tighten the exhaust pipe-to-manifold flange nuts to 12-15 ft. lbs. (16-20 Nm) replace any damaged gaskets with new ones. Check for exhaust leaks.

1975-84 Models

EXCEPT TURBO

An exhaust manifold, as a separate item, is not found on these models. Instead, the Y-shaped exhaust pipe bolts directly to a flange on each cylinder head.

1. Raise and support the vehicle on jackstands.
2. Disengage the electrical connector from the O₂ sensor.

3. From the upper shell cover, remove the air duct.
4. Loosen the front exhaust pipe-to-cylinder head nuts.
5. Remove the front exhaust pipe-to-rear exhaust pipe nuts, then separate the pipes; discard the gasket.
6. Remove the front exhaust pipe-to-bracket bolt. While supporting the front exhaust pipe, unfasten the pipe-to-cylinder head nuts and front exhaust pipe from the vehicle; discard the gaskets.
7. Using a putty knife, clean the gasket mounting surfaces.
To install:
8. Install new gaskets and reverse the removal procedures. Tighten the front exhaust pipe-to-cylinder head nuts to 19-22 ft. lbs. (25-29 Nm), the front exhaust pipe-to-rear exhaust pipe nuts to 9-17 ft. lbs. (12-23 Nm) and the front exhaust pipe-to-bracket to 18-25 ft. lbs. (24-33 Nm) Start the engine and check for exhaust leaks.

TURBO

This model is unique in having a crossover pipe that links both exhaust ports at the cylinder heads and the exhaust inlet at the turbocharger so as to feed all the exhaust through the turbocharger.

1. Disengage the connection at the turbocharger by removing the two nuts and accompanying washers from the top of the turbocharger exhaust inlet flange.
2. From under the car, remove the two nuts at either cylinder head exhaust port and then pull the crossover pipe off the cylinder head studs while guiding the studs integral with the pipe out of the base of the turbocharger. Be careful to pull all three gaskets off.
3. To install, reverse the removal procedure, using new gaskets.

Turbocharger

REMOVAL & INSTALLATION

▶ **See Figure 64**

✳✳WARNING

Do not allow dirt to enter either intake or outlet openings, or the unit may be destroyed at start up.

1. Loosen clamps and remove the air intake duct (leading from the air cleaner to the intake of the flowmeter).
2. Loosen the clamps at either end and at the vacuum hose connector, and remove flowmeter boot (connecting the flowmeter to the turbocharger intake).
3. Remove the mounting bolts from the turbocharger exhaust outlet. Separate the pipe from the turbocharger.
4. Back off the clamp and for the turbocharger drain hose.
5. Disconnect the oil supply line from the top of the turbocharger.
6. Then, loosen and remove the three turbocharger mounting bolts and remove the turbocharger and gasket from the exhaust manifold, disconnecting the drain hose at the same time.
To install:
7. Install the turbocharger using a new gasket.

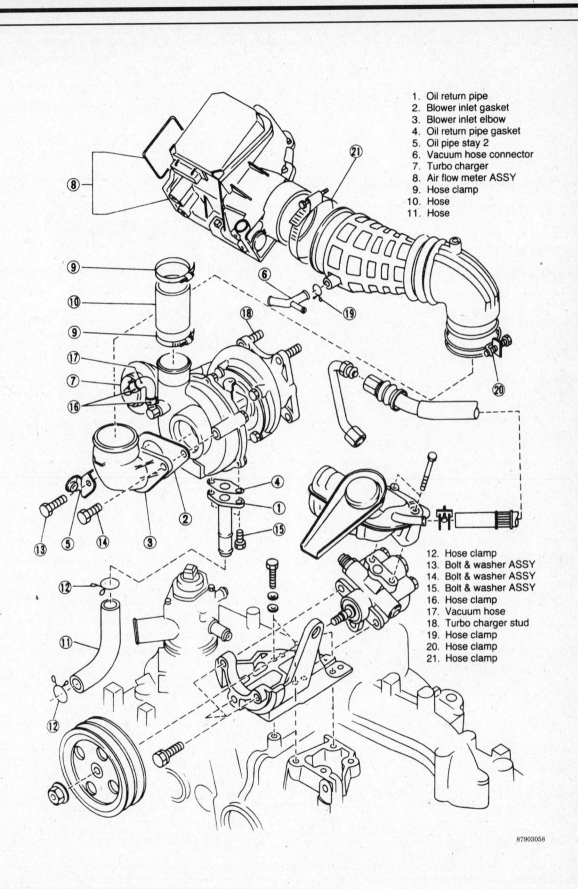

1. Oil return pipe
2. Blower inlet gasket
3. Blower inlet elbow
4. Oil return pipe gasket
5. Oil pipe stay 2
6. Vacuum hose connector
7. Turbo charger
8. Air flow meter ASSY
9. Hose clamp
10. Hose
11. Hose

12. Hose clamp
13. Bolt & washer ASSY
14. Bolt & washer ASSY
15. Bolt & washer ASSY
16. Hose clamp
17. Vacuum hose
18. Turbo charger stud
19. Hose clamp
20. Hose clamp
21. Hose clamp

87903058

Fig. 64 Exploded view of the turbocharger and associated components

8. Connect the oil supply line and tighten the bolts to 8-13 ft. lbs. (10-17 Nm).

9. Install the clamp for the turbocharger drain hose.

10. Install the turbocharger exhaust outlet and fasten the mounting bolts to 31-38 ft. lbs. (42-51 Nm).

11. Install the flowmeter boot and fasten the clamps at the vacuum hose connector.

12. Install the air intake duct and fasten the clamps.

TROUBLESHOOTING

The turbocharger cannot be repaired. The entire unit must be replaced if there is a major mechanical defect. However, you can determine whether or not the seals or bearing are defective, meaning that the unit must be replaced.

Exhaust Side Oil Leak

Inspect the turbocharger exhaust outlet for excessive deposits of hard carbon. These deposits, not to be confused with light layer of normal exhaust soot, indicate oil is leaking past the bearing seal on the exhaust side and forming the carbon due to exhaust heat. Replace the unit.

Intake Side Oil Leak/Bad Bearing

Inspect the intake of the turbocharger for heavy accumulations of fresh oil. There will normally be some oil here because of the PCV system. If you suspect a leak, check axial (in and out) or radial (side-to-side) play in the turbocharger bearing. Use a dial indicator. The limit for axial play is 0.0035 in. (0.88mm) while the limit for radial play is 0.0067 in. (0.170mm)

Checking the Waste Gate

If the engine exhibits severe detonation, the waste gate may be inoperative. Disconnect the waste gate control hose at the waste gate and seal it. Then apply 7-9 psi (48-62 kPa). This must be precisely controlled or the waste gate diaphragm may be damaged. Watch the waste gate to see if it operates. If the waste gate does not move, replace the diaphragm. If this does not cure the malfunction, replace the unit.

If the pressure hose to the waste gate is cracked, replace it.

Radiator

REMOVAL & INSTALLATION

ff-1 and 1300G Models

A main radiator, sub-radiator, and reservoir tank are utilized. They can be removed individually or as an assembly. To remove as an assembly, proceed as follows:

1. Remove the grille.
2. Remove the drain plug, and drain the coolant.

❋❋CAUTION

When draining the coolant, keep in mind that cats and dogs are attracted by ethylene glycol antifreeze, and are quite likely to drink any that is left in an uncovered container or in puddles on the ground. This will prove fatal in sufficient quantity. Always drain the coolant into a sealable container. Coolant should be reused unless it is contaminated or several years old.

3. Disconnect the radiator hoses from the top of the main and sub-radiators, and from the bottom of the main radiator (water pump side).

4. Disconnect the heater control cable, by removing the circlip which retains the inner cable, and the nut which retains the sheath to the bracket. Loosen the clamp which retains the heater duct to the blower casing, and remove the blower casing mounting bolts.

❋❋WARNING

Do not remove the bolt between the radiators.

To remove only the main radiator, proceed as follows:

5. Remove the grille.
6. Remove the drain plug and drain the coolant.
7. Disconnect all hoses from the main radiator.
8. Remove the center and right hand radiator mounting bolts, and the 4 screws which retain the radiator bracket.
9. Remove the main radiator and bracket, leaving the sub-radiator suspended on the left hand mounting bolt and the blower motor casing.

To remove only the sub-radiator:

10. Remove the grille.
11. Remove the drain plug and drain the coolant.
12. Disconnect the radiator shroud from the blower casing.
13. Remove the center and left hand radiator retaining bolts, and remove the sub-radiator.
14. Install in the reverse order of removal.

Except ff-1 and 1300G Models
▶ See Figures 65, 66 and 67

1. On 1982-84 models, remove the cover from underneath, on the right side of the vehicle. You may want to connect a hose to the drain plug to carry coolant away on these models. Drain the cooling system by removing the drain plug in the bottom of the radiator. After loosening the drain plug, remove the radiator cap, which will allow the coolant to drain faster.

2. Loosen the hose clamps and remove the inlet (upper) and outlet (lower) hoses from the radiator. Disconnect inlet and outlet oil cooler lines (automatic transaxle).

3. Remove the two radiator mounting bolts.

4. Before removing the radiator from the vehicle, disconnect the wiring harness of the following items:
   - Thermostat
   - Thermoswitch wiring
   - Oil pressure switch wiring
   - Fan motor wiring
   - Secondary terminal to the distributor

5. Remove the fan and motor assembly from the radiator by removing the 4 bolts which hold the assembly to the radiator.

6. Install the radiator in the reverse order of removal.

Fig. 65 Unfasten the radiator retaining bolts

Fig. 66 Disconnect the thermoswitch wiring

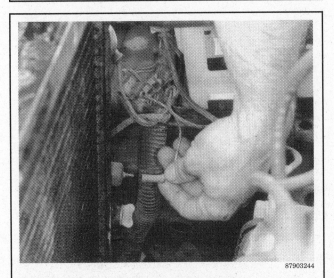

Fig. 67 Remove the radiator from the vehicle

Engine Oil Cooler

REMOVAL & INSTALLATION

1. Put an oil drain pan nearby. Remove the two bolts connecting the oil cooler lines to the bottom of the attachment. Drain oil into the pan.

2. Remove the bolt connecting the bracket for these two oil lines to the block. Pull the oil lines away from the block and drain them into the pan.

3. Remove the three oil cooler mounting bolts and remove it.

4. To install, reverse the above procedure, using new sealing gaskets on the cooler lines. Tighten the piping brace-to-block bolt to 20 ft. lbs. (27 Nm), and the piping-to-attachment bolts to 25 ft. lbs. (33 Nm).

Water Pump

REMOVAL & INSTALLATION

▶ **See Figures 68, 69 and 70**

✲✲CAUTION

Do not perform this operation on a hot engine. Depress the button on the radiator cap to relieve the pressure in the cooling system.

1. Drain the cooling system by loosening the plugs on the radiator and cylinder block.

➡**Place a large, clean container of adequate capacity underneath the drains to catch the coolant for reuse.**

2. Loosen the bolts on the alternator bracket and remove the drive belt.

Fig. 68 Remove the drive belts and disconnect the hoses leading to the water pump

87903249

Fig. 69 Remove the attaching bolts, then remove the water pump from the vehicle

87903250

Fig. 70 Clean the old gasket from the mating surfaces

3. Remove the hoses connected to the pump, which is located on the driver's side at the front of the engine, by unfastening the hose clamps.

4. Remove the bolts which secure the water pump and remove the pump assembly. On the 1800 Turbo, the timing scale plate will come off along with the top left bolts. Note the location of the scale and then remove it with those two bolts.

5. Install the water pump onto the engine. Tighten the water pump bolts securely and attach the hoses. Install the timing scale, if applicable. Install the drive belt. Adjust the drive belt tension at the alternator. Tighten the alternator mounting bolts and replenish the cooling system to the proper level. Run the engine and check for leaks or abnormal noise.

Cylinder Head

REMOVAL & INSTALLATION

▶ **See Figures 71, 72, 73, 74, 75, 76, 77, 78, 79, 80, 81, 82 and 83**

The engine must be removed from the vehicle to remove the cylinder heads. Although it is physically possible (on some models) to remove the cylinder heads with the engine installed, head gasket failure will result upon installation, due to misalignment of the cylinders. The cylinder heads should be removed with the engine cold to prevent warpage.

1. Remove the engine from the vehicle and mount it on a workstand.

2. Unbolt and remove the intake manifold together with the carburetor/throttle body and the various pollution control devices. On 1977 and later models, remove the EGR pipe from the intake manifold and cylinder head. On 1982-84 models, this includes removing the thermostatic water valve and hose and the oil filler pipe brackets. On the turbocharged models, remove the turbocharger and exhaust manifold, and disconnect the fuel injection lines.

➡**Move or disconnect any engine wiring that might impair intake manifold removal.**

3. Remove the spark plugs.

4. Disconnect the crankcase ventilation hose(s) and remove the valve covers.

5. Loosen the alternator adjusting bolts, and unbolt the alternator bracket from the cylinder head.

6. Remove the air injection distributor tubes from the cylinder heads by unscrewing the fittings on models so equipped.

7. On the 1800 Turbo, remove the knock sensor with a 27mm deep well socket only! (A standard socket will damage electrical terminals). Then, remove the fuel injectors.

8. Loosen the valve rocker locknuts and adjusting screws (solid lifter engines only). Loosen the rocker shaft mounting nuts, and remove the rocker arm assembly and pushrods.

➡**If the pushrods are to be reused, keep them in order so that they are installed in the original positions. The pushrods for all engines are identified by knurling (or the absence of knurling). If you are replacing pushrods, make sure knurled patterns are similar or that unmarked pushrods are replaced by unmarked rods. Markings vary from year to year. For example, for 1981 and 1982, 1800cc OHV engines used pushrods with two knurled marks, while 1983-84 engines have 2 knurled marks for 1600cc engines, a single mark for solid lifter, 1800 engines, and no markings for hydraulic lifter engines.**

9. Gradually loosen the head bolts using the correct sequence. If a loosening sequence is not illustrated, reverse the tightening sequence given. Remove the cylinder heads and gaskets.

To install:

➡**The cylinder heads must installed with the cylinders vertical, to avoid misalignment, and to permit the head gasket to crush evenly around the cylinder.**

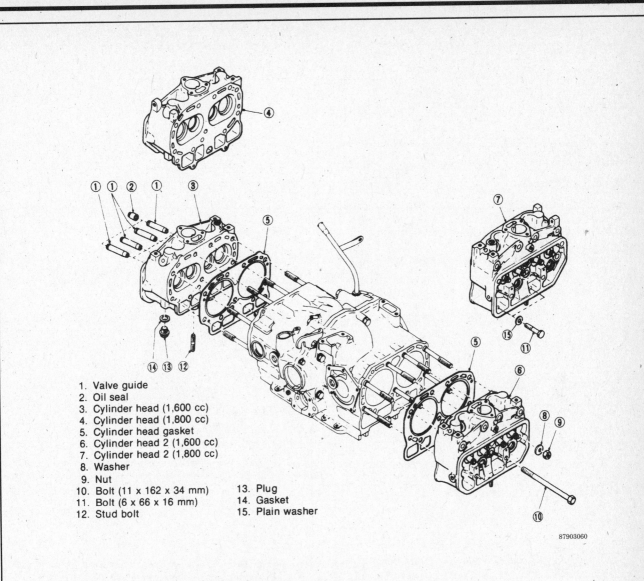

1. Valve guide
2. Oil seal
3. Cylinder head (1,600 cc)
4. Cylinder head (1,800 cc)
5. Cylinder head gasket
6. Cylinder head 2 (1,600 cc)
7. Cylinder head 2 (1,800 cc)
8. Washer
9. Nut
10. Bolt (11 x 162 x 34 mm)
11. Bolt (6 x 66 x 16 mm)
12. Stud bolt
13. Plug
14. Gasket
15. Plain washer

87903060

Fig. 71 Exploded view of a common cylinder head found on Subarus

87903251

Fig. 72 Loosen the head bolts in the reverse order of the tightening sequence . . .

87903252

Fig. 73 . . . then remove the head from the engine

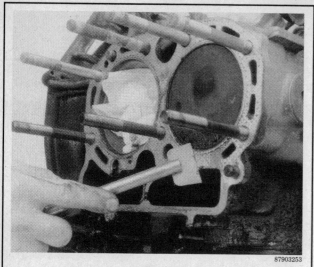

Fig. 74 Clean the old gasket from both mating surfaces

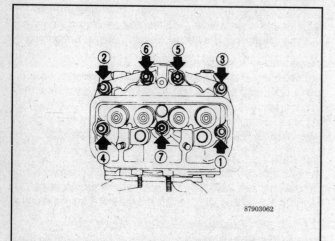

Fig. 75 Loosening sequence of cylinder head bolts — ff-1 models. Use the reverse of this sequence to tighten the bolts

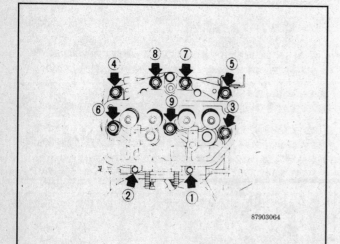

Fig. 76 Loosening sequence for cylinder head bolts — 1980 models

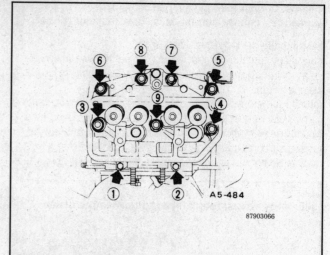

Fig. 77 Loosening sequence for cylinder head bolts — 1981 models

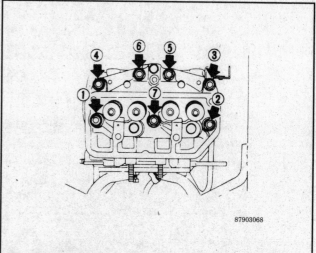

Fig. 78 Loosening sequence for cylinder head bolts — 1982-84 models

10. Construct a cylinder head spacer as shown in the illustration. Assemble the cylinder head on the engine and use the spacer in place of the rocker shaft support. After the cylinder head is tightened to specification following the correct sequence, remove the rocker shaft bolts (or nuts) and spacers, then install the rocker shafts.

11. Install the remaining components in the reverse order of removal.

CLEANING & INSPECTION

Invert the cylinder head and clean the carbon from the valve faces and combustion chambers. Use a permanent felt-tip marker and mark the valves for location.

Use a valve spring compressor and compress the valve springs. Lift out the keepers, release the valve spring compressor and remove the valve, spring and spring retainer. Place all parts removed in order so that they can be reinstalled on the same cylinder.

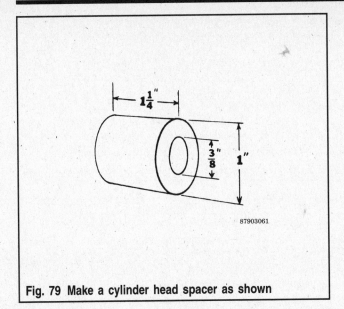

Fig. 79 Make a cylinder head spacer as shown

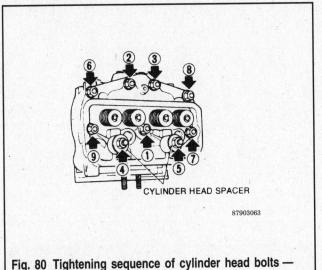

Fig. 80 Tightening sequence of cylinder head bolts — 1970-79 models (except ff-1)

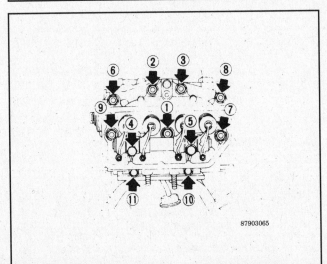

Fig. 81 Tightening sequence of cylinder head bolts — 1980 models

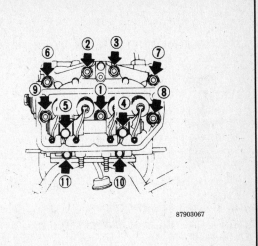

Fig. 82 Tightening sequence for cylinder head bolts — 1981 models

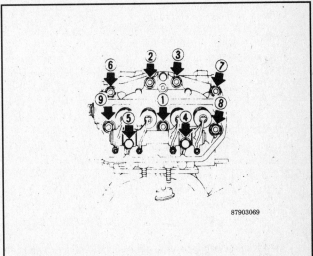

Fig. 83 Tightening sequence for cylinder head bolts — 1982-84 models

Remove the valves from the cylinder head. Chip away any remaining carbon from the valve heads, combustion chambers and ports. Use a rotary wire brush on an electric drill. Be sure that the deposits are actually removed, rather than burned. Clean the valve faces with a wire wheel taking care not to remove the location numbering. Clean the cylinder head and component parts in an engine cleaning solvent.

Remove the pushrods, and, if hollow, clean out the oil passages using fine wire. Roll each pushrod over a piece of clean glass. If a distinct clicking sound is heard as the pushrod rolls, the rod is bent, and must be replaced.

Remove lifters from their bores, and remove gum and varnish, using solvent. Clean walls of lifter bores. Check lifters for concave wear as illustrated. If face is worn concave, replace lifter, and carefully inspect the camshaft. Lightly lubricate lifter and insert it into its bore. If play is excessive, an oversize lifter must be installed (where possible). Consult a machinist concerning feasibility. If play is satisfactory, remove, lubricate, and reinstall the lifter.

RESURFACING

➡**Resurfacing should be performed by a reputable machine shop.**

Check the cylinder head for warpage by placing a straight-edge across the gasket surface. Using feeler gauges, determine the clearance at the center of the straight edge. Measure across the diagonals, along the longitudinal centerline and across the cylinder head at several points. Should the warpage exceed 0.002 in. the cylinder head must be resurfaced, be sure to observe the following grinding limits: ff-1, 0.0197 in.; all other models, 0.020 in.

Valves

REMOVAL & INSTALLATION

▸ **See Figures 84, 85 and 86**

1. Remove the cylinder head from the engine.
2. Remove the pushrods and valve rockers.
3. Using valve spring press assembly (899724100) or its equivalent, compress the valve spring and remove the valve spring retainer key.
4. Mark each valve and spring to prevent confusion during installation.
5. Remove the oil seals from over the valve stems and guide bosses with a pair of pliers
6. Remove the valves.

To install:

7. Lubricate the valve stems, and install the valves in the cylinder head as numbered.
8. Lubricate and position the new seals (if used) and the valve springs.
9. Install the spring retainers, compress the springs, and insert the keys using needlenose pliers or a tool designed for this purpose.

➡**Retain the keys with wheel bearing grease during installation.**

INSPECTION & LAPPING

Clean the valve stems with lacquer thinner. Clean the valve guides using solvent and an expanding wire type valve guide cleaning brush. Insert the valve into the guide it was removed from. With the valve slightly off of the valve seat, rock the valve face and stem back and forth. Excessive wobble means a worn guide, valve stem or both.

Measure the valve stems with a micrometer and compare the reading with the specifications to determine whether valve stem or guide wear is responsible for any excessive clearance. Replace or repair as necessary.

The valves should also be checked for proper seat contact.

1. Apply a thin coat of prussian blue (or white lead) to the valve face and place the valve in the head.
2. Apply light pressure to the valve, but do not rotate it.

3. Carefully remove the valve from the head then check the valve and seat. If blue appears 360 degrees around the valve seat, the seat and valve are concentric.
4. Check that the seat contact is in the middle of the valve face.
5. If the valve and seat are not concentric or the seat contact is not in the middle of the valve face, you should consult a reputable machine shop for proper refacing.
6. After machine work has been performed on valves/seats, it may be necessary to lap the valves to assure proper contact. For this, you should first consult your machine shop to determine if lapping is necessary. Some machine shops will perform this for you as part of the service, but the precision machining which is available today often makes lapping unnecessary. Additionally, the hardened valves/seats used in modern automobiles may make lapping difficult or impossible. If your machine shop recommends that you lap the valves proceed as follows:

   a. Coat the valve face and seat with a light coat of valve grinding compound. Attach the suction cup end of the valve grinding tool to the head of the valve (it helps to moisten it first).

   b. Rotate the tool between the palms, changing position and and lifting the tool often to prevent grooving. Lap in the valve until a smooth, evenly polished surface is evident on both the seat and face.

   c. Remove the valve from the head. Wipe away all traces of grinding compound from the surfaces. Clean out the valve guide with a solvent-soaked rag. Make sure there are NO traces of compound in or on the head.

   d. Proceed through the remaining valves, lapping them one at a time to their seats. Clean the area after each valve is done.

   e. When all the valves have been lapped, thoroughly clean or wash the head with solvent. There must be NO trace of grinding compound present.

Valve Stem Seals

REPLACEMENT

▸ **See Figures 87 and 88**

Due to the pressure differential that exists at the ends of the intake valve guides (atmospheric pressure above, manifold vacuum below), oil is drawn through the valve guides into the intake port. This has been alleviated somewhat since the addition of positive crankcase ventilation, which lowers the pressure above the guides. To reduce blow-by, Subaru employs valve stem seals which must be pressed (or tapped) into position over the valve stem and guide boss.

➡**When installing seals, ensure that a small amount of oil is able to pass the seal to lubricate the valve guides. Otherwise, excessive wear may result.**

Factory seals should be replaced if the seal lip is damaged or the valve is removed.

1. Remove the cylinder head from the engine.
2. Remove the pushrods and valve rockers.

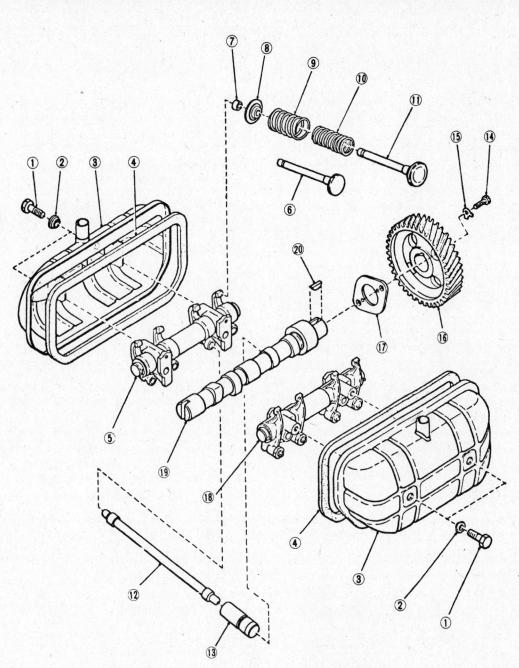

1. Bolt
2. Valve rocker cover seal washer
3. Valve rocker cover
4. Valve rocker cover gasket
5. Valve rocker assembly (R.H.)
6. Exhaust valve
7. Valve spring retainer key
8. Valve spring retainer
9. Valve spring
10. Valve spring 2
11. Intake valve
12. Valve push rod
13. Valve lifter
14. Bolt
15. Lock washer
16. Camshaft gear
17. Camshaft plate
18. Valve rocker assembly
19. Camshaft
20. Woodruff key

87903070

Fig. 84 Exploded view of the valve train components

Fig. 85 Compress the valve spring and remove the spring retainer key

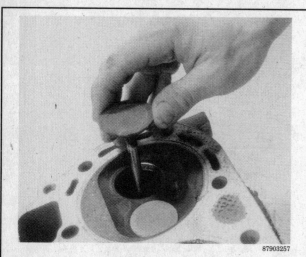

Fig. 86 After the valve springs and seals are removed, invert the head and remove the valves

Fig. 87 After the springs are removed, remove the valve seals from the stems

3. Using valve spring press assembly (899724100) or its equivalent, compress the valve spring and remove the valve spring retainer key.

4. Mark each valve and spring to prevent confusion during installation.

5. Remove the oil seals from over the valve stems and guide bosses with a pair of pliers

To install:

6. Lubricate the new seal prior to installation.

7. Using oil seal installer 898858600 or equivalent press the seal onto the valve stem.

8. Install the valve springs and retainer keys.

9. Install the rockers and pushrods.

10. Install the cylinder heads.

Valve Springs

REMOVAL & INSTALLATION

Valve spring removal and installation is part of the Valves removal and installation procedure covered in this section.

INSPECTION

▶ **See Figure 89**

Place the spring on a flat surface next to a square. Measure the height of the spring, and rotate it against the edge of the square to measure distortion. If spring height varies (by comparison) by more than $1/16$ in. (1.6mm) or if distortion exceeds $1/16$ in. (1.6mm) replace the spring. In addition to evaluating the spring as above, test the spring pressure at the installed and compressed (installed height minus valve lift) height using a valve spring tester.

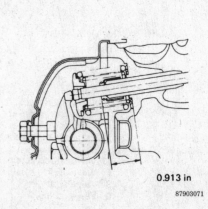

0.913 in

Fig. 88 Install seals over guides by pressing them on until arrowed dimension is shown

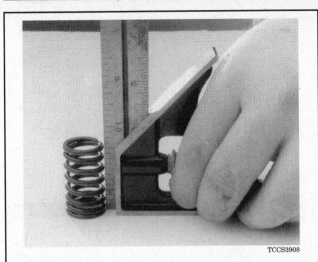

Fig. 89 Check the valve spring for squareness on a flat surface, a carpenters square can be used

VALVE SPRING INSTALLED HEIGHT

Measure the distance between the spring pad and the lower edge of the spring retainer, and compare to specifications. If the installed height is incorrect, add shim washers between the spring pad and the spring. Be sure only to use shims designed for this purpose

Valve Seats

The valve seats in the engines covered in this guide are all non-replaceable and must be recut when service is required. Seat recutting requires special tools and experience, and should be handled at a reputable machine shop. Seat concentricity should also be checked by a machinist.

Valve Guides

REMOVAL & INSTALLATION

Replacing the valve guides involves heating the head to high temperatures and driving the old guide out with the use of special tools. The head may have to be machined for an oversize guide if the bushing bore dimension is over the standard specifications. The new guide is then reamed for the proper valve stem-to-guide clearance. This repair requires a high level of mechanical skill and should only be performed by a reputable machine shop.

Valve guides which are not excessively worn or distorted may, in some cases, be knurled rather than replaced. Knurling is a process in which metal inside the valve guide bore is displaced and raised, thereby reducing clearance. The possibility of knurling rather than replacing the guides should be discussed with a machinist.

Oil Pan

REMOVAL & INSTALLATION

♦ See Figures 90, 91 and 92

To remove the oil pan, it is not necessary that the engine be removed from the vehicle.
1. Remove the drain plug and drain the oil from the engine.
2. Remove the attaching bolts which hold the oil pan to the bottom of the crankcase, and remove the oil pan.
3. Remove the oil pan gasket and clean the mating surfaces of the oil pan and the crankcase.
4. Install in the reverse order of removal using a new gasket. Tighten the bolts until snug

Fig. 90 Remove the oil pan bolts . . .

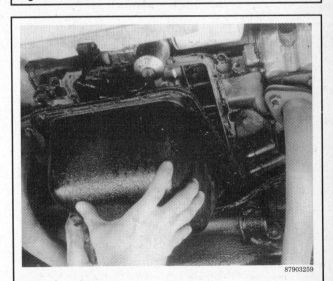

Fig. 91 . . . then lower the oil pan

Fig. 92 Clean the gasket mating surfaces

Oil Pump

REMOVAL & INSTALLATION

▶ See Figure 93

Except 1800 Turbo

The oil pump can be removed with the engine in the vehicle. The oil pump is located on the front of the engine and has the oil filter mounted on it. The pump and filter may be removed as an assembly.

1. Unfasten the 4 bolts which secure the pump to the engine.
2. Remove the pump, complete with the gasket and filter.
3. Remove the filter from the pump.
   To install:
4. Install the oil filter on the pump boss.
5. Using new gaskets and O-rings, fit the pump to the crankcase and carefully engage the pump drive with the slot in the end of the camshaft. Be sure that the pump mounts flush to the block.
6. Secure the pump with the 4 mounting bolts. Tighten the bolts until snug
7. Check the engine oil level and add oil, as necessary, to replace any that was lost.

1800 Turbo

▶ See Figure 94

1. Place a pan underneath oil filter and pump assembly to collect oil, and, using a strap wrench, remove the filter.
2. Next, remove the three bolts which fasten the two oil cooler lines (at bottom) and the turbocharger supply line (at the side) of the attachment. Remove the bolt fastening the brace for the two oil cooler pipes to the block.

3. Support the attachment with one hand while you unscrew the connector which retains it with the other. Now, gently pull the attachment free of the O-rings which seal it. Remove the oil pump attaching bolts, and remove the pump.
   To install:
4. Replace the washers which go over the bolts, as well as the oil pump-to-block O-ring, and the two attachment O-rings. Oil all O-rings. Then, install in reverse order, observing the following specifications:
   - Piping to attachment: 25 ft. lbs. (33 Nm)
   - Attachment connector: 22 ft. lbs. (29 Nm)
   - Piping brace-to-block bolt: 20 ft. lbs. (27 Nm)

Timing Gear Cover

REMOVAL & INSTALLATION

▶ See Figure 95

The timing gears on all 1970-84 OHV Subaru engines are located at the rear of the engine and are covered by the flywheel housing. In order to remove the flywheel housing the engine must be removed from the vehicle. Once this is done proceed in the following order:

1. Separate the engine from the transaxle. If equipped with an automatic transaxle, remove the torque converter with the transaxle.
2. If equipped with a manual transaxle, remove the clutch assembly from the flywheel. Remove the flywheel (MT) or the converter drive plate (AT) from the crankshaft.
3. Remove the flywheel housing-to-engine bolts and work the housing from the two aligning dowels.
4. Using a putty knife, clean the gasket mounting surfaces.
   To install:
5. Use a new gasket (if equipped) and reverse the removal procedures. The flywheel mounting holes are not equally spaced so that the flywheel cannot be incorrectly installed. See Section 7 for proper clutch installation procedures. Tighten the flywheel housing-to-engine bolts to 14-20 ft. lbs. (18-27 Nm), the flywheel-to-crankshaft (MT) bolts to 30-33 ft. lbs. (40-44 Nm) or the drive plate-to-crankshaft (AT) bolts to 36-39 ft. lbs. (48-52 Nm) and the transaxle-to-engine bolts to 34-40 ft. lbs. (46-54 Nm)

OIL SEAL REPLACEMENT

The flywheel housing cover oil seal is pressed in.

1. Remove the engine from the vehicle and separate the engine from the transaxle.
2. Remove the flywheel and clutch assembly from the engine as detailed in Section 7.
3. Remove the flywheel housing from the engine and remove the oil seal from the housing.
4. Install the new oil seal pressing it into place.
5. Reassemble the engine and install it in the reverse order of disassembly and removal.

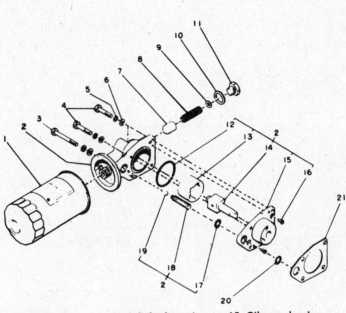

1. Oil filter	8. Relief valve spring	15. Oil pump housing
2. Oil pump body	9. Washer	16. Screw
3. Bolt	10. Washer	17. O-ring
4. Bolt	11. Plug	18. By-pass valve spring
5. Spring washer	12. O-ring	19. Ball
6. Washer	13. Rotor	20. O-ring
7. Oil relief valve	14. Gear	21. Gasket

87903076

Fig. 93 The oil pump and related components

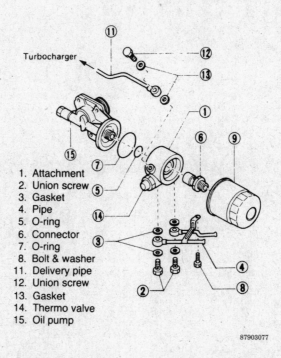

Turbocharger

1. Attachment
2. Union screw
3. Gasket
4. Pipe
5. O-ring
6. Connector
7. O-ring
8. Bolt & washer
11. Delivery pipe
12. Union screw
13. Gasket
14. Thermo valve
15. Oil pump

87903077

Fig. 94 Attachment (1) routes oil to the turbocharger through pipe (11), and to the oil cooler through the pipes at the bottom. A thermostatic valve (14) bypasses the oil cooler when it is not needed

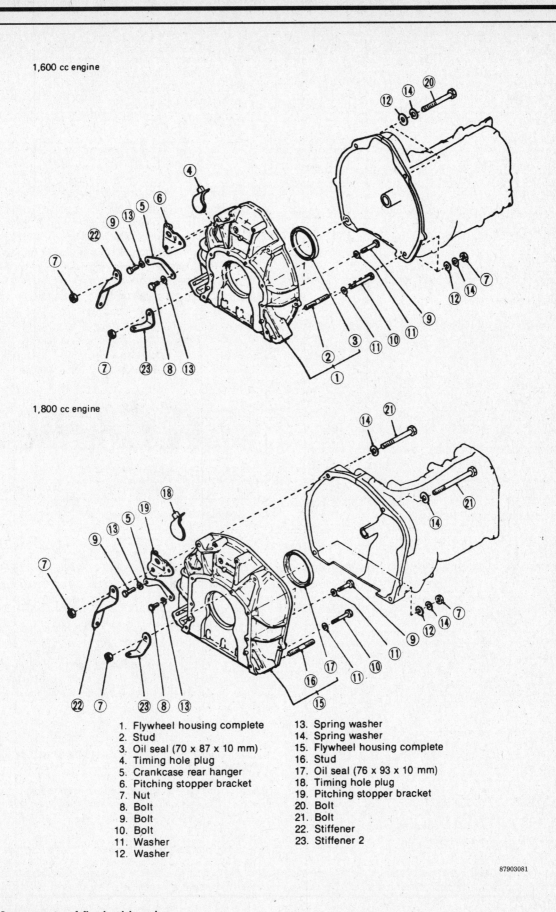

1,600 cc engine

1,800 cc engine

1. Flywheel housing complete
2. Stud
3. Oil seal (70 x 87 x 10 mm)
4. Timing hole plug
5. Crankcase rear hanger
6. Pitching stopper bracket
7. Nut
8. Bolt
9. Bolt
10. Bolt
11. Washer
12. Washer
13. Spring washer
14. Spring washer
15. Flywheel housing complete
16. Stud
17. Oil seal (76 x 93 x 10 mm)
18. Timing hole plug
19. Pitching stopper bracket
20. Bolt
21. Bolt
22. Stiffener
23. Stiffener 2

87903081

Fig. 95 Components of flywheel housing

Camshaft and Bearings

REMOVAL & INSTALLATION

▶ See Figure 96

The camshaft turns on journals that are machined directly into the crankcase.

1. Refer to the engine removal and Installation procedures in this section and remove the engine from the vehicle, then separate the transaxle from the engine.
2. Remove the clutch assembly/flywheel (MT) or the torque converter drive plate (AT).
3. Remove the flywheel housing-to-engine bolts and the housing from the engine.
4. Remove the crankshaft gear from the crankshaft.
5. Straighten the lockwashers and remove the camshaft thrust plate-to-engine bolts.

➡**The lockwashers are straightened and the bolts removed through the access holes in the camshaft gear.**

6. Remove the rocker arm-to-cylinder head covers, the rocker arm-to-cylinder head assemblies, the pushrods and valve lifters.

➡**When removing the pushrods and valve lifters, be sure to keep the items in order for reassembly purposes.**

7. Pull the camshaft toward the rear of the engine and remove it from the engine; be careful not to damage the bearing journals and/or the camshaft lobes.

➡**Remove the oil seal; be sure to replace it with a new one when reassembling the engine.**

8. Inspect the camshaft.
To install:
9. Using a putty knife, clean the gasket mounting surfaces.
10. Install the camshaft and tighten the thrust plate bolts. Using a feeler gauge or a dial indicator, move the camshaft (fore and aft), then measure the end-play, it should be 0.008 in. (0.2032mm) or less.

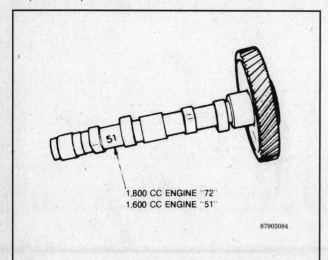

1,800 CC ENGINE "72"
1,600 CC ENGINE "51"

87903084

Fig. 96 The camshaft is stamped by identification marks

11. To complete the installation, use new gaskets and sealant where necessary. Assemble the engine and reverse the removal procedures. Refill the cooling system and the crankcase. Start the engine, allow it to reach normal operating temperatures and check for leaks.

INSPECTION

1. Put the camshaft in V-blocks and have a dial indicator contact the inside face of the cam gear. If run-out exceeds 0.0098 in. (0.24892mm), replace the gear.
2. Using a dial micrometer and a set of V- blocks, measure the camshaft bearing wear and the camshaft bend; the bend limit is 0.002 in. (0.0508mm)
3. Measure the cam gear-to-crankshaft backlash. Mount a dial indicator with its stem resting on a tooth of the camshaft gear. Rotate the gear until all slack is removed, and zero the indicator. Rotate the gear in the opposite direction until slack is removed, and record gear backlash. Mount the indicator with its stem resting on the edge of the camshaft gear, parallel to the axis of the camshaft. Zero the indicator., and turn the camshaft gear one full turn, recording the runout. If either backlash or runout exceeds specifications, replace the worn gear(s).

Crankshaft, Pistons and Connecting Rods

REMOVAL & INSTALLATION

▶ See Figures 97, 98, 99, 100 and 101

1. Refer to the engine removal and Installation procedures in this section and remove the engine from the vehicle. Separate the engine from the transaxle.
2. Remove the intake manifold, the oil pan, the clutch assembly (MT), the flywheel (MT) or drive plate (AT) and the flywheel housing.
3. Remove the rocker arm covers, the rocker arm-to-cylinder head assemblies, the pushrods and the valve lifters.

➡**When removing the pushrods and the valve lifters, be sure to keep them in order for reinstallation purposes. If equipped with solid lifters, install valve lifter retaining clips (Subaru part # 899804100 or equivalent) to keep the lifters from dropping out of the upper crankcase. If equipped with a hydraulic lifter engine, tilt the crankcase and remove the lifters; it is not necessary to loosen the valve rocker adjusting screws.**

4. Remove the cylinder head-to-engine bolts, in the reverse order of the tightening sequence and gaskets. Remove the oil strainer retainer nut/bolt; use a chisel to remove the oil strainer.
5. Using the holes in the camshaft gear, remove the camshaft thrust plate-to-engine lockwashers and bolts.
6. Using a 0.55 in. (13mm) Allen wrench, remove the crankcase plugs (of No. 3 and No. 4 piston side) from the rear of the crankcase.

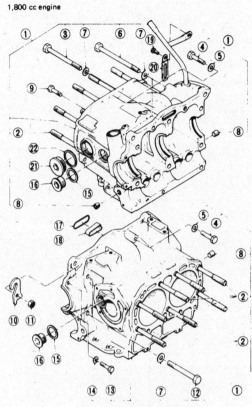

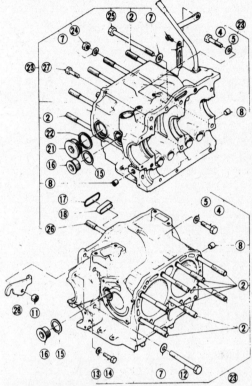

1. Crankcase assembly
2. Stud bolt
3. Bolt (10 x 108 x 28 mm)
4. Bolt
5. Washer
6. Bolt (10 x 145 x 28 mm)
7. Washer (10.5 x 18 x 2 mm)
8. Main gallery plug
9. Bolt
10. Crankcase front hanger
11. Nut
12. Bolt (10 x 70 x 28 mm)
13. Bolt
14. Washer

15. Gasket (26.2 x 31.5 x 1 mm)
16. Crankcase plug
17. Crankcase O-ring
18. Back up ring
19. Bolt & washer (6 x 13 x 13 mm)
20. Clip
21. Crankcase plug
22. Gasket (36.2 x 44 x 1 mm)
23. Crankcase assembly
24. Nut (10 x 8 mm)
25. Bolt (10 x 135 x 28 mm)
26. Stud bolt (10 x 120 x 26 mm)
27. Bolt
28. Crankcase hanger

87903059

Fig. 97 Component parts of crankcase

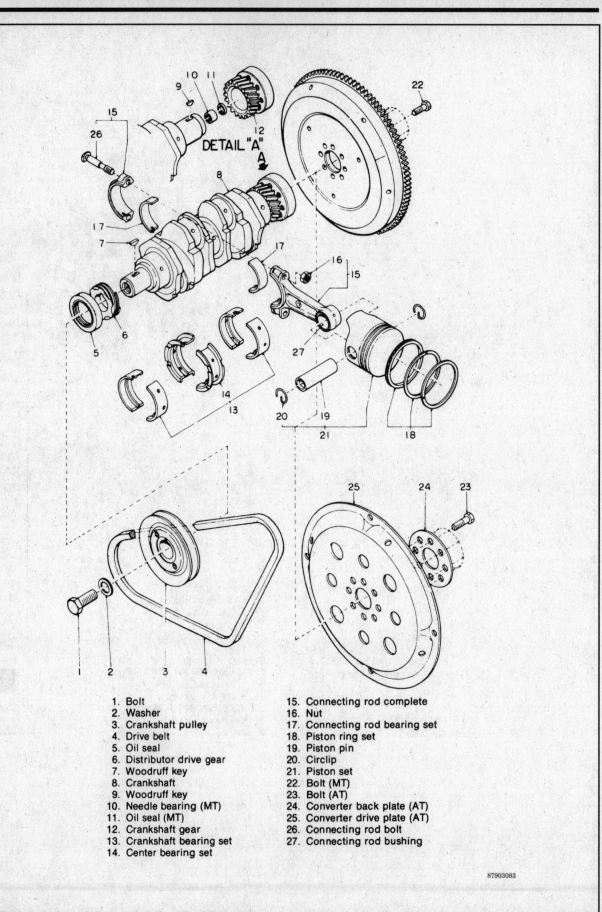

DETAIL "A"

1. Bolt
2. Washer
3. Crankshaft pulley
4. Drive belt
5. Oil seal
6. Distributor drive gear
7. Woodruff key
8. Crankshaft
9. Woodruff key
10. Needle bearing (MT)
11. Oil seal (MT)
12. Crankshaft gear
13. Crankshaft bearing set
14. Center bearing set
15. Connecting rod complete
16. Nut
17. Connecting rod bearing set
18. Piston ring set
19. Piston pin
20. Circlip
21. Piston set
22. Bolt (MT)
23. Bolt (AT)
24. Converter back plate (AT)
25. Converter drive plate (AT)
26. Connecting rod bolt
27. Connecting rod bushing

87903083

Fig. 98 Exploded view of the crankshaft and related parts

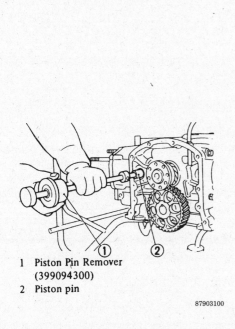

1 Piston Pin Remover
(399094300)
2 Piston pin

87903100

Fig. 99 A special tool is used to remove the piston pins

7. Using a wrench on the crankshaft pulley bolt, rotate the crankshaft so that the No. 3 and No. 4 pistons are at the Bottom Dead Center (BDC) of the their compression stroke.

8. Using the piston circlip (needlenose) pliers, insert them through the crankcase plug holes and remove the wrist pin-to-pistons circlips.

9. Using a Wrist Pin Removal tool No. 399094310 or equivalent, through the rear service holes, remove the wrist pins through the crankcase plug holes.

➡**Keep the circlips and the wrist pins together for each cylinder so that they DO NOT become mixed.**

10. Using a 0.55 in. (13mm) Allen wrench, remove the crankcase plugs (of No. 1 and No. 2 piston side) from the front of the crankcase.

11. Using a wrench on the crankshaft pulley bolt, rotate the crankshaft so that the No. 1 and No. 2 pistons are at the Bottom Dead Center (BDC) of the their compression stroke.

12. Using the piston circlip (needlenose) pliers, insert them through the crankcase plug holes and remove the wrist pin-to-pistons circlips.

13. Using a Wrist Pin Removal tool No. 399094310 or equivalent, through the front service holes, remove the wrist pins through the crankcase plug holes.

➡**Keep the circlips and the wrist pins together for each cylinder so that they do not become mixed.**

14. Rotate the engine, so that the No. 1 and No. 3 piston side is facing upward, then remove the crankcase halves nuts and bolts. If equipped with 4WD, be sure to remove the crankcase hanger and the stiffener.

➡**Before separating the crankcase halves, be sure to pull the camshaft rearward so that it doesn't interfere with the crankcase.**

15. Separate the crankcase halves. Remove the front oil seal, the O-ring and the back-up ring; be sure to replace them with new ones when reassembling the engine.

➡**Keep the pistons and the wrist pins together for each cylinder so that they DO NOT become mixed. Mark the pistons and the connecting rods so that the direction is not changed when they are installed.**

16. Remove the crankshaft together with the connecting rods, the distributor gear and the crankshaft gear as an assembly. Remove the camshaft, the camshaft gear and the thrust plate as an assembly. On the 1970-75 models, remove the cylinder liners, complete with individual gaskets, using a suitable cylinder liner puller.

➡**Keep the gasket from each cylinder with its respective cylinder liner. Mark each cylinder liner flange using a felt tipped pen, with the cylinder number from which it was removed, as an aid to proper installation.**

17. On the 1976-84 models, remove the ridge from the top of the cylinder (unworn area), using a Ridge Reamer tool, to facilitate the removal of the pistons by performing the following procedures:

　　a. Place the piston at the bottom of its bore and cover it with a rag.

　　b. Cut the ridge away using a ridge reamer, exercising extreme care to avoid cutting too deeply.

　　c. Remove the rag and remove the cuttings that remain on the piston.

✳✳WARNING

If the ridge is not removed and new rings are installed, damage to the new rings may result!

18. If the piston rings are to be replaced, remove them with a ring expander. Keep the rings in removal sequence and with the piston from which they were removed.

19. Inspect the pistons, connecting rods and cylinder bores following the procedures outlined in this section.

To install:

20. When assembling the engine, be sure to note the following:

　　a. Rotating or sliding parts should be coated with engine oil prior to installation.

　　b. Coat all oil seal lips with grease prior to installation.

　　c. Always use new gaskets. Apply liquid sealer to the gaskets, where necessary, to prevent leakage.

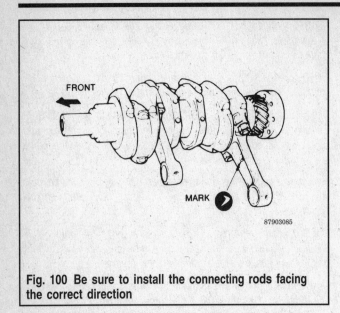

Fig. 100 Be sure to install the connecting rods facing the correct direction

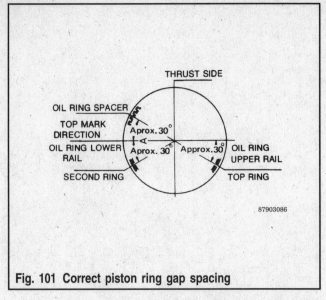

Fig. 101 Correct piston ring gap spacing

d. Replace any worn or defective parts, such as nuts, bolts, washers, etc.

21. Fit the woodruff key(s) on the crankshaft and then install the following components: distributor drive gear, timing gear (if removed), needle bearings, and oil seals.

22. Assemble each connecting rod to the crankshaft throw from which it was originally removed. Tighten the cap bolts or nuts to the figure given in the Torque Specifications chart.

➡ Place each connecting rod on the crankshaft so that the circular Fuji trademark faces the front, and install the rod cap so that the protruding ridge on it also faces front.

Determine the clearance between the sides of the connecting rods and the crankshaft, using feeler gauges. If clearance is below the minimum tolerance, the rod may be machined to provide adequate clearance. If clearance is excessive, substitute an unworn rod, and recheck. If clearance is still outside specifications, the crankshaft must be welded and re-ground, or replaced.

23. Fit the rails of the piston oil control rings by hand, after first installing a ring expander.

a. Use the expander to install the lower and upper compression rings in the same position from which they were removed.

➡ Be sure that the R marked on each of the rings is facing upward.

b. Position the ring gaps, as illustrated.

24. Coat the pistons and cylinder liners with SAE 10W-30 engine oil, compress the rings with a ring compressor, and fit each piston into the liner from which it was removed.

➡ Align the pistons with the marks made during removal so that they face the front of the liner. Be sure that each piston is mated with its original liner. Make sure that the wrist pin hole in the piston aligns with the installation hole in the liner.

25. If they were removed, install the woodruff key and plate on the camshaft. Use a press to install the timing gear on the camshaft.

➡ The camshaft plate should be installed with its protrusion facing away from the cam journals, and the timing gear should be installed with its 1½ in. boss facing toward the journals.

26. Assemble the rocker shafts to the cylinder head.

27. Install any parts which were removed from the intake manifold.

28. Install the crankshaft bearings in the crankcase. Be sure that none of the oil passages are clogged.

29. Install the valve lifters in their respective positions in the crankcase.

30. Install the camshaft and the crankshaft in the crankcase so that the marks on each of their gears are properly aligned.

➡ The bolt hole with the large chamfer on the crankshaft gear should be aligned with the camshaft gear so that the punchmark on the camshaft gear is visible through the chamfered hole.

31. Apply liquid sealer to the joining surfaces of the crankcase halves. Be sure that the surfaces are clean and free of oil or grease.

32. Install clips on the valve lifters to keep them from falling out.

33. Fit the halves of the crankcase together. Install the front crankcase lifting hook (hanger) at the same time.

34. Secure the crankcase halves with the proper fasteners. See the Torque Specifications chart, for the type, size, and torque figures for the different types of fasteners used on each engine.

35. Secure the camshaft mounting plate to the crankcase with the lockwashers and bolts. Work through the holes in the cam gear. Be sure to bend the lockwasher up around the bolt head. Recheck the camshaft gear backlash at this time. With the crankshaft and camshaft installed, and the crankcase halves joined, measure the crankshaft end-play. Mount a dial indicator stand on the front of the block, with the dial indicator stem resting on the nose of the crankshaft, parallel to the

crankshaft axis. Pry the crankshaft the extent of its travel rearward, and zero the indicator. Pry the crankshaft forward and record crankshaft end-play.

➡**Crankshaft end-play also may be measured at the thrust bearing, using feeler gauges. Piston and cylinder liner (if so equipped) installation must be performed with the cylinders in a vertical position.**

36. On EA61, EA62 and EA63 engines:
   a. Set crankcase so that #1 and #3 cylinders face upwards.
   b. Place the connecting rod of #3 piston at TDC.
   c. Install #3 piston and cylinder liner, with a cylinder liner gasket fitted under the cylinder liner.
   d. Check the amount which the cylinder liner protrudes above the crankcase surface. It should be within the following limits:
     • EA61: 0.0024-0.0035 in. (0.06-0.088mm)
     • EA62 and EA63: 0.0028-0.0035 in. (0.07-0.088mm)
   e. If the liner protrusion is not within limits, adjust it by means of a selective fit cylinder liner gasket. Gaskets are available in varying sizes for each type of engine.

✳✳WARNING

Cylinder liner gaskets are not interchangeable between different engine models. Be sure to specify which engine you have when you order selective fit gaskets.

   f. Align the wrist pin hole in the connecting rod with the hole in the piston.
   g. Insert the wrist pin through the crankcase plug hole with a suitable piston pin press. Using circlip pliers, fit the circlip on the wrist pin.
37. Keep the cylinder liners which were just installed, in place with a holding fixture mounted over the stud bolt which is located between the cylinders. A piece of stock, large enough to retain the lips of both installed liners, may be used. Secure the stock with a cylinder head nut.
38. With the cylinder liners secure, invert the engine so that the cylinders on the opposite side of the crankcase are now facing up.
39. On EA71 and EA81 engines:
   a. Position crankcase so that No.2 and No.4 cylinders face downward.
   b. Place the connecting rod of the No.2 piston at bottom dead center and insert the No.2 piston into the cylinder using a piston installation guide.
   c. Line up the hole in the connecting rod with the piston hole.
   d. Install the piston pin and circlip.
   e. Repeat steps b-d for the #4 cylinder.
40. Turn the crankcase upside down so that #1 and #3 cylinders face downward. Install the pistons as described above.
41. Install the cylinder head assembly, on the side of the engine which is facing up. Then invert the engine, remove the cylinder liner holding fixture (on appropriate models) and install

the cylinder head (with the cylinders vertical) on the other side of the engine.

✳✳WARNING

When installing the cylinder heads, pay particular attention to the torque specifications and tightening sequences.

42. Apply liquid sealer to the crankcase plugs and install them, using new gaskets, in the crankcase. Tighten them to 60-70 ft. lbs. (81-94 Nm)
43. If it was removed, fit the oil screen complete with O-ring, by securing it with its stays.
44. Install the flywheel housing and oil seal. Install the rear engine lifting hook at the same time.
45. Install the flywheel, after coating its bolts with liquid sealer. Tighten the bolts to the specifications given in the Torque Specifications chart.
46. Install the clutch assembly, as detailed in Section 7, for manual transaxle models.
47. Attach the oil pan, complete with gasket, to the crankcase.
48. Install the part of the transaxle housing which is retained on the engine.
49. Install the water pump and hoses.
50. Fit the water elbow, pipe, and hose.
51. Attach the oil filler tube, water by-pass tube (if used), and gasket.
52. If it was removed, apply liquid sealer to the threads of the oil pressure light sending unit and screw it into the block.
53. Install the oil pump.
54. Install the front oil seal with a suitable drift.
55. Insert a screwdriver through the hole in the flywheel housing and use it as a brake to keep the crankshaft from turning, then secure the crankshaft pulley. Tighten the pulley bolt to the figure given in the Torque Specifications chart.

➡**Remember to remove the screwdriver.**

56. Adjust the valve clearance. See Section 2.
57. Install the valve covers, with their gaskets.
58. Install the distributor with the No. 1 piston set at TDC. Connect the distributor vacuum line. Install the power steering pump on models so equipped.
59. Attach the halves of the alternator bracket to the cylinder head and crankcase. Be sure to install the water hose clamp along with the bracket.
60. Install the intake manifold assembly, complete with carburetor or throttle body, as detailed above.
61. On models equipped, install the air suction manifold and EGR pipe.
62. Connect the water by-pass hoses if fitted, to the intake manifold connections.
63. Install the alternator and adjust the drive belt tension.
64. Install the spark plugs. Connect all of the spark plug and distributor cables.
65. Install the engine in the car. Remember to replenish the oil and coolant. Adjust the throttle, clutch, and manual choke 1970-73 cables.

CLEANING & INSPECTION

▶ **See Figures 102, 103 and 104**

✷✷WARNING

Do not hot tank clean any aluminum parts or they will be ruined. Use carburetor solvent for cleaning.

Pistons

Using a piston ring expanding tool, remove the piston rings from the pistons; any other method (screwdriver blades, pliers, etc.) usually results in the rings being bent, scratched or distorted and/or the piston itself being damaged.

Clean the varnish from the piston skirts and pins with a cleaning solvent.

DO NOT WIRE BRUSH ANY PART OF THE PISTON.

Clean the ring grooves with a groove cleaner and make sure that the oil ring holes and slots are clean.

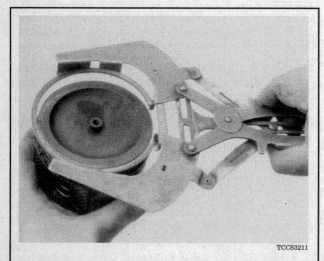

TCCS3211

Fig. 102 Using a ring expander tool to remove the piston rings

TCCS3208

Fig. 103 Clean the piston grooves using a ring groove cleaner

Inspect the piston for cracked ring lands, scuffed or damaged skirts, eroded areas at the top of the piston. Replace the pistons that are damaged or show signs of excessive wear. Inspect the piston ring grooves for nicks or burrs that might cause the rings to hang up.

Measure the piston skirt perpendicular to the piston pin axis and note this figure for the piston clearance check. If installing replacement pistons, follow the manufacturers recommendations on where to measure the piston.

Cylinder Liners and Bores

➡**1970-75 models use cylinder liners. Later model engines use conventional cylinder bores. Refer to the appropriate procedure.**

LINERS

Visually inspect the cylinder bores (liners) for roughness, scoring, or scuffing. If evident, the cylinder bore (liner) must be bored or honed oversize to eliminate imperfections, and the smallest possible oversize piston used. Since 1970-75 model engines use removable cylinder liners these can either be replaced or honed to oversize so long as the honing will not exceed 0.020 in. (0.508mm)

The new pistons should be given to the machinist with the block, so that the cylinders can be bored or honed exactly to the piston size (plus clearance). If no flaws are evident, measure the bore diameter using a telescope gauge and micrometer, or dial gauge, parallel and perpendicular to the engine centerline, at the top (below the ridge) and bottom of the bore. Subtract the bottom measurements from the top to determine taper, and the parallel to the centerline measurements from the perpendicular measurements to determine eccentricity. If the measurements are not within specifications, the cylinder must be bored or honed, and an oversize piston installed. If the measurements are within specifications the cylinder may be used as is, with only finish honing.

BORES

Using a telescoping gauge or an inside micrometer, measure the diameter of the cylinder bore, perpendicular (90°) to the piston pin, at 1-2½ in. (25-64mm) below the surface of the

Cylinder Bore (Liner)

Model	Taper	Eccentricity
FF-1, 1300G	0.0004	0.0004
1972–73 (except 1300G)	0.0008	0.0008
1974–75	0.0004	0.0004
1876	0.0008	0.0008
1977–80	0.0006	0.0004

87903082

Fig. 104 Cylinder bore inspection dimensions

cylinder block. The difference between the two measurements is the piston clearance.

If the clearance is within specifications or slightly below (after the cylinders have been bored or honed), finish honing is all that is necessary, If the clearance is excessive, try to obtain a slightly larger piston to bring the clearance within specifications. If this is not possible, obtain the first oversize piston and hone the cylinder or (if necessary) bore the cylinder to size.

When measuring the cylinder bore, take measurements in several places. If the cylinder bore is tapered or is out-of-round, it is advisable to rebore for the smallest possible oversize piston and rings. After measuring, mark the pistons with a felt-tip pen for reference during assembly.

➡**Boring of the cylinder block should be performed by a reputable machine shop with the proper equipment.**

Connecting Rods and Rod Bearings

Wash the connecting rods in cleaning solvent and dry with compressed air. Check for twisted or bent rods and inspect for nicks or cracks. Replace the connecting rods that are damaged.

Install the cap on the rod and torque to specification. Using an inside micrometer, measure the inside bore diameter perpendicular (90°) to the axis of rod and once again along the axis of the rod. If the two measurements are not within specification, have the rod resized by a competent machine shop.

➡**It is normal for the inside diameter of the rod to be slightly larger when measured perpendicular (90°) to the axis of the rod.**

Replacement bearings are available in standard size and undersize (for re-ground crankshafts). Connecting rod-to-crankshaft bearing clearance is checked using Plastigage® at either the top or the bottom of each crank journal. The Plastigage® has a range of 0.001 0.003 in. (0.0254 0.0762mm).

1. Remove the rod cap with the bearing shell. Completely clean the bearing shell and the crank journal, blow any oil from the oil hole in the crankshaft; place the Plastigage® lengthwise along the bottom center of the lower bearing shell, then install the cap with the shell and torque the bolt or nuts to specification. DO NOT turn the crankshaft with the Plastigage® on the bearing.

2. Remove the bearing cap with the shell. The flattened Plastigage® will be found sticking to either the bearing shell or the crank journal. DO NOT remove it yet.

3. Use the scale printed on the Plastigage® envelope to measure the flattened material at its widest point. The number within the scale which most closely corresponds to the width of the Plastigage® indicates the bearing clearance in thousandths of an inch and millimeters.

4. Check the specifications chart in this section for the desired clearance. It is advisable to install a new bearing if the clearance exceeds specification; however, if the bearing is in good condition and is not being checked because of bearing noise, bearing replacement is not necessary.

5. If you are installing new bearings, try a standard size, then each undersize in order until one is found that is within the specified limits when checked for clearance with Plastigage®; each undersize shell has its size stamped on it.

6. When the proper size shell is found, clean off the Plastigage®, oil the bearing thoroughly, reinstall the cap with its shell and torque the rod bolt nuts to specifications.

➡**With the proper bearing selected and the nuts torqued, it should be possible to move the connecting rod back and forth freely on the crank journal as allowed by the specified connecting rod end clearance. If the rod cannot be moved, either the rod bearing is too far undersize or the rod is misaligned.**

Crankshaft and Main Bearings

Measure the bearing journals at each end twice (90° apart) using a micrometer, to determine diameter, journal taper and eccentricity. The journal diameter is given in the Crankshaft Specifications chart earlier in this section. The taper limit is 0.008 in. (0.20mm) for 1970-76 models, 0.0028 in. (0.071mm) for 1977-84 models. The eccentricity limit is 0.0012 in. (0.030mm) The grinding limit is 0.0098 in. (0.248mm). Using a telescope gauge and micrometer, measure bearing I.D. parallel to piston axis and at 30° on each side of piston axis. Subtract journal O.D. from bearing I.D. to determine oil clearance. If crankshaft journals appear defective, or do not meet tolerances, there is no need to measure bearings, for the crankshaft will require grinding and/or undersize bearings will be required. If bearing appears defective, cause for failure should be determined prior to replacement.

Measure the oil clearance on each crankshaft bearing by means of Plastigage® as follows: Wipe off oil, dust, etc. on the surfaces to be measured. Install the bearings in the crankcase and set the crankshaft in position. Cut the Plastigage® to the bearing width and place it on the journal parallel with the crankshaft axis. Be careful not to put it on the oil hole or groove. Bring together the crankcase halves and tighten the bolts and nut to the specified torque.

➡**During the work, the crankshaft must not be turned nor the crankcase inverted.**

Remove all the bolts and nut and separate the crankcase. Measure the Plastigage® width with the scale printed on the Plastigage® case. If the measurement is not within the specification, replace the defective bearing with an undersize one, and replace or recondition the crankshaft as necessary.

Ring End-Gap

The piston ring end-gap should be checked while the rings are removed from the pistons. Incorrect end-gap indicates that the wrong size rings are being used; ring breakage could result if not corrected.

1. Compress the new piston ring into a cylinder (one at a time).

2. Squirt some clean oil into the cylinder so that the ring and the top 2 in. (51mm) of the cylinder wall are coated.

3. Using an inverted piston, push the ring approximately 1 in. (25mm) below the top of the cylinder.

4. Using a feeler gauge, measure the ring gap and compare it to specification. Carefully remove the ring from the cylinder.

5. If the gap is smaller than specification, file the ring ends using an appropriate piston ring file. If greater, the cylinder bore must be honed to the next oversize or the piston rings are incorrect.

BREAK-IN PROCEDURE

Start the engine, and allow it to run at low speed for a few minutes, while checking for leaks. Stop the engine, check the oil level, and fill as necessary. Restart the engine, and fill the cooling system to capacity. Check the point dwell angle and adjust the ignition timing and the valves. Run the engine at low to medium speed (800-2,500 rpm) for approximately ½ hour, and retorque the cylinder head bolts. Road test the car, and check again for leaks.

Follow the manufacturer's recommended engine break-in procedure and maintenance schedule for new engines.

Rear Main Oil Seal

REPLACEMENT

Refer to the timing gear cover seal replacement procedure in this section.

EXHAUST SYSTEM

General Description

▶ **See Figures 105 and 106**

The exhaust system is suspended by hangers and clamps attached to the frame member. Annoying rattles and noise vibrations in the exhaust system are usually caused by misalignment of parts. When aligning the system, leave all bolts and nuts loose until all parts are properly aligned, then tighten from front to rear. Make sure that you are wearing some form of eye protection when removing or installing the exhaust system, to prevent eye injury. Never work on the exhaust system of a vehicle that has been recently used. Exhaust systems reach extremely high temperatures and can cause severe burns. Always allow the car to cool down before starting any repairs to the exhaust.

The Catalytic Converter is an emission control device added to a gasoline engines exhaust system to reduce hydrocarbon and carbon monoxide pollutants in the exhaust gas stream. The catalyst in the converter is not serviceable.

Periodic maintenance of the exhaust system is not required. However, if the vehicle is raised for other service, it is advisable to check the general condition of the catalytic converter, exhaust pipes and muffler.

Flywheel and Ring Gear

REMOVAL & INSTALLATION

1. Remove the engine and transaxle from the vehicle as previously described.
2. Separate the engine from the transaxle and place the engine on a suitable stand.
3. On models with manual transaxle, remove the clutch cover and clutch disc.

✳✳WARNING

Be careful not to let oil, grease or coolant contact the clutch disc.

4. Install a flywheel stopper (MT), or drive plate stopper (AT), to lock the flywheel or drive plate.
5. Remove the retaining bolts that secure the flywheel (MT), or drive plate (AT), and remove them from the cylinder block.

To install:
6. Install the flywheel or driveplate and tighten the retaining bolts to 30-33 ft.lbs. (40-44 Nm) for the flywheel, 36-39 ft. lbs. (48-52 Nm) for the driveplate, on all 1970-84 1600 engines. On all other engines tighten the flywheel or driveplate to 51-55 ft. lbs. (69-74 Nm).

Exhaust and Y-Pipe

REMOVAL & INSTALLATION

Non-Turbo Models

1. Disconnect the O₂ sensor harness.
2. Remove the air duct from the upper shell cover.
3. Loosen (do not remove) the nuts which hold the front exhaust pipe to the exhaust port of the engine.
4. Disconnect the front and rear exhaust pipes.
5. Disconnect the front exhaust pipe and bracket.
6. While holding the front exhaust pipe with one hand, remove the nuts which hold the front exhaust pipe to the exhaust port. The front exhaust pipe can then be disconnected.
7. During installation, do not tighten any connections more than hand-tight until the entire exhaust system has been installed.

➡**Be sure to install a new gasket at the exhaust port. Use only nuts specified by the manufacturer. Do not remove the gasket placed between the front and rear exhaust pipes. When the front exhaust pipe needs to be replaced, the gasket must be replaced also.**

Turbocharged Models

1. Remove turbocharger covers A and B, and disconnect the center exhaust pipe. Remove the turbocharger unit.

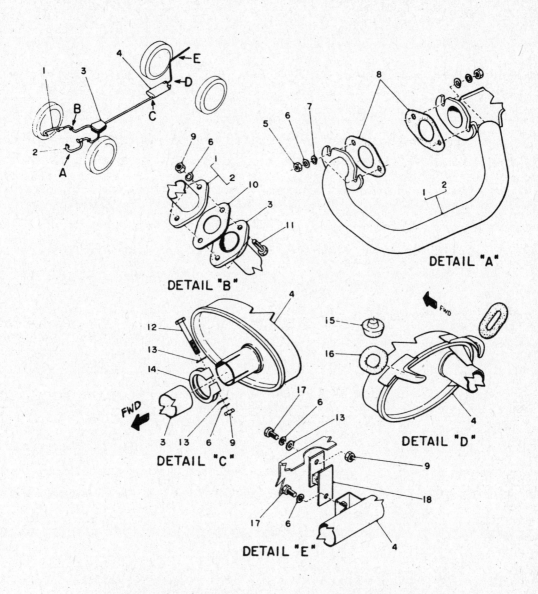

DETAIL "A"

DETAIL "B"

DETAIL "C"

DETAIL "D"

DETAIL "E"

1. Exhaust manifold (RH)
2. Exhaust manifold (LH)
3. Exhaust pipe
4. Muffler assembly
5. Nut
6. Spring washer
7. Washer
8. Gasket
9. Nut
10. Gasket
11. Bolt (8 x 30 mm)
12. Bolt (8 x 55 mm)
13. Washer
14. Clamp A (exhaust pipe)
15. Stopper (exhaust)
16. Cushion (muffler hanger)
17. Bolt (8 x 16 mm)
18. Cushion (tail hanger)

87903087

Fig. 105 Exploded view of the exhaust system used on non-catalytic converter models

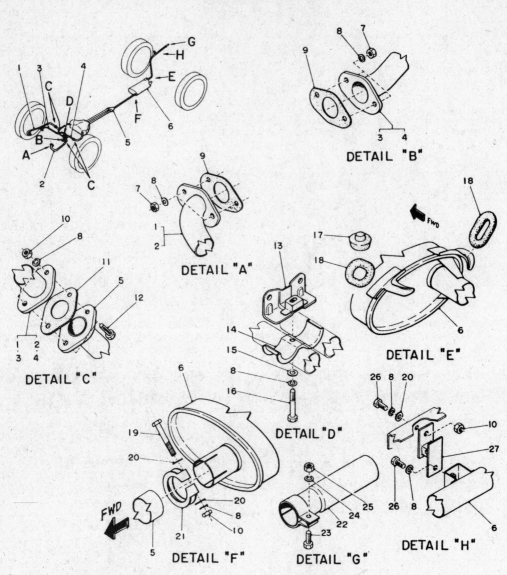

1. Exhaust manifold-A
2. Exhaust manifold-B
3. Exhaust manifold-C
4. Exhaust manifold-D
5. Exhaust pipe
6. Muffler assembly
7. Nut
8. Spring washer
9. Gasket
10. Nut
11. Gasket
12. Bolt (8 x 30 mm)
13. Bracket (exhaust pipe, upper)
14. Bracket (exhaust pipe, lower)
15. Washer
16. Bolt (8 x 50 mm)
17. Stopper (exhaust)
18. Cushion (muffler hanger)
19. Bolt (8 x 55 mm)
20. Washer
21. Clamp (exhaust pipe)
22. Muffler cutter
23. Bolt (8 x 20 mm)
24. Spring washer
25. Nut
26. Bolt (8 x 16 mm)
27. Cushion (tail hanger)

87903088

Fig. 106 Common exhaust system used on models with catalytic converters

2. Remove the nuts which hold the turbocharger bracket to the front exhaust pipe.

3. Remove underguard and right undercover.

4. Loosen the engine mount bracket and pitching stopper. Then slightly raise the engine until the bolts protrude beyond the surface of the crossmember.

5. Disconnect the front exhaust pipe from the engine exhaust port, and remove through the clearance between the crossmember and the cylinder head.

❋❋WARNING

Do not damage power steering pipe which is located along the crossmember. Be sure to remove the bolts only after the engine has cooled off. Before disassembling parts, spray CRC® 5-56 or equivalent on them.

To install:

6. Install the gasket onto the stud bolts at the engine's exhaust port with its flat surface facing the engine. If the gasket is tilted, it may catch on a thread and then will not drop down over the bolt.

➡**Be sure to install a new gasket.**

7. Temporarily tighten the front exhaust pipe to engine's exhaust port with the nuts.

❋❋WARNING

Use only nuts designed by the manufacturer. Be sure to install a new gasket on the inlet of the turbocharger.

8. Lower the engine. Tighten the engine mount bracket and properly adjust the pitching stopper.

9. Install the underguard and right undercover.

10. Connect the front exhaust pipe to the turbocharger bracket.

11. Properly tighten the front exhaust pipe at the engine's exhaust port.

12. Connect the O_2 sensor connector.

13. Install the turbocharger unit, center the exhaust pipe and turbocharger covers A and B.

Center Exhaust Pipe

REMOVAL & INSTALLATION

➡**This procedure applies to turbocharged vehicles only**

1. Remove turbocharger covers A and B.

2. Disconnect the O_2 sensor connector.

3. Remove the flange nuts which hold the center exhaust pipe to turbocharger unit.

❋❋WARNING

Before removing the flange nuts, allow the turbocharger unit and exhaust pipe to cool off and spray CRC 5-56 on the nuts.

4. Remove the flange nuts from the transaxle side.

5. Disconnect the center and rear exhaust pipes.

6. Disconnect the center exhaust pipe from the bracket located on the lower side of the transaxle.

7. Remove the center exhaust pipe from the body.

❋❋WARNING

Do not allow the turbocharger cover mounting bracket to interfere with the brake pipe cover located in the front toeboard. Be sure not to damage the steering universal joint. Do not damage the gasket used on the lower side of the turbocharger unit or turbocharger cover.

To install:

8. Install the gasket onto the stud bolts on the turbocharger unit. Connect the center exhaust pipe flange and temporarily tighten it with nuts.

❋❋WARNING

Be sure not to damage the gasket used on the lower side of the turbocharger unit and turbocharger cover. Use only nuts and bolts designed by the manufacturer and be sure to install a new gasket.

9. Temporarily connect the center exhaust pipe and bracket located on the transaxle side.

10. Temporarily connect the center and rear exhaust pipes, and center exhaust pipe to the bracket located on the lower side of the transaxle with new nuts.

11. Tighten the nuts and bolts at the turbocharger unit bracket, (on the transaxle side) and the bracket (on the lower side of the transaxle), in that order, to specified torque.

➡**Gasket used between the center and rear exhaust pipes may be reused if not removed. When a new center exhaust pipe is installed, replace the old gasket with a new one.**

12. Install turbocharger covers A and B.

Rear Exhaust Pipe

REMOVAL & INSTALLATION

1. Disconnect the Air Suction Valve (ASV) hose from the ASV (49 state 2WD carburetor model only).

2. Disconnect the rear exhaust pipe from the front exhaust pipe (non-turbo), center exhaust pipe (turbocharged models).

3. Disconnect the rear exhaust pipe from the muffler assembly. To prevent damage to the bumper or rear skirt by the muffler, wrap a cloth around the tail pipe.

4. Remove rear exhaust pipe from the rubber cushion. To help in its removal, apply a coat of CRC® 5-56 to the mating surface of the rubber cushion in advance.

To install:

5. Temporarily connect the rear exhaust pipe and the muffler assembly.

6. Temporarily connect the rear exhaust pipe and the front exhaust pipe (non-turbo), center exhaust pipe (turbocharged models).

7. Insert exhaust pipe bracket into the rubber cushion. To aid in installation, apply a coat of CRC® 5-56 to the mating surface of the rubber cushion in advance.

8. Adjust the clearance between the temporarily installed parts and tighten to specified torque.

✳✳WARNING

Be sure to install bolts, springs, and self locking nuts in the order indicated in figure 91. Always install new self locking nuts.

Muffler Assembly

REMOVAL & INSTALLATION

1. Remove the bolts and self locking nuts which hold the rear exhaust pipe to the muffler assembly.

2. Remove the left and right rubber cushions from the muffler assembly and detach the muffler assembly.

3. Installation is in the reverse order of the removal procedure.

➡**Be sure to install new self locking nuts and gaskets.**

ADJUSTMENTS

▶ **See Figure 107**

1. After installing exhaust system parts, check to make sure clearances between parts and car body are at the specified values.

2. If any clearance is not, loosen all connections.

3. Adjust when necessary to obtain proper clearances.

4. Tighten all connections securely.

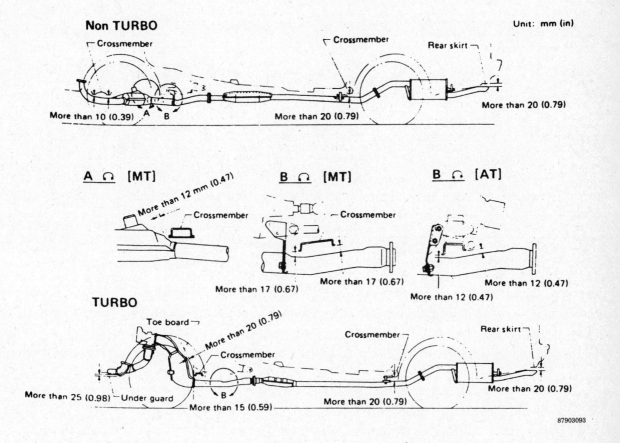

Fig. 107 Always maintain proper exhaust system clearances

Troubleshooting Engine Mechanical Problems

Problem	Cause	Solution
External oil leaks	• Fuel pump gasket broken or improperly seated	• Replace gasket
	• Cylinder head cover RTV sealant broken or improperly seated	• Replace sealant; inspect cylinder head cover sealant flange and cylinder head sealant surface for distortion and cracks
	• Oil filler cap leaking or missing	• Replace cap
	• Oil filter gasket broken or improperly seated	• Replace oil filter
	• Oil pan side gasket broken, improperly seated or opening in RTV sealant	• Replace gasket or repair opening in sealant; inspect oil pan gasket flange for distortion
	• Oil pan front oil seal broken or improperly seated	• Replace seal; inspect timing case cover and oil pan seal flange for distortion
	• Oil pan rear oil seal broken or improperly seated	• Replace seal; inspect oil pan rear oil seal flange; inspect rear main bearing cap for cracks, plugged oil return channels, or distortion in seal groove
	• Timing case cover oil seal broken or improperly seated	• Replace seal
	• Excess oil pressure because of restricted PCV valve	• Replace PCV valve
	• Oil pan drain plug loose or has stripped threads	• Repair as necessary and tighten
	• Rear oil gallery plug loose	• Use appropriate sealant on gallery plug and tighten
	• Rear camshaft plug loose or improperly seated	• Seat camshaft plug or replace and seal, as necessary
	• Distributor base gasket damaged	• Replace gasket
Excessive oil consumption	• Oil level too high	• Drain oil to specified level
	• Oil with wrong viscosity being used	• Replace with specified oil
	• PCV valve stuck closed	• Replace PCV valve

87903C12

Troubleshooting Engine Mechanical Problems (cont.)

Problem	Cause	Solution
Excessive oil consumption	• Valve stem oil deflectors (or seals) are damaged, missing, or incorrect type	• Replace valve stem oil deflectors
	• Valve stems or valve guides worn	• Measure stem-to-guide clearance and repair as necessary
	• Poorly fitted or missing valve cover baffles	• Replace valve cover
	• Piston rings broken or missing	• Replace broken or missing rings
	• Scuffed piston	• Replace piston
	• Incorrect piston ring gap	• Measure ring gap, repair as necessary
	• Piston rings sticking or excessively loose in grooves	• Measure ring side clearance, repair as necessary
	• Compression rings installed upside down	• Repair as necessary
	• Cylinder walls worn, scored, or glazed	• Repair as necessary
	• Piston ring gaps not properly staggered	• Repair as necessary
	• Excessive main or connecting rod bearing clearance	• Measure bearing clearance, repair as necessary
No oil pressure	• Low oil level	• Add oil to correct level
	• Oil pressure gauge, warning lamp or sending unit inaccurate	• Replace oil pressure gauge or warning lamp
	• Oil pump malfunction	• Replace oil pump
	• Oil pressure relief valve sticking	• Remove and inspect oil pressure relief valve assembly
	• Oil passages on pressure side of pump obstructed	• Inspect oil passages for obstruction
	• Oil pickup screen or tube obstructed	• Inspect oil pickup for obstruction
	• Loose oil inlet tube	• Tighten or seal inlet tube
Low oil pressure	• Low oil level	• Add oil to correct level
	• Inaccurate gauge, warning lamp or sending unit	• Replace oil pressure gauge or warning lamp
	• Oil excessively thin because of dilution, poor quality, or improper grade	• Drain and refill crankcase with recommended oil
	• Excessive oil temperature	• Correct cause of overheating engine
	• Oil pressure relief spring weak or sticking	• Remove and inspect oil pressure relief valve assembly
	• Oil inlet tube and screen assembly has restriction or air leak	• Remove and inspect oil inlet tube and screen assembly. (Fill inlet tube with lacquer thinner to locate leaks.)
	• Excessive oil pump clearance	• Measure clearances
	• Excessive main, rod, or camshaft bearing clearance	• Measure bearing clearances, repair as necessary
High oil pressure	• Improper oil viscosity	• Drain and refill crankcase with correct viscosity oil
	• Oil pressure gauge or sending unit inaccurate	• Replace oil pressure gauge
	• Oil pressure relief valve sticking closed	• Remove and inspect oil pressure relief valve assembly
Main bearing noise	• Insufficient oil supply	• Inspect for low oil level and low oil pressure
	• Main bearing clearance excessive	• Measure main bearing clearance, repair as necessary
	• Bearing insert missing	• Replace missing insert
	• Crankshaft end play excessive	• Measure end play, repair as necessary

87903C13

Troubleshooting Engine Mechanical Problems (cont.)

Problem	Cause	Solution
Main bearing noise	· Improperly tightened main bearing cap bolts	· Tighten bolts with specified torque
	· Loose flywheel or drive plate	· Tighten flywheel or drive plate attaching bolts
	· Loose or damaged vibration damper	· Repair as necessary
Connecting rod bearing noise	· Insufficient oil supply	· Inspect for low oil level and low oil pressure
	· Carbon build-up on piston	· Remove carbon from piston crown
	· Bearing clearance excessive or bearing missing	· Measure clearance, repair as necessary
	· Crankshaft connecting rod journal out-of-round	· Measure journal dimensions, repair or replace as necessary
	· Misaligned connecting rod or cap	· Repair as necessary
	· Connecting rod bolts tightened improperly	· Tighten bolts with specified torque
Piston noise	· Piston-to-cylinder wall clearance excessive (scuffed piston)	· Measure clearance and examine piston
	· Cylinder walls excessively tapered or out-of-round	· Measure cylinder wall dimensions, rebore cylinder
	· Piston ring broken	· Replace all rings on piston
	· Loose or seized piston pin	· Measure piston-to-pin clearance, repair as necessary
	· Connecting rods misaligned	· Measure rod alignment, straighten or replace
	· Piston ring side clearance excessively loose or tight	· Measure ring side clearance, repair as necessary
	· Carbon build-up on piston is excessive	· Remove carbon from piston
Valve actuating component noise	· Insufficient oil supply	· Check for: (a) Low oil level (b) Low oil pressure (c) Plugged push rods (d) Wrong hydraulic tappets (e) Restricted oil gallery (f) Excessive tappet to bore clearance
	· Push rods worn or bent	· Replace worn or bent push rods
	· Rocker arms or pivots worn	· Replace worn rocker arms or pivots
	· Foreign objects or chips in hydraulic tappets	· Clean tappets
	· Excessive tappet leak-down	· Replace valve tappet
	· Tappet face worn	· Replace tappet; inspect corresponding cam lobe for wear
	· Broken or cocked valve springs	· Properly seat cocked springs; replace broken springs
	· Stem-to-guide clearance excessive	· Measure stem-to-guide clearance, repair as required
	· Valve bent	· Replace valve
	· Loose rocker arms	· Tighten bolts with specified torque
	· Valve seat runout excessive	· Regrind valve seat/valves
	· Missing valve lock	· Install valve lock
	· Push rod rubbing or contacting cylinder head	· Remove cylinder head and remove obstruction in head
	· Excessive engine oil (four-cylinder engine)	· Correct oil level

87903C14

4

EMISSION CONTROLS

AIR POLLUTION

The earth's atmosphere, at or near sea level, consists approximately of 78 percent nitrogen, 21 percent oxygen and 1 percent other gases. If it were possible to remain in this state, 100 percent clean air would result. However, many varied sources allow other gases and particulates to mix with the clean air, causing our atmosphere to become unclean or polluted.

Certain of these pollutants are visible while others are invisible, with each having the capability of causing distress to the eyes, ears, throat, skin and respiratory system. Should these pollutants become concentrated in a specific area and under certain conditions, death could result due to the displacement or chemical change of the oxygen content in the air. These pollutants can also cause great damage to the environment and to the many man made objects that are exposed to the elements.

To better understand the causes of air pollution, the pollutants can be categorized into 3 separate types, natural, industrial and automotive.

Natural Pollutants

Natural pollution has been present on earth since before man appeared and continues to be a factor when discussing air pollution, although it causes only a small percentage of the overall pollution problem. It is the direct result of decaying organic matter, wind born smoke and particulates from such natural events as plain and forest fires (ignited by heat or lightning), volcanic ash, sand and dust which can spread over a large area of the countryside.

Such a phenomenon of natural pollution has been seen in the form of volcanic eruptions, with the resulting plume of smoke, steam and volcanic ash blotting out the sun's rays as it spreads and rises higher into the atmosphere. As it travels into the atmosphere the upper air currents catch and carry the smoke and ash, while condensing the steam back into water vapor. As the water vapor, smoke and ash travel on their journey, the smoke dissipates into the atmosphere while the ash and moisture settle back to earth in a trail hundreds of miles long. In some cases, lives are lost and millions of dollars of property damage result.

Industrial Pollutants

Industrial pollution is caused primarily by industrial processes, the burning of coal, oil and natural gas, which in turn produce smoke and fumes. Because the burning fuels contain large amounts of sulfur, the principal ingredients of smoke and fumes are sulfur dioxide and particulate matter. This type of pollutant occurs most severely during still, damp and cool weather, such as at night. Even in its less severe form, this pollutant is not confined to just cities. Because of air movements, the pollutants move for miles over the surrounding countryside, leaving in its path a barren and unhealthy environment for all living things.

Working with Federal, State and Local mandated regulations and by carefully monitoring emissions, big business has greatly reduced the amount of pollutant introduced from its industrial sources, striving to obtain an acceptable level. Because of the mandated industrial emission clean up, many land areas and streams in and around the cities that were formerly barren of vegetation and life, have now begun to move back in the direction of nature's intended balance.

Automotive Pollutants

The third major source of air pollution is automotive emissions. The emissions from the internal combustion engines were not an appreciable problem years ago because of the small number of registered vehicles and the nation's small highway system. However, during the early 1950's, the trend of the American people was to move from the cities to the surrounding suburbs. This caused an immediate problem in transportation because the majority of suburbs were not afforded mass transit conveniences. This lack of transportation created an attractive market for the automobile manufacturers, which resulted in a dramatic increase in the number of vehicles produced and sold, along with a marked increase in highway construction between cities and the suburbs. Multi-vehicle families emerged with a growing emphasis placed on an individual vehicle per family member. As the increase in vehicle ownership and usage occurred, so did pollutant levels in and around the cities, as suburbanites drove daily to their businesses and employment, returning at the end of the day to their homes in the suburbs.

It was noted that a smoke and fog type haze was being formed and at times, remained in suspension over the cities, taking time to dissipate. At first this "smog," derived from the words "smoke" and "fog," was thought to result from industrial pollution but it was determined that automobile emissions shared the blame. It was discovered that when normal automobile emissions were exposed to sunlight for a period of time, complex chemical reactions would take place.

It is now known that smog is a photo chemical layer which develops when certain oxides of nitrogen (NOx) and unburned hydrocarbons (HC) from automobile emissions are exposed to sunlight. Pollution was more severe when smog would become stagnant over an area in which a warm layer of air settled over the top of the cooler air mass, trapping and holding the cooler mass at ground level. The trapped cooler air would keep the emissions from being dispersed and diluted through normal air flows. This type of air stagnation was given the name "Temperature Inversion."

TEMPERATURE INVERSION

In normal weather situations, surface air is warmed by heat radiating from the earth's surface and the sun's rays. This causes it to rise upward, into the atmosphere. Upon rising it will cool through a convection type heat exchange with the cooler upper air. As warm air rises, the surface pollutants are carried upward and dissipated into the atmosphere.

When a temperature inversion occurs, we find the higher air is no longer cooler, but is warmer than the surface air, causing the cooler surface air to become trapped. This warm air blanket can extend from above ground level to a few hundred or even a few thousand feet into the air. As the surface air is trapped, so are the pollutants, causing a severe smog condition. Should this stagnant air mass extend to a few thousand feet high, enough air movement with the inversion takes place to allow the smog layer to rise above ground level but the pollutants still cannot dissipate. This inversion can remain for days over an area, with the smog level only rising or lowering from ground level to a few hundred feet high. Meanwhile, the pollutant levels increase, causing eye irritation, respiratory problems, reduced visibility, plant damage and in some cases, even disease.

This inversion phenomenon was first noted in the Los Angeles, California area. The city lies in terrain resembling a basin and with certain weather conditions, a cold air mass is held in the basin while a warmer air mass covers it like a lid.

Because this type of condition was first documented as prevalent in the Los Angeles area, this type of trapped pollution was named Los Angeles Smog, although it occurs in other areas where a large concentration of automobiles are used and the air remains stagnant for any length of time.

HEAT TRANSFER

Consider the internal combustion engine as a machine in which raw materials must be placed so a finished product comes out. As in any machine operation, a certain amount of wasted material is formed. When we relate this to the internal combustion engine, we find that through the input of air and fuel, we obtain power during the combustion process to drive the vehicle. The by-product or waste of this power is, in part, heat and exhaust gases with which we must dispose.

The heat from the combustion process can rise to over 4000°F (2204°C). The dissipation of this heat is controlled by a ram air effect, the use of cooling fans to cause air flow and a liquid coolant solution surrounding the combustion area to transfer the heat of combustion through the cylinder walls and into the coolant. The coolant is then directed to a thin-finned, multi-tubed radiator, from which the excess heat is transferred to the atmosphere by 1 of the 3 heat transfer methods, conduction, convection or radiation.

The cooling of the combustion area is an important part in the control of exhaust emissions. To understand the behavior of the combustion and transfer of its heat, consider the air/fuel charge. It is ignited and the flame front burns progressively across the combustion chamber until the burning charge reaches the cylinder walls. Some of the fuel in contact with the walls is not hot enough to burn, thereby snuffing out or quenching the combustion process. This leaves unburned fuel in the combustion chamber. This unburned fuel is then forced out of the cylinder and into the exhaust system, along with the exhaust gases.

Many attempts have been made to minimize the amount of unburned fuel in the combustion chambers due to quenching, by increasing the coolant temperature and lessening the contact area of the coolant around the combustion area. However, design limitations within the combustion chambers prevent the complete burning of the air/fuel charge, so a certain amount of the unburned fuel is still expelled into the exhaust system, regardless of modifications to the engine.

AUTOMOTIVE EMISSIONS

Before emission controls were mandated on internal combustion engines, other sources of engine pollutants were discovered along with the exhaust emissions. It was determined that engine combustion exhaust produced approximately 60 percent of the total emission pollutants, fuel evaporation from the fuel tank and carburetor vents produced 20 percent, with the final 20 percent being produced through the crankcase as a by-product of the combustion process.

Exhaust Gases

The exhaust gases emitted into the atmosphere are a combination of burned and unburned fuel. To understand the exhaust emission and its composition, we must review some basic chemistry.

When the air/fuel mixture is introduced into the engine, we are mixing air, composed of nitrogen (78 percent), oxygen (21 percent) and other gases (1 percent) with the fuel, which is 100 percent hydrocarbons (HC), in a semi-controlled ratio. As the combustion process is accomplished, power is produced to move the vehicle while the heat of combustion is transferred to the cooling system. The exhaust gases are then composed of nitrogen, a diatomic gas (N_2), the same as was introduced in the engine, carbon dioxide (CO_2), the same gas that is used in beverage carbonation, and water vapor (H_2O). The nitrogen (N_2), for the most part, passes through the engine unchanged, while the oxygen (O_2) reacts (burns) with the hydrocarbons (HC) and produces the carbon dioxide (CO_2) and the water vapors (H_2O). If this chemical process would be the only process to take place, the exhaust emissions would be harmless. However, during the combustion process, other compounds are formed which are considered dangerous. These pollutants are hydrocarbons (HC), carbon monoxide (CO), oxides of nitrogen (NOx) oxides of sulfur (SOx) and engine particulates.

HYDROCARBONS

Hydrocarbons (HC) are essentially fuel which was not burned during the combustion process or which has escaped into the atmosphere through fuel evaporation. The main sources of incomplete combustion are rich air/fuel mixtures, low engine temperatures and improper spark timing. The main sources of hydrocarbon emission through fuel evaporation on most vehicles used to be the vehicle's fuel tank and carburetor float bowl.

To reduce combustion hydrocarbon emission, engine modifications were made to minimize dead space and surface area in the combustion chamber. In addition, the air/fuel mixture was made more lean through the improved control which feedback carburetion and fuel injection offers and by the addition of external controls to aid in further combustion of the hydrocarbons outside the engine. Two such methods were the addition of air injection systems, to inject fresh air into the exhaust manifolds and the installation of catalytic converters, units that are able to burn traces of hydrocarbons without affecting the internal combustion process or fuel economy.

To control hydrocarbon emissions through fuel evaporation, modifications were made to the fuel tank to allow storage of the fuel vapors during periods of engine shut-down. Modifications were also made to the air intake system so that at specific times during engine operation, these vapors may be purged and burned by blending them with the air/fuel mixture.

CARBON MONOXIDE

Carbon monoxide is formed when not enough oxygen is present during the combustion process to convert carbon (C) to carbon dioxide (CO_2). An increase in the carbon monoxide (CO) emission is normally accompanied by an increase in the hydrocarbon (HC) emission because of the lack of oxygen to completely burn all of the fuel mixture.

Carbon monoxide (CO) also increases the rate at which the photo chemical smog is formed by speeding up the conversion of nitric oxide (NO) to nitrogen dioxide (NO_2). To accomplish this, carbon monoxide (CO) combines with oxygen (O_2) and nitric oxide (NO) to produce carbon dioxide (CO_2) and nitrogen dioxide (NO_2). ($CO + O_2 + NO = CO_2 + NO_2$).

The dangers of carbon monoxide, which is an odorless and colorless toxic gas are many. When carbon monoxide is inhaled into the lungs and passed into the blood stream, oxygen is replaced by the carbon monoxide in the red blood cells, causing a reduction in the amount of oxygen supplied to the many parts of the body. This lack of oxygen causes headaches, lack of coordination, reduced mental alertness and, should the carbon monoxide concentration be high enough, death could result.

NITROGEN

Normally, nitrogen is an inert gas. When heated to approximately 2500°F (1371°C) through the combustion process, this gas becomes active and causes an increase in the nitric oxide (NO) emission.

Oxides of nitrogen (NOx) are composed of approximately 97-98 percent nitric oxide (NO). Nitric oxide is a colorless gas but when it is passed into the atmosphere, it combines with oxygen and forms nitrogen dioxide (NO_2). The nitrogen dioxide then combines with chemically active hydrocarbons (HC) and when in the presence of sunlight, causes the formation of photo-chemical smog.

Ozone

To further complicate matters, some of the nitrogen dioxide (NO_2) is broken apart by the sunlight to form nitric oxide and oxygen. ($NO_2 + sunlight = NO + O$). This single atom of oxygen then combines with diatomic (meaning 2 atoms) oxygen (O_2) to form ozone (O_3). Ozone is one of the smells associated with smog. It has a pungent and offensive odor, irritates the eyes and lung tissues, affects the growth of plant life and causes rapid deterioration of rubber products. Ozone

can be formed by sunlight as well as electrical discharge into the air.

The most common discharge area on the automobile engine is the secondary ignition electrical system, especially when inferior quality spark plug cables are used. As the surge of high voltage is routed through the secondary cable, the circuit builds up an electrical field around the wire, which acts upon the oxygen in the surrounding air to form the ozone. The faint glow along the cable with the engine running that may be visible on a dark night, is called the "corona discharge." It is the result of the electrical field passing from a high along the cable, to a low in the surrounding air, which forms the ozone gas. The combination of corona and ozone has been a major cause of cable deterioration. Recently, different and better quality insulating materials have lengthened the life of the electrical cables.

Although ozone at ground level can be harmful, ozone is beneficial to the earth's inhabitants. By having a concentrated ozone layer called the "ozonosphere," between 10 and 20 miles (16-32 km) up in the atmosphere, much of the ultra violet radiation from the sun's rays are absorbed and screened. If this ozone layer were not present, much of the earth's surface would be burned, dried and unfit for human life.

OXIDES OF SULFUR

Oxides of sulfur (SOx) were initially ignored in the exhaust system emissions, since the sulfur content of gasoline as a fuel is less than $1/10$ of 1 percent. Because of this small amount, it was felt that it contributed very little to the overall pollution problem. However, because of the difficulty in solving the sulfur emissions in industrial pollutions and the introduction of catalytic converter to the automobile exhaust systems, a change was mandated. The automobile exhaust system, when equipped with a catalytic converter, changes the sulfur dioxide (SO_2) into the sulfur trioxide (SO_3).

When this combines with water vapors (H_2O), a sulfuric acid mist (H_2SO_4) is formed and is a very difficult pollutant to handle since it is extremely corrosive. This sulfuric acid mist that is formed, is the same mist that rises from the vents of an automobile battery when an active chemical reaction takes place within the battery cells.

When a large concentration of vehicles equipped with catalytic converters are operating in an area, this acid mist may rise and be distributed over a large ground area causing land, plant, crop, paint and building damage.

PARTICULATE MATTER

A certain amount of particulate matter is present in the burning of any fuel, with carbon constituting the largest percentage of the particulates. In gasoline, the remaining particulates are the burned remains of the various other compounds used in its manufacture. When a gasoline engine is in good internal condition, the particulate emissions are low but as the engine wears internally, the particulate emissions increase. By visually inspecting the tail pipe emissions, a determination can be made as to where an engine defect may exist. An engine with light gray or blue smoke emitting from the tail pipe normally indicates an increase in the oil consumption through burning due to internal engine wear. Black smoke would indicate a defective fuel delivery system, causing the engine to operate in a rich mode. Regardless of the color of the smoke, the internal part of the engine or the fuel delivery system should be repaired to prevent excess particulate emissions.

Diesel and turbine engines emit a darkened plume of smoke from the exhaust system because of the type of fuel used. Emission control regulations are mandated for this type of emission and more stringent measures are being used to prevent excess emission of the particulate matter. Electronic components are being introduced to control the injection of the fuel at precisely the proper time of piston travel, to achieve the optimum in fuel ignition and fuel usage. Other particulate after-burning components are being tested to achieve a cleaner emission.

Good grades of engine lubricating oils should be used, which meet the manufacturers specification. Cut-rate oils can contribute to the particulate emission problem because of their low flash or ignition temperature point. Such oils burn prematurely during the combustion process causing emission of particulate matter.

The cooling system is an important factor in the reduction of particulate matter. The optimum combustion will occur, with the cooling system operating at a temperature specified by the manufacturer. The cooling system must be maintained in the same manner as the engine oiling system, as each system is required to perform properly in order for the engine to operate efficiently for a long time.

Crankcase Emissions

Crankcase emissions are made up of water, acids, unburned fuel, oil fumes and particulates. These emissions are classified as hydrocarbons (HC) and are formed by the small amount of unburned, compressed air/fuel mixture entering the crankcase from the combustion area (between the cylinder walls and piston rings) during the compression and power strokes. The head of the compression and combustion help to form the remaining crankcase emissions.

Since the first engines, crankcase emissions were allowed into the atmosphere through a road draft tube, mounted on the lower side of the engine block. Fresh air came in through an open oil filler cap or breather. The air passed through the crankcase mixing with blow-by gases. The motion of the vehicle and the air blowing past the open end of the road draft tube caused a low pressure area (vacuum) at the end of the tube. Crankcase emissions were simply drawn out of the road draft tube into the air.

To control the crankcase emission, the road draft tube was deleted. A hose and/or tubing was routed from the crankcase to the intake manifold so the blow-by emission could be burned with the air/fuel mixture. However, it was found that

intake manifold vacuum, used to draw the crankcase emissions into the manifold, would vary in strength at the wrong time and not allow the proper emission flow. A regulating valve was needed to control the flow of air through the crankcase.

Testing, showed the removal of the blow-by gases from the crankcase as quickly as possible, was most important to the longevity of the engine. Should large accumulations of blow-by gases remain and condense, dilution of the engine oil would occur to form water, soots, resins, acids and lead salts, resulting in the formation of sludge and varnishes. This condensation of the blow-by gases occurs more frequently on vehicles used in numerous starting and stopping conditions, excessive idling and when the engine is not allowed to attain normal operating temperature through short runs.

Evaporative Emissions

Gasoline fuel is a major source of pollution, before and after it is burned in the automobile engine. From the time the fuel is refined, stored, pumped and transported, again stored until it is pumped into the fuel tank of the vehicle, the gasoline gives off unburned hydrocarbons (HC) into the atmosphere. Through the redesign of storage areas and venting systems, the pollution factor was diminished, but not eliminated, from the refinery standpoint. However, the automobile still remained the primary source of vaporized, unburned hydrocarbon (HC) emissions.

Fuel pumped from an underground storage tank is cool but when exposed to a warmer ambient temperature, will expand. Before controls were mandated, an owner might fill the fuel tank with fuel from an underground storage tank and park the vehicle for some time in warm area, such as a parking lot. As the fuel would warm, it would expand and should no provisions or area be provided for the expansion, the fuel would spill out of the filler neck and onto the ground, causing hydrocarbon (HC) pollution and creating a severe fire hazard. To correct this condition, the vehicle manufacturers added overflow plumbing and/or gasoline tanks with built in expansion areas or domes.

However, this did not control the fuel vapor emission from the fuel tank. It was determined that most of the fuel evaporation occurred when the vehicle was stationary and the engine not operating. Most vehicles carry 5-25 gallons (19-95 liters) of gasoline. Should a large concentration of vehicles be parked in one area, such as a large parking lot, excessive fuel vapor emissions would take place, increasing as the temperature increases.

To prevent the vapor emission from escaping into the atmosphere, the fuel systems were designed to trap the vapors while the vehicle is stationary, by sealing the system from the atmosphere. A storage system is used to collect and hold the fuel vapors from the carburetor (if equipped) and the fuel tank when the engine is not operating. When the engine is started, the storage system is then purged of the fuel vapors, which are drawn into the engine and burned with the air/fuel mixture.

CRANKCASE AND EVAPORATIVE EMISSION CONTROLS

▶ See Figures 1 and 2

Crankcase Ventilation System

OPERATION

▶ See Figures 3 and 4

1970-71 EA61 Engines

On EA61 engines (ff-1) the closed crankcase ventilation system consists of a sealed oil filler cap, a valve cover with a hose outlet, an oil separator, and a special oil pan.

Blow-by gases pass from the outlet in the valve cover to the oil separator, where they are sucked into the air cleaner

through a hose, and the oil is returned to the oil pan via another hose. The gases sucked into the air cleaner are burned along with the regular air/fuel mixture.

1971-78 EA62, EA63 and EA71 Engines

The crankcase ventilation system used on the EA62 and EA63 engines (1300G, GL, and DL models) is similar to that described above for EA61 engines. Only two hoses are used instead of one and the oil separator is integral with the air cleaner.

Blow-by gases from the crankcase are routed to the air cleaner via the two hoses, where they are pulled into the carburetor and burned with the air/fuel mixture.

The oil, which is trapped by the oil separator in the air cleaner, returns through the crankcase ventilation system hoses to the valve covers, where it is mixed with the oil used to lubricate the valve train.

1977-84 1200, 1600 and 1800 Engines

A sealed crankcase emission system is used, which prevents blow-by gases from being emitted into the air.

The system consists of a sealed oil filler cap, valve covers with an emission outlet and a fresh air inlet, connecting hoses, a Positive Crankcase Ventilation (PCV) valve and an air cleaner.

Strong intake vacuum at part throttle suck blow-by gases from the crankcase, through a connecting hose (on the single valve cover on the 1200 engine, the #2 and #4 valve cover on the 1600 and 1800 engines), into the intake manifold via the PCV valve.

However, at wide open throttle, the increase in volume of blow-by and the decrease in manifold vacuum make the flow through the PCV valve inadequate. Under these conditions excess vapors are drawn into the air cleaner (via a connecting hose from the #1 and #3 valve cover on the 1600 and 1800 engines) and pass through the carburetor into the engine.

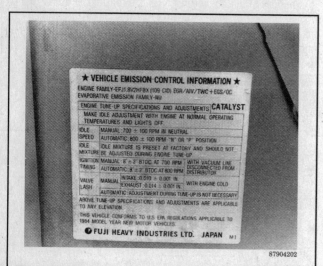

Fig. 1 Somewhere under the hood you should have a vehicle emission control information tag . . .

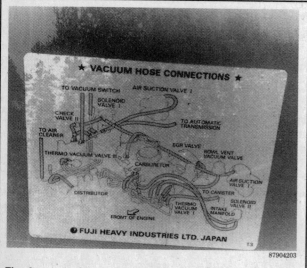

Fig. 2 . . . and a vacuum hose routing tag

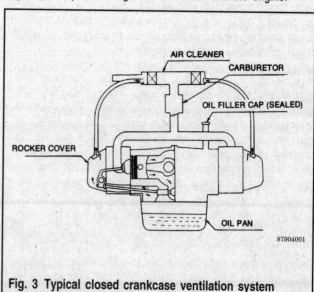

Fig. 3 Typical closed crankcase ventilation system

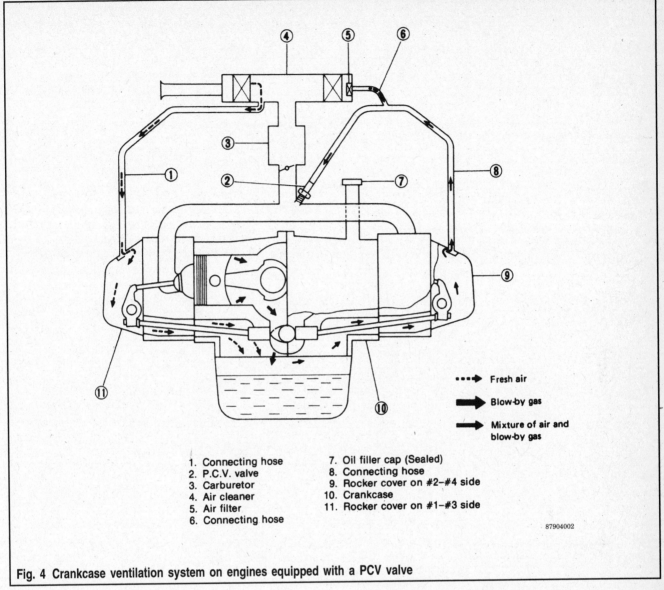

Fresh air

Blow-by gas

Mixture of air and blow-by gas

1. Connecting hose
2. P.C.V. valve
3. Carburetor
4. Air cleaner
5. Air filter
6. Connecting hose
7. Oil filler cap (Sealed)
8. Connecting hose
9. Rocker cover on #2–#4 side
10. Crankcase
11. Rocker cover on #1–#3 side

87904002

Fig. 4 Crankcase ventilation system on engines equipped with a PCV valve

SERVICE

See section 1 for crankcase ventilation system air cleaner and PCV valve servicing procedures and intervals.

REMOVAL & INSTALLATION

Closed System Components

In the closed crankcase ventilation system removal and installation is limited to unfastening the hose clamps and removing the hoses from their connections.

Positive Crankcase Ventilation (PCV) Systems

In the closed crankcase ventilation system removal and installation is limited to unfastening the hose clamps and removing the hoses from their connections. On some 1600 engines the oil separator may be detached by removing its securing bolts.

On the Positive Crankcase Ventilation (PCV) valve system:
1. Remove the hose connected to the PCV valve at the base of the air cleaner.
2. Remove the PCV valve.
3. Installation is the reverse of removal.

Evaporative Emission Control System

OPERATION

▶ **See Figures 5, 6 and 7**

1970-72 Models

Evaporative gas from the fuel tank is not discharged into the surrounding atmosphere but conducted to the air cleaner unit and then burned in the combustion chamber. No absorbent (charcoal) is used.

The system consists of a sealed fuel tank and filler cap, two reservoir tanks on the station wagon, an air breather valve, breather hoses, breather pipe and the air cleaner with fixtures to receive the breather hoses.

While the engine is running, evaporative gas is absorbed into the intake manifold due to the suction pressure of the manifold, and never discharged directly into the atmosphere.

While the engine is stopped, the gases collect on the inner wall of the element of the air cleaner.

There is an air breather valve located at the filler cap. When the flap (door) is opened, a spring exerts pressure on the rubber breather hose and pinches it shut.

1973 Models

The evaporative emission control system remains much the same as for 1970-72 models, except that an orifice on the sedans and thin nylon tube on wagons, replaces the air breather valve (which functioned as an overflow limiter). Also, a vacuum relief gas filler cap is used.

1974-76 Models

On 1974-76 models, the orifice and thin nylon tube (1973) are replaced by an overflow limiter valve. The overflow limiter has two functions:

1. To prevent fuel from flowing into the air cleaner.
2. To vent the gas tank to fresh air from the air cleaner when pressure decreases in the tank (as it empties).

1977-84 Models

The EEC system was revised to include a vapor canister which collects the fuel vapor before it reaches the carburetor. Once in the canister, the fuel vapor is absorbed on a supply of activated charcoal particles. These particles hold the vapor until the engine idle speed increases to a point where the carburetor vacuum is sufficient to open the purge control valve on the canister. On late models a solenoid controls the vacuum flow. With the valve open the fuel vapor is sucked out of the charcoal particles and into the intake manifold. Fresh air is

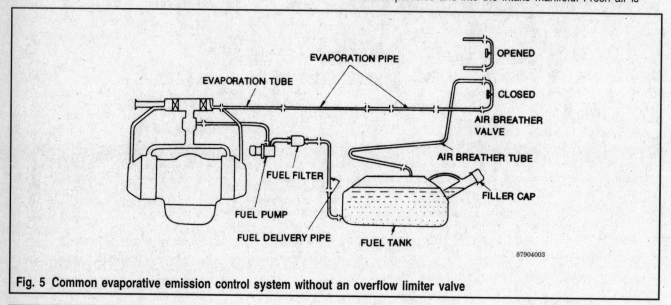

Fig. 5 Common evaporative emission control system without an overflow limiter valve

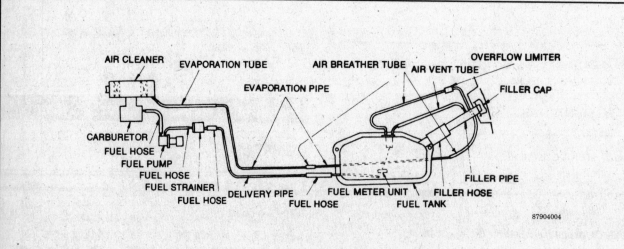

Fig. 6 Common evaporative emission control system with an overflow limiter valve

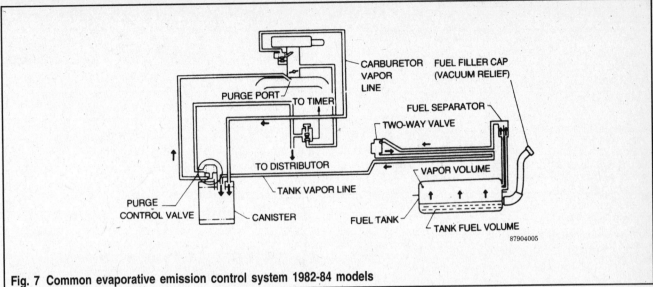

Fig. 7 Common evaporative emission control system 1982-84 models

drawn through a filter at the bottom of the canister to displace the escaping fuel vapor.

The system also incorporates two orifices located on the line between the fuel tank and vapor canister. These prevent fuel spillage in the event of impact. On station wagons (1977-79), two small reserve tanks on both sides of the fuel tank are employed to prevent liquid fuel from flowing into the air cleaner in case of an abrupt stop, etc. Some models have a check valve on the line between the canister and the intake manifold to prevent a build-up of vapor in the manifold when the engine is stopped. A carburetor vapor line connects the float chamber and canister as well as a tank vapor line. A two-way valve is located between the fuel tank and canister. It functions to control the flow of fuel vapor to the canister according to pressure in the fuel tank.

SERVICE

The EEC system requires little service as a part of normal maintenance. Every 24 months/24,000 miles (38,000 km) the hoses should be visually checked for cracks and leaks. At the same interval, change the bottom filter on the vapor canister on 1977-79 models.

REMOVAL & INSTALLATION

▶ **See Figures 8 and 9**

Removal and installation of the various evaporative emission control system components consists of unfastening hoses, loosening securing screws, and removing the part which is to be replaced from its mounting bracket.

✳✳WARNING

When replacing any EEC system hoses, always use hoses that are fuel resistant or are marked EVAP.

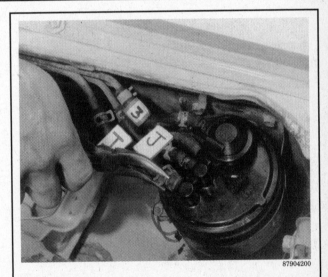

Fig. 8 Tag and remove the hoses at the canister . . .

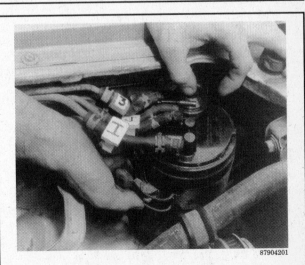

Fig. 9 . . . then loosen the retaining bracket and remove the canister from the vehicle

TESTING

EEC System Troubleshooting

There are several things which may be checked if a malfunction of the evaporative emission control system is suspected.

1. Leaks may be traced by using a hydrocarbon tester. Run the test probe along the lines and connections. The meter will indicate the presence of a leak by a high hydrocarbon (HC) reading. This method is much more accurate than visual inspection which would only indicate the presence of a leak large enough to pass liquid.

2. Leaks may be caused by any of the following:
   a. Defective or worn hoses.
   b. Disconnected or pinched hoses.
   c. Improperly routed hoses.

   d. A defective filler cap or safety valve (sealed cap system).

✳✳WARNING

If it becomes necessary to replace any of the hoses used in the evaporative emission control system, use only hoses which are fuel resistant or are marked EVAP.

3. If the fuel tank collapses, it may be the fault of clogged or pinched vent lines, a defective vapor separator, or a plugged or incorrect filler cap.

4. To test the filler cap (if it is the safety valve type), clean it and place it against the mouth. Blow into the relief valve housing. If the cap passes pressure with light blowing or if it fails to release with hard blowing, it is defective and must be replaced.

✳✳WARNING

Use the proper cap for the type of system used; either a sealed cap or safety valve cap, as required.

EXHAUST EMISSION CONTROLS

The purpose of this system is to prevent excessive amounts of Carbon Monoxide (CO), Hydrocarbon (HC) and Nitrous Oxide (NOx) emissions from being given off with the normal engine exhaust. The methods employed to accomplish this purpose have been revised and varied over the past several years in order to meet stricter government standards, while at the same time maintaining or improving vehicle performance. From 1970 Subaru has made a number of changes in its exhaust emission control system. Some changes are minor, others involve adding or eliminating major components.

There are four basic systems within the Subaru exhaust emission control system. Despite variations in terminology from year-to-year, they can be classified as: engine modification system, air injection (suction) system, exhaust gas recirculation system and on selected models, a catalytic converter system or a three-way catalyst attended with an Electronically Controlled Carburetor (ECC) system.

Hot Air Control System

The purpose of the hot air control system is to reduce HC emissions and improve engine performance during warm-up. This is accomplished by deflecting either cool outside air or warm engine-heated air into the carburetor, depending upon engine operating conditions.

On 1970-76 models a two position control valve, mounted in the air cleaner snorkel, allows either underhood air or preheated air to flow into the air cleaner. The valve is controlled by a lever marked **HOT** and **COLD**, or **WINTER** and **SUMMER**.

When the ambient temperature is below 59°F (15°C), set the lever to the **HOT** or **WINTER** position. If the temperature is above 59°F (15°C), move the lever to the **COLD** or **SUMMER** position.

On the 1977-84 system works automatically be means of a temperature sensor and vacuum motor. The temperature sensor detects the inlet air temperature and controls the flow of vacuum to the vacuum motor. Together they regulate the air control valve, mounted in the air horn. The possible combinations of inlet (underhood) air temperatures and vacuum readings, and the resulting valve operation are shown on the Operation of the Air Control Valve chart.

REMOVAL & INSTALLATION

▶ **See Figures 10 and 11**

Temperature Sensor

1. Remove the air cleaner cover and filter.
2. Using pliers, flatten the clip securing the vacuum hose to the temperature sensor and remove the hose.
3. Now pull the same clip completely away from the sensor. Lift the sensor off the air cleaner.

➡**The gasket between the sensor and air cleaner is glued to the air cleaner and should be removed. Always install a new clip when the temperature sensor is reinstalled.**

Vacuum Motor

▶ **See Figures 12, 13 and 14**

1. Detach the connected to the vacuum motor.
2. Remove the screws securing the vacuum motor to the air cleaner.
3. Disconnect the vacuum motor valve shaft from the air control valve, and remove the vacuum motor from the air cleaner.

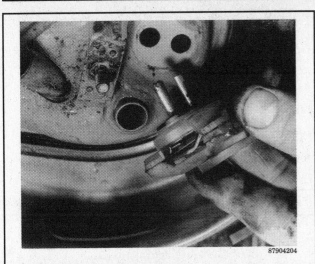

Fig. 10 The air temperature sensor is mounted to the air cleaner

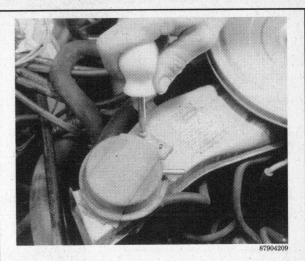

Fig. 13 Remove the screws securing the vacuum motor to the air cleaner

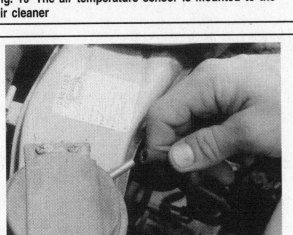

Fig. 12 Unplug the hose connected to the vacuum motor

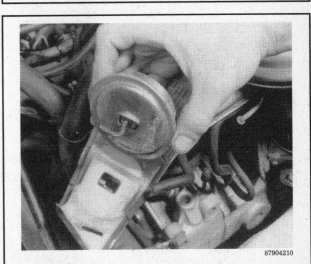

Fig. 14 Disconnect the valve shaft from the control valve, then remove the vacuum motor

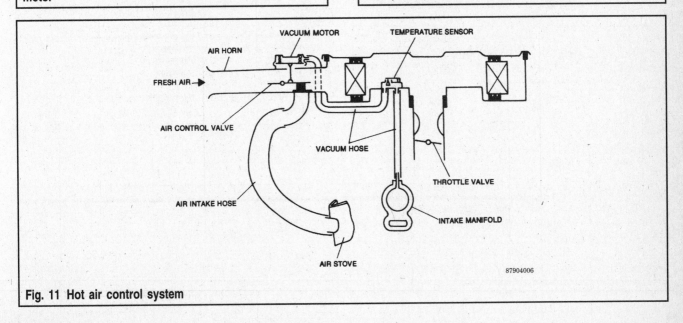

Fig. 11 Hot air control system

TROUBLESHOOTING & INSPECTION

▶ **See Figures 15 and 16**

Air Control Valve

1. If the car is running, turn **OFF** engine.
2. Place a mirror at the end of the air cleaner.
3. Inspect the position of the air control valve. The proper position is with the fresh air vent open and the hot air inlet closed.
4. If the position is not as described in Step 3, check the air control valve linkage for sticking.

Vacuum Motor

1. Keep mirror in position and engine **OFF**.
2. Remove the vacuum hose from the vacuum motor.
3. Connect a separate piece of the same type of hose to the now vacant vacuum motor. Insert the other end of the new

hose into your mouth and draw in a breath, creating a vacuum in the vacuum motor.
4. Check the position of the air control valve. The fresh air vent should be closed and the hot air inlet open.
5. Now, pinch the hose attached to the vacuum motor so that the vacuum is not instantly lost. The valve position described in Step 4 should be maintained for more than 30 seconds.

➡**If the conditions described in Steps 4 and 5 are not observed, replace the vacuum motor.**

Temperature Sensor

✳✳WARNING

Engine must be cold before starting this test.

1. Keep the mirror in position in front of the air horn as shown in Fig. 7.
2. Start the engine and keep it idling.
3. Check the position of the air control valve immediately after starting. The fresh air vent should be closed and the hot air inlet open.
4. Continue to watch the air control valve as the engine warms up. The fresh air vent should gradually open.

➡**If the conditions described in Steps 2 and 3 are not observed, replace the temperature sensor.**

Engine Modification System

IGNITION CONTROL

▶ **See Figures 17 and 18**

The operating principal of this system is not only to obtain correct air/fuel mixture while the vehicle is decelerating, but also to promote complete combustion by advancing or retard-

87904007

Fig. 15 Inspect the position of the air control valve with a mirror

Operation of the Air Control Valve

Under Hood Air Temperature	Vacuum Reading at Vacuum Motor Diaphragm	Temperature Sensor Valve Operations	Air Control Valve Operation
Below 100 F	Below 1.57 inHg	Closed	Cool air admission
	Above 6.30 inHg		Hot air admission
100–127 F	Varies	Open	Cool and hot air mixture admission
Above 127 F	No vacuum*	Open	Cool air admission

*Vacuum connection is broken when valve inside temperature sensor fully opens

87904008

Fig. 16 Air control valve operating conditions

ing the ignition timing, thus reducing the amount of emissions released into the atmosphere.

→**This system is found, with variations, on almost all models from 1972.**

While the vehicle is decelerating, the primary throttle valve is closed, causing a high vacuum condition to occur in the intake manifold. This vacuum is conducted through a vacuum control valve and on to the carburetor where a by-pass jet is opened and extra mixture is allowed to enter the venturi below the throttle plates. This enriches the mixture and promotes cleaner combustion.

The vacuum is also routed to the distributor vacuum control. After passing through an air damper (1972-73 only) which regulates the vacuum to a smooth application, the distributor vacuum control advances or retards the ignition spark in order to promote complete combustion in the cylinders.

While the primary throttle plate is opened during acceleration, cruising or idling, the by-pass air valve in the carburetor does not open because the vacuum does not reach the specified measure. However, the distributor vacuum control operates at a much lower vacuum condition. Thus it is operating more often than the by-pass valve in the carburetor.

There is an anti-dieseling solenoid switch mounted on the side opposite the float bowl on the carburetor. The purpose of this switch is to prevent the engine from dieseling when the ignition switch is turned OFF. When the ignition switch is turned off, the electrical current which supplies an electromagnet in the switch is also cut off. A spring inside of the housing forces a plunger into position, blocking the fuel passages leading to the opening below the throttle plates. When the ignition switch is turned ON, it energizes the electromagnet in the switch and pulls the plunger out of the fuel passage, thus allowing fuel to reach the opening below the throttle plates.

On some models there is a solenoid valve located on the line to the distributor vacuum control. It is an electrically operated switch which receives a signal from the coolant temperature switch. At coolant temperatures below 100°F (38°C), the solenoid valve prevents engine vacuum from actuating the distributor retard mechanism. This allows for improved engine starting in cold weather.

On 1982-84 models, this system operates the vacuum advance diaphragm of the distributor via a thermal vacuum valve. The valve opens the entire vacuum advance circuit to atmospheric pressure in a certain temperature range. This range (measured at the intake manifold cooling water circuit) is 59°F (15°C) to 95°F (35°C) on all but the turbocharged engine. On the 1800 Turbo, this range is 113°F (45°C) to 131°F (55°C).

The valve simultaneously activates the EGR valve so that when vacuum advance is turned off the EGR valve does not work either. If this system is operating improperly, the car would exhibit very poor operation when cold. Symptoms such as very poor fuel mileage and performance with the engine hot, or slow warm-up may also occur.

The system draws its vacuum supply from a port in the carburetor (or throttle body) above the throttle, so vacuum advance is not present at normal hot engine idle speed, but begins as the throttle is opened past idle. On certain models, advance is also desirable at idle. These incorporate a port located under the lower edge of the throttle plate which becomes ineffective above idle throttle opening. A check valve connects this port to the rest of the system. These models are:

1800 Turbo, 1982 1600 2-door Hatchback GL (5MT), 4-door GL (5MT) and Hardtop GLF (5MT), and all 1983-84 1600cc models. If the check valve fails, symptoms would include slow or erratic idle and, possibly, a slight hesitation.

TESTING

Thermal Vacuum Valve (TVV)

To check the function of the thermal vacuum valve:
1. Drain a little coolant and remove the air cleaner.
2. Disconnect the hoses and remove the valve from the intake manifold.
3. Cap off the center (EGR) port and connect hoses to the upper and lower ports. These hoses must seal tightly so no water will get into the top part of the valve. The tops of the hoses must also stay dry.

❊❊CAUTION

When draining the coolant, keep in mind that cats and dogs are attracted by ethylene glycol antifreeze, and are quite likely to drink any that is left in an uncovered container or in puddles on the ground. This will prove fatal in sufficient quantity. Always drain the coolant into a sealable container. Coolant should be reused unless it is contaminated or several years old.

4. Immerse the valve in a pan of water that also contains a 200°F (93°C) thermometer. If necessary, use ice to cool the water below 59°F (15°C) unless your car is an 1800 Turbo.
5. Heat the water while blowing into the air cleaner hose connection.
6. The valve should seal at first. As the temperature passes the 59°F (15°C) mark, or as it passes the 113°F (45°C) mark on the Turbo, the valve should open and you should be able to blow air through it freely.
7. Again, at 104°F (40°C), 131°F (55°C) on the Turbo, the valve should seal tightly.
8. If it fails any of these tests, replace the valve.
9. Coat the valve with sealer before screwing it back into the intake manifold.
10. To check for proper functioning of the check valve, install a timing light and idle the engine after it is fully warmed up.
11. Accelerate the engine up to about 2000 rpm and then slowly return the throttle to normal idle position while watching the point at which the ignition fires.
12. The timing should remain fully advanced right down to idle speed. If the check valve is stuck shut, timing will retard fairly suddenly at idle speed.
13. If the check valve is stuck open, the timing will abruptly retard slightly above idle speed.
14. If the valve fails these tests, note which end of the valve is connected to vacuum lines leading to the distributor, and then pull off the vacuum lines on either end of the valve.
15. To confirm your test results, blow through the valve in the direction of flow from the carburetor lower port toward the distributor. Air should flow freely.
16. Then, turn the valve around and blow through it in the other direction. The valve should seal tightly.

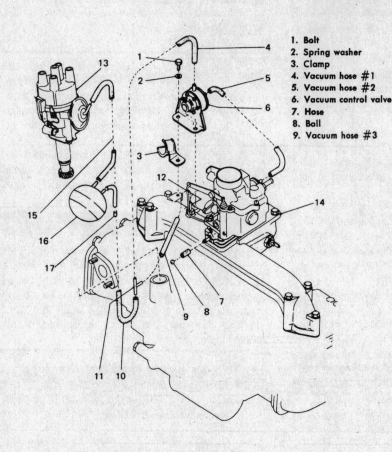

1. Bolt
2. Spring washer
3. Clamp
4. Vacuum hose #1
5. Vacuum hose #2
6. Vacuum control valve
7. Hose
8. Ball
9. Vacuum hose #3
10. Vacuum hose #4
11. Connector
12. Connector
13. Distributor
14. Carburetor
15. Air dumper (accumulator)
16. Vacuum hose #5
17. Orifice

87904009

Fig. 17 Engine modification system component locations

17. Replace the valve if either test is failed.

REMOVAL & INSTALLATION

▶ **See Figure 19**

➡**Remove the spare tire and the air cleaner assembly from the engine compartment to gain access to the various components of the engine modifications system.**

Vacuum Control Valve

1. Detach the vacuum hoses from the distributor retard unit, carburetor by-pass servo diaphragm, automatic choke main diaphragm (if so equipped), and the intake manifold.
2. Remove the bolts which secure the vacuum control valve to the intake manifold.
3. Lift the valve assembly off the manifold. On 1972-73 models, the air damper (accumulator) is connected to the valve bracket and can be removed at the same time.

4. When installing the valve, be sure to route the vacuum hoses correctly.

Anti-Dieseling Solenoid

1972-73 MODELS

1. Disconnect the lead which runs to the anti-dieseling solenoid.
2. Remove the 3 screws which secure the solenoid to the carburetor.
3. Carefully remove the solenoid assembly from the carburetor.

1974-82 MODELS

1. Disconnect the solenoid electrical lead.
2. Unscrew the solenoid assembly.
3. Remove it, complete with gasket from the carburetor body.
4. Be sure to install the gasket before installing the solenoid assembly.

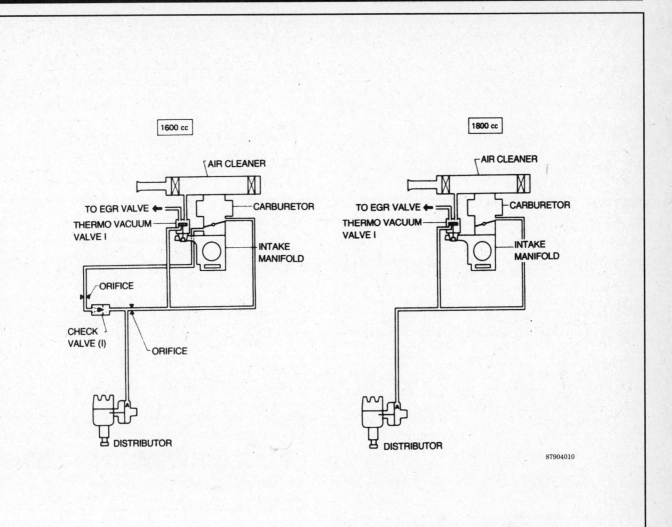

Fig. 18 The ignition control system for the 1982-84 models have two versions, pictured here. See text for exact model delineation

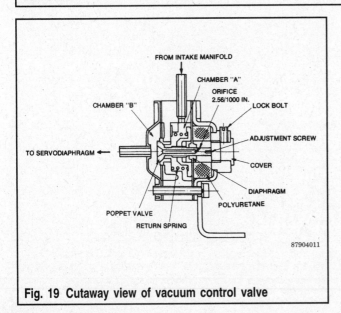

Fig. 19 Cutaway view of vacuum control valve

Carburetor By-pass Servo Diaphragm

✳✳WARNING

Be careful not to confuse the servo diaphragm with the choke diaphragm used on 1974 and later carburetors.

1. Remove the vacuum hose from the servo diaphragm.
2. Remove the 3 screws that attach the diaphragm to the carburetor.
3. Remove the servo diaphragm.
4. Installation is performed in the reverse order of removal.

Electrically Assisted Automatic Choke

Starting in 1974, a vacuum operated automatic choke replaces the manual choke previously used. The automatic choke uses a choke cap which contains a heating element, to speed up choke valve opening, and thus reduce CO emissions during warm-up.

The heating element gets its power from a special tap on the voltage regulator, when the ignition is on and the engine running.

REMOVAL & INSTALLATION

1. Remove the air cleaner assembly from the carburetor.
2. Remove the electrical lead which runs from the choke cap to the voltage regulator.
3. Disconnect the setting piston from the auxiliary choke diaphragm.
4. Remove the 3 screws which secure the choke cap to the carburetor and remove the cap.
5. Be sure that the choke lever is positioned in the middle of the bi-metal before installing the cap.

After installation, check to see that the carburetor choke valve closes when the cap is turned counterclockwise. Align the setting marks on the choke housing and cap. See the Carburetor Section for further choke adjustments.

TESTING

1. Disconnect the choke lead from the voltage regulator.
2. Connect an ohmmeter between the lead that you just disconnected and a good ground. The ohmmeter should read about 9 ohms.
3. Replace the choke cap if the reading shows an opened (no resistance) or shorted (infinite resistance) heating coil.
4. If the choke coil is working properly, but a fault is suspected in the choke heater system, substitute a new voltage regulator to see if it will solve the problem.

Carburetor Dashpot

ADJUSTMENT

ff-1 and 1300G

1. Be sure that the throttle valve is in the idle (closed) position.
2. The dashpot stem should be able to move about 4mm beyond the throttle lever's idle position.
3. If the stem does not move the correct distance, adjust the dashpot by loosening its locknut and rotating the dashpot assembly until the proper amount of movement is obtained.
4. Tighten the locknut and recheck dashpot stem movement.

Air Injection System

ff-1, 1300G AND ALL 1975 MODELS

▶ See Figure 20

An air injection system is used on ff-1, 1300G and all 1975 models

A belt driven air pump is used to supply air, under pressure, to air distribution manifolds which have openings at each exhaust port. Injection of air at this point causes combustion of the unburned hydrocarbons in the exhaust manifolds, rather than allowing them to escape into the atmosphere. An anti-backfire valve controls the flow of air from the pump to prevent backfiring which results from an overly rich mixture under closed throttle conditions.

Check valves prevent hot exhaust gas backflow into the pump and hoses in case of pump failure or when the anti-backfire valve is not working.

Air pumps are equipped with a relief valve to discharge excess air which the pump produces at high engine speed.

On 1300G models, an additional air by-pass valve is used. When the manual choke is pulled out, the air by-pass causes the air from the pump to flow into the air cleaner rather than the exhaust manifolds, which prevents the manifolds from being overheated.

REMOVAL & INSTALLATION

▶ See Figure 21

Air Pump

1. Disconnect the air hoses from the pump.
2. Loosen the bolt on the adjusting link and remove the drive belt.
3. Remove the mounting bolts and remove the pump.

✳✳CAUTION

Do not pry on the pump housing. It may become distorted.

To install:

4. Install the pump, fasten the mounting bolts and fasten the bolt on the adjusting link. Connect the hoses.
5. Adjust the drive belt tension. Belt deflection should be 3.5 in. (9mm) with 22 lbs. (29 Nm) pressure.

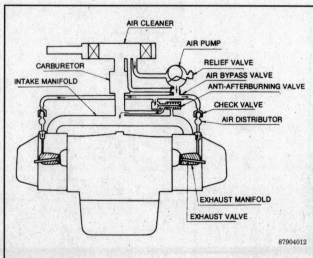

Fig. 20 1300G air injection system — ff-1 and 1975 models similar

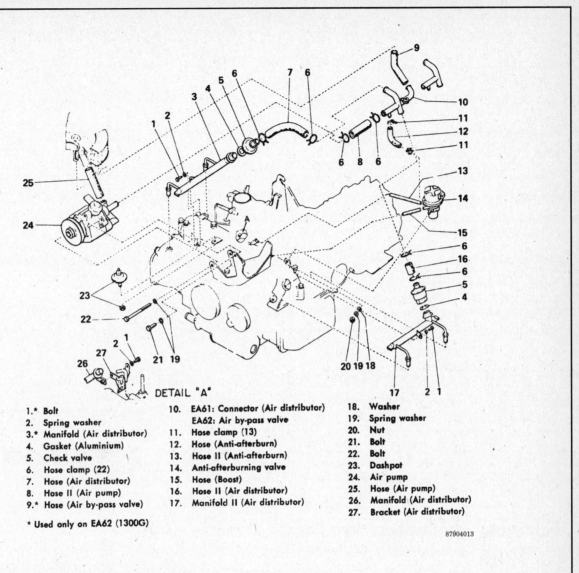

Fig. 21 Components of the air injection system

1.* Bolt	10. EA61: Connector (Air distributor)
2. Spring washer	EA62: Air by-pass valve
3.* Manifold (Air distributor)	11. Hose clamp (13)
4. Gasket (Aluminium)	12. Hose (Anti-afterburn)
5. Check valve	13. Hose II (Anti-afterburn)
6. Hose clamp (22)	14. Anti-afterburning valve
7. Hose (Air distributor)	15. Hose (Boost)
8. Hose II (Air pump)	16. Hose II (Air distributor)
9.* Hose (Air by-pass valve)	17. Manifold II (Air distributor)

18. Washer
19. Spring washer
20. Nut
21. Bolt
22. Bolt
23. Dashpot
24. Air pump
25. Hose (Air pump)
26. Manifold (Air distributor)
27. Bracket (Air distributor)

* Used only on EA62 (1300G)

87904013

Anti-Backfire Valve

1. Detach the air hoses from the valve.
2. Remove the valve securing bolt.
3. Remove the valve.
4. Installation is the reverse of removal.

Check Valves

1. Detach the intake hoses from the valves.
2. Use an open end wrench to remove the valve from its mounting. Be sure to save the aluminum gasket.

Relief Valve

1. Remove the air pump from the car.
2. Support the pump so that it cannot rotate.

✳✳CAUTION

Never clamp the pump in a vise. The aluminum case will be distorted.

3. Remove the relief valve from the top of the pump.
To install:
4. Position the new relief valve over the opening in the pump.

➡The air outlet should be pointing toward the left.

5. Gently tap the relief valve home, using a block of wood and a hammer.
6. Install the pump on the engine, as outlined above.

Air Injection Manifold

1. Remove the check valve, as outlined above.
2. Detach the air supply hose from the check valve.
3. Remove the manifold.

Air By-pass Valve (1971-72 EA62 Only)

1. Disconnect the hoses from the air by-pass valve.
2. Detach the cable from the valve butterfly operating lever.
3. Remove the valve.

TESTING

▶ **See Figure 22**

Belt Tension and Air Leaks

1. Before proceeding with the tests, check the pump drive belt tension to see if it is within specifications.

2. Turn the pump by hand. If it has seized, the belt will slip, making a noise. Disregard any chirping, squealing, or rolling sounds from inside the pump. These are normal when it is turned by hand.

3. Check the hoses and connections for leaks. Hissing or a blast of air is indicative of a leak. Soapy water, applied lightly around the area in question, is a good method for detecting leaks.

Air Output

1. Disconnect the air supply hose at the anti-backfire valve.

2. Connect a vacuum gauge, using a suitable adaptor, to the air supply hose.

➡ **If there are two hoses, plug the second one.**

3. With the engine at normal operating temperature, increase the idle speed and watch the vacuum gauge.

4. The air flow from the pump should be steady and fall between 1.5-6 psi (10-41 kPa). If it is unsteady or falls below this, the pump is defective and must be replaced.

Pump Noise Diagnosis

The air pump is normally noisy. As engine speed increases, the noise of the pump will rise in pitch. The rolling sound the pump bearings make is normal. But if this sound becomes objectionable at certain speeds, the pump is defective and will have to be replaced.

A continual hissing sound from the air pump pressure relief valve at idle, indicates a defective valve. Replace the relief valve.

If the pump rear bearing fails, a continual knocking sound will be heard.

Anti-Backfire Valve

1. Detach the air supply hose which runs between the pump and the gulp valve.

2. Connect a tachometer and run the engine to 1500-2000 rpm.

3. Allow the throttle to snap closed. This should produce a loud sucking sound from the gulp valve.

4. Repeat this operation several times. If no sound is present, the valve is not working, or the vacuum connections are loose.

Check Valve Test

1. Before starting the test, check all of the hoses and connections for leaks.

2. Detach the air supply hose from the check valve.

3. Insert a suitable probe into the check valve and depress the plate. Release it. The plate should return to its original position against the valve seat. If binding is evident, replace the valve.

4. With the engine running at normal operating temperature, gradually increase its speed to 1500 rpm. Check for exhaust gas leakage. If any is present, replace the valve assembly.

Air By-pass valve (EA62 Only)

Check the air by-pass valve to be sure that it is open when the choke is closed.

If the by-pass valve is not operating in this manner, adjust its operating cable.

Air Suction System

OPERATION

▶ **See Figure 23**

The air suction system is very similar to the air injection system, except it does not use an air pump. It is used on 1976-84 models.

Air Injection System Diagnosis

Problem	Cause	Cure
1. Noisy drive belt	Loose belt	Tighten belt
	Seized pump	Replace
2. Noisy pump	Leaking hose	Trace and fix leak
	Loose hose	Tighten hose clamp
	Hose contacting other parts	Reposition hose
	Diverter or check valve failure	Replace
	Pump mounting loose	Tighten securing bolts
	Defective pump	Replace
3. No air supply	Loose belt	Tighten belt
	Leak in hose or at fitting	Trace and fix leak
	Defective antibackfire valve	Replace
	Defective check valve	Replace
	Defective pump	Replace
4. Exhaust backfire	Vacuum or air leaks	Trace and fix leak
	Defective antibackfire valve	Replace
	Sticking choke	Service choke
	Choke setting rich	Adjust choke

87904019

Fig. 22 Troubleshooting the air injection system

To operate, the system utilizes the vacuum created by exhaust gas pulsation and normal intake manifold vacuum. Each exhaust port is connected to the air suction valve by air suction manifolds. When a vacuum is created in the exhaust ports a reed in the suction valve opens allowing fresh air to be sucked through the air cleaner and silencer (1976-79 models) or the secondary air cleaner (1980-84 models) and into the exhaust ports. When there is pressure rather than vacuum in the exhaust ports, the reed in the air suction valve closes, preventing the flow of exhaust gases.

The fresh air sucked through the air suction valve is used for oxidation of HC and CO in the exhaust passages and partly for combustion in the cylinders

1982-84 models incorporate an electronically controlled solenoid that either deactivates this system entirely, or partially a short time after the engine is started cold. The only way to determine that there is a problem with this system is to remove the solenoid and test it electrically. See the test procedure below.

These models also incorporate an Air Suction Valve which can be disassembled and serviced. See the procedure below for service.

Port Liner

Various models from 1980-84 have an exhaust port liner made from stainless steel plate built into the cylinder head as one unit.

The port liner has a built in air layer which decreases heat transfer to the cylinder head while keeping the exhaust port at a higher temperature. The insulation of the exhaust port helps oxidation of residual HC and CO with the help of the remaining air in the exhaust gases.

Anti-afterburning Valve

The anti-afterburning valve prevents afterburning that occurs on cold starts. Below about 50°C the temperature valve has an open passage connecting the afterburning valve with the intake manifold via a vacuum line. The vacuum line remains opened and the afterburning valve in operation until the coolant temperature becomes hot enough to shut off the vacuum and override the afterburning system.

REMOVAL & INSTALLATION

▶ See Figure 24

Silencer

1. Loosen the sleeve nut which mounts the silencer to the top of the air suction valve.
2. Pull the silencer from the hose connecting it to the air cleaner.

➡ **Be careful not to lose the small tapered sleeve below the sleeve nut when lifting off the silencer.**

3. Installation is the reverse of removal.

Secondary Air Cleaner

On late model EA71 and EA81 engines, the air flowing to the air suction valve passes through a secondary air cleaner instead of the carburetor air cleaner and silencer. Do not attempt to clean the filter element. Replace the cleaner element every 30 months or 30,000 miles (48,000 km), whichever occurs first.

Air Suction Valve

1. Remove the air silencer or secondary air cleaner.
2. Remove the four bolts which run through the air suction valve, mounting it between the two air suction manifolds.
3. Pull the suction valve from between the manifolds. Take care not to damage the reeds.

➡ **If the gaskets on the sides of the air suction valve are worn or damaged, replace them.**

Air Suction Manifolds
▶ See Figure 25

1. Remove the air silencer or secondary air cleaner and the air suction valve.
2. Remove the clamp which supports the right side suction manifold by loosening the mounting bolt.
3. Loosen the threaded sleeves (two on each manifold) which mount the suction manifolds to the engine. Lift off the manifolds.
4. Remember to lightly oil the threaded sleeves before mounting the suction manifold to the engine.

TESTING

Solenoid Valve (1982-84 Only)

1. Remove the valve from the engine. Using an ohmmeter, test the resistance between the electrical terminals. It must be 32.7-39.9 ohms. If not, replace it.
2. If resistance is o.k., check the resistance between each terminal and the solenoid body. It must be 1,000 ohms. or more in both places, or the valve should be replaced.
3. Apply 12 volts between the plus and minus terminals (positive battery terminal to positive solenoid terminal). When current is on, you should be able to blow through the solenoid from A to B. When it is off, it must seal off tight from A to B and open from B to C. Otherwise, replace the solenoid.

DISASSEMBLY

Air Suction Valve (1982-87 only)
▶ See Figure 26

1. Remove the three screws, and separate the control valve assembly, seat, and reed valve cover.
2. Separate the reed valve assembly by pulling it and its gasket from the inside of the valve cover.
3. Remove the O-ring from the control valve assembly.
4. Now, inspect the valve parts as follows:
   a. Apply vacuum to the vacuum inlet. The valve should retract fully. Release the vacuum. The valve should extend fully.
   b. Check the O-ring for cracks or other damage.
   c. Inspect the reed valve gasket for damage. Then, clean the reed valve in a safe, non-volatile solvent and inspect it for any damage such as waviness, cracks or dents, or rust.

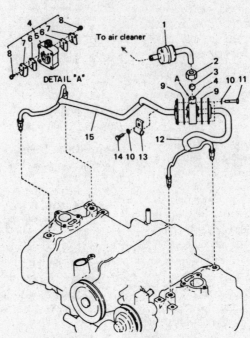

To air cleaner

DETAIL "A"

1. Silencer
2. Sleeve nut
3. Tapered sleeve
4. Air suction valve
5. Valve body
6. Reed valve
7. Valve stopper
8. Screw
9. Gasket
10. Spring washer
11. Bolt
12. Air suction manifold II
13. Clamp
14. Bolt
15. Air suction manifold I

87904014

Fig. 23 Exploded view of the air suction system

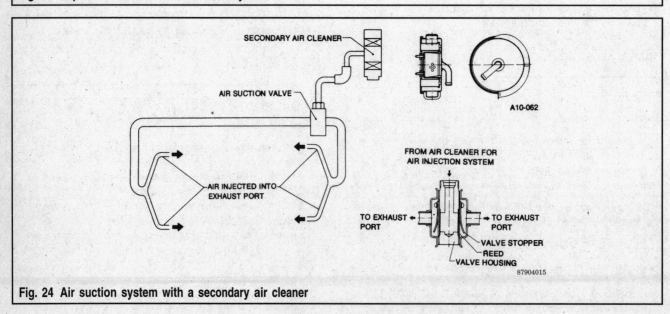

SECONDARY AIR CLEANER

AIR SUCTION VALVE

AIR INJECTED INTO
EXHAUST PORT

A10-062

FROM AIR CLEANER FOR
AIR INJECTION SYSTEM

TO EXHAUST
PORT

TO EXHAUST
PORT

VALVE STOPPER
REED
VALVE HOUSING

87904015

Fig. 24 Air suction system with a secondary air cleaner

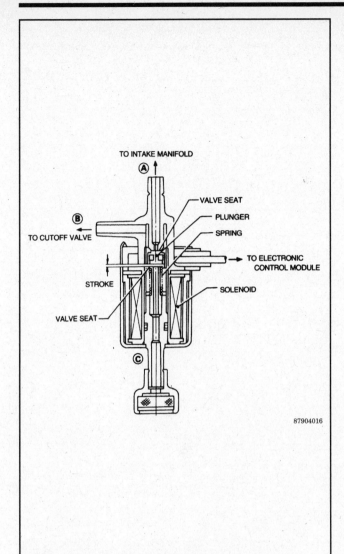

Fig. 25 Solenoid valve for the 1982-84 air suction systems. See text for a description of which passages (A, B, C) are open under various conditions

5. Replace parts that are damaged, reassemble the valve in reverse order, and reinstall it.

Exhaust Gas Recirculation (EGR) System

OPERATION

▶ **See Figure 27**

An Exhaust Gas Recirculation system (EGR) is used on 1974-76 California models and all models from 1977 to reduce the Oxides of Nitrogen (NOx) emissions by lowering peak flame temperature during combustion. A small portion of the exhaust gases are routed into the intake manifold via a vacuum operated EGR control valve.

1974 California Models

A solenoid vacuum valve controls the flow of vacuum from a port on the carburetor (above the primary throttle valve) to the

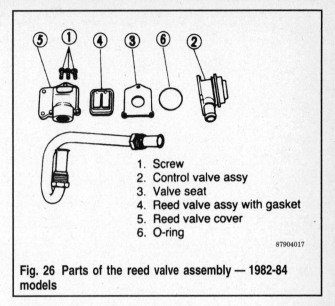

1. Screw
2. Control valve assy
3. Valve seat
4. Reed valve assy with gasket
5. Reed valve cover
6. O-ring

Fig. 26 Parts of the reed valve assembly — 1982-84 models

EGR valve vacuum diaphragm. The solenoid, in turn, is operated by a coolant temperature switch.

When the coolant temperature reaches 122°F (50°C), the temperature switch breaks the current flow to the vacuum solenoid valve. The valve closes, permitting the throttle port vacuum to operate the EGR valve diaphragm. This causes the EGR valve to open under conditions other than idle or wide open throttle.

Below 122°F (50°C), the vacuum solenoid valve is energized to vent the vacuum from the throttle port into the atmosphere through a filter. By preventing exhaust gas recirculation from occurring before the engine has warmed up, cold driveability is greatly improved.

1975-84 Models

Unlike the 1974 California models, this EGR system does not use a solenoid valve. Instead, the amount of exhaust gas recirculated is controlled by the EGR valve itself, according to the amount of vacuum at the carburetor.

REMOVAL & INSTALLATION

Vacuum Solenoid Valve

1. Disconnect the vacuum solenoid wiring from the coolant temperature switch.
2. Remove the EGR vacuum hose from the carburetor throttle port.
3. Remove its two securing screws and take the solenoid off the intake manifold.
4. Be sure to connect the coolant temperature switch wiring after the vacuum solenoid is installed.

EGR Valve

▶ **See Figures 28, 29 and 30**

1. Detach the vacuum hose from the EGR valve.
2. Remove the two nuts which secure the EGR bracket and valve to the intake manifold.
3. Remove the valve, bracket and gasket from the manifold.

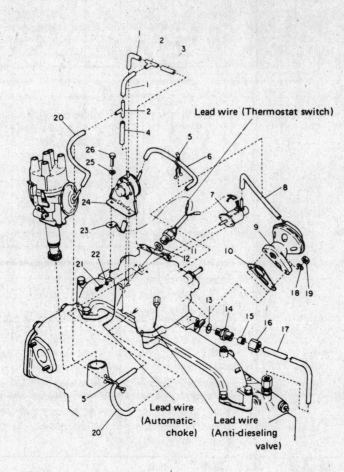

Lead wire (Thermostat switch)

1. Vacuum hose
2. T-connector
3. Vacuum hose
4. Vacuum hose
5. Clamp
6. Vacuum hose
7. Solenoid valve
8. Vacuum hose
9. EGR valve
10. Gasket
11. Thermostat switch
12. Washer
13. Spring washer
14. Nut
15. Spacer
16. Nut
17. EGR pipe
18. Spring washer
19. Nut
20. Vacuum hose
21. Screw
22. Washer
23. Clamp
24. Vacuum Control valve
25. Washer
26. Bolt

Lead wire (Automatic-choke)

Lead wire (Anti-dieseling valve)

87904018

Fig. 27 Common EGR system components

4. Tighten the EGR valve securing nuts to 17-19 ft. lbs. (23-25 Nm)

Coolant Temperature Switch

1. Disconnect the leads which run to the coolant temperature switch.
2. Use an open-end wrench to unscrew the switch from the intake manifold water passage.
3. Remove the temperature switch, complete with gasket.
4. Tighten the switch to 17-19 ft. lbs. (23-25 Nm)

TESTING

EGR System and Valve

1. Start the engine and allow it to reach normal operating temperature.
2. Increase the engine speed to 3000-3500 rpm (no load). The valve shaft should move upward. On 1983-84 California, 2

87904205

Fig. 28 Common EGR valve location

Fig. 29 Remove the vacuum hose and the EGR valve retainers . . .

Fig. 30 . . . then remove the EGR valve and bracket

wheel drive cars, the EGR system does not function until the engine has run for eight minutes.

3. Decrease speed to idle, the shaft should go down.

4. If the valve shaft fails to raise in Step 2, check the vacuum lines, connections, and the carburetor throttle vacuum port. Replace any clogged or damaged hoses, and clean the throttle port if it is clogged.

5. On 1974 models, connect the EGR vacuum hose directly to the carburetor throttle port. Speed the engine up and return it to idle as in Steps 2 and 3. If the valve works, the fault is in the vacuum solenoid valve or temperature switch.

6. If the EGR valve doesn't work:

a. Remove the EGR valve from the intake manifold.

b. Plug the vacuum inlet on the top of the valve diaphragm.

c. Depress and release the diaphragm several times.

d. The diaphragm should remain depressed while the vacuum inlet is plugged. If not, the diaphragm is leaking and the valve must be replaced.

e. If the valve stem seems stuck, clean the diaphragm with a wire brush or spark plug cleaner (NOT solvents).

f. Install the valve and test it again. If it still does not work, replace it.

VACUUM SOLENOID VALVE AND COOLANT TEMPERATURE SWITCH (1974 ONLY)

1. Disconnect the vacuum solenoid leads.

2. Connect the solenoid directly to a 12 volt power source. The solenoid should click on. Disconnect the solenoid, it should go off. If not, it is defective. Replace it and perform the system test again.

3. If the solenoid is working properly and everything else in the system is in proper operating order, replace the coolant temperature switch, then perform the system tests again.

THERMAL VACUUM VALVE (1982-84)

▶ **See Figure 31**

This valve actuates both vacuum spark advance and the EGR valve. It turns the EGR valve off until the engine is warmed up to help ensure smooth cold engine performance.

Drain some coolant out of the system, disconnect the vacuum hoses, and remove the valve from the intake manifold.

❋❋CAUTION

When draining coolant, keep in mind that cats and dogs are attracted by ethylene glycol antifreeze, and are quite likely to drink any that is left in an uncovered container or in puddles on the ground. This will prove fatal in sufficient quantity. Always drain coolant into a sealable container. Coolant should be reused unless it is contaminated or several years old.

Cap off the top (air cleaner) port and install hoses on the other two ports (to keep the top of the valve dry). Then, immerse the valve in cool water. Use a thermometer to measure water temperature. Blow into either hose and warm the water (for example, on a stove). The valve must open when water rises past 68°F (20°C). Now, remove the water from heat and chill with ice cubes. The valve must close as the temperature drops below 50°F (10°C). If not, replace the valve.

ECC SYSTEM

An Electronically Controlled Carburetor (ECC) is used on late models in conjunction with a three-way catalyst, EGR system, air injection system, ignition control system and (in some cases) a high altitude kit.

The three-way catalyst reduces HC, CO and NOx in exhaust gases and permits simultaneous oxidation. The concentration of exhaust gas pollutants varies with the air/fuel mixture (ratio).

The air/fuel ratio needs to be controlled to a value within a very narrow range to purify the exhaust gas components. The ECC system is employed to control the air/fuel ratio. Improper air/fuel ratios such as a rich mixture can damage the catalytic convertor which can also lead to dangerous emission levels.

The system includes: an oxygen sensor, and Electronic Control Module (ECM), a duty solenoid and a carburetor. The

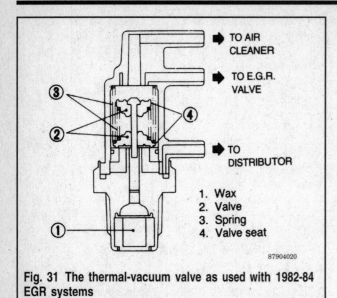

TO AIR CLEANER

TO E.G.R. VALVE

TO DISTRIBUTOR

1. Wax
2. Valve
3. Spring
4. Valve seat

87904020

Fig. 31 The thermal-vacuum valve as used with 1982-84 EGR systems

components provide feedback to control the air/fuel ratio during operation by supplying a measured amount of air into the carburetor air bleeders. Vacuum switches, a thermosensor and an engine speed sensing circuit are used to avoid feedback during certain driving conditions.

Oxygen (O₂) Sensor

The oxygen sensor is installed on the exhaust manifold and provides information to the ECM on the exhaust gases from a rich or lean air/fuel ratio.

The oxygen sensor is a kind of concentration cell that generates electromotive force according to the ratio of oxygen concentration in the air to that in the exhaust gases, and has a characteristic that the electromotive force is charged drastically with respect to the stoichiometric air fuel ratio. The force is larger on the rich side (smaller air-fuel ratio) and smaller on the lean side (larger air-fuel ratio) of the mixture.

Electronic Control Module (ECM)

Upon receiving information from the O_2 sensor the ECM signals the duty solenoid to allow either more or less air into the carburetor to maintain the correct air/fuel mixture.

Duty Solenoid

The Duty Solenoid(s) is (are) controlled by the ECM. At a given signal, the Duty Solenoid will admit more or less air to the carburetor, maintaining the proper air/fuel ratio.

➡ **On late models equipped with a Hitachi carburetor, two duty solenoids are installed on the exhaust manifold. Models equipped with a C-W carburetor have the duty solenoid mounted on the carburetor.**

Vacuum Switches and Thermosensor

Vacuum switches, thermosensors (and speed sensing circuits) signal the ECM to help determine the air/fuel ratio.

SERVICE

To insure proper performance of the ECC system, make sure all vacuum and air hoses are connected tightly. Check the air lines and hoses to make sure no cracks, splits or hardening exists. Replace any vacuum line or hose that is suspect. Check all electrical connections for tightness. Check all electrical wiring for cuts or burns. Repair as necessary.

REMOVAL & INSTALLATION

1. Disconnect the O_2 sensor cord.
2. Remove the exhaust manifold plate.
3. Apply CRC® (004301003) or its equivalent to the threaded portion of the oxygen (O_2) sensor, and let is soak.
4. Loosen the O_2 sensor by turning it 10-40° with a wrench.
5. Apply CRC® (004301003) or its equivalent to the threaded portion of the oxygen (O_2) sensor again, and let is soak.
6. Remove the O_2 sensor.

✳✳WARNING

When removing, do not force the O_2 sensor, especially when the exhaust manifold is cold, otherwise it will damage the exhaust manifold.

To install:
7. Apply an anti-seize compound only to the threaded portion of the O_2 sensor.
8. Install the O_2 sensor into the exhaust manifold and torque it 18-25 ft. lbs. (24-33 Nm).
9. Install the exhaust manifold plate, and securely connect the O_2 sensor cord.

VACUUM DIAGRAMS

Following is a listing of vacuum diagrams for most of the engine and emissions package combinations covered by this manual. Because vacuum circuits will vary based on various engine and vehicle options, always refer first to the emissions label found in the engine compartment, if present. Should the label be missing, or should your vehicle be equipped with a

different engine from original equipment, refer to the diagrams below for the same or a similar configuration.

If you wish to obtain a replacement emissions label, most manufacturers make the labels available for purchase. The labels can usually be ordered from a local dealer.

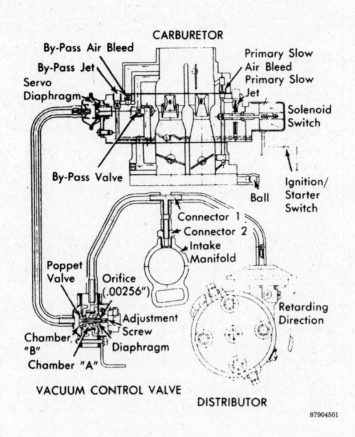

CARBURETOR

By-Pass Air Bleed

By-Pass Jet

Servo Diaphragm

Primary Slow Air Bleed

Primary Slow Jet

Solenoid Switch

By-Pass Valve

Ball

Ignition/ Starter Switch

Connector 1

Connector 2

Intake Manifold

Poppet Valve

Orifice (.00256")

Retarding Direction

Adjustment Screw

Chamber "B"

Diaphragm

Chamber "A"

VACUUM CONTROL VALVE

DISTRIBUTOR

87904501

Fig. 32 1972 ff-1 and 1300G engines

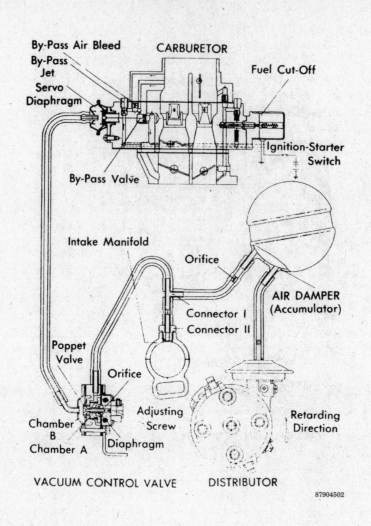

By-Pass Air Bleed
By-Pass Jet
Servo Diaphragm
CARBURETOR
Fuel Cut-Off
By-Pass Valve
Ignition-Starter Switch
Intake Manifold
Orifice
AIR DAMPER (Accumulator)
Connector I
Connector II
Poppet Valve
Orifice
Chamber B
Chamber A
Diaphragm
Adjusting Screw
Retarding Direction
VACUUM CONTROL VALVE
DISTRIBUTOR
87904502

Fig. 33 1972 1300 and 1973 1400 engines

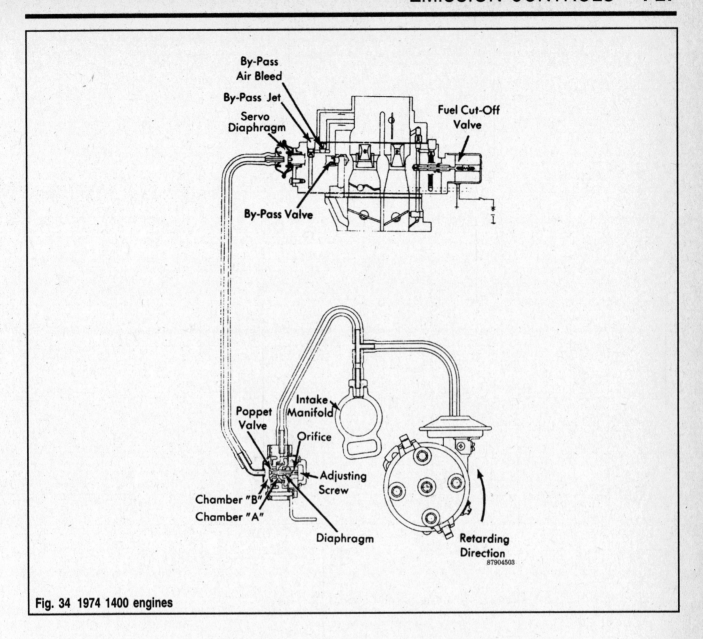

Fig. 34 1974 1400 engines

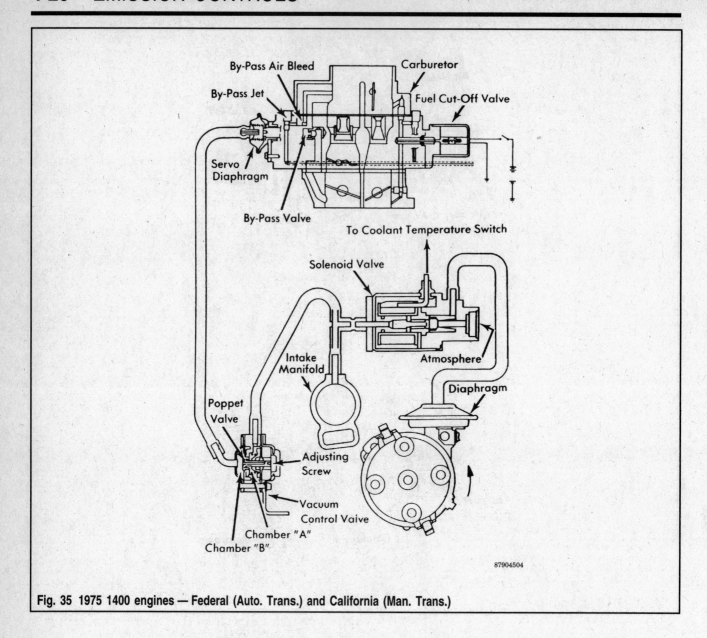

Fig. 35 1975 1400 engines — Federal (Auto. Trans.) and California (Man. Trans.)

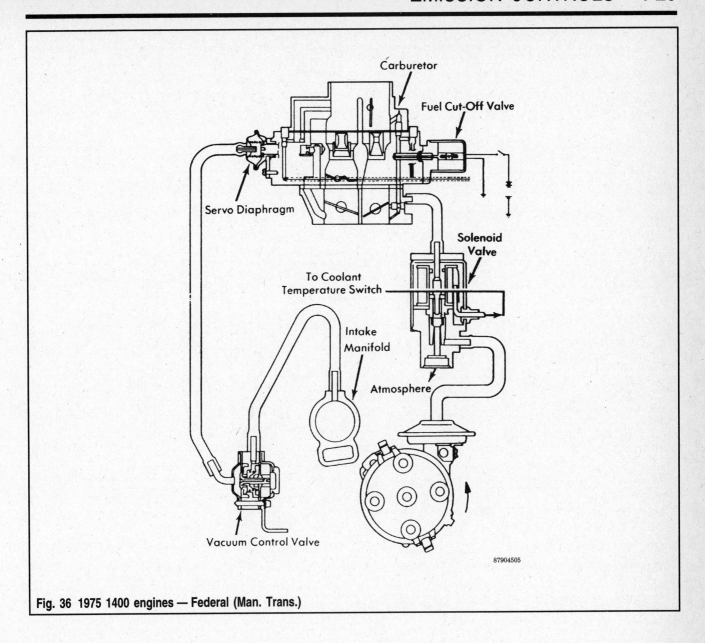

Carburetor

Fuel Cut-Off Valve

Servo Diaphragm

Solenoid Valve

To Coolant Temperature Switch

Intake Manifold

Atmosphere

Vacuum Control Valve

87904505

Fig. 36 1975 1400 engines — Federal (Man. Trans.)

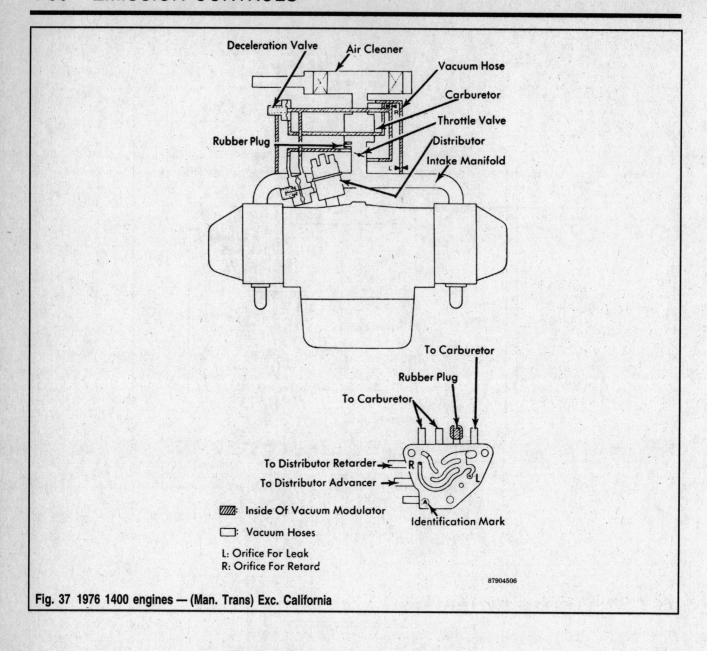

Deceleration Valve Air Cleaner Vacuum Hose Carburetor Throttle Valve Distributor Intake Manifold Rubber Plug

To Carburetor
Rubber Plug
To Carburetor
To Distributor Retarder →
To Distributor Advancer →
Identification Mark

▨: Inside Of Vacuum Modulator
▢: Vacuum Hoses

L: Orifice For Leak
R: Orifice For Retard

87904506

Fig. 37 1976 1400 engines — (Man. Trans) Exc. California

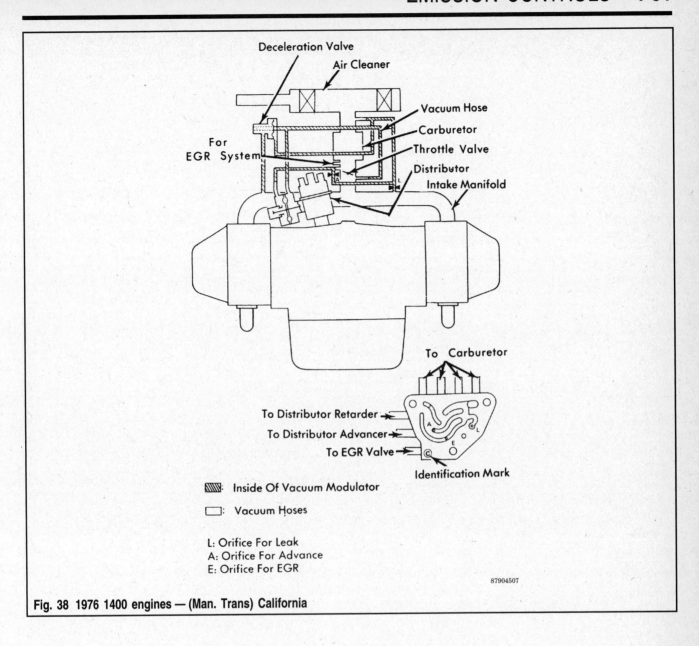

Deceleration Valve
Air Cleaner
Vacuum Hose
Carburetor
Throttle Valve
For EGR System
Distributor
Intake Manifold

To Carburetor
To Distributor Retarder
To Distributor Advancer
To EGR Valve
Identification Mark

▨: Inside Of Vacuum Modulator

☐: Vacuum Hoses

L: Orifice For Leak
A: Orifice For Advance
E: Orifice For EGR

87904507

Fig. 38 1976 1400 engines — (Man. Trans) California

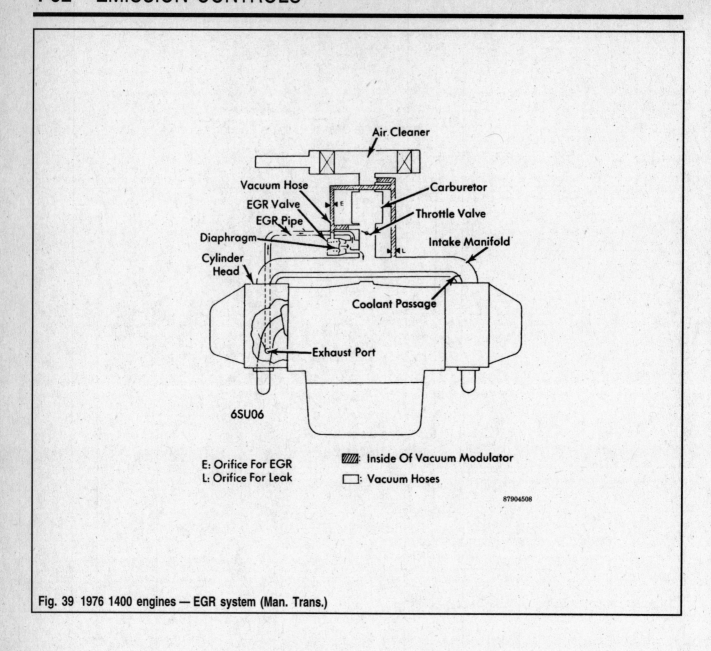

6SU06

E: Orifice For EGR
L: Orifice For Leak

▨ : Inside Of Vacuum Modulator
☐ : Vacuum Hoses

87904508

Fig. 39 1976 1400 engines — EGR system (Man. Trans.)

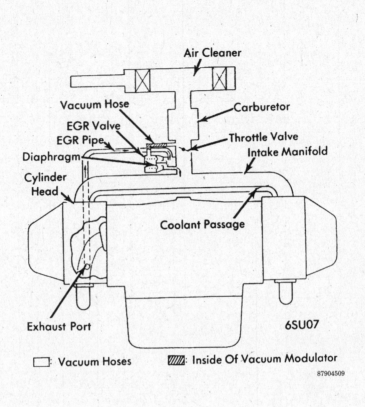

Fig. 40 1976 1600 engines — EGR system (Auto. Trans.)

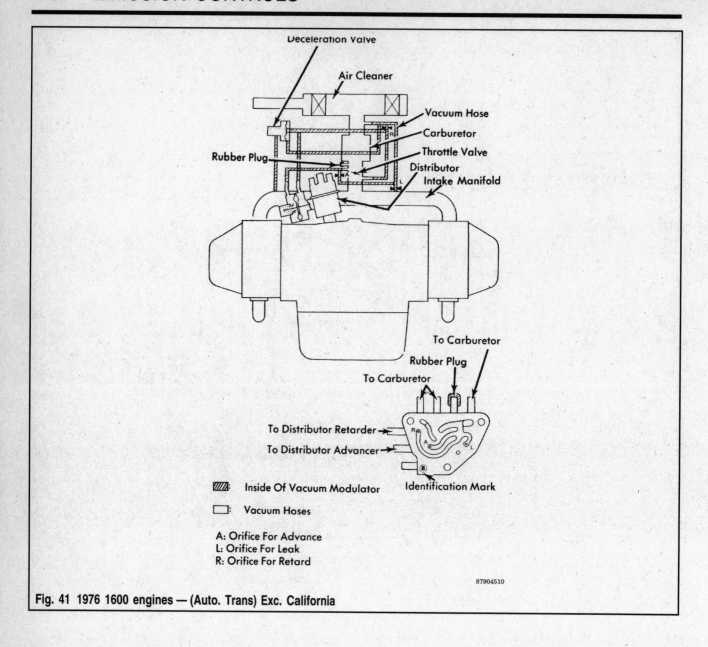

Fig. 41 1976 1600 engines — (Auto. Trans) Exc. California

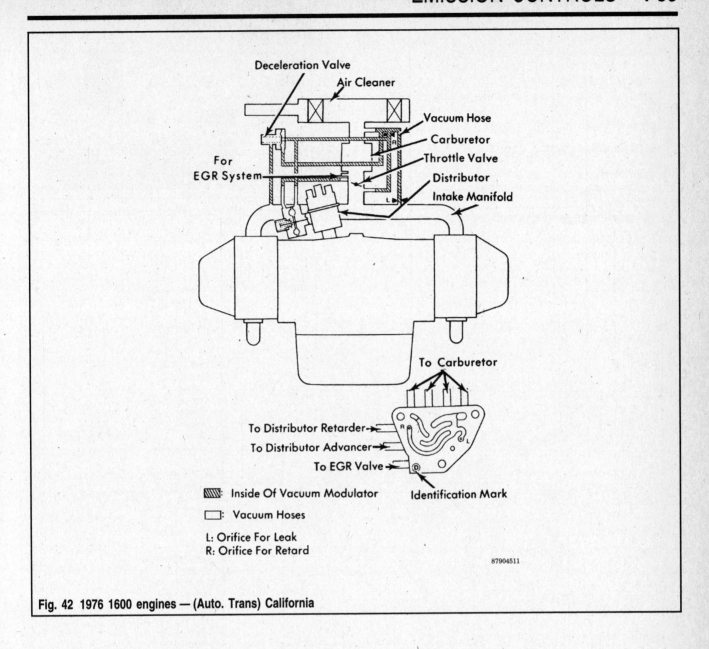

Fig. 42 1976 1600 engines — (Auto. Trans) California

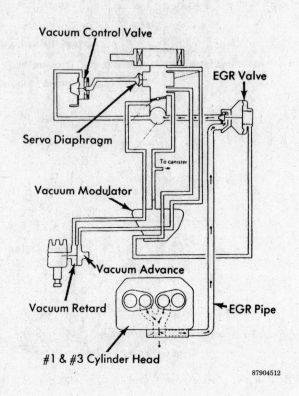

Vacuum Control Valve

EGR Valve

Servo Diaphragm

To canister

Vacuum Modulator

Vacuum Advance

Vacuum Retard

EGR Pipe

#1 & #3 Cylinder Head

87904512

Fig. 43 1977 1600 engines — high altitude (Auto. Trans.)

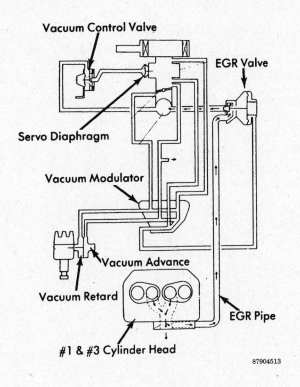

Vacuum Control Valve

EGR Valve

Servo Diaphragm

Vacuum Modulator

Vacuum Advance

Vacuum Retard

#1 & #3 Cylinder Head

EGR Pipe

87904513

Fig. 44 1977 1600 engines — Federal (Auto. Trans.) and 4WD

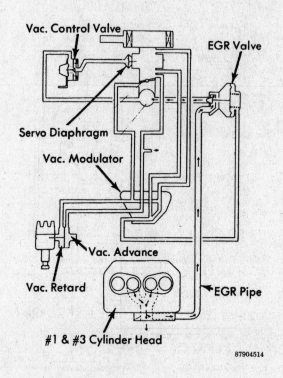

Vac. Control Valve

EGR Valve

Servo Diaphragm

Vac. Modulator

Vac. Advance

Vac. Retard

EGR Pipe

#1 & #3 Cylinder Head

87904514

Fig. 45 1977 1600 engines — Federal (Exc. Auto. Trans.) and 4WD

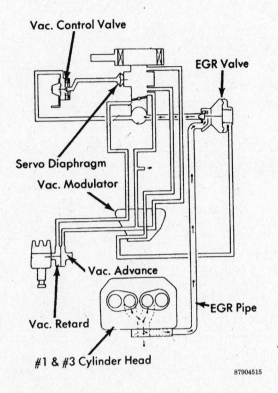

Fig. 46 1977 1600 engines — California (Auto. Trans) and high altitude 4WD

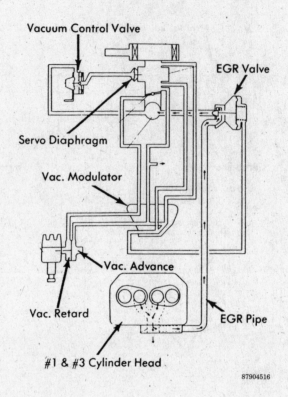

Vacuum Control Valve

EGR Valve

Servo Diaphragm

Vac. Modulator

Vac. Advance

Vac. Retard

EGR Pipe

#1 & #3 Cylinder Head

87904516

Fig. 47 1977 1600 engines — California (Exc. Auto. Trans.) and high altitude (Exc. Auto. Trans. and 4WD)

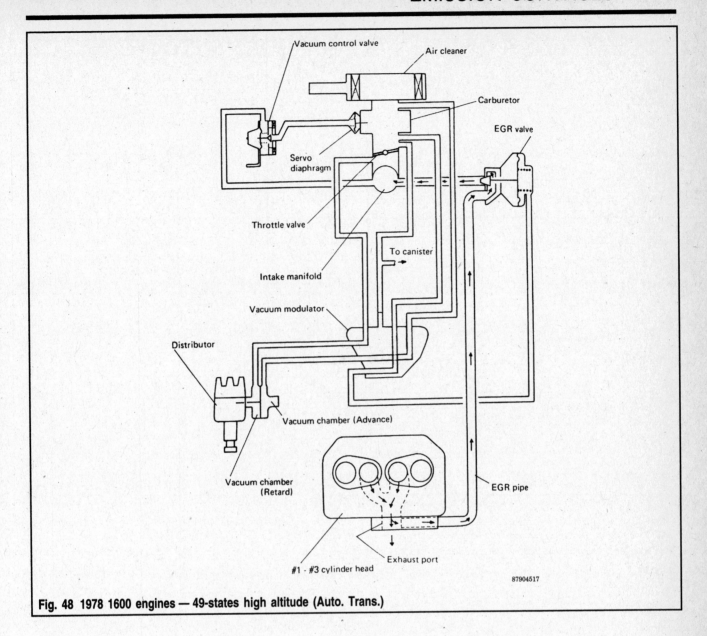

Fig. 48 1978 1600 engines — 49-states high altitude (Auto. Trans.)

87904517

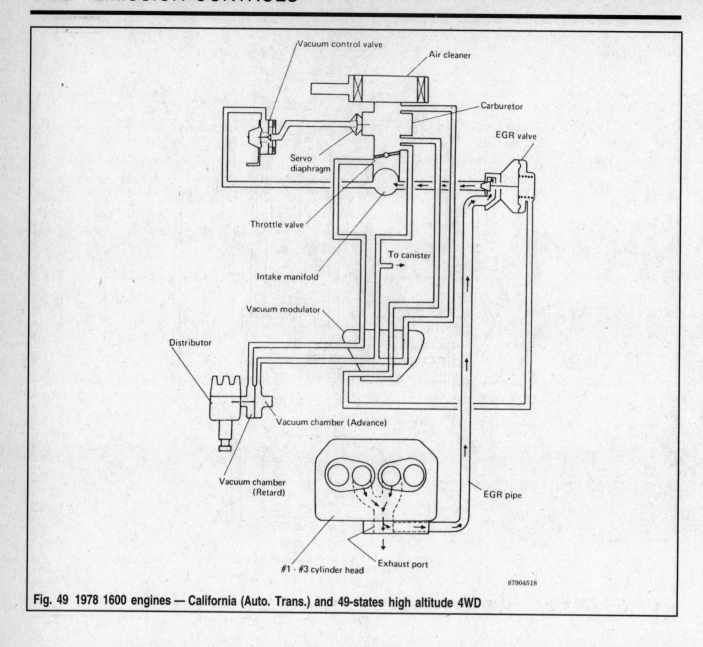

Fig. 49 1978 1600 engines — California (Auto. Trans.) and 49-states high altitude 4WD

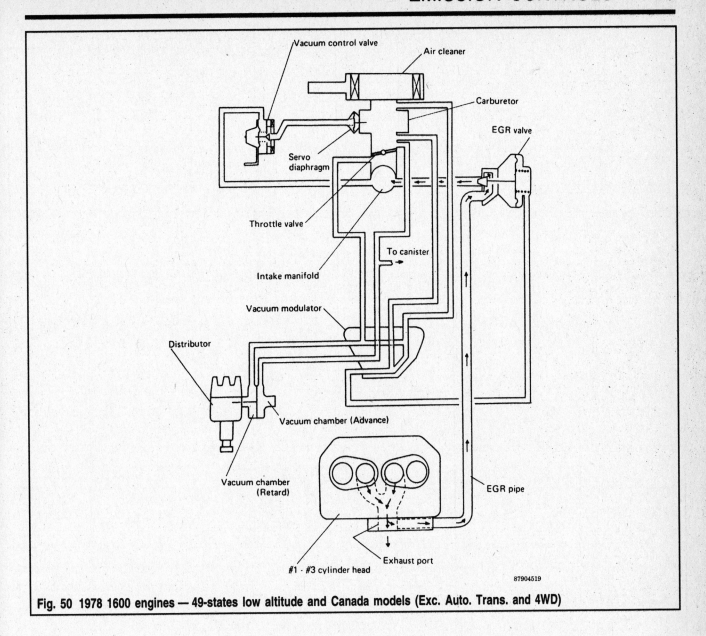

Fig. 50 1978 1600 engines — 49-states low altitude and Canada models (Exc. Auto. Trans. and 4WD)

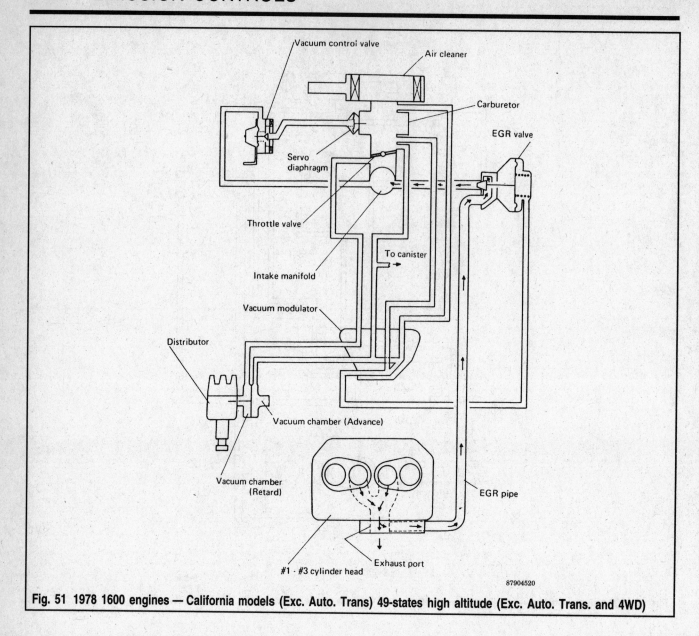

Fig. 51 1978 1600 engines — California models (Exc. Auto. Trans) 49-states high altitude (Exc. Auto. Trans. and 4WD)

87904520

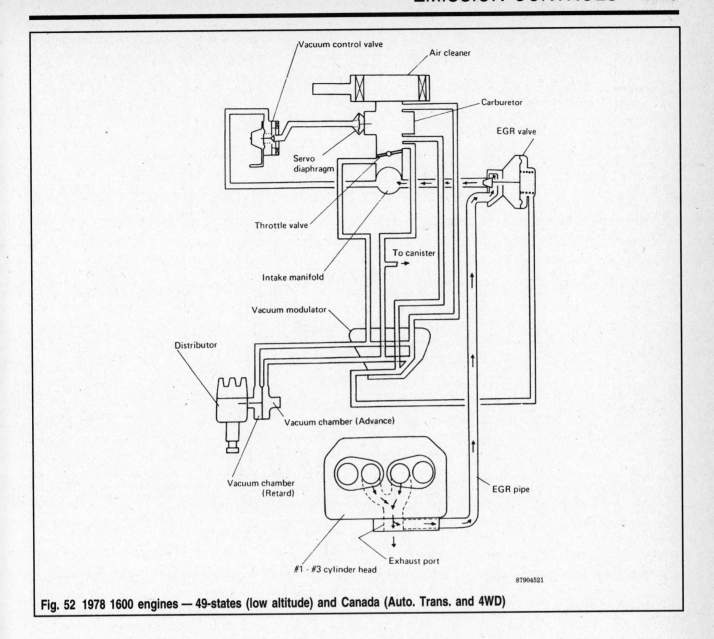

Fig. 52 1978 1600 engines — 49-states (low altitude) and Canada (Auto. Trans. and 4WD)

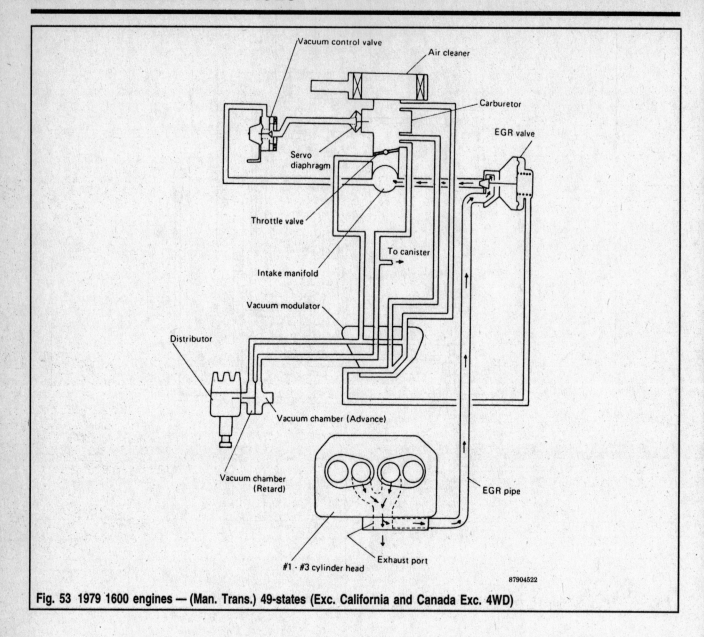

Fig. 53 1979 1600 engines — (Man. Trans.) 49-states (Exc. California and Canada Exc. 4WD)

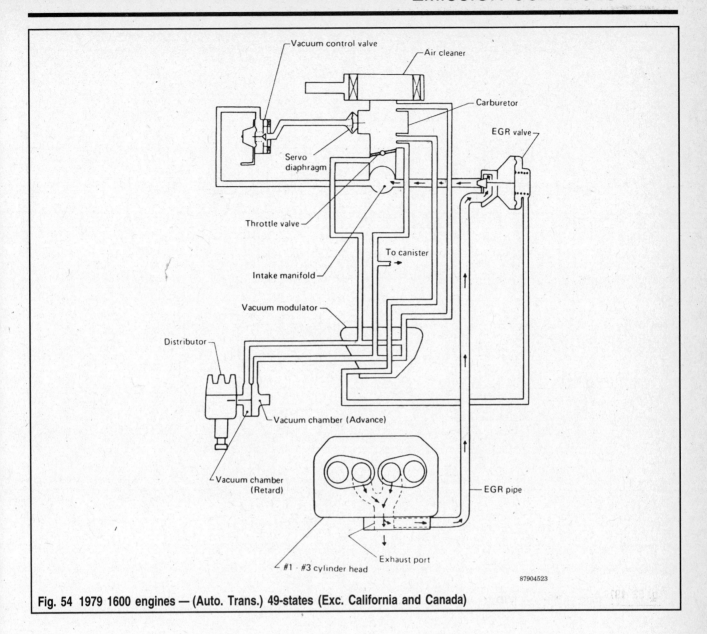

Fig. 54 1979 1600 engines — (Auto. Trans.) 49-states (Exc. California and Canada)

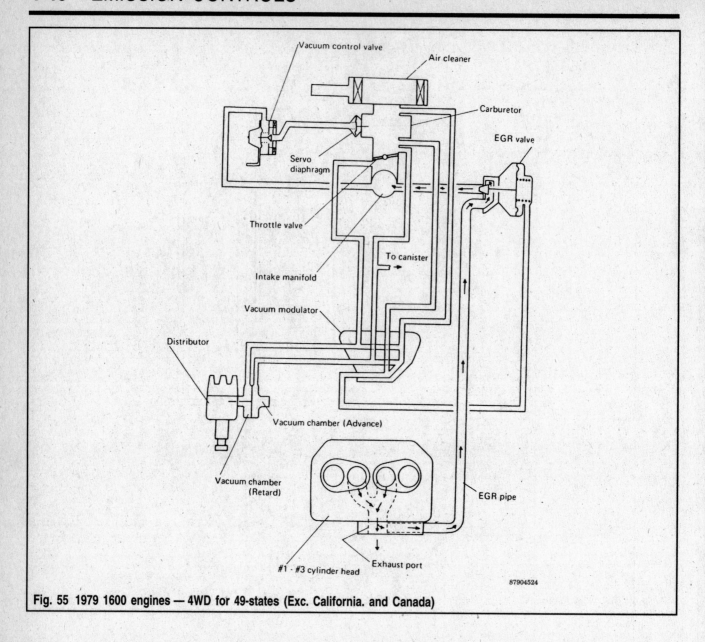

Fig. 55 1979 1600 engines — 4WD for 49-states (Exc. California. and Canada)

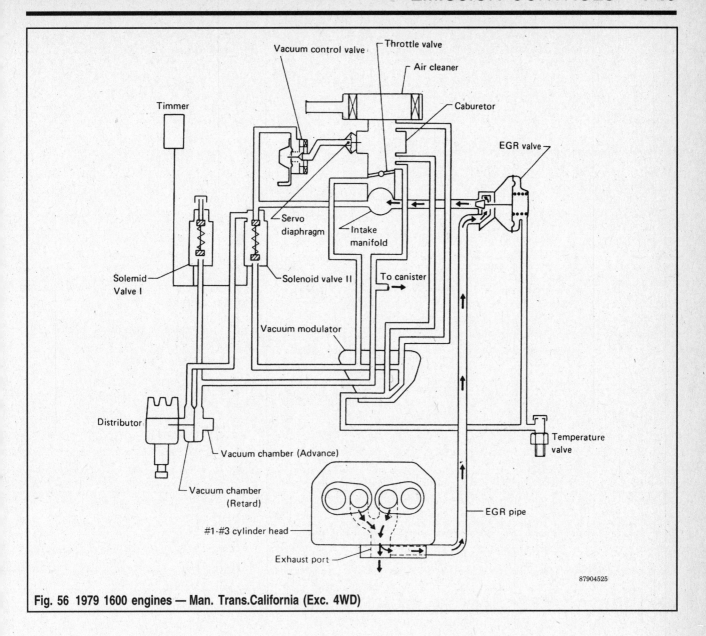

Fig. 56 1979 1600 engines — Man. Trans.California (Exc. 4WD)

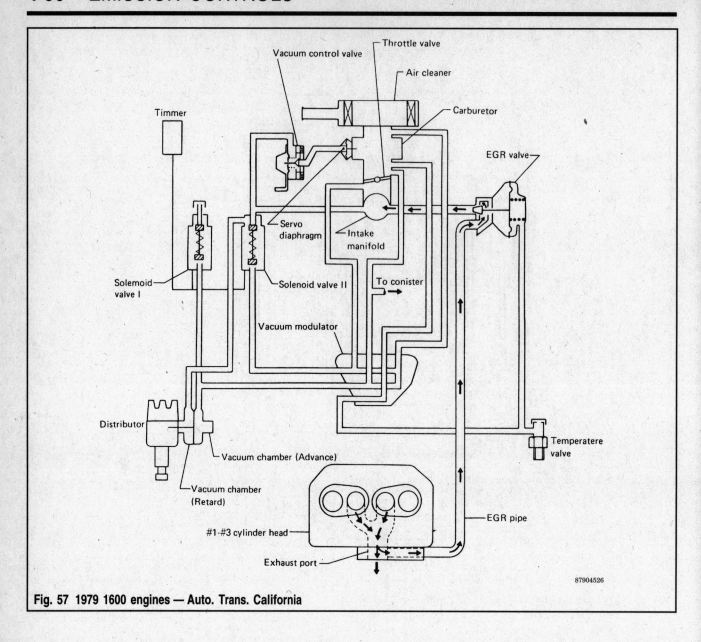

Fig. 57 1979 1600 engines — Auto. Trans. California

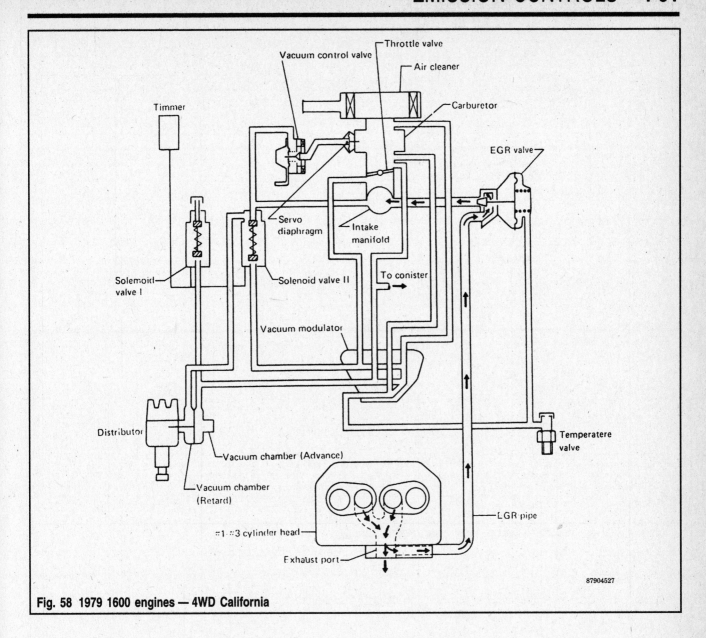

Fig. 58 1979 1600 engines — 4WD California

● All models except Hatchback STD, DL, Sedan DL, Hardtop DL and other Cal. models.

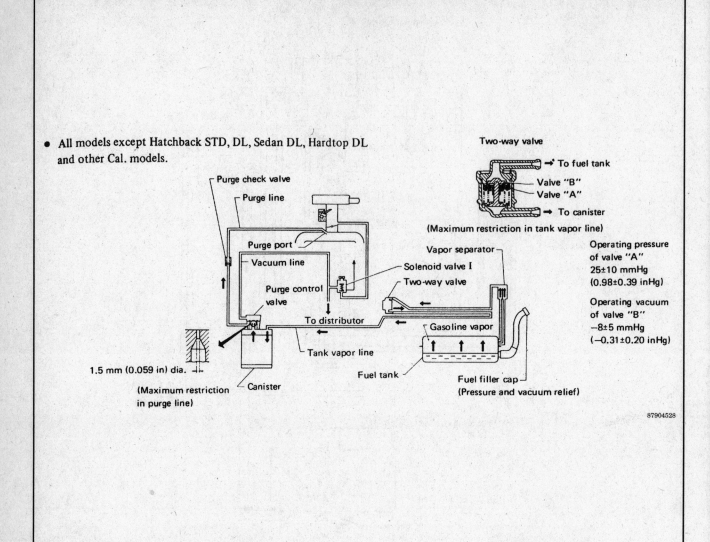

Fig. 59 !980 1600 and 1800 engines — (Exc. Hatchback STD, DL, Sedan, DL, Hardtop DL) and other California models

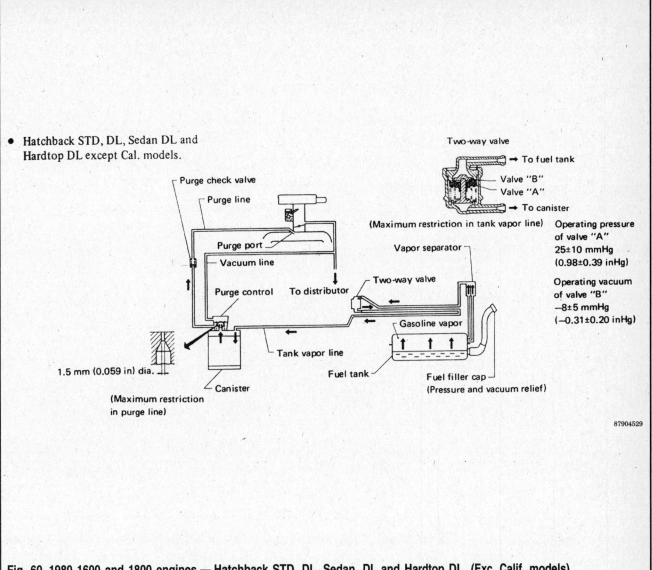

- Hatchback STD, DL, Sedan DL and Hardtop DL except Cal. models.

Purge check valve
Purge line
Purge port
Vacuum line
Purge control
To distributor
1.5 mm (0.059 in) dia.
Canister
(Maximum restriction in purge line)
Tank vapor line
Fuel tank
Two-way valve
Vapor separator
Gasoline vapor
Fuel filler cap
(Pressure and vacuum relief)

Two-way valve
→ To fuel tank
Valve "B"
Valve "A"
→ To canister
(Maximum restriction in tank vapor line)
Operating pressure of valve "A" 25±10 mmHg (0.98±0.39 inHg)
Operating vacuum of valve "B" −8±5 mmHg (−0.31±0.20 inHg)

87904529

Fig. 60 1980 1600 and 1800 engines — Hatchback STD, DL, Sedan, DL and Hardtop DL, (Exc. Calif. models)

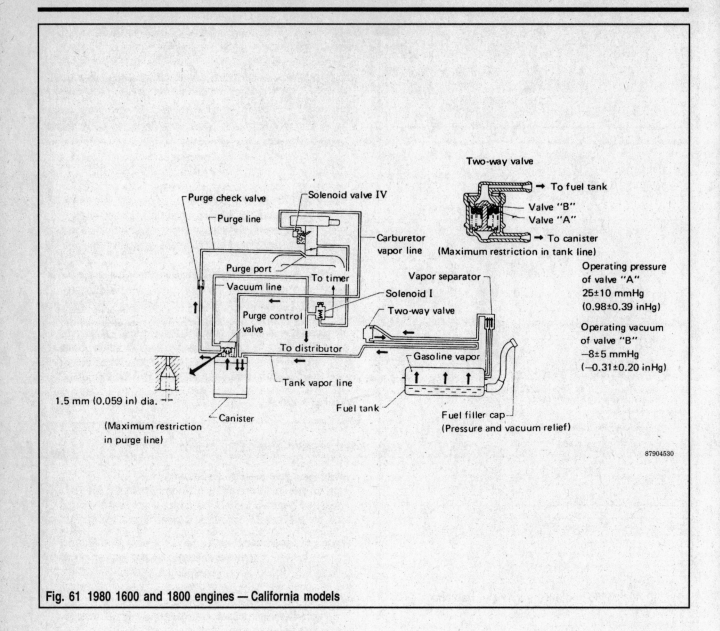

Two-way valve
→ To fuel tank
Valve "B"
Valve "A"
→ To canister
(Maximum restriction in tank line)

Purge check valve
Purge line
Solenoid valve IV
Carburetor vapor line
Purge port
Vacuum line
To timer
Vapor separator
Solenoid I
Two-way valve
Purge control valve
To distributor
Gasoline vapor
Tank vapor line
1.5 mm (0.059 in) dia.
Canister
Fuel tank
Fuel filler cap
(Pressure and vacuum relief)
(Maximum restriction in purge line)

Operating pressure of valve "A"
25±10 mmHg
(0.98±0.39 inHg)

Operating vacuum of valve "B"
−8±5 mmHg
(−0.31±0.20 inHg)

87904530

Fig. 61 1980 1600 and 1800 engines — California models

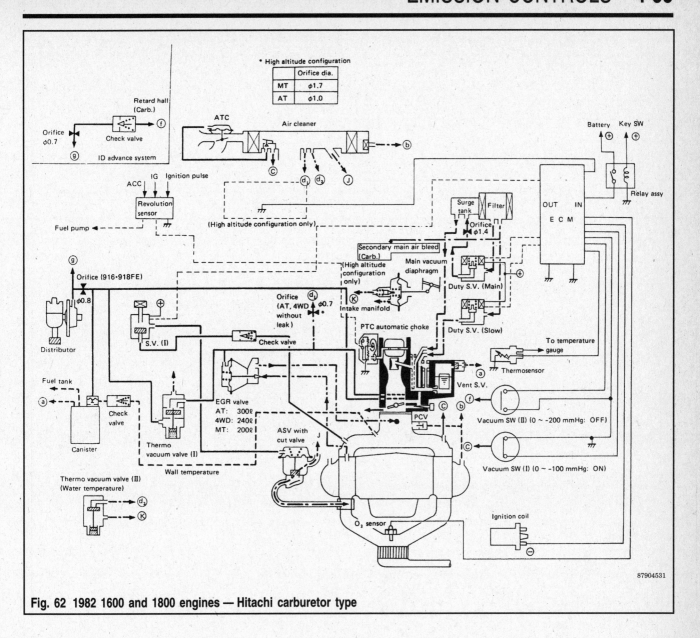

Fig. 62 1982 1600 and 1800 engines — Hitachi carburetor type

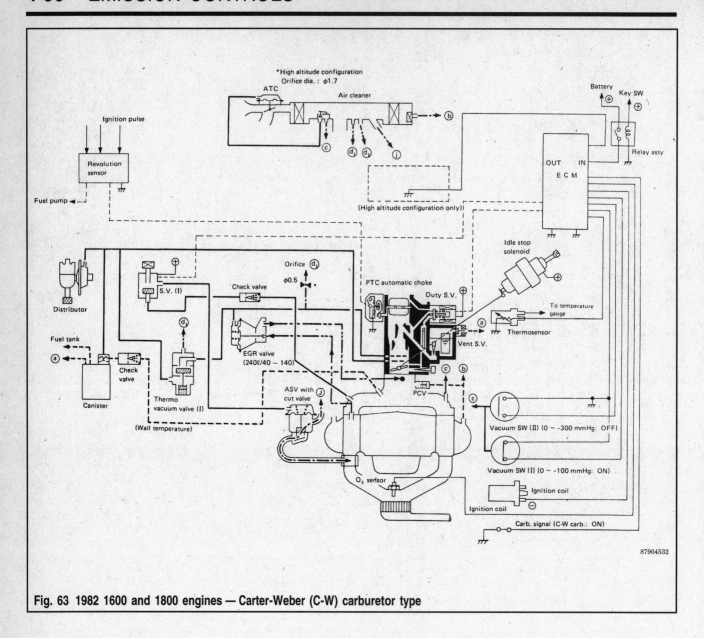

Fig. 63 1982 1600 and 1800 engines — Carter-Weber (C-W) carburetor type

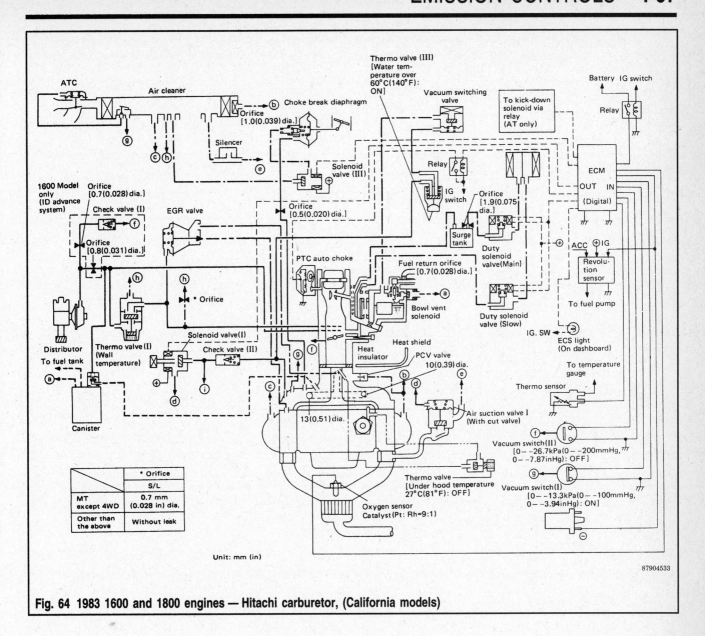

Fig. 64 1983 1600 and 1800 engines — Hitachi carburetor, (California models)

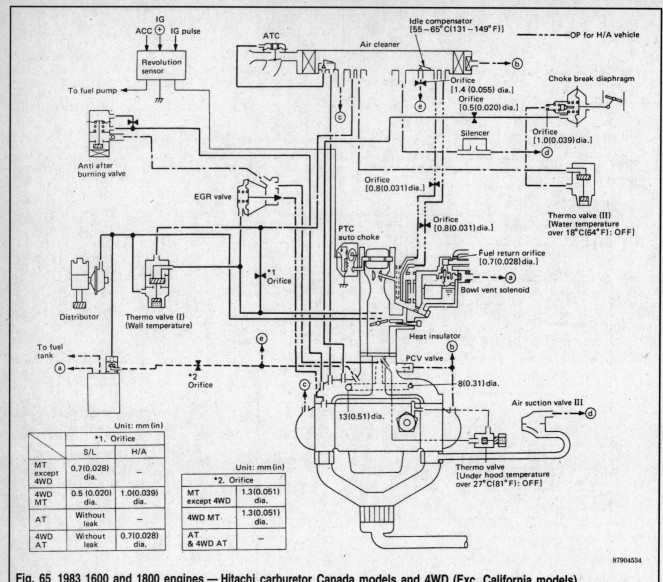

Fig. 65 1983 1600 and 1800 engines — Hitachi carburetor Canada models and 4WD (Exc. California models)

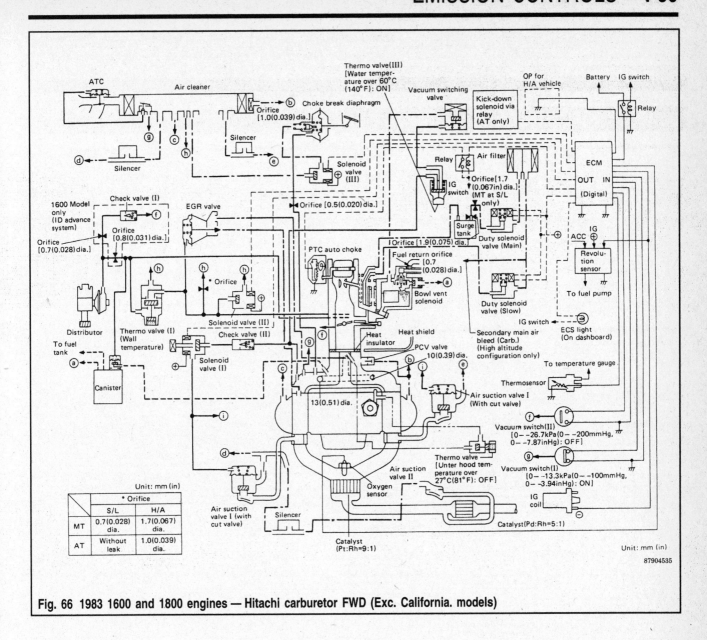

Fig. 66 1983 1600 and 1800 engines — Hitachi carburetor FWD (Exc. California. models)

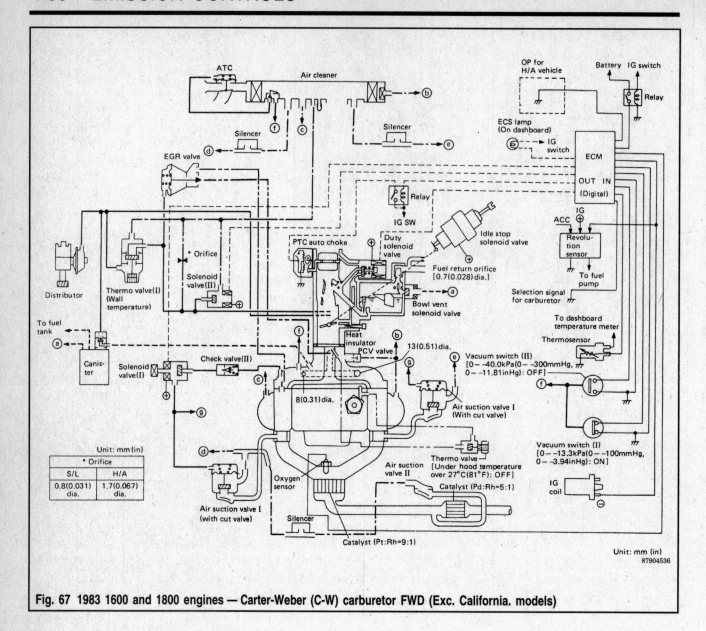

Fig. 67 1983 1600 and 1800 engines — Carter-Weber (C-W) carburetor FWD (Exc. California. models)

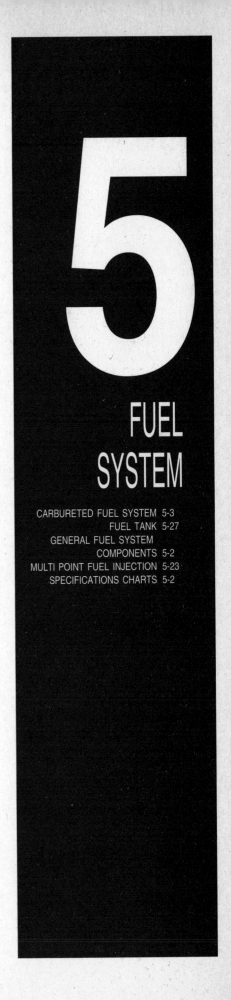

5

FUEL
SYSTEM

GENERAL FUEL SYSTEM COMPONENTS

Understanding the Fuel System

An automotive fuel system consists of everything between the fuel tank and the carburetor or injection system. This includes the tank itself, all the lines, one or more fuel filters, a fuel pump, and the carburetor, fuel rail or injectors.

With the exception of the carburetor, fuel rail or injectors the fuel system is quite simple in operation. Fuel is drawn from the tank through the fuel line by the fuel pump, which forces it to the fuel filter, and from there to the carburetor, fuel rail or injectors, where it is distributed to the cylinders.

➡**For a description of the injection system used on the 1800 Turbo, turn to the section devoted to it behind carburetor adjustments. Repair procedures are also located there.**

Fuel Pump

The fuel pump is located in the engine compartment, next to the strut tower, on the left side 1970-83 models or under the center of the vehicle 1984.

Two different types of electromagnetic fuel pumps are used: ff-1 and 1300G sedans use a Bendix type fuel pump, while ff-1 and 1300G station wagons and all other models use a diaphragm type electromagnetic pump

If either type of pump fails, it must be replaced as an assembly, since it cannot be rebuilt.

Fuel Filters

All fuel systems have at least one filter located somewhere between the fuel tank and the carburetor, fuel rail or injectors. On some models the filter is part of the fuel pump itself, on others it is located in the fuel line

The fuel filter screens out impurities in the fuel before it has a chance to reach the carburetor or injector.

Troubleshooting Basic Fuel System Problems

Problem	Cause	Solution
Engine cranks, but won't start (or is hard to start) when cold	• Empty fuel tank • Incorrect starting procedure • Defective fuel pump • No fuel in carburetor • Clogged fuel filter • Engine flooded • Defective choke	• Check for fuel in tank • Follow correct procedure • Check pump output • Check for fuel in the carburetor • Replace fuel filter • Wait 15 minutes; try again • Check choke plate
Engine cranks, but is hard to start (or does not start) when hot— (presence of fuel is assumed)	• Defective choke	• Check choke plate
Rough idle or engine runs rough	• Dirt or moisture in fuel • Clogged air filter • Faulty fuel pump	• Replace fuel filter • Replace air filter • Check fuel pump output
Engine stalls or hesitates on acceleration	• Dirt or moisture in the fuel • Dirty carburetor • Defective fuel pump • Incorrect float level, defective accelerator pump	• Replace fuel filter • Clean the carburetor • Check fuel pump output • Check carburetor
Poor gas mileage	• Clogged air filter • Dirty carburetor • Defective choke, faulty carburetor adjustment	• Replace air filter • Clean carburetor • Check carburetor
Engine is flooded (won't start accompanied by smell of raw fuel)	• Improperly adjusted choke or carburetor	• Wait 15 minutes and try again, without pumping gas pedal • If it won't start, check carburetor

87905C03

CARBURETED FUEL SYSTEM

Electric Fuel Pump

REMOVAL & INSTALLATION

▶ See Figures 1, 2 and 3

1. Loosen the fuel pump bracket-to-chassis nuts or bolts and lower the pump; be careful not to lose any washers or cushions.
2. Remove the fuel delivery hoses from the fuel pump.
3. Disengage the electrical harness connector from the fuel pump.
4. Remove the pump.
5. Inspect the fuel pump; if found to be defective, it should be replaced.

To install:

6. Reverse the removal procedures. Be sure the ground wire does not contact the pump body or the unit may vibrate. Start the engine and check for leaks.

PRESSURE TESTING

1. Raise and support the vehicle on jackstands.
2. Using a fuel pressure gauge, connect into the fuel line.
3. Turn the ignition switch On and observe the fuel pressure; it should be 2.6-3.3 psi (15-22 kPa) in carbureted vehicles. If the fuel pump does not meet specifications, replace the pump.
4. After testing, disconnect the pressure gauge and reconnect the fuel line.

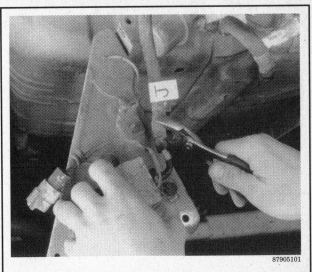

Fig. 2 Remove the fuel delivery hoses from the pump

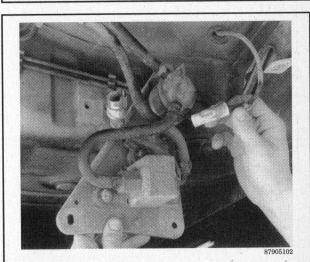

Fig. 3 Disengage the electrical harness connector from the fuel pump

PUMP FILTER REPLACEMENT

▶ See Figures 4 and 5

The Bendix type fuel pump used on these models has an internal filter in addition to an inline fuel filter. To change the filter element, proceed in the following manner:

1. Remove the pump from the car.
2. Invert the pump assembly so that the end cover is facing up. Otherwise, when you remove the cover the parts could fall out.
3. Remove the ground lead screw from the end cover.
4. Carefully remove the end cover from the pump body by turning the cover.
5. Remove the gasket and filter elements from the pump.
6. Insert a new filter element and reassemble the end cover to the pump in the reverse order of its removal.

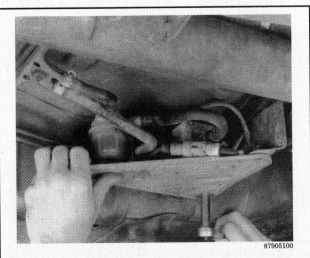

Fig. 1 Loosen the fuel pump bracket-to-chassis nuts or bolts and lower the pump

87905103

Fig. 4 Invert the pump assembly so that the end cover is facing up

Carburetor

The carburetor supplies the correct mixture of fuel and air to the engine under varying conditions.

Despite their complexity in design, carburetors function because of a simple physical principle (the venturi principle). Air is drawn into the engine by the pumping action of the pistons. As the air enters the top of the carburetor it passes through a venturi, which is nothing more than a restriction in the throttle bore. The air speeds up as it passes through the venturi causing a slight drop in pressure. The pressure drop pulls fuel from the float bowl through a nozzle into the throttle bore, where it mixes with the air and forms a fine mist which is distributed to the cylinders through the intake manifold.

All carburetors except the C-W are 2-barrel, down-draft carburetors which supplies the best air/fuel mixture under any operating condition. The C-W is a 1-barrel carburetor.

The carburetor uses a progressive linkage between the primary and secondary circuit. For optimum performance plus fuel economy, the secondary circuit of the carburetor is used only

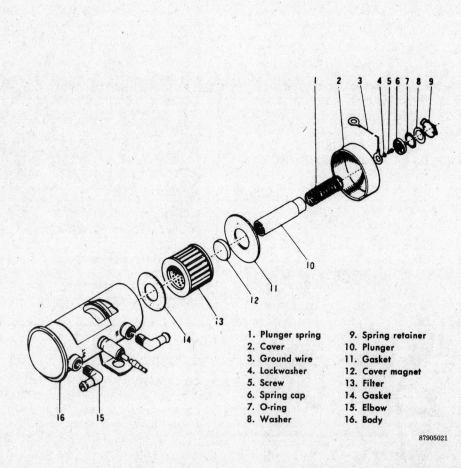

1. Plunger spring
2. Cover
3. Ground wire
4. Lockwasher
5. Screw
6. Spring cap
7. O-ring
8. Washer
9. Spring retainer
10. Plunger
11. Gasket
12. Cover magnet
13. Filter
14. Gasket
15. Elbow
16. Body

87905021

Fig. 5 Fuel pump and filter used on ff-1 and 1300G models

at high engine rpm. Normal low speed operation is handled by the primary circuit.

On later models, the carburetor is provided with a coasting by-pass system which helps control exhaust emissions during deceleration.

A hand control (manual) choke was used on Subaru models until 1973. From 1974 until present an automatic control choke is used. The automatic choke and a throttle chamber heated by engine coolant, to prevent throttle bore icing, help the Subaru start and run well in the coldest conditions.

The basic systems of the carburetor are:
1. The float system
2. The primary side
   a. Slow system
   b. Main system
   c. Accelerator pump
   d. Power system
   e. Choke system
   f. Slow float shut-off system
3. Secondary side
   a. Step system
   b. Main system
4. Coasting by-pass system.

On the following pages illustrations will help you better understand the systems and what functions they perform.

If you are planning to clean, rebuild or replace your carburetor be sure you understand what is necessary. Read all instructions, have all parts/tools on hand and keep everything as clean as possible. Remember the gasoline mileage and the performance of your Subaru depend on how well you do the job.

ADJUSTMENTS

▶ **See Figures 6, 7 and 8**

Fast Idle

1970-73 MODELS

1. With the carburetor removed from the engine, make sure that the choke valve is fully closed.
2. Measure the clearance between the upper edge of the primary throttle valve and its bore with a wire gauge. It should be the appropriate figure given in the chart at the end of this Section.
3. If the clearance is incorrect, adjust it by bending the choke adjusting rod.
4. Check the operation of the linkage for smoothness after adjustment is completed.

1974 AND LATER MODELS (EXCEPT C-W)

1. With the carburetor removed from the engine, set the fast idle cam adjusting lever on the fourth highest step of the fast idle cam.
2. Check to be sure that the choke valve is fully closed.
3. Measure the clearance between the lower edge of the primary throttle valve and its bore. The clearance should be the value specified in the Fast Idle chart in this section.
4. If the clearance is incorrect, turn the fast idle adjusting screw to bring it within specifications. Turning the screw in increases the throttle clearance and vice-versa.

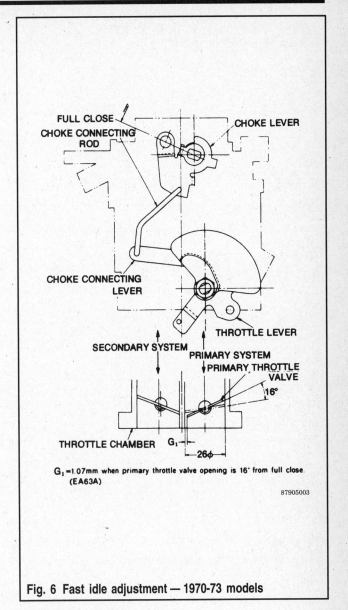

G₁ =1.07mm when primary throttle valve opening is 16° from full close. (EA63A)

87905003

Fig. 6 Fast idle adjustment — 1970-73 models

Float and Fuel Level
▶ **See Figure 9**

ALL MODELS

Float level adjustments are unnecessary, on models equipped with a sight glass on the carburetor float bowl, if the fuel is level within 0.05 in. (1.5mm) with the dot on its center, when the engine is running.

The float level may be adjusted with the carburetor installed on the engine, by removing the air horn as follows:
1. Disconnect the accelerator pump actuating rod from the pump lever.
2. Remove the throttle return spring.
3. Disconnect the choke cable from the choke lever, and remove it from the spring hanger.
4. Remove the spring hanger, the choke bellcrank and the remaining air horn retaining screws.
5. Lift the air horn slightly, disconnect the choke connecting rod, and remove the air horn.
6. Invert the air horn (float up), and measure the distance between the surface of the air horn and the float.

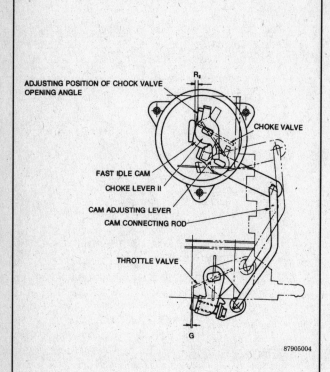

Fig. 7 Fast idle adjustment from 1974 — except C-W

Fast Idle

Model	Primary Throttle-to-Bore Clearance
FF-1	0.038 in.
1971–72 (except FF-1)	0.046 in.
1973–74	0.050 in.
1975	0.039 in.
1976	0.056 in.
1977–79	0.047 in.①
1980–82 all auto. trans.	0.060 in.
manual trans. (exc. C-W)	0.050 in.②
1983–84	
DCP 306-17	.0386 in.
DCP 306-18	
DCP 306-21	.0480 in.
DCP 306-19	
DCP 306-22	.0528 in.

① California models and 49 state high altitude models—
0.060 in.
② HB-STD, HB-DL, SD-DL, and HT-DL use 0.041 in.

87905c01

Fig. 8 Fast idle adjustment specifications

7. Bend the float arm until the clearance is approximately 10mm.

8. Invert the air horn to its installed position, and measure the distance between the float arm and the needle valve stem. This dimension should be 0.05-0.06 in. (1.3-1.7mm), and is adjusted by bending the float stops.

Primary/Secondary Throttle Linkage

▶ See Figure 10

ALL MODELS

1. With the carburetor removed from the engine, operate the linkage so that the connecting rod contacts the groove on the end of the secondary actuating lever.

2. Measure the clearance between the lower end of the primary throttle valve and its bore. It should be about 6mm (the size of the shank of a ¼ in. drill bit) for all models.

3. Adjust the clearance by bending the connecting rod.

4. Check to make sure that the linkage operates smoothly after performing the adjustment.

Manual Choke Cable

▶ See Figure 11

1970-73 MODELS

1. Pull the choke knob on the instrument panel out all the way. Remove the air cleaner and check the position of the choke valve. If the choke valve is fully closed, the cable is adjusted properly.

2. If the choke valve is not fully closed, adjust the cable by loosening its retaining nut and pulling on the cable lightly to take up any slack.

3. Tighten the retaining nut.

4. Check to see that the choke valve is now fully opened when the choke knob is pushed all the way in.

Automatic Choke

▶ See Figure 12

1974 AND LATER (EXCEPT C-W)

➡The choke is not adjustable on 1982-84 models

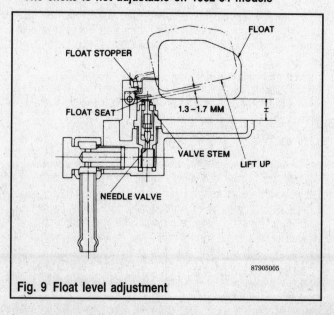

Fig. 9 Float level adjustment

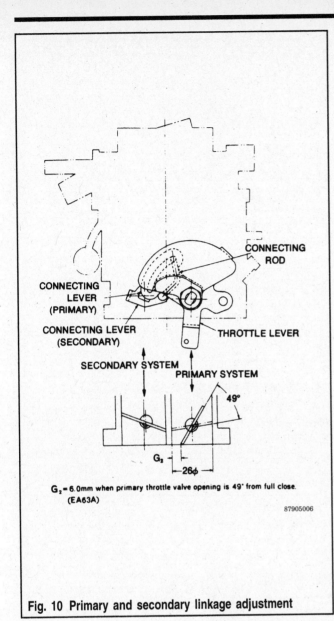

Fig. 10 Primary and secondary linkage adjustment

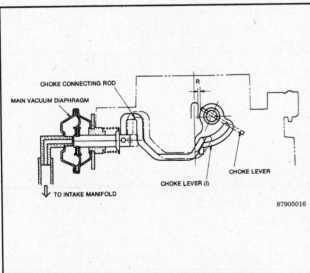

Fig. 11 Main diaphragm and linkage adjustment

1. Adjust the fast idle as detailed in this section, and perform the adjustments which follow, in the sequence given.

2. Pull the main choke diaphragm lever as far as it will go to the left and measure the clearance between the upper end of the choke valve and its bore with a wire gauge. The clearance should be 0.04-0.05 in. (1.2-1.4mm). Adjust, as necessary, by bending the diaphragm-to-choke connecting rod.

3. Apply 8-9 in.Hg of vacuum to the main diaphragm, it should operate the choke valve. If it does not, replace the diaphragm with a new one.

4. Place the fast idle cam adjusting lever on the third step of the fast idle cam. Measure the clearance between the upper end of the choke valve and its bore. The clearance should be 0.06-0.07 in. (1.6-1.9mm) for 1974-76 cars; 0.025-0.037 in.(0.66-0.94mm) for cars from 1977. Carefully bend (turn) the fast idle cam to obtain the correct clearance, as necessary. To obtain the clearance, bend the cam clockwise. To decrease it, bend the cam counter clockwise.

5. Loosen the 3 choke cap securing screws, and match the line on it up with the longest line on the choke coil housing. Tighten the retaining screws.

✳✳CAUTION

Do not loosen the screw which secures the choke lever.

6. Fit the tank on the bi-metal lever, which is connected to the auxiliary diaphragm, against the stop in the choke coil housing. Pull the setting piston of the auxiliary diaphragm back and, with the piston in this position, tighten the compensator adjusting screw so that it contacts the tang on the bi-metal lever. The gap should be 0.1 in. (5mm), on 1974-76 cars and 0.03 in.(0.86mm) on 1977 and later models.

7. Apply vacuum from an outside source to the auxiliary diaphragm. It should take 9.5-11.8 in.Hg of vacuum to operate the diaphragm on 1974-76 cars and 6.9-9.2 in.Hg of vacuum in 1977 and later models. To adjust the vacuum setting, bend the diaphragm rod. Vacuum is reduced when the rod is bent to shorten it and increased when the rod is bent to lengthen it.

➡**When the setting piston is released, there should be no clearance between the tan on the bi-metal lever and the stop on the coil housing. If they don't contact, the bi-metal lever has been bent too much.**

REMOVAL & INSTALLATION

1970-73 Models

1. Remove the spare tire from the engine compartment.

2. Disconnect the emission control system hoses from the air cleaner case, unfasten the bracket bolts, unscrew the wing nut, and remove the air cleaner assembly from the carburetor.

3. Disconnect the fuel lines from the carburetor. Unfasten the vacuum hoses from the distributor port (ff-1 and 1300G) or the servo diaphragm (DL and GL).

4. On DL and GL models, disconnect the anti-dieseling solenoid wiring.

5. Detach the choke cable from the choke lever and spring hanger, then remove the throttle cable from the throttle lever.

6. Remove the 4 carburetor mounting bolts and lift the carburetor, with gasket, off the intake manifold. Be sure to cover

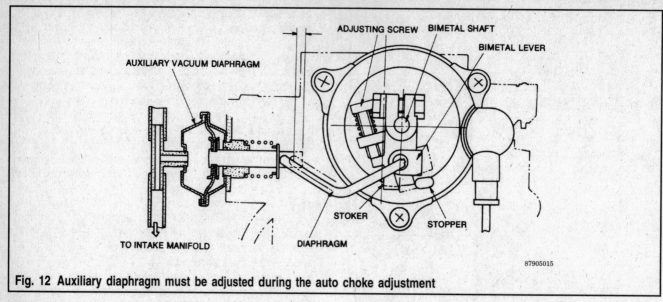

Fig. 12 Auxiliary diaphragm must be adjusted during the auto choke adjustment

the manifold opening, to prevent anything from being dropped down it.

7. Install the new or rebuilt carburetor and gasket onto the intake manifold.

8. Install the 4 carburetor mounting bolts and tighten them securely.

➡**Do not over-tighten the carburetor bolts. Carburetors are made of soft metal and can be easily cracked.**

9. Install the throttle cable, choke cable and anti-dieseling solenoid wiring onto the carburetor.

10. Connect the vacuum hoses to either the distributor port or servo diaphragm, depending on the model.

11. Connect the fuel lines, install the air cleaner, connect the emission control hoses and replace the spare tire.

12. Be sure to adjust the choke cable, idle speed (see Section 2), and make any other necessary adjustments.

1974-81 Models

1. Remove the air cleaner emission control system hoses, mounting bracket screws, wing nut or nuts, and lift the air cleaner assembly off the carburetor.

2. Disconnect the fuel lines from the carburetor.

3. Unfasten the vacuum hoses from the servo diaphragm, automatic choke diaphragms, distributor, and the EGR port (if so equipped).

4. Disconnect the anti-dieseling switch and automatic choke heater electrical leads. On California vehicles and some other models disconnect switch vent solenoid valve wire and hose to canister.

5. Remove the accelerator cable from the throttle lever.

6. Unfasten the 4 nuts which secure the carburetor and take it off the intake manifold. Cover the hole in the intake manifold, to prevent anything from falling in.

7. Install the new or rebuilt carburetor and gasket onto the intake manifold.

8. Install the 4 carburetor mounting bolts and tighten them securely.

➡**Do not over-tighten the carburetor bolts. Carburetors are made of soft metal and can be easily cracked.**

9. Install the vacuum hoses from the servo diaphragm, automatic choke diaphragms, distributor, and the EGR port (if so equipped).

10. Connect the anti-dieseling switch and automatic choke heater electrical leads. On California and some other models, connect switch vent solenoid valve wire and hose to the canister.

11. Connect the fuel lines, install the air cleaner, connect the emission control hoses and replace the spare tire.

12. Be sure to adjust the choke cable, idle speed (see Section 2), and make any other necessary adjustments.

1982-84 Models

▶ **See Figures 13, 14, 15, 16 and 17**

1. Remove the air cleaner.

2. Disconnect fuel supply and return lines at the carburetor.

3. Disconnect the carburetor vent hose for the ECC system.

4. Disconnect remaining vacuum hoses to distributor, etc.

5. Disconnect the EGR tube.

6. On the Hitachi carburetor:

  a. Disconnect the ignition retard, if applicable.

  b. Disconnect vacuum hoses for solenoid valves, the main diaphragm, and, on high altitude carburetors, the secondary main air bleed.

  c. Disconnect the duty solenoid valve connector on those models so equipped.

7. On both types of carburetor, disconnect the harness connectors and then disengage the accelerator cable from the throttle lever.

Fig. 13 Remove the air cleaner

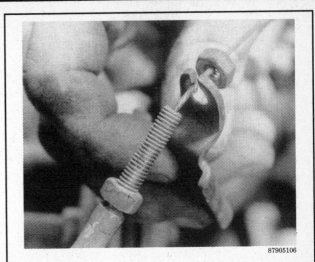

Fig. 15 Disengage the accelerator cable from the throttle lever

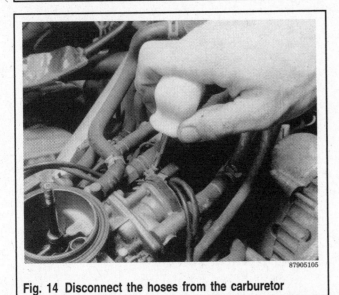

Fig. 14 Disconnect the hoses from the carburetor

Fig. 16 Remove the carburetor from the intake manifold

8. Drain some coolant out of the radiator so as to drain water out of the water heated throttle bore.

❋❋CAUTION

When draining the coolant, keep in mind that cats and dogs are attracted by ethylene glycol antifreeze, and are quite likely to drink any that is left in an uncovered container or in puddles on the ground. This will prove fatal in sufficient quantity. Always drain the coolant into a sealable container. Coolant should be reused unless it is contaminated or several years old.

9. Remove the four mounting nuts on the Hitachi or two nuts on the C-W, and remove the carburetor. On the C-W, disconnect the vent hose and remove its connector with the spacer and gasket. Cover the intake manifold opening.
   To install:
10. Clean the carburetor mounting surface.
11. Install the carburetor onto the intake manifold and tighten the mounting bolts.

Fig. 17 Clean the carburetor mounting surface

12. On the C-W, connect the vent hose, spacer and gasket.

13. Engage the accelerator cable to the throttle lever and the harness connector to the carburetor.

14. On the Hitachi carburetor:

a. Connect the duty solenoid valve connector on those models so equipped.

b. Connect vacuum hoses for solenoid valves, the main diaphragm, and, on high altitude carburetors, the secondary main air bleed.

c. Connect the ignition retard, if applicable.

15. Connect the EGR tube.

16. Connect the vacuum hoses to the distributor.

17. Connect the carburetor vent hose for the ECC system.

18. Connect the fuel lines to the carburetor and install the air cleaner.

19. Make any necessary adjustments to the carburetor, check fuel lines for leaks and refill the radiator with coolant.

OVERHAUL NOTES

▶ **See Figures 18, 19, 20, 21, 22, 23, 24, 25, 26, 27 and 28**

Generally, when a carburetor requires major service, a rebuilt one is purchased on an exchange basis, or a kit may be bought for overhauling the carburetor

The kit contains the necessary parts which varies on the kit type and some form of instructions for carburetor rebuilding. The instructions may vary from a simple exploded view to detailed step-by-step rebuilding instructions. Unless you are familiar with carburetor overhaul, the latter should be used.

There are some general overhaul procedures which should always be observed:

Efficient carburetion depends greatly on careful cleaning and inspection during overhaul since dirt, gum, water, or varnish in or on the carburetor parts are often responsible for poor performance.

Overhaul your carburetor in a clean, dust-free area. Carefully disassemble the carburetor, referring often to the exploded views. Keep all similar and look-alike parts segregated during disassembly and cleaning to avoid accidental interchange during assembly. Make a note of all jet sizes.

When the carburetor is disassembled, wash all parts (except diaphragms, electric choke units, pump plunger, and any other plastic, leather, fiber, or rubber parts) in clean carburetor solvent. Do not leave parts in the solvent any longer than is necessary to sufficiently loosen the deposits. Excessive cleaning may remove the special finish from the float bowl and choke valve bodies, leaving these parts unfit for service. Rinse all parts in clean solvent and blow them dry with compressed air or allow them to air dry. Wipe clean all cork, plastic, leather, and fiber parts with a clean, lint-free cloth.

Blow out all passages and jets with compressed air and be sure that there are no restrictions or blockages. Never use wire or similar tools to clean jets, fuel passages, or air bleeds. Clean all jets and valves separately to avoid accidental interchange.

Check all parts for wear or damage. If wear or damage is found, replace the defective parts. Especially check the following:

1. Check the float needle and seat for wear. If wear is found, replace the complete assembly.

2. Check the float hinge pin for wear and the float(s) for dents or distortion. Replace the float if fuel has leaked into it.

3. Check the throttle and choke shaft bores for wear or an out-of-round condition. Damage or wear to the throttle arm, shaft, or shaft bore will often require replacement of the throttle body. These parts require a close tolerance. Wear may allow air leakage, which could affect starting and idling.

➡**Throttle shafts and bushings are usually not included in overhaul kits. They can be usually purchased separately.**

4. Inspect the idle mixture adjusting needles for burrs or grooves. Any such condition requires replacement of the needle, since you will not be able to obtain a satisfactory idle.

5. Test the accelerator pump check valves. They should pass air one way but not the other. Test for proper seating by blowing and sucking on the valve. Replace the valve if necessary. If the valve is satisfactory, wash the valve again to remove breath moisture.

6. Check the bowl cover for warped surfaces with a straightedge.

7. Closely inspect the valves and seats for wear and damage, replacing as necessary.

8. After the carburetor is assembled, check the choke valve for freedom of operation.

Carburetor overhaul kits are recommended for each overhaul. These kits contain all gaskets and new parts to replace those that deteriorate most rapidly. Failure to replace all parts supplied with the kit (especially gaskets) can result in poor performance later.

Most carburetor manufacturers supply overhaul kits of three basic types: minor repair, major repair, and gasket kits. Basically, they contain the following:

Minor Repair Kits:
- All gaskets
- Float needle valve
- Volume control screw
- All diaphragms
- Spring for the pump diaphragm

Major Repair Kits:
- All jets and gaskets
- All diaphragms
- Float needle valve
- Volume control screw
- Pump ball valve
- Main jet carrier
- Float
- Complete intermediate rod
- Intermediate pump lever
- Complete injector tube
- Some cover hold-down screws and washers

Gasket Kits:
- All gaskets

After cleaning and checking all components, reassemble the carburetor, using new parts and referring to the exploded view. When reassembling, make sure that all screws and jets are tight in their seats, but do not overtighten, as the tips will be distorted. Tighten all screws gradually, in rotation. Do not tighten needle valves into their seats. Uneven jetting will result. Always use new gaskets. Be sure to adjust the float level when reassembling.

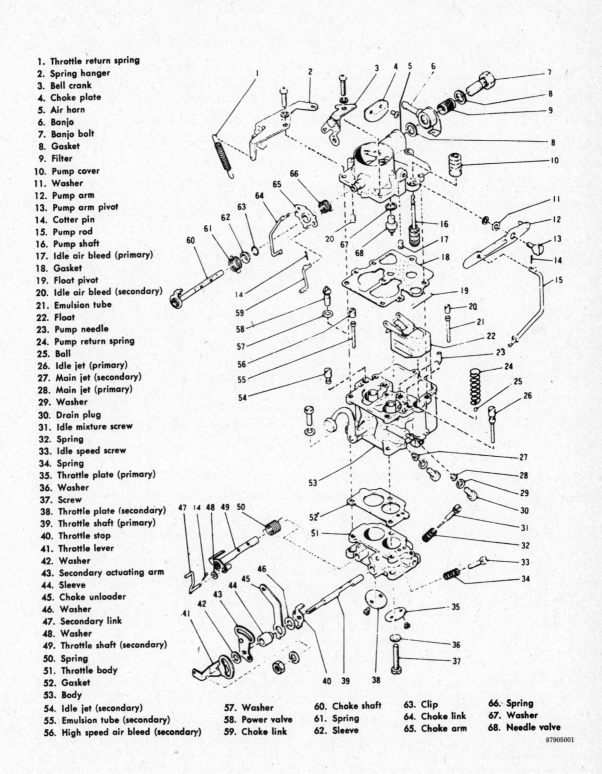

1. Throttle return spring
2. Spring hanger
3. Bell crank
4. Choke plate
5. Air horn
6. Banjo
7. Banjo bolt
8. Gasket
9. Filter
10. Pump cover
11. Washer
12. Pump arm
13. Pump arm pivot
14. Cotter pin
15. Pump rod
16. Pump shaft
17. Idle air bleed (primary)
18. Gasket
19. Float pivot
20. Idle air bleed (secondary)
21. Emulsion tube
22. Float
23. Pump needle
24. Pump return spring
25. Ball
26. Idle jet (primary)
27. Main jet (secondary)
28. Main jet (primary)
29. Washer
30. Drain plug
31. Idle mixture screw
32. Spring
33. Idle speed screw
34. Spring
35. Throttle plate (primary)
36. Washer
37. Screw
38. Throttle plate (secondary)
39. Throttle shaft (primary)
40. Throttle stop
41. Throttle lever
42. Washer
43. Secondary actuating arm
44. Sleeve
45. Choke unloader
46. Washer
47. Secondary link
48. Washer
49. Throttle shaft (secondary)
50. Spring
51. Throttle body
52. Gasket
53. Body
54. Idle jet (secondary)
55. Emulsion tube (secondary)
56. High speed air bleed (secondary)

57. Washer
58. Power valve
59. Choke link

60. Choke shaft
61. Spring
62. Sleeve

63. Clip
64. Choke link
65. Choke arm

66. Spring
67. Washer
68. Needle valve

87905001

Fig. 18 Exploded view ff-1 and 1300G carburetor

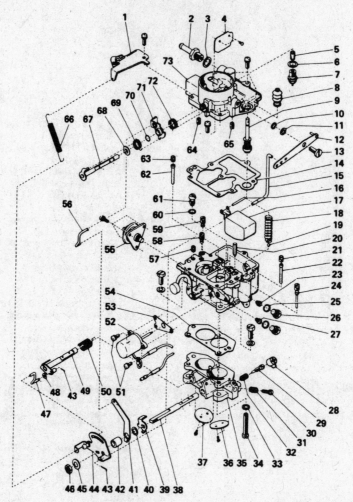

1. Spring hanger	25. Washer	49. Secondary throttle shaft
2. Nipple	26. Drain plug (Float chamber)	50. Spring (Secondary throttle)
3. Washer	27. Secondary main pet (#155)	51. Screw
4. Choke valve	28. Cap (Idle limiter)	52. Anti-dieseling solenoid
5. Filter	29. Idle adjustment screw	53. Gasket
6. Washer	30. Throttle adjustment screw	54. Gasket (throttle chamber)
7. Needle valve	31. Spring (Throttle adjustment screw)	55. Servo diaphragm
8. Cover (Pump)	32. Spring (Idle adjustment screw)	56. Connecting rod (Choke)
9. Piston	33. Washer	57. Bypass air bleed (#320)
10. Spring washer	34. Screw	58. Secondary slow jet (#60)
11. Washer	35. Throttle chamber	59. Bypass slow jet (#55)
12. Lever (Pump)	36. Primary throttle-valve	60. Washer
13. Shaft (Pump lever)	37. Secondary throttle valve	61. Power valve (#4)
14. Gasket (Float chamber)	38. Primary throttle shaft	62. Secondary emulsion tube
15. Connecting rod (Pump)	39. Adjusting plate	63. Secondary main air bleed (#90)
16. Shaft (Float)	40. Washer	64. Secondary slow air bleed (#70)
17. Float	41. Connecting lever	65. Primary slow air bleed (#200)
18. Piston return spring	42. Sleeve	66. Throttle return spring
19. Ball (5/32 in.)	43. Cotter pin	67. Choke shaft
20. Weight A (Injector)	44. Throttle lever	68. Sleeve (A)
21. Primary main air bleed (#60)	45. Spring washer	69. Choke valve spring
22. Primary emulsion tube	46. Nut	70. Clip
23. Primary main jet (#95)	47. Connecting rod	71. Choke lever
24. Primary slow jet (#43)	48. Washer	72. Choke spring
		73. Choke chamber

87905002

Fig. 19 Exploded view 1972-73 GL and DL carburetor

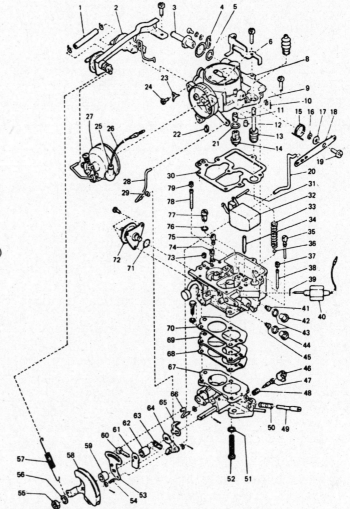

1. Vacuum hose
2. Vacuum diaphragm
3. Nipple (fuel inlet)
4. Stopper
5. Washer
6. Nipple guide
7. Pump cover
8. Choke chamber
9. Washer
10. Cotter pin
11. Filter
12. Primary slow air bleed (#200)
13. Piston
14. Needle valve
15. Pump lever spring
16. Spring washer
17. Washer
18. Pump lever
19. Shaft (pump lever)
20. Connecting rod (accelerator pump)
21. Washer
22. Secondary slow air bleed (#70)
23. Spring washer
24. Screw
25. Boot
26. Heater lead
27. Bimetal cover
28. Cam connecting rod
29. Washer
30. Gasket (float chamber)
31. Shaft (float)
32. Float
33. Piston return spring
34. Weight (injector)
35. Primary slow jet (#43)
36. Ball (5/32 in.)
37. Primary main air bleed (#60)
38. Primary emulsion tube
39. Washer
40. Anti-dieseling solenoid

41. Primary main jet (#95, #93)
42. Drain plug (primary)
43. Washer
44. Drain plug (secondary)
45. Secondary main jet (#155)
46. Idle limiter cap
47. Idle adjust screw
48. Spring (idle adjust screw)
49. Throttle adjust screw
50. Spring (throttle adjust screw)
51. Washer
52. Screw
53. Connecting lever
54. Spring
55. Nut
56. Spring washer
57. Throttle return spring
58. Throttle lever
59. Sleeve
60. First idle adjust screw

61. Lever A (fast idle)
62. Sleeve
63. Spring (throttle adjust screw)
64. Lever B (fast idle)
65. Plate
66. Connecting rod
67. Throttle chamber
68. Gasket (throttle chamber)
69. Insulator
70. Gasket (throttle chamber)
71. O-ring
72. Servo diaphragm
73. Air bleed (coasting)
74. Secondary slow jet (#60)
75. Slow jet (coasting) (#50)
76. Washer
77. Power valve (#45)
78. Secondary emulsion tube
79. Secondary main air bleed (#90)

87905007

Fig. 20 1974 carburetor (1975-79 differs in jet size only)

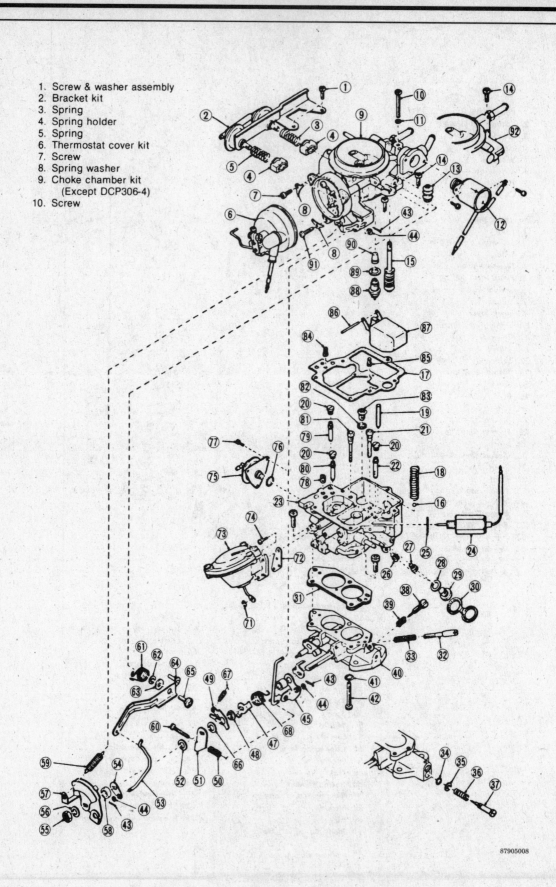

1. Screw & washer assembly
2. Bracket kit
3. Spring
4. Spring holder
5. Spring
6. Thermostat cover kit
7. Screw
8. Spring washer
9. Choke chamber kit
   (Except DCP306-4)
10. Screw

Fig. 21 1980 DCP306-1, DCP306-3, DCP306-4 and DCP306-5 carburetors

87905008

11. Spring washer
12. Switch vent solenoid valve
    (DCP306-1)
    (DCP306-2)
    (DCP306-5)
13. Pump cover
14. Screw & washer assembly
15. Piston
16. Ball
17. Float chamber gasket
18. Piston return spring
19. Injector weight
20. Plug
21. Primary main air bleed (#95)
22. Primary slow jet
    DCP306-1 .... #52
    DCP306-2 ┐
    DCP306-3 │
    DCP306-5 ┘
    DCP306-4
23. Float chamber
24. Anti-dieseling switch
25. Washer
26. Secondary main jet (#145)
27. Primary main jet
    DCP306-1 ┐ .... #113
    DCP306-2 ┘
    DCP306-3 ┐ .... #111
    DCP306-5 ┘
    DCP306-4 .... #106
28. Washer
29. Float chamber drain plug
30. Lock plate
31. Insulator
32. Throttle adjusting screw
33. Throttle adjusting spring
34. O-ring
    (DCP306-1)
    (DCP306-2)
35. Washer
    (DCP306-1)
    (DCP306-2)
36. Idle adjusting spring
    (DCP306-1)
    (DCP306-2)
37. Idle adjusting screw
    (DCP306-1)
    (DCP306-2)
38. Idle adjusting screw
    (DCP306-3)
    (DCP306-4)
    (DCP306-5)
39. Idle adjusting spring
    (DCP306-3)
    (DCP306-4)
    (DCP306-5)
40. Throttle chamber kit
41. Washer
42. Screw
43. Cotter pin
44. Washer
45. Fast idle level A
46. Sleeve
47. Connecting level (P)
48. Sleeve A
49. Return plate
50. Idle adjusting spring

51. Fast idle level B
52. Washer
53. Pump connecting rod
54. Connecting lever
55. Nut
56. Spring washer
57. Throttle level
58. Collar
59. Throttle return spring
60. Screw
61. Pump lever spring
62. Spring washer
63. Washer
64. Pump lever
65. Pump lever shaft
66. Washer
67. Return spring (S)
68. Spring
69. Cam connecting rod
70. Adjust plate
71. E-ring
72. Diaphragm gasket
73. Secondary diaphragm
74. Screw & washer assembly
75. Diaphragm chamber
76. O-ring
77. Screw & washer assembly
78. Coasting by-pass air bleed
    DCP306-1 ┐
    DCP306-2 │ .... #260
    DCP306-3 │
    DCP306-5 ┘
    DCP306-4 .... #200
79. Coasting by-pass jet
    DCP306-1 ┐
    DCP306-2 │ .... #40
    DCP306-3 │
    DCP306-5 ┘
    DCP306-4 .... #50
80. Secondary slow jet
    DCP306-1 ┐
    DCP306-2 │ .... #70
    DCP306-3 │
    DCP306-5 ┘
    DCP306-4 .... #80
81. Secondary main air bleed
    (#80)
82. Washer
    (DCP306-4)
83. Power valve
    (#45) (DCP306-4)
84. Secondary slow air bleed
    DCP306-1 ┐
    DCP306-2 │ .... #100
    DCP306-3 │
    DCP306-5 ┘
    DCP306-4 .... #80
85. Primary slow air bleed
    (#160)
86. Float shaft
87. Float
88. Needle valve
89. Washer
90. Filter
91. Screw
92. Choke chamber kit (DCP306-4)

87905009

Fig. 22 Components, 1980 DCP306-1, DCP306-3, DCP306-4 and DCP306-5 carburetors

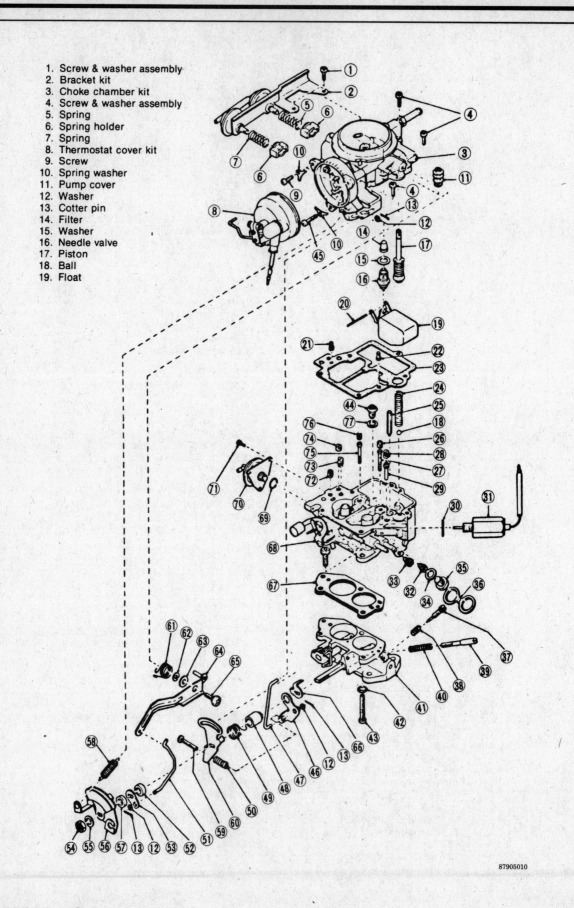

1. Screw & washer assembly
2. Bracket kit
3. Choke chamber kit
4. Screw & washer assembly
5. Spring
6. Spring holder
7. Spring
8. Thermostat cover kit
9. Screw
10. Spring washer
11. Pump cover
12. Washer
13. Cotter pin
14. Filter
15. Washer
16. Needle valve
17. Piston
18. Ball
19. Float

Fig. 23 DCJ306-15 carburetor used in 1980

87905010

20. Float shaft
21. Secondary slow air bleed (#70)
22. Primary slow air bleed (#170)
23. Float chamber gasket
24. Piston return spring
25. Injector weight
26. Primary main air bleed (#75)
27. Primary emulsion tube
28. Plug
29. Primary slow jet (#48)
30. Washer
31. Anti-dieseling switch
32. Primary main jet (#114)
33. Secondary main jet (#145)
34. Washer
35. Float chamber drain plug
36. Lock plate
37. Idle adjusting screw
38. Idle adjusting spring
39. Throttle adjusting screw
40. Throttle adjusting spring
41. Throttle chamber kit
42. Washer
43. Screw
44. Power valve (#35)
45. Screw
46. Fast idle level A
47. Cam connecting rod
48. Sleeve

49. Spring
50. Idle adjusting spring
51. Pump connecting rod
52. Sleeve A
53. Connecting level
54. Nut
55. Spring washer
56. Throttle lever
57. Collar
58. Throttle return spring
59. Screw
60. Connecting level (P)
61. Pump lever spring
62. Spring washer
63. Washer
64. Pump lever
65. Pump lever shaft
66. Adjust plate
67. Insulator
68. Float chamber
69. O-ring
70. Diaphragm chamber
71. Screw & washer assembly
72. Coasting by-pass air bleed (#260)
73. Secondary slow jet (#70)
74. Coasting by-pass jet (#40)
75. Secondary emulsion tube
76. Secondary main air bleed (#80)
77. Washer

87905011

Fig. 24 Components, DCJ306-15 carburetor used in 1980

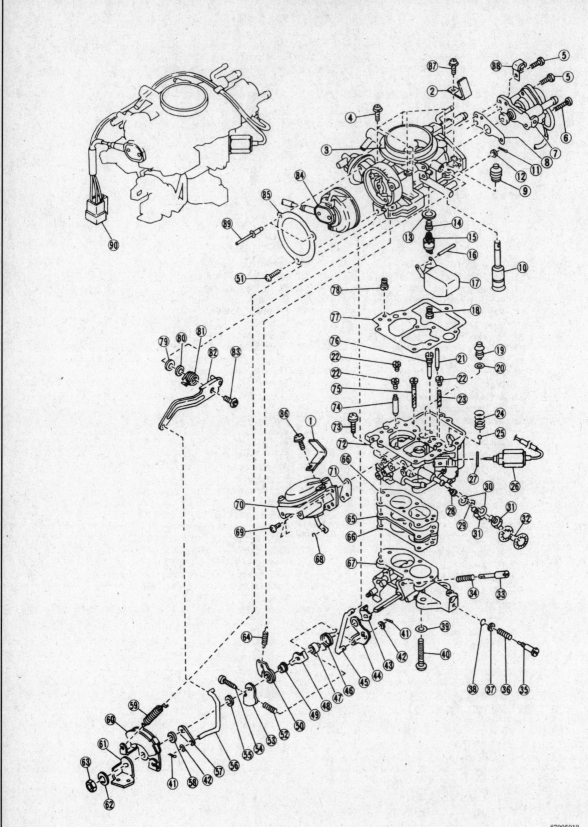

Fig. 25 1983-84 Hitachi carburetor

87905012

1. Clip
2. Lead wire holder
3. Choke chamber kit
4. Screw & washer
5. Screw & washer
6. Screw
7. Switch vent solenoid valve
8. Gasket
9. Pump cover
10. Piston
11. Cotter pin
12. Washer
13. Washer
14. Filter
15. Needle valve
16. Float shaft
17. Float
18. Primary slow air bleed
19. Power jet
20. Washer
21. Injector weight
22. Plug
23. Primary slow jet
24. Piston return spring
25. Ball
26. Solenoid valve CP
27. Washer
28. Secondary main jet
29. Primary main jet
30. Washer
31. Float chamber plug

32. Lock plate
33. Throttle adjust screw
34. Throttle adjust spring
35. Idle adjust screw
36. Idle adjust spring
37. Washer
38. O-ring
39. Washer
40. Screw
41. Cotter pin
42. Washer
43. Adjust plate
44. Fast idle lever A
45. Cam connecting rod
46. Spring
47. Sleeve
48. Connecting lever
49. Sleeve A
50. Return plate
51. Screw & washer
52. Idle adjust spring
53. Fast idle lever B
54. Screw
55. Washer
56. Pump connecting rod
57. Connecting lever
58. Collar
59. Throttle return spring
60. Throttle lever
61. F.I.C.D. lever
62. Spring washer

63. Nut
64. Return spring
65. Insulator
66. Gasket
67. Throttle chamber
68. "E" ring
69. Screw & washer
70. Diaphragm chamber
71. Gasket
72. Float chamber
73. Screw & washer
74. Secondary slow jet
75. Secondary main air bleed
76. Primary main air bleed
77. Gasket
78. Secondary slow air bleed
79. Spring washer
80. Washer
81. Pump lever spring
82. Pump lever
83. Pump lever shaft
84. P.T.C. bimetal CP
85. Bimetal cover
86. Screw & washer
87. Screw & washer
88. Lead wire holder
89. Blind rivet
90. Connector

87905013

Fig. 26 Components, 1983-84 Hitachi carburetor

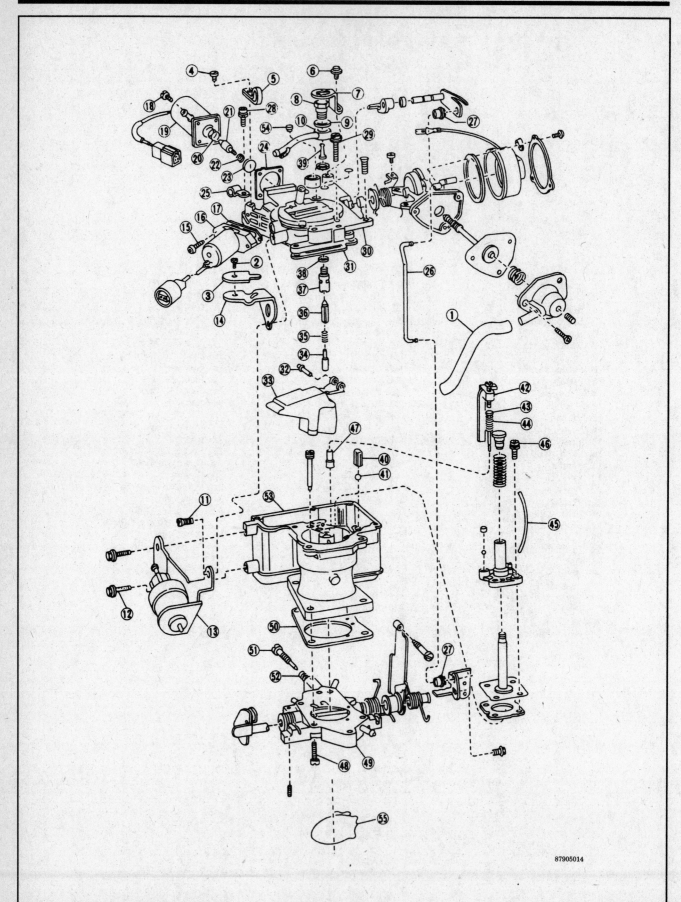

Fig. 27 1983-84 Carter-Weber carburetor

87905014

1. Choke vacuum hose
2. Fuel line clamp screw (outer)
3. Fuel line clamp (outer)
4. Fuel line clamp screw (inner)
5. Fuel line clamp (inner)
6. Banjo lock screw
7. Banjo lock
8. Banjo fuel bolt
9. Banjo gasket
10. Banjo fuel line ASSY
11. Fuel line bracket attaching screw
12. Idle stop solenoid attaching screw
13. Idle stop solenoid
14. Fuel line bracket
15. Feedback solenoid attaching screw
16. Feedback solenoid
17. Feedback solenoid gasket
18. Bowl vent solenoid attaching screw
19. Bowl vent solenoid
20. Bowl vent armature spring
21. Bowl vent armature
22. Bowl vent armature spring retainer
23. Bowl vent valve
24. Bowl vent gasket
25. Wire support(s)
26. Connector rod
27. Connector rod bushing
28. Air horn attaching screw (short)
29. Air horn attaching screw (long)
30. Air horn
31. Air horn gasket
32. Float hinge pin
33. Float
34. Fuel inlet needle pin
35. Fuel inlet needle pin spring
36. Fuel inlet needle
37. Fuel inlet needle seat
38. Fuel inlet needle seat gasket
39. Fuel inlet filter
40. Pump discharge weight
41. Pump discharge check ball
42. Lifter link
43. Metering rod
44. Metering rod spring
45. Pump delivery hose
46. Pump assembly attaching screw
47. Main jet
48. Flange attaching screws
49. Flange
50. Flange gasket
51. Idle mixture screw
52. Idle mixture screw spring
53. Body casting
54. Metering rod adjustment hole plug
55. Flange O-ring

87905a15

Fig. 28 Components, 1983-84 Carter-Weber carburetor

Carburetor Jet Specifications Chart

	1975 Primary	1975 Secondary	1976 Primary	1976 Secondary	1977–79 Primary	1977–79 Secondary
Main jet	#93	#155	#103	#155	#103 ①	#155 ②
Slow jet	#43	#60	#45	#70	#46	#70
Main air bleed	#60	#90	#75	#80	#75	#80
Slow air bleed	#200	#70	#200	#70	#170	#70
Power valve	#35		#45		#45	
By-pass jet	#55		#45		#45	
By-pass air bleed	#320		#200		#200	

① 49 state high altitude models are #95
② 49 state high altitude models are #135

	1980-81 All Primary	1980-81 All Secondary	1982 1600 Sedan-Man. trans. Primary	1982 1600 Sedan-Man. trans. Secondary	1982 Sta Wag, 4WD Primary	1982 Sta Wag, 4WD Secondary	1982 Automatic Primary	1982 Automatic Secondary
Main jet	#110	#150	#116	#145	#114	#145	#116	#145
Slow jet	#43	#80	#43	#80	#43	#80	#43	#80
Main air bleed	#60	#80	#60	#80	#60	#80	#60	#80
Slow air bleed	#100	#90	#150	#50	#150	#50	#150	#50
Power valve	#40		#50		#50		#50	
Econ. bleed	#95		#95	#90	#95	#90	#95	#90
Acc. Pump Nozzle	.020		.020		.020		.020	

1983–84	DCP306-17 ① Primary	DCP306-17 ① Secondary	DCP306-18 ② Primary	DCP306-18 ② Secondary	DCP306-19 ③ Primary	DCP306-19 ③ Secondary	DCP306-21 ④ Primary	DCP306-21 ④ Secondary	DCP306-22 ⑤ Primary	DCP306-22 ⑤ Secondary
Main jet	#116	#145	#114	#145	#114	#145	#109	#140	#109	#145
Slow jet	#43	#80	#43	#80	#43	#80	#43	#80	#43	#80
Main air bleed	#60	#80	#60	#80	#60	#80	#70	#80	#70	#80
Slow air bleed	#50	#150	#50	#150	#50	#150	#160	#90	#150	#90
Power valve	#50		#50		#50		#35		plugged	
Econ. Bleed	#95	#90	#95	#90	#95	#90	#95	#90	#95	#90
Acc. Pump Nozzle	.020		.020		.020		.020		.020	

① 1600 engines only
② 1800 man. Cal and 2WD 49 states
③ 1800 auto. Cal and 2WD 49 states
④ 1800 man. Canada and 4WD 49 states
⑤ 1800 auto. Canada and 4WD 49 states

MULTI POINT FUEL INJECTION

Operation

▶ **See Figures 29 and 30**

The Subaru 1800 Turbo comes equipped with Multi-Port Electronic Fuel Injection system. The Electronic Fuel Injection System is particularly suited for use with the turbocharger because it requires no venturi restriction. That means that it has a greater capacity for total power than an equivalent carburetor since air flows through it more freely.

Also, carburetors are limited in their ability to accurately measure airflow because they do not compensate for changes in barometric pressure or temperature, and cannot accurately and quickly respond to throttle changes. This system overcomes those limitations.

Additionally, by injecting the fuel with nearly 40 psi (275 kPa) pressure right at the intake ports, the engine is fed a more consistently atomized mixture with the injection system. This improves performance and fuel economy, especially during cold engine operation.

The heart of the system is a fuel supply loop which consists of a fuel pump and damper which supply fuel under a relatively smooth and constant pressure through a filter. Fuel is supplied to a loop which passes by each fuel injector (one for each cylinder). The loop returns to the fuel tank via a pressure regulator which measures the pressure or vacuum (depending upon throttle opening and turbocharger performance) that exists in the intake manifold. The pressure regulator, by precisely controlling the return of fuel to the tank, maintains exactly 36.3 psi (250 kPa) above the pressure in the intake manifold.

Each fuel injector consists of a nozzle and a tiny electric solenoid valve. The system employs electronics to determine how long the solenoid should be open each time it inputs fuel. By varying the electric pulse sent to the injector and, therefore, the time each injector stays open, the system can precisely supply the amount of fuel the engine requires. For example, if the driver should open the throttle and double the amount of airflow to the engine, the injectors would stay open just twice as long as before the driver decelerated. Air flowing into the system flows through the air cleaner, and then enters the air flow meter. This device measures the flow of air through a precisely designed flap, which opens or closes with airflow against the tension of a spring. A temperature measuring device compensates for the increased density of cold air.

From here, the air passes through the turbocharger into the throttle body. This part contains the throttle which controls airflow according to the driver's demands, much as in an ordinary carburetion system. It has switches which tell the electronic microprocessor which controls the system when the car is at full throttle or at idle, for appropriate changes in fuel/air mixture. When the driver releases the throttle, the throttle body closes off entirely, and air for engine idle is routed through the auxiliary air valve to the engine.

Whenever there is a change in airflow, it is reflected in a change in the air flow meter's signal to the microprocessor and a change in the width (or time) of the pulse the microprocessor sends to the injectors.

The system is extremely complex and requires specialized training and equipment to fully service and repair. You can, however, make a few simple checks and adjustments, provided you adhere to the safety precautions in this section.

FUEL DELIVERY

The MPFI system supplies the optimum air/fuel mixture to the engine under all various operating conditions. System fuel, which is pressurized at a constant pressure, is injected into the intake air passage of the cylinder head. The amount of fuel injected is controlled by the intermittent injection system where the electromagnetic injection valve (fuel injector) opens only for a short period of time, depending on the amount of air required for 1 cycle of operation. During system operation, the amount injection is determined by the duration of an electric pulse sent to the fuel injector, which permits precise metering of the fuel.

All the operating conditions of the engine are converted into electric signals, resulting in additional features of the system, such as improved adaptability and easier addition of compensating element. The MPFI system also incorporates the following features:

- Reduced emission of exhaust gases
- Reduction in fuel consumption
- Increased engine output
- Superior acceleration and deceleration
- Superior starting and warm-up performance in cold weather since compensation is made for coolant and intake air temperature
- Improved performance with turbocharger, if equipped

Safety Precautions

1. Do not connect the battery, or jumper cables, with reverse polarity.
2. Never disconnect the battery while the engine is running.
3. Turn **OFF** the ignition switch before disengaging any connector in the system.
4. Keep all connectors dry.
5. If handling electronic parts, do not drop them or permit them to be banged against another part while removing or installing them.

Relieving The Fuel System Pressure

➡**This procedure must be performed prior to servicing any component of the fuel injection system which contains fuel because of the high pressures in the fuel lines.**

1. Disengage the fuel pump connector at the fuel pump.
2. Crank the engine for 5 seconds or more to relieve the fuel pressure. If the engine starts during this time, allow it to run until it stalls.
3. Engage the fuel pump connector.

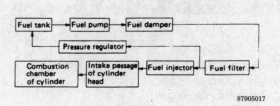

Fig. 29 The fuel passes from the tank, through a pump, damper and filter to the fuel injectors. It returns through a fuel pressure regulator.

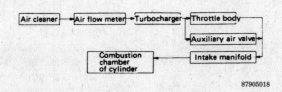

Fig. 30 Air entering the system passes through the air cleaner to the air flow meter, where the system measures how much air the engine is actually getting. From here, the air goes through the turbocharger to the throttle body, which actually controls airflow.

Electric Fuel Pump

The fuel pump is located under the center of the vehicle, in front of the fuel tank (1984 models).

A diaphragm type electromagnetic pump is used. If the pump fails, it must be replaced as an assembly, since it cannot be rebuilt.

REMOVAL & INSTALLATION

▶ See Figures 31 and 32

1. Release the fuel system pressure and disconnect the negative battery cable.

2. Keep the fuel pump harness disconnected after releasing the fuel system pressure.

3. Raise and support the vehicle safely.

4. Clamp the middle portion of the thick hose connecting the pipe and the pump to prevent fuel from flowing out of the tank.

5. Loosen the hose clamp and disconnect the hose.

6. Remove the three pump bracket mounting bolts and remove the pump together with the pump damper.

To Install:

7. If the pump and damper have been removed from the bracket, reinstall and tighten the bolts securely.

8. Install the hose and tighten the clamp screw to 0.7-1.1 ft. lbs. (1.0-1.5 Nm).

9. Install the pump bracket in position to the vehicle body and secure it with the bolts.

➡**Take care to position the rubber cushion properly.**

10. Connect the pump harness connector.

11. Connect the negative battery cable and test the fuel pump for proper operation.

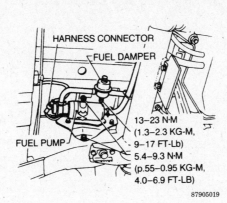

Fig. 31 Fuel pump and damper on the 1800 Turbo Brat

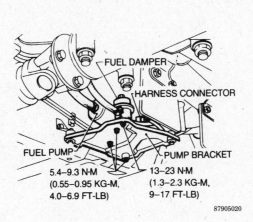

Fig. 32 Fuel pump and damper on the 1800 Turbo wagon

TESTING

1. Turn the ignition **ON** and listen for the fuel pump to make a growling sound. Turn the ignition **OFF**.

2. Release the fuel system pressure. Disconnect the pump connector and crank the engine for 5 seconds or more. If the engine starts, allow it to run until it stops. Turn the ignition **OFF** and install the fuel pump connector.

3. Disconnect the fuel hose at the fuel pump.

4. Connect a gauge in-line using a T-fitting.

5. Start the engine and measure the fuel pressure.

6. Release the fuel system pressure and remove the gauge.

Throttle Body

REMOVAL & INSTALLATION

1. Disconnect the negative battery cable.

2. Remove the air intake duct assembly.

3. Remove the engine cover, as required.

4. Drain the cooling system.

5. Remove the water hoses leading to the throttle body.

6. Remove the emissions gas hoses and as required, the auxiliary air hose.

7. Label and disengage all electrical connectors from the throttle body.

8. Remove the bracket holding the throttle body to the cylinder head.

9. Disconnect the accelerator cable, and cruise control cable if equipped.

10. Remove the bolts attaching the throttle body to the air plenum.

11. Remove the throttle body and discard the gasket.

To install:

12. Using a new gasket, install the throttle body and tighten the bolts to 17-20 ft. lbs. (23-26 Nm).

13. Install the throttle body bracket and tighten the bolts to 10-13 ft. lbs. (14-17 Nm).

14. Connect the accelerator cable, and cruise control cable if equipped.

15. Engage all electrical connectors to the throttle body.

16. Install the blow-by gas hose.

17. Install the water hoses leading to the throttle body.

18. Fill the cooling system.

19. Install the air intake duct assembly.

20. Connect the negative battery cable.

Fuel Injector

REMOVAL & INSTALLATION

1. Relieve the fuel system pressure.
2. Disconnect the negative battery cable.

➡**On some engines, it may be necessary to remove the intake plenum to gain access to the fuel lines connecting the injectors.**

3. Remove the fuel lines connecting the injectors.

4. Disengage the fuel injector electrical connectors.

5. Remove the injectors by pulling with a slight twist. Discard the gaskets and O-rings.

6. Remove the injector holder plate, insulator, holder and seal. Discard the insulator and seal.

To install:

7. Install the injectors using new gaskets, seals (insulators) and O-rings. Lubricate the O-rings prior to installation.

8. Install the fuel lines connecting the injectors.

9. Engage the injector electrical connectors.

10. Install the intake plenum if removed.

11. Connect the negative battery cable.

12. Start the engine and check for leaks.

Pressure Regulator

REMOVAL & INSTALLATION

▶ **See Figure 33**

1. Locate the pressure regulator on the fuel rail near the injectors.

2. Relieve the fuel system pressure.

3. Disconnect the negative battery cable.

4. Remove the vacuum line leading to the regulator.

5. Loosen the fuel line nuts and remove the regulator.

To install:

6. Install the regulator and tighten the fuel line nuts securely.

7. Install the vacuum line on the regulator.

8. Connect the negative battery cable.

9. Start the engine and check for leaks.

10. Check for correct fuel pressure.

Airflow Meter

REMOVAL & INSTALLATION

1. Disconnect the negative battery cable.

2. Disengage the connector from the airflow meter.

3. Remove the engine harness from the clip.

4. Loosen the hose clamps securing the air intake boot and remove the air intake boot assembly.

5. Loosen the bolts attaching the air flow meter to the air cleaner assembly and remove the airflow meter.

To install:

6. Install the airflow meter and tighten the bolts to 3-5 ft. lbs. (4-7 Nm).

7. Install the air intake boot assembly and tighten the attaching clamps to securely.

8. Install the engine harness on the clip and engage the airflow meter connector.

9. Connect the negative battery cable.

Throttle Sensor

REMOVAL & INSTALLATION

1. Disconnect the negative battery cable.

2. Disengage the throttle sensor connector.

3. Loosen the throttle sensor attaching screws.

4. Remove the throttle sensor.

To install:

5. Install the throttle sensor and loosely tighten the screws.

6. Engage the throttle sensor electrical connector.

7. Connect the negative battery cable.

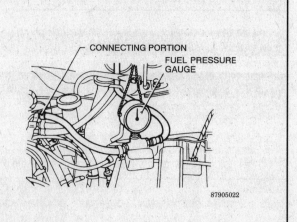

CONNECTING PORTION
FUEL PRESSURE GAUGE

87905022

Fig. 33 Connecting the fuel pressure gauge to test the pressure regulator

8. Adjust the throttle sensor to the correct specifications and tighten the sensor attaching screws securely.

Auxiliary Air Valve

REMOVAL & INSTALLATION

1. Disconnect the negative battery cable.
2. Disengage the air valve electrical connector.
3. Disconnect the hose leading to the air valve.
4. Remove the air valve retaining screws, then remove the air valve.
   To Install:
5. Install the air valve and tighten the retaining screws securely.
6. Connect the air valve hose.
7. Engage the air valve electrical connector.
8. Connect the negative battery cable.

TESTING

1. Pinch the hose connecting the air intake duct and the auxiliary air valve, then note engine rpm change. With the engine cold, engine idle speed drops as the hose is pinched. With the engine hot, reduction in engine rpm is within 100.
2. When the engine is started, the auxiliary air valve is heated by the built-in heater and its shutter valve gradually closes. This causes engine rpm to lower gradually until the specified idling rpm is reached. If the engine speed does not drop to the idling rpm smoothly, the heater circuit or the heater power supply circuit may be faulty. Proceed as follows:
   a. Disconnect the auxiliary air valve electrical connector.
   b. Using an ohmmeter, measure the resistance between the 2 terminals on the auxiliary air valve. Ohmmeter should read other than 0 ohms and infinity.
   c. If ohmmeter reads 0 ohms or infinity, replace the auxiliary air valve.
   d. Disconnect the auxiliary air valve electrical connector.
   e. Using a voltmeter, check the voltage on the auxiliary air valve connector.
   f. With the engine running, voltmeter should read 12 volts or more. If specifications are not within parameters, check the harness and connector for faults.

Fuel Tank

▶ **See Figure 34**

The fuel tanks are located at the rear of the vehicle. The tank itself also contains a fuel gauge sending unit, and a filler tube. In most tanks, there is also a screen of some sort in the bottom of the tank near the pickup to filer out impurities. Since the advent of emission controls, tanks are equipped with a control system to prevent fuel vapor from being discharged into the atmosphere. A vent line in the tank is connected to a filter in the engine compartment. Vapors from the tank are trapped in the filter canister, where they are routed back to the fuel tank, making the system a closed loop. All the fumes are prevented from escaping to the atmosphere. These systems also require the use of a special gas cap which makes an airtight seal.

Tank Assembly

REMOVAL & INSTALLATION

Mounted Behind Rear Seat

1. Disconnect the ground cable from the negative (-) terminal of the battery.
2. Remove the rear seat and luggage shelf.

Fig. 34 Typical mounting of an under vehicle fuel tank assembly

3. Disconnect the gas line running to the fuel pump and drain the gas tank. Removing the gas filler cap will enable the gas to drain faster.

✳✳CAUTION

When draining the gas tank try to avoid making sparks, also avoid smoking or open flames! Use a safe container to store the gas.

Plug the gas line with a bolt (8mm) to prevent drain back from the fuel pump.

4. Disconnect the evaporation hose from the tank pipes.

5. Remove the hardboard from the trunk.

6. Loosen the clamps holding the filler hose to the filler pipe. Remove the filler hose.

7. Disconnect the wiring harness from the fuel sending unit.

8. Remove the bolts from the right and left side of the fuel tank. Remove the tank by pulling it out of the brackets.

9. During installation, be sure to connect the filler hose after the tank has been mounted, to prevent leakage at the connection. Be careful not to kink hoses or overtighten fittings when reconnecting.

Mounted Under Vehicle

▶ **See Figures 35 and 36**

1. Disconnect the ground cable from the negative (-) terminal of the battery.

2. Block the front wheels of the vehicle. Raise the rear of the vehicle.

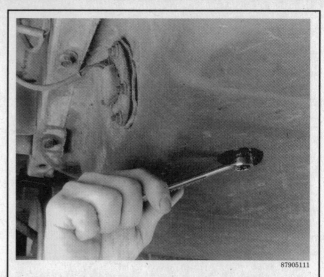

Fig. 36 Remove the drain plug to drain the fuel tank

✳✳WARNING

Refer to the correct jacking points, as mentioned in earlier Section 1. Make sure to support the vehicle with stands.

3. Remove the right rear wheel.

4. Disconnect the fuel tank sending unit wiring harness.

5. Drain the gas tank, by removing the drain plug, or disconnecting the fuel feed line to the fuel pump.

✳✳CAUTION

No smoking while draining the gas tank! Use a safe container to store the gas.

6. Plug the gas line to fuel pump to prevent drain back from the pump. If the drain plug was removed, replace and tighten.

7. Disconnect all remaining small diameter fuel and evaporating system hoses.

8. Loosen clamps and remove the fuel filler hose.

➡**On some earlier models, it may help to loosen the fuel tank mounting bolts before trying to disconnect the small hoses.**

9. Remove mounting bolts evenly (one from each side) while supporting the tank.

10. Remove the gas tank.

11. During installation, be sure to connect the filler hose after the tank has been mounted, to prevent leakage at the connection.

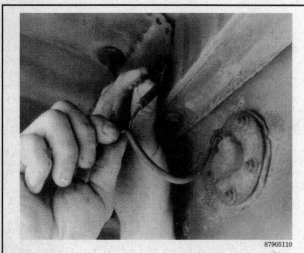

Fig. 35 Disconnect the fuel tank sending unit wiring harness

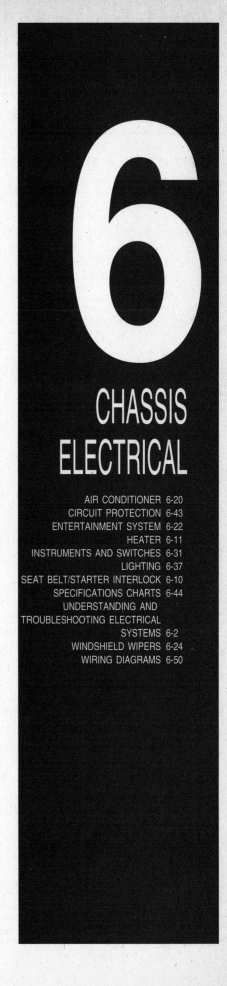

6

CHASSIS ELECTRICAL

UNDERSTANDING AND TROUBLESHOOTING ELECTRICAL SYSTEMS

Over the years import and domestic manufacturers have incorporated electronic control systems into their production lines. In fact, electronic control systems are so prevalent that all new cars and trucks built today are equipped with at least one on-board computer. These electronic components (with no moving parts) should theoretically last the life of the vehicle, provided that nothing external happens to damage the circuits or memory chips.

While it is true that electronic components should never wear out, in the real world malfunctions do occur. It is also true that any computer-based system is extremely sensitive to electrical voltages and cannot tolerate careless or haphazard testing/service procedures. An inexperienced individual can literally cause major damage looking for a minor problem by using the wrong kind of test equipment or connecting test leads/connectors with the ignition switch **ON**. When selecting test equipment, make sure the manufacturer's instructions state that the tester is compatible with whatever type of system is being serviced. Read all instructions carefully and double check all test points before installing probes or making any test connections.

The following section outlines basic diagnosis techniques for dealing with automotive electrical systems. Along with a general explanation of the various types of test equipment available to aid in servicing modern automotive systems, basic repair techniques for wiring harnesses and connectors are also given. Read the basic information before attempting any repairs or testing. This will provide the background of information necessary to avoid the most common and obvious mistakes that can cost both time and money. Although the replacement and testing procedures are simple in themselves, the systems are not, and unless one has a thorough understanding of all components and their function within a particular system, the logical test sequence these systems demand cannot be followed. Minor malfunctions can make a big difference, so it is important to know how each component affects the operation of the overall system in order to find the ultimate cause of a problem without replacing good components unnecessarily. It is not enough to use the correct test equipment; the test equipment must be used correctly.

Safety Precautions

✳✳CAUTION

Whenever working on or around any electrical or electronic systems, always observe these general precautions to prevent the possibility of personal injury or damage to electronic components.

• Never install or remove battery cables with the key **ON** or the engine running. Jumper cables should be connected with the key **OFF** to avoid power surges that can damage electronic control units. Engines equipped with computer controlled systems should avoid both giving and getting jump starts due to the possibility of serious damage to components from arcing in the engine compartment if connections are made with the ignition **ON**.

• Always remove the battery cables before charging the battery. Never use a high output charger on an installed battery or attempt to use any type of "hot shot" (24 volt) starting aid.

• Exercise care when inserting test probes into connectors to insure good contact without damaging the connector or spreading the pins. Always probe connectors from the rear (wire) side, NOT the pin side, to avoid accidental shorting of terminals during test procedures.

• Never remove or attach wiring harness connectors with the ignition switch **ON**, especially to an electronic control unit.

• Do not drop any components during service procedures and never apply 12 volts directly to any component (like a solenoid or relay) unless instructed specifically to do so. Some component electrical windings are designed to safely handle only 4 or 5 volts and can be destroyed in seconds if 12 volts are applied directly to the connector.

• Remove the electronic control unit if the vehicle is to be placed in an environment where temperatures exceed approximately 176°F (80°C), such as a paint spray booth or when arc/gas welding near the control unit location.

Understanding Basic Electricity

Understanding the basic theory of electricity makes electrical troubleshooting much easier. Several gauges are used in electrical troubleshooting to see inside the circuit being tested. Without a basic understanding, it will be difficult to understand testing procedures.

THE WATER ANALOGY

Electricity is the flow of electrons — hypothetical particles thought to constitute the basic stuff of electricity. Many people have been taught electrical theory using an analogy with water. In a comparison with water flowing in a pipe, the electrons would be the water. As the flow of water can be measured, the flow of electricity can be measured. The unit of measurement is amperes, frequently abbreviated amps. An ammeter will measure the actual amount of current flowing in the circuit.

Just as the water pressure is measured in units such as pounds per square inch, electrical pressure is measured in volts. When a voltmeter's two probes are placed on two live portions of an electrical circuit with different electrical pressures, current will flow through the voltmeter and produce a reading which indicates the difference in electrical pressure between the two parts of the circuit.

While increasing the voltage in a circuit will increase the flow of current, the actual flow depends not only on voltage, but on the resistance of the circuit. The standard unit for measuring circuit resistance is an ohm, measured by an ohmmeter. The ohmmeter is somewhat similar to an ammeter, but incorporates its own source of power so that a standard voltage is always present.

CIRCUITS

An actual electric circuit consists of four basic parts. These are: the power source, such as a generator or battery; a hot wire, which conducts the electricity under a relatively high voltage to the component supplied by the circuit; the load, such as a lamp, motor, resistor or relay coil; and the ground wire, which carries the current back to the source under very low voltage. In such a circuit the bulk of the resistance exists between the point where the hot wire is connected to the load, and the point where the load is grounded. In an automobile, the vehicle's frame or body, which is made of steel, is used as a part of the ground circuit for many of the electrical devices.

Remember that, in electrical testing, the voltmeter is connected in parallel with the circuit being tested (without disconnecting any wires) and measures the difference in voltage between the locations of the two probes; that the ammeter is connected in series with the load (the circuit is separated at one point and the ammeter inserted so it becomes a part of the circuit); and the ohmmeter is self-powered, so that all the power in the circuit should be off and the portion of the circuit to be measured contacted at either end by one of the probes of the meter.

For any electrical system to operate, it must make a complete circuit. This simply means that the power flow from the battery must make a complete circle. When an electrical component is operating, power flows from the battery to the component, passes through the component causing it to perform it to function (such as lighting a light bulb) and then returns to the battery through the ground of the circuit. This ground is usually (but not always) the metal part of the vehicle on which the electrical component is mounted.

Perhaps the easiest way to visualize this is to think of connecting a light bulb with two wires attached to it to your vehicle's battery. The battery in your car has two posts (negative and positive). If one of the two wires attached to the light bulb was attached to the negative post of the battery and the other wire was attached to the positive post of the battery, you would have a complete circuit. Current from the battery would flow out one post, through the wire attached to it and then to the light bulb, where it would pass through causing it to light. It would then leave the light bulb, travel through the other wire, and return to the other post of the battery.

AUTOMOTIVE CIRCUITS

The normal automotive circuit differs from this simple example in two ways. First, instead of having a return wire from the bulb to the battery, the light bulb return the current to the battery through the chassis of the vehicle. Since the negative battery cable is attached to the chassis and the chassis is made of electrically conductive metal, the chassis of the vehicle can serve as a ground wire to complete the circuit. Secondly, most automotive circuits contain switches to turn components on and off.

Some electrical components which require a large amount of current to operate also have a relay in their circuit. Since these circuits carry a large amount of current, the thickness of the wire in the circuit (gauge size) is also greater. If this large wire were connected from the component to the control switch on the instrument panel, and then back to the component, a voltage drop would occur in the circuit. To prevent this potential drop in voltage, an electromagnetic switch (relay) is used. The large wires in the circuit are connected from the car battery to one side of the relay, and from the opposite side of the relay to the component. The relay is normally open, preventing current from passing through the circuit. An additional, smaller wire is connected from the relay to the control switch for the circuit. When the control switch is turned on, it grounds the smaller wire from the relay and completes the circuit.

SHORT CIRCUITS

If you were to disconnect the light bulb (from the previous example of a light-bulb being connected to the battery by two wires) from the wires and touch the two wires together (please take our word for this; don't try it), the result will be a shower of sparks. A similar thing happens (on a smaller scale) when the power supply wire to a component or the electrical component itself becomes grounded before the normal ground connection for the circuit. To prevent damage to the system, the fuse for the circuit blows to interrupt the circuit — protecting the components from damage. Because grounding a wire from a power source makes a complete circuit — less the required component to use the power — the phenomenon is called a short circuit. The most common causes of short circuits are: the rubber insulation on a wire breaking or rubbing through to expose the current carrying core of the wire to a metal part of the car, or a shorted switch.

Some electrical systems on the car are protected by a circuit breaker which is, basically, a self-repairing fuse. When either of the described events takes place in a system which is protected by a circuit breaker, the circuit breaker opens the circuit the same way a fuse does. However, when either the short is removed from the circuit or the surge subsides, the circuit breaker resets itself and does not have to be replaced as a fuse does.

Electrical Troubleshooting

When diagnosing a specific problem, organized troubleshooting is a must. The complexity of a modern automobile demands that you approach any problem in a logical, organized manner. There are certain troubleshooting techniques that are standard:

1. Establish when the problem occurs. Does the problem appear only under certain conditions? Were there any noises, odors, or other unusual symptoms?

2. Isolate the problem area. To do this, make some simple tests and observations; then eliminate the systems that are working properly. Check for obvious problems such as broken wires, dirty connections or split/disconnected vacuum hoses. Always check the obvious before assuming something complicated is the cause.

3: Test for problems systematically to determine the cause once the problem area is isolated. Are all the components functioning properly? Is there power going to electrical switches and motors? Is there vacuum at vacuum switches and/or actuators? Is there a mechanical problem such as bent linkage or loose mounting screws? Performing careful, systematic checks will often turn up most causes on the first inspection without wasting time checking components that have little or no relationship to the problem.

4. Test all repairs after the work is done to make sure that the problem is fixed. Some causes can be traced to more than one component, so a careful verification of repair work is important in order to pick up additional malfunctions that may cause a problem to reappear or a different problem to arise. A blown fuse, for example, is a simple problem that may require more than another fuse to repair. If you don't look for a problem that caused a fuse to blow, a shorted wire (for example) may go undetected.

Experience has shown that most problems tend to be the result of a fairly simple and obvious cause, such as loose or corroded connectors or air leaks in the intake system. This makes careful inspection of components during testing essential to quick and accurate troubleshooting.

BASIC TROUBLESHOOTING THEORY

Electrical problems generally fall into one of three areas:
• The component that is not functioning is not receiving current.
• The component itself is not functioning.
• The component is not properly grounded.

Problems that fall into the first category are by far the most complicated. It is the current supply system to the component which contains all the switches, relay, fuses, etc.

The electrical system can be checked with a test light and a jumper wire. A test light is a device that looks like a pointed screwdriver with a wire attached to it. It has a light bulb in its handle. A jumper wire is a piece of insulated wire with an alligator clip attached to each end.

If a light bulb is not working, you must follow a systematic plan to determine which of the three causes is the villain.

1. Turn on the switch that controls the inoperable bulb.
2. Disconnect the power supply wire from the bulb.
3. Attach the ground wire to the test light to a good metal ground.
4. Touch the probe end of the test light to the end of the power supply wire that was disconnected from the bulb. If the bulb is receiving current, the test light will go on.

➡If the bulb is one which works only when the ignition key is turned on (turn signal), make sure the key is turned on.

If the test light does not go on, then the problem is in the circuit between the battery and the bulb. As mentioned before, this includes all the switches, fuses, and relays in the system. Turn to a wiring diagram and find the bulb on the diagram. Follow the wire that runs back to the battery. The problem is an open circuit between the battery and the bulb. If the fuse is blown and, when replaced, immediately blows again, there is a short circuit in the system which must be located and repaired. If there is a switch in the system, bypass it with a jumper wire. This is done by connecting one end of the jumper wire to the power supply wire into the switch and the other end of the jumper wire to the wire coming out of the switch. If the test

light illuminates with the jumper wire installed, the switch or whatever was bypassed is defective.

➡Never substitute the jumper wire for the bulb, as the bulb is the component required to use the power from the power source.

5. If the bulb in the test light goes on, then the current is getting to the bulb that is not working in the car. This eliminates the first of the three possible causes. Connect the power supply wire and connect a jumper wire from the bulb to a good metal ground. Do this with the switch which controls the bulb works with jumper wire installed, then it has a bad ground. This is usually caused by the metal area on which the bulb mounts to the car being coated with some type of foreign matter.

6. If neither test located the source of the trouble, then the light bulb itself is defective.

The above test procedure can be applied to any of the components of the chassis electrical system by substituting the component that is not working for the light bulb. Remember that for any electrical system to work, all connections must be clean and tight.

TEST EQUIPMENT

➡Pinpointing the exact cause of trouble in an electrical system can sometimes only be accomplished by the use of special test equipment. The following describes different types of commonly used test equipment and explains how to use them in diagnosis. In addition to the information covered below, the tool manufacturer's instructions booklet (provided with the tester) should be read and clearly understood before attempting any test procedures.

Jumper Wires

Jumper wires are simple, yet extremely valuable, pieces of test equipment. They are basically test wires which are used to bypass sections of a circuit. The simplest type of jumper wire is a length of multi-strand wire with an alligator clip at each end. Jumper wires are usually fabricated from lengths of standard automotive wire and whatever type of connector (alligator clip, spade connector or pin connector) that is required for the particular vehicle being tested. The well equipped tool box will have several different styles of jumper wires in several different lengths. Some jumper wires are made with three or more terminals coming from a common splice for special purpose testing. In cramped, hard-to-reach areas it is advisable to have insulated boots over the jumper wire terminals in order to prevent accidental grounding, sparks, and possible fire, especially when testing fuel system components.

Jumper wires are used primarily to locate open electrical circuits, on either the ground (-) side of the circuit or on the hot (+) side. If an electrical component fails to operate, connect the jumper wire between the component and a good ground. If the component operates only with the jumper installed, the ground circuit is open. If the ground circuit is good, but the component does not operate, the circuit between the power feed and component may be open. By moving the jumper wire successively back from the lamp toward the power source, you can isolate the area of the circuit where the open is located. When the component stops functioning, or the power is cut off, the open is in the segment of wire between the jumper and the point previously tested.

You can sometimes connect the jumper wire directly from the battery to the hot terminal of the component, but first make sure the component uses 12 volts in operation. Some electrical components, such as fuel injectors, are designed to operate on about 4 volts and running 12 volts directly to the injector terminals can cause damage.

By inserting an in-line fuse holder between a set of test leads, a fused jumper wire can be used for bypassing open circuits. Use a 5 amp fuse to provide protection against voltage spikes. When in doubt, use a voltmeter to check the voltage input to the component and measure how much voltage is normally being applied.

✳✳CAUTION

Never use jumpers made from wire that is of lighter gauge than that which is used in the circuit under test. If the jumper wire is of too small a gauge, it may overheat and possibly melt. Never use jumpers to bypass high resistance loads in a circuit. Bypassing resistances, in effect, creates a short circuit. This may, in turn, cause damage and fire. Jumper wires should only be used to bypass lengths of wire.

Unpowered Test Lights

The 12 volt test light is used to check circuits and components while electrical current is flowing through them. It is used for voltage and ground tests. Twelve volt test lights come in different styles but all have three main parts; a ground clip, a probe, and a light. The most commonly used 12 volt test lights have pick-type probes. To use a 12 volt test light, connect the ground clip to a good ground and probe wherever necessary with the pick. The pick should be sharp so that it can be probed into tight spaces.

✳✳CAUTION

Do not use a test light to probe electronic ignition spark plug or coil wires. Never use a pick-type test light to probe wiring on computer controlled systems unless specifically instructed to do so. Any wire insulation that is pierced by the test light probe should be taped and sealed with silicone after testing.

Like the jumper wire, the 12 volt test light is used to isolate opens in circuits. But, whereas the jumper wire is used to bypass the open to operate the load, the 12 volt test light is used to locate the presence of voltage in a circuit. If the test light glows, you know that there is power up to that point; if the 12 volt test light does not glow when its probe is inserted into the wire or connector, you know that there is an open circuit (no power). Move the test light in successive steps back toward the power source until the light in the handle does

glow. When it glows, the open is between the probe and point which was probed previously.

➡**The test light does not detect that 12 volts (or any particular amount of voltage) is present; it only detects that some voltage is present. It is advisable before using the test light to touch its terminals across the battery posts to make sure the light is operating properly.**

Self-Powered Test Lights

The self-powered test light usually contains a 1.5 volt penlight battery. One type of self-powered test light is similar in design to the 12 volt unit. This type has both the battery and the light in the handle, along with a pick-type probe tip. The second type has the light toward the open tip, so that the light illuminates the contact point. The self-powered test light is a dual purpose piece of test equipment. It can be used to test for either open or short circuits when power is isolated from the circuit (continuity test). A powered test light should not be used on any computer controlled system or component unless specifically instructed to do so. Many engine sensors can be destroyed by even this small amount of voltage applied directly to the terminals.

Voltmeters

A voltmeter is used to measure voltage at any point in a circuit, or to measure the voltage drop across any part of a circuit. It can also be used to check continuity in a wire or circuit by indicating current flow from one end to the other. Analog voltmeters usually have various scales on the meter dial and a selector switch to allow the selection of different voltages. The voltmeter has a positive and a negative lead. To avoid damage to the meter, always connect the negative lead to the negative (-) side of the circuit (to ground or nearest the ground side of the circuit) and connect the positive lead to the positive (+) side of the circuit (to the power source or the nearest power source). Note that the negative voltmeter lead will always be black and that the positive voltmeter will always be some color other than black (usually red).

Depending on how the voltmeter is connected into the circuit, it has several uses. A voltmeter can be connected either in parallel or in series with a circuit and it has a very high resistance to current flow. When connected in parallel, only a small amount of current will flow through the voltmeter current path; the rest will flow through the normal circuit current path and the circuit will work normally. When the voltmeter is connected in series with a circuit, only a small amount of current can flow through the circuit. The circuit will not work properly, but the voltmeter reading will show if the circuit is complete or not.

Ohmmeters

The ohmmeter is designed to read resistance (which is measured in ohms or Ω) in a circuit or component. Although there are several different styles of ohmmeters, all analog meters will usually have a selector switch which permits the measurement of different ranges of resistance (usually the selector switch allows the multiplication of the meter reading by 10, 100, 1000, and 10,000). A calibration knob allows the meter to be set at zero for accurate measurement. Since all ohmmeters are powered by an internal battery, the ohmmeter can be used as a self-powered test light. When the ohmmeter is connected, current from the ohmmeter flows through the circuit or component being tested. Since the ohmmeter's internal resistance and voltage are known values, the amount of current flow through the meter depends on the resistance of the circuit or component being tested.

The ohmmeter can be used to perform a continuity test for opens or shorts (either by observation of the meter needle or as a self-powered test light), and to read actual resistance in a circuit. It should be noted that the ohmmeter is used to check the resistance of a component or wire while there is no voltage applied to the circuit. Current flow from an outside voltage source (such as the vehicle battery) can damage the ohmmeter, so the circuit or component should be isolated from the vehicle electrical system before any testing is done. Since the ohmmeter uses its own voltage source, either lead can be connected to any test point.

➡**When checking diodes or other solid state components, the ohmmeter leads can only be connected one way in order to measure current flow in a single direction. Make sure the positive (+) and negative (-) terminal connections are as described in the test procedures to verify the one-way diode operation.**

In using the meter for making continuity checks, do not be concerned with the actual resistance readings. Zero resistance, or any ohm reading, indicates continuity in the circuit. Infinite resistance indicates an open in the circuit. A high resistance reading where there should be none indicates a problem in the circuit. Checks for short circuits are made in the same manner as checks for open circuits except that the circuit must be isolated from both power and normal ground. Infinite resistance indicates no continuity to ground, while zero resistance indicates a dead short to ground.

Ammeters

An ammeter measures the amount of current flowing through a circuit in units called amperes or amps. Amperes are units of electron flow which indicate how fast the electrons are flowing through the circuit. Since Ohms Law dictates that current flow in a circuit is equal to the circuit voltage divided by the total circuit resistance, increasing voltage also increases the current level (amps). Likewise, any decrease in resistance will increase the amount of amps in a circuit. At normal operating voltage, most circuits have a characteristic amount of amperes, called "current draw" which can be measured using an ammeter. By referring to a specified current draw rating, measuring the amperes, and comparing the two values, one can determine what is happening within the circuit to aid in diagnosis. An open circuit, for example, will not allow any current to flow so the ammeter reading will be zero. More current flows through a heavily loaded circuit or when the charging system is operating.

An ammeter is always connected in series with the circuit being tested. All of the current that normally flows through the circuit must also flow through the ammeter; if there is any other path for the current to follow, the ammeter reading will not be accurate. The ammeter itself has very little resistance to current flow and therefore will not affect the circuit, but it will measure current draw only when the circuit is closed and electricity is flowing. Excessive current draw can blow fuses

and drain the battery, while a reduced current draw can cause motors to run slowly, lights to dim and other components to not operate properly. The ammeter can help diagnose these conditions by locating the cause of the high or low reading.

Multimeters

Different combinations of test meters can be built into a single unit designed for specific tests. Some of the more common combination test devices are known as Volt/Amp testers, Tach/Dwell meters, or Digital Multimeters. The Volt/Amp tester is used for charging system, starting system or battery tests and consists of a voltmeter, an ammeter and a variable resistance carbon pile. The voltmeter will usually have at least two ranges for use with 6, 12 and/or 24 volt systems. The ammeter also has more than one range for testing various levels of battery loads and starter current draw. The carbon pile can be adjusted to offer different amounts of resistance. The Volt/Amp tester has heavy leads to carry large amounts of current and many later models have an inductive ammeter pickup that clamps around the wire to simplify test connections. On some models, the ammeter also has a zero-center scale to allow testing of charging and starting systems without switching leads or polarity. A digital multimeter is a voltmeter, ammeter and ohmmeter combined in an instrument which gives a digital readout. These are often used when testing solid state circuits because of their high input impedance (usually 10 megohms or more).

The tach/dwell meter that combines a tachometer and a dwell (cam angle) meter is a specialized kind of voltmeter. The tachometer scale is marked to show engine speed in rpm and the dwell scale is marked to show degrees of distributor shaft rotation. In most electronic ignition systems, dwell is determined by the control unit, but the dwell meter can also be used to check the duty cycle (operation) of some electronic engine control systems. Some tach/dwell meters are powered by an internal battery, while others take their power from the vehicle battery in use. The battery powered testers usually require calibration (much like an ohmmeter) before testing.

TESTING

Open Circuits

To use the self-powered test light or a multimeter to check for open circuits, first isolate the circuit from the vehicle's 12 volt power source by disconnecting the battery or wiring harness connector. Connect the test light or ohmmeter ground clip to a good ground and probe sections of the circuit sequentially with the test light. (start from either end of the circuit). If the light is out/or there is infinite resistance, the open is between the probe and the circuit ground. If the light is on/or the meter shows continuity, the open is between the probe and end of the circuit toward the power source.

Short Circuits

By isolating the circuit both from power and from ground, and using a self-powered test light or multimeter, you can check for shorts to ground in the circuit. Isolate the circuit from power and ground. Connect the test light or ohmmeter ground clip to a good ground and probe any easy-to-reach test point in the circuit. If the light comes on or there is continuity, there is a short somewhere in the circuit. To isolate the short, probe a test point at either end of the isolated circuit (the light should be on/there should be continuity). Leave the test light probe engaged and open connectors, switches, remove parts, etc., sequentially, until the light goes out/continuity is broken. When the light goes out, the short is between the last circuit component opened and the previous circuit opened.

➡**The battery in the test light and does not provide much current. A weak battery may not provide enough power to illuminate the test light even when a complete circuit is made (especially if there are high resistances in the circuit). Always make sure that the test battery is strong. To check the battery, briefly touch the ground clip to the probe; if the light glows brightly the battery is strong enough for testing. Never use a self-powered test light to perform checks for opens or shorts when power is applied to the electrical system under test. The 12 volt vehicle power will quickly burn out the light bulb in the test light.**

Available Voltage Measurement

Set the voltmeter selector switch to the 20V position and connect the meter negative lead to the negative post of the battery. Connect the positive meter lead to the positive post of the battery and turn the ignition switch **ON** to provide a load. Read the voltage on the meter or digital display. A well charged battery should register over 12 volts. If the meter reads below 11.5 volts, the battery power may be insufficient to operate the electrical system properly. This test determines voltage available from the battery and should be the first step in any electrical trouble diagnosis procedure. Many electrical problems, especially on computer controlled systems, can be caused by a low state of charge in the battery. Excessive corrosion at the battery cable terminals can cause a poor contact that will prevent proper charging and full battery current flow.

Normal battery voltage is 12 volts when fully charged. When the battery is supplying current to one or more circuits it is said to be "under load." When everything is off the electrical system is under a "no-load" condition. A fully charged battery may show about 12.5 volts at no load; will drop to 12 volts under medium load; and will drop even lower under heavy load. If the battery is partially discharged the voltage decrease under heavy load may be excessive, even though the battery shows 12 volts or more at no load. When allowed to discharge further, the battery's available voltage under load will decrease more severely. For this reason, it is important that the battery be fully charged during all testing procedures to avoid errors in diagnosis and incorrect test results.

Voltage Drop

When current flows through a resistance, the voltage beyond the resistance is reduced (the larger the current, the greater the reduction in voltage). When no current is flowing, there is no voltage drop because there is no current flow. All points in the circuit which are connected to the power source are at the same voltage as the power source. The total voltage drop always equals the total source voltage. In a long circuit with many connectors, a series of small, unwanted voltage drops due to corrosion at the connectors can add up to a total loss of voltage which impairs the operation of the normal loads in the circuit. The maximum allowable voltage drop under load is critical, especially if there is more than one high resistance problem in a circuit because all voltage drops are cumulative. A small drop is normal due to the resistance of the conductors.

INDIRECT COMPUTATION OF VOLTAGE DROPS

1. Set the voltmeter selector switch to the 20 volt position.
2. Connect the meter negative lead to a good ground.
3. While operating the circuit, probe all loads in the circuit with the positive meter lead and observe the voltage readings. A drop should be noticed after the first load. But, there should be little or no voltage drop before the first load.

DIRECT MEASUREMENT OF VOLTAGE DROPS

1. Set the voltmeter switch to the 20 volt position.
2. Connect the voltmeter negative lead to the ground side of the load to be measured.
3. Connect the positive lead to the positive side of the resistance or load to be measured.
4. Read the voltage drop directly on the 20 volt scale.

Too high a voltage indicates too high a resistance. If, for example, a blower motor runs too slowly, you can determine if perhaps there is too high a resistance in the resistor pack. By taking voltage drop readings in all parts of the circuit, you can isolate the problem. Too low a voltage drop indicates too low a resistance. Take the blower motor for example again. If a blower motor runs too fast in the MED and/or LOW position, the problem might be isolated in the resistor pack by taking voltage drop readings in all parts of the circuit to locate a possibly shorted resistor.

HIGH RESISTANCE TESTING

1. Set the voltmeter selector switch to the 4 volt position.
2. Connect the voltmeter positive lead to the positive post of the battery.
3. Turn on the headlights and heater blower to provide a load.
4. Probe various points in the circuit with the negative voltmeter lead.
5. Read the voltage drop on the 4 volt scale. Some average maximum allowable voltage drops are:
- FUSE PANEL: 0.7 volts
- IGNITION SWITCH: 0.5 volts
- HEADLIGHT SWITCH: 0.7 volts
- IGNITION COIL (+): 0.5 volts
- ANY OTHER LOAD: 1.3 volts

➡**Voltage drops are all measured while a load is operating; without current flow, there will be no voltage drop.**

Resistance Measurement

The batteries in an ohmmeter will weaken with age and temperature, so the ohmmeter must be calibrated or "zeroed" before taking measurements. To zero the meter, place the selector switch in its lowest range and touch the two ohmmeter leads together. Turn the calibration knob until the meter needle is exactly on zero.

➡️**All analog (needle) type ohmmeters must be zeroed before use, but some digital ohmmeter models are automatically calibrated when the switch is turned on. Self-calibrating digital ohmmeters do not have an adjusting knob, but its a good idea to check for a zero readout before use by touching the leads together. All computer controlled systems require the use of a digital ohmmeter with at least 10 megohms impedance for testing. Before any test procedures are attempted, make sure the ohmmeter used is compatible with the electrical system or damage to the on-board computer could result.**

To measure resistance, first isolate the circuit from the vehicle power source by disconnecting the battery cables or the harness connector. Make sure the key is **OFF** when disconnecting any components or the battery. Where necessary, also isolate at least one side of the circuit to be checked in order to avoid reading parallel resistances. Parallel circuit resistances will always give a lower reading than the actual resistance of either of the branches. When measuring the resistance of parallel circuits, the total resistance will always be lower than the smallest resistance in the circuit. Connect the meter leads to both sides of the circuit (wire or component) and read the actual measured ohms on the meter scale. Make sure the selector switch is set to the proper ohm scale for the circuit being tested to avoid misreading the ohmmeter test value.

✳✳WARNING

Never use an ohmmeter with power applied to the circuit. Like the self-powered test light, the ohmmeter is designed to operate on its own power supply. The normal 12 volt automotive electrical system current could damage the meter!

Wiring Harnesses

The average automobile contains about ½ mile of wiring, with hundreds of individual connections. To protect the many wires from damage and to keep them from becoming a confusing tangle, they are organized into bundles, enclosed in plastic or taped together and called wiring harnesses. Different harnesses serve different parts of the vehicle. Individual wires are color coded to help trace them through a harness where sections are hidden from view.

Automotive wiring or circuit conductors can be in any one of three forms:

1. Single strand wire
2. Multi-strand wire
3. Printed circuitry

Single strand wire has a solid metal core and is usually used inside such components as alternators, motors, relays and other devices. Multi-strand wire has a core made of many small strands of wire twisted together into a single conductor. Most of the wiring in an automotive electrical system is made up of multi-strand wire, either as a single conductor or grouped together in a harness. All wiring is color coded on the insulator, either as a solid color or as a colored wire with an identification stripe. A printed circuit is a thin film of copper or other conductor that is printed on an insulator backing. Occasionally, a printed circuit is sandwiched between two sheets of plastic for more protection and flexibility. A complete printed circuit, consisting of conductors, insulating material and connectors for lamps or other components is called a printed circuit board. Printed circuitry is used in place of individual wires or harnesses in places where space is limited, such as behind instrument panels.

Since automotive electrical systems are very sensitive to changes in resistance, the selection of properly sized wires is critical when systems are repaired. A loose or corroded connection or a replacement wire that is too small for the circuit will add extra resistance and an additional voltage drop to the circuit. A ten percent voltage drop can result in slow or erratic motor operation, for example, even though the circuit is complete. The wire gauge number is an expression of the cross-section area of the conductor. The most common system for expressing wire size is the American Wire Gauge (AWG) system.

Gauge numbers are assigned to conductors of various cross-section areas. As gauge number increases, area decreases and the conductor becomes smaller. A 5 gauge conductor is smaller than a 1 gauge conductor and a 10 gauge is smaller than a 5 gauge. As the cross-section area of a conductor decreases, resistance increases and so does the gauge number. A conductor with a higher gauge number will carry less current than a conductor with a lower gauge number.

➡️**Gauge wire size refers to the size of the conductor, not the size of the complete wire. It is possible to have two wires of the same gauge with different diameters because one may have thicker insulation than the other.**

12 volt automotive electrical systems generally use 10, 12, 14, 16 and 18 gauge wire. Main power distribution circuits and larger accessories usually use 10 and 12 gauge wire. Battery cables are usually 4 or 6 gauge, although 1 and 2 gauge wires are occasionally used. Wire length must also be considered when making repairs to a circuit. As conductor length increases, so does resistance. An 18 gauge wire, for example, can carry a 10 amp load for 10 feet without excessive voltage drop; however if a 15 foot wire is required for the same 10 amp load, it must be a 16 gauge wire.

An electrical schematic shows the electrical current paths when a circuit is operating properly. It is essential to understand how a circuit works before trying to figure out why it doesn't. Schematics break the entire electrical system down into individual circuits and show only one particular circuit. In a schematic, no attempt is made to represent wiring and components as they physically appear on the vehicle; switches and other components are shown as simply as possible. Face views of harness connectors show the cavity or terminal locations in all multi-pin connectors to help locate test points.

If you need to backprobe a connector while it is on the component, the order of the terminals must be mentally reversed. The wire color code can help in this situation, as well as a keyway, lock tab or other reference mark.

WIRING REPAIR

Soldering is a quick, efficient method of joining metals permanently. Everyone who has the occasion to make wiring repairs should know how to solder. Electrical connections that are soldered are far less likely to come apart and will conduct electricity much better than connections that are only "pigtailed" together. The most popular (and preferred) method of soldering is with an electrical soldering gun. Soldering irons are available in many sizes and wattage ratings. Irons with higher wattage ratings deliver higher temperatures and recover lost heat faster. A small soldering iron rated for no more than 50 watts is recommended, especially on electrical systems where excess heat can damage the components being soldered.

There are three ingredients necessary for successful soldering; proper flux, good solder and sufficient heat. A soldering flux is necessary to clean the metal of tarnish, prepare it for soldering and to enable the solder to spread into tiny crevices. When soldering, always use a rosin core solder which is non-corrosive and will not attract moisture once the job is finished. Other types of flux (acid core) will leave a residue that will attract moisture and cause the wires to corrode. Tin is a unique metal with a low melting point. In a molten state, it dissolves and alloys easily with many metals. Solder is made by mixing tin with lead. The most common proportions are 40/60, 50/50 and 60/40, with the percentage of tin listed first. Low priced solders usually contain less tin, making them very difficult for a beginner to use because more heat is required to melt the solder. A common solder is 40/60 which is well suited for all-around general use, but 60/40 melts easier and is preferred for electrical work.

Soldering Techniques

Successful soldering requires that the metals to be joined be heated to a temperature that will melt the solder, usually 360-460°F (182-238°C). Contrary to popular belief, the purpose of the soldering iron is not to melt the solder itself, but to heat the parts being soldered to a temperature high enough to melt the solder when it is touched to the work. Melting flux-cored solder on the soldering iron will usually destroy the effectiveness of the flux.

➡**Soldering tips are made of copper for good heat conductivity, but must be "tinned" regularly for quick transference of heat to the project and to prevent the solder from sticking to the iron. To "tin" the iron, simply heat it and touch the flux-cored solder to the tip; the solder will flow over the hot tip. Wipe the excess off with a clean rag, but be careful as the iron will be hot.**

After some use, the tip may become pitted. If so, simply dress the tip smooth with a smooth file and "tin" the tip again. Flux-cored solder will remove oxides but rust, bits of insulation and oil or grease must be removed with a wire brush or emery cloth. For maximum strength in soldered parts, the joint must start off clean and tight. Weak joints will result in gaps too wide for the solder to bridge.

If a separate soldering flux is used, it should be brushed or swabbed on only those areas that are to be soldered. Most solders contain a core of flux and separate fluxing is unnecessary. Hold the work to be soldered firmly. It is best to solder on a wooden board, because a metal vise will only rob the piece to be soldered of heat and make it difficult to melt the solder. Hold the soldering tip with the broadest face against the work to be soldered. Apply solder under the tip close to the work, using enough solder to give a heavy film between the iron and the piece being soldered, while moving slowly and making sure the solder melts properly. Keep the work level or the solder will run to the lowest part and favor the thicker parts, because these require more heat to melt the solder. If the soldering tip overheats (the solder coating on the face of the tip burns up), it should be retinned. Once the soldering is completed, let the soldered joint stand until cool. Tape and seal all soldered wire splices after the repair has cooled.

Wire Harness Connectors

Most connectors in the engine compartment or that are otherwise exposed to the elements are protected against moisture and dirt which could create oxidation and deposits on the terminals.

These special connectors are weather-proof. All repairs require the use of a special terminal and the tool required to service it. This tool is used to remove the pin and sleeve terminals. If removal is attempted with an ordinary pick, there is a good chance that the terminal will be bent or deformed. Unlike standard blade type terminals, these weather-proof terminals cannot be straightened once they are bent. Make certain that the connectors are properly seated and all of the sealing rings are in place when connecting leads. On some models, a hinge-type flap provides a backup or secondary locking feature for the terminals. Most secondary locks are used to improve connector reliability by retaining the terminals if the small terminal lock tangs are not positioned properly.

Molded-on connectors require complete replacement of the connection. This means splicing a new connector assembly into the harness. All splices should be soldered to insure proper contact. Use care when probing the connections or replacing terminals in them as it is possible to short between opposite terminals. If this happens to the wrong terminal pair, it is possible to damage certain components. Always use jumper wires between connectors for circuit checking and never probe through weatherproof seals.

Open circuits are often difficult to locate by sight because corrosion or terminal misalignment are hidden by the connectors. Merely wiggling a connector on a sensor or in the wiring harness may correct the open circuit condition. This should always be considered when an open circuit or a failed sensor is indicated. Intermittent problems may also be caused by oxidized or loose connections. When using a circuit tester for diagnosis, always probe connections from the wire side. Be careful not to damage sealed connectors with test probes.

All wiring harnesses should be replaced with identical parts, using the same gauge wire and connectors. When signal wires are spliced into a harness, use wire with high temperature insulation only. It is seldom necessary to replace a complete harness. If replacement is necessary, pay close attention to insure proper harness routing. Secure the harness with suitable plastic wire clamps to prevent vibrations from causing the harness to wear in spots or contact any hot components.

➡**Weatherproof connectors cannot be replaced with standard connectors. Instructions are provided with replacement connector and terminal packages. Some wire harnesses have mounting indicators (usually pieces of colored tape) to mark where the harness is to be secured.**

In making wiring repairs, its important that you always replace damaged wires with wiring of the same gauge as the wire being replaced. The heavier the wire, the smaller the gauge number. Wires are color-coded to aid in identification and whenever possible the same color coded wire should be used for replacement. A wire stripping and crimping tool is necessary to install solderless terminal connectors. Test all crimps by pulling on the wires; it should not be possible to pull the wires out of a good crimp.

Wires which are open, exposed or otherwise damaged are repaired by simple splicing. Where possible, if the wiring harness is accessible and the damaged place in the wire can be located, it is best to open the harness and check for all possible damage. In an inaccessible harness, the wire must be bypassed with a new insert, usually taped to the outside of the old harness.

When replacing fusible links, be sure to use fusible link wire, NOT ordinary automotive wire. Make sure the fusible segment is of the same gauge and construction as the one being replaced and double the stripped end when crimping the terminal connector for a good contact. The melted (open) fusible link segment of the wiring harness should be cut off as close to the harness as possible, then a new segment spliced in as described. In the case of a damaged fusible link that feeds two harness wires, the harness connections should be replaced with two fusible link wires so that each circuit will have its own separate protection.

➡**Most of the problems caused in the wiring harness are due to bad ground connections. Always check all vehicle ground connections for corrosion or looseness before performing any power feed checks to eliminate the chance of a bad ground affecting the circuit.**

Hard-Shell Connectors

Unlike molded connectors, the terminal contacts in hard-shell connectors can be replaced. Weatherproof hard-shell connectors with the leads molded into the shell have non-replaceable terminal ends. Replacement usually involves the use of a special terminal removal tool that depresses the locking tangs (barbs) on the connector terminal and allows the connector to be removed from the rear of the shell. The connector shell should be replaced if it shows any evidence of burning, melting, cracks, or breaks. Replace individual terminals that are burnt, corroded, distorted or loose.

➡**The insulation crimp must be tight to prevent the insulation from sliding back on the wire when the wire is pulled. The insulation must be visibly compressed under the crimp tabs, and the ends of the crimp should be turned in for a firm grip on the insulation.**

The wire crimp must be made with all wire strands inside the crimp. The terminal must be fully compressed on the wire strands with the ends of the crimp tabs turned in to make a firm grip on the wire. Check all connections with an ohmmeter to insure a good contact. There should be no measurable resistance between the wire and the terminal when connected.

Add-On Electrical Equipment

The electrical system in your vehicle is designed to perform under reasonable operating conditions without interference between components. Before any additional electrical equipment is installed, it is recommended that you consult your dealer or a reputable repair facility that is familiar with the vehicle and its systems.

If the vehicle is equipped with mobile radio equipment and/or mobile telephone, it may have an effect upon the operation of the ECM. Radio Frequency Interference (RFI) from the communications system can be picked up by the vehicle's wiring harnesses and conducted into the ECM, giving it the wrong messages at the wrong time. Although well shielded against RFI, the ECM should be further protected by taking the following measures:

• Install the antenna as far as possible from the ECM. For instance, if the ECM is located behind the center console area, then the antenna should be mounted at the rear of the vehicle.

• Keep the antenna wiring a minimum of eight inches away from any wiring running to the ECM and from the ECM itself. NEVER wind the antenna wire around any other wiring.

• Mount the equipment as far from the ECM as possible. Be very careful during installation not to drill through any wires or short a wire harness with a mounting screw.

• Insure that the electrical feed wire(s) to the equipment are properly and tightly connected. Loose connectors can cause interference.

• Make certain that the equipment is properly grounded to the vehicle. Poor grounding can damage expensive equipment.

SEAT BELT/STARTER INTERLOCK

General Information

▶ **See Figure 1**

In addition to the light and buzzer used in 1972-73, a starter interlock was incorporated into the seat belt warning system in 1974.

The car cannot be started unless the seat belts are fastened in a specific order. The driver (and front seat passenger) must get into the car, close the door(s), sit down, and then fasten the seat belts. If the seat belts are not fastened, or if they are fastened before the driver (and passenger) sit down, the car will not start, and the light and buzzer will operate. This prevents the belts from being permanently fastened and shoved behind the seats.

In case of a system failure and to make it easier for mechanics working on a car, a manual bypass button is located under the hood. Pushing this button allows one free

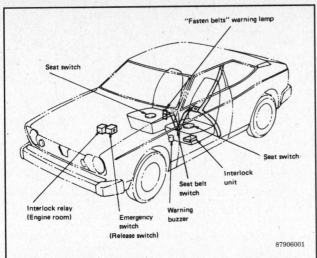

Seat switch

"Fasten belts" warning lamp

Seat switch

Interlock unit

Seat belt switch

Interlock relay (Engine room)

Emergency switch (Release switch)

Warning buzzer

87906001

Fig. 1 Component location — 1974 seat belt interlock system

start, i.e., without fastening the seat belt. Each additional free start requires that the button be pushed again.

➡If a package, handbag, etc., is placed on the passenger's seat, the car may not start, and the light and buzzer may come on as well, even if there is no one sitting in the seat. Either fasten the seat belt or remove the item.

The following components are used for the seat belt/starter interlock system: a logic module (transistorized), two pressure sensitive front seat switches, a starter relay, a bypass (emergency start button, two seat belt buckle switches, a warning buzzer, and a warning light.

SERVICE

Repair of the seat belt interlock components is limited to their replacement. Testing the system requires the use of a special tester, which connects to the seat belt/starter interlock system at several points. About the only place that you are likely to find the tester is at your local Subaru dealer's. Because of this, repair and testing are best left to a dealer.

If the warning light bulb burns out, access to it may be gained by removing the instrument cluster.

HEATER

Blower Motor

REMOVAL & INSTALLATION

ff-1 and 1300G Models

▶ **See Figure 2**

1. Disconnect the negative (-) battery cable.
2. Detach the heater control cable at the blower housing in the front of the engine compartment by removing the cable retaining circlip and the sheath securing nut.
3. Disengage the blower motor connections at the blower motor.
4. Remove its clamps and take the hot air duct off the blower housing.
5. Unbolt the sub-radiator shroud at the housing.
6. Remove the bolts which secure the housing and lift it out of the car.
7. To remove the motor and fan assembly from the housing, unfasten the motor securing screws.

To install:

8. Install the motor into the housing.
9. Position the blower housing into the vehicle and secure with the retainer fasteners.
10. Install the sub-radiator shroud.
11. Install the hot air duct onto the blower housing and engage the electrical connections.

12. Install the heater control cable.
13. Connect the battery cable.

Except ff-1 and 1300G Models

▶ **See Figures 3, 4, 5, 6, 7 and 8**

1. Disconnect the negative (-) battery cable.
2. Remove the luggage shelf and glovebox.
3. Detach the heater duct at the blower case.
4. Set the mode lever to CIRC for access and then disconnect the vacuum hose at the actuator.
5. Disengage the blower electrical connector.
6. Remove the actuator from the blower case by removing two screws and a clip.
7. Remove the blower case assembly from the body of the heater unit.
8. Remove the two bolts, and remove the blower and motor assembly and seal from the case.
9. If you're replacing the motor, remove the attaching nut and washers, and pull the blower off the motor shaft. Transfer these parts to the new motor.
10. Before installation, make sure the seal is in good condition or, if necessary, replace it.
11. Installation is in the reverse of removal.

➡Some Subaru owners report that the blower may sometimes rub the case in which it is mounted as it warms up. If this seems to be the case (you hear a rubbing noise after the blower has run for a while), ascertain that the blower is properly mounted to the shaft. If so, replace the motor assembly.

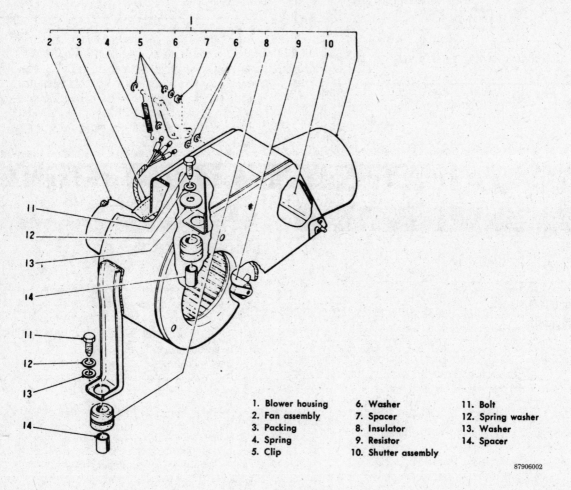

1. Blower housing
2. Fan assembly
3. Packing
4. Spring
5. Clip
6. Washer
7. Spacer
8. Insulator
9. Resistor
10. Shutter assembly
11. Bolt
12. Spring washer
13. Washer
14. Spacer

87906002

Fig. 2 Blower assembly used on ff-1 and 1300G models

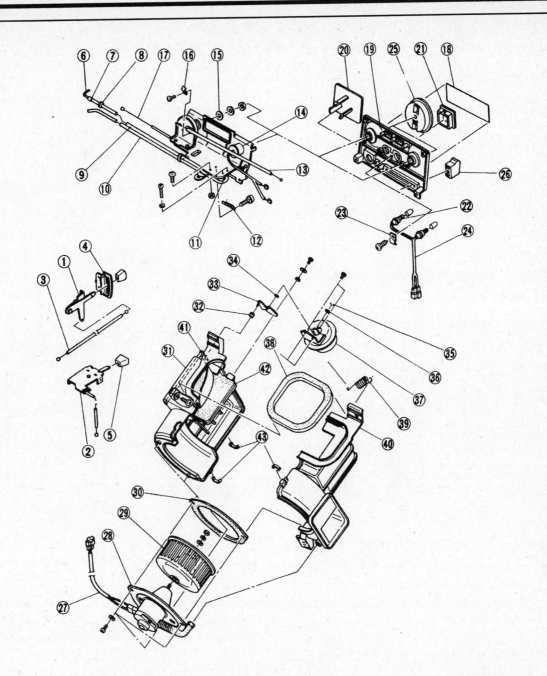

1	Fresh air ventilation lever (Standard type)
2	Fresh air ventilation lever (Multi type)
3	Ventilation cable
4	Ventilation grille
5	Ventilation knob
6	Vacuum pipe
7	Vacuum hose
8	Check valve
9	Vacuum hose
10	Vacuum hose
11	Vacuum switch
12	Spring
13	Temperature control cable
14	Fan switch
15	Bushing
16	Cable clamp
17	Mode control cable
18	Plate
19	Panel
20	Cigarette lighter cap
21	Rear defogger switch
22	Bulbs
23	Cord clamp
24	Cord assembly
25	Fan and temperature control knobs
26	Mode lever knob
27	Harness
28	Motor assembly
29	Blower
30	Packing
31	Blower case (R.H.)
32	Bushing
33	Intake shutter lever
34	Spacer
35	Clip
36	Bushing
37	Actuator
38	Packing
39	Intake shutter return spring
40	Blower case (L.H.)
41	Intake shutter shaft
42	Intake shutter
43	Springs

87906003

Fig. 3 Blower assembly and control system — all models similar except ff-1 and 1300G

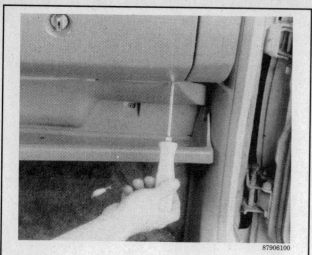

Fig. 4 Remove the screws securing the luggage shelf . . .

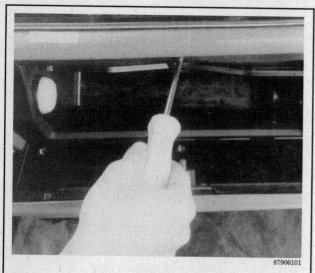

Fig. 5 . . . and the glovebox

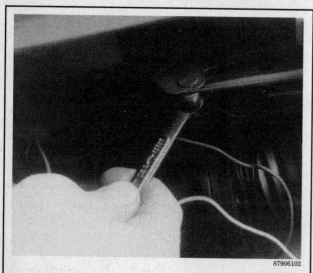

Fig. 6 Detach the heater duct at the case . . .

Fig. 7 . . . then remove the blower assembly

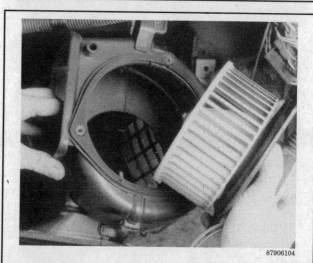

Fig. 8 Separate the blower and motor assembly from its mount

Heater Assembly

REMOVAL & INSTALLATION

1972-73 GL and DL Models
▶ See Figure 9

❊❊CAUTION

When draining the coolant, keep in mind that cats and dogs are attracted by ethylene glycol antifreeze, and are quite likely to drink any that is left in an uncovered container or in puddles on the ground. This will prove fatal in sufficient quantity. Always drain the coolant into a sealable container. Coolant should be reused unless it is contaminated or several years old.

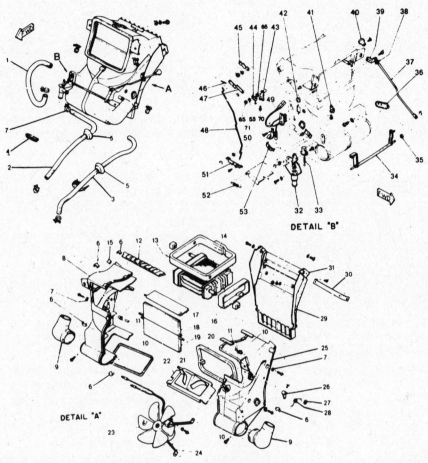

DETAIL "B"

DETAIL "A"

1. Hose	14. Heater core	27. Speed nut
2. Heater inlet hose	15. Gasket	28. Return spring
3. Heater outlet hose	16. Gasket	29. Case (C)
4. Cushion	17. Shutter	30. Bracket
5. Grommet	18. Shutter	31. Gasket
6. Spring	19. Shuter	32. Water valve
7. Grommet	20. Gasket	33. Spring
8. Case (B)	21. Gasket	34. Water valve connecting rod
9. Duct	22. Shutter	35. Washer
10. Grommet	23. Heater fan	36. Bracket
11. Spacer	24. Bracket	37. Water valve rod
12. Guide	25. Case (A)	38. Spacer
13. Gasket	26. Shutter lever	39. Bracket

40. Water valve knob
41. Shutter lever
42. Grommet (register)
43. Shutter lever
44. Return spring
45. Shutter lever
46. Return spring
47. Shutter lever
48. Shutter rod
49. Register
50. Clip
51. Shutter lever
52. Return spring

87906004

Fig. 9 Exploded view of the GL and DL heater assembly

The blower motor and the heater core are located in the heater unit. In order to service either of these components, the heater unit must be removed from the vehicle. In order to remove the heater unit from the vehicle, the entire instrument panel has to be removed.

1. Disconnect the negative (-) terminal of the battery.
2. Unscrew the nuts which retain the instrument panel to the body at both ends.
3. Remove the screws which hold the upper panel face of the instrument panel to the body bracket which is attached to the firewall.
4. Remove the bolts which retain the steering bracket and the steering shaft.
5. Loosen the nuts which hold the lower side of the instrument panel to the steering bracket.
6. Disconnect the defroster hoses.
7. Disconnect the heater control rod and wiring harness.
8. Disconnect and tag the following wiring and cables:
   a. Remove the speedometer cable hanger spring.
   b. Disconnect the speedometer cable from the speedometer.
   c. Disengage all of the electrical wiring connected to the instrument panel.
   d. Disconnect the antenna lead.
9. Remove the instrument panel from the vehicle being careful of interference between the side end of the instrument panel and the front pillars.
10. Drain the coolant from the radiator.
11. Disconnect the heater hoses on the engine side, both the inlet and the outlet hoses.
12. Remove the console by removing the six attaching screws.
13. Disconnect the heater control assembly and the heater unit by disengaging the room shutter cable and the two air inlet control rods.
14. Disconnect the wiring harnesses of the fan motor, the main harness, and the motor control switch wirings.
15. Remove the heater unit mounting bolts.
16. Lift the assembly to the side being careful of the stopper at the bottom of the unit.
17. Remove the grommet on the firewall at this time.
18. Remove the unit assembly.
19. Remove the blower fan motor, and the heater core.

To install:
20. Install the blower fan motor and heater core, then secure the unit with the mounting bolts.
21. Connect the motor control switch wiring, the main harness and the fan motor harness.
22. Install the air inlet control rods, and the room shutter cable to the heater unit, then connect the heater control assembly.
23. Install the console and tighten the six attaching screws securely.
24. Install the heater hoses.
25. Install the instrument panel and front pillars.
26. Engage the antenna lead and all electrical wiring connected to the instrument panel.
27. Connect the heater control rod and wiring harness.
28. Install the upper panel face to the instrument panel.
29. Install the steering bracket and shaft and tighten securely.

30. Install and tighten the nuts on both ends of the instrument panel.
31. Connect the negative battery cable.
32. Fill the cooling system, start the engine then check the heater system to make sure it is operating properly and does not leak.

1974 Models

The heater unit contains the core and blower. The entire assembly must be removed from the car before either the blower or core can be serviced. To remove the heater unit:
1. Disconnect the negative (-) battery cable.
2. Drain the coolant from the radiator.

✳✳CAUTION

When draining the coolant, keep in mind that cats and dogs are attracted by ethylene glycol antifreeze, and are quite likely to drink any that is left in an uncovered container or in puddles on the ground. This will prove fatal in sufficient quantity. Always drain the coolant into a sealable container. Coolant should be reused unless it is contaminated or several years old.

3. Disconnect the heater water hoses at the engine.
4. Remove the console by unfastening its screws and lifting it out.
5. Unfasten the screws which secure the parcel shelf and remove it from under the instrument panel.
6. Remove the instrument cluster.
7. Pull the knob off the ventilator lever.
8. Remove the ventilator grille by unfastening the two screws at each end.
9. Disconnect the control cables from the heater valve by unfastening the cable clamp and retaining nut.
10. Detach the control rod from the heater shutter (door).
11. Disengage the heater blower multi-connector.
12. Unfasten the heater housing securing bolts and remove the housing from underneath the dash.
13. Unfasten the two housing screws and spring, then remove the housing.
14. Separate the defroster duct from the heater assembly.
15. Remove the water hoses.
16. Unfasten the two heater valve screws and remove the valve.
17. Remove the shutter control rod from the link.
18. Unfasten the link screws, and remove the link.
19. Remove the heater core assembly.
20. Disconnect the fan motor wiring harness, loosen its 3 retaining screws, and separate it from the core, complete with blower.

To install:
21. Connect the heater core and blower to the fan motor wiring harness then secure the unit with the 3 retaining screws.
22. Connect the shutter control rod to the heater control link.
23. Install the heater valve and connect the water hoses.
24. Connect the defroster duct to the heater assembly.
25. Reassemble the heater housing and install it into the vehicle.
26. Engage the heater blower multi-connector.
27. Connect the heater control rod to the shutter.

28. Connect the control cable to the heater valve.
29. Position the vent grill and install the retainer screws.
30. Place the vent knob onto the lever.
31. Install the instrument cluster and parcel shelf.
32. Install the console.
33. Connect the heater water hoses.
34. Fill the radiator with coolant.
35. Connect the negative battery cable.
36. Start the engine and check for leaks.
37. Adjust the shutter control rod as follows:

   a. Loosen the screw which attaches the air intake shutter (door) control rod to its link.

   b. Push the link down as far as it will go.

   c. Slide the heater control lever to CIRC.

   d. Fasten the shutter control rod and link securing screw.

38. Adjust the heater valve cable as follows:

   a. Slide the temperature control lever to COOL.

   b. Pull the lever on the heater valve toward the driver's side and secure the control cable to it with the clamp.

   c. Slide the temperature control to WARM and push the heater valve lever outward.

   d. Fasten the outer cable to the heater valve cable with the clamp.

1975-79 Models

The heater unit contains the core and blower. The entire assembly must be removed from the car before either the blower or core can be serviced. To remove the heater unit:

1. Disconnect the the negative (-) battery cable.
2. Remove the console, luggage shelf, meter and visor assembly, and center ventilation grill.
3. Drain the coolant and disconnect the two heater hoses in the engine compartment.
4. Disconnect the heater control cable and the fan motor harness.
5. Disengage the control rod connecting the air flow fan switch control lever on the instrument panel to the heater unit, on the right side.
6. Unfasten the two mounting bolts and remove the heater unit.

To install:

7. Install the heater unit and tighten the mounting bolts securely.
8. To reconnect the control rod push up the link provided at the side of the heater unit to its full stroke, set the air/fan switch control lever to vent and then connect the rod to the link.
9. To reconnect the heater control cable set the temperature control lever to cold, the heater control lever on the heater unit to off then engage the cock cable.
10. Install the console, and luggage shelf.
11. Install the meter and visor assembly.
12. Install center ventilation grill.
13. Fill the radiator with coolant.
14. Connect the negative battery cable.
15. Start the vehicle and check for leaks.

1980-84 Models

▶ See Figures 10 and 11

The heater unit contains the core and blower. The entire assembly must be removed from the car before either the blower or core can be serviced.

To remove the heater unit:

1. Disconnect the negative battery cable.
2. Drain the engine coolant through the radiator drain plug.
3. Disconnect the heater hoses in the engine compartment.
4. Remove the rubber grommet the heater hoses run through on the kick panel inside the car. The location is slightly above and to the right of the accelerator pedal.
5. Remove the radio box or console.
6. Remove the instrument panel.
7. Remove the luggage shelf, if equipped.
8. Disconnect the heater control cables and fan motor harness.
9. Disconnect the duct between the heater unit and blower assembly.
10. Remove the right and left defroster nozzles.
11. Remove the two mounting bolts at the top sides of the heater unit.
12. Remove the retaining bracket and screws at the bottom of the heater unit.
13. Lift the heater unit up and out.

To install:

14. Install retaining bracket and screws at the bottom of the heater unit.
15. Install the heater unit and tighten the two mounting bolts securely.
16. Connect the duct between the heater unit and blower assembly.
17. Install the left and right defroster nozzles.
18. Connect the fan motor harness and heater control cables.
19. Install the luggage shelf, if equipped.
20. Install the instrument panel, console and radio box.
21. Install the heater hose rubber grommets and connect the heater hoses.
22. Fill the radiator with coolant.
23. Connect the negative battery cable.
24. Start the engine and check for leaks.

Heater Core

REMOVAL & INSTALLATION

ff-1 and 1300G Models

The sub-radiator also functions as the heater core. Sub-radiator removal and installation are given in Section 3.

Except ff-1 and 1300G Models

▶ See Figures 12 and 13

➡The heater unit must be removed from the car to service the heater core.

1. Disconnect the negative (-) battery cable.

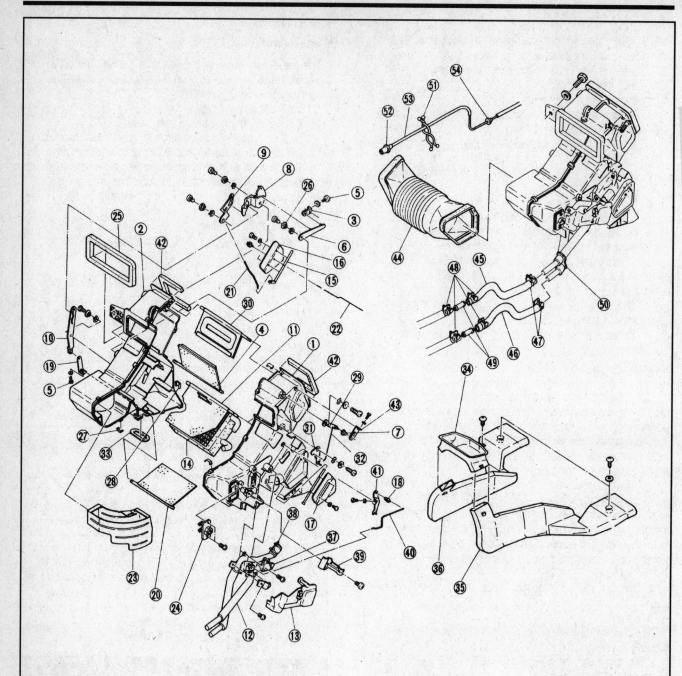

1	Heater case (L.H.)	15	Defroster shaft
2	Heater case (R.H.)	16	Defroster shutter (R.H.)
3	Upper lever	17	Defroster shutter (L.H.)
4	Upper shutter	18	Rod clamp
5	Screw	19	Lower lever
6	Upper link	20	Lower shutter
7	Bushing	21	Defroster rod
8	Mode lever	22	Defroster shutter shaft
9	Defroster link	23	Guide
10	Lower link	24	Resistor
11	Air mixing shutter	25	Intake packing
12	Heater cock CP	26	Shaft bushing
13	Protector	27	Hold spring A
14	Heater core	28	Hold spring B

29	Ventilation link A	43	Ventilation lever
30	Ventilation shutter	44	Heater duct
31	Ventilation link B	45	Heater inlet hose
32	Ventilation rod	46	Heater outlet hose
33	Cushion	47	Hose clamp
34	Lower duct	48	Hose clamp
35	Rear duct (L.H.)	49	Connector
36	Rear duct (R.H.)	50	Heater hose grommet
37	Hose clamp A	51	Clip
38	Hose clamp B	52	Vacuum connector
39	Hose bracket	53	Vacuum hose
40	Heater cock rod	54	Vacuum hose grommet
41	Air mixing lever		
42	Ventilation packing		

87906005

Fig. 10 Exploded view of the heater unit and duct assembly

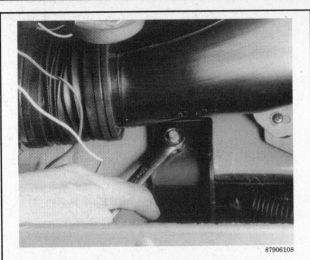

Fig. 11 Remove the two mounting bolts at the top sides of the heater unit

2. Remove water valve cover and disconnect the water valve.

3. Disconnect the control rod that operates the defroster doors.

4. Separate the heater case by disengaging the retaining tabs.

5. Disconnect the air intake shutter return spring.

6. Remove the heater core.

7. Installation is the reverse of removal.

8. After Installation, be sure to check the operation of the intake shutter return spring.

Heater Water Control Valve

✷✷CAUTION

When draining the coolant, keep in mind that cats and dogs are attracted by ethylene glycol antifreeze, and are quite likely to drink any that is left in an uncovered

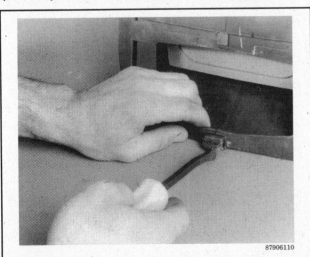

Fig. 12 Use a prybar to disengage the retaining tabs of the heater unit

Fig. 13 Separate the case, then remove the heater core from the case

container or in puddles on the ground. This will prove fatal in sufficient quantity. Always drain the coolant into a sealable container. Coolant should be reused unless it is contaminated or several years old.

REMOVAL & INSTALLATION

The water control valve may be replaced without removing the heater unit from the car.

1. Disconnect the negative (-) battery cable.

2. Drain the engine coolant through the radiator drain plug.

3. Disconnect the heater hoses in the engine compartment.

4. Remove the rubber grommet that the heater hoses pass through on the kick panel inside the car. The location is slightly above and to the right of the accelerator pedal.

5. Remove the dash panel on the driver's side.

6. Remove the left defroster duct.

7. Remove the two screws that secure the control valve cover. One screw is located on the top, the other in the center of the cover.

8. Disconnect the control rod.

9. Loosen the hose clamps and remove the heater hoses.

10. Unfasten the three screws holding the water control in place and remove the valve.

To install:

11. Install the water control valve and tighten the three retaining screws securely.

12. Connect the heater hoses and tighten the hose clamps.

13. Connect the heater control rod.

14. Position the heater control valve cover and tighten the retaining screws.

15. Install the defroster ducts.

16. Install the dash panel.

17. Install the heater hose rubber grommets and connect the heater hoses.

18. Fill the radiator with coolant.

19. Connect the negative battery cable.

20. Start the engine and check for leaks.

AIR CONDITIONER

▶ **See Figure 14**

➡ Consult laws in your area before servicing the air conditioning system. In most areas it is illegal to perform repairs involving refrigerant unless the work done by a certified technician

Compressor

REMOVAL & INSTALLATION

1. Discharge air conditioning system using a recovery/recycling machine.
2. Disconnect the flexible hose.
3. Disconnect the compressor mounting bolts.
4. Remove the compressor.
5. Installation is the reverse of removal.
6. After the compressor is installed evacuate, charge and leak test the system.

Evaporator Core

REMOVAL & INSTALLATION

1. Open the hood and remove the spare tire (if necessary).
2. Disconnect the negative (-) battery terminal.
3. Discharge the system using a proper recycling/recovery system. Precise control is possible only when using a proper A/C refrigerant recovery station. If you do not have access to these tools, this service should be performed by a reputable shop.

4. Disconnect the evaporator discharge pipe, suction pipe and grommets.
5. Remove the evaporator core under cover.
6. Remove the pocket assembly.
7. Disengage the harness connector from the evaporator.
8. Unfasten the two retaining bands and remove the evaporator.
9. Installation is in the reverse of removal.

➡ When installing the evaporator into the car body, make sure that the wiring harness and vacuum hose do not get caught between the body parts.

Air Conditioner Blower

REMOVAL & INSTALLATION

▶ **See Figure 15**

1. Disconnect the negative battery cable.
2. Disengage the vacuum hose and the electrical connector.
3. Unfasten the bolt(s) and remove the blower cage unit.
4. Unfasten the bolts mounting the motor to the blower case and remove it.

To install:

5. Transfer the blower wheel to the new motor (if you're replacing the motor) by removing the attaching nut and washers.
6. Install these parts on the new motor.
7. Install new seals if necessary.
8. Install the motor and fasten the mounting bolts.
9. Install the blower cage unit and fasten the bolt(s).
10. Engage the electrical connector and the vacuum hose.
11. Connect the negative battery cable.

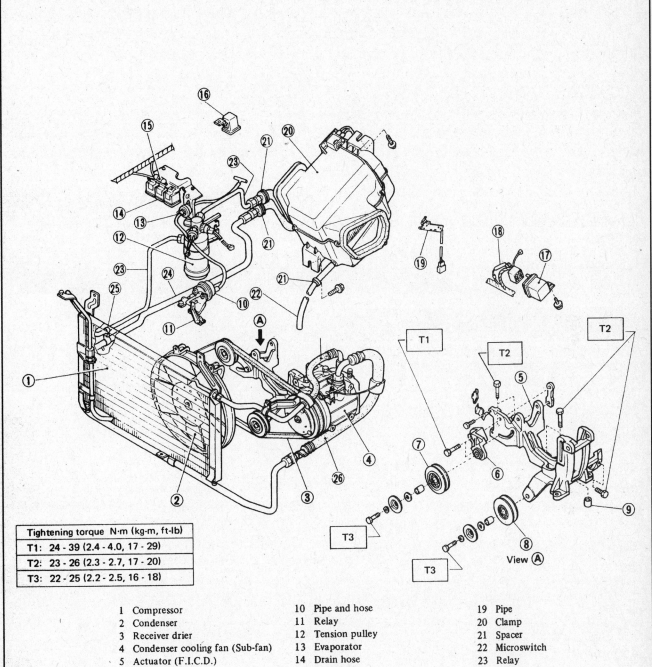

Tightening torque N·m (kg-m, ft-lb)
T1: 24 - 39 (2.4 - 4.0, 17 - 29)
T2: 23 - 26 (2.3 - 2.7, 17 - 20)
T3: 22 - 25 (2.2 - 2.5, 16 - 18)

1 Compressor
2 Condenser
3 Receiver drier
4 Condenser cooling fan (Sub-fan)
5 Actuator (F.I.C.D.)
6 Belt
7 Compressor bracket
8 F.I.C.D. lever
9 Pipe and hose

10 Pipe and hose
11 Relay
12 Tension pulley
13 Evaporator
14 Drain hose
15 Grommet
16 Grommet
17 Grommet
18 Pipe

19 Pipe
20 Clamp
21 Spacer
22 Microswitch
23 Relay
24 Fuse (A)
25 Fuse (B)
26 Relay

87906007

Fig. 14 A common air conditioning system found on Subarus

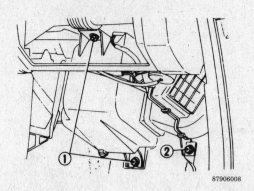

Fig. 15 The air conditioning blower is removed by unfastening the bolt at (2). Do not disturb the evaporator mounting bolts (1)

ENTERTAINMENT SYSTEM

Radio

Never operate the radio without a speaker. Damage to the output transistors will result. If the speaker must be replaced, use a speaker of correct ohm impedance or else the output transistors will require replacement in short order. Never operate the radio with the speaker leads shorted together.

REMOVAL & INSTALLATION

ff-1 and 1300G Models

1. Disconnect the negative (-) battery cable.
2. Pull the two radio knobs off their shafts and remove the nuts from the shafts.
3. Unfasten the two bezel retaining screws and remove the radio bezel.
4. Remove the lower heater duct cover and the ash tray, then unfasten the radio securing screw which is located underneath them.
5. Disconnect the radio power, speaker, and antenna leads.
6. Pull the radio out of the dash.
7. Installation is the reverse of removal.

1971-73 GL and DL Models

1. Disconnect the negative (-) battery cable.
2. Remove the center panel of the instrument panel:
   a. Removing the radio installing nut.
   b. Remove the bolt which holds the center panel to the instrument panel. It can be reached by removing the ash tray.
   c. Remove the lighting switch and the wiper switch knobs by loosening the screw and removing the dress nut.
   d. Remove the heater control knobs by loosening the screws.
   e. Remove the hanger spring of the speedometer cable.

f. Disconnect the speedometer cable from the back side of the instrument cluster.
   g. Disconnect the junction block from the back side of the instrument cluster.
   h. Disconnect the wiring harness from the cigar lighter. Remove the center panel from the instrument panel.
3. Remove the speaker grille by loosening the two attaching screws.
4. Pull out the feed cord from the radio plug.
5. Loosen the radio mounting bolt.
6. Loosen the radio mounting screws.
7. Disconnect the radio wiring and remove the radio.
8. Reverse the procedure to install the unit.

1974-76 Models

1. Disconnect the negative (-) battery cable.

➡**Steps 2 and 3 do not apply to 1976 models.**

2. Use a Phillips screwdriver with a short shank to unfasten the screws holding the speaker grille down.
3. Remove the grille.
4. Disengage the speaker lead from the radio connector.
5. Remove the instrument cluster bezel screws at the radio end.
6. Remove its screws and lift out the console, if so equipped.
7. Pull the knob off the fresh air lever and unfasten the two securing screws at either end.
8. Remove the center outlet grille.
9. Pull both knobs off the radio shafts.
10. Remove the ash tray.
11. Pull the knobs off the heater controls.
12. Remove the nuts from the radio control shafts.
13. Loosen the screws which secure the radio surround panel and remove the panel.
14. Remove the radio bracket screws.
15. Disconnect the radio leads and pull the radio out of the dash.

To install:

16. Install the radio leads onto the radio and place the unit in the dash.

17. Install the radio bracket screws and tighten securely.

18. Install the cover panel and tighten the retaining screws.

19. Install the radio control shaft nuts.

20. Install the heater control knobs, the radio control knobs and the ash tray.

21. Install the center outlet grille and tighten the two retaining screws.

22. Install the fresh air lever knob.

23. Install the console.

24. Install the instrument cluster bezel.

25. Install the speaker leads to the radio connector.

26. Install the speaker grille.

27. Connect the negative battery cable.

1977-84 Models

▶ **See Figures 16, 17 and 18**

1. Disconnect the (-) battery cable.

2. Remove the center console assembly by removing the mounting screws.

3. Disconnect the wire harness and antenna cable.

4. Pull off the radio control knobs.

5. Remove the radio mounting nuts from the control stems.

6. Remove the radio mounting screw from the back of the radio.

7. Lift out the radio.

8. Installation is the reverse of removal.

ANTENNA TRIMMER ADJUSTMENT

The antenna trimmer should always be adjusted when the antenna and/or its lead are replaced. It is a good idea to adjust it if the radio has been removed from the car for any reason.

1. Remove the radio from the car, as necessary, to gain access to the trimmer.

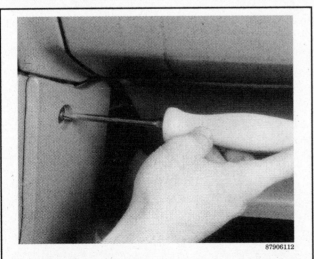

Fig. 16 Remove the screws securing the center console . . .

Fig. 17 . . . then remove the center console

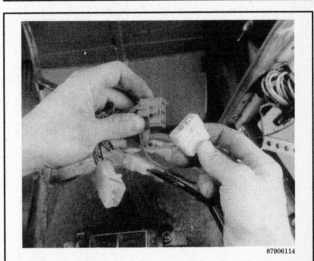

Fig. 18 Disengage the radio electrical connections and remove the radio

2. Be sure that the speaker and antenna leads are connected to the radio, and that the antenna is pulled up all the way.

3. Select a weak station around 1400 kHz on the dial.

4. Turn the trimmer screw either right or left until the signal become's the strongest (volume the loudest).

5. Install the radio after the adjustment is completed.

Speakers

REMOVAL & INSTALLATION

▶ **See Figure 19**

Front Speakers

1. Disconnect the negative battery cable.

2. Remove the speaker cover retaining screws.

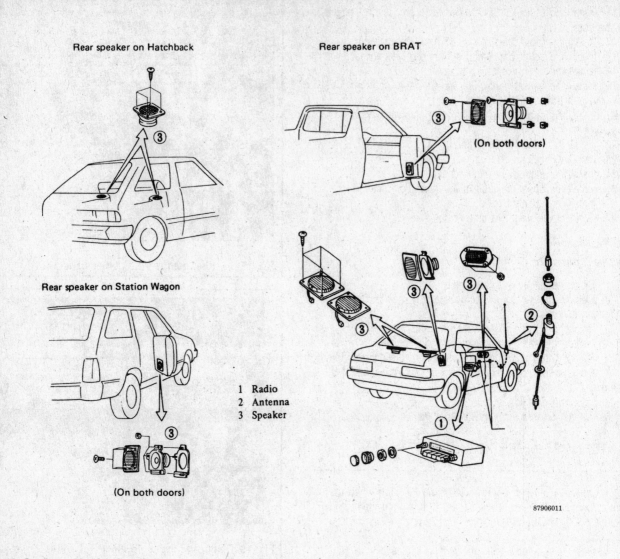

Rear speaker on Hatchback

Rear speaker on BRAT

(On both doors)

Rear speaker on Station Wagon

1 Radio
2 Antenna
3 Speaker

(On both doors)

87906011

Fig. 19 Common speaker locations

3. Remove the cover from the speaker and remove the attaching fasteners.

4. Remove the speaker and disengage the electrical connector.

5. Installation is the reverse of removal.

Rear Speakers

1. Disconnect the negative battery cable.
2. Remove the speaker cover retaining screws.
3. Remove the cover from the speaker and remove the attaching fasteners.
4. Disengage the electrical connector.
5. Installation is the reverse of removal.

WINDSHIELD WIPERS

Wipers Blades and Arms

REMOVAL & INSTALLATION

▶ **See Figures 20, 21 and 22**

1. To replace the complete wiper blade, lift up on the locking lever and slide the blade off of the wiper arm.

2. The wiper arms are held on by a cap nut. If the cap nut is covered by a boot, slide the boot back and away from the wiper arm base.

3. Loosen the nut and apply upward pressure to remove the wiper arm.

4. Place the new wiper arm in position and reverse the above procedure.

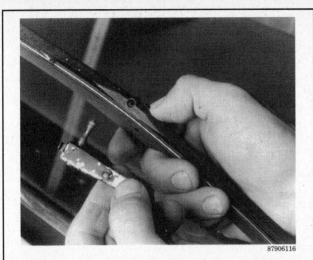

Fig. 20 Press down on the spring to remove the wiper blade

Fig. 21 Pull the boot back to uncover the cap nut

Fig. 22 Loosen the cap nut while applying upward pressure

Windshield Wiper Motor

REMOVAL & INSTALLATION

ff-1 and 1300G

On ff-1 and 1300G models, the wiper linkage is attached to the wiper motor, and the two are removed as a complete assembly.

1. Disconnect the negative (-) battery cable.
2. Unfasten the Phillips screw retaining the arms, and remove the arms.
3. Remove the pivot installing nuts, rubber boots, and washers.
4. Remove the instrument cluster, as detailed in this section. Disconnect the wiper motor wiring.
5. Remove both windshield wiper assembly retaining bolts and slide the motor and linkage assembly out from behind the dash.
6. Installation is the reverse of removal.

1972-79 Models (Except 1300G)

▶ See Figure 23

1. Disconnect the negative (-) battery cable.
2. Remove the spare tire if it is in the way.
3. Remove the windshield washer reservoir.
4. Remove the screws which secure the motor to the firewall.
5. Remove the wiper arms and cowl by unfastening their respective securing nuts and screws.
6. Disconnect the wiper motor wiring.
7. Detach the clip which attaches the motor to the link, and remove the motor.

✳✳WARNING

On 1976-79 models the clip is secured by means of plastic prongs. BE EXTREMELY CAREFUL WHEN WORKING WITH THESE PRONGS. If they are bent too far they will become broken or distorted.

1980-84 Models

▶ See Figures 24, 25, 26 and 27

1. Disconnect the negative (-) battery cable.
2. Remove the wiper blades from the wiper arms by pulling the retainer lever up and sliding the blade away from the arm.
3. Slide the covering boot up the wiper arm.
4. Remove the retaining nuts that hold the wiper arms to the linkage and remove the arms.
5. Disconnect the electric wires to the wiper motor.
6. Remove the screws holding the cowl to the body. Remove the cowl.
7. Find or fabricate a ring which has the same diameter as the outer diameter of the plastic joint that retains the linkage to the wiper motor. Force the ring down over the joint to force the four plastic retaining jaws inward, and then disconnect and remove the linkage.
8. Loosen the bolts securing the wiper motor, and remove it.

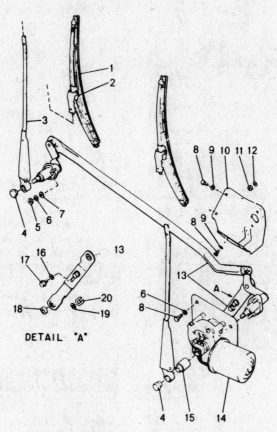

DETAIL "A"

1. Wiper blade
2. Blade holder
3. Wiper arm
4. Special nut
5. Nut
6. Spring washer
7. Washer
8. Bolt
9. Spring washer
10. Bracket
11. Nut
12. Spring washer
13. Link assembly
14. Wiper motor
15. Cap
16. Spring washer
17. Flange bolt
18. Packing
19. Washer
20. Clip

87906017

Fig. 23 Wiper assembly used on 1972-79 models

Fig. 24 Unfasten the screws holding the cowl panel and remove the panel

Fig. 25 Disconnect the harness for the wiper motor

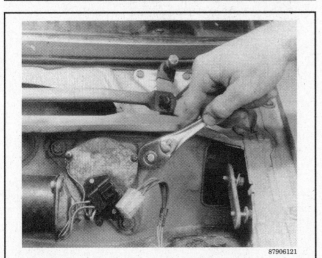

Fig. 26 After disconnecting the linkage, loosen the bolts retaining the wiper motor . . .

Fig. 27 . . . the remove the wiper motor

To install:

9. Install the wiper motor and cycle the motor before installing the arms.

10. Install the arms after the ignition switch has been on (wiper switch off) for a few seconds to put the linkage in park position. Install the wiper unit with the red marking on the driver's side.

Rear Window Wiper Motor

REMOVAL & INSTALLATION

▶ See Figures 28 and 29

1. At the rear window, pull the wiper blade outward from the arm and press down on the clip, then remove the blade from the arm.

2. Remove the wiper arm cover.

3. Loosen the wiper arm-to-wiper assembly nut, then remove the nut and the arm from the assembly.

4. Remove the wiper assembly-to-rear gate cap, nut and cushion.

5. From inside of the rear gate, remove the wiper motor assembly trim panel.

6. Disengage the electrical connector from the wiper motor assembly.

7. Remove the wiper motor assembly-to-rear gate bolts and the motor assembly from the rear gate.

8. If necessary, replace the wiper motor.

9. To install, reverse the above procedures. With the rear wiper motor switch in the **OFF** position, install the wiper arm blade so that it is positioned 0.98 in. (25mm) above the rear glass molding.

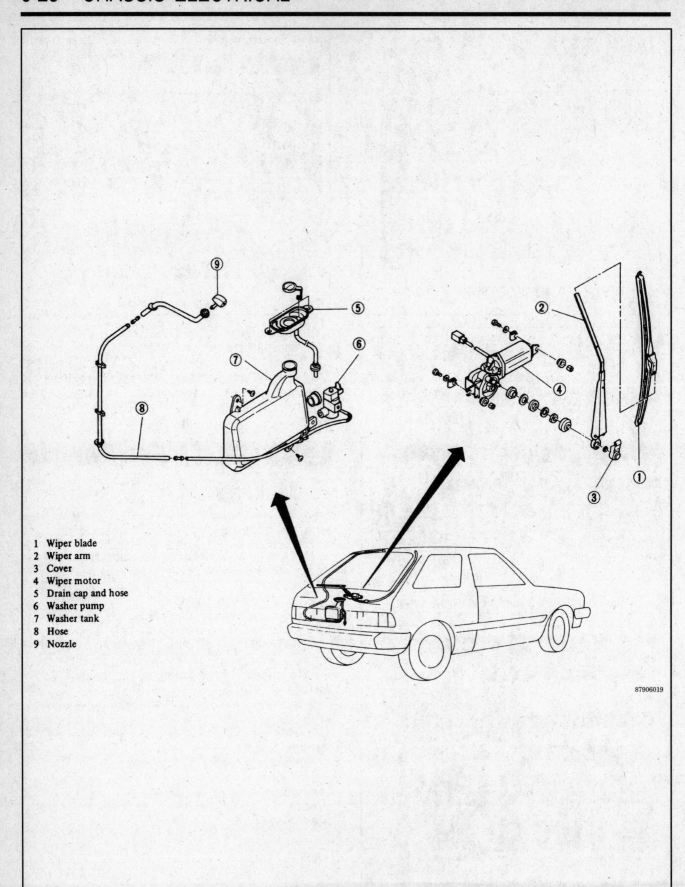

1 Wiper blade
2 Wiper arm
3 Cover
4 Wiper motor
5 Drain cap and hose
6 Washer pump
7 Washer tank
8 Hose
9 Nozzle

87906019

Fig. 28 Rear wiper and washer components on the Hatchback

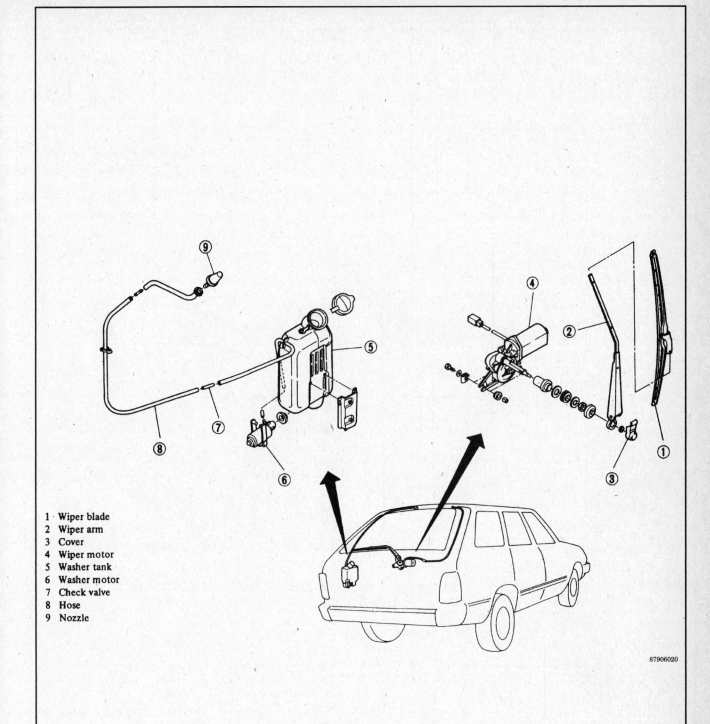

1 Wiper blade
2 Wiper arm
3 Cover
4 Wiper motor
5 Washer tank
6 Washer motor
7 Check valve
8 Hose
9 Nozzle

87906020

Fig. 29 Rear wiper and washer components on the Station Wagon

Wiper Linkage

REMOVAL & INSTALLATION

ff-1 and 1300G Models

See the wiper motor removal and installation procedure in this section, for linkage removal and installation.

Except ff-1 and 1300G Models

1. Disconnect the negative (-) battery cable. Remove the spare tire if it is in the way.
2. Remove the nuts which secure the wiper arms to the pivots. Lift the arms off the pivots.
3. Loosen the self-tapping screws and remove the cowl panel.
4. Remove the nuts which secure the wiper link.
5. Remove the wiper bracket attaching bolts.
6. Remove the clip which secures the linkage to the motor.

✳WARNING

On models from 1976, the clip is secured by means of plastic prongs. BE EXTREMELY CAREFUL WHEN WORKING WITH THESE PRONGS. If they are bent too far they will become broken or distorted.

7. Remove the linkage through the cowl opening.
8. Place the new linkage into the cowl opening and reverse the above procedure.

Windshield Washer Fluid Reservoir

REMOVAL & INSTALLATION

▶ **See Figures 30 and 31**

1. Disconnect the negative (-) battery cable.
2. Disengage the hoses from the fluid reservoir.
3. Remove the reservoir retaining fasteners.
4. Disengage the electrical connections.
5. Remove the tank by pulling it up.
To install:
6. Install the tank and engage the electrical connections.
7. Fasten the reservoir retaining fasteners and connect the hoses.
8. Connect the negative battery cable.

Windshield Washer Motor

REMOVAL & INSTALLATION

▶ **See Figures 30 and 32**

The windshield washer motor is located on the windshield fluid reservoir.

1. Disconnect the negative (-) battery cable.

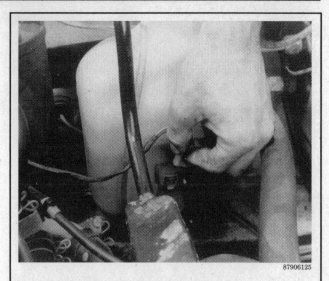

Fig. 30 Disengage the electrical connection . . .

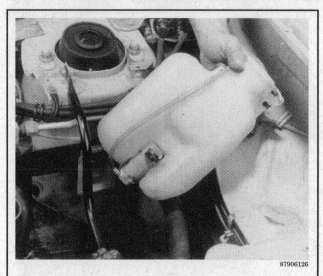

Fig. 31 . . . then remove the tank by pulling it up

2. Disengage the hoses from the fluid reservoir.
3. Remove the reservoir retaining fasteners.
4. Disengage the electrical connections.
5. Remove the washer motor from the tank.
To install:
6. Install the washer motor.
7. Install the tank and engage the electrical connections.
8. Fasten the reservoir retaining fasteners and connect the hoses.
9. Connect the negative battery cable.

Rear Windshield Washer Fluid Reservoir

REMOVAL & INSTALLATION

The rear windshield washer fluid reservoir on the hatchback is located behind the hatchback door panel. On the station

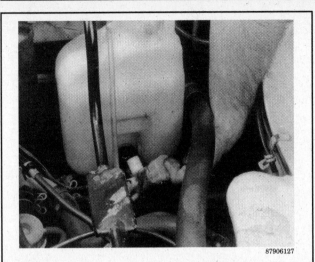

Fig. 32 Remove the washer motor by pulling it out of the tank

wagon it is located behind the trim panel at rear left wheel well.

1. Disconnect the negative (-) battery cable.
2. Unfasten the screws and remove the trim panel.
3. Disconnect the hose from the washer tank and nozzle.
4. Take out the drain hose by removing the grommet of the hose.
5. Unfasten the washer fluid tank retaining screws and disengage the electrical connector.
6. Remove the washer fluid tank.

To install:
7. Install the washer fluid tank and fasten the retaining screws.
8. Engage the electrical connector and install the drain hose.
9. Connect the drain hose to the washer tank and nozzle.
10. Connect the negative battery cable.

Rear Windshield Washer Motor

REMOVAL & INSTALLATION

The rear windshield washer motor is located on the rear windshield washer fluid reservoir. On the hatchback is located behind the hatchback door panel. On the station wagon it is located behind the trim panel at rear left wheel well.

1. Disconnect the negative (-) battery cable.
2. Unfasten the screws and remove the trim panel.
3. Disconnect the hose from the washer tank and nozzle.
4. Unfasten the washer fluid tank retaining screws and disengage the electrical connector.
5. Remove the washer fluid tank.
6. Remove the washer motor.

To install:
7. Install the washer motor.
8. Install the washer fluid tank and fasten the retaining screws.
9. Engage the electrical connector and install the drain hose.
10. Connect the drain hose to the washer tank and nozzle.
11. Connect the negative battery cable.

INSTRUMENTS AND SWITCHES

Instrument Cluster

REMOVAL & INSTALLATION

1970 ff-1and 1300G
▶ See Figure 33

1. Disconnect the negative (-) battery cable.
2. Disconnect the speedometer cable, by reaching up behind the dash panel and loosening its securing nut.
3. Carefully pull the instrument cluster wiring connector straight back, away from the cluster.
4. Loosen the cluster retaining springs and pull the cluster forward, out of the dash panel.
5. Installation is the reverse of removal.

1972-73 GL and DL

1. Disconnect the negative (-) battery cable.
2. Pull the knobs off the radio shafts and remove the shaft securing nuts.
3. Remove the ash tray and the instrument panel securing nut which is located behind it.

4. Remove the set screw which secures the light switch (GL Coupe only) and the wiper switch (all models) knobs. Pull the knob(s) off and remove the retaining nut(s) from the switch(es).
5. Working from underneath the dash, remove the speedometer cable securing spring. Push the hook on the speedometer up, while pulling the cable back in order to disengage it.
6. Disconnect the junction block at the back of the instrument cluster.
7. Disengage the cigar lighter wiring connectors.
8. Remove the complete instrument panel surround from the car and separate the cluster from it, by removing the cluster securing screws.
9. On GL models only, remove the tachometer in the following manner:
    a. Remove the tachometer surround panel by loosening its two attaching screws.
    b. Remove the tachometer securing screws.
    c. Disconnect the tachometer leads.
    d. Remove the tachometer from the dash.

To install:
10. Install the tachometer leads and secure the tachometer to the surround panel (GL models only).
11. Secure the instrument cluster to the instrument panel and install the panel into the dashboard.

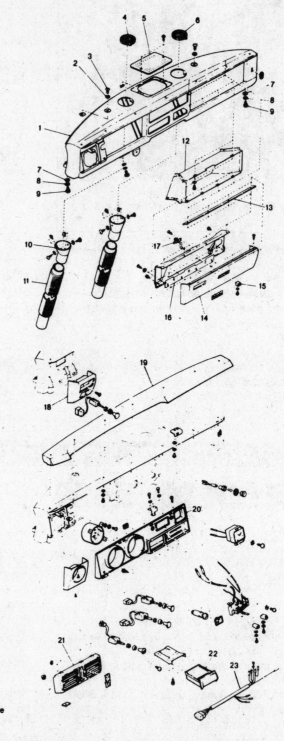

1. Instrument panel
2. Trim washer
3. Screw
4. Defroster grille (L)
5. Speaker grille
6. Defroster grille (R)
7. Washer
8. Spring washer
9. Bolt
10. Defroster duct
11. Defroster hose
12. Pocket
13. Base
14. Cover
15. Knob
16. Plate
17. Lock assembly
18. Side cover
19. Pad
20. Center panel
21. Ventilator grille
22. Ash tray
23. Wiring cord

87906021

Fig. 33 Instrument panel components — 1972-73 GL and DL

12. Connect the cigar lighter wiring and the junction block to the back of the instrument cluster.

13. Install the speedometer cable and all switches and knobs that were removed.

14. Connect the negative battery cable.

1974-76 Models

1. Disconnect the negative (-) battery cable.

2. Detach the driver's side fresh air vent duct by loosening its securing clamp.

3. On GL Coupe models, perform the following, working from underneath the dash:

   a. Disconnect the rear window defogger switch leads.

   b. Disconnect the tachometer lead.

   c. Loosen the trip odometer reset knob setscrew and pull the knob off.

4. On all models, reach up underneath the dash and disconnect the speedometer cable and the junction block.

5. Remove the screws which secure the instrument cluster bezel.

6. On GL Coupes, pull the cluster/bezel assembly out just far enough to disconnect the following electrical leads:

   a. Clock

   b. Brake warning lamp

   c. Seat belt warning lamp

7. Pull the cluster/bezel assembly out, away from the dash and lift it out of the car. Separate the cluster from the bezel by removing its attaching screws.

To install:

8. Connect the instrument cluster/bezel assembly and install all electrical leads that were removed.

9. Install the cluster/bezel assembly into the dash.

10. Connect the speedometer cable and junction block to the instrument cluster.

11. Connect the rear window defogger switch leads, the tachometer lead and the trip odometer reset knob.

12. Attach the drivers side fresh air vent duct.

13. Connect the negative battery cable.

1977-79 Models

1. Disconnect the negative (-) battery cable.

2. Remove the instrument cluster bezel, with rear window defogger switch, by removing the mounting screws.

3. Remove the screws mounting the instrument cluster.

4. Disconnect the speedometer cable and wiring harness from the back of the instrument cluster.

5. Remove the instrument cluster.

6. Reverse the above procedure to install the cluster.

1980-84 Models

▶ **See Figures 34, 35, 36, 37, 38 and 39**

1. Disconnect the negative (-) battery cable.

2. Remove the two bolts under the dash which fasten the steering column to the dash.

3. Lower the steering column until the wheel rests on the seat.

4. Remove the screws securing the visor.

5. Disengage the electrical connectors and remove the visor.

6. On GL models, to remove the visor perform the following:

   a. Remove the center ventilator control lever by pulling it.

   b. Remove the three screws accessible through the ventilator grill to the right of the cluster and the one screw accessible through the grill on the left.

   c. Remove the visor.

7. Remove the four screws holding the instrument cluster in place.

8. Pull the meter out a little and disengage the speedometer cable and electrical connectors behind the cluster.

9. Remove the cluster.

10. Installation is the reverse of the removal.

Speedometer Cable

REMOVAL & INSTALLATION

▶ **See Figure 40**

1. Working from under the hood, remove the retaining bolt that secures the speedometer cable to the transaxle.

2. Remove the cable from the retaining clamps.

3. Working from inside the car, remove the instrument panel as describer earlier.

4. Unscrew the speedometer cable from the back of the speedometer.

5. Again, working from under the hood, pull the speedometer cable from the vehicle.

6. Installation is the reverse of removal.

Center Panel

REMOVAL & INSTALLATION

The center panel is installed by spring clips attached to it. It can be detached by pulling both sides with your hands.

Console Box and Handbrake Cover

REMOVAL & INSTALLATION

▶ **See Figures 41 and 42**

1. Apply the handbrake lever.

2. Lift the tray while pushing it forward.

3. Remove the screws which hold the handbrake cover and the console box.

4. Open the handbrake cover lid. Remove the screws from the bottom of the console box and detach the handbrake cover.

5. Remove the shift knob on manual transaxles.

6. Remove the screws which hold the console box, and detach the console box.

7. Reverse the above procedure to install the console box and handbrake cover. Be careful not to pinch any harnesses during installation.

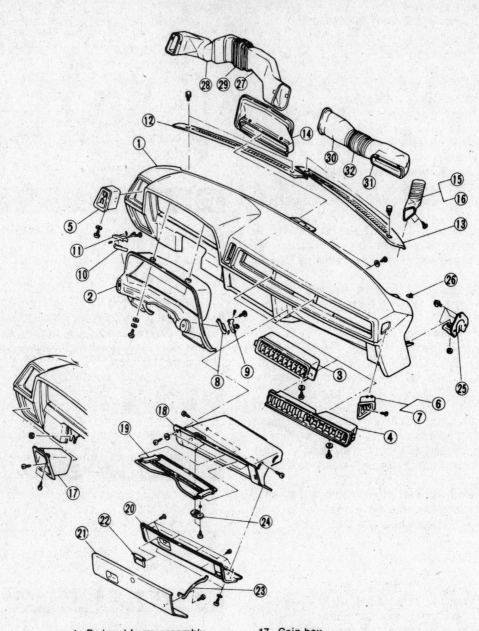

1. Pad and frame assembly
2. Visor and switch box
3. Center grille
4. Side grille
5. Side ventilation grille
6. Side defroster grille L.H.
7. Side defroster grille R.H.
8. Wiper plate
9. Wiper indicator lamp
10. Lighting plate
11. Lighting indicator lamp
12. Defroster grille L.H.
13. Defroster grille R.H.
14. Center duct
15. Side defroster duct L.H.
16. Side defroster duct R.H.
17. Coin box
18. Glove box
19. Shelf
20. Panel
21. Glove box lid
22. Lock assembly
23. Stay
24. Striker
25. Instrument panel bracket
26. Speed nut
27. Side ventilation duct A (L.H.)
28. Side ventilation duct B (L.H.)
29. Joint L.H.
30. Side ventilation duct O (R.H.)
31. Side ventilation duct D (R.H.)
32. Joint R.H.)

87906024

Fig. 34 Instrument panel components — 1980-84 models

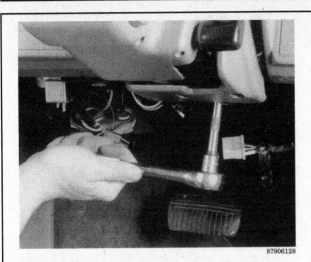

Fig. 35 Remove the two bolts under the dash which fasten the steering column to the dash

Fig. 38 Unfasten the screws retaining the instrument cluster and pull the instrument panel forward so that you may gain access to wiring

Fig. 36 Remove the screws securing the visor

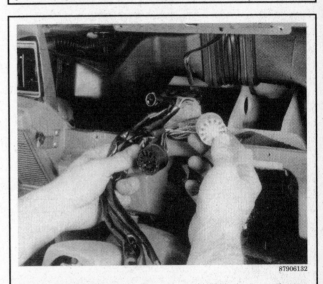

Fig. 39 Disengage the wires from the instrument cluster

Fig. 37 Remove the visor from the instrument panel

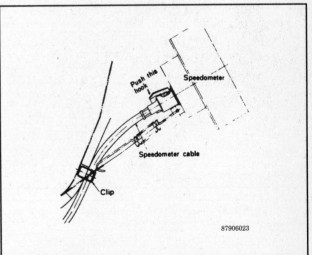

Fig. 40 Push on the hook to disengage the speedometer cable

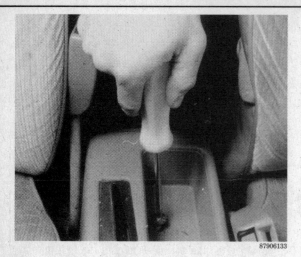

Fig. 41 Remove the screws securing the handbrake cover . . .

Fig. 42 . . . then remove the handbrake cover

Windshield Wiper Switches

REMOVAL & INSTALLATION

1. Disconnect the negative (-) battery cable.
2. Remove the necessary dash-to-chassis screws in order to gain access to the wiper switch retaining screws.
3. Remove the windshield wiper switch-to-dash screws.
4. Remove the wiper switch(es).
5. Installation is the reverse of removal.

Headlight Switch

REMOVAL & INSTALLATION

The switch is located at the left side of the instrument panel and is combined with the illumination intensity control switch.
1. Disconnect the negative (-) battery cable.
2. Remove the steering column-to-dash screws and pull downward on the steering column.
3. Remove the instrument cluster visor-to-dash screws and the visor from the instrument cluster.
4. Disengage the electrical harness connector from the headlight switch assembly.
5. Pull the headlight knob out.
6. Remove the headlight switch-to-visor nut and the switch from the visor.
7. Installation is the reverse of removal. Check the operation of the headlights.

Combination Switch

The combination switch is fitted on the steering column and is combined with the dimmer switch, turn signal switch, hazard warning light switch, and the horn switch.

REMOVAL & INSTALLATION

1. Disconnect the negative (-) battery cable.
2. Remove the screws and detach the lower cover.
3. Remove the fixing screws and detach the column covers (upper and lower).
4. Take out the steering wheel cover and remove the nut. Then, detach the steering wheel.
5. Detach the clip and band fitting the harness to the steering column, and disconnect the connectors.
6. Remove the screws fixing the combination switch to the control wing bracket.
7. Remove the combination switch.
8. Installation is the reverse of removal.

Switch Panel

There are many switches provided in the switch panel, i.e. rear window defogger switch, cruise control switch, height control switch and 4WD AT auto switch.

REMOVAL & INSTALLATION

1. Disconnect the negative (-) battery cable.
2. Detach all knobs using a small prybar.
3. Remove the retaining screws, and pull out switch panel.
4. Disengage the electrical connectors.
5. Remove the switch panel.
6. Installation is the reverse of removal.

Ignition Switch

REMOVAL & INSTALLATION

The ignition switch is installed on the steering column on some models and on the dash on others. For steering column and switches refer to Section 8. A steering column lock mech- anism is provided on all models. To remove the dash mounted ignition switch perform the following procedures.

1. Disconnect the negative (-) battery cable.
2. Disengage the electrical connection.
3. Pull the key plate out of the ignition. The key plate can only be removed in the **LOCK** position.
4. Remove the ignition switch.

To install:

5. Install the ignition switch.
6. Engage the electrical connection and install the key plate.
7. Connect the negative battery cable.

LIGHTING

Headlights

REMOVAL & INSTALLATION

▶ **See Figures 43, 44, 45, 46, 47 and 48**

1. Remove the headlight bezels, by unfastening their attaching screws.

➡**On some models it may be necessary to remove the grille first. To remove, unscrew the grille securing screws.**

2. Loosen and remove the retaining ring screws, then remove the ring.

➡**Be careful not to disturb the headlight aiming screws.**

3. Pull the headlight out and disengage the connector from the back of the sealed beam unit.
4. Reverse the procedure to install the headlight.

AIMING

The headlights must be properly aimed to provide the best, safest road illumination. The lights should be checked for

Fig. 44 . . . then carefully remove the grille from the vehicle

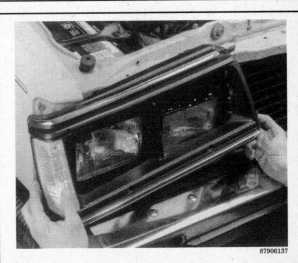

Fig. 45 Loosen the retaining screws and remove the headlight bezel

Fig. 43 If necessary, remove the grille retaining screws . . .

proper aim, and adjusted if necessary, after installing a new sealed beam unit or if the front end sheet metal has been replaced. The headlamps should be aimed by a professional with a special alignment tool. Certain state and local authorities

Fig. 46 Remove the headlight retaining screws . . .

Fig. 47 . . . and the retainer

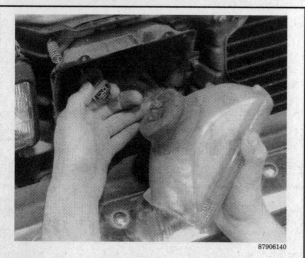

Fig. 48 Pull the headlight out and disengage the electrical connection

may require professional adjustment, but use the procedure below for temporary adjustments.

➡**The vehicle's fuel tank should be about half full when adjusting the headlights. Tires should be properly inflated, and if a heavy load is carried in the trunk or in the cargo area of station wagons, it should remain there.**

Horizontal and vertical aiming of each sealed beam unit is provided by two adjusting screws, which move the mounting ring in the body against the tension of the coil spring.

1. Place the car on a level floor with headlamps 25 ft. (7.62m)from a light colored wall.
2. Tape three vertical lines on the wall, one for the vertical center of the car and two for the vertical center of the headlamps. Then, tape one horizontal line for the horizontal and vertical center of the headlamps.
3. Adjust the low beams so the high intensity zone is just below the horizontal line and to the right of the outboard vertical lines.
4. Adjust the high beams so the high intensity zone is centered where the outboard lines intersect with the horizontal line.

Signal and Marker Lights

REMOVAL & INSTALLATION

Front Turn Signal and Parking Lights
▶ **See Figures 49, 50 and 51**

1. Disconnect the negative (-) battery cable.
2. Remove the two screws which secure the lens cover and gasket to the vehicle.
3. Remove the lens cover and gasket.
4. Grasp the bulb firmly and remove it from the electrical connector.
   To install:
5. Install the new bulb in the electrical connector.

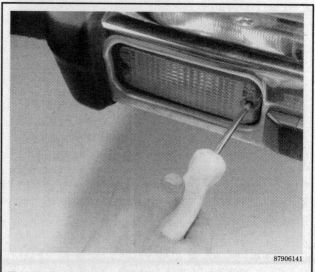

Fig. 49 Remove the lens retaining screws

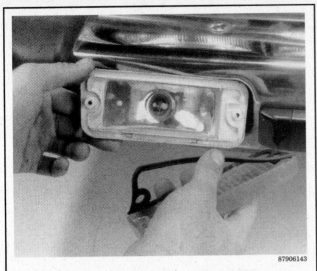

Fig. 50 Remove the lens cover and the gasket

Fig. 52 Remove the lens retaining screws

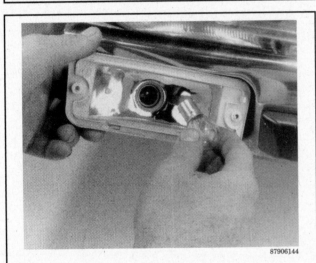

Fig. 51 Grasp the bulb firmly and remove it from the electrical connector

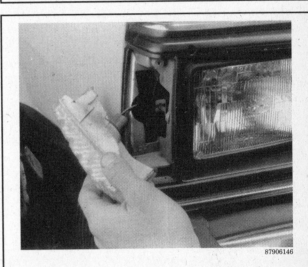

Fig. 53 Remove the light assembly away from the vehicle

6. Install the gasket and lens cover, then fasten the two screws.

7. Connect the negative battery cable.

Side Marker Lights

▶ **See Figures 52, 53, 54 and 55**

1. Disconnect the negative (-) battery cable.

2. Remove the two screws which secure the lens cover and gasket to the vehicle.

3. Pull the lens cover, with the electrical wire, away from the vehicle.

4. Remove the lens cover from the bulb receptacle.

5. Grasp the bulb firmly and pull it from the electrical connector.

To install:

6. Install the new bulb in the electrical connector.

7. Install the lens and gasket cover, then fasten the retaining screws.

8. Connect the negative battery cable.

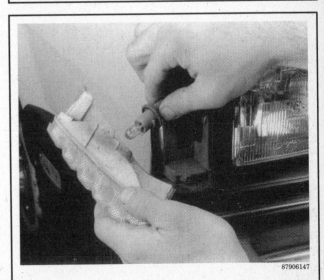

Fig. 54 Remove the bulb and socket from the light lens

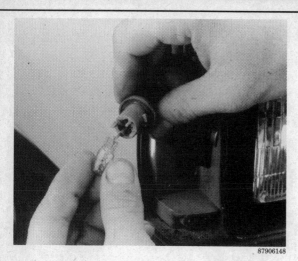

Fig. 55 Grasp the bulb firmly and pull it from the electrical connector

Rear Turn Signal, Brake and Parking Lights
▶ **See Figures 56, 57, 58 and 59**

On Subaru vehicles there are two different ways of removing the rear turn signal, brake and parking light bulbs. On the station wagon the lens is retained by exterior screws. On the coupe and sedan the fasteners are reached from the trunk.
1. Disconnect the negative (-) battery cable.

2. Remove the lens or cover retaining fasteners.
3. Remove the old bulb from the electrical connector.
To install:
4. Install the new bulb in the electrical connector.
5. Fasten the lens or cover retaining fasteners.
6. Connect the negative battery cable.

Dome Light
▶ **See Figure 60**

1. The lens can be removed by turning the mark on the lens towards the dome light switch on the dome light.
2. Pull off the dome light cover by hand.
3. Remove the bulb.
4. Installation is the reverse of removal.

Passenger Area Lamps

To replace the courtesy and glove box lamps, simply remove the bulb through the access hole. To replace the ashtray lamp, it is necessary to remove the ashtray and the ashtray retainer first.

License Plate Lights
▶ **See Figure 61**

1. Remove the lamp attaching bolts or screws.
2. Remove the lens fasteners.
3. Remove the lamp socket then remove the bulb.
4. Installation is the reverse of removal.

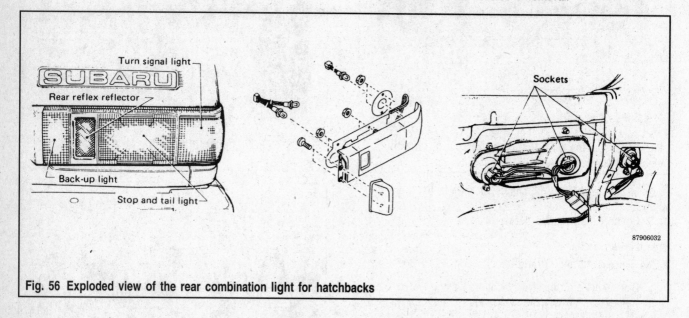

Fig. 56 Exploded view of the rear combination light for hatchbacks

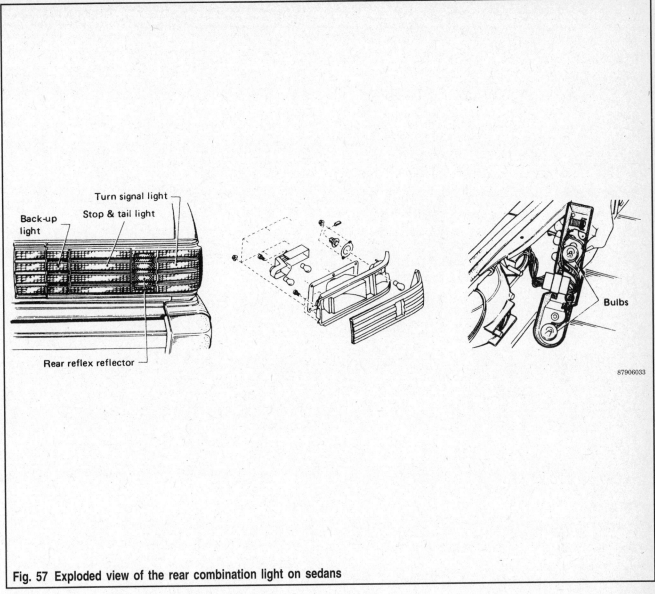

Fig. 57 Exploded view of the rear combination light on sedans

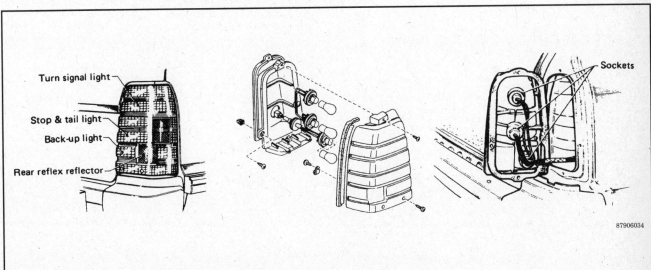

Fig. 58 Exploded view of the rear combination light on station wagons

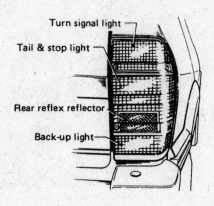
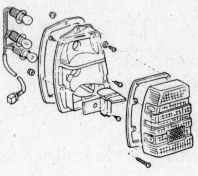

Turn signal light

Tail & stop light

Rear reflex reflector

Back-up light

87906035

Fig. 59 Exploded view of the rear combination light for the Brat

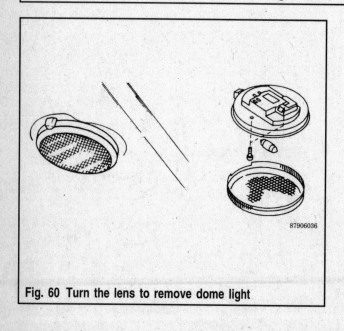

87906036

Fig. 60 Turn the lens to remove dome light

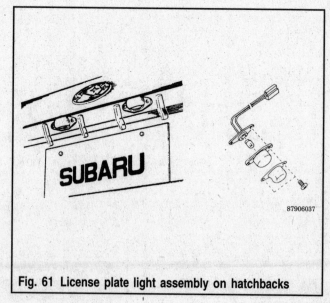

SUBARU

87906037

Fig. 61 License plate light assembly on hatchbacks

CIRCUIT PROTECTION

Fuses

▶ **See Figure 62**

On ff-1 and 1300G models, the fuse box is located in the engine compartment, on the left front fender.

On all other models until 1978, it is located on the right front wheel arch in the engine compartment. From 1978-84 it is located underneath the instrument panel, on the left side.

The amperage for each fuse is stamped on the fuse box cover.

If equipped with 4WD, a fuse holder is located near the ignition coil. For servicing purposes, to change 4WD to FWD, insert a 15A fuse into the FWD fuse holder. The FWD pilot lamp (on the instrument panel) will turn ON to indicate the the vehicle is set in the FWD mode.

ff-1 and 1300G models have two spare fuses tied to the wiring harness which runs between the battery and voltage regulator. The spare fuses are inside the fuse box cover on all other models.

REMOVAL & INSTALLATION

▶ **See Figures 63 and 64**

1. Open the cover to the fuse panel.
2. Select the fuse to be removed and using a fuse puller tool remove the fuse.
3. Check that the new fuse is of the proper amperage.
4. Installation of the fuse is the reverse of removal

Fig. 63 Open the fuse panel cover . . .

Fusible Link

LOCATION

▶ **See Figure 65**

The fusible link is located next to the battery positive terminal. All current except for the starter motor flows through it. If excessive current flows through the fusible link the fusible metal melts, thus breaking the circuit and protecting the electrical equipment from damage.

REMOVAL & INSTALLATION

1. Disconnect the negative battery cable.

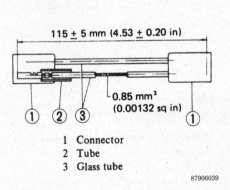

115 ± 5 mm (4.53 ± 0.20 in)

0.85 mm²
(0.00132 sq in)

1 Connector
2 Tube
3 Glass tube

Fig. 62 Components of a glass tube fuse

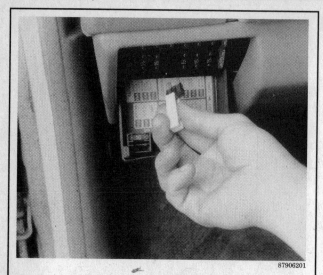

Fig. 64 . . . then use a fuse puller to remove the fuse

2. Cut the damaged fuse link from the wiring harness and discard it. If the fuse link is one of three circuits feed by a single feed wire, cut it out of harness at each splice end and discard.

3. Identify and obtain proper fuse link and butt connectors for attaching the fuse link to the harness.

4. Strip away approximately ½ in. of insulation from the two wiring ends. Attach the replacement fuse link to stripped wire ends with two proper size butt connectors.

5. Solder the connectors and wires and insulate with electrical tape.

Circuit Breaker

Circuit breakers provide a similar protection to fuses. Unlike fuses most circuit breakers only have to be reset, and not replaced. Circuit breakers are used only in models equipped with power windows, and are located underneath the front seat.

REMOVAL & INSTALLATION

1. Remove the malfunctioning circuit breaker by pulling it out of its cavity.

2. Replace the circuit breaker with one of proper amp rating for the circuit, by pushing straight in until the fuse or circuit breaker seats itself fully into the cavity.

Flashers

REPLACEMENT

The turn signal flasher and hazard units are usually located located under the dash either to the left or right of the steering column on most models.

1. Remove the turn signal flasher unit or hazard unit by pulling them up from the electrical connection.

2. To install push the unit(s) into the electrical connector.

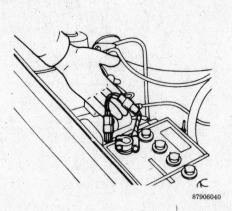

Fig. 65 The fusible link can be found next to the battery

Troubleshooting Basic Turn Signal and Flasher Problems

Most problems in the turn signals or flasher system, can be reduced to defective flashers or bulbs, which are easily replaced. Occasionally, problems in the turn signals are traced to the switch in the steering column, which will require professional service.

F = Front   R = Rear   ● = Lights off   o = Lights on

Problem		Solution
Turn signals light, but do not flash		• Replace the flasher
No turn signals light on either side		• Check the fuse. Replace if defective. • Check the flasher by substitution • Check for open circuit, short circuit or poor ground
Both turn signals on one side don't work		• Check for bad bulbs • Check for bad ground in both housings
One turn signal light on one side doesn't work		• Check and/or replace bulb • Check for corrosion in socket. Clean contacts. • Check for poor ground at socket
Turn signal flashes too fast or too slow		• Check any bulb on the side flashing too fast. A heavy-duty bulb is probably installed in place of a regular bulb. • Check the bulb flashing too slow. A standard bulb was probably installed in place of a heavy-duty bulb. • Check for loose connections or corrosion at the bulb socket
Indicator lights don't work in either direction		• Check if the turn signals are working • Check the dash indicator lights • Check the flasher by substitution
One indicator light doesn't light		• On systems with 1 dash indicator: See if the lights work on the same side. Often the filaments have been reversed in systems combining stoplights with taillights and turn signals. Check the flasher by substitution • On systems with 2 indicators: Check the bulbs on the same side Check the indicator light bulb Check the flasher by substitution

87906C01

Troubleshooting Basic Lighting Problems

Problem	Cause	Solution
Lights		
One or more lights don't work, but others do	· Defective bulb(s) · Blown fuse(s) · Dirty fuse clips or light sockets · Poor ground circuit	· Replace bulb(s) · Replace fuse(s) · Clean connections · Run ground wire from light socket housing to car frame
Lights burn out quickly	· Incorrect voltage regulator setting or defective regulator · Poor battery/alternator connections	· Replace voltage regulator · Check battery/alternator connections
Lights go dim	· Low/discharged battery · Alternator not charging · Corroded sockets or connections · Low voltage output	· Check battery · Check drive belt tension; repair or replace alternator · Clean bulb and socket contacts and connections · Replace voltage regulator
Lights flicker	· Loose connection · Poor ground · Circuit breaker operating (short circuit)	· Tighten all connections · Run ground wire from light housing to car frame · Check connections and look for bare wires
Lights "flare"—Some flare is normal on acceleration—if excessive, see "Lights Burn Out Quickly"	· High voltage setting	· Replace voltage regulator
Lights glare—approaching drivers are blinded	· Lights adjusted too high · Rear springs or shocks sagging · Rear tires soft	· Have headlights aimed · Check rear springs/shocks · Check/correct rear tire pressure
Turn Signals		
Turn signals don't work in either direction	· Blown fuse · Defective flasher · Loose connection	· Replace fuse · Replace flasher · Check/tighten all connections
Right (or left) turn signal only won't work	· Bulb burned out · Right (or left) indicator bulb burned out · Short circuit	· Replace bulb · Check/replace indicator bulb · Check/repair wiring
Flasher rate too slow or too fast	· Incorrect wattage bulb · Incorrect flasher	· Flasher bulb · Replace flasher (use a variable load flasher if you pull a trailer)
Indicator lights do not flash (burn steadily)	· Burned out bulb · Defective flasher	· Replace bulb · Replace flasher
Indicator lights do not light at all	· Burned out indicator bulb · Defective flasher	· Replace indicator bulb · Replace flasher

87906C02

Troubleshooting Basic Dash Gauge Problems

Problem	Cause	Solution
Coolant Temperature Gauge		
Gauge reads erratically or not at all	· Loose or dirty connections · Defective sending unit	· Clean/tighten connections · Bi-metal gauge: remove the wire from the sending unit. Ground the wire for an instant. If the gauge registers, replace the sending unit.
	· Defective gauge	· Magnetic gauge: disconnect the wire at the sending unit. With ignition ON gauge should register COLD. Ground the wire; gauge should register HOT.
Ammeter Gauge—Turn Headlights ON (do not start engine). Note reaction		
Ammeter shows charge Ammeter shows discharge Ammeter does not move	· Connections reversed on gauge · Ammeter is OK · Loose connections or faulty wiring · Defective gauge	· Reinstall connections · Nothing · Check/correct wiring · Replace gauge
Oil Pressure Gauge		
Gauge does not register or is inaccurate	· On mechanical gauge, Bourdon tube may be bent or kinked	· Check tube for kinks or bends preventing oil from reaching the gauge
	· Low oil pressure	· Remove sending unit. Idle the engine briefly. If no oil flows from sending unit hole, problem is in engine.
	· Defective gauge	· Remove the wire from the sending unit and ground it for an instant with the ignition ON. A good gauge will go to the top of the scale.
	· Defective wiring	· Check the wiring to the gauge. If it's OK and the gauge doesn't register when grounded, replace the gauge.
	· Defective sending unit	· If the wiring is OK and the gauge functions when grounded, replace the sending unit
All Gauges		
All gauges do not operate	· Blown fuse · Defective instrument regulator	· Replace fuse · Replace instrument voltage regulator
All gauges read low or erratically	· Defective or dirty instrument voltage regulator	· Clean contacts or replace
All gauges pegged	· Loss of ground between instrument voltage regulator and car · Defective instrument regulator	· Check ground · Replace regulator
Warning Lights		
Light(s) do not come on when ignition is ON, but engine is not started	· Defective bulb · Defective wire	· Replace bulb · Check wire from light to sending unit
	· Defective sending unit	· Disconnect the wire from the sending unit and ground it. Replace the sending unit if the light comes on with the ignition ON.
Light comes on with engine running	· Problem in individual system · Defective sending unit	· Check system · Check sending unit (see above)

87906C03

Troubleshooting the Ignition Switch

Problem	Cause	Solution
Ignition switch electrically inoperative	• Loose or defective switch connector • Feed wire open (fusible link) • Defective ignition switch	• Tighten or replace connector • Repair or replace • Replace ignition switch
Engine will not crank	• Ignition switch not adjusted properly	• Adjust switch
Ignition switch wil not actuate mechanically	• Defective ignition switch • Defective lock sector • Defective remote rod	• Replace switch • Replace lock sector • Replace remote rod
Ignition switch cannot be adjusted correctly	• Remote rod deformed	• Repair, straighten or replace

87906C06

Troubleshooting the Turn Signal Switch

Problem	Cause	Solution
Turn signal will not cancel	• Loose switch mounting screws • Switch or anchor bosses broken • Broken, missing or out of position detent, or cancelling spring	• Tighten screws • Replace switch • Reposition springs or replace switch as required
Turn signal difficult to operate	• Turn signal lever loose • Switch yoke broken or distorted • Loose or misplaced springs • Foreign parts and/or materials in switch • Switch mounted loosely	• Tighten mounting screws • Replace switch • Reposition springs or replace switch • Remove foreign parts and/or material • Tighten mounting screws
Turn signal will not indicate lane change	• Broken lane change pressure pad or spring hanger • Broken, missing or misplaced lane change spring • Jammed wires	• Replace switch • Replace or reposition as required • Loosen mounting screws, reposition wires and retighten screws
Turn signal will not stay in turn position	• Foreign material or loose parts impeding movement of switch yoke • Defective switch	• Remove material and/or parts • Replace switch
Hazard switch cannot be pulled out	• Foreign material between hazard support cancelling leg and yoke	• Remove foreign material. No foreign material impeding function of hazard switch—replace turn signal switch.
No turn signal lights	• Inoperative turn signal flasher • Defective or blown fuse • Loose chassis to column harness connector • Disconnect column to chassis connector. Connect new switch to chassis and operate switch by hand. If vehicle lights now operate normally, signal switch is inoperative • If vehicle lights do not operate, check chassis wiring for opens, grounds, etc.	• Replace turn signal flasher • Replace fuse • Connect securely • Replace signal switch • Repair chassis wiring as required
Instrument panel turn indicator lights on but not flashing	• Burned out or damaged front or rear turn signal bulb • If vehicle lights do not operate, check light sockets for high	• Replace bulb • Repair chassis wiring as required

87906C07

Troubleshooting the Turn Signal Switch (cont.)

Problem	Cause	Solution
Instrument panel turn indicator lights on but not flashing	resistance connections, the chassis wiring for opens, grounds, etc. • Inoperative flasher • Loose chassis to column harness connection • Inoperative turn signal switch • To determine if turn signal switch is defective, substitute new switch into circuit and operate switch by hand. If the vehicle's lights operate normally, signal switch is inoperative.	• Replace flasher • Connect securely • Replace turn signal switch • Replace turn signal switch
Stop light not on when turn indicated Stop light not on when turn indicated (cont.)	• Loose column to chassis connection • Disconnect column to chassis connector. Connect new switch into system without removing old. Operate switch by hand. If brake lights work with switch in the turn position, signal switch is defective. • If brake lights do not work, check connector to stop light sockets for grounds, opens, etc.	• Connect securely • Replace signal switch • Repair connector to stop light circuits using service manual as guide
Turn indicator panel lights not flashing	• Burned out bulbs • High resistance to ground at bulb socket • Opens, ground in wiring harness from front turn signal bulb socket to indicator lights	• Replace bulbs • Replace socket • Locate and repair as required
Turn signal lights flash very slowly	• High resistance ground at light sockets • Incorrect capacity turn signal flasher or bulb • If flashing rate is still extremely slow, check chassis wiring harness from the connector to light sockets for high resistance • Loose chassis to column harness connection • Disconnect column to chassis connector. Connect new switch into system without removing old. Operate switch by hand. If flashing occurs at normal rate, the signal switch is defective.	• Repair high resistance grounds at light sockets • Replace turn signal flasher or bulb • Locate and repair as required • Connect securely • Replace turn signal switch
Hazard signal lights will not flash—turn signal functions normally	• Blow fuse • Inoperative hazard warning flasher • Loose chassis-to-column harness connection • Disconnect column to chassis connector. Connect new switch into system without removing old. Depress the hazard warning lights. If they now work normally, turn signal switch is defective. • If lights do not flash, check wiring harness "K" lead for open between hazard flasher and connector. If open, fuse block is defective	• Replace fuse • Replace hazard warning flasher in fuse panel • Conect securely • Replace turn signal switch • Repair or replace brown wire or connector as required

87906C08

WIRING DIAGRAMS

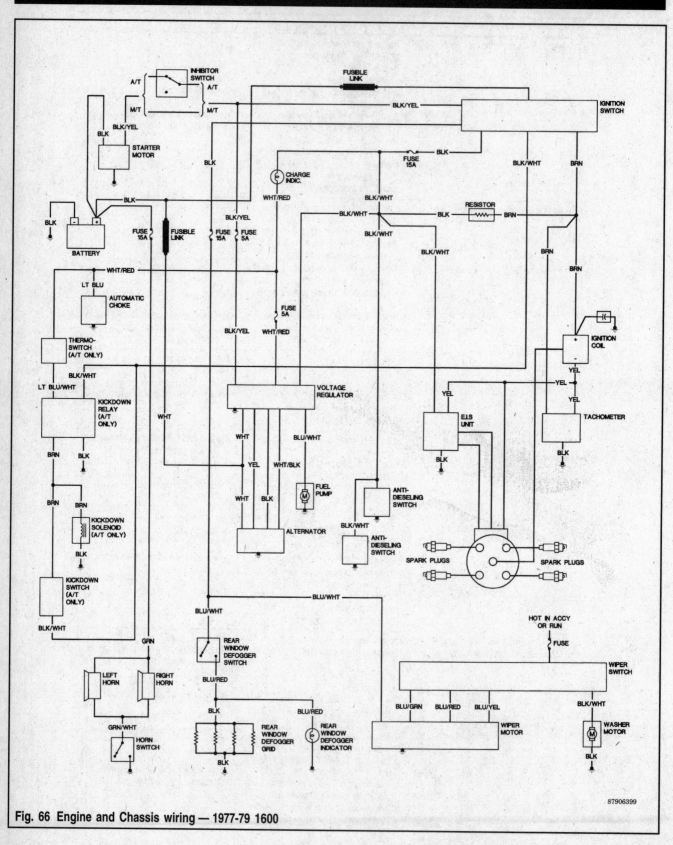

Fig. 66 Engine and Chassis wiring — 1977-79 1600

87906399

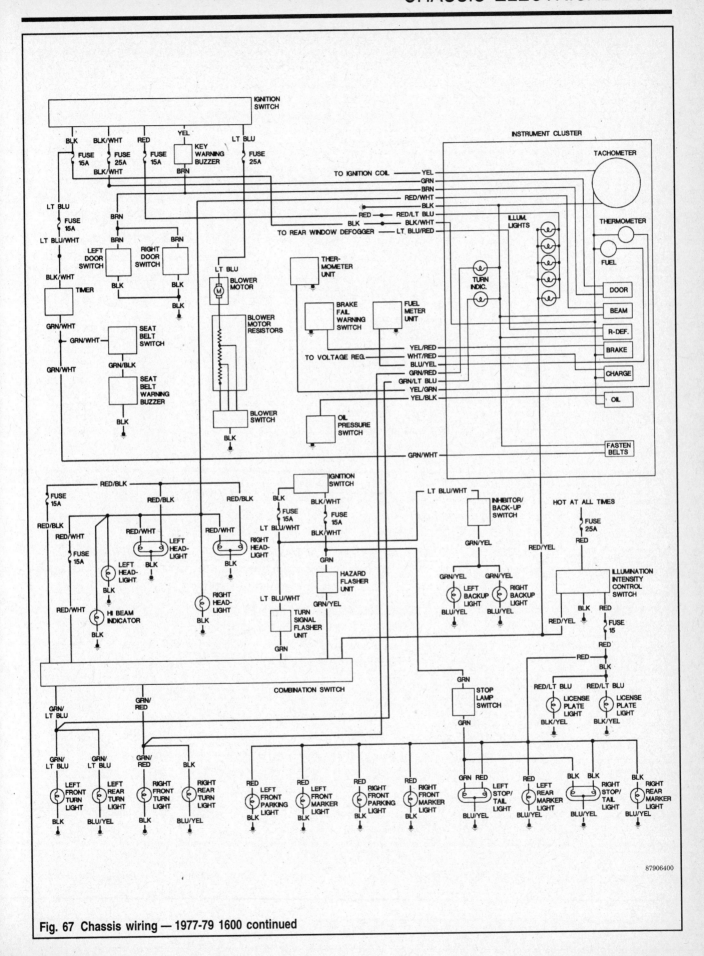

Fig. 67 Chassis wiring — 1977-79 1600 continued

87906400

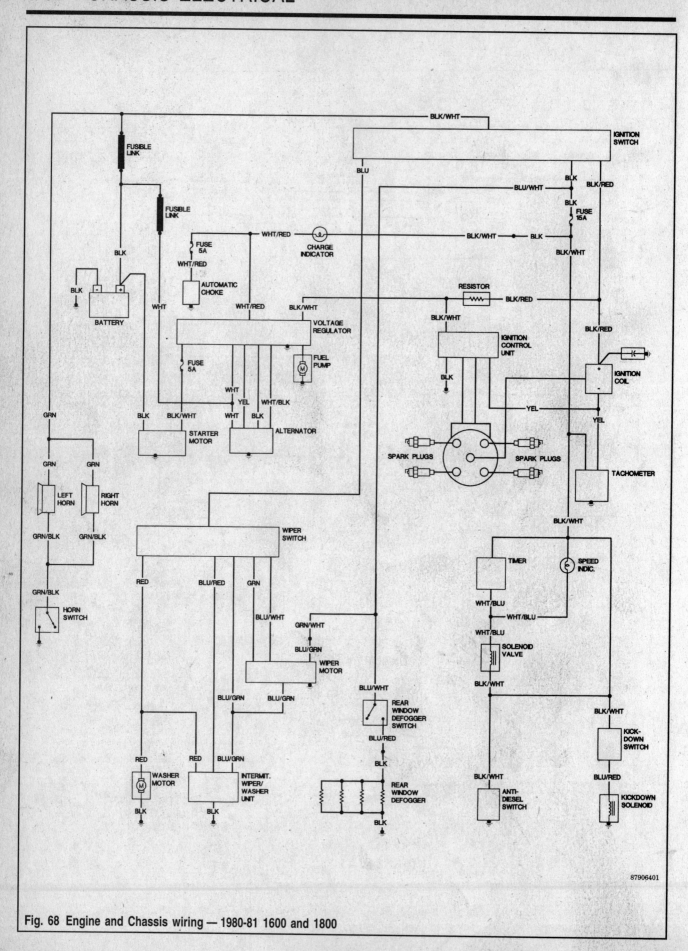

Fig. 68 Engine and Chassis wiring — 1980-81 1600 and 1800

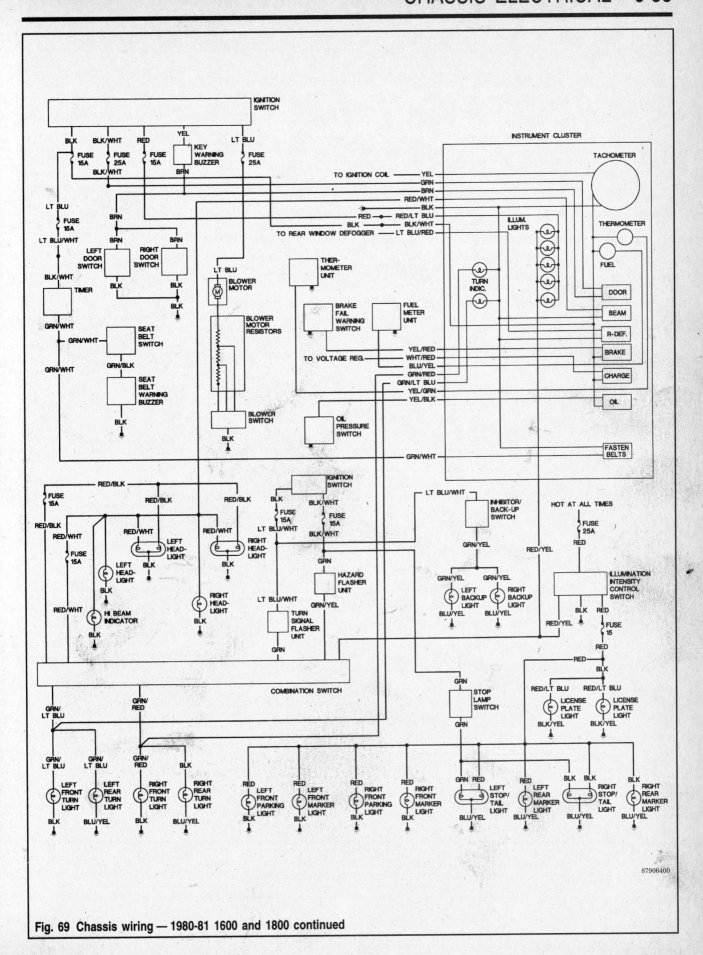

Fig. 69 Chassis wiring — 1980-81 1600 and 1800 continued

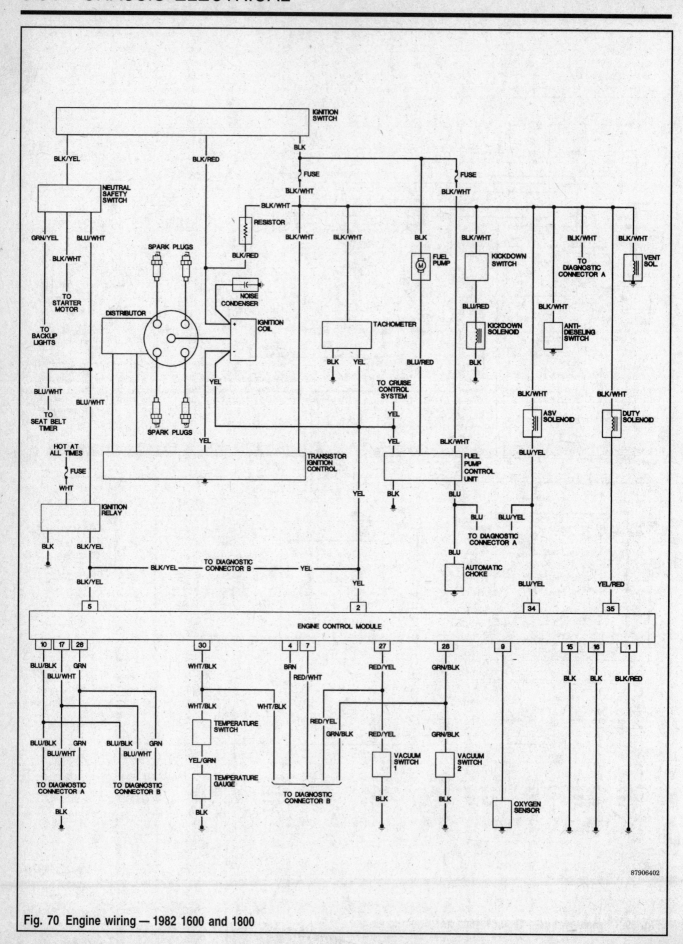

Fig. 70 Engine wiring — 1982 1600 and 1800

87906402

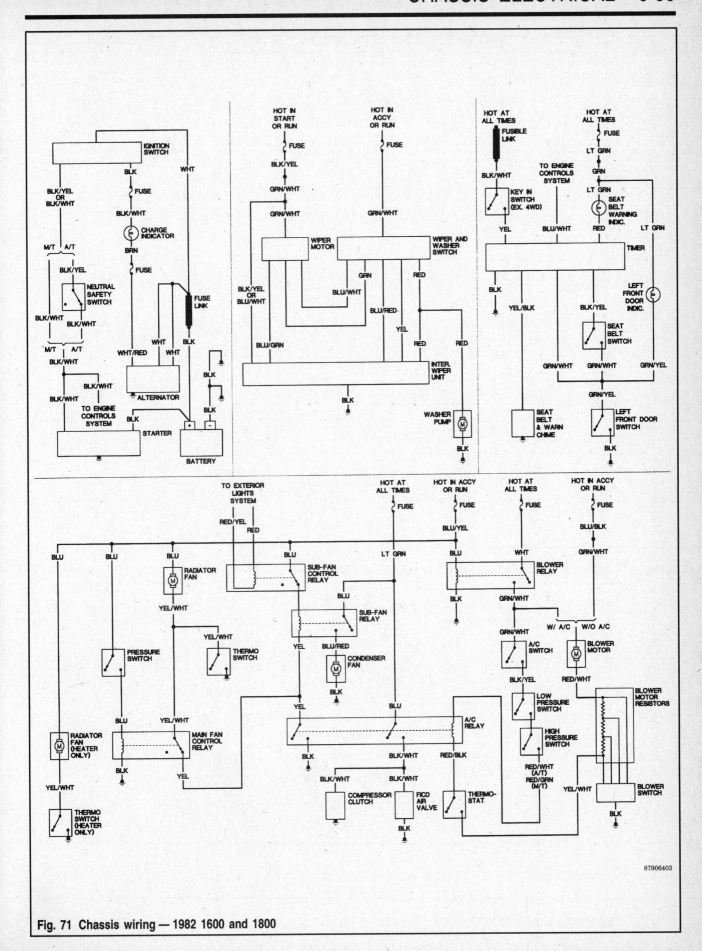

Fig. 71 Chassis wiring — 1982 1600 and 1800

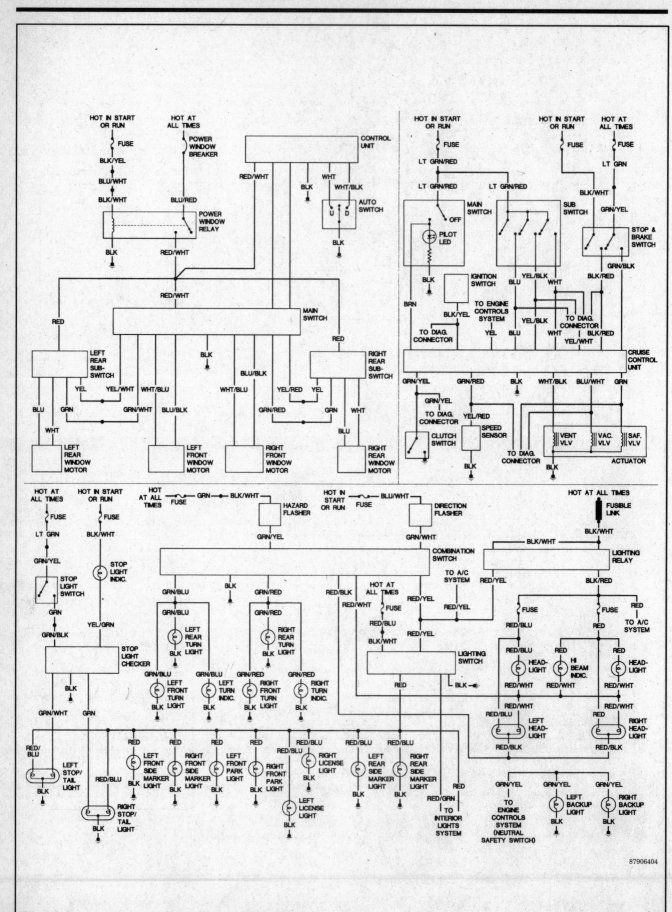

Fig. 72 Chassis wiring — 1982 1600 and 1800 continued

87906404

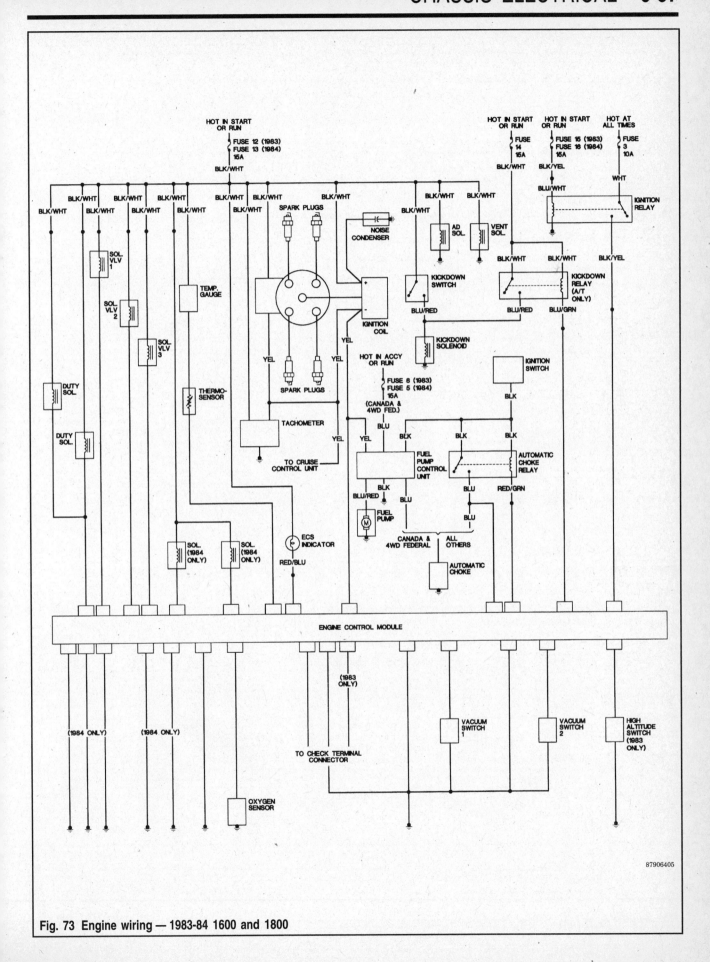

Fig. 73 Engine wiring — 1983-84 1600 and 1800

87906405

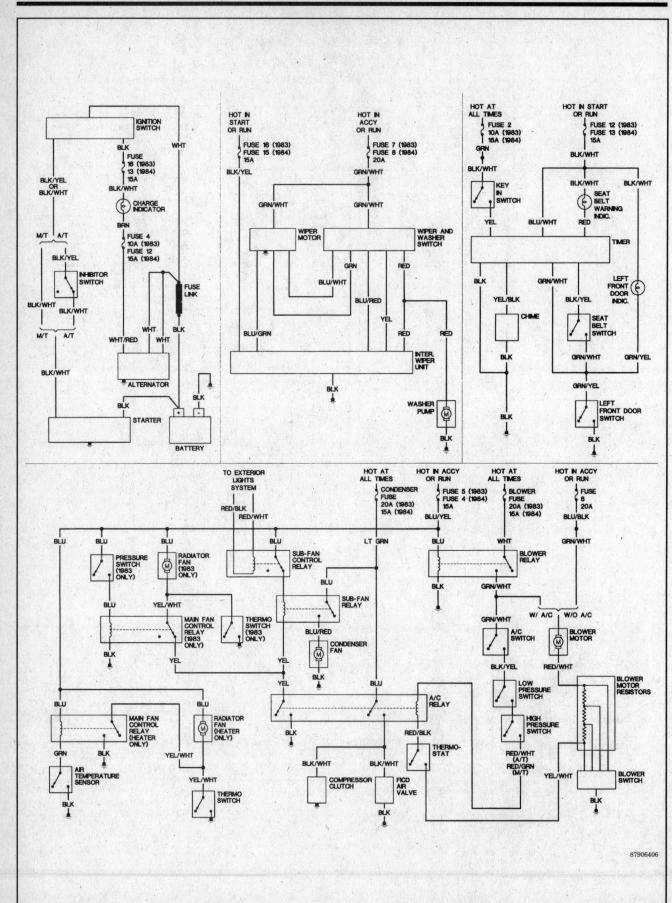

Fig. 74 Chassis wiring — 1983-84 1600 and 1800

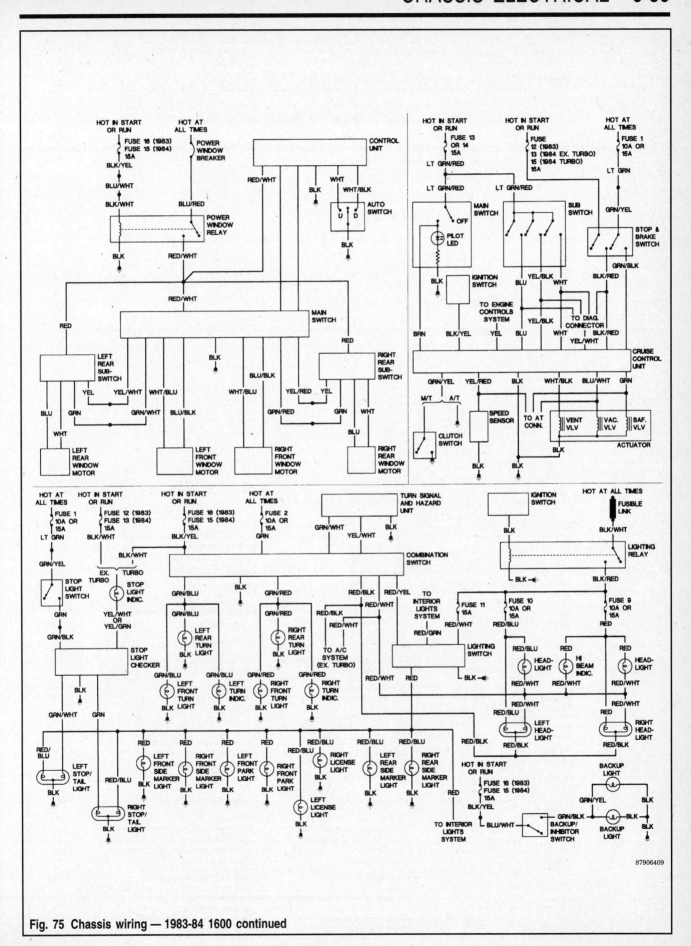

Fig. 75 Chassis wiring — 1983-84 1600 continued

87906409

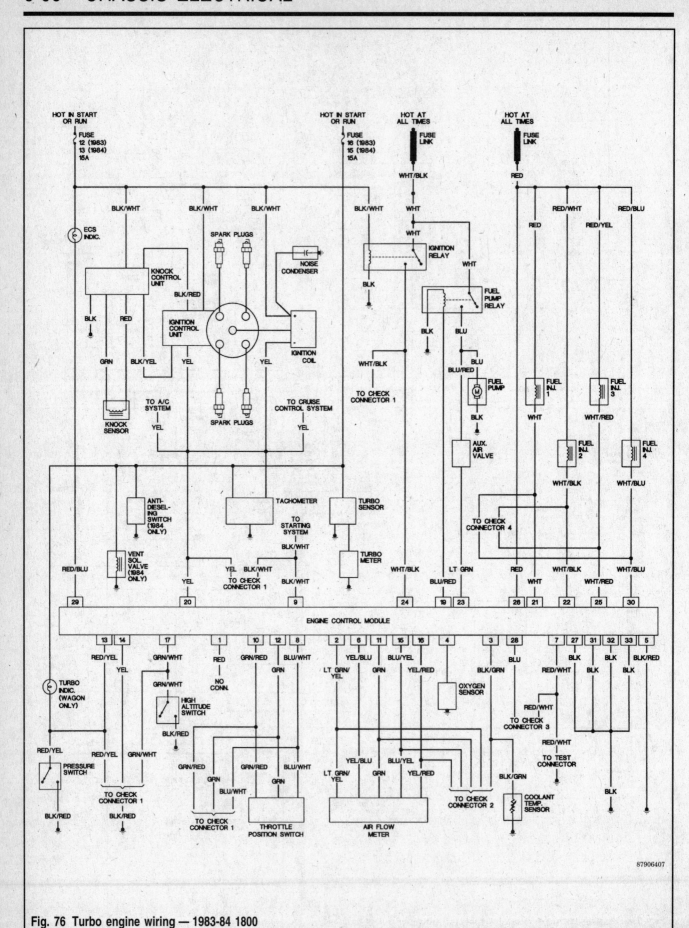

Fig. 76 Turbo engine wiring — 1983-84 1800

87906407

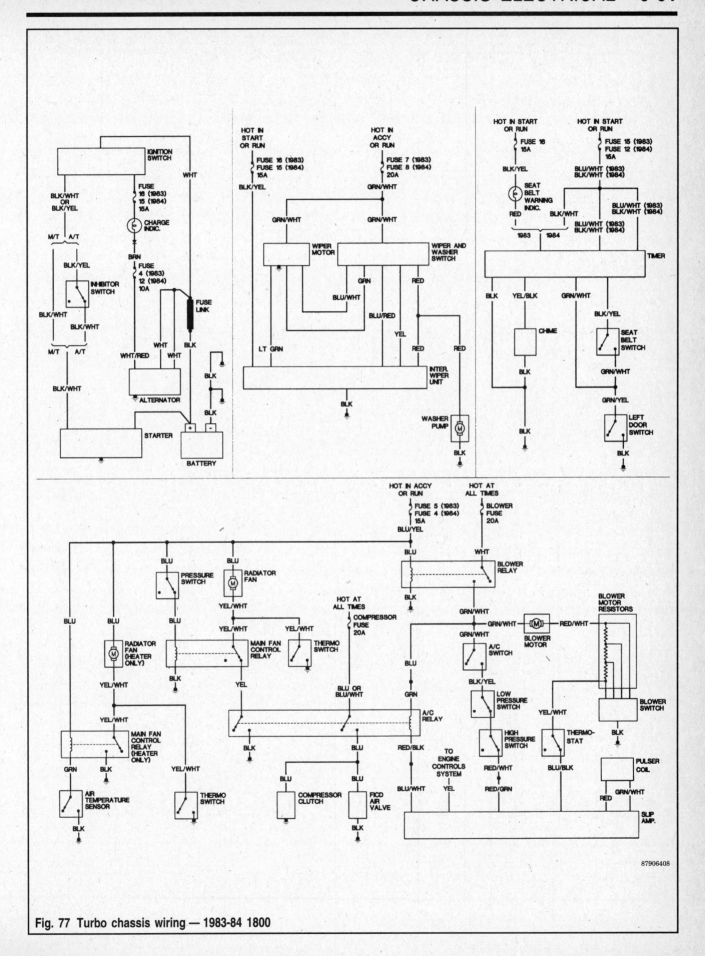

Fig. 77 Turbo chassis wiring — 1983-84 1800

87906408

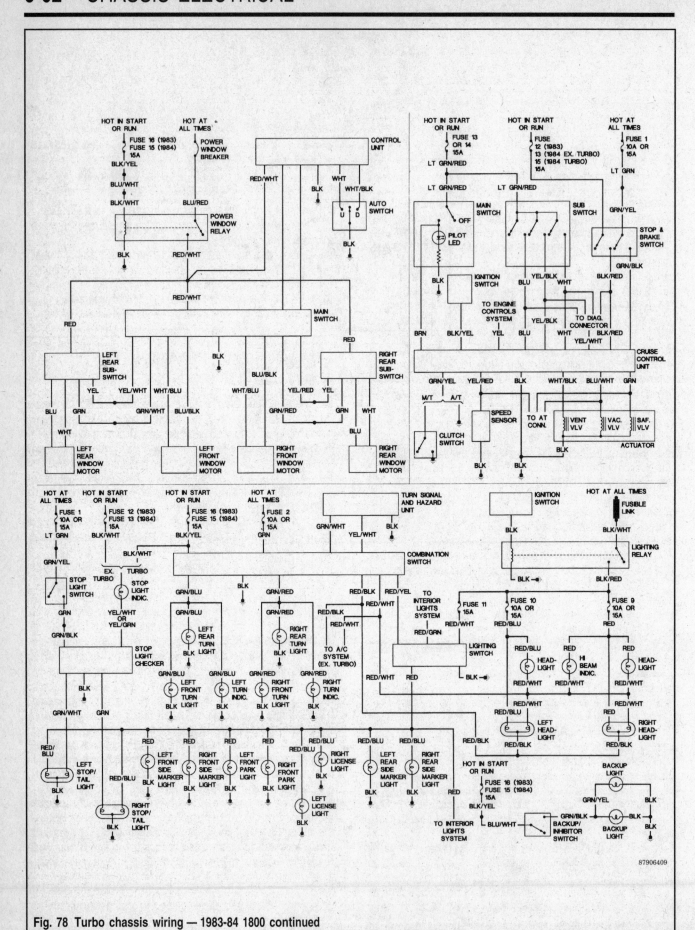

Fig. 78 Turbo chassis wiring — 1983-84 1800 continued

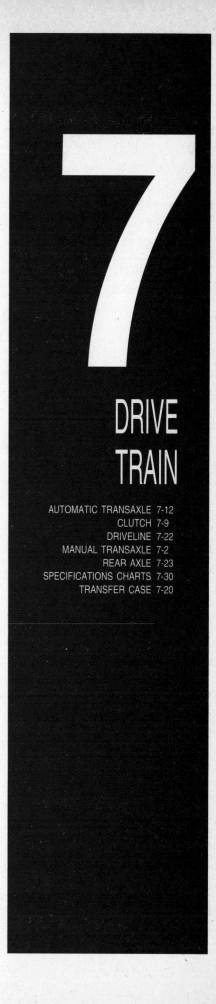

7

DRIVE
TRAIN

MANUAL TRANSAXLE

Identification

Each of the Subaru transaxles can be identified by locating the number on the transaxle housing.

Adjustments

There are no adjustments that can be made on the shift linkage for standard transaxles or for the rear drive system. If you experience looseness or too much play in shifting it is a sign of worn parts, which should be replaced.

Back-Up Light Switch

REMOVAL & INSTALLATION

➡**When removing the back-up light switch fluid may leak from the transaxle. You should first loosen the back-up light switch a few turns to see if any fluid leaks out. If this does occur retighten the switch and place an oil pan under the switch to catch the fluid before continuing with the removal and installation of the switch.**

This switch is mounted on the transaxle lever shaft and is bolted to the transaxle.

1. Disconnect the negative battery cable.
2. Disconnect the electrical connector and remove the old switch.
3. Install a new switch and reconnect the electrical connector.
4. Install the negative battery cable.

Transaxle

REMOVAL & INSTALLATION

ff-1 and 1300G,

The transaxle and engine are removed as an assembly on these models. The transaxle is then separated from the engine. For these procedures, see Section 3.

Except ff-1 and 1300G

▸ See Figures 1, 2, 3, 4 and 5

➡**The transaxle can be removed separately from the engine.**

1. Open the hood and secure it.
2. Remove the spare wheel from engine compartment, if equipped.
3. Disconnect the negative battery cable.
4. Remove the spare wheel supporter.

5. Disengage the clutch cable as follows:
   a. Remove the clutch cable return spring.
   b. Remove both the locknut and adjusting nut from the clutch cable.
   c. Unfasten the clip which retains the outer cable.
   d. Detach the rubber boot.
6. Disconnect the speedometer cable from the transaxle. Unfasten the clip on the speedometer cable.
7. Disengage the following wiring connections.
   a. Back-up lamp switch connector.
   b. Ground cable (on the car body).
   c. Starter harness (black and white).
8. Remove the starter with the battery cable, and put the starter on the bulkhead.
9. Remove the upper bolts which secure the engine to the transaxle. Loosen the lower nuts.
10. Loosen the nut retaining the pitching stopper to the transaxle side, and tighten the nut by an equal amount on the engine side. Slightly tilt the engine backward in order to facilitate removal of the transaxle.

✳✳WARNING

Do not loosen or tighten the nuts more than 0.39 in. (10mm).

11. On the 4WD model, separate both the 4WD selector system and gearshift system from transaxle as follows:
    a. Remove hand brake tray cover, and the hand brake cover.
    b. Remove rod cover.
    c. Set the drive selector lever at 4WD position.
    d. Remove the nut connecting the two rods.
    e. Remove the two nuts to separate the rod and drive selector lever from the plate.
    f. Remove the boot installing screws.
    g. Remove nut connecting gearshift lever with lever, and pull up gearshift lever with boot.
12. Disconnect O$_2$ sensor harness and unclamp it, if equipped.
13. Block the rear wheels, raise the front end of the car and support it with jackstands.
14. Remove the front exhaust pipe assembly as follows:
    a. Disconnect the hot air intake hose.
    b. Loosen the nuts which secure the exhaust pipe assembly to the exhaust port of the engine.
    c. Remove the bolts which secure the front exhaust pipe to the rear exhaust pipe.
    d. Remove the bolts which secure the front exhaust pipe to the bracket on the car body.
    e. Supporting the front exhaust pipe assembly, remove the nuts from the exhaust port of the engine. The exhaust pipe assembly can now be removed.

➡**Be careful not to strike the oxygen sensor against any adjacent parts during removal, if equipped.**

15. Drain the transaxle fluid.
16. On the 4WD models remove the transaxle shield.

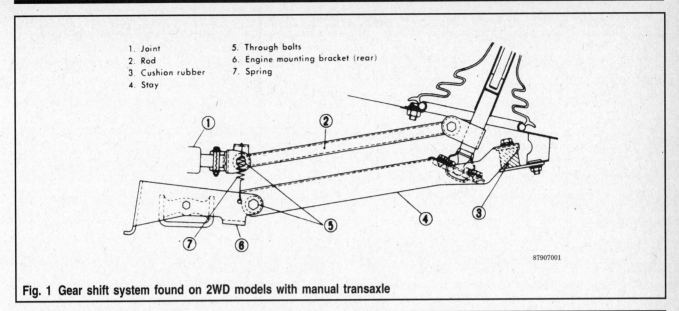

1. Joint
2. Rod
3. Cushion rubber
4. Stay
5. Through bolts
6. Engine mounting bracket (rear)
7. Spring

87907001

Fig. 1 Gear shift system found on 2WD models with manual transaxle

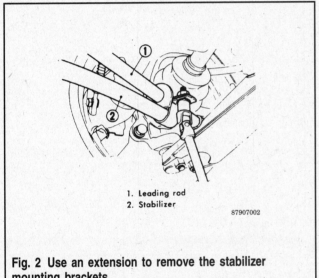

1. Leading rod
2. Stabilizer

87907002

Fig. 2 Use an extension to remove the stabilizer mounting brackets

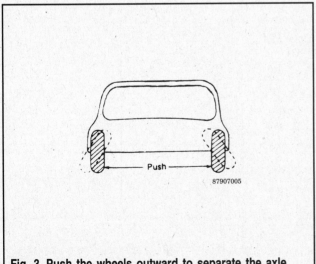

Push

87907005

Fig. 3 Push the wheels outward to separate the axle shafts from the transaxle

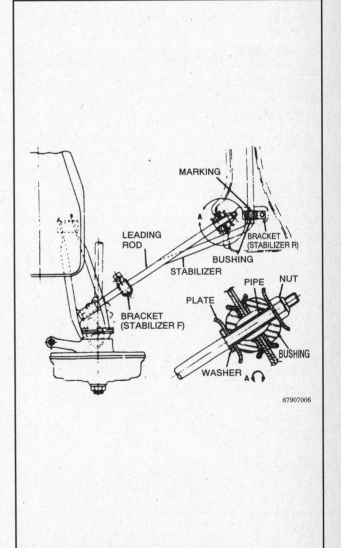

MARKING

LEADING ROD

BRACKET (STABILIZER R)

BUSHING

STABILIZER

PLATE

PIPE

NUT

BRACKET (STABILIZER F)

BUSHING

WASHER A

87907006

Fig. 4 Position the bushings for the stabilizer and leading rod as shown

Torque Specifications
(ft. lbs.)

	1972-74	1975-84
Transverse link to front cross member	80	50
Stabilizer to leading rod and rear cross member	26	15
Rear cross member to vehicle body	60	60
Front cross member to vehicle body	30	40
Front engine mount to cross member	20	20
Rear engine mount to cross member	20	20
Propeller shaft to rear differential (4WD)	—	15

87907007

Fig. 5 Torque specifications for installing the transaxle

17. On the 4WD models, remove the bolts which secure the propeller shaft to the rear differential gear, and detach the propeller shaft.

✳✳WARNING

When disconnecting the propeller shaft, plug the open end of the driveshaft with a cap to prevent the oil from running out. Be careful not to damage the oil seal located at the end of the propeller shaft.

18. Remove the exhaust cover, if equipped.
19. Remove the bolts which secure the gearshift system to free it from the transaxle. (All manual transaxle models except 4WD).
20. Remove the stabilizer.
21. Remove the bolts which secure the left and right transverse links to the front crossmember, and lower the transverse links.
22. Drive both the left and right spring pins out of the axle shaft.

✳✳WARNING

Discard and do not re-use the spring pins.

23. Push the wheels toward the outer side, separate the axle shaft from the driveshaft.
24. Unfasten the clamp on the left side of the hand brake cable, in order to facilitate the removal of the center crossmember.
25. Remove the nuts which secure the left and right transaxle mount rubber cushions.
26. Securely support the transaxle by placing a jack under it.
27. Remove the crossmember.
28. Remove the two nuts which secure the engine to transaxle
29. Move the transaxle away from the engine just enough so that the transaxle mainshaft does not interfere with the engine. Lower the jack and remove the transaxle.

To install:

30. Position the transaxle on the jack and raise it up into the vehicle. Align the transaxle mainshaft with the engine. Attach the transaxle to the engine and tighten the two attaching nuts to 34-40 ft. lbs. (46-54 Nm)

➡**Apply a slight coat of grease on the transaxle mainshaft before installation. If the mainshaft is hard to align, turn the left and right shafts until the mainshaft engages.**

31. Install the crossmember and tighten the retaining nuts to 7-13 ft. lbs. (9-17 Nm) for the 8mm nuts and 65-87 ft. lbs. (88-117 Nm) for 12mm nuts.
32. Install the left and right transaxle mount cushions and tighten the retaining nuts securely.
33. Fasten the clamp on the left side of the hand brake cable.
34. Install the axle shafts into the drive shaft and install new spring retainer pins.
35. Install the left and right transverse links to the front crossmember and tighten the retaining bolts to 13-16 ft. lbs. (17-21 Nm)
36. Install the stabilizer.
37. Install the bolts which secure the gearshift system to the transaxle and tighten securely. (All manual transaxle models except 4WD).
38. Install the exhaust cover.
39. On the 4WD models, connect the propeller shaft to the rear differential gear, install the bolts and tighten securely.
40. Install the transaxle shield (4WD models only).
41. Fill the transaxle using the proper fluid.
42. Install the exhaust assembly and the hot air intake hose.
43. Remove the jackstands and lower the front end of the vehicle.
44. Connect the O_2 sensor.
45. On the 4WD model, connect both the 4WD selector system and gearshift system to the transaxle.

✳✳WARNING

Do not tighten the nuts more than 0.39 in. (10mm).

46. Loosen the nut on the engine side and tighten the nut retaining the pitching stopper on the transaxle side by an equal amount.
47. Tighten the pitcher stopper to 6.5-9.4 ft. lbs. (8-12 Nm) and adjust the clearance to 0.07 in. (2mm).
48. Install the upper and lower bolts and nuts which secure the engine to the transaxle. Tighten the transaxle-to-engine nuts to 34-40 ft. lbs. (46-54 Nm)
49. Install the starter and battery cable. Tighten the starter-to-transaxle and engine to 34-40 ft. lbs. (46-54 Nm).
50. Engage the starter harness (black and white), ground cable (on the car body), and back-up lamp switch connector.
51. Connect the speedometer cable to the transaxle.
52. Connect the clutch cable on the transaxle.
53. Install the spare wheel supporter.
54. Place the spare tire in the engine compartment.
55. Connect the negative battery cable.

Additional torque figures are:
- Driveshaft bolts/nuts: 13-18 ft. lbs. (17-24 Nm)
- Rear mount nuts: 14-25 ft. lbs. (18-33 Nm)
- Transverse link bolts (use new self-locking nuts): 13-16 ft. lbs. (17-21 Nm)
- Stabilizer (make sure slits on bushings face inward): 13-16 ft. lbs. (17-21 Nm)
- Linkage rod nut: 5.8-8.7 ft. lbs. (7-11 Nm)

Drive Axle/HalfShafts

REMOVAL & INSTALLATION

The halfshaft consists of a Double Offset Joint (DOJ), an axle shaft, a constant velocity joint, and a stub axle.

ff-1 and 1300G Models
▶ See Figures 6, 7 and 8

1. Engage the parking brake. Remove the wheel cover and loosen the lug nuts.
2. Flatten the lockplate on the hub nut and loosen the hub nut.
3. Raise the car and support it with jackstands.

✳✳CAUTION

Be sure that the car is securely supported.

4. Remove the lug nuts, wheel and tire.
5. Remove the hub nut.
6. Remove the 3 retaining bolts and separate the double offset joint from the brake drum.
7. Remove the inner panel from the wheel well.
8. Turn the steering knuckle to full lock and pull the stub axle out of the hub.
9. Slide the drive axle assembly out of the wheel well.
To install:
10. Reverse the above process and assemble the drive axle to the vehicle.
11. Tighten the hub nut to 87-101 ft. lbs. (117-136 Nm) and secure it by bending the tabs of the lockplate up around it.

✳✳CAUTION

Excessive torque applied to the hub nut will cause bearing damage.

Except ff-1 and 1300G Models

1. Engage the parking brake.
2. Remove the wheel cover (sedans and wagon), and loosen the lug nuts.
3. Raise the car and support it with jackstands.

✳✳CAUTION

Be sure that the car is securely supported.

4. Remove the lug nuts, wheel and tire.
5. Remove the drum brake or disc brake rotor as outlined in Section 8.

6. On drum brake equipped cars, remove the 4 backing plate installing bolts and safety wire the backing plate to the suspension without disconnecting the hydraulic line.

➡**Remove the bracket which secures the brake hose to the shock absorber strut in order to gain enough free movement of the hose to perform Step 5.**

7. Drive out the spring pin, which fastens the double offset joint end of the axle shaft to the driveshaft, by lightly tapping the pin out with a hammer. Throw the old spring pin away. Do not reuse it.
8. Remove the self locking nuts which attach the ends of the control arm to the stabilizer bar and the crossmember inner pivot.
9. Separate the control arm from the crossmember pivot by prying it rearward with a suitable lever.
10. To disconnect the control arm from the stabilizer bar, swing the link forward.
11. Pull the axle shaft out of the driveshaft (double offset joint side) by pushing outward on the front suspension assembly.

✳✳WARNING

Be careful not to damage the boots on the double offset and constant velocity joints.

12. Remove the other end of the drive axle out of the housing, while holding the shaft so that it doesn't drop. Do not hammer on the end of the drive axle to remove it. Damage to both the bearing and the splines will result.
To install:
13. Thread a suitably sized metric bolt or rod, which is long enough to fit through the axle housing, into the end of the stub axle.
14. Fit the bolt through the axle housing, using care not to damage the oil seal, splines, or the bearing. Draw the drive axle assembly into place by grasping the end of the bolt with a puller.
15. On GL Coupes, install the brake disc and hub, as outlined in Section 8.
16. On drum brake equipped models, perform the following steps:
    a. Secure the backing plate with its 4 bolts. Tighten the bolts to 22-37 ft. lbs. (29-50 Nm) each.
    b. Install the brake drum assembly as detailed in Section 8.
17. Install the hub nut:
    a. On 1972-73 models, install the spacer, lockwasher, and hub nut.
    b. Tighten the nut to 145-181 ft. lbs. (196-245 Nm) and secure it with the lockwasher.
    c. On 1974-84 models, install the spacer, conical spring washer and the hub nut.
    d. Tighten the nut to 160-180 ft. lbs. (216-244 Nm), (174 ft. lbs. (244 Nm) preferred).
    e. Secure the hub nut to the axle shaft by using a punch to stake the flange on the nut to the groove in the end of the axle shaft.
18. Connect the double offset joint side of the axle shaft to the driveshaft and secure them with a new spring pin.

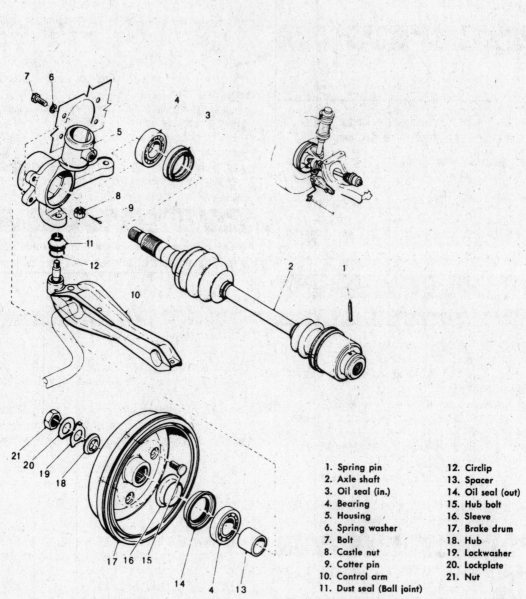

1. Spring pin	12. Circlip
2. Axle shaft	13. Spacer
3. Oil seal (in.)	14. Oil seal (out)
4. Bearing	15. Hub bolt
5. Housing	16. Sleeve
6. Spring washer	17. Brake drum
7. Bolt	18. Hub
8. Castle nut	19. Lockwasher
9. Cotter pin	20. Lockplate
10. Control arm	21. Nut
11. Dust seal (Ball joint)	

87907010

Fig. 6 Exploded view axle shaft assembly — ff-1 and 1300G models with drum brakes

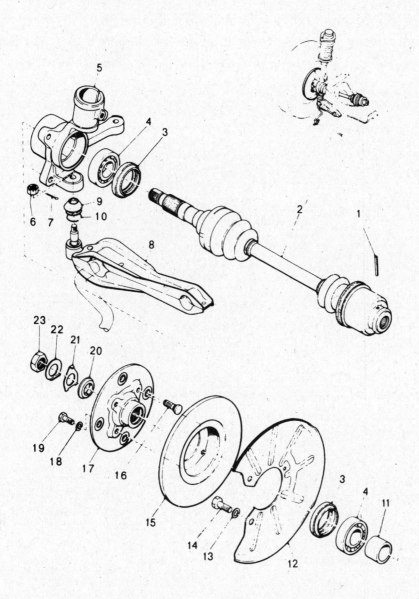

1. Spring pin
2. Axle shaft
3. Oil seal
4. Bearing
5. Housing
6. Castle nut
7. Cotter pin
8. Control arm
9. Dust seal (Ball joint)
10. Circlip
11. Spacer
12. Disc cover
13. Spring washer
14. Bolt
15. Disc
16. Hub bolt
17. Disc hub
18. Spring washer
19. Bolt
20. Center piece
21. Lockwasher
22. Lockplate
23. Nut

87907009

Fig. 7 Exploded view axle shaft assembly — ff-1 and 1300G models with disc brakes

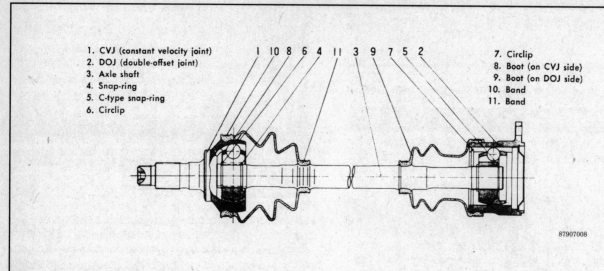

1. CVJ (constant velocity joint)
2. DOJ (double-offset joint)
3. Axle shaft
4. Snap-ring
5. C-type snap-ring
6. Circlip
7. Circlip
8. Boot (on CVJ side)
9. Boot (on DOJ side)
10. Band
11. Band

1 10 8 6 4 11 3 9 7 5 2

87907008

Fig. 8 Axle shaft components — ff-1 and 1300G models

19. Fit the washer and bushing over the end of the stabilizer bar and then connect the transverse link to the end of the stabilizer.

20. Install the remaining washer and bushing and temporarily secure them with a new self-locking nut.

21. Install the control arm to the crossmember pivot in the same way it was attached to the stabilizer bar in Step 7. Temporarily secure them with another new self-locking nut.

22. On disc brake models, install the dust cover, caliper, and parking brake cable, as detailed in section 8.

23. Install the wheel with the lug nuts, remove the jackstands, and lower the car to the ground.

24. Tighten the new self-locking nuts used at each end of the transverse link to 72-87 ft. lbs. (97-117 Nm) with the car resting on its wheels.

CV-JOINT OVERHAUL

▶ **See Figures 9 and 10**

1. Remove the bands from the boots at both the constant velocity and double offset joints, and slide the boots away from the joints.

2. Pry the circlip out of the double offset joint, and slide the outer race of the joint off the shaft.

3. Remove the balls from the cage, rotate the cage slightly, and slide the cage inward on the axle shaft.

4. Using snaping pliers, remove the outer snaping which retains the inner race to the shaft.

5. Slide the inner race, cage, and boot off the axle shaft.

✳✳WARNING

Exercise care to avoid damaging the boot on the inner snaping.

6. Pull back the constant velocity joint boot and pivot the stub axle around the joint far enough to expose a ball.

7. Remove the exposed ball, and continue this procedure until all balls are removed, at which time the outer race (stub axle) may be removed from the axle shaft.

TCCS7031

Fig. 9 Pry up on the outer band of the CV-boot

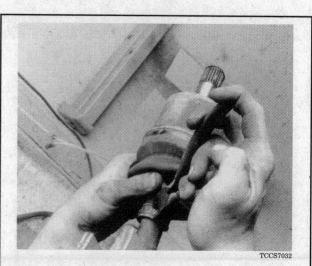

TCCS7032

Fig. 10 Use pliers to remove the inner band from the CV-boot

8. Remove the retaining snapring, and slide the inner race off the shaft.

9. Inspect the parts of both joints for wear, damage, or corrosion, and replace if necessary. Examine the axle shaft for bending or distortion, and replace if evident. Should the boots be dried out, cracked, or distorted, they must be replaced.

To install:

10. Install the constant velocity joint inner race on the axle shaft, and retain with a snapring.

11. Assemble the joint in the opposite order of disassembly.

12. Slide the double offset joint cage onto the shaft, with the counterbore toward the end of the shaft.

13. Install the inner race on the shaft.

14. Install the retaining snapring.

15. Position the cage over the inner race, and fill the cage pockets with grease.

16. Insert the balls into the cage.

17. Fill the well in the outer race with approximately 1 oz. (28 g) grease, and slide the outer race onto the axle shaft.

18. Install the retaining circlip, and add 1 oz. more grease to the interior of the joint. Fill the boot with approximately 1 oz. (28 g), grease, and slide it into position over the double offset joint.

19. Fill the constant velocity joint boot with 3 oz. grease, and install the boot over the joint.

20. Band the boots on both joints tightly enough that they cannot be turned by hand.

✳✳WARNING

Use only grease specified for use in constant velocity joints.

CLUTCH

✳✳CAUTION

The clutch driven disc may contain asbestos, which has been determined to be a cancer causing agent. Never clean clutch surfaces with compressed air! Avoid inhaling any dust from any clutch surface! When cleaning any clutch surfaces, use a commercially available brake cleaning fluid.

Adjustments

CABLE

The clutch cable can be adjusted at the cable bracket where the cable is attached to the side of the transaxle housing. To adjust the length of the cable, remove the circlip and clamp, slide the cable end in the direction desired and then replace the circlip and clamp into the nearest gutters on the cable end. The cable should not be stretched out straight nor should it have right angle kinks in it. Any curves should be gradual.

PEDAL HEIGHT

▶ **See Figure 11**

Adjust the pedal with the return stop bolt, so that its pad is on the same level as the brake pedal pad.

Check to be sure that the stroke of the pedal is 3-5.4 in. (128-138mm). Check the clutch release fork stroke. It should be 0.67 in. (17mm).

FREE-PLAY ADJUSTMENT

▶ **See Figure 12**

1. Remove the clutch fork return spring and loosen the locknut on the fork adjusting nut.

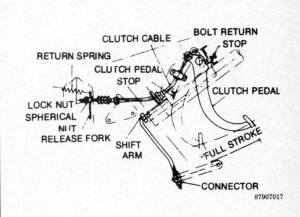

Fig. 11 Clutch pedal and linkage assembly

2. Turn the adjusting nut (wing nut) until a release fork free-play of 0.13-0.17 in. (3.5-4.5mm) is obtained.

3. Tighten the locknut.

4. Check the pedal free-play. It should be one of the following.

- ff-1 and 1300G: 1.18-1.4 in. (30-38mm)
- All other models 1970-84: 0.07-0.11 in. (2-3mm)

5. Adjust the pedal free-play, as necessary, with the pedal adjusting bolt.

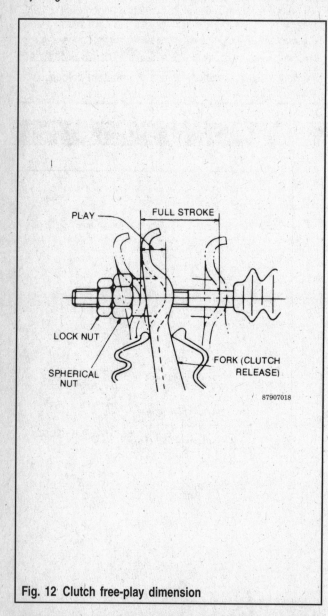

Fig. 12 Clutch free-play dimension

Clutch Cable

REMOVAL & INSTALLATION

The clutch cable is connected to the clutch pedal at one end and to the clutch release lever at the other end. The cable conduit is retained by a bolt and clamp on a bracket mounted on the flywheel housing.

1. If necessary, raise and support the vehicle safely.

2. Disconnect both ends of the cable and the conduit, then remove the assembly from under the vehicle.

3. Using engine oil, lubricate the clutch cable. If the cable is defective, replace it.

4. Installation is the reverse the removal procedure.

Driven Disc and Pressure Plate

REMOVAL & INSTALLATION

▶ See Figures 13, 14, 15, 16 and 17

✷✷CAUTION

The clutch driven disc may contain asbestos, which has been determined to be a cancer causing agent. Never clean clutch surfaces with compressed air! Avoid inhaling any dust from any clutch surface! When cleaning clutch surfaces, use a commercially available brake fluid.

1. Disconnect the negative (-) battery cable.

2. Depending on model, remove the engine and transaxle or just the transaxle as outlined earlier in this section.

3. Gradually unscrew the six bolts (6mm) which hold the pressure plate assembly on the flywheel. Loosen the bolts only one turn at a time, working around the pressure plate. Do not unscrew all the bolts on one side at one time.

4. When all of the bolts have been removed, remove the clutch plate and disc.

5. Remove the two retaining springs and remove the throwout bearing and the release fork.

➡**Do not disassemble either the clutch cover or disc. Inspect the parts for wear or damage and replace any parts as necessary. Replace the clutch disc if there is any oil or grease on the facing. Do not wash or attempt to lubricate the throwout bearing. If it requires replacement, the bearing may be removed and a new one installed in the holder by means of a press.**

To install:

6. Fit the release fork boot on the front of the transaxle housing.

7. Install the release fork.

8. Insert the throwout bearing assembly and secure it with the two springs.

9. Coat the inside diameter of the bearing holder and the fork-to-holder contact points with grease.

10. Insert a pilot shaft through the clutch cover and disc, then insert the end of the pilot into the needle bearing.

11. 1970-76 models should be tightened to 7-9 ft . lbs. (9-12 Nm), 1977-84 models to 12 ft. lbs. (16 Nm)

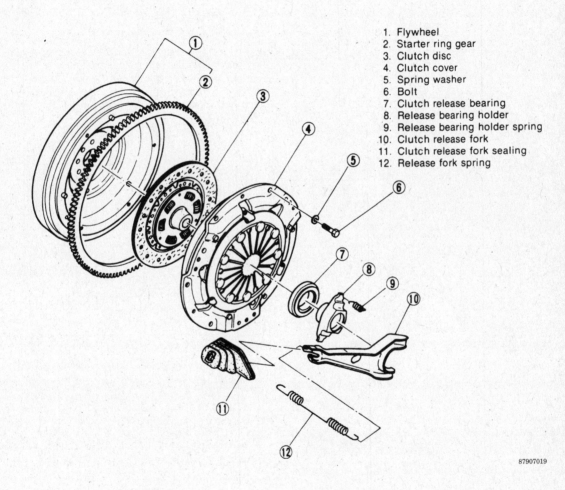

1. Flywheel
2. Starter ring gear
3. Clutch disc
4. Clutch cover
5. Spring washer
6. Bolt
7. Clutch release bearing
8. Release bearing holder
9. Release bearing holder spring
10. Clutch release fork
11. Clutch release fork sealing
12. Release fork spring

87907019

Fig. 13 Exploded view of the clutch assembly found on Subarus

Fig. 14 Removing the clutch and pressure plate bolts

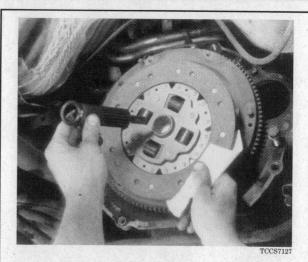

Fig. 16 Install a clutch alignment arbor, to align the clutch assembly during installation

Fig. 15 Removing the clutch and pressure plate

Fig. 17 Be sure to use a torque wrench to tighten all bolts

12. Tighten the pressure plate bolts gradually, one turn at a time, until the proper torque is reached.

✳✳WARNING

When installing the clutch pressure plate assembly, make sure that the O marks on the flywheel and the clutch pressure plate assembly are at least 120° apart. These marks indicate the direction of residual unbalance. Also, make sure that the clutch disc is installed properly, noting the FRONT and REAR markings.

13. After installation of the transaxle and engine in the car, perform the necessary adjustments.

AUTOMATIC TRANSAXLE

Understanding Automatic Transaxles

The automatic transaxle allows engine torque and power to be transmitted to the rear wheels within a narrow range of engine operating speeds. It will allow the engine to turn fast enough to produce plenty of power and torque at very low speeds, while keeping it at a sensible rpm at high vehicle speeds (and it does this job without driver assistance). The transaxle uses a light fluid as the medium for the transmission of power. This fluid also works in the operation of various hydraulic control circuits and as a lubricant. Because the transmission fluid performs all of these functions, trouble within the unit can easily travel from one part to another. For this reason, and because of the complexity and unusual operating principles of the transaxle, a very sound understanding of the basic principles of operation will simplify troubleshooting.

TORQUE CONVERTER

The torque converter replaces the conventional clutch. It has three functions:

1. It allows the engine to idle with the vehicle at a standstill, even with the transaxle in gear.

2. It allows the transaxle to shift from range-to-range smoothly, without requiring that the driver close the throttle during the shift.

3. It multiplies engine torque to an increasing extent as vehicle speed drops and throttle opening is increased. This has the effect of making the transaxle more responsive and reduces the amount of shifting required.

The torque converter is a metal case which is shaped like a sphere that has been flattened on opposite sides. It is bolted to the rear end of the engine's crankshaft. Generally, the entire metal case rotates at engine speed and serves as the engine's flywheel.

The case contains three sets of blades. One set is attached directly to the case. This set forms the torus or pump. Another set is directly connected to the output shaft, and forms the turbine. The third set is mounted on a hub which, in turn, is mounted on a stationary shaft through a one-way clutch. This third set is known as the stator.

A pump, which is driven by the converter hub at engine speed, keeps the torque converter full of transmission fluid at all times. Fluid flows continuously through the unit to provide cooling.

Under low speed acceleration, the torque converter functions as follows:

The torus is turning faster than the turbine. It picks up fluid at the center of the converter and, through centrifugal force, slings it outward. Since the outer edge of the converter moves faster than the portions at the center, the fluid picks up speed.

The fluid then enters the outer edge of the turbine blades. It then travels back toward the center of the converter case along the turbine blades. In impinging upon the turbine blades, the fluid loses the energy picked up in the torus.

If the fluid was now returned directly into the torus, both halves of the converter would have to turn at approximately the same speed at all times, and torque input and output would both be the same.

In flowing through the torus and turbine, the fluid picks up two types of flow, or flow in two separate directions. It flows through the turbine blades, and it spins with the engine. The stator, whose blades are stationary when the vehicle is being accelerated at low speeds, converts one type of flow into another. Instead of allowing the fluid to flow straight back into the torus, the stator's curved blades turn the fluid almost 90° toward the direction of rotation of the engine. Thus the fluid does not flow as fast toward the torus, but is already spinning when the torus picks it up. This has the effect of allowing the torus to turn much faster than the turbine. This difference in speed may be compared to the difference in speed between the smaller and larger gears in any gear train. The result is that engine power output is higher, and engine torque is multiplied.

As the speed of the turbine increases, the fluid spins faster and faster in the direction of engine rotation. As a result, the ability of the stator to redirect the fluid flow is reduced. Under cruising conditions, the stator is eventually forced to rotate on its one-way clutch in the direction of engine rotation. Under these conditions, the torque converter begins to behave almost like a solid shaft, with the torus and turbine speeds being almost equal.

PLANETARY GEARBOX

The ability of the torque converter to multiply engine torque is limited. Also, the unit tends to be more efficient when the turbine is rotating at relatively high speeds. Therefore, a planetary gearbox is used to carry the power output of the turbine to the driveshaft.

Planetary gears function very similarly to conventional transaxle gears. However, their construction is different in that three elements make up one gear system, and, in that all three elements are different from one another. The three elements are: an outer gear that is shaped like a hoop, with teeth cut into the inner surface; a sun gear, mounted on a shaft and located at the very center of the outer gear; and a set of three planet gears, held by pins in a ring-like planet carrier, meshing with both the sun gear and the outer gear. Either the outer gear or the sun gear may be held stationary, providing more than one possible torque multiplication factor for each set of gears. Also, if all three gears are forced to rotate at the same speed, the gearset forms, in effect, a solid shaft.

Most automatics use the planetary gears to provide various reductions ratios. Bands and clutches are used to hold various portions of the gearsets to the transaxle case or to the shaft on which they are mounted. Shifting is accomplished, then, by changing the portion of each planetary gearset which is held to the transaxle case or to the shaft.

SERVOS AND ACCUMULATORS

The servos are hydraulic pistons and cylinders. They resemble the hydraulic actuators used on many other machines, such as bulldozers. Hydraulic fluid enters the cylinder, under pressure, and forces the piston to move to engage the band or clutches.

The accumulators are used to cushion the engagement of the servos. The transmission fluid must pass through the accumulator on the way to the servo. The accumulator housing contains a thin piston which is sprung away from the discharge passage of the accumulator. When fluid passes through the accumulator on the way to the servo, it must move the piston against spring pressure, and this action smooths out the action of the servo.

HYDRAULIC CONTROL SYSTEM

The hydraulic pressure used to operate the servos comes from the main transaxle oil pump. This fluid is channeled to the various servos through the shift valves. There is generally a manual shift valve which is operated by the transaxle selector lever and an automatic shift valve for each automatic upshift the transaxle provides.

There are two pressures which affect the operation of these valves. One is the governor pressure which is effected by vehicle speed. The other is the modulator pressure which is effected by intake manifold vacuum or throttle position. Governor pressure rises with an increase in vehicle speed, and modulator pressure rises as the throttle is opened wider. By responding to these two pressures, the shift valves cause the upshift points to be delayed with increased throttle opening to make the best use of the engine's power output.

Most transaxles also make use of an auxiliary circuit for downshifting. This circuit may be actuated by the throttle linkage the vacuum line which actuates the modulator, by a cable or by a solenoid. It applies pressure to a special downshift surface on the shift valve or valves.

The transaxle modulator also governs the line pressure, used to actuate the servos. In this way, the clutches and bands will be actuated with a force matching the torque output of the engine.

Oil Pan and Filter

REMOVAL & INSTALLATION

▶ See Figures 18 and 19

The fluid should be changed with the transaxle warm. A 20 minute drive at highway speeds should accomplish this.

➡**Normal maintenance does not require removal of the transaxle oil pan, or changing or cleaning of the oil strainer. However, if a leak is detected at the transaxle oil pan gasket it must be replaced.**

1. Park the car on a level surface. Turn the engine **OFF**.
2. Raise the vehicle and support it with jackstands.
3. Remove the drain plug and drain the transaxle fluid into a suitable container.
4. Remove the mounting bolts and lower the oil pan and gasket.

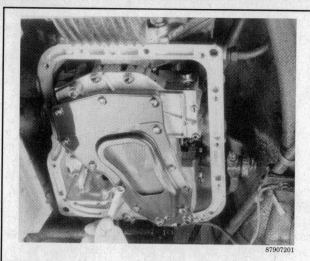

87907201

Fig. 19 Unbolt and remove the oil strainer from the valve body

5. Clean the pan thoroughly with solvent and air dry it. Be very careful not to get any lint from rags in the pan.

➡**It is normal to find a SMALL amount of metal shavings in the pan. An excessive amount of metal shavings indicates transaxle damage which must be handled by a professional automatic transaxle mechanic.**

6. Unbolt the oil strainer from the valve body.

➡**The strainer can be cleaned in fresh solvent and dried with compressed air or allowed to air dry.**

To install:
7. Install the oil strainer and fasten the retaining bolts.
8. Install the pan. Always use a new pan gasket.
9. Remove the jackstands and lower the vehicle.
10. Start the vehicle and let it run for five minutes. Check for leaks.

Adjustments

SHIFT LINKAGE

▶ See Figure 20

The linkage adjustment is important for the automatic transaxle. Great care should be exercised because improper adjustment will result in damage to the transaxle.

To determine if adjustment is necessary, check the shifting operation with the engine off and the parking brake applied. While holding in the release button with your thumb, move the selector lever forward until you can feel that the transaxle is in park. Then move the lever back and feel for the five remaining positions. If the gear selector indicator points to the proper gear at each stop, and if the selector lever does not jump when the release button is let go, the shift linkage is properly adjusted. If this is not the case adjustment is necessary.

1. Place the gear selector in Neutral position.
2. Loosen the adjusting nuts on the linkage rod.
3. Check that the manual lever on the transaxle is in the **N** detent position.

87907200

Fig. 18 Loosen and remove the mounting bolts, then lower the oil pan and gasket

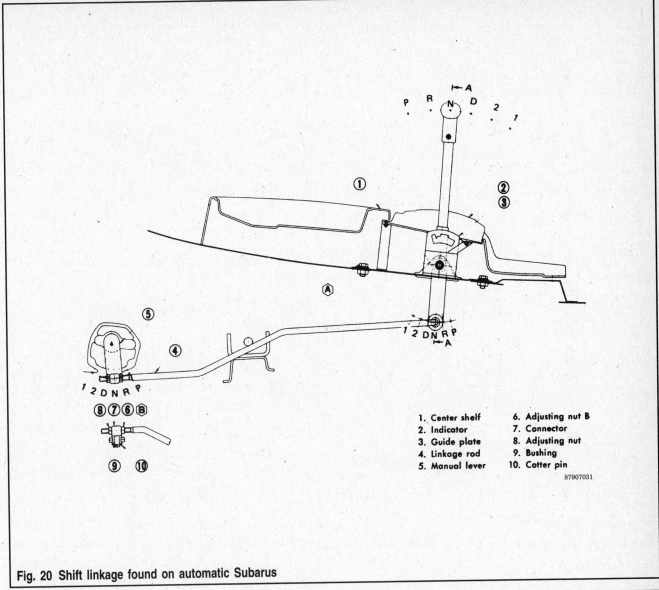

Fig. 20 Shift linkage found on automatic Subarus

1. Center shelf
2. Indicator
3. Guide plate
4. Linkage rod
5. Manual lever
6. Adjusting nut B
7. Connector
8. Adjusting nut
9. Bushing
10. Cotter pin

87907031

4. Set the gear selector lever so that it clicks in the Neutral position.

5. Tighten the adjusting nuts.

BRAKE BAND ADJUSTMENT

▶ **See Figure 21**

This adjustment can be performed on the outside of the transaxle.

1. Park the car on a level surface.

2. Raise the vehicle and support it with jackstands, engine OFF.

3. Locate the adjusting screw above the pan on the left side of the transaxle.

4. Loosen the locknut.

5. On models 1970-80, tighten the adjusting screw to 6.5 ft. lbs. (8 Nm), then turn it back exactly 2 full turns.

6. On 1981-84 models, tighten the adjusting screw to 18 ft. lbs. (24 Nm), then turn it back exactly ¾ turn.

7. Tighten the locknut.

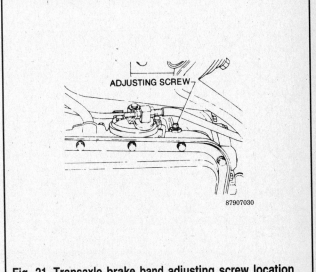

Fig. 21 Transaxle brake band adjusting screw location

Following the above procedure will adjust the transaxle brake band to the factory specified setting. However, if any of the following conditions are detected the adjusting screw can be moved ¼ turn in either direction:

Turn ¼ turn clockwise if the transaxle:

- Jolts when shifting from 1st to 2nd
- Engine speed abruptly rises from 2nd to 3rd, or,
- Shift delays in kickdown from 3rd to 2nd.

Turn ¼ turn counterclockwise if:

- Car slips from 1st to 2nd, or
- There is braking action at shift from 2nd to 3rd.

THROTTLE LINKAGE

The control valve assembly of the automatic transaxle is governed by intake manifold vacuum rather than throttle position, therefore, there is no linkage which requires adjustment.

KICKDOWN SOLENOID

The kickdown solenoid is located on the right side of the transaxle case. The switch is operated by the upper part of the accelerator lever inside the car, and its position can be varied to give slower or quicker kickdown response. To test its function press the accelerator to the floor with the engine off and the ignition switch on. An audible click should be heard from the solenoid.

Neutral Safety Switch (Inhibitor Switch)

REMOVAL & INSTALLATION

▶ **See Figure 22**

This switch is mounted on the transaxle lever shaft and is bolted to the transaxle. It functions to prevent the car from starting in any gear position but Park or Neutral, and to activate the back-up lights when in Reverse. Adjustment is as follows.

1. Disconnect the linkage rod from the transaxle manual lever.

➡**Refer to the illustration of the shift linkage system earlier in this section.**

2. Make sure that the manual lever on the transaxle is in the neutral detent position.
3. Remove the manual lever by taking off the mounting nut.
4. Remove the two safety switch mounting bolts and the setscrew from the lower face of the switch.
5. Disconnect the wire harness from the switch.

To install:

6. Connect the wire harness from the switch.
7. Bolt the switch in place.
8. Reinstall the setscrew and the manual lever.
9. Connect the linkage rod and adjust, if necessary, according to the procedure given earlier in this section.

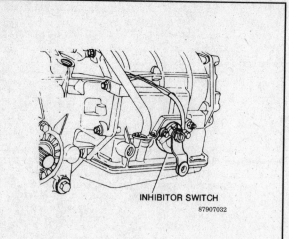

Fig. 22 Location of the neutral safety switch (inhibitor switch)

ADJUSTMENT

1. Disconnect the linkage rod from the transaxle manual lever.

➡**Refer to the illustration of the shift linkage system earlier in this section.**

2. Make sure that the manual lever on the transaxle is in the neutral detent position.
3. Remove the manual lever by taking off the mounting nut.
4. Remove the two safety switch mounting bolts and the setscrew from the lower face of the switch.
5. Insert a 1.5mm drill bit through the set screw hole. Turn the switch slightly so that the drill bit passes through into the back part of the switch.
6. Bolt the switch in place and remove the drill bit.
7. Reinstall the setscrew and the manual lever.
8. Connect the linkage rod and adjust, if necessary, according to the procedure given earlier in this section.

Transaxle

REMOVAL & INSTALLATION

Except Turbo Engines

➡**The transaxle can be removed separately from the vehicle.**

1. Raise and secure the hood.
2. If equipped, remove the spare wheel from engine compartment.
3. Disconnect the negative (-) battery cable.
4. Remove the spare wheel supporter clamps and the supporter from the vehicle.
5. If equipped with a carburetor, remove the air duct.
6. Disconnect the diaphragm vacuum hose (2WD) and/or the air breather hose (4WD).

7. From the transaxle, disconnect and remove the speedometer cable.

8. Disconnect the speedometer cable clip.

9. Disengage the electrical wiring connectors from the back-up lamp switch.

10. Disconnect the O_2 sensor (exhaust pipe), the transaxle-to-chassis ground strap and starter.

11. Remove the starter and move it aside.

12. If equipped with a turbocharger, perform the following procedures:

    a. Remove the accelerator cable cover from the transaxle.

    b. Remove the turbo covers from the turbocharger and the center exhaust pipe.

    c. Disconnect the exhaust pipe-to-turbocharger bolts.

    d. Raise and support the front of the vehicle with jackstands.

    e. Disconnect the center exhaust pipe-to-rear pipe nuts/bolts.

    f. Remove the center exhaust pipe-to-vehicle hanger bolt.

    g. Disconnect the exhaust pipe from the transaxle.

    h. Remove the center exhaust pipe and lower the vehicle to the floor.

13. Remove the timing hole from the flywheel housing.

14. Working through the timing plug hole, remove the torque converter-to-drive plate bolts.

➡ **Be careful that the bolts do not fall into the converter housing.**

15. Disconnect and plug the oil cooler hoses from the transaxle; be careful not to damage the O-ring.

16. From the right-side, remove the engine/transaxle assembly-to-chassis support (pitching stopper rod) nut/bolt and loosen the lower nuts.

17. Remove the exhaust pipe-to-cylinder head nuts, the exhaust pipe-to-rear pipe nuts/bolts, the exhaust pipe-to-hanger bracket and the front exhaust pipe from the vehicle.

18. If equipped with 4WD, disconnect the driveshaft from the rear of the transaxle and plug the opening to prevent oil from draining from the opening.

19. Disconnect the linkage rod from the shift lever.

20. Loosen the stabilizer-to-transverse link nuts and bolts, on the lower side of the plate.

21. Remove the transverse link by performing the following procedures:

    a. Remove the hand brake cable bracket from the transverse link.

    b. Remove the transverse link-to-crossmember nut/bolt and the link from the vehicle.

22. Using a hammer and the pin punch, drive the spring pin (discard it) from the axle shaft/drive shaft assembly.

23. Push the tire outward to separate the axle shaft from the driveshaft; perform this procedures on each side.

24. Remove the engine-to-transaxle nuts.

25. Position a transmission jack under the transaxle and secure the jack to the transaxle. Remove the rear rubber cushion mounting nuts.

26. Remove the rear crossmember-to-chassis bolts and the crossmember from the vehicle.

27. Moving the floor jack rearward and downward, remove the transaxle from the vehicle.

To install:

28. Align the chamfered holes of the axle shaft with the driveshaft (install a new spring pin) and reverse the removal procedures.

29. Tighten the crossmember-to-chassis bolts to 27-49 ft. lbs. (36-66 Nm), the rubber cushion-to-crossmember bolts to 20-35 ft. lbs. (27-47 Nm).

30. Tighten the lower engine-to-transaxle bolts to 34-40 ft. lbs. (46-54 Nm) and the transverse link-to-front crossmember nuts/bolts (use new self-locking nuts) to 43-51 ft. lbs. (58-69 Nm).

31. Tighten the transverse link-to-stabilizer bolts to 14-22 ft. lbs. (18-29 Nm) and the pitching stopper rod-to-engine/transaxle assembly nut/bolt to 34-40 ft. lbs. (46-54 Nm)

Turbo Engines

1. Open the front hood and support it securely. Remove the spare tire.

2. Disconnect the negative battery cable.

3. Remove the spare tire mounting bracket.

4. Remove the thermosensor.

5. Disconnect vacuum hoses from the air intake shutter, transaxle breather, and vacuum control diaphragm.

6. Disconnect the accelerator cable and link and move them out of the way.

7. Disconnect the speedometer cable at the transaxle and move it out of the way.

8. Disengage wiring harnesses at the transfer solenoid connector.

9. Disengage transaxle kickdown solenoid connector.

10. Disengage the body ground and O_2 sensor connector.

11. Disengage the starter connector.

12. Remove the upper cover from the turbocharger.

13. Remove the center exhaust pipe by:

    a. Detaching it at the turbocharger body.

    b. Removing the rear cover.

    c. Removing the bolt supporting the pipe at the transaxle and disconnecting it from the rear exhaust pipe.

    d. Removing the hanger bolt from the bottom of the transaxle.

    e. Disengage the pipe from the attaching studs and remove it.

14. Loosen (do not remove) the attaching bolts and remove the front exhaust pipe cover.

15. Remove the turbocharger as follows:

    a. Remove the intake duct.

    b. Remove the air flow meter boot.

    c. Disconnect the inlet oil pipe.

    d. Unfasten the mounting bolts and remove the turbocharger together with the outlet oil hose.

    e. Lower cover and gasket. (You may want to refer to the Turbocharger Removal and Installation procedure in Section 3 for more detail).

16. Raise the car and support it with jackstands.

17. Remove the bolts attaching the tighten converter to the drive plate.

18. Remove the bolts joining the engine and transaxle to one another.

19. Remove the bolts joining the starter to the transaxle. The starter-to-battery cable may be left connected.

20. Disconnect both oil cooler lines at the transaxle.

21. Loosen the retaining bolt on the transaxle side of the pitching stopper about 0.39 in. (10mm) and tighten the nut on the opposite side a corresponding amount. This will tilt the engine backward to aid in transaxle removal. Do not loosen/tighten the nuts more than the specified amount!

22. Drain the torque converter.

23. Remove the oil supply pipe, being careful not to damage the O-ring.

24. Mark the position of the transaxle shift rod nut. Remove the nut for the transaxle shift rod and disconnect the rod. Set the selector lever on the transaxle to Park position if it is not already there.

25. Remove the stabilizer by removing the two bolts and nut.

26. Remove the right and left side hand brake clamps.

27. Remove the inner transverse link by removing the nut and bolt on both sides that fastens it to the front suspension crossmember. Lower the link and remove it.

28. Separate the right and left side axle shafts from the transaxle driveshaft.

29. On each side, remove the spring pin, and then separate the axle shaft from the driveshaft by pushing the rear of either front wheel outward.

30. Remove the lower engine-to-transaxle nuts. Do not loosen upper nuts yet.

31. Remove the rear transaxle mount nuts.

32. Disconnect the driveshaft, and cap off the opening to retain transaxle fluid.

33. Support the transaxle securely with a jack.

34. Remove the rear crossmember.

35. Remove the upper transaxle-to-engine mounting nuts.

36. Move the jack rearward until the front of the transaxle is no longer in contact with the front crossmember.

37. Lower the transaxle and pull it out.

To install:

38. Use new spring pins in the axle shafts.

39. When installing the rear crossmember, make sure it's positioned properly on the rubber bushings. There are guides on the crossmember and bushings. Tighten the 8mm nuts to 7-13 ft. lbs. (9-17 Nm), and the 12mm nuts to 65-87 ft. lbs. (88-117 Nm).

40. Additional torque figures are:
- Lower transaxle-to-engine nuts: 34-40 ft. lbs. (46-54 Nm)
- Driveshaft bolts/nuts: 13-18 ft. lbs. (17-24 Nm)
- Rear mount nuts: 14-25 ft. lbs. (18-33 Nm)
- Transverse link bolts (use new self-locking nuts): 13-16 ft. lbs. (17-21 Nm)
- Stabilizer (make sure slits on bushings face inward) 13-16 ft. lbs. (17-21 Nm)
- Linkage rod nut: 5.8-8.7 ft. lbs. (7-11 Nm)
- Pitching stopper (adjusted to 2mm clearance): 6.5-9.4 ft. lbs. (8-12 Nm)
- Starter-to-transaxle and engine: 34-40 ft. lbs. (46-54 Nm)
- Torque converter to drive plate: 17-20 ft. lbs. (23-27 Nm)

Make sure the transaxle fluid level is correct with the engine idling.

Halfshaft

REMOVAL & INSTALLATION

▶ **See Figures 23, 24, 25, 26, 27, 28 and 29**

1. Disconnect the negative (-) battery cable.

2. Engage the parking brake. Remove the front wheel grease cap and the cotter pin.

3. Loosen the wheel hub nuts and the halfshaft castle nut.

4. Raise and support the front of the vehicle with jackstands.

5. Remove the wheel lug nuts, the wheel/tire assembly and the hub nut.

6. Release the parking brake.

7. Remove the parking brake cable bracket from the transverse link.

8. Using a pin punch, drive out the Double-Offset Joint (DOJ)-to-transaxle shaft, spring (roll) pin; discard the old pin.

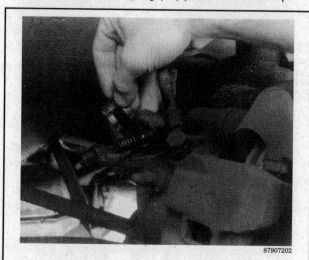

87907202

Fig. 23 Remove the parking brake cable bracket from the transverse link

87907101

Fig. 24 Using a pin punch, drive out the spring (roll) pin

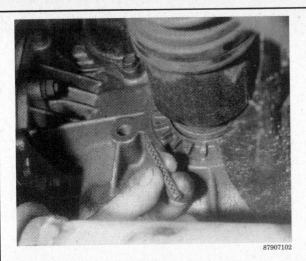

Fig. 25 Close-up of the spring pin. Always use new pins when installing the shafts

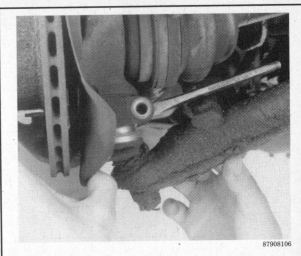

Fig. 28 Lower the transverse link from the steering knuckle

Fig. 26 Using a ball joint puller tool, separate the tie-rod end from the steering knuckle

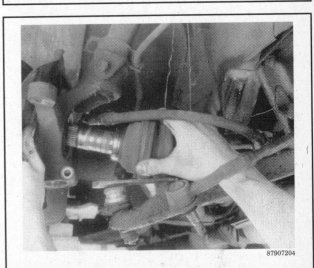

Fig. 29 Push out on the housing to remove the halfshaft from the steering knuckle housing

9. Remove the disc brake caliper-to-steering knuckle bolts and the brake caliper from the steering knuckle; using a wire, suspend it (DO NOT disconnect the brake hose) from the strut tower.

10. Remove the damper strut-to-steering knuckle bolts.

11. At the tie-rod end ball stud, remove the cotter pin and the castle nut.

12. Using a Ball Joint Puller tool, remove the tie-rod end from the steering knuckle.

13. Remove the transverse link ball stud-to-steering knuckle bolt. Using a cold chisel, drive it into the slit on the steering knuckle housing (to expand the joint), then lower the transverse link from the steering knuckle.

14. Using the Puller tool No. 926470000 or equivalent, press the halfshaft from the steering knuckle housing.

15. Clean and inspect the parts for wear and/or damage.

To install:

16. Install the halfshaft into the steering knuckle housing and attach the Installation Spacer tool No. 925130000 or

Fig. 27 Using a cold chisel, drive it into the slit on the steering knuckle housing to expand the joint

922430000 or equivalent, onto the outer bearing inner race; be careful not to damage the oil seal lip.

17. Use a new spring pin and reverse the removal procedures.

18. Tighten the transverse link ball joint-to-housing bolts to 22-29 ft. lbs. (29-39 Nm) and the damper strut-to-housing bolts to 22-29 ft. lbs. (29-39 Nm).

19. Tighten the disc cover-to-housing bolts to 4-19 ft. lbs. (5-25 Nm) and the steering knuckle housing-to-halfshaft nut to 145 ft. lbs. (196 Nm)

➡**After tightening the halfshaft nut to specifications, re-tighten it another 30 degrees further.**

OVERHAUL

1. Remove the bands from the boots at both the constant velocity and double offset joints, and slide the boots away from the joints.

2. Pry the circlip out of the double offset joint, and slide the outer race of the joint off the shaft.

3. Remove the balls from the cage, rotate the cage slightly, and slide the cage inward on the axle shaft.

4. Using snapring pliers, remove the outer snapring which retains the inner race to the shaft.

5. Slide the inner race, cage, and boot off the axle shaft.

✳✳WARNING

Exercise care to avoid damaging the boot on the inner snapring.

6. Pull back the constant velocity joint boot and pivot the stub axle around the joint far enough to expose a ball.

7. Remove the exposed ball, and continue this procedure until all balls are removed, at which time the outer race (stub axle) may be removed from the axle shaft.

8. Remove the retaining snapring, and slide the inner race off the shaft.

9. Inspect the parts of both joints for wear, damage, or corrosion, and replace if necessary. Examine the axle shaft for bending or distortion, and replace if evident. Should the boots be dried out, cracked, or distorted, they must be replaced.

To install:

10. Install the constant velocity joint inner race on the axle shaft, and retain with a snapring.

11. Assemble the joint in the opposite order of disassembly.

12. Slide the double offset joint cage onto the shaft, with the counterbore toward the end of the shaft.

13. Install the inner race on the shaft, and install the retaining snapring.

14. Position the cage over the inner race, and fill the cage pockets with grease.

15. Insert the balls into the cage.

16. Fill the well in the outer race with approximately 1 oz. (28 g) grease, and slide the outer race onto the axle shaft.

17. Install the retaining circlip, and add 1 oz. (28 g) more grease to the interior of the joint. Fill the boot with approximately 1 oz. (28 g) grease, and slide it into position over the double offset joint.

18. Fill the constant velocity joint boot with 3 oz. grease, and install the boot over the joint.

19. Band the boots on both joints tightly enough that they cannot be turned by hand.

✳✳WARNING

Use only grease specified for use in constant velocity joints.

TRANSFER CASE

▶ **See Figure 30**

The transfer case provides a direct drive (1:1 gear ratio) coupling to the rear differential. This means that when the 4WD unit is engaged, the transaxle provides equal power to the front and rear differentials. When the 4WD unit is not engaged power is transmitted to only the front wheels. In either case shifting of the transaxle remains the same. Late models have dual range 4WD.

The drive selector can be shifted at any time, with or without clutching. However, if you shift the drive selector while the car is moving the steering wheel should be in the straight forward position. This minimizes the load on the rear drive system and shifting is made easier.

➡**You may feel a braking action when turning a sharp corner in four wheel drive. This is a normal phenomenon which arises from the difference in turning radius between the front wheels and the rear wheels, and will not occur when running in front wheel drive.**

The transfer case is integral with the transaxle and must be serviced as a unit.

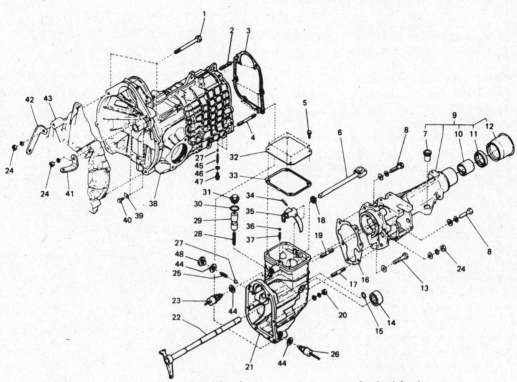

1. Bolt
2. Stud bolt
3. Transmission cover gasket
4. Stud bolt
5. Bolt and washer
6. Shifter fork rail 3
7. Change rod bushing
8. Bolt
9. Transmission case 4
10. Rear extension bushing
11. Extension oil seal
12. Transmission cover 4
13. Bolt
14. Needle bearing
15. O-ring
16. Transmission case gasket
17. Stud bolt

18. Oil seal
19. Stud bolt
20. Nut
21. Transmission case 3
22. Shifter arm
23. Back-up light switch assembly
    (4WD selector)
24. Nut
25. Reverse accent spring
26. Back-up switch assembly
27. Ball
28. Reverse return spring
29. Reverse accent shaft
30. Aluminum gasket *
31. Plug
32. Transmission case cover 3
33. Transmission case gasket 3

34. Straight pin
35. Shifter fork 3
36. Ball
37. Shifter rail spring
38. Transmission case assembly
39. Release spring bracket
40. Bolt
41. Stiffener 2
42. Stiffener
43. Flywheel housing
44. Gasket
45. Shifter fork rail spring
46. Aluminum gasket
47. Shifter rail spring plug
48. Filler

* Selective part

87907034

Fig. 30 Transaxle/transfer case assembly found on 4WD Subarus

DRIVELINE

Rear Driveshaft and U-Joints

REMOVAL & INSTALLATION

1. Raise and support the vehicle with jackstands.
2. Position a drain pan under the rear of the transaxle, to catch the excess oil from the transaxle; plug the transaxle opening (if necessary).
3. Remove the driveshaft flange-to-rear differential flange bolts and separate the driveshaft from the differential flange.
4. While supporting the rear of the driveshaft, gently pull it rearward to remove it from the vehicle.
5. To install, reverse the above process. Tighten the center bearing-to-chassis bolts to 25-33 ft. lb. (33-44 Nm) and the driveshaft-to-rear differential flange bolts to 13-20 ft. lbs. (17-27 Nm) Check and/or refill the transaxle.

OVERHAUL

▶ **See Figures 31 and 32**

Selective snaprings are used to provide proper clearance of the gearing cap-to-yoke. The clearance should be 0.0007 in. (0.02mm) and the opposing snaprings must be of the same thickness.

As a rule, the driveshaft U-joints should not be removed since the driveshaft is balanced at the factory and the U-joints are constructed to be maintenance free. However, if removal and overhaul of the U-joints should become necessary, proceed as follows.

1. Remove the driveshaft as outlined.
2. Matchmark the flange yoke, sleeve yoke and U-joint in such a way that it can be reassembled exactly as it was.
3. Remove the snaprings which retain the bearing races one at a time by using a flat-blade prybar.
4. Remove the bearing race by tapping on the other side of the yoke with a hammer.
5. Repeat Steps 3 and 4 until the U-joint is free.
6. Reassemble in the reverse order of removal.
7. Be sure to align the matchmarks and to use new grease.
8. It is also necessary to measure the side play of the U-joints in each direction. The proper play, after installation of

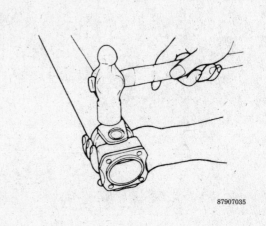

87907035

Fig. 31 Removing the bearing race

the U-joint, is 0.0003 in. (0.1mm). Snaprings of various sizes are available to achieve this tolerance (they range from 0.07-0.08 in. (1.9-2.1mm). Also, the opposing snaprings must be of the same thickness.

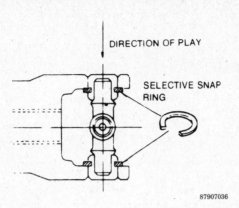

DIRECTION OF PLAY

SELECTIVE SNAP RING

87907036

Fig. 32 Selective snaprings are used to obtain the proper clearance between the bearing cap and yoke

REAR AXLE

The rear drive system of the four wheel drive models contains a differential unit, a driveshaft connected to the output shaft of the transfer case, and an axle shaft running to each rear wheel. The driveshaft is equipped with two maintenance free universal joints and a ball spline at the transfer case connection. To aid in reducing drive train noise and vibration, the differential is mounted to the vehicle body with three or four rubber bushings, one or two at the front and two at the rear of the differential carrier.

Understanding Drive Axles

Power enters the axle from the driveshaft via the companion flange. The flange is mounted on the drive pinion shaft. The drive pinion shaft and gear which carry the power into the differential turn at engine speed. The gear on the end of the pinion shaft drives a large ring gear the axis of rotation of which is 90° away from the of the pinion. The pinion and gear reduce the gear ratio of the axle, and change the direction of rotation to turn the axle shafts which drive both wheels. The axle gear ratio is found by dividing the number of pinion gear teeth into the number of ring gear teeth.

The ring gear drives the differential case. The case provides the two mounting points for the ends of a pinion shaft on which are mounted two pinion gears. The pinion gears drive the two side gears, one of which is located on the inner end of each axle shaft.

By driving the axle shafts through the arrangement, the differential allows the outer drive wheel to turn faster than the inner drive wheel in a turn.

The main drive pinion and the side bearings, which bear the weight of the differential case, are shimmed to provide proper bearing preload, and to position the pinion and ring gears properly.

❋❋WARNING

The proper adjustment of the relationship of the ring and pinion gears is critical. It should be attempted only by those with extensive equipment and/or experience.

Limited slip differentials include clutches which tend to link each axle shaft to the differential case. Clutches may be engaged either by spring action or by pressure produced by the torque on the axles during a turn. During turning on a dry pavement, the effects of the clutches are overcome, and each wheel turns at the required speed. When slippage occurs at either wheel, however, the clutches will transmit some of the power to the wheel which has the greater amount of traction. Because of the presence of clutches, limited slip units require a special lubricant.

Determining Axle Ratio

The drive axle is said to have a certain axle ratio. This number (usually a whole number and a decimal fraction) is actually a comparison of the number of gear teeth on the ring gear and the pinion gear. For example, a 4.11 rear means that theoretically, there are 4.11 teeth on the ring gear and one tooth on the pinion gear or, put another way, the driveshaft must turn 4.11 times to turn the wheels once. Actually, on a 4.11 rear, there might be 37 teeth on the ring gear and 9 teeth on the pinion gear. By dividing the number of teeth on the pinion gear into the number of teeth on the ring gear, the numerical axle ratio (4.11) is obtained. This also provides a good method of ascertaining exactly what axle ratio one is dealing with.

Another method of determining gear ratio is to jack up and support the car so that both rear wheels are off the ground. Make a chalk mark on the rear wheel and the driveshaft. Put the transaxle in neutral. Turn the rear wheel one complete turn and count the number of turns that the driveshaft makes. The number of turns that the driveshaft makes in one complete revolution of the rear wheel is an approximation of the rear axle ratio.

Rear Differential Carrier

REMOVAL & INSTALLATION

▶ See Figures 33 and 34

1. Drain the differential oil as outlined in Section 1.
2. Raise the rear wheels and support the car with jackstands.
3. Remove the exhaust pipe and muffler as outlined in Section 3.
4. Remove the driveshaft and axle shafts.
5. Support the differential carrier with a jack.
6. Remove the two nuts securing the differential to the rear mounting bracket.
7. Remove the two bolts securing the differential to the front mounting bracket.
8. Lower the jack and remove the differential.
9. Installation is the reverse of removal.
10. Observe the following torque specifications:
    - Rear mounting nuts: 48 ft. lbs. (65 Nm)
    - Front mounting bolts: 60 ft. lbs. (81 Nm)

Rear Halfshafts

REMOVAL & INSTALLATION

Sleeve Yoke Type

▶ See Figure 35

1. Drain the differential oil as outlined in Section 1.
2. Raise the rear wheels and support the car with jackstands.
3. Remove the four mounting bolts which secure the halfshaft to the wheel.
4. Remove the side yoke retaining bolt which secures the halfshaft to the differential.
5. Lower the halfshaft assembly, being careful not to damage the rubber boot.
6. Reverse the above process to install the halfshaft.

Double Offset Joint Type

1. Firmly apply the parking brake.
2. Remove the rear wheel cap and the cotter pin, then loosen the castle nut.
3. Disconnect the shock absorber from the inner arm.
4. Loosen the crossmember outer bushing lock bolts.
5. Remove the inner trailing arm-to-chassis bolt and the inner arm.
6. Raise and support the rear of the vehicle with jackstands.
7. Remove the rear wheel assemblies.

8. Using a 6mm diameter. steel rod or a pin punch, drive the inner/outer spring pins from the DOJ's (Double Offset Joint).
9. With the trailing arm fully lowered, remove the ball joint from the trailing arm spindle and the inner DOJ from the differential spindle.
10. Remove the castle nut and the brake drum
11. Disconnect and plug the brake hose from the inner arm bracket.
12. Remove the brake assembly from the trailing arm.
13. Disconnect the inner arm from the outer arm and remove the inner arm from the vehicle.
14. Secure the inner arm in a vise, then using a hammer and a punch, straighten the staked portion of the ring nut. Using tool No. 925550000 or equivalent, remove the ring nut.
15. Using a plastic hammer on the outside of the spindle, drive it inward to remove it.

To install:

16. Clean, inspect and/or replace the necessary parts.
17. Using an arbor press and a piece of 35mm pipe, insert the spindle from the inside and press the outer bearing's inner race from outside.
18. Using tool No. 925550000 or equivalent, tighten the axle shaft ring nut to 127-163 ft. lbs. (172-220 Nm). Using a punch and a hammer, stake the ring nut, facing the ring nut groove.
19. To complete the installation, use new spring pins and reverse the removal procedures.
20. Tighten the backing plate-to-axle housing bolts to 34-43 ft. lbs. (46-58 Nm).
21. Tighten the axle spindle-to-axle housing nut to 145 ft. lbs. (196 Nm) and the shock absorber-to-inner arm bolt to 65-87 ft. lbs. (88-117 Nm).
22. Bleed the brake system.

➡After tightening the rear axle halfshaft-to-axle housing nut, tighten the axle shaft nut 30 degrees further.

Rear Halfshaft Bearing And Seal

REMOVAL & INSTALLATION

1. Refer to the rear halfshaft removal and installation procedures in this section and remove the halfshaft.
2. From the inner arm housing, remove the oil seal.
3. From outside the housing, insert the spindle and extract the inner bearing's outer race and the spacer. Using an arbor press and the spindle, push the outer bearing's inner race from the housing.
4. Using an arbor press, press the inner bearing's inner race from the spindle.
5. Clean, inspect and/or replace the necessary parts.

To install:

6. Using an arbor press, install the inner bearing's inner race onto the spindle and the outer races (inner and outer bearings) into the housing.
7. Inside the housing, grease the bearing outer race.
8. Using an arbor press and a piece of 35mm pipe, insert the spindle from the inside and press the outer bearing's inner race from outside.

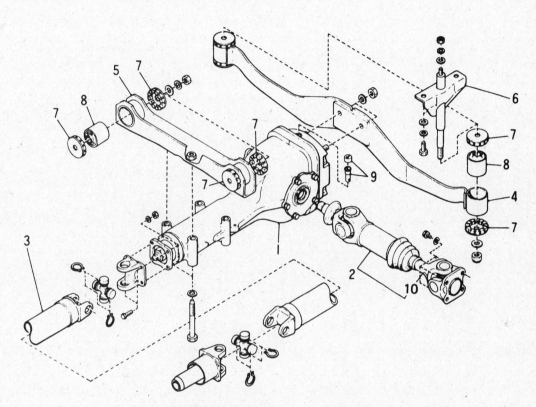

1. Differential assembly
2. Drive shaft assembly
3. Propeller shaft assembly
4. Mounting member
5. Mounting bracket
6. Bracket
7. Stopper
8. Bushing
9. Breather cap
10. Flange yoke

87907037

Fig. 33 Exploded view of the rear differential mounting and components

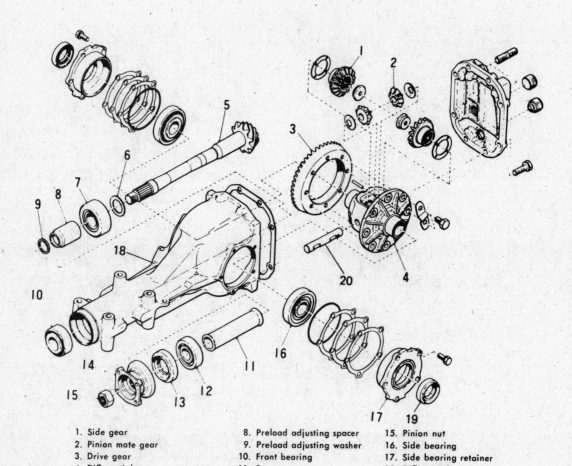

1. Side gear
2. Pinion mate gear
3. Drive gear
4. Differential case
5. Drive pinion
6. Pinion height adjusting washer
7. Rear bearing
8. Preload adjusting spacer
9. Preload adjusting washer
10. Front bearing
11. Spacer
12. Pilot bearing
13. Oil seal
14. Companion flange
15. Pinion nut
16. Side bearing
17. Side bearing retainer
18. Differential carrier
19. Side oil seal
20. Differential pinion shaft

87907045

Fig. 34 Exploded view of the differential carrier

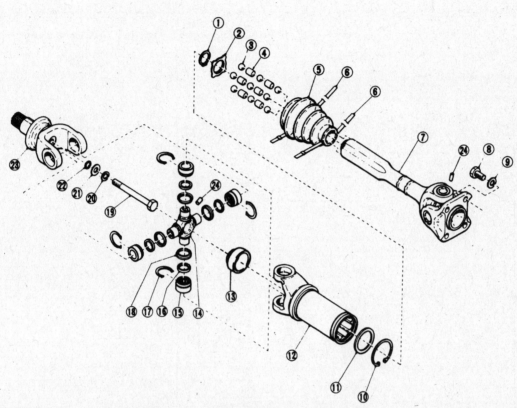

1. Snap—ring	9. Spring washer	17. Snap—ring
2. Stopper	10. Snap ring	18. Dust cover (oil seal)
3. Ball	11. Stopper	19. Bolt
4. Ball spacer	12. Sleeve yoke	20. Spring washer
5. Rubber boot	13. Cap	21. Washer
6. Boot band	14. Cross	22. O-ring
7. Yoke	15. Bearing race	23. Side yoke
8. Bolt	16. Oil seal	24. Grease nipple

87907046

Fig. 35 Exploded view of the sleeve yoke halfshaft assembly

9. Using tool No. 925550000 or equivalent, tighten the axle shaft ring nut to 127-163 ft. lbs. (172-220 Nm) Using a punch and a hammer, stake the ring nut, facing the ring nut groove.

10. Using the Oil Seal Installation tool No. 925530000 or equivalent, and a new oil seal, install a new oil seal into the housing.

11. To complete the installation, use new spring pins and reverse the removal procedures.

12. Tighten the backing plate-to-axle housing bolts to 34-43 ft. lbs. (46-58 Nm).

13. Tighten the axle spindle-to-axle housing nut to 145 ft. lbs. (196 Nm) and the shock absorber-to-inner arm bolt to 65-87 ft. lbs. (88-117 Nm).

14. Bleed the brake system.

➡ **After tightening the rear axle halfshaft-to-axle housing nut, tighten the axle shaft nut 30 degrees further.**

Differential Oil Seals

REMOVAL & INSTALLATION

Front Oil Seal

▶ **See Figures 36, 37 and 38**

1. Drain the differential gear oil as outlined in Section 1.
2. Raise the rear wheels and support the car with jackstands.
3. Remove the driveshaft as outlined earlier in this section.
4. Measure the turning resistance of the differential companion flange. To do this, attach either a spring scale or an inch pound torque wrench to one of the mounting holes. Make sure that the flange turns smoothly, and then turn the flange through one complete revolution using the scale or torque wrench. Mark down the reading registered. It will be used during installation.
5. Remove the drive pinion nut while holding the companion flange with a flange or pipe wrench.
6. Remove the companion flange and oil seal with a puller.
7. Using a drift, tap in a new oil seal.

To install:

8. Install the companion flange.
9. Tighten the pinion nut to 123-145 ft. lbs. (167-196 Nm). The proper torque has been reached when the turning resistance of the companion flange is the same as it was when measured in Step 4.
10. Stake the pinion nut with a punch.

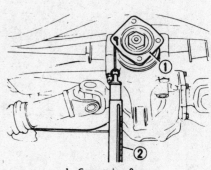

1. Companion flange
2. Spring scale

87907038

Fig. 36 Measuring the turning resistance of the companion flange

Side Oil Seal

▶ **See Figure 39**

1. Drain the differential oil as outlined in Section 1.
2. Raise the rear wheels and support the car with jackstands.
3. Remove the side yoke retaining bolt and pull the side yoke out of the differential carrier.
4. Extract the oil seal with a puller.

To install:

5. Using a drift, tap in a new oil seal.
6. Install the side yoke and tighten the retaining bolt.

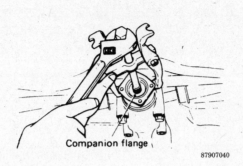

Fig. 37 Use a puller to remove the companion flange

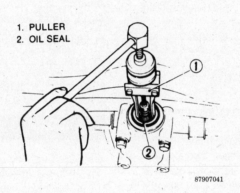

1. PULLER
2. OIL SEAL

Fig. 38 a special puller is also used to remove the front oil seal

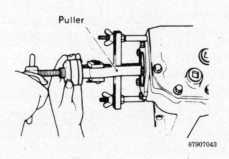

Puller

Fig. 39 Pulling the side seal from the differential housing

Troubleshooting the Manual Transmission and Transfer Case

Problem	Cause	Solution
Transmission shifts hard	· Internal bind in transmission caused by shift forks, selector plates, or synchronizer assemblies	· Remove, dissemble and inspect transmission. Replace worn or damaged components as necessary.
	· Clutch housing misalignment	· Check runout at rear face of clutch housing
	· Incorrect lubricant	· Drain and refill transmission
	· Block rings and/or cone seats worn	· Blocking ring to gear clutch tooth face clearance must be 0.030 inch or greater. If clearance is correct it may still be necessary to inspect blocking rings and cone seats for excessive wear. Repair as necessary.
Gear clash when shifting from one gear to another	· Clutch adjustment incorrect	· Adjust clutch
	· Clutch linkage or cable binding	· Lubricate or repair as necessary
	· Clutch housing misalignment	· Check runout at rear of clutch housing
	· Lubricant level low or incorrect lubricant	· Drain and refill transmission and check for lubricant leaks if level was low. Repair as necessary.
	· Gearshift components, or synchronizer assemblies worn or damaged	· Remove, disassemble and inspect transmission. Replace worn or damaged components as necessary.
Transmission noisy	· Lubricant level low or incorrect lubricant	· Drain and refill transmission. If lubricant level was low, check for leaks and repair as necessary.
	· Clutch housing-to-engine, or transmission-to-clutch housing bolts loose	· Check and correct bolt torque as necessary
	· Dirt, chips, foreign material in transmission	· Drain, flush, and refill transmission
	· Gearshift mechanism, transmission gears, or bearing components worn or damaged	· Remove, disassemble and inspect transmission. Replace worn or damaged components as necessary.
	· Clutch housing misalignment	· Check runout at rear face of clutch housing
Jumps out of gear	· Clutch housing misalignment	· Check runout at rear face of clutch housing
	· Gearshift lever loose	· Check lever for worn fork. Tighten loose attaching bolts.
	· Offset lever nylon insert worn or lever attaching nut loose	· Remove gearshift lever and check for loose offset lever nut or worn insert. Repair or replace as necessary.
	· Gearshift mechanism, shift forks, selector plates, interlock plate, selector arm, shift rail, detent plugs, springs or shift cover worn or damaged	· Remove, disassemble and inspect transmission cover assembly Replace worn or damaged components as necessary.
	· Clutch shaft or roller bearings worn or damaged	· Replace clutch shaft or roller bearings as necessary
Jumps out of gear (cont.)	· Gear teeth worn or tapered, synchronizer assemblies worn or damaged, excessive end play caused by worn thrust washers or output shaft gears	· Remove, disassemble, and inspect transmission. Replace worn or damaged components as necessary.
	· Pilot bushing worn	· Replace pilot bushing
Will not shift into one gear	· Gearshift selector plates, interlock plate, or selector arm, worn, damaged, or incorrectly assembled	· Remove, disassemble, and inspect transmission cover assembly. Repair or replace components as necessary.

87907C04

Troubleshooting the Manual Transmission and Transfer Case (cont.)

Problem	Cause	Solution
Will not shift into one gear	• Shift rail detent plunger worn, spring broken, or plug loose	• Tighten plug or replace worn or damaged components as necessary
	• Gearshift lever worn or damaged	• Replace gearshift lever
	• Synchronizer sleeves or hubs, damaged or worn	• Remove, disassemble and inspect transmission. Replace worn or damaged components.
Locked in one gear—cannot be shifted out	• Shift rail(s) worn or broken, shifter fork bent, setscrew loose, center detent plug missing or worn	• Inspect and replace worn or damaged parts
	• Broken gear teeth on countershaft gear, clutch shaft, or reverse idler gear	• Inspect and replace damaged part
	Gearshift lever broken or worn, shift mechanism in cover incorrectly assembled or broken, worn damaged gear train components	• Disassemble transmission. Replace damaged parts or assemble correctly.
Transfer case difficult to shift or will not shift into desired range	• Vehicle speed too great to permit shifting	• Stop vehicle and shift into desired range. Or reduce speed to 3–4 km/h (2–3 mph) before attempting to shift.
	• If vehicle was operated for extended period in 4H mode on dry paved surface, driveline torque load may cause difficult shifting	• Stop vehicle, shift transmission to neutral, shift transfer case to 2H mode and operate vehicle in 2H on dry paved surfaces
	• Transfer case external shift linkage binding	• Lubricate or repair or replace linkage, or tighten loose components as necessary
	• Insufficient or incorrect lubricant	• Drain and refill to edge of fill hole with SAE 85W-90 gear lubricant only
	• Internal components binding, worn, or damaged	• Disassemble unit and replace worn or damaged components as necessary
Transfer case noisy in all drive modes	• Insufficient or incorrect lubricant	• Drain and refill to edge of fill hole with SAE 85W-90 gear lubricant only. Check for leaks and repair if necessary. Note: If unit is still noisy after drain and refill, disassembly and inspection may be required to locate source of noise.
Noisy in—or jumps out of four wheel drive low range	• Transfer case not completely engaged in 4L position	• Stop vehicle, shift transfer case in Neutral, then shift back into 4L position
	• Shift linkage loose or binding	• Tighten, lubricate, or repair linkage as necessary
	• Shift fork cracked, inserts worn, or fork is binding on shift rail	• Disassemble unit and repair as necessary
Lubricant leaking from output shaft seals or from vent	• Transfer case overfilled	• Drain to correct level
	• Vent closed or restricted	• Clear or replace vent if necessary
	• Output shaft seals damaged or installed incorrectly	• Replace seals. Be sure seal lip faces interior of case when installed. Also be sure yoke seal surfaces are not scored or nicked. Remove scores, nicks with fine sandpaper or replace yoke(s) if necessary.
Abnormal tire wear	• Extended operation on dry hard surface (paved) roads in 4H range	• Operate in 2H on hard surface (paved) roads

87907C05

Troubleshooting Basic Clutch Problems

Problem	Cause
Excessive clutch noise	Throwout bearing noises are more audible at the lower end of pedal travel. The usual causes are: · Riding the clutch · Too little pedal free-play · Lack of bearing lubrication A bad clutch shaft pilot bearing will make a high pitched squeal, when the clutch is disengaged and the transmission is in gear or within the first 2" of pedal travel. The bearing must be replaced. Noise from the clutch linkage is a clicking or snapping that can be heard or felt as the pedal is moved completely up or down. This usually requires lubrication. Transmitted engine noises are amplified by the clutch housing and heard in the passenger compartment. They are usually the result of insufficient pedal free-play and can be changed by manipulating the clutch pedal.
Clutch slips (the car does not move as it should when the clutch is engaged)	This is usually most noticeable when pulling away from a standing start. A severe test is to start the engine, apply the brakes, shift into high gear and SLOWLY release the clutch pedal. A healthy clutch will stall the engine. If it slips it may be due to: · A worn pressure plate or clutch plate · Oil soaked clutch plate · Insufficient pedal free-play
Clutch drags or fails to release	The clutch disc and some transmission gears spin briefly after clutch disengagement. Under normal conditions in average temperatures, 3 seconds is maximum spin-time. Failure to release properly can be caused by: · Too light transmission lubricant or low lubricant level · Improperly adjusted clutch linkage
Low clutch life	Low clutch life is usually a result of poor driving habits or heavy duty use. Riding the clutch, pulling heavy loads, holding the car on a grade with the clutch instead of the brakes and rapid clutch engagement all contribute to low clutch life.

87907C06

Troubleshooting Basic Automatic Transmission Problems

Problem	Cause	Solution
Fluid leakage	· Defective pan gasket	· Replace gasket or tighten pan bolts
	· Loose filler tube	· Tighten tube nut
	· Loose extension housing to transmission case	· Tighten bolts
	· Converter housing area leakage	· Have transmission checked professionally
Fluid flows out the oil filler tube	· High fluid level	· Check and correct fluid level
	· Breather vent clogged	· Open breather vent
	· Clogged oil filter or screen	· Replace filter or clean screen (change fluid also)
	· Internal fluid leakage	· Have transmission checked professionally
Transmission overheats (this is usually accompanied by a strong burned odor to the fluid)	· Low fluid level · Fluid cooler lines clogged	· Check and correct fluid level · Drain and refill transmission. If this doesn't cure the problem, have cooler lines cleared or replaced.
	· Heavy pulling or hauling with insufficient cooling	· Install a transmission oil cooler
	· Faulty oil pump, internal slippage	· Have transmission checked professionally

87907C07

Troubleshooting Basic Automatic Transmission Problems (cont.)

Problem	Cause	Solution
Buzzing or whining noise	· Low fluid level · Defective torque converter, scored gears	· Check and correct fluid level · Have transmission checked professionally
No forward or reverse gears or slippage in one or more gears	· Low fluid level · Defective vacuum or linkage controls, internal clutch or band failure	· Check and correct fluid level · Have unit checked professionally
Delayed or erratic shift	· Low fluid level · Broken vacuum lines · Internal malfunction	· Check and correct fluid level. · Repair or replace lines · Have transmission checked professionally

87907C08

Lockup Torque Converter Service Diagnosis

Problem	Cause	Solution
No lockup	· Faulty oil pump · Sticking governor valve · Valve body malfunction 　(a) Stuck switch valve 　(b) Stuck lockup valve 　(c) Stuck fail-safe valve · Failed locking clutch · Leaking turbine hub seal · Faulty input shaft or seal ring	· Replace oil pump · Repair or replace as necessary · Repair or replace valve body or its internal components as necessary · Replace torque converter · Replace torque converter · Repair or replace as necessary
Will not unlock	· Sticking governor valve · Valve body malfunction 　(a) Stuck switch valve 　(b) Stuck lockup valve 　(c) Stuck fail-safe valve	· Repair or replace as necessary · Repair or replace valve body or its internal components as necessary
Stays locked up at too low a speed in direct	· Sticking governor valve · Valve body malfunction 　(a) Stuck switch valve 　(b) Stuck lockup valve 　(c) Stuck fail-safe valve	· Repair or replace as necessary · Repair or replace valve body or its internal components as necessary
Locks up or drags in low or second	· Faulty oil pump · Valve body malfunction 　(a) Stuck switch valve 　(b) Stuck fail-safe valve	· Replace oil pump · Repair or replace valve body or its internal components as necessary
Sluggish or stalls in reverse	· Faulty oil pump · Plugged cooler, cooler lines or fittings · Valve body malfunction 　(a) Stuck switch valve 　(b) Faulty input shaft or seal ring	· Replace oil pump as necessary · Flush or replace cooler and flush lines and fittings · Repair or replace valve body or its internal components as necessary
Loud chatter during lockup engagement (cold)	· Faulty torque converter · Failed locking clutch · Leaking turbine hub seal	· Replace torque converter · Replace torque converter · Replace torque converter

87907C09

Lockup Torque Converter Service Diagnosis (cont.)

Problem	Cause	Solution
Vibration or shudder during lockup engagement	• Faulty oil pump	• Repair or replace oil pump as necessary
	• Valve body malfunction	• Repair or replace valve body or its internal components as necessary
	• Faulty torque converter	• Replace torque converter
	• Engine needs tune-up	• Tune engine
Vibration after lockup engagement	• Faulty torque converter	• Replace torque converter
	• Exhaust system strikes underbody	• Align exhaust system
	• Engine needs tune-up	• Tune engine
	• Throttle linkage misadjusted	• Adjust throttle linkage
Vibration when revved in neutral Overheating oil blows out of dip stick tube or pump seal	• Torque converter out of balance	• Replace torque converter
	• Plugged cooler, cooler lines or fittings	• Flush or replace cooler and flush lines and fittings
	• Stuck switch valve	• Repair switch valve in valve body or replace valve body
Shudder after lockup engagement	• Faulty oil pump	• Replace oil pump
	• Plugged cooler, cooler lines or fittings	• Flush or replace cooler and flush lines and fittings
	• Valve body malfunction	• Repair or replace valve body or its internal components as necessary
	• Faulty torque converter	• Replace torque converter
	• Fail locking clutch	• Replace torque converter
	• Exhaust system strikes underbody	• Align exhaust system
	• Engine needs tune-up	• Tune engine
	• Throttle linkage misadjusted	• Adjust throttle linkage

87907C10

Transmission Fluid Indications

The appearance and odor of the transmission fluid can give valuable clues to the overall condition of the transmission. Always note the appearance of the fluid when you check the fluid level or change the fluid. Rub a small amount of fluid between your fingers to feel for grit and smell the fluid on the dipstick.

If the fluid appears:	It indicates:
Clear and red colored	• Normal operation
Discolored (extremely dark red or brownish) or smells burned	• Band or clutch pack failure, usually caused by an overheated transmission. Hauling very heavy loads with insufficient power or failure to change the fluid, often result in overheating. Do not confuse this appearance with newer fluids that have a darker red color and a strong odor (though not a burned odor).
Foamy or aerated (light in color and full of bubbles)	• The level is too high (gear train is churning oil) • An internal air leak (air is mixing with the fluid). Have the transmission checked professionally.
Solid residue in the fluid	• Defective bands, clutch pack or bearings. Bits of band material or metal abrasives are clinging to the dipstick. Have the transmission checked professionally
Varnish coating on the dipstick	• The transmission fluid is overheating

87907C11

Special Tools, Manual Transmission and Differential:

398405200	398507703	398663600	398791600
STAND	DUMMY COLLAR	PLIERS	REMOVER II
Rear drive shaft.	Oil seal of input shaft holder	Input shaft snap ring.	Straight pin (Transfer shifter fork).
4WD	4WD Dual-range	4WD Dual-range	2WD · 4WD

398791700	399295120	399411700	399513600
REMOVER II	STAND SET	INSTALLER	INSTALLER
Spring pin (5-speed)	Transmission main case	Reverse shifter rail arm	Extension rear oil seal.
2WD 4WD	2WD 4WD	2WD 4WD	4WD
	1 STAND CP (399935120) 2 BOLT (016510600) 10 x 60mm 3 BOLT (016510700) 10 x 70mm 4 BOLT (016510400) 10 x 40mm ST 169		

399520105	399527700	399780104	399790110
SEAT	PULLER SET	WEIGHT	INSTALLER
Roller bearing (Differential)	Roller bearing (Differential)	Preload on roller bearing	Roller bearing, (Differential) Axle shaft oil seal
2WD Non-TURBO	2WD TURBO 4WD	2WD 4WD	2WD Non-TURBO
	1 BOLT (899621412) 2 PULLER (399527702) 3 HOLDER (399527703) 4 ADAPTER (398497701) 5 BOLT (899520107) 6 NUT (021008000)		

87907C12

Special Tools, Manual Transmission and Differential:

899714110	899754110	899754112	899858600
RETAINER	PRESS ASSY	PRESS	RETAINER II
Transmission main shaft, Drive pinion, Rear drive shaft	Transmission main shaft, Needle bearing (transfer case), Rear drive shaft	Clutch release bearing holder (Except 4WD)	Transmission main shaft, Drive pinion.
2WD · 4WD	4WD	2WD Non-TURBO	2WD Non-TURBO

899864100	899874100	899884100	899904100
REMOVER	INSTALLER	HOLDER	REMOVER
Transmission main shaft, Drive pinion.	Transmission main shaft, Drive pinion, Transfer drive gear bushing.	Drive pinion, Rear drive shaft, Extension ASSY	Straight pin (Differential).
2WD · 4WD	2WD · 4WD	2WD · 4WD	2WD · 4WD

899988608
SOCKET WRENCH (27)
Transmission main shaft (2WD) Rear drive shaft (4WD)
2WD · 4WD

87907C13

Special Tools, Manual Transmission and Differential:

498937000	499267200	499277000	499277100
TRANSMISSION HOLDER	STOPPER PIN	INSTALLER	BUSH 1–2 INSTALLER
Transmission main shaft lock nut	Transfer case and fork high-low rod	Drive pinion.	1st driven gear thrust plate. 1st–2nd driven gear bush
2WD TURBO 4WD	4WD Dual-range	2WD Non-TURBO	2WD TURBO · 4WD

499277200	499747000	499747100	499757001
INSTALLER	GUIDE	CLUTCH DISC GUIDE	SNAP RING GUIDE
For press fitting the 2nd driven gear, roller bearings, & 5th driven gear onto the driven shaft	Clutch disc	Clutch disc.	Snap ring (OUT 25)
	2WD Non TURBO	2WD TURBO · 4WD	4WD Dual-range

499757002	499787000	499797000	499827000
SNAP RING PRESS	WRENCH ASSY	OIL SEAL INSTALLER	PRESS
Snap ring (OUT 25) Ball bearing (25 x 62 x 17)	Differential side retainer	Differential side retainer oil seal.	Oil seal (Speedometer).
4WD Dual-range	2WD · 4WD	2WD TURBO · 4WD	2WD · 4WD

87907C14

Special Tools, Manual Transmission and Differential:

499857000	499877000	499917100	499917500
REMOVER ASSY	RACE 4 - 5 INSTALLER	GAUGE ASSY 2	DRIVE PINION GAUGE ASSY
To remove the driven gear ASSY 5th gear	Needle bearing 4th and 5th races. Transmission main shaft rear ball bearing	Drive pinion shim.	Drive pinion shim adjustment.
	2WD TURBO 4WD	2WD Non-TURBO	2WD TURBO · 4WD
			1 Plate 2 Scale

499927000	499927100	499987003	499987300
HANDLE	HANDLE	SOCKET WRENCH (35)	SOCKET WRENCH (50)
Transmission main shaft	Transmission main shaft.	Drive pinion lock nut (2WD · 4WD) Main shaft lock nut (4WD)	To remove the driven gear ASSY lock nut
2WD Non TURBO	2WD TURBO 4WD	2WD · 4WD	

898938600	899474100	899524100	899580100
HOLDER	EXPANDER	PULLER SET	INSTALLER
Transmission main shaft	Snap ring (Transmission main shaft)	Roller bearing (Differential)	Transmission main shaft. Drive pinion, Ball bearing (Rear drive shaft)
2WD Non-TURBO	2WD 4-speed · 4WD Dual-range	2WD Non-TURBO	2WD · 4WD

87907C15

Special Tools, Manual Transmission and Differential:

498057000	498057100	498057200	498067000
OIL SEAL INSTALLER	INSTALLER	OIL SEAL INSTALLER	TRANSFER RACE PRESS
Transfer case oil seal	Transfer front oil seal	Transfer rear oil seal.	Transfer race
4WD	4WD Dual-range	4WD Dual-range	4WD
498077000	498147000	498247001	498247100
5TH DRIVE GEAR REMOVER	DEPTH GAUGE	MAGNET BASE	DIAL GAUGE
5th driven gear.	Main shaft axial end play adjustment	Backlash between side gear and pinion. Hypoid gear backlash	Backlash between side gear and pinion. Hypoid gear backlash
2WD TURBO 4WD	2WD 4WD	2WD 4WD	2WD 4WD
498427000	498517000	498787000	498787100
STOPPER	REPLACER	STOPPER	MAIN SHAFT STOPPER
For securing the drive pinion shaft ASSY and driven gear ASSY when removing the drive pinion shaft ASSY lock nut (18 x 13.5)	Drive pinion thrust plate and needle bearing race	Transmission main shaft.	Transmission main shaft.
	2WD Non-TURBO	2WD Non TURBO	2WD TURBO 4WD

87907C16

Special Tools, Automatic Transmission and Differential:

398437700	398643600	398653600	398781600
DRIFT	GAUGE	SHAFT	STOPPER
Drive pinion front bearing cup	Low & reverse brake, total endplay, oil pump, drive pinion height	Drive pinion and reduction drive gear.	Reduction drive gear.
398833600	399513600	399520105	399703600
GUIDE	INSTALLER	SEAT	PULLER
Needle bearing	Drive pinion rear bearing cup	Roller bearing (Differential)	Axle shaft bearing cup.
399780111	399790110	399913601	399913603
WRENCH	INSTALLER	MASTER	HOLDER
Axle shaft oil seal holder	Roller bearing (Differential) Axle shaft oil seal	Drive pinion	Drive pinion.
		A13-190	

87907C17

Special Tools, Automatic Transmission and Differential:

3999T3604	498247001	498247100	498477000
SPACER	MAGNET BASE	DIAL GAUGE	HANDLE
Drive pinion.	Backlash of gears.	Backlash of gears.	Bearing cup, needle bearing, drive pinion front bearing retainer and impeller bushing.
498517000	498567000	498807000	498847000
REPLACER	PULLEY	BEARING GUIDE	OIL SEAL GUIDE
Drive pinion front bearing core.	Preload check	Needle bearing.	Oil seal holder
499247000	499247100	499247200	499267100
INSTALLER	OIL SEAL INSTALLER	INSTALLER	SPACER
Drive pinion oil seal	Oil seal holder	Final reduction case.	Oil seal holder.
4WD			

87907C18

Special Tools, Automatic Transmission and Differential:

499427000	499827000	499867000	499897000
INSTALLER	PRESS	REMOVER	PLIERS
Drive pinion front bearing cup, axle shaft bearing cup and thrust bearing retainer	Speedometer shaft oil seal	Needle bearing at reduction drive gear	Snap ring
499917400	499937000	499987100	899524100
MASTER 2	DIFFERENTIAL STAND	SOCKET WRENCH (35)	PULLER SET
Drive pinion	Final reduction section	Drive pinion	Roller bearing (Differential)
899580100	899904100	899924100	
INSTALLER	REMOVER	HANDLE	
Drive pinion	Differential case	Reduction drive gear	

87907C19

Special Tools, Automatic Transmission and Differential:

398308700	398534800	398573600	398603610
PULLER	ADAPTER 2	OIL PRESSURE GAUGE ASSY	SOCKET
Transmission case oil seal.	Line pressure	Line pressure and governor pressure.	Brake band.

398663600	398673600	398863600	398893600
PLIER	COMPRESSOR	INSTALLER 2	ADAPTER
Governor valve.	Reverse clutch, forward clutch and low & reverse brake.	Needle bearing on oil pump carrier.	Line pressure and governor pressure.

399248700	399543600	399793600	399893600
INSTALLER 2	INSTALLER	INSTALLER	PLIER
Transmission case oil seal.	Needle bearing and bushing on oil pump housing.	Final reduction case.	Reverse clutch, forward clutch and low & reverse brake.

87907C20

Special Tools, Automatic Transmission and Differential:

399903600	498107000	498147000	498597000
REMOVER 2	REPLACER	DEPTH GAUGE	SOCKET WRENCH (7)
Needle bearing and bushing on oil pump carrier	Impeller bushing on converter housing	Low & reverse brake	Plug
498627000	**498797000**	**498897000**	**499257100**
SEAT	REMOVER	ADAPTER	OIL SEAL GUIDE
Center support snap ring	Pin for bush of oil pump shaft.	Measure the line pressure.	Drive pinion oil seal. 4WD
499337000	**499527000**	**499667000**	**499687100**
VERNIER CALLIPER	PULLER SET	THICKNESS GAUGE	BASE
Vacuum diaphragm rod selection.	Final reduction case.	Forward clutch, reverse clutch, low & reverse brake and oil pump etc.	Low & reverse brake.

87907C21

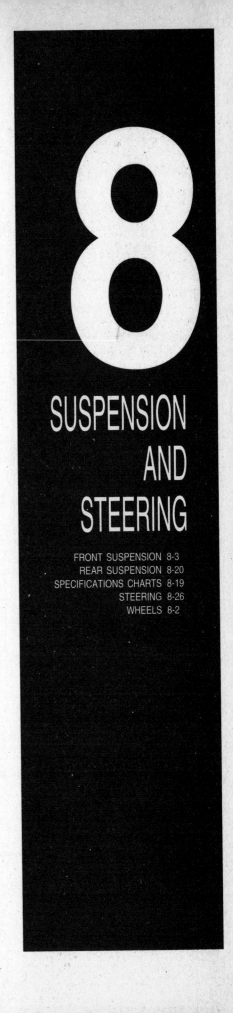

8

SUSPENSION AND STEERING

WHEELS

Wheel Assembly

REMOVAL & INSTALLATION

▶ **See Figures 1, 2 and 3**

1. If using a lug wrench, loosen the lug nuts slightly before raising the vehicle.
2. Raise the vehicle and support it safely.
3. Remove the lug nuts and wheel from the vehicle.

To install:

4. Install the wheel and hand tighten the lug nuts until they are snug.
5. Lower the vehicle and torque the lug nuts evenly to 58-72 ft. lbs (78-97 Nm).

INSPECTION

1. Before installing the wheels check for any cracks on the wheels or enlarged bolt holes, remove any corrosion on the mounting surfaces with a wire brush. Installation of wheels without a good metal-to-metal contact at the mounting surface can cause wheel nuts to loosen.
2. Recheck the wheels after 1000 miles of driving.

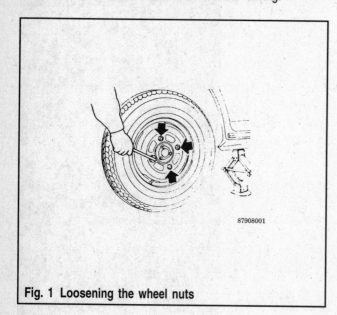

Fig. 1 Loosening the wheel nuts

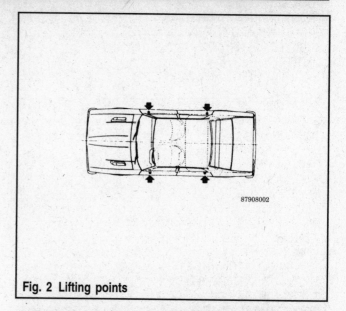

Fig. 2 Lifting points

Wheel Lug Studs

REPLACEMENT

Front Wheels

The brake disc must be supported properly before pressing the wheel stud in or out.

1. Remove the rotor assembly from the car.
2. Remove the damaged bolt with a press. Do not damage the wheel mounting surface on the hub flange.

To install:

3. Install a new serrated bolt into the hole in the hub. Tap lightly with a hammer to start the bolt serrations in the hole, make sure the bolt is square with the hub flange.

Rear Wheels

1. Raise and support the car. Remove the wheels from the vehicle.
2. ark the relationship of the wheel assembly to the axle flange and remove the brake drum.
3. Using a press remove the wheel stud from the axle flange.

To install:

4. Insert a new wheel stud in the axle flange hole. Rotate the bolt slowly to assure the serrations are aligned with those made with the original bolt.
5. Place a flat washer over the outside end of the wheel stud and thread a standard wheel nut with the flat side against the washer. Tighten the wheel nut until the bolt head seats against the axle flange.

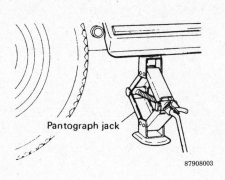

Fig. 3 Raising the vehicle using the pantograph jack

FRONT SUSPENSION

The ff-1 and 1300G models have a wishbone type independent front suspension, with torsion bar mounted upper control arms. They also have inboard drum type front brakes, utilized for stress reduction on the torsion bars and weight reduction on the suspension as a whole.

In 1972, a MacPherson strut front suspension was incorporated on all GL and DL models. This system has a double action shock absorber (damper strut) located inside a coil spring, both of which are mounted on the transverse links (control arms). This eliminates the torsion bars. The transverse link (control arm) has a maintenance free ball joint riveted at the outer end, and a stabilizer bar runs from both control arms to a body mount. The advantage of using this system is in overall weight reduction and improved stability and handling.

In 1975, the MacPherson suspension system was slightly modified to include a leading rod between the transverse link and the rear crossmember. This further improved stability.

Torsion Bars

REMOVAL & INSTALLATION

ff-1 and 1300G

▶ **See Figure 4**

1. Raise the vehicle and support it with jackstands.
2. Loosen the ride height adjusting cam retainer.
3. Remove the shock absorber upper retaining nuts.
4. Flatten the locktab, and remove the upper ball joint upper nut.
5. Remove both torsion bar lockbolts and nuts at the adjuster arm and the upper control arm.
6. Rotate the upper control arm away from the ball joint, and then down, to fully relax the torsion bar.
7. Remove the adjuster arm, and slide the torsion bar out.
8. To install the torsion bar, reverse Steps 1 through 6.
9. Do not interchange torsion bars side-to-side.

Index the missing tooth on the torsion bar splines with the double tooth on the anchor arm. Following installation, adjust ride height.

Shock Absorber

REMOVAL & INSTALLATION

ff-1 and 1300G

1. Raise the vehicle body and remove the wheels.

➡**Prior to shock removal, loosen the ride height adjusting cam, and adjust ride height after shock absorber installation is completed.**

2. Remove the shock absorber upper double nut, the washer, and the upper rubber bushing.
3. Remove the nut from the damping pin at the bottom of the mount.
4. Remove the shock absorber.
   To install:
5. Install the upper rubber bushing and insert the bolt section into the bracket hole.
6. Temporarily tighten the locknut through the upper side of the rubber and washer.
7. Install the upper mounting section on the mounting pin.
8. Install the washer, spring washer and nut.
9. Tighten the nut until the washer and shoulder of the pin contact.
10. Tighten the upper nut and locknut.

TESTING

Visually inspect the shock absorber. If there is evidence of leakage and the shock absorber is covered with oil, the shock is defective and should be replaced.

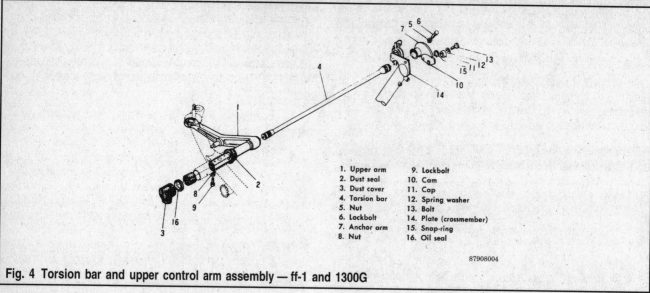

1. Upper arm
2. Dust seal
3. Dust cover
4. Torsion bar
5. Nut
6. Lockbolt
7. Anchor arm
8. Nut
9. Lockbolt
10. Cam
11. Cap
12. Spring washer
13. Bolt
14. Plate (crossmember)
15. Snap-ring
16. Oil seal

87908004

Fig. 4 Torsion bar and upper control arm assembly — ff-1 and 1300G

If there is no sign of excessive leakage (a small amount of weeping is normal) bounce the car at one corner by pressing down on the fender or bumper and releasing. When you have the car bouncing as much as you can, release the fender or bumper. The car should stop bouncing after the first rebound. If the bouncing continues past the center point of the bounce more than once, the shock absorbers are worn and should be replaced.

Except ff-1 and 1300G

1970-79 MODELS

➡Use this procedure if only shock absorber (strut) or spring removal is desired.

1. Remove the wheel cover (DL models) and loosen the lug nuts.
2. Raise the front of the car and support it with jackstands.

❋❋CAUTION

Secure the spring with a spring compressor before loosening the upper strut nut.

3. Remove the lug nuts and wheels.
4. Remove the bolts which secure the bottom of the strut assembly to the axle housing.
5. Remove the bolts which attach the strut bracket to the axle housing.
6. Detach the end of the tie rod from the axle housing in order to prevent ball joint damage.
7. Remove the strut from the housing, gradually and carefully, by lowering the housing.
8. Remove the nuts which attach the upper end of the strut assembly to the wheel arch.
9. Remove the strut (shock and spring) from the body.

10. Use a coil spring compressor to compress the coil spring until it can move freely.

❋❋CAUTION

Do not suddenly release the tension on the coil spring by removing the compressor too rapidly.

11. Use a spanner or a large open end wrench to keep the upper spring seat from turning, while removing the shock nut with a box wrench.
12. Remove the components from the top of the shock, being careful to note their order, and remove the spring in its compressed state.

❋❋CAUTION

Use care not to strike the upper shock absorber stud.

13. Test the operation of the shock absorber by placing it in an upright position. Push and pull on the shock, if it presents little resistance or binds, replace it with a new shock.
14. Examine the shock for leaks, a bent mounting stud, or other signs of wear or damage to it. Replace it as necessary.
   To install:
15. Compress the spring and place the shock into the spring housing.
16. Place the retaining components on the top of the shock in the reverse order from which they were removed and tighten the shock nut.
17. Place the strut into the body of the vehicle.
18. Install the nuts which attach the upper end of the strut to the wheel arch.
19. Slowly and carefully release the spring compressor and guide the strut into the axle housing.
20. Gradually raise the axle housing and attach the tie rod ends.
21. Install the bolts which attach the strut bracket to the axle housing.
22. Install the bolts which secure the bottom of the strut assembly to the axle housing.
23. Install the wheels, lug nuts and wheel covers.

24. Lower the vehicle. Be sure to assemble the components on the top of the shock in the correct order.

25. Lubricate the oil seal lips and the thrust washers with a light coating of grease.

26. Tighten the shock absorber-to-mount locknut nut to 43-54 ft. lbs. (58-73 Nm).

1980-84 MODELS

▶ **See Figures 5, 6, 7, 8 and 9**

1. Disconnect the negative (-) battery cable.
2. Loosen the wheel nuts just slightly. Then, raise up the car and support it with jackstands.
3. Remove the wheels.
4. Release the handbrake.

➡**When loosening the union bolt on the caliper, use a flare nut wrench only.**

5. Disconnect the brake hose first at the pipe where it comes out of the body and then at the caliper. Plug the brake line coming out of the body.

6. Remove the clip and detach the brake hose from the damper strut.

7. Remove the two damper strut attaching bolts (these attach the strut to a housing to which the lower control arm, the other major front suspension components, and the wheel spindle, are also attached). This will loosen the grip of the housing on the lower strut, but you may have to use a solvent to free the strut from the housing if there is corrosion.

8. Remove the two nuts that pass through the fender well and fasten the strut at the top. Then, pull the strut downward and out of the body.

To install:

9. Installation is the reverse of removal.
10. Torque the strut-to-body nuts to 22-29 ft. lbs. (29-39 Nm) and the strut-to-housing bolts to 22-29 ft. lbs. (29-39 Nm).
11. Torque the brake line nut to 9-13 ft. lbs. (12-17 Nm) and the brake line-to-caliper nut to 11-14 ft. lbs. (14-18 Nm).
12. Torque the wheel nuts to 58-72 ft. lbs. (78-97 Nm).
13. Bleed the brakes.

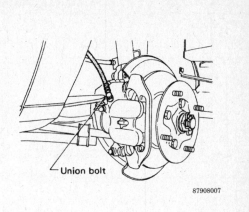

Fig. 6 When loosening the union bolt on the caliper, use a flare nut wrench only

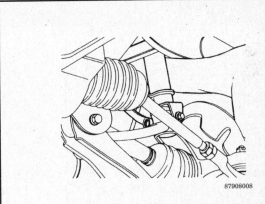

Fig. 7 The damper strut attaching bolts attach the strut to a housing to which the lower control arm, the other major front suspension components, and the wheel spindle, are also attached

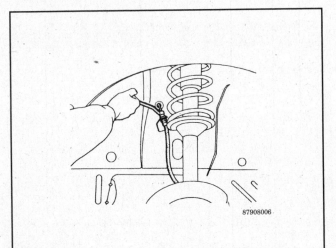

Fig. 5 Always use a flare nut wrench to remove the brake hose

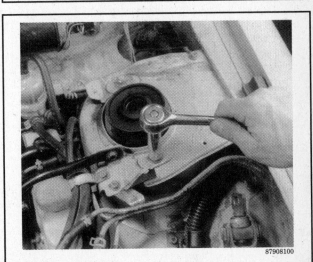

Fig. 8 Using a socket remove the damper strut mounting nut

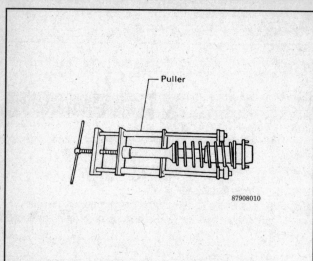

Fig. 9 Use the puller to compress the spring when disassembling the damper strut assembly

MacPherson Strut Assembly

REMOVAL & INSTALLATION

Except ff-1 and 1300G

▶ See Figures 10, 11, 12, 13, 14, 15, 16 and 17

➡Use this procedure to remove the entire suspension assembly. If only shock and/or spring removal are desired, use the procedure given under Shock Absorbers.

It is desirable that removal and installation of the front suspension be performed with the car up on a lift or over a pit. If this is not possible, then you will need a jack and jackstands to raise and support the vehicle.

1. Remove the negative (-) battery cable.
2. Remove the hub caps and loosen the lug nuts.
3. Raise the vehicle until the tire clears the ground and remove the lug nuts and the wheel/tire assembly.
4. Place the jackstands under the vehicle and remove the jack. Perform this operation on the other side also if the suspension is to be removed from both sides of the vehicle.
5. Remove the hand brake cable bracket and the hand-brake cable hanger from the transverse link and the tie rod end.
6. Remove the hand brake cable end.
7. Remove the axle nut, lockplate, washer, and center piece.
8. Remove the front brake drums by using a puller.
9. Disconnect the brake hoses from the brake fluid pipes. Plug the openings to prevent fluid loss.
10. Remove the backing plates with the brake assemblies attached.
11. On cars equipped with front disc brakes, remove the hand brake cable end from the caliper lever.
12. Disengage the outer cable clip from the cable end support bracket at the caliper.
13. Disengage the brake line from the caliper and remove it from the bracket.

14. Unfasten the hand brake cable bracket from the housing mount by loosening the nuts.
15. Drive out the spring pins of the double offset joint side by using a drift pin and a hammer. The double offset side of the axle is the side closest to the transaxle.
16. Remove the transverse link (lower control arm) by loosening the locknut nut which holds the transverse link to the inner pivot shaft of the crossmember.
17. Loosen and remove the nuts which clamp the transverse link to the stabilizer.
18. Remove the transverse link rearward from the crossmember by using a lever and pulling the transverse link out from the end of the stabilizer.
19. Remove the cotter pin from the castle nut.
20. Remove the nuts and ball stud from the knuckle arm of the tie rod end ball joint housing. Take care not to bend the housing.
21. On models from 1975-84, disconnect the leading rod from the rear crossmember by removing the self-locking-nut, washers, plates, bushings and pipe.
22. On models from 1975-84, disconnect the stabilizer by removing the bolt at the bracket connecting one end of the stabilizer to the leading rod, and then removing the nuts fixing the bracket to the rear crossmember.

✳✳CAUTION

Secure the spring with a spring compressor before loosening the upper strut nut.

23. Remove the nuts which hold the strut mount to the body (suspension assembly upper mounting nut to the top of the shock absorber tower).
24. Pull the double offset joint out of the driveshaft and then remove the suspension assembly from the body.
25. Reverse the above process to install the suspension assembly, and torque the components to the following specifications:
   • Strut-to-body nuts to 22-29 ft. lbs. (29-39 Nm).
   • Strut-to-steering knuckle housing bolts to 22-29 ft. lbs. (29-39 Nm).

Upper Ball Joint

INSPECTION

Inspect the upper ball joint with the vehicle raised and supported with jackstands, as follows:

1. Separate the ball stud from the steering knuckle.
2. Move the stud with your finger.
3. If there is excessive play present, replace the lower ball joint.
4. Check the ball joint boots for tears or other damage. Replace the boots, if they are damaged.
5. Repack with a long lasting chassis grease, if the boots are being replaced.
6. Apply 0.28-0.35 oz. (8-10g) of grease to the stud neck, 0.11 oz. (3g) to the boot interior, and a small amount of grease to the inner lip of the boot.

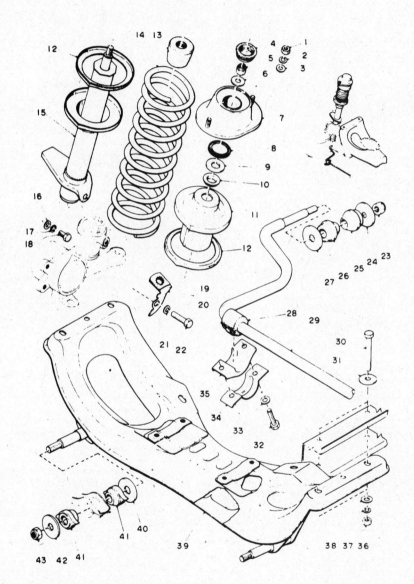

1. Nut
2. Spring washer
3. Washer
4. Cap (strut mount)
5. Self-locking nut
6. Washer
7. Strut mount
8. Oil seal (strut mount)
9. Washer (thrust bearing)
10. Thrust washer
11. Spring retainer (upper)
12. Rubber seat (coil spring)
13. Helper
14. Coil spring
15. Shock absorber
16. Washer
17. Spring washer
18. Bolt
19. Bracket compl.
     (brake hose: RH)
20. Bracket compl.
     (brake hose: LH)
21. Spring washer
22. Bolt
23. Self-locking nut
24. Washer
25. Bushing (link outer)
26. Bushing (link outer)
27. Washer
28. Bushing (stabilizer)
29. Stabilizer bar
30. Bolt
31. Washer
32. Bolt (10 x 40)
33. Washer
34. Lockplate
35. Bracket (stabilizer)
36. Nut
37. Spring washer
38. Washer
39. Crossmember
40. Washer
41. Bushing (inner pivot)
42. Washer
43. Self-locking nut

87908011

Fig. 10 Exploded view of the MacPherson strut front suspension — 1972-74 models

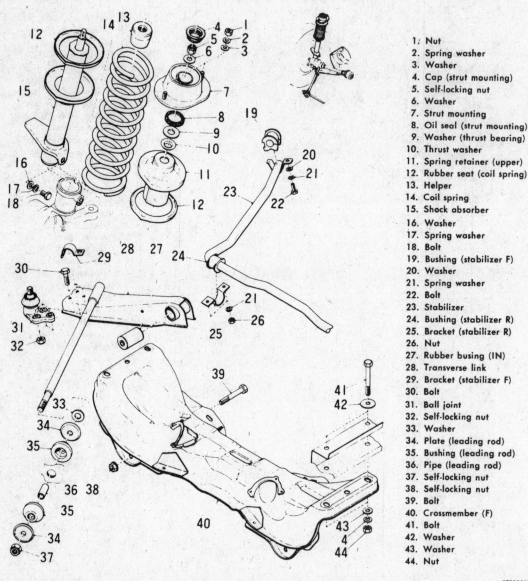

1. Nut
2. Spring washer
3. Washer
4. Cap (strut mounting)
5. Self-locking nut
6. Washer
7. Strut mounting
8. Oil seal (strut mounting)
9. Washer (thrust bearing)
10. Thrust washer
11. Spring retainer (upper)
12. Rubber seat (coil spring)
13. Helper
14. Coil spring
15. Shock absorber
16. Washer
17. Spring washer
18. Bolt
19. Bushing (stabilizer F)
20. Washer
21. Spring washer
22. Bolt
23. Stabilizer
24. Bushing (stabilizer R)
25. Bracket (stabilizer R)
26. Nut
27. Rubber busing (IN)
28. Transverse link
29. Bracket (stabilizer F)
30. Bolt
31. Ball joint
32. Self-locking nut
33. Washer
34. Plate (leading rod)
35. Bushing (leading rod)
36. Pipe (leading rod)
37. Self-locking nut
38. Self-locking nut
39. Bolt
40. Crossmember (F)
41. Bolt
42. Washer
43. Washer
44. Nut

87908012

Fig. 11 Exploded view of the MacPherson strut suspension — 1975-79 models

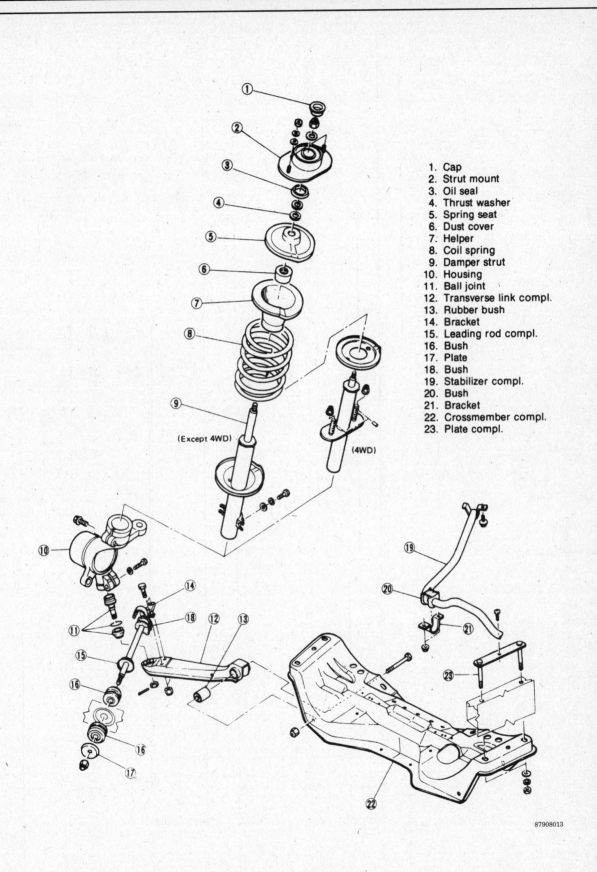

1. Cap
2. Strut mount
3. Oil seal
4. Thrust washer
5. Spring seat
6. Dust cover
7. Helper
8. Coil spring
9. Damper strut
10. Housing
11. Ball joint
12. Transverse link compl.
13. Rubber bush
14. Bracket
15. Leading rod compl.
16. Bush
17. Plate
18. Bush
19. Stabilizer compl.
20. Bush
21. Bracket
22. Crossmember compl.
23. Plate compl.

(Except 4WD)

(4WD)

87908013

Fig. 12 Exploded view of the MacPherson strut suspension — 1980-84 models

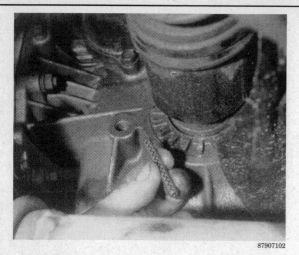

Fig. 13 Remove the spring pin from the double offset joint and discard it

Fig. 14 Remove the transverse link (lower control arm) by loosening the locknut nut which holds the transverse link to the inner pivot shaft of the crossmember

Fig. 15 Remove the nuts and ball stud from the knuckle arm of the tie rod end ball joint housing

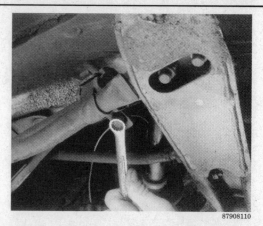

Fig. 16 Disconnect the stabilizer by removing the bolt at the bracket connecting one end of the stabilizer to the leading rod, and then removing the nuts fixing the bracket to the rear crossmember

Fig. 17 Pull the double offset joint out of the driveshaft and then remove the suspension assembly from the body

REMOVAL & INSTALLATION

1. Raise and support the front of the vehicle with jackstands. Remove the wheels.

2. Remove the cotter pin and the castellated nut from the ball joint.

3. Remove the steering knuckle-to-ball joint bolt and the ball joint from the vehicle.

4. Inspect the ball joint for damage to the boot that retains grease for stress cracks.

To install:

5. Use a new the ball joint and reverse Steps 1 through 4.

6. Torque the ball joint stud-to-steering knuckle housing bolt to 22-29 ft. lbs. (29-39 Nm).

7. Connect the ball joint to the transverse link and install the castellated nut.

8. Torque the ball joint-to-lower control arm nut to 29 ft. lbs. (39 Nm). Then, torque the nut further, just until the castellations are aligned with the hole in the end of the ball stud.

9. Install a new cotter pin and bend it around the nut.

Lower Ball Joint

INSPECTION

ff-1 and 1300G

Inspect the lower ball joint next, with the vehicle still raised and supported with jackstands, as follows:
1. Grasp the wheel and move it up and down (vertically).
2. Move the wheel back and forth.
3. If play is excessive in either or both directions, replace the upper ball joint.

➡**Excessive wheel play may also be caused by a worn wheel bearing or an improperly installed bearing nut.**

1972-74 GL and DL
▶ **See Figure 18**

The lower control arm (transverse link) must be removed from the vehicle, in order to check the ball joint; see below.
1. Use a pull scale to apply a force of 154 ft. lbs. (208 Nm) to the ball joint stud.
2. The ball joint should have no more than 0.3mm play when this force is applied.
3. Replace the entire control arm assembly if the ball joint is defective.
4. Check the boot for wear, tears, or other signs of damage. Replace it, as necessary.
5. Lubricate the ball stud with 0.28-0.35 oz. (8-10g) of long life chassis grease and apply 0.11 oz. (3g) of grease to the inside of the boot.

1975-84

INSPECTION

Inspect the lower ball joint, with the vehicle still raised and supported with jackstands, as follows:
1. Grasp the wheel and move it up and down (vertically).

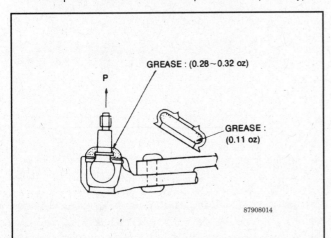

Fig. 18 Lubricate the ball stud with 0.28-0.35 oz. (8-10g) of long life chassis grease and apply 0.11 oz. (3g) of grease to the inside of the boot. 1972-74 model shown

2. Move the wheel back and forth.
3. If play is excessive in either or both directions, replace the upper ball joint.

➡**Excessive wheel play may also be caused by a worn wheel bearing or an improperly installed bearing nut.**

REMOVAL & INSTALLATION

ff-1 and 1300G

In order to remove the ball joints, it will be necessary to remove the steering knuckle/hub assembly from the car first. See the Knuckle and Spindle removal and installation procedures later in this section for the correct procedure. Knuckle and spindle removal is also necessary for bearing service. After completing removal, perform the following Steps:
1. Remove the cotter pin from the castellated nut. Unfasten the nut.
2. Extract the ball joint with a puller.
3. Repeat for the other ball joint.
4. Reverse the above steps to install the ball joint.
5. Torque the ball joint stud nuts to 43-65 ft. lbs. (58-88 Nm).

1972-74 GL and DL

The single ball joint on these models is integral with the lower control arm (transverse link). If the ball joint is defective, the entire assembly must be replaced. See control arm removal and installation in this section.

1975-79 Models

1. Raise the front wheel and use a jackstand to safely support the vehicle.
2. Remove the cotter pin and castle nut from the stud on top of the ball joint.
3. Remove the bolts and self-locking nuts which attach the ball joint to the transverse link. Detach the ball joint.
4. Reverse the above process to install the ball joint.
5. Tighten the self-locking nuts to 38 ft. lbs. (51 Nm) and the castle nut to 90 ft. lbs. (122 Nm).

➡**Use new self-locking nuts, the old ones may not be reused.**

1980-84
▶ **See Figures 19, 20 and 21**

1. Raise the front of the car and support it with jackstands. Remove the wheels.
2. Remove the cotter pin and the castellated nut.
3. Remove the bolt on the steering knuckle.
4. Remove the ball joint.
5. If you're considering reusing it, inspect the joint for damage to the grease, boot or stress cracks.
   To install:
6. Insert the ball stud, ungreased, into the steering knuckle, install the bolt, and torque it to 22-29 ft. lbs. (29-39 Nm)
7. Connect the joint to the transverse link and install the castellated nut, torquing to 29 ft. lbs. (39 Nm). Then, torque the nut further, just until the castellations are aligned with the hole in the end of the ballstud.

87908101

Fig. 19 Use a pair of pliers to remove the cotter pin

87908102

Fig. 20 Use a wrench or socket to remove the castellated nut

8. Install a new cotter pin and bend it around the nut.

Upper Control Arm

REMOVAL & INSTALLATION

ff-1 and 1300G

1. Remove the wheel cover and loosen the lug nuts.
2. Raise the car and support it with jackstands. Block the rear wheels.

✳✳CAUTION

Be sure that the car is securely supported.

3. Remove the lug nuts and wheels.
4. Remove the end bolt on the ride height adjusting cam, in order to loosen the cam.

87908104

Fig. 21 Use a puller to separate the ball joint from the steering knuckle

5. Remove the two nuts and washers from the shock absorber upper mounting stud.
6. Straighten out the lockwasher on the upper ball joint securing nut and remove the nut.
7. Remove the dust cover and the locknut from the upper arm.
8. Push the upper control arm downward, in order to release the tension from the torsion bar.
9. Pull on the upper anchor arm in order to disengage the upper control arm from the torsion bar. Remove the control arm.

To install:

10. Install the upper control arm to the torsion bar.
11. Install the dust cover and lock nut to the upper control arm.
12. Install the upper ball joint securing nut and lock washer.
13. Install the retaining nuts and washers to the upper mounting stud of the shock absorber.
14. Install the end bolt to the ride height adjusting cam and tighten the bolt securely.
15. Install the wheels, lug nuts and wheel cover.
16. Lower the vehicle. Adjust the ride height as detailed in this section, after installation is completed.

Lower Control Arm

REMOVAL & INSTALLATION

ff-1 and 1300G

1. Remove the wheel cover and loosen the lug nuts.
2. Raise the car and support it with jackstands. Block the rear wheels.

✳✳CAUTION

Be sure that the car is securely supported.

3. Remove the lug nuts and wheels.

4. Remove the nut which secures the lower control arm shaft to its front crossmember bracket.

5. Disconnect the lower control arm from the front crossmember.

6. Separate the arm from the ball joint and remove the arm from the steering knuckle.

7. Remove the nuts and the spring washers which attach the control arm to the body mounting bracket.

To install:

8. Installation is the reverse of removal.

9. Tighten the nuts which secure the arm to the body bracket to 26-32 ft. lbs. (35-43 Nm), and the lower arm shaft nut to 33-43 ft. lbs. (44-58 Nm)

1972-79 Models

EXCEPT 1300G

These models have only one control arm which may be referred to either as the lower control arm or as the transverse link. To remove and install it, proceed as follows:

1. Remove the wheel cover (DL models) and loosen the lug nuts.

2. Raise the car and support it with jackstands. Block the rear wheels.

✳✳CAUTION

Be sure that the car is securely supported.

3. Remove the lug nuts and the wheel.

4. Remove the parking brake cable clamp from the control arm by unfastening its nut.

5. Remove the self-locking nut which attaches the control arm to the crossmember. Be sure to note the installation sequence of the washers.

6. Remove the locknut nut which secures the stabilizer bar to the control arm. Again, note the installation sequence of the washers.

7. On models from 1975-79, unbolt the leading rod from the rear crossmember.

8. Pry the control arm off the crossmember with a suitable lever.

9. Push the control arm forward and detach it from the end of the stabilizer bar.

10. Remove the cotter pin from the castle nut. Unfasten the nut and remove the ball joint from the axle housing with a suitable puller.

11. Remove the control arm from under the car.

To install:

12. Installation is the reverse of removal.

13. Do not grease the upper ball joint stud which fits into the axle housing.

14. Torque the castle nut to 30-40 ft. lbs. (40-54 Nm). Use new self-locking nuts on the crossmember and stabilizer bar mounts.

15. Torque the new self-locking nuts to 73-87 ft. lbs. (98-117 Nm) with the vehicle weight resting on the wheels.

1980-84 Models

▶ **See Figures 22 and 23**

1. Raise the vehicle, support it with jackstands, and remove the front wheel.

2. Remove the two nuts and two bolts fastening the leading rod and stabilizer bar to the center of the transverse link.

3. Remove the cotter pin and castellated nut which fasten the lower ball joint to the transverse link and pull (or press, if necessary) the ball joint stud out of the link.

4. Remove the nut and bolt fastening the link and bushing to the crossmember. Pull (or pry, if necessary) the link and bushing out of the crossmember.

5. Remove the bushing from the link. Replace if damaged.

To install:

6. Reverse Steps 1 through 4 to install the unit using the following torque figures:

- Link-to-crossmember nut/bolt: 43-51 ft. lbs. (58-69 Nm)
- Ball joint stud nut: 29 ft. lbs. (39 Nm)

7. After torquing, tighten the nut further just until the cotter pin can be installed.

8. Install the cotter pin and bend it around the nut.

Knuckle and Spindle

REMOVAL & INSTALLATION

▶ **See Figures 24, 25, 26, 27, 28, 29 and 30**

1. Disconnect the negative (-) battery cable.

2. Apply the parking brake.

3. Remove the front wheel cap and cotter pin, and loosen the castle nut and wheel nut.

4. Raise the vehicle, support it with jackstands and remove the front tires and wheels.

5. Release the parking brake.

6. Pull out the parking brake cable outer clip from the caliper.

7. Disconnect the parking brake cable end from the caliper lever.

8. Loosen the two nuts and remove the disc brake assembly from the housing.

9. Remove the two nuts which connect the housing and damper strut.

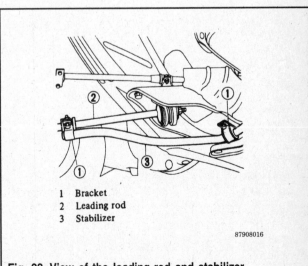

1 Bracket
2 Leading rod
3 Stabilizer

87908016

Fig. 22 View of the leading rod and stabilizer assemblies

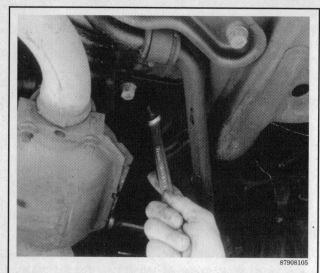

Fig. 23 Loosen and remove the leading rod retainer

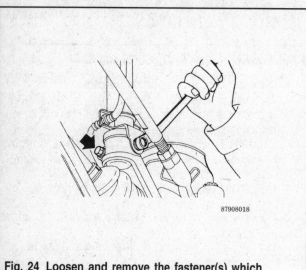

Fig. 24 Loosen and remove the fastener(s) which connect the housing and damper strut.

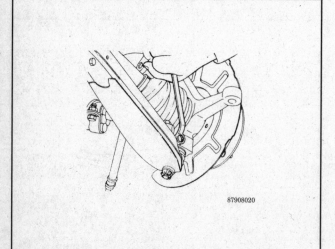

Fig. 25 Loosen and remove the fastener(s) which connect the tie rod end ball stud

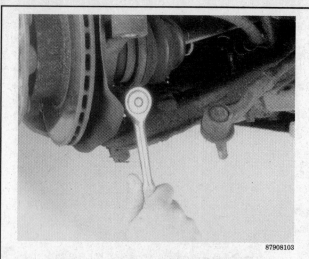

Fig. 26 Loosen and remove the fastener(s) which connect the transverse link to the housing

Fig. 27 Expand the slit of the housing using a hammer and chisel. Do not expand the slit more than 0.15 in. (4mm)

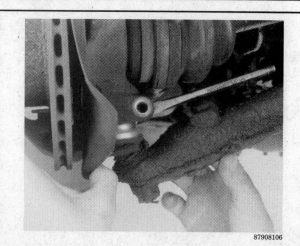

Fig. 28 When you have expanded the slit, lower the housing gradually, being careful not to damage the ball joint boot

10. Remove the cotter pin and castle nut, then disconnect the the tie rod end ball joint from the housing knuckle arm by using a puller.

11. Disconnect the strut from the housing by opening the slit of the housing and lowering the housing gradually, being careful not to damage the ball joint boot.

➡ Do not expand the slit of the housing more than 0.15 in. (4mm). If the housing is hard to remove from the strut, lightly tap the hub and disc with a large rubber mallet.

12. Remove the castle nut, washer spring center piece on the axle shaft, and take out the hub and disc assembly.

13. Remove the disc cover.

14. Attach puller 921121000 or equivalent to the housing and drive the axle shaft out of the housing toward the engine at the bearing location.

➡ If the inner bearing and/or oil seal are left on the axle shaft, remove them with a puller.

15. Disconnect the transverse link from the housing, and detach the housing.

To install:

16. Fit the housing onto the axle shaft and attach spacer installer 925130000 or 922430000 or their equivalents, on the outer bearing inner race taking care not to damage the oil seal lip. Then, connect the rod of the installer to the thread of the axle shaft so that the housing does not drop off the axle shaft.

17. Install the transverse link ball joint to the housing and torque the ball joint-to housing nut to 22-29 ft. lbs. (29-39 Nm).

18. Turn the handle while holding the rod end, by means of a spanner, thus pushing in the housing.

19. Connect the damper strut and housing by installing the two damper strut-to-housing bolts and torque to 22-29 ft. lbs. (29-39 Nm).

20. Connect the tie rod end ball joint and housing knuckle arm. Torque the castle nut 18-22 ft. lbs. (24-29 Nm).

21. After tightening the nut to the specified torque, further torque the nut just enough to align the holes of the nut and ball stud. Then insert a cotter pin into the ball stud and bend it around the castle nut.

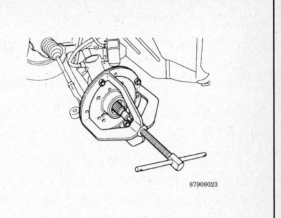

Fig. 30 Attach puller 921121000 or equivalent to the housing and drive the axle shaft out of the housing toward the engine at the bearing location

22. Install the disc cover to housing and torque the cover-to-housing nut to 4.3-10.1 ft. lbs. (5-13 Nm).

23. Install the hub and disc assembly onto the axle shaft.

➡ Be sure to press the hub and disc assembly onto the axle shaft until the end surface of the hub contacts the ball bearing. If the assembly is hard to press, rotate it to locate the point where it is easily pressed.

24. Install the disc brake to housing assembly and torque the two bolts 36-51 ft. lbs. (48-69 Nm).

25. Connect the parking brake cable to the brake assembly.

26. Apply the parking brake.

27. Position the center piece, washer spring and castle nut in this order onto the axle shaft and tighten the castle nut to 145 ft. lbs. (196 Nm).

28. Insert a new cotter pin and bend it around the nut.

➡ After tightening the nut to the specified torque, retighten it further until a slot of the castle nut is aligned to the hole in the axle shaft.

29. Install the wheel and hub cap.
30. Remove the jackstands and lower the vehicle.
31. Connect the negative battery cable.

Front Hub and Bearing

REMOVAL PACKING & INSTALLATION

▶ See Figures 31, 32, 33, 34 and 35

✳✳CAUTION

Asbestos, a known cancer causing agent, is still present in many types of brake lining. Do not use compressed air to clean accumulated dust from your brake system. A safer method is to use rags soaked with a safe solvent so that dust will not be able to enter your throat and lungs.

1. Refer to the "Front Halfshaft, Removal and Installation" procedures in this section and remove the halfshaft from the

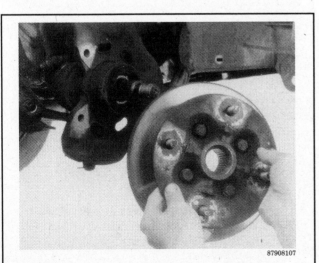

Fig. 29 Remove the disc and hub assembly being careful not to damage the splines on the axle shaft

vehicle; be sure to remove the steering knuckle from the vehicle.

2. Using your finger, move the spacer (inside the steering knuckle) in the radial direction.

3. Using a brass bar, insert it through the inner race of the outer bearing, then tap the bar with a hammer to drive out the bearing (with the oil seal); discard the bearing and the oil seal.

4. Remove the spacer and the inner bearing.

5. Position the brass bar through the outer race of the inner bearing, then using a hammer, drive the out the bearing (with the oil seal); discard the bearing and the oil seal.

6. Clean and inspect the parts for wear, cracks and/or damage; if necessary, replace the damaged parts.

To install:

7. Using new bearings, pack them with wheel bearing grease as follows.

a. Place some high temperature grease in the palm of your hand.

b. Thoroughly work the grease into the bearing until it protrudes from the other side of the bearing.

c. Turn the bearing with your hand to ensure that the bearing is thouroughly packed.

8. Using the Die tool No. 925140000 or equivalent, install the steering knuckle onto the die.

9. Using a press and the Punch tool No. 925140000 or equivalent, press the outer bearing into the housing until it contacts the housing stopper.

10. Using 3 oz. (85 g) of wheel bearing grease, pack the inside of the housing.

11. Invert the housing on the Die tool No. 925140000 or equivalent, and install the spacer.

12. Using a press and the Punch tool No. 925140000 or equivalent, press the inner bearing into the housing until it contacts the housing stopper.

13. Using a press and the Punch tool No. 925140000 or equivalent, position the new outer oil seal in the punch tool so that the lip faces the groove, then press it into the steering

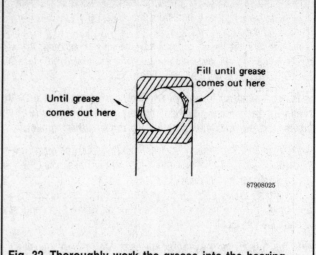

Fig. 32 Thoroughly work the grease into the bearing until it protrudes from the other side of the bearing

knuckle housing, until it comes in contact with the bearing end face.

14. Invert the steering knuckle housing onto the Punch tool No. 925140000 or equivalent, so that the seal lip faces the groove.

15. Using a press and the Die tool No. 925140000 or equivalent, press the new inner oil seal into the steering knuckle housing, until it comes in contact with the bearing end face.

16. To install the steering knuckle, fit the housing onto the axle shaft and attach a spacer of the Installation tool No. 925130000 or equivalent, on the outer bearing inner race; be careful not to damage the oil seal. Thread the axle shaft onto the installation tool, then turn the handle to draw the axle into the housing, until it is seated.

17. To complete the installation, reverse the remaining removal procedures.

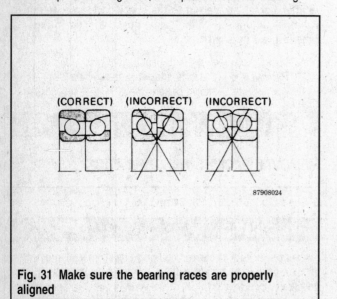

Fig. 31 Make sure the bearing races are properly aligned

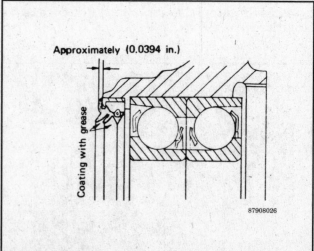

Fig. 33 Be sure to install the bearing outer oil seal to the proper depth

Item	Torque (ft. lbs.)
Backing plate securing bolts	22–35
Lower control arm nut	25–29
Tie-rod end nut	18–22
Shock-to-axle housing	22–29
Axle shaft nut (1972–73)	145–181
Axle shaft nut (1974–75)	170

87908027

Fig. 34 Front bearing and hub torque specifications — 1972-75

Item	Torque (ft. lbs.)
Lower control arm nut	25–29
Tie-rod end nut	18–22
Shock-to-axle housing	22–29
Caliper bracket-to-hub	36–51
Axle shaft nut	145–181

87908028

Fig. 35 Front bearing and hub torque specifications — 1976-84

Front End Alignment

➡The procedure for checking and adjusting front wheel alignment requires specialized equipment and professional skills. The following descriptions and adjustment procedures are for general reference only.

Front wheel alignment is the position of the front wheels relative to each other and to the vehicle. It is determined, and must be maintained to provide safe, accurate steering with minimum tire wear. Many factors are involved in wheel alignment, and adjustments are provided to return those that might change due to normal wear to their original value. The factors which determine wheel alignment are dependent on one another; therefore, when one of the factors is adjusted, the others must be adjusted to compensate. Descriptions of these factors and their affects on the vehicle are provided below.

➡Do not attempt to check and adjust the front wheel alignment without first making a thorough inspection of the front suspension components.

CASTER AND CAMBER

Caster angle is the number of degrees that a line drawn through the steering knuckle pivots is inclined from the vertical, toward the front or rear of the vehicle. Caster improves directional stability and decreases susceptibility to crosswinds or road surface deviations.

Camber angle is the number of degrees that the centerline of the wheel is inclined from the vertical. Camber reduces loading of the outer wheel bearing and improves the tire contact patch while cornering.

ff-1 and 1300G

Caster and camber are controlled by hexagonal cams which control the position of the lower ball joint on the control arm. Rotating the inner (caster) or outer (camber) cam by two flats changes caster or camber by 1°.

Except ff-1 and 1300G

Caster and camber are not adjustable on these models. If either of these specifications is not within the factory recommended range, this would indicate bent or damaged parts that must be replaced.

TOE-IN

▶ See Figure 36

Toe-in is the difference of the distance between the centers of the front and rear of the front wheels. It is most commonly measured in inches, but is occasionally referred to as an angle between the wheels. Toe-in is necessary to compensate for the tendency of the wheels to deflect rearward while in motion. Due to this tendency, the wheels of a vehicle, with properly adjusted toe-in, are traveling straight forward when the vehicle itself is traveling straight forward, resulting in directional stability and minimum tire wear.

➡The Do-it-Yourself mechanic should not attempt to perform any wheel alignment procedures. Expensive alignment tools are needed and would not be cost efficient to purchase these tools. The wheel alignment should be performed by a certified alignment technician using the proper alignment tools.

Toe-in is adjusted by loosening the locknuts on the tie rods, and turning the tie rods until the proper specification is obtained.

✳✳WARNING

Before performing the toe-in adjustment, be sure that the steering gear is centered by aligning the marks on it, and that the wheels are straight ahead.

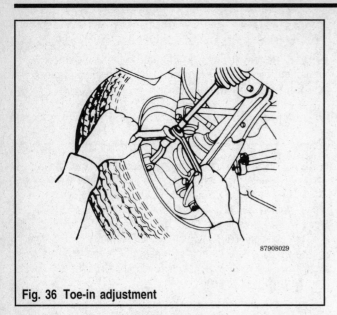

Fig. 36 Toe-in adjustment

Tighten the locknuts after the toe-in adjustment is completed.

STEERING AXIS INCLINATION

Steering axis inclination is the number of degrees that a line drawn through the steering knuckle pivots is inclined from the vertical, when viewed from the front of the vehicle. This, in combination with caster, is responsible for directional stability and self-centering of the steering. As the steering knuckle swings from lock to lock, the spindle generates an arc, the high point being the straight-ahead position of the wheel. Due to this arc, as the wheel turns, the front of the vehicle is raised. The weight of the vehicle acts against this lift and attempts to return the spindle to the high point of the arc, resulting in self-centering, when the steering wheel is released, and straight line stability.

RIDE HEIGHT

♦ See Figure 37

ff-1 and 1300G

Ride height is measured from the center of the lower control arm to the ground. It should be 8-9 in. (227-238mm). Adjust it by turning the adjustment cam on the front of each torsion bar. Turning the cam clockwise raises, and counterclockwise lowers ride height. Each notch in the cam corresponds to an 3 in. (8mm) change in height.

Access to the cams is obtained through the cooling slots located on either side, below the bumper.

ADJUSTING FRONT ROAD CLEARANCES

4-Wheel Drive Vehicles
♦ See Figure 38

1. Check and even out the tire pressure in both front wheels.
2. Park vehicle on a level surface and measure the height of the vehicle from the ground. Measurement is taken from the transverse link mounting bolt to the ground.
3. Adjustment is made by turning the two adjusting nuts on the bottom of each strut. Turn both nuts at the same time and the same amount.
4. Adjust the other side following the instructions in Step 3.
5. Re-measure the ground clearance to be sure both sides are even. Recheck and if necessary, adjust toe-in.

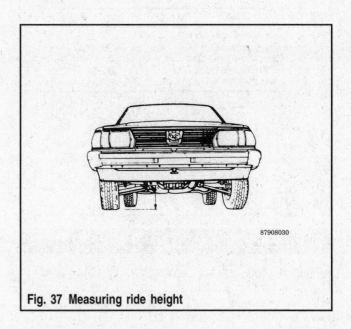

Fig. 37 Measuring ride height

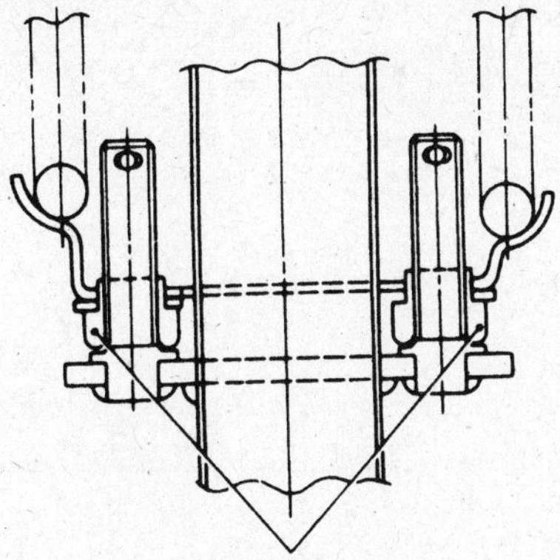

Fig. 38 Adjusting ride height 4WD vehicles — 1980 models

Wheel Alignment Specifications

Year	Model	Caster Range (deg)	Caster Preferred Setting (deg)	Camber Range (deg)	Camber Preferred Setting (deg)	Toe-in (in.)
1970–72	FF-1 and 1300G	1½P–2P	2P	1¼P–1¾P	1¾P	.20
1972	GL and DL	0–1½P	1P	¾P–1¾P	1¼P	.08–.32
1973–74	All	0–1½P	¾P	—	1½P	.09–.32
1975–76	Sedan, Coupe, H.T.	0–1½P	¾P	1P–2P	1½P	.08–.32
	Station Wagon	0–1½P	¾P	1P–2P	1½P	.08–.32
	4WD	0–1½P	¾P	2P–3P	2½P	.24–.47
1977–79	Sedan, Coupe, H.T.	1½N–5N	3¼N	¾P–2¼P	1½P	.08–.32
	Station Wagon	1N–½P	¼N	1P–2½P	1P	.08–.32
	4WD	1½N–5N	3¼N	1½P–3P	2¼P	.24–.47
1980–81	Sedan and H.T.	1⅙N–⅓P	—	¾P–2¼P	—	.08–.31
	Station Wagon	⅚N–⅔P	—	1P–2½P	—	.08–.31
	Sedan 4WD	1¼N–¼P	—	1⅚P–3⅓P	—	.24–.47
	4WD	1⅓N–1/12P	—	1⅚P–3⅓P	—	.24–.47
1982	exc. 4WD and Station Wagon	−1°10′ to 20′	—	45′ to 2°30′	—	.04 ± .04
	exc. 4WD Station Wagon	−50′ to 40′	—	1° to 2°30′	—	.04 ± .04
	4WD Hatchback	−1°15′ to 15′	—	1°15′ to 3°20′	—	.08 ± .04
	4WD exc. Hatchback	−1°25′ to 5′	—	1°50′ to 3°20′	—	.08 ± .04
'83–'84	Hatchback, Sedan, Hardtop	−1°10′ to 20′	—	45′ to 2°15′	—	.04 ± .04
	Station Wagon	−50′ to 40′	—	1° to 2°30′	—	.04 ± .04
	Hatchback 4WD, Sedan 4WD	−1°15′ to 15′	—	1°40′ to 3°10′	—	.2 ± .04 ①
	Wagon 4WD, Brat	−1°25′ to 5′	—	1°40′ to 3°10′	—	.2 ± .04 ①
	Turbo	−1°15′ to 15′	—	1°25′ to 2°55′	—	.2 ± .04 ①

Not adjustable—MacPherson Strut
① Refers to Toe-out

87908C01

REAR SUSPENSION

Torsion Bars

REMOVAL AND INSTALLATION

1970-72 Models

▶ See Figure 39

1. Raise the rear of the vehicle and support it with jackstands.
2. Remove the wheel.
3. Using a hex key (8mm), loosen the center arm and spring to relax the torsion bars.
4. Remove the nut and retaining plate from the cross-member mounting bracket.
5. Back out the lockbolts at each end of the torsion bar to be removed, thread a bolt into the bar, and pull it out of the crossmember.

☀☀WARNING

Torsion bars are marked R or L, and must be installed on the correct side. Installation on the incorrect side will result in premature failure of the bars.

6. To install reverse Steps 1 through 5, and adjust ride height.

1972-1979 Models

▶ See Figure 40

1. Remove the shock absorber lower retaining nut, and separate the shock absorber from the trailing arm.
2. Raise the vehicle, support it with jackstands, and remove the wheels.
3. Index mark the splines on the outside and inside of the torsion bar, to indicate mounting position for installation.

4. Remove the lockbolt from the outer torsion bar bushing.
5. Position the trailing arm so as to remove all load from the torsion bar, and tap the torsion bar out.

To install:

6. When installing the torsion bars, reverse Steps 1 through 5.
7. Each torsion bar is marked R or L, on the outer end, to indicate on which side it is installed.

☀☀WARNING

Installation on the incorrect side will result in premature failure of the bars.

8. Index the splines according to the marks made during removal, install the wheel and check ride height.
9. If necessary, adjust ride height as indicated below.
10. Remount the shock absorber after the vehicle has been lowered.

1980-84 Models

▶ See Figure 41

1. Raise the vehicle and support it with jackstands.
2. Remove the rear wheel.
3. Support the brake drum in a position eliminating load from the torsion bar.
4. Remove the lockbolt for the outer bushing and the three outer arm to inner arm connecting bolts.
5. Pull the outer arm and torsion bar out of the crossmember. The torsion bar may not be removed from the outer arm.

To install:

6. Installation is the reverse of removal, keeping the following points in mind:

    a. The torsion bar's splines must be aligned with those in the outer arm and crossmember so that the outer arm lines up with the inner arm as it did during removal, or ride height will be affected.

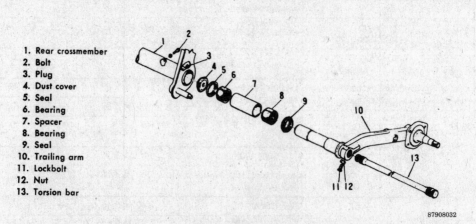

1. Rear crossmember
2. Bolt
3. Plug
4. Dust cover
5. Seal
6. Bearing
7. Spacer
8. Bearing
9. Seal
10. Trailing arm
11. Lockbolt
12. Nut
13. Torsion bar

87908032

Fig. 39 Exploded view of a typical trailing arm and torsion bar assembly — 1970-72 ff-1 sedans and wagons, 1300G wagons

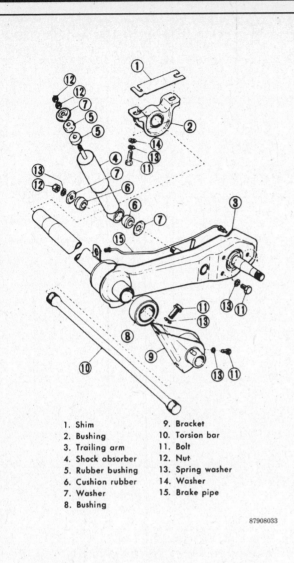

1. Shim	9. Bracket
2. Bushing	10. Torsion bar
3. Trailing arm	11. Bolt
4. Shock absorber	12. Nut
5. Rubber bushing	13. Spring washer
6. Cushion rubber	14. Washer
7. Washer	15. Brake pipe
8. Bushing	

87908033

Fig. 40 Exploded view of a typical rear suspension (except ff-1 and 1300G and 4WD)

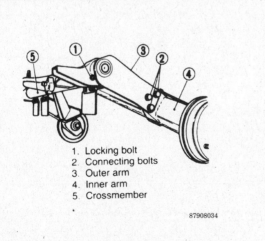

1. Locking bolt
2. Connecting bolts
3. Outer arm
4. Inner arm
5. Crossmember

87908034

Fig. 41 Rear torsion bar suspension components — 1980-84 models

b. If you are removing both torsion bars, make sure the markings (R or L) correspond with the side of the car you're installing the bar on.

c. Use the following torques:
- Inner arm to outer arm: 87-101 ft. lbs. (117-136 Nm)
- Outer bushing lockbolt: 23-29 ft. lbs. (31-39 Nm)

Shock Absorbers

REMOVAL & INSTALLATION

1970-80 Models

1. Remove the wheel cover and loosen the lug nuts.
2. Set the parking brake and block the rear wheels. Raise the rear of the car and support it with jackstands.

✳✳CAUTION

Be sure that the car is securely supported.

3. Remove the lug nuts and the rear wheels.
4. Fully loosen the ride height adjustment bolt on all 1971 ff-1 models and on 1971-72 ff-1 and 1300G station wagons.
5. Loosen the two upper shock absorber mounting nuts. Remove the washer and the bushing, being sure to note their correct assembly sequence for installation.
6. Remove the nut on the trailing arm pin (nut and bolt on later models) and remove the shock absorber. Note the installing positions of the washers.

To install:

7. Reverse Steps 1 through 5.
8. Do not fully tighten the upper mounting nuts until the lower shock nut has been installed with the washer and the pin shoulder contacting each other.
9. Torque the upper nuts to 22-32 ft. lbs. (29-43 Nm). Adjust ride height bolts, if so equipped.

1981-84 Models

▶ See Figures 42, 43 and 44

Semi-trailing arms mounted to torque tubes, which act on an internal torsion bar, are used. Shock absorbers are mounted to the trailing arm, close to the stub axle.

1. Raise and support the rear of the vehicle with jackstands.
2. Set the parking brake and blocking the front wheels. Remove the wheel cover and loosen the lug nuts.
3. Remove the lug nuts and the rear wheels.
4. Loosen the upper shock absorber-to-chassis nuts.
5. Remove the washer and the bushing, being sure to note their correct assembly sequence for installation.
6. Remove the shock absorber-to-trailing arm pin nut (nut and bolt on later models) and the shock absorber. Note the installation positions of the washers.
7. To install, reverse Steps 1 through 6.

8. Torque the shock absorber-to-chassis nuts to 22-32 ft. lbs. (29-43 Nm). Adjust the ride height bolts, if equipped.

➡DO NOT fully tighten the upper mounting nuts until the lower shock nut has been installed with the washer and the pin shoulder contracting each other.

Rear Control (Inner) Arms

REMOVAL & INSTALLATION

➡The vehicle must be in the unloaded condition. Remove all cargo from the vehicle, there should be no weight bearing down on the rear suspension.

1. Loosen the rear wheel lug nuts.
2. Raise and support the rear of the vehicle with jackstands; position the jackstands under the crossmember.
3. Remove the wheel/tire assemblies.

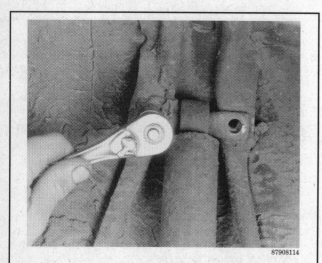

Fig. 42 Loosen the upper shock absorber-to-chassis nuts

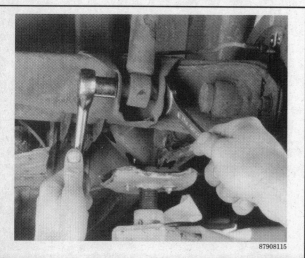

Fig. 43 Loosen and remove the lower shock absorber nut and bolt

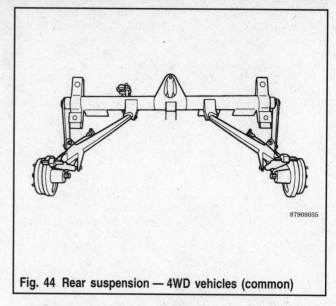

Fig. 44 Rear suspension — 4WD vehicles (common)

4. Remove the shock absorber/strut-to-inner arm nut/bolt and separate the shock absorber/strut from the inner arm.
5. If equipped with 4WD, perform the following procedures:
    a. Using a 6mm pin punch, drive the spring pins from the halfshaft-to-axle shaft and the halfshaft-to-differential assembly.
    b. While pushing downward on the inner arm, separate the halfshaft from the axle shaft.
    c. Pull the halfshaft from the differential and position it out of the way.
6. Disconnect and plug the brake hose from the brake pipe on each inner arm.
7. Remove the outer arm-to-inner arm nuts/bolts, then separate the inner arm from the outer arm and support the inner arm with a jackstand.
8. Remove the inner arm-to-crossmember nut/bolt and the inner arm from the vehicle.
   To install:
9. Use new spring pins (4WD) and reverse the above process.
10. Torque the inner arm-to-crossmember nuts/bolts to 54-69 ft. lbs. (73-93 Nm) and the inner arm-to-outer arm bolts to 87-108 ft. lbs. (117-146 Nm).
11. Torque the shock absorber-to-inner arm nut/bolt to 65-87 ft. lbs. (88-117 Nm).
12. Bleed the brake system. Check and/or adjust the rear vehicle height and the rear wheel alignment.

Rear Wheel Bearings — FWD Only

➡For wheel bearing removal and installation procedure on all 4WD models, refer to the Rear Axle section.

REMOVAL & INSTALLATION

1. Apply the hand brake and loosen the rear wheel lug nuts.
2. Raise and support the rear of the vehicle with jackstands. Remove the rear wheel assemblies.

3. If equipped with rear disc brakes, remove the caliper and support it on a wire.

4. Using a small prybar, remove the rear wheel grease cap.

5. Using a hammer and a punch, flatten the lock washer and loosen the axle nut. Remove the lock washer and the thrust plate.

6. When removing the drum or disc, be careful not to drop the inner race from the outer bearing.

7. Using a gear puller, remove the spacer and the inner race of the inner bearing.

8. Using a brass drift and a hammer, drive the outer race of the inner bearing (with the oil seal) from the drum or disc.

9. Using a brass drift and a hammer, drive the outer race of the outer bearing from the drum or disc.

10. Clean and inspect the parts for damage, wear and/or corrosion; replace the parts, if necessary.

To install:

11. Using the Bearing Installation tool No. 925220000 or equivalent, press the outer race of the inner bearing into the drum or disc until it seats against the shoulder.

➡**When pressing the bearing, be sure not to exceed the load to the bearing, so as not to damage it.**

12. Apply a small amount of grease to the oil seal lips, then install the oil seal until it is flush with the drum or disc.

13. Using the Bearing Installation tool No. 921130000 or equivalent, press the outer race of the outer bearing into the drum or disc until it seats against the shoulder.

14. Apply approximately ⅛ oz. (3.5 g) of wheel bearing grease to the inner and the outer bearings. Fill the disc or drum hub with 1 oz. (28 g) of wheel bearing grease.

15. Install a new spacer O-ring, the spacer and the inner race of the inner bearing onto the trailing arm spindle.

➡**When installing the spacer, be sure to face the stepped surface toward the bearing. Use a new thrust plate and lock washer.**

16. To complete the installation, reverse the remaining removal procedures. Adjust the wheel bearing.

ADJUSTMENT

1. Temporarily tighten the axle nut to 36 ft. lbs. 48 Nm), turn the drum or disc (back and forth) several times to ensure that the bearings are properly seated.

2. Rotate the nut backwards ⅛ turn in order to obtain the correct starting force.

3. Using a spring gauge, at a 90° angle to the wheel lug, check the rotating force; the force should be 1.9-3.2 ft. lbs. (2-4 Nm).

4. After adjustment is complete, bend the lock washer.

5. After installing a new O-ring to the grease cap, install the cap with a plastic hammer.

Independent Rear Suspension

ADJUSTMENTS

Frequent checks and adjustment of the rear independent suspension should not be necessary. However, under the following conditions the rear suspension alignment should be checked and adjusted:
- Uneven tire wear.
- Insufficient ground clearance.
- One side of the rear is higher than the other.
- Rear suspension components are replaced or overhauled.

Be sure to check the following prior to checking rear suspension alignment.
- Tire inflation pressures.
- Tire condition and wear.
- Ground clearance.
- Wheel and tire runout.

Ride Height

1970-72 ff-1 SEDANS, WAGONS AND 1300G WAGONS

Adjust rear ride height by turning a socket head bolt (8mm), clockwise to raise, and counterclockwise to lower the vehicle. The bolt is accessible through a port in the trunk.

EXCEPT 1970-72 ff-1 SEDANS, WAGONS AND 1300G WAGONS

No routine ride height adjustment is provided. Should it be necessary to adjust ride height, the torsion bar(s) must be removed as described in this section. To increase ride height, turn the outer end of the torsion bar in the direction of the arrow (on the end of the bar). Decrease ride height by reversing the above.

Shifting the torsion bar one tooth will alter ride height approximately (0.19 in. (5mm).All 4 wheel drive vehicles have a unique adjusting device that will alter the ride height. (In addition to adjust the torsion bars) refer to rear road clearance for instructions.

Rear Road Clearance
▶ **See Figures 45 and 46**

4-WHEEL DRIVE VEHICLES

Although the ride height is adjustable on all torsion bar equipped vehicles — 1980-84 4WD vehicles incorporated a built-in adjuster to make this easier.

1. Measure the height of the vehicle from the lowest point of the rear axle crossmember to the ground.

2. To adjust the rear height remove the access cover from the service hole located in the vehicle floor above the rear axle. Turn the adjusting bolt, clockwise to increase the height; counterclockwise to lower it.

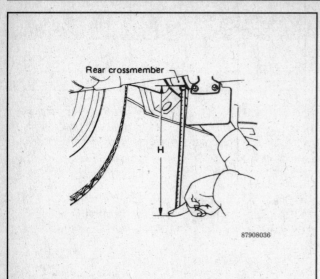

87908036

Fig. 45 Measuring rear road clearance height

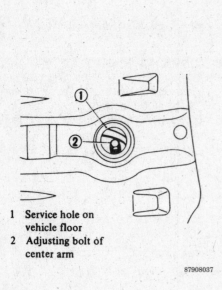

1 Service hole on vehicle floor
2 Adjusting bolt of center arm

87908037

Fig. 46 Remove the access cover from the service hole located in the vehicle floor above the rear axle. Turn the adjusting bolt, clockwise to increase the height; counterclockwise to lower it

Rear Camber

1970-79 MODELS

◗ **See Figure 47**

Camber is adjusted by changing the number of shims mounted between the inner torsion bar bushing assembly and the body. Each shim corresponds to $1/4°$ of change. Adding shims decreases the camber. Removing shims increases it.

➡**Camber on 1980-84 models is not adjustable. If any of the rear suspension components become worn or damaged, they must be replaced in order to bring the rear alignment back within specification.**

Rear Wheel Toe-In

1970-79 MODELS

◗ **See Figure 48**

Rear wheel toe-in is changed by loosening the inner torsion bar bushing assembly bolts and sliding the bushing assembly forward or backward. Forward movement decreases toe-in and backward movement increases it. The range of adjustment is 6mm. Tighten the bolts after completing the adjustment.

➡**Rear wheel toe-in on 1980-84 models is not adjustable. If any of the rear suspension components become worn or damaged, they must be replaced in order to bring the rear alignment back within specification.**

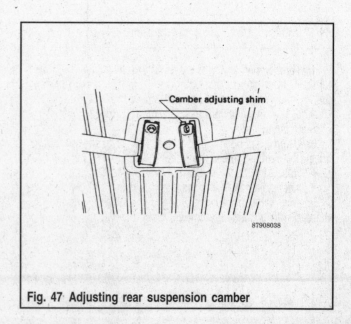

87908038

Fig. 47 Adjusting rear suspension camber

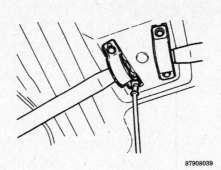

87908039

Fig. 48 Rear wheel toe-in is changed by loosening the inner torsion bar bushing assembly bolts and sliding the bushing assembly forward or backward. Forward movement decreases toe-in and backward movement increases it

Rear End Alignment

Year	Model	Body Type	Ride* Height (in.)	Camber (deg)	Toe-In (in.)	Tracking (in.)▲
1970–72	FF-1, 1300G	Sedans	12.1–12.6	1P ± ½	.04–.20	–.12– +.12
	FF-1, 1300G	Wagon	13.0–13.4	1P ± ½	.04–.20	–.12– +.12
1972	GL	Coupe	11.1–11.7	¼P–1½P	.04–.20	–.12– +.12
	DL	All	11.3–11.9	½P–1½P	.04–.20	–.12– +.12
1973–74	GL, DL	Coupe, Sedan	11.3–11.9	¼P–1½P	.04–.20	–.12– +.12
	DL	Wagon	11.2–12.0	¼P–1½P	.04–.20	–.12– +.12
1975–76	DL, GL, GF	Sedan, Coupe, H.T.	11.3–11.9	¼P–1½P	.04–.20	–.12– +.12
	DL	Wagon	12.2–12.8	1P–2P	.08–.24	–.12– +.12
	4WD	Wagon	14.2–14.8	1½P–2¼P	.08–.24	0– +.16
1977–79	DL, GL, GF	Sedan, Coupe, H.T.	11.2–12.0	¼N–1P	.04–.20	–.12– +.12
	DL	Wagon	12.2–13.0	¼P–2P	.08–.24	–.12– +.12
	4WD	Wagon	13.6–14.4	½P–2P	.08–.24	0– +.16
1980–81	exc. 4WD	Sedan, H.T.	10.2–11.0	¾N–¾P	—	–.20– +.20
	exc. 4WD	Station Wagon	11.0–11.8	¾N–¾P	—	–.20– +.20
	4WD	Sedan	12.6–13.4	¾N–¾P	—	–.20– +.20
	4WD	exc. Sedan	13.1–13.9	⅓N–1P	—	–.20– +.20
1982	exc. 4WD	Hatchback, Sedan and Hardtop	10.3–11.1	–45'–45'	–.12 to .12	–.20– +.20
	exc. 4WD	Station Wagon	11.1–11.9	–45'–45'	–.12 to .12	–.20– +.20
	4WD	Hatchback	12.6–13.4	–45'–45'	–.12 to .12	–.20– +.20
	4WD	Exc. Hatchback	13.2–14.0	–25'–1°05'	–.12 to .12	–.20– +.20
1983–84	2WD	Hatchback Sedan Hardtop, XT Coupe	10.24–11.02	–45' to 45'	0 ± .12	–.20– +.20
		Station Wagon	11.02–11.81	–45' to 45'	0 ± .12	–.20– +.20
	4WD	Hatchback, Sedan	12.80–13.58 ①	–45' to 45'	0 ± .12	–.20– +.20
	4WD	Station Wagon, Brat	13.19–14.17 ②	–25' to 1°05'	0 ± .12	–.20– +.20
		Turbo	12.80–13.58	–1° to 30'	0 ± .12	–.20– +.20

* Measured from outer center of torsion bar
▲ Measured with one passenger aboard
① —on '83 models, 12.60–11.81
② —on '83 models, 13.19–14.17

87908C02

STEERING

Steering Wheel

REMOVAL & INSTALLATION

▶ See Figures 49, 50 and 51

1. Disconnect the negative (-) battery cable.
2. Remove the horn lead from the wiring harness which is located beneath the instrument panel.
3. Working from behind the steering wheel, remove the two or three (depending upon the number of spokes) horn assembly retaining screws.
4. On ff-1 and 1300G models, depress the horn bar as far as you can, and slide it away from the wheel.
5. On all other models, lift the crash pad assembly off the front of the wheel.
6. Matchmark the steering wheel and the column for installation.
7. Remove the steering wheel retaining nut and remove the wheel from the column with a puller.

To install:

8. Installation is the reverse of removal.
9. Index the matchmarks and torque the retaining nut to 20-29 ft. lbs. (27-39 Nm).

❄CAUTION

Do not hammer on the steering wheel or the steering column. Damage to the collapsible column could result.

Fig. 49 Loosen the screws that retain the horn pad and remove the horn pad

Fig. 50 Matchmark the steering wheel and the column to aid during installation.

Fig. 51 Loosen the steering wheel retaining nut and remove the wheel from the column with a puller

Turn Signal (Combination) Switch

REMOVAL & INSTALLATION

▶ See Figure 52

1. Disconnect the negative (-) battery cable.
2. Perform the Steering Wheel Removal procedure.
3. Separate the steering column wiring connectors which are located underneath the instrument panel.
4. Remove the turn signal (combination) switch securing screws and unscrew the hazard warning switch knob.
5. Remove the contact plate, cancelling cam, and switch assembly from the steering column housing.

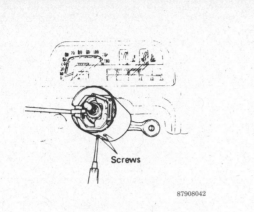

87908042

Fig. 52 Remove the turn signal (combination) switch securing screws and unscrew the hazard warning switch knob

6. Installation is the reverse of removal.

✳✳CAUTION

Do not hammer on the steering wheel or column. Damage to the collapsible column could result.

Ignition Switch

REMOVAL & INSTALLATION

The ignition switch is mounted to the steering column using shear bolts. These bolts are constructed so that the head is sheared off when the bolt is tightened. For this reason removal of the ignition switch is rather complicated.

1. Disconnect the negative (-) battery cable.
2. Remove the steering wheel as previously outlined.
3. Disconnect the steering shaft from the universal joint (located near the steering gear box) by loosening the locking bolt.
4. Remove the steering shaft installing bolt from the instrument panel.
5. Pull the steering shaft assembly from the hole in floor board and remove the assembly from the car.
6. Loosen the screws holding the column cover and hazard knob, then pull the steering shaft out of the column cover.
7. Drill into the shaft of the shear bolts and extract them with a screw extractor. Remove the switch.
8. Installation is the reverse of removal.

➡**Be sure to use new shear bolts to install the ignition switch.**

Steering Column

REMOVAL & INSTALLATION

▶ **See Figure 53**

1. Disconnect the negative (-) battery terminal.
2. Unfasten the universal joint connecting bolts and remove the universal.
3. Disengage the connector to the ignition switch.
4. Disengage the combination switch wiring harness under the instrument panel.
5. Remove the steering shaft installing bolts under the instrument panel.
6. Pull out the steering shaft assembly from the hole in the toe board.

✳✳WARNING

Be sure to remove the steering shaft assembly installing bolts when removing the steering shaft assembly or leaving it downward for servicing of other parts.

7. Installation is the reverse of removal.

Tie Rod Ends

REMOVAL & INSTALLATION

1. Raise the front end of the car and support it with jackstands.
2. Remove the front wheels.
3. Remove the cotter pin and castle nut from the tie rod end stud. Detach the tie rod end using a suitable puller or extracting tool.
4. Reverse the above process to install the tie rod ends.
5. Torque the castle nut to 20 ft. lbs. (27 Nm).

Manual Steering Gear

All Subaru models are quipped with rack and pinion steering, which provides light, positive steering and good road feel.

Backlash is automatically adjusted to zero, and therefore no maintenance is required.

REMOVAL & INSTALLATION

1. Raise the front of the vehicle and support it with jackstands. Remove the front wheels.
2. Remove the cotter pin and loosen the castle nut.
3. Remove the tie rod end from the knuckle arm of the housing.
4. Remove the hand brake cable hanger from the tie rod.
5. Pull out the cotter pins and remove the rubber coupling connecting bolts.
6. Disconnect the pinion with the gearbox from the steering shaft.

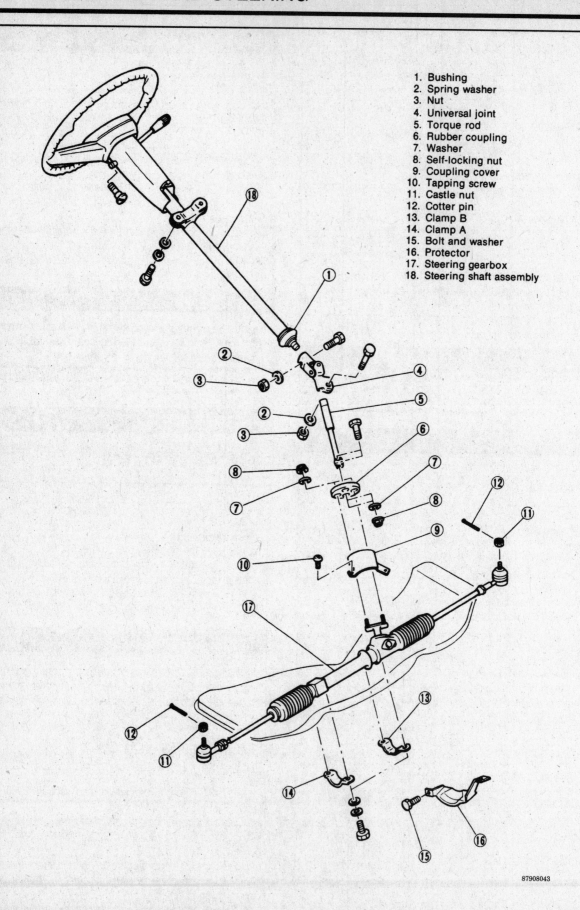

1. Bushing
2. Spring washer
3. Nut
4. Universal joint
5. Torque rod
6. Rubber coupling
7. Washer
8. Self-locking nut
9. Coupling cover
10. Tapping screw
11. Castle nut
12. Cotter pin
13. Clamp B
14. Clamp A
15. Bolt and washer
16. Protector
17. Steering gearbox
18. Steering shaft assembly

87908043

Fig. 53 Exploded view of a typical steering system

7. Straighten the lockplate and remove the bolts which hold the gearbox bracket to the crossmember.

8. On DL and GL models, loosen the front engine mounting bolts and lift up the engine by about 0.19 in. (5mm) to avoid touching the gearbox with the engine. Remove the gearbox from the vehicle.

To install:

9. Reverse Steps 1 through 6 to install the steering gear.

10. Torque the rack and pinion assembly securing bolts to 33-40 ft. lbs. (44-54 Nm) and torque the tie rod end castellated nuts to 18-22 ft. lbs. (24-29 Nm).

11. Adjust the rear wheel toe-in after completing installation.

Power Steering Gear

▶ **See Figure 54**

The power steering gearbox is a rack and pinion type integral system. The power cylinder is built in the gearbox, using the rack shaft as a piston. The control valve is arranged around the pinion shaft.

REMOVAL & INSTALLATION

1. Disconnect the negative (-) battery cable.
2. Remove the spare tire.
3. If necessary, disconnect the thermo sensor connector.
4. Raise and support the front of the vehicle with jackstands.
5. Remove the front wheels.
6. Disengage the electrical connector from the O_2 sensor, then remove the front exhaust pipe assembly.

➡ **If equipped with an air stove, remove it.**

7. Remove the tie rod end cotter pin and loosen the castle nut.
8. Using a Ball Joint Puller tool, separate the tie rod ends from the steering knuckle arm.
9. Remove the jack-up plate and the clamp.
10. From the power steering gear, remove the center pressure pipe, connect a vinyl hose to the pipe and joint, then turn the steering wheel to discharge the fluid into a container.

➡ **When discharging the power steering fluid, turn the steering wheel fully, left and right. Be sure to disconnect the other pipe and drain the fluid in the same manner.**

11. Make alignment marks on the steering shaft universal joint assembly-to-power steering unit and the steering shaft-to-universal joint assembly.

12. Remove the lower/upper universal joint-to-shaft bolts. Lift the universal joint assembly upward and secure it out of the way.

13. From the control valve of the gearbox assembly, remove the power steering pressure pipes.

14. Remove the power steering pressure pipes from the control valve of the gearbox assembly.

15. Remove the power steering gearbox-to-crossmember assembly bolts and the gearbox assembly from the vehicle.

➡ **When installing the universal joint assembly, be sure to align the matchmarks.**

To install:

16. Installation is the reverse of removal.

17. Torque the power steering gearbox-to-crossmember bolts to 33-40 ft. lbs. (44-54 Nm) and the power steering pressure pipes to 7-12 ft. lbs. (9-16 Nm).

18. Torque the universal joint assembly-to-power steering gearbox bolts to 16-19 ft. lbs. (21-25 Nm) and the universal joint assembly-to-steering shaft bolts to 16-19 ft. lbs. (21-25 Nm).

19. Torque the tie rod end-to-steering knuckle nut to 18-22 ft. lbs. (24-29 Nm), (after torquing, turn it 60° further) and the wheel lug nuts to 58-72 ft. lbs. (78-97 Nm).

20. Refill and bleed the power steering system. Check and/or adjust the toe-in and the steering angle.

ADJUSTMENT

Tighten the backlash adjuster until it bottoms, back off the screw 30° and torque the locknut to 22-36 ft. lbs. (29-48 Nm). There should be 0.004 in. (0.124mm) clearance between the screw tip and the sleeve plate.

Power Steering Pump

REMOVAL & INSTALLATION

Except Turbo Models

1. Remove the negative (-) battery cable.
2. Remove the spare tire from the engine compartment.
3. Raise the front of the vehicle and safely support it with jackstands.
4. Drain the fluid from the system by removing the line flare nuts from the center of the power steering gearbox and turning the steering wheel from left to right.
5. Loosen and remove the drive belt. See the belt adjustment procedure that follows.
6. Disengage the hoses connected to the air cleaner and remove the air cleaner assembly.
7. Remove the engine oil dipstick.
8. Remove any other interference that will prevent pump removal.
9. Disconnect the fluid hoses from the back of the pump.
10. Unfasten the pump mounting bolts/nuts and remove the pump.
11. Installation is the reverse of removal.
12. Fill the pump with fluid before starting the engine.

Turbo Models

1. Disconnect the negative (-) battery cable.
2. Remove the spare tire.
3. Drain the power steering fluid from the oil reservoir located on the pump by siphoning the oil out.
4. Loosen but do not remove the power steering pump pulley nut.
5. Loosen the alternator mounting bolts, move the alternator toward the power steering pump, and remove the belts.
6. Remove the nut and pull off the pump pulley.

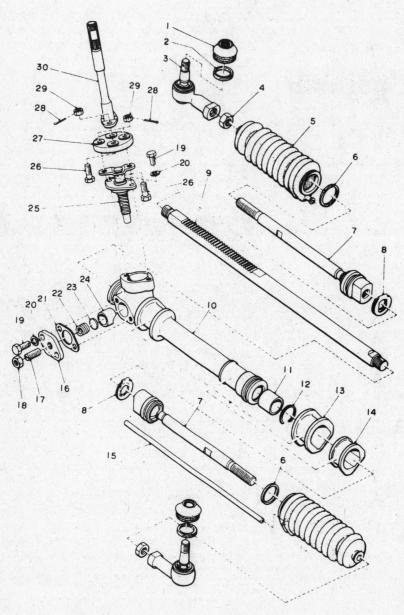

1. Dust seal
2. Snap-ring
3. Tie-rod end
4. Locknut
5. Boot
6. Snap-ring (boot)
7. Ball joint
8. Lockwasher
9. Rack
10. Gearbox unit
11. Bushing-A
12. Clip
13. Adapter-A
14. Adapter-B
15. Air vent tube
16. Cap (steering gear box)
17. Adjusting screw
18. Locknut
19. Bolt
20. Spring washer
21. Packing
22. Spring (sleeve)
23. Plate (sleeve)
24. Sleeve
25. Pinion
26. Bolt
27. Rubber coupling
28. Cotter pin
29. Castle nut
30. Torque rod

87908044

Fig. 54 Exploded view of a common steering gear

7. Disconnect the oil pump line at the pipe using two wrenches. Use one wrench to hold the pipe nut in place and use the other wrench to turn the other nut, this prevents twisting or kinking the pipe.

8. Loosen the clamp and disengage the line where it connects to the tank. Be sure to keep oil off the belts.

9. Unfasten the three bolts attaching the front of the pump to the mount and remove it.

10. To install reverse the removal process, but keep these points in mind:

   a. Do not twist hoses.

   b. Install and adjust the belts before tightening the power steering pulley bolt.

   c. Fill the fluid reservoir with the specified fluid and have someone keep it filled (use new fluid only). Idle the engine and turn the steering wheel from lock-to-lock to force air out of the system.

DRIVE BELT ADJUSTMENT

1. Using a pair of adjustable jawed pliers (with a piece of rag between the jaws), turn and pull to remove the idler cover cap.

2. Turn the adjusting bolt until the correct belt tension is obtained.

3. If disengaging the belt, loosen the adjusting bolt until the drive belt can be removed.

4. After a new belt is installed and the correct tension obtained, replace the idler cap cover by pushing in and turning.

SYSTEM BLEEDING

1. Raise and support the front of the vehicle with jackstands.

2. Refill the reservoir with power steering fluid.

3. With the engine running, turn the steering wheel (back and forth), from lock-to-lock, until the air is removed from the fluid.

4. Lower the vehicle, recheck the reservoir fluid level and replace the reservoir cap.

Noise Diagnosis

The Noise Is	Most Probably Produced By
· Identical under Drive or Coast	· Road surface, tires or front wheel bearings
· Different depending on road surface	· Road surface or tires
· Lower as the car speed is lowered	· Tires
· Similar with car standing or moving	· Engine or transmission
· A vibration	· Unbalanced tires, rear wheel bearing, unbalanced driveshaft or worn U-joint
· A knock or click about every 2 tire revolutions	· Rear wheel bearing
· Most pronounced on turns	· Damaged differential gears
· A steady low-pitched whirring or scraping, starting at low speeds	· Damaged or worn pinion bearing
· A chattering vibration on turns	· Wrong differential lubricant or worn clutch plates (limited slip rear axle)
· Noticed only in Drive, Coast or Float conditions	· Worn ring gear and/or pinion gear

87908C03

Troubleshooting Basic Steering and Suspension Problems

Problem	Cause	Solution
Hard steering (steering wheel is hard to turn)	· Low or uneven tire pressure	· Inflate tires to correct pressure
	· Loose power steering pump drive belt	· Adjust belt
	· Low or incorrect power steering fluid	· Add fluid as necessary
	· Incorrect front end alignment	· Have front end alignment checked/adjusted
	· Defective power steering pump	· Check pump
	· Bent or poorly lubricated front end parts	· Lubricate and/or replace defective parts
Loose steering (too much play in the steering wheel)	· Loose wheel bearings	· Adjust wheel bearings
	· Loose or worn steering linkage	· Replace worn parts
	· Faulty shocks	· Replace shocks
	· Worn ball joints	· Replace ball joints
Car veers or wanders (car pulls to one side with hands off the steering wheel)	· Incorrect tire pressure	· Inflate tires to correct pressure
	· Improper front end alignment	· Have front end alignment checked/adjusted
	· Loose wheel bearings	· Adjust wheel bearings
	· Loose or bent front end components	· Replace worn components
	· Faulty shocks	· Replace shocks
Wheel oscillation or vibration transmitted through steering wheel	· Improper tire pressures	· Inflate tires to correct pressure
	· Tires out of balance	· Have tires balanced
	· Loose wheel bearings	· Adjust wheel bearings
	· Improper front end alignment	· Have front end alignment checked/adjusted
	· Worn or bent front end components	· Replace worn parts
Uneven tire wear	· Incorrect tire pressure	· Inflate tires to correct pressure
	· Front end out of alignment	· Have front end alignment checked/adjusted
	· Tires out of balance	· Have tires balanced

87908C04

Troubleshooting the Steering Column

Problem	Cause	Solution
Will not lock	• Lockbolt spring broken or defective	• Replace lock bolt spring
High effort (required to turn ignition key and lock cylinder)	• Lock cylinder defective	• Replace lock cylinder
	• Ignition switch defective	• Replace ignition switch
	• Rack preload spring broken or deformed	• Replace preload spring
	• Burr on lock sector, lock rack, housing, support or remote rod coupling	• Remove burr
	• Bent sector shaft	• Replace shaft
	• Defective lock rack	• Replace lock rack
	• Remote rod bent, deformed	• Replace rod
	• Ignition switch mounting bracket bent	• Straighten or replace
	• Distorted coupling slot in lock rack (tilt column)	• Replace lock rack
Will stick in "start"	• Remote rod deformed	• Straighten or replace
	• Ignition switch mounting bracket bent	• Straighten or replace
Key cannot be removed in "off-lock"	• Ignition switch is not adjusted correctly	• Adjust switch
	• Defective lock cylinder	• Replace lock cylinder
Lock cylinder can be removed without depressing retainer	• Lock cylinder with defective retainer	• Replace lock cylinder
	• Burr over retainer slot in housing cover or on cylinder retainer	• Remove burr
High effort on lock cylinder between "off" and "off-lock"	• Distorted lock rack	• Replace lock rack
	• Burr on tang of shift gate (automatic column)	• Remove burr
	• Gearshift linkage not adjusted	• Adjust linkage
Noise in column	• One click when in "off-lock" position and the steering wheel is moved (all except automatic column)	• Normal—lock bolt is seating
	• Coupling bolts not tightened	• Tighten pinch bolts
	• Lack of grease on bearings or bearing surfaces	• Lubricate with chassis grease
	• Upper shaft bearing worn or broken	• Replace bearing assembly
	• Lower shaft bearing worn or broken	• Replace bearing. Check shaft and replace if scored.
	• Column not correctly aligned	• Align column
	• Coupling pulled apart	• Replace coupling
	• Broken coupling lower joint	• Repair or replace joint and align column
	• Steering shaft snap ring not seated	• Replace ring. Check for proper seating in groove.
	• Shroud loose on shift bowl. Housing loose on jacket—will be noticed with ignition in "off-lock" and when torque is applied to steering wheel.	• Position shroud over lugs on shift bowl. Tighten mounting screws.
High steering shaft effort	• Column misaligned	• Align column
	• Defective upper or lower bearing	• Replace as required
	• Tight steering shaft universal joint	• Repair or replace
	• Flash on I.D. of shift tube at plastic joint (tilt column only)	• Replace shift tube
	• Upper or lower bearing seized	• Replace bearings
Lash in mounted column assembly	• Column mounting bracket bolts loose	• Tighten bolts
	• Broken weld nuts on column jacket	• Replace column jacket
	• Column capsule bracket sheared	• Replace bracket assembly

87908C05

Troubleshooting the Steering Column (cont.)

Problem	Cause	Solution
Lash in mounted column assembly (cont.)	· Column bracket to column jacket mounting bolts loose	· Tighten to specified torque
	· Loose lock shoes in housing (tilt column only)	· Replace shoes
	· Loose pivot pins (tilt column only)	· Replace pivot pins and support
	· Loose lock shoe pin (tilt column only)	· Replace pin and housing
	· Loose support screws (tilt column only)	· Tighten screws
Housing loose (tilt column only)	· Excessive clearance between holes in support or housing and pivot pin diameters	· Replace pivot pins and support
	· Housing support-screws loose	· Tighten screws
Steering wheel loose—every other tilt position (tilt column only)	· Loose fit between lock shoe and lock shoe pivot pin	· Replace lock shoes and pivot pin
Steering column not locking in any tilt position (tilt column only)	· Lock shoe seized on pivot pin	· Replace lock shoes and pin
	· Lock shoe grooves have burrs or are filled with foreign material	· Clean or replace lock shoes
	· Lock shoe springs weak or broken	· Replace springs
Noise when tilting column (tilt column only)	· Upper tilt bumpers worn	· Replace tilt bumper
	· Tilt spring rubbing in housing	· Lubricate with chassis grease
One click when in "off-lock" position and the steering wheel is moved	· Seating of lock bolt	· None. Click is normal characteristic sound produced by lock bolt as it seats.
High shift effort (automatic and tilt column only)	· Column not correctly aligned	· Align column
	· Lower bearing not aligned correctly	· Assemble correctly
	· Lack of grease on seal or lower bearing areas	· Lubricate with chassis grease
Improper transmission shifting— automatic and tilt column only	· Sheared shift tube joint	· Replace shift tube
	· Improper transmission gearshift linkage adjustment	· Adjust linkage
	· Loose lower shift lever	· Replace shift tube

87908C06

Troubleshooting the Manual Steering Gear

Problem	Cause	Solution
Hard or erratic steering	· Incorrect tire pressure	· Inflate tires to recommended pressures
	· Insufficient or incorrect lubrication	· Lubricate as required (refer to Maintenance Section)
	· Suspension, or steering linkage parts damaged or misaligned	· Repair or replace parts as necessary
	· Improper front wheel alignment	· Adjust incorrect wheel alignment angles
	· Incorrect steering gear adjustment	· Adjust steering gear
	· Sagging springs	· Replace springs
Play or looseness in steering	· Steering wheel loose	· Inspect shaft spines and repair as necessary. Tighten attaching nut and stake in place.
	· Steering linkage or attaching parts loose or worn	· Tighten, adjust, or replace faulty components
	· Pitman arm loose	· Inspect shaft splines and repair as necessary. Tighten attaching nut and stake in place
	· Steering gear attaching bolts loose	· Tighten bolts
	· Loose or worn wheel bearings	· Adjust or replace bearings
	· Steering gear adjustment incorrect or parts badly worn	· Adjust gear or replace defective parts

87908C07

Troubleshooting the Manual Steering Gear (cont.)

Problem	Cause	Solution
Wheel shimmy or tramp	· Improper tire pressure	· Inflate tires to recommended pressures
	· Wheels, tires, or brake rotors out-of-balance or out-of-round	· Inspect and replace or balance parts
	· Inoperative, worn, or loose shock absorbers or mounting parts	· Repair or replace shocks or mountings
	· Loose or worn steering or suspension parts	· Tighten or replace as necessary
	· Loose or worn wheel bearings	· Adjust or replace bearings
	· Incorrect steering gear adjustments	· Adjust steering gear
	· Incorrect front wheel alignment	· Correct front wheel alignment
Tire wear	· Improper tire pressure	· Inflate tires to recommended pressures
	· Failure to rotate tires	· Rotate tires
	· Brakes grabbing	· Adjust or repair brakes
	· Incorrect front wheel alignment	· Align incorrect angles
	· Broken or damaged steering and suspension parts	· Repair or replace defective parts
	· Wheel runout	· Replace faulty wheel
	· Excessive speed on turns	· Make driver aware of conditions
Vehicle leads to one side	· Improper tire pressures	· Inflate tires to recommended pressures
	· Front tires with uneven tread depth, wear pattern, or different cord design (i.e., one bias ply and one belted or radial tire on front wheels)	· Install tires of same cord construction and reasonably even tread depth, design, and wear pattern
	· Incorrect front wheel alignment	· Align incorrect angles
	· Brakes dragging	· Adjust or repair brakes
	· Pulling due to uneven tire construction	· Replace faulty tire

87908C08

Troubleshooting the Power Steering Gear

Problem	Cause	Solution
Hissing noise in steering gear	· There is some noise in all power steering systems. One of the most common is a hissing sound most evident at standstill parking. There is no relationship between this noise and performance of the steering. Hiss may be expected when steering wheel is at end of travel or when slowly turning at standstill.	· Slight hiss is normal and in no way affects steering. Do not replace valve unless hiss is extremely objectionable. A replacement valve will also exhibit slight noise and is not always a cure. Investigate clearance around flexible coupling rivets. Be sure steering shaft and gear are aligned so flexible coupling rotates in a flat plane and is not distorted as shaft rotates. Any metal-to-metal contacts through flexible coupling will transmit valve hiss into passenger compartment through the steering column.
Rattle or chuckle noise in steering gear	· Gear loose on frame	· Check gear-to-frame mounting screws. Tighten screws to 88 N·m (65 foot pounds) torque.
	· Steering linkage looseness	· Check linkage pivot points for wear. Replace if necessary.
	· Pressure hose touching other parts of car	· Adjust hose position. Do not bend tubing by hand.
	· Loose thrust bearing preload adjustment	· Adjust to specification with gear out of vehicle

87908C09

Troubleshooting the Power Steering Gear (cont.)

Problem	Cause	Solution
Rattle or chuckle noise in steering gear	NOTE: A slight rattle may occur on turns because of increased clearance off the "high point." This is normal and clearance must not be reduced below specified limits to eliminate this slight rattle. • Loose pitman arm	• Tighten pitman arm nut to specifications
Squawk noise in steering gear when turning or recovering from a turn	• Damper O-ring on valve spool cut	• Replace damper O-ring
Poor return of steering wheel to center	• Tires not properly inflated • Lack of lubrication in linkage and ball joints • Lower coupling flange rubbing against steering gear adjuster plug • Steering gear to column misalignment • Improper front wheel alignment • Steering linkage binding • Ball joints binding • Steering wheel rubbing against housing • Tight or frozen steering shaft bearings • Sticking or plugged valve spool • Steering gear adjustments over specifications • Kink in return hose	• Inflate to specified pressure • Lube linkage and ball joints • Loosen pinch bolt and assemble properly • Align steering column • Check and adjust as necessary • Replace pivots • Replace ball joints • Align housing • Replace bearings • Remove and clean or replace valve • Check adjustment with gear out of car. Adjust as required. • Replace hose
Car leads to one side or the other (keep in mind road condition and wind. Test car in both directions on flat road)	• Front end misaligned • Unbalanced steering gear valve NOTE: If this is cause, steering effort will be very light in direction of lead and normal or heavier in opposite direction	• Adjust to specifications • Replace valve
Momentary increase in effort when turning wheel fast to right or left	• Low oil level • Pump belt slipping • High internal leakage	• Add power steering fluid as required • Tighten or replace belt • Check pump pressure. (See pressure test)
Steering wheel surges or jerks when turning with engine running especially during parking	• Low oil level • Loose pump belt • Steering linkage hitting engine oil pan at full turn • Insufficient pump pressure • Pump flow control valve sticking	• Fill as required • Adjust tension to specification • Correct clearance • Check pump pressure. (See pressure test). Replace relief valve if defective. • Inspect for varnish or damage, replace if necessary
Excessive wheel kickback or loose steering	• Air in system • Steering gear loose on frame • Steering linkage joints worn enough to be loose • Worn poppet valve • Loose thrust bearing preload adjustment	• Add oil to pump reservoir and bleed by operating steering. Check hose connectors for proper torque and adjust as required. • Tighten attaching screws to specified torque • Replace loose pivots • Replace poppet valve • Adjust to specification with gear out of vehicle

87908C10

Troubleshooting the Power Steering Gear (cont.)

Problem	Cause	Solution
Excessive wheel kickback or loose steering	· Excessive overcenter lash	· Adjust to specification with gear out of car
Hard steering or lack of assist	· Loose pump belt · Low oil level **NOTE:** Low oil level will also result in excessive pump noise · Steering gear to column misalignment · Lower coupling flange rubbing against steering gear adjuster plug · Tires not properly inflated	· Adjust belt tension to specification · Fill to proper level. If excessively low, check all lines and joints for evidence of external leakage. Tighten loose connectors. · Align steering column · Loosen pinch bolt and assemble properly · Inflate to recommended pressure
Foamy milky power steering fluid, low fluid level and possible low pressure	· Air in the fluid, and loss of fluid due to internal pump leakage causing overflow	· Check for leak and correct. Bleed system. Extremely cold temperatures will cause system aeriation should the oil level be low. If oil level is correct and pump still foams, remove pump from vehicle and separate reservoir from housing. Check welsh plug and housing for cracks. If plug is loose or housing is cracked, replace housing.
Low pressure due to steering pump	· Flow control valve stuck or inoperative · Pressure plate not flat against cam ring	· Remove burrs or dirt or replace. Flush system. · Correct
Low pressure due to steering gear	· Pressure loss in cylinder due to worn piston ring or badly worn housing bore · Leakage at valve rings, valve body-to-worm seal	· Remove gear from car for disassembly and inspection of ring and housing bore · Remove gear from car for disassembly and replace seals

87908C11

Troubleshooting the Power Steering Pump

Problem	Cause	Solution
Chirp noise in steering pump	· Loose belt	· Adjust belt tension to specification
Belt squeal (particularly noticeable at full wheel travel and stand still parking)	· Loose belt	· Adjust belt tension to specification
Growl noise in steering pump	· Excessive back pressure in hoses or steering gear caused by restriction	· Locate restriction and correct. Replace part if necessary.
Growl noise in steering pump (particularly noticeable at stand still parking)	· Scored pressure plates, thrust plate or rotor · Extreme wear of cam ring	· Replace parts and flush system · Replace parts
Groan noise in steering pump	· Low oil level · Air in the oil. Poor pressure hose connection.	· Fill reservoir to proper level · Tighten connector to specified torque. Bleed system by operating steering from right to left—full turn.
Rattle noise in steering pump	· Vanes not installed properly · Vanes sticking in rotor slots	· Install properly · Free up by removing burrs, varnish, or dirt
Swish noise in steering pump	· Defective flow control valve	· Replace part

87908C12

Troubleshooting the Power Steering Pump (cont.)

Problem	Cause	Solution
Whine noise in steering pump	• Pump shaft bearing scored	• Replace housing and shaft. Flush system.
Hard steering or lack of assist	• Loose pump belt • Low oil level in reservoir **NOTE:** Low oil level will also result in excessive pump noise • Steering gear to column misalignment • Lower coupling flange rubbing against steering gear adjuster plug • Tires not properly inflated	• Adjust belt tension to specification • Fill to proper level. If excessively low, check all lines and joints for evidence of external leakage. Tighten loose connectors. • Align steering column • Loosen pinch bolt and assemble properly • Inflate to recommended pressure
Foaming milky power steering fluid, low fluid level and possible low pressure	• Air in the fluid, and loss of fluid due to internal pump leakage causing overflow	• Check for leaks and correct. Bleed system. Extremely cold temperatures will cause system aeriation should the oil level be low. If oil level is correct and pump still foams, remove pump from vehicle and separate reservoir from body. Check welsh plug and body for cracks. If plug is loose or body is cracked, replace body.
Low pump pressure	• Flow control valve stuck or inoperative • Pressure plate not flat against cam ring	• Remove burrs or dirt or replace. Flush system. • Correct
Momentary increase in effort when turning wheel fast to right or left	• Low oil level in pump • Pump belt slipping • High internal leakage	• Add power steering fluid as required • Tighten or replace belt • Check pump pressure. (See pressure test)
Steering wheel surges or jerks when turning with engine running especially during parking	• Low oil level • Loose pump belt • Steering linkage hitting engine oil pan at full turn • Insufficient pump pressure	• Fill as required • Adjust tension to specification • Correct clearance • Check pump pressure. (See pressure test). Replace flow control valve if defective.
Steering wheel surges or jerks when turning with engine running especially during parking (cont.)	• Sticking flow control valve	• Inspect for varnish or damage, replace if necessary
Excessive wheel kickback or loose steering	• Air in system	• Add oil to pump reservoir and bleed by operating steering. Check hose connectors for proper torque and adjust as required.
Low pump pressure	• Extreme wear of cam ring • Scored pressure plate, thrust plate, or rotor • Vanes not installed properly • Vanes sticking in rotor slots • Cracked or broken thrust or pressure plate	• Replace parts. Flush system. • Replace parts. Flush system. • Install properly • Freeup by removing burrs, varnish, or dirt • Replace part

87908C13

Special Tools, Suspension

926110000	926500000	926510000	926520000
COIL SPRING COMPRESSOR	ADAPTER	SPANNER	AIR PIPE REMOVER
Used to remove and install coil spring.	Camber & caster gauge.	Used to disassemble and assemble front strut ASSY or front air suspension ASSY.	Used to disconnect air pipe from joint.
Except Air Suspension	All models	All models	For Air Suspension

*926940000
3-WAY JOINT ASSY
Used as an adapter for gauge manifold of air conditioning system to measure pressure.

* Newly adopted tool

87908C14

Special Tools, Manual Steering System

925640000 *3	926530000	926540000
SPANNER	BUSH A INSTALLER	BUSH A REMOVER
Big end: Used to loosen and tighten the lock nut when adjusting gear backlash of steering gearbox.	Used to install bush A into steering gearbox unit.	Used to remove bush A from VGR (Variable Gear Ratio) steering gearbox unit.
		For VGR steering gearbox

*3 SPANNER (926230000) for power steering can be used instead of this tool.

87908C15

Special Tools, Manual Steering System

926720000	926730000	926740000
CLAMP	INSTALLER	STAND
Used when assembling steering column ASSY. Attach this tool to STAND.	Used to remove and install steering boss of pipe ASSY.	Used when disassembling and assembling steering column ASSY.

87908C16

Special Tools, Power Steering System

926320000	926330000	926420000	*926970000
INSTALLER	REMOVER	PLUG	INSTALLER
Attach this tool to the left side of rack when press-fitting back-up ring and oil seal to steering body ASSY.	Used to remove back-up ring and oil seal from steering body.	When oil leaks from pinion side of gearbox ASSY, remove pipe B from valve housing, attach this tool and check oil leaking points.	Oil seal of oil pump.

*926980000
GUIDE
Shaft and bearing ASSY of oil pump.

* Newly adopted tool

87908C17

Special Tools, Power Steering System

925700000	925711000 *4	926200000	926210000
WRENCH	PRESSURE GAUGE	STAND	ADAPTER A
Used to remove and install tie-rod. Apply this tool to rack.	Oil pump.	Used when inspection characteristic of gearbox ASSY and disassembling it. Vise this tool and secure gearbox ASSY using gearbox clamps.	Used with PRESSURE GAUGE.
			To Gauge

926220000	926230000	926240000	926250000
ADAPTER B	SPANNER	INSTALLER	GUIDE
Used with PRESSURE GAUGE.	For the lock nut when adjusting backlash of gearbox. Removal and installation of tie-rod. Measurement of rotating resistance of gearbox ASSY.	Oil seal of steering body ASSY.	Fit this tool to the left side of rack when installing seal holder ASSY into steering body ASSY.
To Gauge		INSTALLER A / INSTALLER B / INSTALLER C	

926260000	926290000	926300000	926310000
REMOVER	REMOVER	INSTALLER	GUIDE
Seal holder snap ring.	Used to remove dust seal, back-up ring, Y-packing and ball bearing from valve housing. Used to install ball bearing into valve housing	Used to install dust seal, back-up ring and Y-packing into valve housing.	Input shaft.

*4 Interchangeable with former PRESSURE GAUGE (925710000).

87908C18

Special Tools, Power Steering System

926220000	926230000	926340000	926350000
ADAPTER B	SPANNER	WRENCH	INSTALLER
Used with PRESSURE GAUGE.	For the lock nut when adjusting backlash of gearbox. Removal and installation of tie-rod. Measurement of rotating resistance of gear box ASSY.	Used to remove and install circlip which secures rack stopper.	Used to install oil seal into valve housing.
To Gauge			
926360000	926370000	926380000	*926390001
INSTALLER	INSTALLER	INSTALLER	COVER & REMOVER ASSY
Oil seal valve ASSY.	Ball bearing of valve ASSY.	Oil seal and back-up washer of rack housing.	Left side of rack.
INSTALLER B / INSTALLER A	INSTALLER B	INSTALLER A / INSTALLER B	REMOVER (926410001) / COVER
926400000	*926410001	926420000	926790000
GUIDE	REMOVER	PLUG	INSTALLER
Right side of rack when installing rack bush.	Oil seal and back-up washer of rack housing.	When oil leaks from pinion side of gearbox ASSY, remove pipe B from valve housing, attach this tool and check oil leaking points.	Oil seal and shaft of oil pump.

87908C19

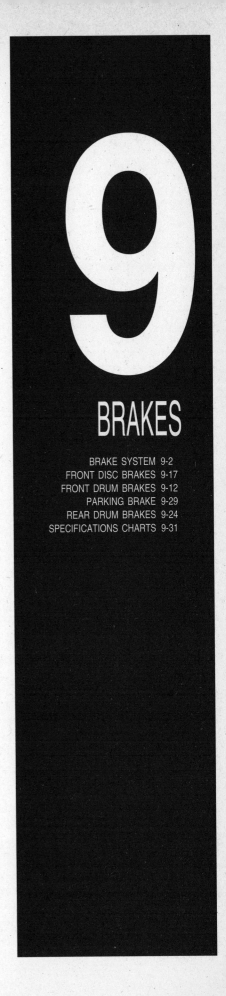

9

BRAKES

BRAKE SYSTEM

❊❊CAUTION

Asbestos, a known cancer causing agent, is still present in many types of brake lining. Do not use compressed air to clean accumulated dust from your brake system. A safer method is to use rags soaked with a safe solvent so that dust will not be able to enter your throat and lungs.

The hydraulic brake system employed by Subaru has gone through several changes since 1970.

In 1970 through 1972, the front brakes on the ff-1 and 1300G models were a duo servo, single anchor type drum brake. This system employs brake shoes as do the rear brakes, but the duo servo action provides better braking effect. Also, the front brakes were mounted inboard (on either side of the differential housing) to improve handling.

Since the front suspension system on the GL and DL models was changed in 1972 to a MacPherson strut type, inboard front brakes were no longer necessary as a suspension improvement. Thus, the front brakes were mounted at the ends of the axle shafts (outboard) for easier serviceability. The duo servo type brake was continued for all sedans and wagons through 1975, although GL and G models were equipped with front disc brakes.

Since 1976, all models were equipped with front disc brakes. This system employs piston pressure to force two pads against both surfaces of a disc, or rotor. The advantages of disc brakes are in over all braking effect, road stability during braking and service life of the brakes.

The master cylinder used on ff-1 and 1300G models is a conventional, single chamber master cylinder which supplies hydraulic pressure to all four wheel cylinders. All other models are equipped with a tandem master cylinder, which employs a dual hydraulic circuit with each circuit supplying pressure to diagonally opposed wheels. This is a safety feature which allows for at least 50% braking action in case of fluid leak at any one wheel.

The final improvement of the hydraulic brake system was the incorporation of a vacuum, suspended type power brake unit, which provides better response than manual brakes. Since the power unit uses engine vacuum for its operation, it cannot function when the engine stalls out. This does not mean, however, that all braking power is lost, rather, the brake pedal will simply require greater foot pressure to stop the vehicle. Power brakes are standard from 1975 except on the 1975 2-door sedan.

On all models the handbrake is mechanically operated and attached to the front wheels by means of a cable.

❊❊CAUTION

The brake system is one of the most important safety related components of your car. Therefore, extreme care and attention to detail should be observed whenever performing service to it.

Adjustments

FRONT DRUM BRAKES

The front drum brakes are self adjusting and very rarely, if ever, require a manual adjustment. For this reason, prior to adjustment, be sure that the self adjusters are working and that the brake linings are not excessively worn.

The front drum brakes on the ff-1 and 1300G are mounted inboard, however, they are adjusted in the same manner as the outboard drums used on the DL sedans and wagons.

If manual adjustment becomes necessary, proceed as follows:

1. Block the rear wheels and fully release the parking brake.

2. Raise the front of the car and support it with jackstands.

❊❊CAUTION

Be sure that the car is securely supported.

3. Remove the rubber inspection plug from the backing plate.

4. Adjustment to tighten:

   a. Insert a brake adjusting spoon into the hole.

   b. Turn the star-shaped adjusting screw inside the drum with the spoon, until the wheel has a slight drag. Do this to both wheels until there is equal drag on each wheel. DO NOT make the adjustment over-tight!

5. Adjustment to loosen and remove the drum:

   a. Insert a brake adjusting spoon and small prybar to hold the adjusting lever away from the sprocket.

   b. Back off each adjusting screw until the drum turns freely. If the brake shoes drag with the adjusters backed off all the way, the parking brake cables could be excessively tight.

DISC BRAKES

The front disc brakes require no adjustment, as disc brakes are inherently self-adjusting.

➡**The brake fluid level in the master cylinder should be checked regularly.**

REAR DRUM BRAKES

▶ See Figures 1 and 2

Perform the rear brake adjustment every 6 months/6000 miles (9600 km) whichever occurs first. Adjust the rear brakes by turning the wedge, which is located on the bottom of the backing plate.

1. Chock the front wheels and set the parking brake.

2. Raise the rear of the car and support it with jackstands.

✵✵CAUTION

Be sure that the car is securely supported.

3. Loosen the locknut on the wedge.
4. While rotating the wheel, turn the wedge clockwise until the brakes lock.
5. Turn the wedge back 180° (½ turn) from the locked position.
6. Tighten the locknut and perform the adjustment on the other rear drum.

Brake Light Switch

If the operation of the brake light switch is not smooth and/or the stroke is not within specified value, replace the switch with a new one.

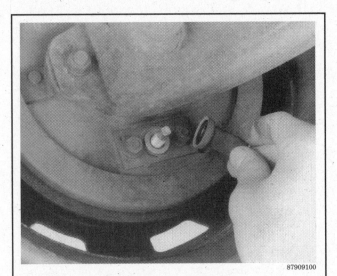

Fig. 1 Remove the adjusting wedge cover

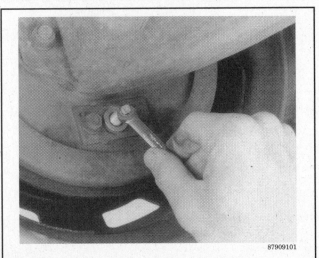

Fig. 2 While rotating the wheel, turn the wedge clockwise until the brakes lock

REMOVAL & INSTALLATION

1. Disengage the electrical connector from the brake light switch.
2. Remove the switch from the brake pedal bracket.
   To install:
3. Install the switch on the brake pedal bracket.
4. Engage the electrical connector. Then check to make sure that the stoplamps work within 0.07-0.12 in. (1.8-3.3mm) of pedal travel.

Master Cylinder

REMOVAL & INSTALLATION

ff-1 and 1300G Models
▶ See Figure 3

1. Separate the brake line below the master cylinder, at the three way connector.
2. Remove the connecting tube from the master cylinder and drain the fluid from the reservoir into a suitable container.

✵✵WARNING

Avoid spilling brake fluid on painted surfaces.

3. Remove the two master cylinder retaining bolts.
4. Remove the master cylinder from the bracket.
   To install:
5. Bench bleed the master cylinder prior to installation.
6. Install the master cylinder and fasten the retaining bolts.
7. Install the connecting tube.
8. Engage the brake line below the master cylinder, at the three way connector.
9. Refill the master cylinder with fresh brake fluid and bleed the system.

1970-80 Models (Except ff-1 and 1300G)

✵✵WARNING

Avoid spilling brake fluid on painted surfaces.

1. Disconnect the negative (-) battery cable.
2. Remove the brake line or lines from the master cylinder and drain the fluid into a suitable container.
3. If equipped with a fluid level indicator, disengage the electrical harness connector from the master cylinder.
4. On 1972-74 models and on 1975 2-door sedans, remove the nuts which connect the master cylinder to the pedal bracket.
5. On models from 1975-80 (except 1975 2-door sedan), remove the nuts connecting the master cylinder to the power brake unit.
6. Pull the master cylinder assembly forward and out.
   To install:
7. Bench bleed the master cylinder prior to installation.
8. Install the master cylinder and fasten the retaining nuts.

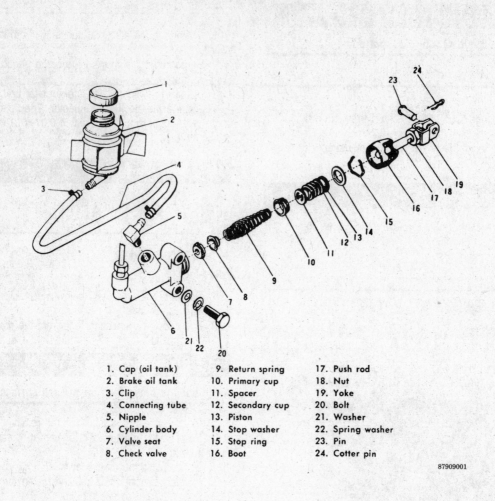

1. Cap (oil tank)
2. Brake oil tank
3. Clip
4. Connecting tube
5. Nipple
6. Cylinder body
7. Valve seat
8. Check valve
9. Return spring
10. Primary cup
11. Spacer
12. Secondary cup
13. Piston
14. Stop washer
15. Stop ring
16. Boot
17. Push rod
18. Nut
19. Yoke
20. Bolt
21. Washer
22. Spring washer
23. Pin
24. Cotter pin

87909001

Fig. 3 Exploded view of the master cylinder — ff-1 and 1300G

9. Engage the fluid level indicator harness connector (if equipped).

10. Engage the brake line or lines to the master cylinder.

11. Connect the negative battery cable.

12. Refill the master cylinder with fresh brake fluid and bleed the system.

➡ Do not use the old brake fluid drained from the master cylinder to refill it after installation. Use new fluid. See Section 1 for the correct type.

1980-84 Models

▶ See Figures 4, 5 and 6

❋❋CAUTION

Avoid spilling brake fluid on painted surfaces, it will lift the paint.

1. Disconnect the negative (-) battery cable.

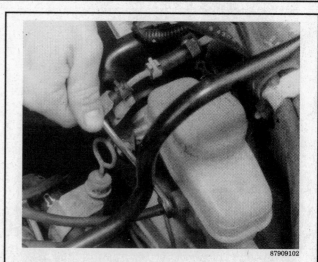

87909102

Fig. 4 Use a flare nut wrench to disconnect the brake lines. Be sure to plug them to prevent the entry of dirt

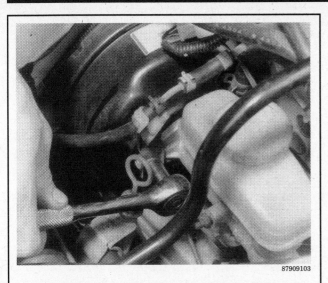

Fig. 5 Remove the master cylinder retaining fasteners

2. Disconnect and plug the brake lines at the master cylinder.

➡It is advised to thoroughly drain the fluid from the master cylinder before performing any removal procedures.

3. If equipped with fluid level indicator, disengage the electrical harness connector from the master cylinder.

4. Remove the master cylinder-to-power booster nuts and the master cylinder from the vehicle.

To install:

5. Bench bleed the master cylinder prior to installation.

6. Install the master cylinder on the power booster and tighten the nuts to 7-13 ft. lbs. (10-18 Nm).

7. Connect the fluid level indicator.

8. Connect the brake lines and tighten the flare nut to 9-13 ft. lbs. (13-18 Nm).

9. Connect the negative battery cable.

10. Refill the master cylinder with fresh brake fluid and bleed the system.

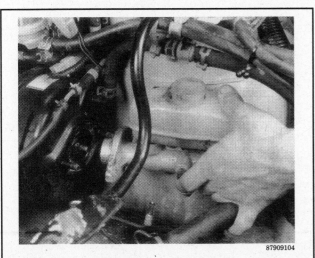

Fig. 6 When removing the master cylinder from the vehicle be, careful not to spill any brake fluid

11. Bleed the brake system as required.

OVERHAUL

Rebuilding the master cylinder is a tedious, time consuming job. You can save yourself time and trouble by buying a rebuilt master cylinder from your dealer or a parts supply house. The small difference in cost between a rebuilding kit and a rebuilt part usually makes it more economical, in terms of time and work, to buy the rebuilt part.

ff-1 and 1300G Models

1. Remove the master cylinder from the vehicle and mount it securely on a bench.

2. Remove the boot from the cylinder body.

3. Remove the connecting tube nipple.

4. Remove the brake pipe joint and drain any fluid remaining in the master cylinder.

5. Remove the stop ring and stop washer, and pull out the piston assembly.

6. Pull out the primary cup, return spring, check valve and valve seat.

7. Inspect the master cylinder as follows:

a. Make sure that the bore of the master cylinder is smooth and perfectly round. If the bore is worn or scarred, replace the master cylinder.

✳✳WARNING

It is not advisable to correct the bore by honing with emery cloth or a cylinder hone. Use only genuine rubber parts. The sliding parts used in the cylinder should be washed in clean brake fluid before assembling. Do not allow dust or other foreign matter to enter the cylinder.

b. Check the following tolerances: the inside diameter of the master cylinder should be 0.741-0.742 in. (19.02-19.05mm), the outside diameter of the piston should be 0.740-0.742 in. (18.99-19.03mm), the cylinder-to-piston clearance should be 0.0007-0.0058 in. (0.02-0.15mm).

c. Check the master cylinder rubber cup for scars, splits, wear and other damage. Even if the damage is only slight in the case of the rubber cup, the cup must be replaced.

d. Replace the return spring if it is excessively worn. The free length of the primary spring should be 2.31 in. (59mm). The free length of the secondary spring should be 2 in. (51mm).

e. Check the brake fluid reservoir for cracks and replace if any cracks are found.

8. Install the Valve seat, check valve, return spring and the primary cup.

9. Install the piston assembly, stop washer and the stop ring.

10. Install the brake pipe joint and the connecting tube nipple.

11. Install the boot in the cylinder body.

12. Bench bleed the master cylinder and install it on the vehicle.

13. Refill the master cylinder with fresh fluid and bleed the system.

!970-79 Models (Except ff-1 and 1300G)

▶ **See Figure 7**

1. Remove the master cylinder from the car.
2. Remove the reservoir caps, filters and drain the brake fluid.
3. Pry the piston stopper snapring from the open end of the master cylinder with a screwdriver.
4. Remove the stopper screw and washer from the side or bottom of the master cylinder while applying rearward pressure on the piston.
5. Remove the primary and secondary piston assemblies from the master cylinder bore.
6. Remove the caps on the underside of the master cylinder to gain access to the check valves for cleaning.

❊❊WARNING

Do not disassemble the brake fluid level gauge, if equipped.

7. Discard all used rubber parts and gaskets. These parts should be replaced with the new components included in the rebuilding kit.

❊❊WARNING

Do not remove the master cylinder reservoir tank(s) unless leaking. If removed for any reason, replacement is necessary.

8. Clean all the parts in clean brake fluid. Do not use mineral oil or alcohol for cleaning.
9. Check the cylinder bore and piston for wear, scoring, corrosion, or any other damage.
10. The bore can be dressed with crocus cloth or a cylinder hone soaked in brake fluid.
11. Wash both the cylinder bore and the piston with clean brake fluid.
12. Soak all of the components in clean brake fluid before assembling them.
13. Assemble the master cylinder in the reverse order of disassembly.
14. Bench bleed the master cylinder.
15. Install the master cylinder and fill it with fresh clean brake fluid.
16. Bleed the system.

1980-84 Models

▶ **See Figures 8, 9, 10, 11 and 12**

1. Remove the level indicator assemblies from the reservoir(s) by turning them counterclockwise to unlock.
2. Drain out and properly discard the fluid.
3. Remove the stopper screw while simultaneously holding the pistons fully back in the cylinder.
4. Keeping the pistons fully pushed in, remove the stopper washer with a screwdriver.
5. Remove the stopper washer, both piston assemblies, and the return spring.
6. Inspect all parts for wear or cracks. If rubber cups are worn, you must replace the piston assembly it is a part of. Leave pistons assembled.

7. The check valve can be disassembled by removing the check valve cap and then removing the valve, spring, and seat.
8. Wash all parts in clean, approved brake fluid. Check the cylinder and other parts for scoring, damage or corrosion, and check springs for deformation or fatigue.
   To install:
9. Assembly is the reverse of disassembly.
10. Coat all wear surfaces with clean, approved fluid.
11. Make sure the primary piston is pushed all the way into the cylinder before installing the stopper screw.
12. Tighten the check valve cap to 18-25 ft. lbs. (24-33 Nm) and the stopper screw to 13-26 inch lbs. (1.4-2.9 Nm). Do not remove the reservoir unless it is leaking. It must be replaced if disassembled.

Power Brake Booster

▶ **See Figure 13**

The power brake booster uses engine manifold vacuum against a diaphragm to assist in the application of the brakes. The vacuum is regulated to be proportional to the pressure placed on the pedal.

If brake performance is questionable and the booster unit suspect, conduct the following tests.

TESTING

Air Tightness

1. Apply handbrake and start engine.
2. Run the engine for one or two minutes, then turn it off.
3. Apply brakes several times using the same force as in normal braking.
4. The pedal stroke should be greatest on the first application and become smaller with each additional stroke. If no change occurs in the pedal height while it is applied the power brake unit could be faulty.

Operational Check

1. With the engine **OFF**.
2. Apply the brakes several times using normal pedal pressure, make sure the pedal height does not vary on each stroke.
3. With the brakes applied, start the engine.
4. When the engine starts the brake pedal should move slightly toward the floor.
5. If no change in the pedal height occurs the power brake unit could be faulty.

Component Inspection

Inspect the vacuum hose and check valve periodically, the hose for cracking or brittleness. The check valve (engine running and brakes applied) for air leaks. Replace hose or valve if necessary. Sometimes a stuck check valve can act like a bad power booster. If this is suspected, replace the check valve.

Rebuilding a power brake booster or doing a complete pressure test requires special gauges and tools. It is just not practical for the car owner to attempt servicing the unit except to remove and replace it.

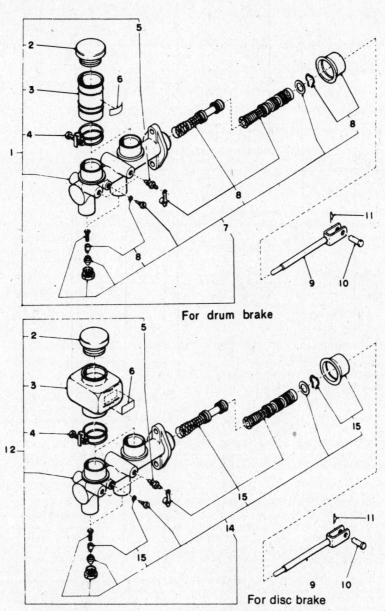

For drum brake

For disc brake

1. Master cylinder
2. Cap complete (resorvoir)
3. Brake fluid reservoir (master cylinder)
4. Reservoir band (master cylinder)
5. Bleeder screw
6. Level (brake fluid tank)
7. Master cylinder repair kit (B)
8. Master cylinder repair kit (A)
9. Pushrod
10. Head pin
11. Cotter pin (master cylinder)
12. Master cylinder ass'y
13. Brake fluid reservoir
14. Master cylinder repair kit (B)
15. Master cylinder repair kit (A)

87909002

Fig. 7 Exploded view of a master cylinder found on 1970-79 models

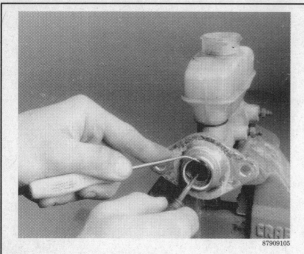

Fig. 8 When overhauling the master cylinder, it is better to mount it in a vise for stability

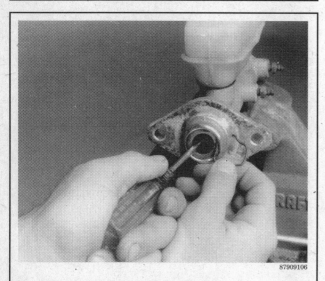

Fig. 9 Remove the snapring and washer

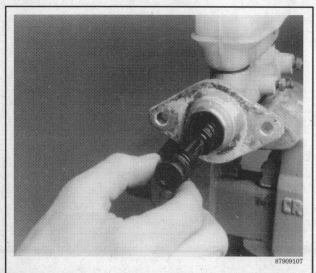

Fig. 10 Remove the primary piston assembly

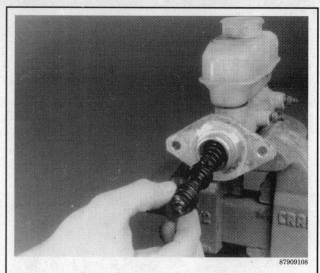

Fig. 11 Remove the secondary piston assembly

REMOVAL & INSTALLATION

1. Remove the master cylinder.
2. Disconnect the vacuum hose.
3. Disconnect the brake pedal from the power booster push rod by removing the clevis pin.
4. Remove the four nuts that mount the booster to the firewall.
5. Remove the booster.
6. Installation is the reverse of removal.

Brake Fluid Level Warning Indicator

The low brake fluid warning device (cars equipped) is contained in the reservoir of the master cylinder. If the brake fluid level falls about 0.70 in. (18mm) below the MAX line, a float closes an electrical circuit which causes the warning lamp on the dash panel to light.

Refilling the master cylinder will cause the warning lamp to go out. However, the entire brake system should be inspected for signs of leakage so the loss of brake fluid can be accounted for.

Proportioning Valve

REMOVAL & INSTALLATION

1. Remove the brake pipes from the proportioning valve.
2. Remove the proportioning valve from its bracket.

❋❋WARNING

Do not attempt to disassemble or adjust the proportioning valve. If defective, the valve must be replaced as a unit.

To install:
3. Make sure that the brake pipes are properly connected to the proportioning valve after installation.

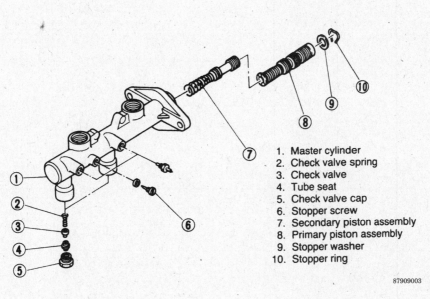

1. Master cylinder
2. Check valve spring
3. Check valve
4. Tube seat
5. Check valve cap
6. Stopper screw
7. Secondary piston assembly
8. Primary piston assembly
9. Stopper washer
10. Stopper ring

87909003

Fig. 12 Exploded view of a common master cylinder found on 1980-84 models

4. Tighten the brake pipe flare nut 9-13 ft. lbs. (12-17 Nm), tighten the proportioning valve to bracket 14-21 ft. lbs. (18-28 Nm)

5. Bleed the system of air, then check each joint or brake pipe for leaks.

Brake Lines and Hoses

Metal lines and rubber brake hoses should be checked frequently for leaks and external damage. Metal lines are particularly prone to crushing and kinking under the car. Any such deformation can restrict the proper flow of fluid and therefore impair braking at the wheels. Rubber hoses should be checked for cracking or scraping; such damage can create a weak spot in the hose and it could fail under pressure.

Any time the lines are removed or disconnected, extreme cleanliness must be observed. Clean all joints and connections before disassembly (use a stiff bristle brush and clean brake fluid); be sure to plug the lines and ports as soon as they are opened. New lines and hoses should be flushed clean with brake fluid before installation to remove any contamination.

REMOVAL & INSTALLATION

1. Elevate and safely support the car on jackstands.
2. Remove the wheel(s) as necessary for access.
3. Clean the surrounding area at the joints to be disconnected.
4. Place a catch pan under the joint to be disconnected.
5. Using two wrenches (one to hold the joint and one to turn the fitting), disconnect the hose or line to be replaced.
6. Disconnect the other end of the line or hose, moving the drain pan if necessary. Always use two wrenches if possible.
7. Disconnect any retaining clips or brackets holding the line and remove the line.
8. If the system is to remain open for more time than it takes to swap lines, tape or plug each remaining line and port to keep dirt out and fluid in.
9. Install the new line or hose, starting with the end farthest from the master cylinder. Connect the other end, then confirm that both fittings are correctly threaded and turn smoothly using finger pressure. Make sure the new line will not rub

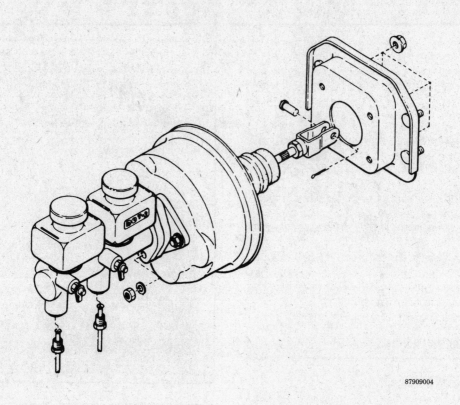

87909004

Fig. 13 Common power booster and master cylinder mounting

against any other part. Brake lines must be at least ½ in. (13mm) from the steering column and other moving parts. Any protective shielding or insulators must be reinstalled in the original location.

✳✳WARNING

If the new metal line requires bending, do so gently using a pipe bending tool. Do not attempt to bend the tubing by hand; it will kink the pipe and render it useless.

10. Using two wrenches as before, tighten each fitting until snug.
11. Install any retaining clips or brackets on the lines.
12. Refill the brake reservoir with clean, fresh brake fluid.
13. Bleed the brake system.
14. Install the wheels and lower the car to the ground.

BRAKE PIPE FLARING

Flaring steel lines is a skill which needs to be practiced before it should be done on a line which is to be used on a vehicle. A special flaring kit with double flaring adapters is required. It is essential that the flare is formed evenly to prevent any leaks when the brake system is under pressure. Only steel lines, not copper lines, should be used. It is also mandatory that the flare be a double flare. With the supply of parts available today, a pre-flared steel brake line should be available to fit your needs. Due to the high pressures in the brake system and the serious injuries that could occur if the flare should fail, it is strongly advised that pre-flared lines should be installed when repairing the braking system. If a line were to leak brake fluid due to a defective flare, and the leak were to go undetected, brake failure would result.

❋❋WARNING

A double flaring tool must be used, as single flaring tools cannot produce a flare strong enough to hold the necessary pressure.

1. Determine the length of pipe needed. Allow 1/8 in. (3.2 mm) for each flare. Cut using an appropriate tool.
2. Square the end of the tube with a file and chamfer the edges. Remove any burrs.
3. Install the required fittings on the pipe.
4. Install the flaring tool into a vice and install the handle into the operating cam.
5. Loosen the die clamp screw and rotate the locking plate to expose the die carrier.
6. Select the required die set and install in the carrier.
7. Insert the prepared line through the rear of the die and push forward until the line end is flush with the die face.
8. Make sure the rear of both halves of the die are resting against the hexagonal die stops. Then, rotate the locking plate to the fully closed position and clamp the die firmly by tightening the clamp screw.
9. Rotate the punch turret until the appropriate size points toward the open end of the line to be flared.
10. Pull the operating handle against the line resistance in order to create the flare, then return the handle to the original position.
11. Release the clamp screw and rotate the locking plate to the open position.
12. Remove the die set and the line, then separate by gently tapping both halves on the bench. Inspect the flare for proper size and shape.

Bleeding the System

▶ See Figure 14

The purpose of bleeding the brakes is to expel air trapped in the hydraulic system. The system must be bled whenever the pedal feels spongy, indicating that compressible air has entered the system. It must also be bled whenever the system has been opened or repaired. You will need a helper for this job.

❋❋CAUTION

Never reuse brake fluid which has been bled from the system.

Start with the longest brake line (usually the wheel furthest from the master cylinder):

1. Clean all dirt from around the master cylinder reservoir caps.

2. Remove the caps and fill the master cylinder to the proper level with clean, fresh brake fluid meeting DOT 3 specifications.

❋❋WARNING

Brake fluid picks up moisture from the air, which reduces its effectiveness and causes brake line corrosion. Don't leave the master cylinder or the fluid container open any long than necessary. Be careful not to spill brake fluid on painted surfaces. Wipe up any spilled fluid immediately and rinse the area with clear water.

3. Clean all the bleeder screws. You may want to give each one a shot of penetrating solvent to loosen it up. Seizure is a common problem with bleeder screws, which then break off, requiring replacement.
4. Attach a length of clear vinyl tubing to the bleeder screw on the wheel cylinder (or master cylinder). Insert the other end of the tube into a clear, clean plastic bottle half filled with brake fluid.
5. Have your helper slowly depress the brake pedal.
6. As this is being done, open the bleeder screw 1/3-1/2 of a turn, and allow the fluid to run through the tube.
7. Close the bleeder screw before the pedal reaches the end of its travel.
8. Have your assistant slowly release the pedal.
9. Repeat this process until no air bubbles appear in the expelled fluid.
10. Repeat the procedure on the other three brakes, checking the fluid level in the master cylinder reservoirs often.
11. Do not allow the reservoirs to run dry, or the bleeding process will have to be repeated.
12. Upon completion of bleeding all four wheels, check the level of the brake fluid in the master cylinder reservoir and add fluid to the level line, if necessary.

Hill-Holder®

The Hill-Holder, introduced on late model cars, is a device that prevents the car from drifting backwards when starting up

87909109

Fig. 14 When bleeding the brake system use a clear container and fresh clean brake fluid — watch the hose for bubble-free fluid

an incline from a stop. The Hill-Holder holds the brake on, temporarily, until the clutch pedal is released and the car is in forward motion.

A Pressure Hold Valve (PHV) is connected to one of the service brake lines. A clutch connected cable opens or closes the valve. When the vehicle is stopped and the clutch depressed hydraulic pressure is maintained even when the brake pedal is released.

REMOVAL & INSTALLATION

To remove the Hill-Holder PHV:
1. Drain the fluid from the master cylinder primary side.
2. Remove the cable adjusting nut, clamp and cable mounting bracket from the engine mounting.
3. Detach the PHV cable from the mounting clips.
4. Separate the connector bracket from the PHV support.
5. Disconnect the brake line from the PHV. Use a flare wrench to prevent damage to the line nut.
6. Remove the PHV.

FRONT DRUM BRAKES

✳✳CAUTION

Brake shoes may contain asbestos, which has been determined to be a cancer causing agent. Never clean the brake surfaces with compressed air! Avoid inhaling any dust from any brake surface! When cleaning brake surfaces, use a commercially available brake cleaning fluid.

Brake Drums

REMOVAL & INSTALLATION

ff-1 and 1300G

1. Raise the front of the vehicle and support it with jackstands.
2. Remove the front wheels.
3. Loosen the 3 bolts on the Double Offset Joint (DOJ) side, and remove the DOJ from the drum.
4. Remove the drum cover attached to the brake assembly.
5. Remove the interior portion of the handbrake cable assembly into the engine compartment.
6. Straighten the brake drum locking cotter pin and remove it.
7. Unscrew the nut and remove the drum in parallel with the splined shaft.

✳✳WARNING

Do not depress the brake pedal while the drum is removed.

8. Installation is the reverse of removal.
9. Tighten the brake retaining nut to 116-134 ft. lbs. (157-181 Nm) and lock with the cotter pin.

7. Installation is the reverse of removal.
8. Bleed the brake system after installing the PHV.

ADJUSTMENT

1. Inspect the clutch pedal free play adjust as necessary.
2. Test the Hill-Holder on a grade of 3° or higher.
3. If the vehicle moves when the Hill-Holder is applied or the engine stalls when the Hill-Holder is released:
   a. Engine stalls: The Hill-Holder is releasing after the clutch. Loosen the adjusting nut gradually until smooth starting and no stalling is enabled.
   b. Vehicle slips backwards: The Hill-Holder is releasing before the clutch. Tighten the adjusting nut so that the Hill-Holder is released after the clutch engages.

✳✳WARNING

When adjusting the control cable nut be sure to prevent the cable from turning.

1972-75 DL Sedans and Wagons

1. Apply the parking brake. Remove the wheel cover and loosen the lug nuts.
2. Either straighten out the locktabs with pliers or straighten the staked portion of the axle shaft nut with a chisel, depending upon model year. Loosen, but do not remove the axle shaft nut.
3. Raise the front of the car and support it with jackstands, making sure that it is securely supported.
4. Remove the lug nuts and the wheel.
5. Unfasten the axle shaft nut, and release the parking brake.
6. Remove the brake drum with a suitable puller.

✳✳CAUTION

Do not depress the brake pedal while the drum is removed.

7. Reverse Steps 1 through 6 to install the brake drums.
8. Install the axle shaft nut and tighten to the following specifications:
   - 1972-73: 145-181 ft. lbs.(196-245 Nm)
   - 1974-75: 170 ft. lbs. (230 Nm)
9. Secure the nut with either the nut lock (1972-73) or by staking it (1974-75).

INSPECTION

1. Clean the drum.
2. Inspect the drum for scoring, grooves, cracks or out-of-roundness. Replace or turn the drum, as required.
3. Light scoring may be removed by dressing the drum with fine emery cloth.
4. Heavy scoring will require the use of a brake drum lathe to turn the drums. Turn the drums from both sides of the car

an equal amount to avoid uneven braking. The service limits of the inside drum diameter are as follows:

- ff-1, 1300G sedans: 8 in. (205mm)
- All others: 9 in. (230mm)

✳✳WARNING

On ff-1 and 1300G models when the drum is turned, the automatic adjusters may reach the end of their travel when the brake linings are only half worn. Replacement of the drums is the only cure.

Brake Shoes

INSPECTION

Inspect the brake shoes for excessive or uneven wear, fluid contamination, bent and/or broken parts and cracks. If any of these conditions exist, replace the brake shoes.Inspect the shoes for wear, rust or damage. On ff-1 and 1300G models, if the lining is worn down to 0.07 in. (1.8mm) or less, replace the shoes. On other models, the primary shoe lining limit is 0.03 (1mm) and the secondary shoe lining limit is 0.05 in. (1.5mm). Replace both brake shoes on the other side, as well, to prevent uneven braking.

REMOVAL & INSTALLATION

▶ **See Figure 15**

➡ **It is a good idea to remove the shoes one side at a time. This way you can refer to the brake on the other side for the correct order of shoe installation.**

ff-1 and 1300G

▶ **See Figure 16**

1. Remove the brake drums.

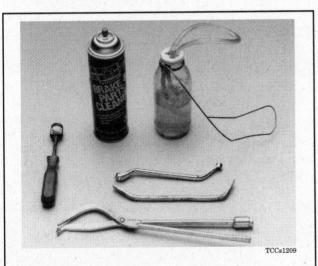

Fig. 15 Although not always necessary, using specialized brake tools will save time

TCCs1209

2. Loosen and remove the brake line from the rear of the backing plate.

3. Unscrew the 4 brake backing plate bolts and remove the brake assembly from the vehicle.

4. Before disassembling, make sure that the automatic adjuster assembly movement is correct by pulling the cable.

5. Lift the automatic adjuster assembly cable by pulling it out from the shoe side and removing it from the shoe hole.

6. Remove the automatic adjuster assembly from the shoe.

7. Remove the shoe return spring and cable from the anchor pin by using a brake tool.

8. Remove the shoe set spring with a brake tool to release the shoe.

9. Remove the handbrake cable from the shoe.

10. Remove the handbrake shoe strut and shoes.

11. Clean the adjuster and grease its threads. Remove excess grease from its outside.

   To install:

12. Install the primary shoe on the backing plate and secure it with its retaining spring.

13. Attach the parking brake lever and cable assembly to the secondary shoe.

14. Install the secondary shoe and secure it with its retaining spring.

15. Coat the backing plate surfaces with a small amount of brake grease where it contacts the brake shoes.

✳✳CAUTION

Be careful not to get any grease on the lining surfaces.

16. Position the parking brake strut between the shoes.

17. Using a brake tool, fit the automatic adjuster cable over the anchor pin.

18. Install the primary shoe return spring, adjuster cable, and the cable guide on the secondary shoe.

19. After making sure that the cable guide is installed in its positioning hole, attach the secondary shoe return spring.

20. Adjust the length of the automatic adjuster, so that it will position the shoes 2 in. (58mm) apart.

21. Move the automatic adjuster lever toward the cable and install the adjuster spring.

22. Be sure that all of the parts are correctly assembled. Check the brake on the other side, if in doubt.

23. Apply brake grease between the cable and the guide, using care not to get any on the linings.

24. Install the automatic adjuster between the shoes and into its hole. Make sure that the lever engages with the starwheel properly.

25. Measure the outside diameter of the shoes against the inside diameter of the drum. The shoes should have 0.01-0.02 in. (0.3-0.6mm) clearance from the drum.

26. Move the adjuster to obtain proper clearance as necessary.

27. Install the baffle over the end of the driveshaft, if it was removed.

28. Connect the brake line to the wheel cylinder.

29. Insert the parking brake cable.

30. Install the brake and backing plate assembly. Tighten the backing plate attaching bolts to 30 ft. lbs. (40 Nm)

31. See the appropriate section above for the brake drum installing procedure.

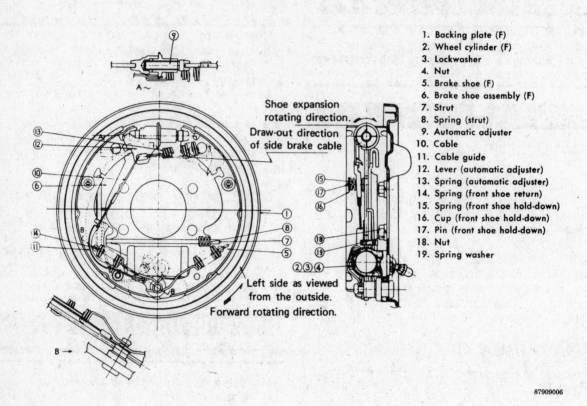

Fig. 16 Drum brake assembly — ff-1 and 1300G models

1. Backing plate (F)
2. Wheel cylinder (F)
3. Lockwasher
4. Nut
5. Brake shoe (F)
6. Brake shoe assembly (F)
7. Strut
8. Spring (strut)
9. Automatic adjuster
10. Cable
11. Cable guide
12. Lever (automatic adjuster)
13. Spring (automatic adjuster)
14. Spring (front shoe return)
15. Spring (front shoe hold-down)
16. Cup (front shoe hold-down)
17. Pin (front shoe hold-down)
18. Nut
19. Spring washer

Shoe expansion rotating direction.

Draw-out direction of side brake cable

Left side as viewed from the outside.
Forward rotating direction.

87909006

32. Bleed the brake system after performing the shoe removal and installation procedure to the other side.

1972-75 DL Sedans and Wagons

▶ See Figure 17

1. Raise the vehicle and support it with jackstands.
2. Remove the wheel, tire and the brake drum.
3. Remove the automatic adjuster spring with a screwdriver.
4. Remove the automatic adjuster lever.
5. Remove the lower shoe return spring.
6. Remove the handbrake cable end from the handbrake lever. Loosen the clamp nut with a box wrench. Separate the washer and pull the handbrake cable out.
7. Remove the upper shoe return springs from the anchor pin with a brake tool.
8. Remove the automatic adjuster.

9. Remove the shoe set springs with the brake tool and free the brake shoes.

To install:

10. Install the shoes and the shoe set springs.
11. Install the automatic adjuster and the upper shoe return spring.
12. Install the handbrake cable and the lower shoe return spring.
13. Install the automatic adjuster spring and the brake drum.
    a. The shoe-to-drum clearance should be 0.003-0.009 (0.10-0.25mm). Check this by measuring the outside diameter of the installed shoes and comparing against the inside diameter of the drum. Use the adjuster to obtain the correct clearance.
14. Install the wheel and lower, tighten the lug nuts and lower the vehicle.
15. Perform the operation to the front brake on the other side, and then bleed the brake system.

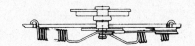

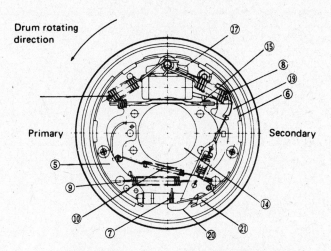

Drum rotating direction

Primary

Secondary

1. Backing plate
2. Wheel cylinder
3. Spring washer
4. Nut
5. Brake shoe (Primary)
6. Brake shoe (Secondary)
7. Automatic adjuster
8. Spring (Shoe return, upper)
9. Spring (Shoe return, lower)
10. Spring (Shoe return)
11. Spring (Shoe hold-down)
12. Pin (Shoe hold-down)
13. Cup (shoe hold-down)
14. Lever (handbrake)
15. Strut
16. Spring (Strut)
17. Anchor
18. Adjuster cable
19. Cable guide
20. Adjuster lever
21. Adjuster spring
22. Plug

87909007

Fig. 17 Drum brake assembly — 1972-75 DL models

Wheel Cylinders

REMOVAL & INSTALLATION

▶ See Figure 18

1. Raise the vehicle and support it with jackstands.
2. Remove the wheel.
3. Remove the brake drum and the brake shoes from the backing plate.
4. Disconnect and plug the fluid line for the wheel cylinder at the backing plate.
5. Remove the wheel cylinder from the backing plate by unscrewing the attaching bolts.

6. Remove the rubber boots from both ends of the wheel cylinder, then push out the inner pistons and spring together with the rubber cups.
7. Inspect the inside of the wheel cylinder bore. If it is worn or scratched in any way, it should be honed with a wheel cylinder hone or a piece of crocus cloth until the scratches are removed.

To install:

8. Replace the rubber cups with new ones. The internal replacement parts are usually supplied in a wheel cylinder rebuilding kit.
9. Reassemble the wheel cylinder and replace it on the backing plate in the reverse order of removal.
10. After reinstalling the brake line and the brake assembly, together with the brake drum, bleed the brake system.

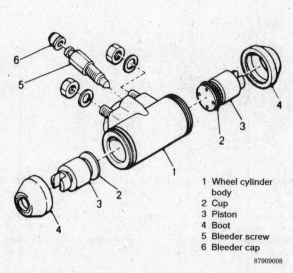

1 Wheel cylinder body
2 Cup
3 Piston
4 Boot
5 Bleeder screw
6 Bleeder cap

87909008

Fig. 18 Exploded view of the wheel cylinder assembly

FRONT DISC BRAKES

✳✳CAUTION

Brake pads may contain asbestos, which has been determined to be a cancer causing agent. Never clean the brake surfaces with compressed air! Avoid inhaling any dust from any brake surface! When cleaning brake surfaces, use a commercially available brake cleaning fluid.

Brake Pads

INSPECTION

▶ **See Figure 19**

Inspect the brake pads for excessive or uneven wear, fluid contamination, bent and/or broken parts and cracks. If any of these conditions exist, replace the brake shoes.

Check the brake pads for wear and replace them if the thickness is less than 0.058 in. (1.5mm) on 1975-79 models. On later models, the usable thickness including the backing should be no less than 0.29 in. (7.5mm). Replace all 4 brake pads together to prevent the braking from being uneven.

REMOVAL & INSTALLATION

1975-79 Models
▶ **See Figure 20**

1. Raise the front of the car and support it with jackstands. Remove the wheel and tire.

✳✳CAUTION

Be sure that the car is securely supported.

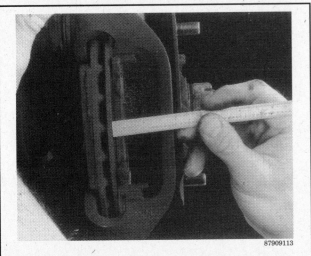

87909113

Fig. 19 Measure the pad thickness, if it is not within specifications they must be replaced

2. Remove the parking brake cable by disengaging the outer cable clip.

3. Remove the 4 pins from the caliper guides.

4. Fit the tip of a screwdriver on the guide and tap lightly to drive the guide out. When one is removed, the other one can be easily removed.

➡ **It is not necessary to remove the brake line.**

5. Remove the caliper by firmly holding the caliper body and pulling the lower part out while pushing the upper part in. Safety wire the caliper out of the way.

6. Remove the disc brake pad.

To install:

✳✳CAUTION

Do not try to force the piston back into the caliper body without turning as damage to the threaded spindle may occur.

7. Remove a small portion of brake fluid from the master cylinder reservoir. With an appropriate tool, turn the caliper piston clockwise into the cylinder bore and align the notches. Be sure the boot is not twisted or pinched.

8. Install the disc brake pads into the caliper.

9. Fit the caliper into the caliper housing and install the guides and pins.

10. Install the parking brake cable and outer cable clip.

11. Install the wheel and tighten the lug nuts.

12. Lower the vehicle and make sure that the brake pedal is firm.

1980-84 Models
▶ **See Figures 21, 22, 23 and 24**

1. Block the rear wheels. Raise the vehicle and the vehicle with jackstands.

2. Remove the wheel and tire.

3. Release the handbrake and disconnect the cable from the caliper lever.

4. On 1980-82 models, remove the 6mm lock pin bolt, (lower front of the caliper). Unfasten and disengage the lock pin. Make sure the lock pin is fully loosened before you try to remove it.

5. On 1983-84 models, simply unscrew and remove the lock pin, which is simply a long bolt.

6. The caliper will now pivot on its support. Swing the caliper up and away from the support and remove the pads.

To install:

7. Remove a small portion of brake fluid from the master cylinder reservoir. With an appropriate tool, turn the caliper

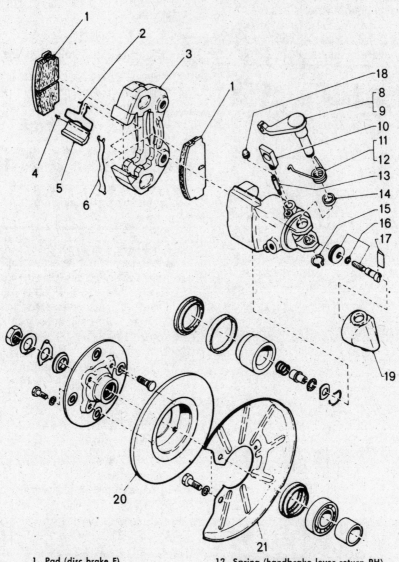

1. Pad (disc brake F)
2. Spring (caliper)
3. Bracket (mounting)
4. Pin (caliper)
5. Guide
6. Spring (pad)
7. Body caliper
8. Lever & spindle ass'y (LH)
9. Lever & spindle ass'y (RH)
10. Bracket (handbrake)
11. Spring (handbrake lever return LH)
12. Spring (handbrake lever return RH)
13. Bleeder screw (wheel cylinder)
14. Bushing (handbrake)
15. Retaining spring
16. Spindle
17. Connecting link
18. Cap (air bleeder)
19. Cap (lever)
20. Brake disc (F)
21. Cover (disc)

87909023

Fig. 20 Exploded view of the disc brake assembly-1975-79 models

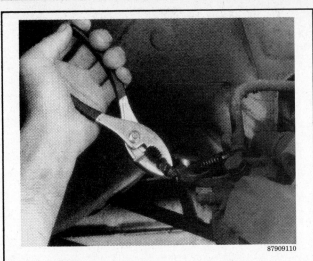

Fig. 21 Release the handbrake and disconnect the cable from the caliper lever

Fig. 22 Unscrew and remove the lock pin, which is simply a long bolt

Fig. 23 Swing the caliper up and away from the support and inspect the pads

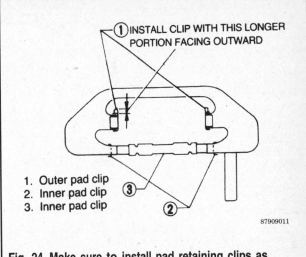

1. Outer pad clip
2. Inner pad clip
3. Inner pad clip

Fig. 24 Make sure to install pad retaining clips as shown

piston clockwise into the cylinder bore and align the notches. Be sure the boot is not twisted or pinched.

✳✳WARNING

Do not force the piston into the caliper body. The piston must be rotated clockwise at a rapid rate as it is forced in gently. Make sure the piston seal is not twisted. If it is, straighten it using a smooth, rounded screwdriver blade. Also, make sure the dowel on the back of the pad fits into the piston notch.

   8. Install the disc brake pads into the caliper.
   9. Install the caliper.
  10. Connect the handbrake cable to the caliper lever.
  11. Install the wheel and tighten the lug nuts.
  12. Lower the vehicle.
  13. Pump the brake pedal until piston-to-pad clearance is taken up (keep reservoir full).
  14. Make sure the brake pedal is firm before operating the car.

Disc Brake Calipers

REMOVAL & INSTALLATION

▶ See Figures 25 and 26

   1. Raise and support the vehicle with jackstands. Remove the front wheels.
   2. Remove the brake hose from the caliper body and plug the hose to prevent the entrance of dirt or moisture.
   3. Remove the handbrake cable and brake pads.
   4. Remove the caliper assembly by pulling it out of the support. Do not remove the guide pin unless it damaged.
  To install:
   5. Rotate the piston until the notch at the head of the piston is vertical.
   6. Install the handbrake cable and brake pads.
   7. Install the caliper assembly on the support and tighten the support bolt.

Fig. 25 Remove the brake hose from the caliper body

Fig. 26 Remove the caliper assembly from the vehicle

8. Fit the caliper into the caliper housing and install the mouting bolts/lock pins. Tighten the mounting bolts on 1975-79 models to 36-50 ft. lbs. (48-67 Nm). Tighten the lock pins to 33-54 ft. lbs. (44-73 Nm) on 1980-82 models and 12-17 ft. lbs. (16-23 Nm) on 1983-84 models.

9. Connect the brake hose and tighten the fitting.

10. Bleed the brake system.

11. Install the wheels and lower the vehicle.

12. Check the fluid level in the master cylinder.

OVERHAUL

▶ **See Figures 27, 28, 29, 30, 31, 32, 33, 34, 35, 36 and 37**

1. Follow the removal procedure outlined previously.

2. Remove any sludge and dirt from the outer part of the caliper.

3. On 1983-84 models, remove the sleeve and then the lock pin boot.

❋❋WARNING

Do not allow dirt to enter the brake fluid inlet.

4. Remove the boot ring and piston boot.

5. 1980-84 models, remove the guide pin boot from the caliper by alternately tapping both dowels on the boot.

6. Draw out the piston by applying compressed air at the brake fluid inlet. Excessive pressure is not necessary.

7. Remove the piston seal. Be careful not to scratch the inner wall of the cylinder.

8. Remove the cap ring and lever cap.

9. Remove the snapring from the spindle.

10. Compress the spring washers with a puller to eliminate the force retaining the handbrake lever and spindle, then slide out the lever and spindle.

11. Remove the connecting link.

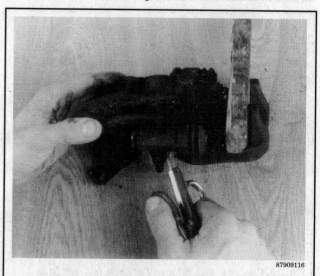

Fig. 27 Use compressed air to draw out the piston . . .

Fig. 28 . . . then remove the piston from the caliper

Fig. 29 Avoid scratching the bore when extracting the piston seal

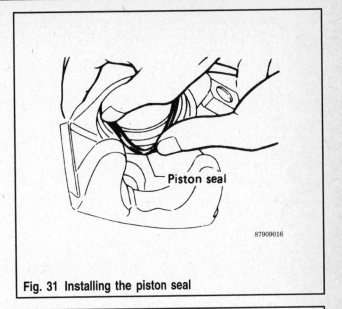

Fig. 31 Installing the piston seal

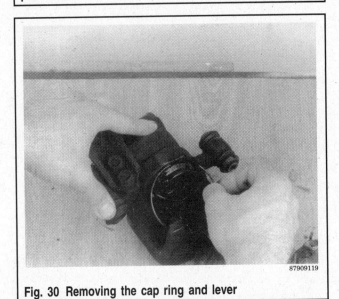

Fig. 30 Removing the cap ring and lever

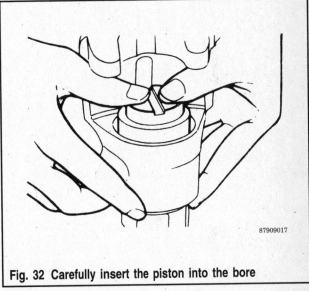

Fig. 32 Carefully insert the piston into the bore

To install:

12. Clean the inner part of the cylinder with fresh brake fluid and make sure that the inner wall of the brake cylinder is not scratched or corroded.

13. Apply a thin coat of silicon lubricant to a new piston seal and insert the seal into the groove.

14. After inspecting the piston for scratches, apply a thin coat of brake fluid to the piston and insert it into the cylinder.

15. Inspect the piston boot for scratches and replace if necessary.

16. Apply a thin coating of grease to the rim of the boot and attach it in the cylinder grooves on 1975-79 models.

17. On 1980-84 models, apply the grease into the grooves in the cylinder and those along the circumference of the piston head.

18. Attach the boot in the cylinder grooves. Make sure the boot is not twisted anywhere.

19. Attach the outer boot ring.

20. Apply a thin coat of silicone lubricant to the spindle assembly O-ring and insert the spindle assembly.

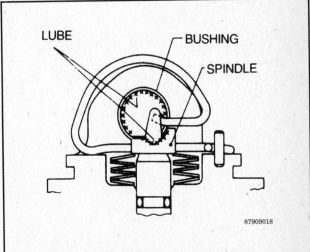

Fig. 33 Be sure the spring hooks and fits into the groove into the lever and spindle as shown

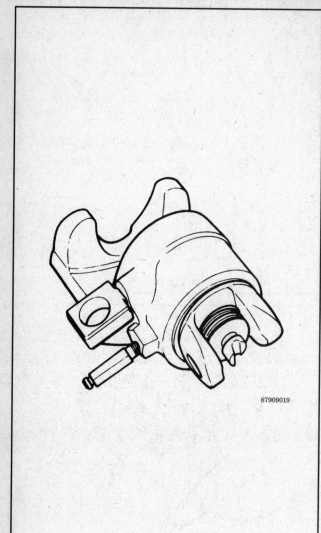

Fig. 34 Inserting the spindle

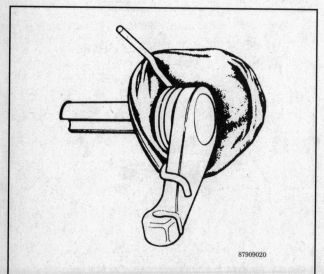

Fig. 35 Lever, shaft spring and cap as an assembly

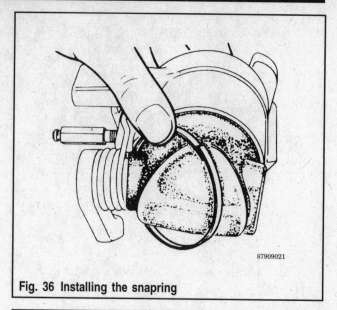

Fig. 36 Installing the snapring

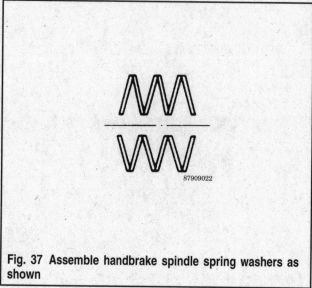

Fig. 37 Assemble handbrake spindle spring washers as shown

21. On 1980-84 models, apply the silicone to the section of the spindle where the spring washers go, into the spaces between the spring washers, and onto the caliper body surface where the washers bear.

22. Apply the same lubricant to the recess in the caliper body where the O-ring fits.

23. If replacing the spring washers, assemble them in the sequence shown.

24. Insert the spindle assembly into the cylinder by turning it clockwise from the opening at the bottom of the caliper body.

25. On 1975-79 models, insert the handbrake lever and spindle shaft assembly at the rear of the caliper. Be careful not to knock the connecting link out of place.

26. On 1980-84 models, you'll need some sort of tapered mandrel to install the O-ring.

27. Coat the O-ring with silicone compound and install it into the recess carefully.

28. Apply a grease designed for this type of service (example: NIGLUBE RX-2) to the head of the spindle assembly and onto the inner wall of the caliper body.

29. Install the connecting link and return spring.

30. Now, press in a set of spring washers and hold them there with a puller.

31. Apply the grease to the grooves in the lever and spindle in which the lever cap and connecting link are to be fitted.

32. Make sure the caliper bore is clean.

33. Then, fit the connecting link into the groove at the head of the spindle. Insert the lever and spindle complete with the lever cap and garter spring.

34. Make sure the inner tip of the return spring hooks and that it fits into the groove in the lever and spindle. Then remove the puller.

35. Insert the handbrake lever and spindle shaft assembly at the rear of the caliper. Be careful not to knock the connecting link out of place.

36. Apply silicone grease to the groove of the caliper body where the lever cap will go. Apply it also to the snapring.

37. Install the snapring at the end of the lever and spindle shaft. Then apply sufficient silicone grease to the space around the connecting link and lever and spindle to fill the inside of the lever cap after it is installed.

38. Fit the lever cap into the slot at the rear of the caliper body and anchor it in place with the cap ring. Make sure you don't damage the lever cap with the sharp edge of the cap ring.

39. On late model calipers with guide pins, make sure the hole the guide pin slides into is clean. Install a new guide pin boot by evenly tapping all around the metal periphery.

40. Make sure to rotate the caliper piston to the proper position.

41. On 1980-84 calipers, which use guide pins and lock pins, coat the entire guide pin, and all but the outer end of the lockpin, with silicone grease.

42. Make sure both boots fit properly in the guide pin and lock pin grooves. If the boots get full of air during installation, simply squeeze them gently to release excess air.

43. Install the calipers.

44. Bleed the system.

Brake Disc (Rotor)

REMOVAL & INSTALLATION

▶ **See Figures 38, 39, 40 and 41**

1. Raise the vehicle and support it with jackstands.

2. Remove the front wheel, handbrake cable, guides, caliper and caliper support in the same manner as outlined in this section.

3. Safety wire the caliper to a suspension member, so that it is out of the way.

4. Unfasten the two bolts which hold the caliper bracket to the housing and remove the bracket from the housing.

5. Remove the axle shaft nut and pull the disc off the axle shaft with a puller.

6. Remove the 4 bolts which hold the disc to the hub.

7. Reverse the above process to install the rotor.

8. Tighten caliper bracket bolts to 36-51 ft. lbs. (48-69 Nm).

INSPECTION

1. Check the disc for any obvious defects such as excessive rust, chipping, or deep scoring. Light scoring is normal on disc brakes.

2. Install a dial indicator on the caliper so that its feeler will contact the disc about 0.20 in. (5 mm) from the outer edge of the rotor.

3. Turn the disc and observe the runout reading. If the reading exceeds 0.0039 in. (0.10 mm), the disc should be replaced.

➡**All brake rotors (discs) have a minimum thickness dimension cast into them, on the hub between the lugs. This is the minimum wear dimension and not a refinish dimension. Do not reuse a brake rotor that will not meet specifications. Replace with a new rotor.**

Refinishing of brake rotors can be handled at machine shops equipped for brake work.

87909122

Fig. 38 Loosen the two bolts which hold the caliper bracket to the housing, then remove the bracket

87909123

Fig. 39 Remove the axle shaft nut and pull the disc off the axle shaft with a puller

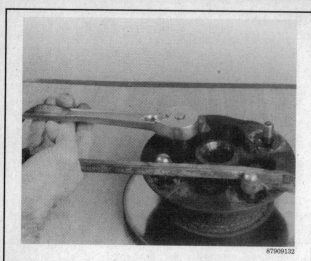

Fig. 40 Remove the 4 bolts which hold the disc to the hub

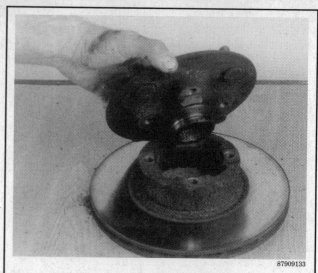

Fig. 41 Separate the disc from the hub

REAR DRUM BRAKES

✳✳CAUTION

Brake shoes may contain asbestos, which has been determined to be a cancer causing agent. Never clean the brake surfaces with compressed air! Avoid inhaling any dust from any brake surface! When cleaning brake surfaces, use a commercially available brake cleaning fluid.

Brake Drums

REMOVAL & INSTALLATION

Except 4WD Models

◗ **See Figures 42, 43 and 44**

1. Block the front wheels. Raise the vehicle and support it with jackstands.
2. Remove the wheel and tire.
3. Remove the 3 cap retaining bolts, spring washers, cap, bearing retaining plate (if equipped), or the covering cap.
4. Remove the cotter pin or straighten out the lockwasher, and loosen and unfasten the nut taking care not to damage the bearing seal.
5. Remove the lockwasher and lockplate on 1980-84 models.
6. Remove the brake drum with a puller.

✳✳WARNING

Do not depress the brake pedal with the brake drum removed.

To install:

7. Reverse the above process to install the drums.
8. On 1970-73 models, tighten the axle shaft castle nut to 80-145 ft. lbs. (108-196 Nm).

Fig. 42 Remove the dust cap and seal

9. On all 1974-84 models and on ff-1 and 1300G station wagons, do not tighten the bearing adjusting nut. Instead perform the bearing preload adjustment as detailed in this section.
10. Tighten the 3 bearing cap securing plate bolts to 20-50 inch lbs. (2-5 Nm) on models so equipped.

4WD Models

◗ **See Figures 45 and 46**

1. Block the front wheels. Raise the rear of the vehicle and support it with jackstands.
2. Remove the wheel and tire.
3. On 1980-84 models, straighten and disengage the cotter pin, then remove the castellated nut, spring washer, spacer and pull off the brake drum. Note parts orientation. If necessary to use a puller, its center should bear on the center of the rear spindle only.

Fig. 43 Remove the axle shaft nut

Fig. 44 Remove the lockwasher and lockplate

4. On 1970-79 models, using a chisel with a flat blade about 0.23 in. (6mm) across, straighten the staked portion of the axle nut.

5. Apply oil on the threads and groove in the axle shaft. Have someone hold the brakes on while you repeatedly loosen and tighten the nut just 0.23 in. (6mm) or so. This is done to force metal chips created in straightening the staked portion of the nut into the groove.

6. Then, loosen the nut. Remove the spring washer and spacer and then pull the drum off the spindle. If you need a puller, bear on the center of the spindle, only.

To install:

7. Put the drum onto the spindle.

8. Install the spacer, spring washer (in original position), and the plain or castellated nut onto the spindle.

9. Note that on late model cars, the spring washer has a paint mark on one side which must face outward.

10. On models 1970-79, install the nut and tighten it to 174 ft. lbs. (235 Nm), with someone holding the brakes on.

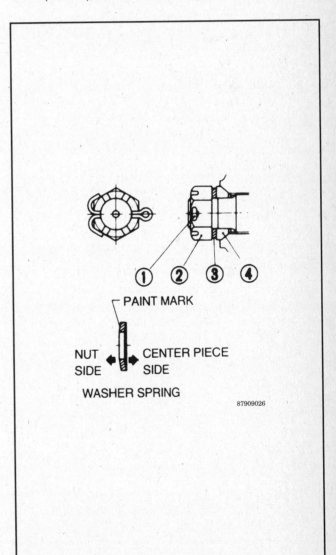
Fig. 46 On 1980-84 4WD cars, install the cotter pin (1), castellated nut (2), spring washer (3), and spacer (4) as shown

1. Brake drum
2. Outer oil seal
3. Spindle

Fig. 45 Brake drum and spindle assembly

11. Then, stake the flanged portion of the retaining nut down into the groove in the spindle until it touches the bottom of the groove, using a center punch.

12. On 1980-84 models, tighten the castellated nut, with the brakes applied, to 145 ft. lbs. (196 Nm).

13. Then tighten the castellated nut just enough further to align holes on nut and spindle.

14. Install a new cotter pin and bend its ends until it's firmly secured.

INSPECTION

After removing the brake drum, inspect the inner braking surface for excessive wear or damage. If it is unevenly worn, streaked, or cracked, have it resurfaced or replaced. The standard inside diameter of the brake drum is 7 in. (180mm). The maximum allowed diameter is 7.15 in. (182mm).

BEARING PRELOAD ADJUSTMENT

▶ **See Figure 47**

1. On 1979 and earlier models, tighten the adjusting nut until it is just snug while rotating the drum back and forth to seat the bearing.

2. On 1980-83 models, tighten the nut to 36 ft. lbs. (48 Nm), or 29 ft. lbs. (39 Nm) on 1984 models, while rotating the drum back and forth to seat the bearing. Loosen the nut about 0.11 in. (3mm).

3. Then, attach a spring scale to one of the wheel studs. Pull on the spring scale at a 90° angle to the diameter of the brake drum and measure the force required to start the drum turning.

4. It should be 6-9 ft. lbs. (8-12 Nm) on 1970-77 cars, 2.2-3.1 ft. lbs. (3-4 Nm) on 1978-83 cars, and 2.6-4.0 ft. lbs. (3.5-5 Nm) on 1984 cars.

5. Loosen or tighten the nut slightly to get the right rolling resistance.

6. When the rolling resistance is right, bend the lockwasher over to hold the nut in place.

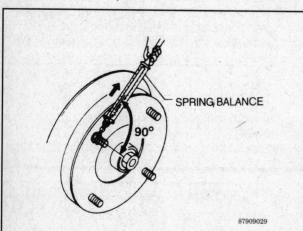

SPRING BALANCE

90°

87909029

Fig. 47 Turn the rear brake drum with a spring scale at 90° to the diameter of the drum to measure the starting force

Brake Shoes

INSPECTION

Inspect the brake shoes for excessive or uneven wear, fluid contamination, bent and/or broken parts and cracks. If any of these conditions exist, replace the brake shoes.

Measure the lining thickness. Replace the linings if they are below minimum service thickness limits. See the Brake Specifications Chart in this section. Replace the leading and trailing shoes on both sides at the same time. Replacement of the shoes one side or one shoe at a time, will cause uneven braking.

REMOVAL & INSTALLATION

▶ **See Figures 48, 49, 50, 51, 52 and 53**

1. Raise the vehicle and support it with jackstands. Remove the wheels.

2. Remove the brake drums.

3. Remove both return springs carefully with a pair of brake pliers.

4. Remove both retaining clips by first turning them 90° with a pair of pliers to line up the slot in the lip with the flat end of the pin and then pulling them off the pins.

5. Disconnect shoes on the adjuster side first and then on the wheel cylinder side, and pull them off the backing plate.

To install:

6. Apply brake grease to the backing plate where the brake shoes contact it.

7. Install shoes to the wheel cylinder and then to the adjuster.

8. Install the two retaining clips.

✹✹WARNING

Be careful to keep the grease off the linings.

9. Assemble the return springs. The upper spring is thinner.

10. Use the wedge to adjust the brake shoe diameter to 7 in. (180mm). Measure the diameter in at least 3 places around the shoes.

11. Install the drum and adjust the brakes as outlined below.

12. Perform the operation for the brake shoes on the other side.

ADJUSTMENT

▶ **See Figure 54**

1. Raise the vehicle and support it with jackstands.

2. Spin the wheel rapidly and then tighten the adjusting screw until the wheel stops rotating.

3. Then, turn the adjusting screw back just ½ turn.

4. Turn the wheel to make sure it rotates without dragging.

5. Readjust if necessary.

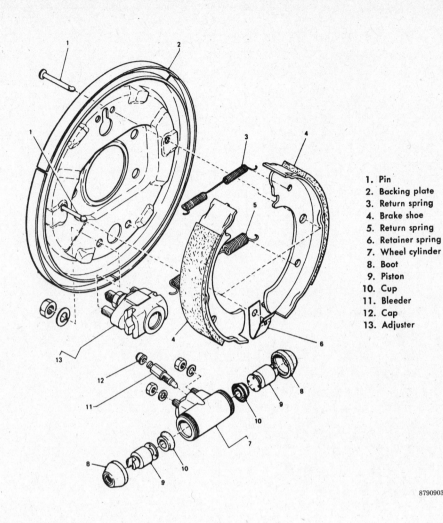

1. Pin
2. Backing plate
3. Return spring
4. Brake shoe
5. Return spring
6. Retainer spring
7. Wheel cylinder
8. Boot
9. Piston
10. Cup
11. Bleeder
12. Cap
13. Adjuster

87909030

Fig. 48 Exploded view of the rear brake assembly found on Subarus

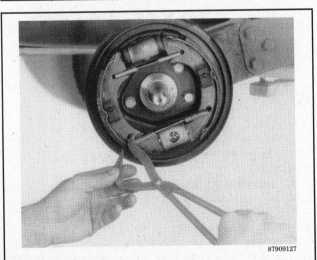

87909127

Fig. 49 Use a pair of brake pliers to free the brake return springs. . .

87909128

Fig. 50 . . . then remove the springs from the show assembly

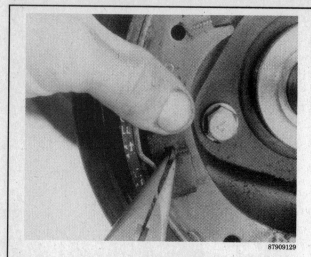

Fig. 51 Line up the slot in the lip with the flat end of the pin, then pull them off the pins

Fig. 52 Remove the brake shoes from the vehicle

Fig. 53 Apply brake grease to the backing plate where the brake shoes contact it

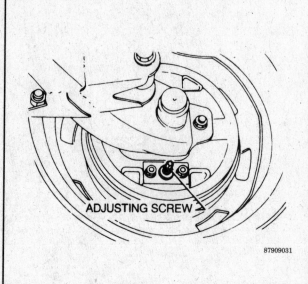

ADJUSTING SCREW

Fig. 54 Location of the rear drum adjusting screw

Wheel Cylinders

REMOVAL & INSTALLATION

▶ See Figure 55

1. Raise the vehicle and support it with jackstands.
2. Remove the wheel.
3. Remove the brake drum and the brake shoes from the backing plate.
4. Disconnect and plug the fluid line for the wheel cylinder at the backing plate.
5. Remove the wheel cylinder from the backing plate by unscrewing the attaching bolts.
6. Remove the rubber boots from both ends of the wheel cylinder, then push out the inner pistons and spring together with the rubber cups.
7. Inspect the inside of the wheel cylinder bore. If it is worn or scratched in any way, it should be honed with a wheel

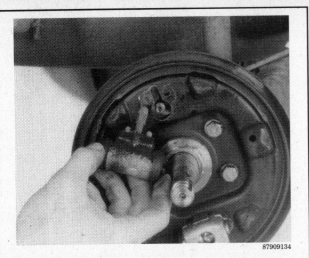

Fig. 55 Remove the wheel cylinder from the backing plate by unscrewing the attaching bolts

cylinder hone or a piece of crocus cloth until the scratches are removed.

To install:

8. Replace the rubber cups with new ones. The internal replacement parts are usually supplied in a wheel cylinder re-building kit.

9. Reassemble the wheel cylinder and replace it on the backing plate in the reverse order of removal.

10. After reinstalling the brake line and the brake assembly, together with the brake drum, bleed the brake system.

PARKING BRAKE

Cable

REMOVAL & INSTALLATION

ff-1 and 1300G Models

1. Loosen the cable turnbuckle locknut.
2. Separate the halves of the cable.
3. Withdraw the clip, pin, pulley, and the cable.
4. Loosen the nut and remove the cable from its bracket.
5. Remove the nut, washer, bushing, and turnbuckle from the cable.
6. Withdraw the cable boot from the engine compartment side of the floorboard.
7. Remove the brake cable.

To install:

8. Install the cable boot to the engine compartment side of the floorboard.
9. install the turnbuckle, bushing, washer and the nut on the cable.
10. Install the cable in the bracket and fasten the nut.
11. Install the cable, pulley, pin, and the clip.
12. Engage the halves of the cable.
13. Fasten the turnbuckle locknut.

1970-79 Models (Except ff-1 and 1300G)

▶ **See Figure 56**

1. Raise the vehicle and support it with jackstands.
2. Remove the wheel and tire.
3. Remove the brake drum.
4. Remove the handbrake cover and console.
5. Loosen the cable adjusting nut.
6. Remove the cable end from the equalizer.
7. Remove the cable end tightening clip.
8. Remove the service hole cover on the tunnel.

9. Remove the cable clamp from the crossmember.
10. Remove the cable installing bracket from the control arm.
11. Remove the handbrake cable hanger from the tie rod end.
12. Disconnect the handbrake cable end from the handbrake lever by removing the secondary shoe.
13. Remove the cable end nut, washer, and spring washer from the inside of the backing plate and pull the handbrake cable out from the backing plate.
14. Pull the handbrake cable assembly from the engine compartment and remove it from the body together with the grommet.

To install:

15. Install the handbrake cable through the engine compartment and into the body together with the grommet.
16. Install the brake cable end into the lever and spindle assembly and secure it with the hose clamp.
17. Install the handbrake cable into the backing plate and install the spring washer, washer and cable end nut.
18. Install the secondary brake shoe and connect the handbrake cable end.
19. Install the handbrake cable hanger to tie rod end.
20. Connect the cable installing bracket to the control arm.
21. Install the cable clamp to the crossmember and the service hole cover to the tunnel.
22. Install the cable end tightening clip.
23. Install the cable end from the equalizer.
24. Tighten the cable adjusting nut.
25. Install the handbrake cover and console.
26. Install the brake drum.
27. Install the wheel and tire and lower the vehicle.

1980-84 Models

1. Raise the front of the vehicle and support it with jackstands.
2. Remove the front wheels.

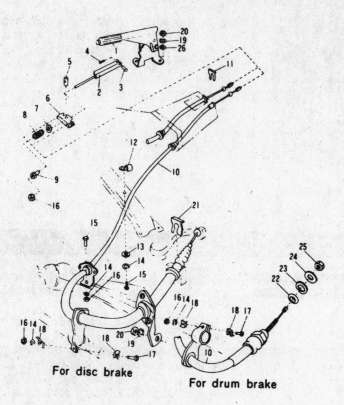

1. Lever assembly
2. Rod
3. Clevis pin
4. Cotter pin
5. Pin
6. Equalizer
7. Washer
8. Spring
9. Adjuster
10. Parking brake cable assembly
11. Clamp
12. Clamp
13. Washer
14. Spring washer
15. Bolt
16. Nut
17. Bolt
18. Washer
19. Spring washer
20. Nut
21. Clamp
22. O-ring
23. Spring washer
24. Washer
25. Nut
26. Washer

For disc brake

For drum brake

87909033

Fig. 56 1970-79 parking brake assembly (except ff-1 and 1300G)

3. Remove the parking brake cover.

4. Unfasten the locknut and then loosen the parking brake adjuster until tension is almost gone.

5. Disconnect the inner cable ends from the equalizer.

6. Remove the clips that fasten the cable grommets in place where the cable passes through the body.

7. Pull the parking brake cable clamp out of the caliper and disconnect the end of the cable.

8. On 1980 vehicles disconnect the front exhaust pipe and remove it.

9. On 1980-81 vehicles, remove the front-most exhaust system cover.

10. Loosen the attaching bolt and remove the bracket holding the cable to the transverse link.

11. Unfasten the bolt and remove the bracket attaching the cable to the crossmember bracket.

12. Detach the cable from the guide to the rear crossmember.

13. Pull the cable out of the passenger compartment.

14. To install, reverse this procedure, making sure the cable passes through the guide inside the driveshaft tunnel. Adjust the brake as described in this section.

ADJUSTMENT

ff-1 and 1300G Models
▶ **See Figures 57 and 58**

1. Pull the parking brake lever up forcefully. Release it and repeat several times.

2. It should take 7-8 notches to apply the parking brake.

3. Loosen the locknut on the turnbuckle and adjust the length of the cable, so that the parking brake is applied within specifications.

4. Tighten the locknut and recheck operation of the parking brake lever.

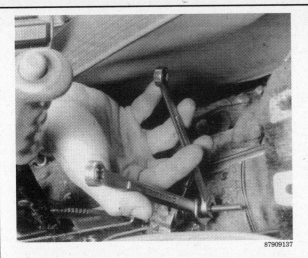

Fig. 57 Adjust the cable by loosening the locknut, then turning the cable adjusting nut

Except ff-1 and 1300G Models

The parking brake adjusting procedure is similar to that given above for ff-1 and 1300G models. Adjust the number of ratchet notches necessary to apply the parking brake to the following specifications:

- 1972-73: 9-10 notches
- 1974-76: 6-7 notches
- 1977-82: 6-9 notches
- 1983-84: 3-5 notches

Adjust the cable by loosening the lock and turning the cable adjusting nut. Tighten the adjusting nut to 36-48 inch lbs. (4-5 Nm). Make sure the front wheels turn freely when the handbrake is released.

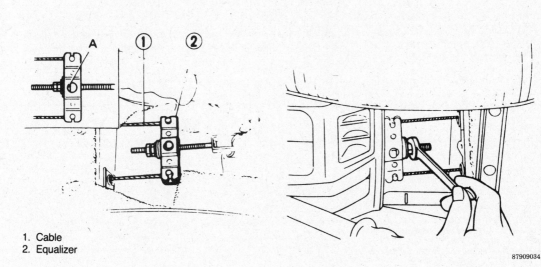

1. Cable
2. Equalizer

Fig. 58 Adjusting the handbrake on ff-1 and 1300G models

Brake Specifications

All measurements given are (in.) unless noted

Year	Model	Lug Nut Torque (ft. lbs.)	Master Cylinder Bore	Brake Disc		Diameter	Brake Drum		Minimum Lining Thickness	
				Minimum Thickness	Maximum Run-Out		Maximum Machine O/S	Maximum Wear Limit	Front	Rear
1970–72	FF-1 & 1300G Sedan	40–54	.75	—	—	8.01-F 7.09-R	8.08-F 7.17-R	8.08-F 7.17-R	.067	.067
	FF-1 & 1300G Wagon	40–54	.75	—	—	9.01-F 7.09-R	9.08-F 7.17-R	9.08-F 7.17-R	.067	.067
1972–75	DL Sedan & Wagon	40–54 ①	.75	—	—	9.01-F 7.09-R	9.08-F 7.17-R	9.08-F 7.17-R	.04-P .06-S	.06
	GL & GF Coupe	40–54 ①	.75	.33	.006	7.09	7.17	7.17	.06	.06
1976–79	All Models	58–72	.75	.33	.006	7.09	7.17	7.17	.06	.06
1980–82	All Models	58–72	.8125	.394	.0039	7.09	7.17	7.17	.295 ②	.06
1982–84	All Models	58–72	.8125	.610 ③	.0039	7.24	7.17	7.17	.295	.059

① 1975 models: 58–72 ft. lbs.
② Includes back metal
  F—Front
  R—Rear

P—Primary
S—Secondary
③ On unventilated, 1983 discs, minimum thickness is .39

NOTE: *Minimum lining thickness is as recommended by the manufacturer. Because of variations in state inspection regulations, the minimum allowable thickness may be different than recommended by the manufacturer.*

87909C01

Troubleshooting the Brake System

Problem	Cause	Solution
Low brake pedal (excessive pedal travel required for braking action.)	• Excessive clearance between rear linings and drums caused by inoperative automatic adjusters	• Make 10 to 15 alternate forward and reverse brake stops to adjust brakes. If brake pedal does not come up, repair or replace adjuster parts as necessary.
	• Worn rear brakelining	• Inspect and replace lining if worn beyond minimum thickness specification
	• Bent, distorted brakeshoes, front or rear	• Replace brakeshoes in axle sets
	• Air in hydraulic system	• Remove air from system. Refer to Brake Bleeding.
Low brake pedal (pedal may go to floor with steady pressure applied.)	• Fluid leak in hydraulic system	• Fill master cylinder to fill line; have helper apply brakes and check calipers, wheel cylinders, differential valve tubes, hoses and fittings for leaks. Repair or replace as necessary.
	• Air in hydraulic system	• Remove air from system. Refer to Brake Bleeding.
	• Incorrect or non-recommended brake fluid (fluid evaporates at below normal temp).	• Flush hydraulic system with clean brake fluid. Refill with correct-type fluid.
	• Master cylinder piston seals worn, or master cylinder bore is scored, worn or corroded	• Repair or replace master cylinder
Low brake pedal (pedal goes to floor on first application—o.k. on subsequent applications.)	• Disc brake pads sticking on abutment surfaces of anchor plate. Caused by a build-up of dirt, rust, or corrosion on abutment surfaces	• Clean abutment surfaces
Fading brake pedal (pedal height decreases with steady pressure applied.)	• Fluid leak in hydraulic system	• Fill master cylinder reservoirs to fill mark, have helper apply brakes, check calipers, wheel cylinders, differential valve, tubes, hoses, and fittings for fluid leaks. Repair or replace parts as necessary.
	• Master cylinder piston seals worn, or master cylinder bore is scored, worn or corroded	• Repair or replace master cylinder
Decreasing brake pedal travel (pedal travel required for braking action decreases and may be accompanied by a hard pedal.)	• Caliper or wheel cylinder pistons sticking or seized	• Repair or replace the calipers, or wheel cylinders
	• Master cylinder compensator ports blocked (preventing fluid return to reservoirs) or pistons sticking or seized in master cylinder bore	• Repair or replace the master cylinder
	• Power brake unit binding internally	• Test unit according to the following procedure: (a) Shift transmission into neutral and start engine (b) Increase engine speed to 1500 rpm, close throttle and fully depress brake pedal (c) Slow release brake pedal and stop engine (d) Have helper remove vacuum check valve and hose from power unit. Observe for backward movement of brake pedal. (e) If the pedal moves backward, the power unit has an internal bind—replace power unit

87909C02

Troubleshooting the Brake System (cont.)

Problem	Cause	Solution
Spongy brake pedal (pedal has abnormally soft, springy, spongy feel when depressed.)	• Air in hydraulic system	• Remove air from system. Refer to Brake Bleeding.
	• Brakeshoes bent or distorted	• Replace brakeshoes
	• Brakelining not yet seated with drums and rotors	• Burnish brakes
	• Rear drum brakes not properly adjusted	• Adjust brakes
Hard brake pedal (excessive pedal pressure required to stop vehicle. May be accompanied by brake fade.)	• Loose or leaking power brake unit vacuum hose	• Tighten connections or replace leaking hose
	• Incorrect or poor quality brakelining	• Replace with lining in axle sets
	• Bent, broken, distorted brakeshoes	• Replace brakeshoes
	• Calipers binding or dragging on mounting pins. Rear brakeshoes dragging on support plate.	• Replace mounting pins and bushings. Clean rust or burrs from rear brake support plate ledges and lubricate ledges with molydisulfide grease. **NOTE:** If ledges are deeply grooved or scored, do not attempt to sand or grind them smooth—replace support plate.
	• Caliper, wheel cylinder, or master cylinder pistons sticking or seized	• Repair or replace parts as necessary
	• Power brake unit vacuum check valve malfunction	• Test valve according to the following procedure: (a) Start engine, increase engine speed to 1500 rpm, close throttle and immediately stop engine (b) Wait at least 90 seconds then depress brake pedal (c) If brakes are not vacuum assisted for 2 or more applications, check valve is faulty
	• Power brake unit has internal bind	• Test unit according to the following procedure: (a) With engine stopped, apply brakes several times to exhaust all vacuum in system (b) Shift transmission into neutral, depress brake pedal and start engine (c) If pedal height decreases with foot pressure and less pressure is required to hold pedal in applied position, power unit vacuum system is operating normally. Test power unit. If power unit exhibits a bind condition, replace the power unit.
	• Master cylinder compensator ports (at bottom of reservoirs) blocked by dirt, scale, rust, or have small burrs (blocked ports prevent fluid return to reservoirs).	• Repair or replace master cylinder **CAUTION:** Do not attempt to clean blocked ports with wire, pencils, or similar implements. Use compressed air only.
	• Brake hoses, tubes, fittings clogged or restricted	• Use compressed air to check or unclog parts. Replace any damaged parts.
	• Brake fluid contaminated with improper fluids (motor oil, transmission fluid, causing rubber components to swell and stick in bores	• Replace all rubber components, combination valve and hoses. Flush entire brake system with DOT 3 brake fluid or equivalent.
	• Low engine vacuum	• Adjust or repair engine

87909C03

Troubleshooting the Brake System (cont.)

Problem	Cause	Solution
Grabbing brakes (severe reaction to brake pedal pressure.)	· Brakelining(s) contaminated by grease or brake fluid	· Determine and correct cause of contamination and replace brakeshoes in axle sets
	· Parking brake cables incorrectly adjusted or seized	· Adjust cables. Replace seized cables.
	· Incorrect brakelining or lining loose on brakeshoes	· Replace brakeshoes in axle sets
	· Caliper anchor plate bolts loose	· Tighten bolts
	· Rear brakeshoes binding on support plate ledges	· Clean and lubricate ledges. Replace support plate(s) if ledges are deeply grooved. Do not attempt to smooth ledges by grinding.
	· Incorrect or missing power brake reaction disc	· Install correct disc
	· Rear brake support plates loose	· Tighten mounting bolts
Dragging brakes (slow or incomplete release of brakes)	· Brake pedal binding at pivot	· Loosen and lubricate
	· Power brake unit has internal bind	· Inspect for internal bind. Replace unit if internal bind exists.
	· Parking brake cables incorrrectly adjusted or seized	· Adjust cables. Replace seized cables.
	· Rear brakeshoe return springs weak or broken	· Replace return springs. Replace brakeshoe if necessary in axle sets.
	· Automatic adjusters malfunctioning	· Repair or replace adjuster parts as required
	· Caliper, wheel cylinder or master cylinder pistons sticking or seized	· Repair or replace parts as necessary
	· Master cylinder compensating ports blocked (fluid does not return to reservoirs).	· Use compressed air to clear ports. Do not use wire, pencils, or similar objects to open blocked ports.
Vehicle moves to one side when brakes are applied	· Incorrect front tire pressure	· Inflate to recommended cold (reduced load) inflation pressure
	· Worn or damaged wheel bearings	· Replace worn or damaged bearings
	· Brakelining on one side contaminated	· Determine and correct cause of contamination and replace brakelining in axle sets
	· Brakeshoes on one side bent, distorted, or lining loose on shoe	· Replace brakeshoes in axle sets
	· Support plate bent or loose on one side	· Tighten or replace support plate
	· Brakelining not yet seated with drums or rotors	· Burnish brakelining
	· Caliper anchor plate loose on one side	· Tighten anchor plate bolts
	· Caliper piston sticking or seized	· Repair or replace caliper
	· Brakelinings water soaked	· Drive vehicle with brakes lightly applied to dry linings
	· Loose suspension component attaching or mounting bolts	· Tighten suspension bolts. Replace worn suspension components.
	· Brake combination valve failure	· Replace combination valve
Chatter or shudder when brakes are applied (pedal pulsation and roughness may also occur.)	· Brakeshoes distorted, bent, contaminated, or worn	· Replace brakeshoes in axle sets
	· Caliper anchor plate or support plate loose	· Tighten mounting bolts
	· Excessive thickness variation of rotor(s)	· Refinish or replace rotors in axle sets
Noisy brakes (squealing, clicking, scraping sound when brakes are applied.)	· Bent, broken, distorted brakeshoes	· Replace brakeshoes in axle sets
	· Excessive rust on outer edge of rotor braking surface	· Remove rust

87909C04

Troubleshooting the Brake System (cont.)

Problem	Cause	Solution
Noisy brakes (squealing, clicking, scraping sound when brakes are applied.) (cont.)	• Brakelining worn out—shoes contacting drum of rotor	• Replace brakeshoes and lining in axle sets. Refinish or replace drums or rotors.
	• Broken or loose holdown or return springs	• Replace parts as necessary
	• Rough or dry drum brake support plate ledges	• Lubricate support plate ledges
	• Cracked, grooved, or scored rotor(s) or drum(s)	• Replace rotor(s) or drum(s). Replace brakeshoes and lining in axle sets if necessary.
	• Incorrect brakelining and/or shoes (front or rear).	• Install specified shoe and lining assemblies
Pulsating brake pedal	• Out of round drums or excessive lateral runout in disc brake rotor(s)	• Refinish or replace drums, re-index rotors or replace

87909C05

Special Tools, Brake System

925460000	925471000	925600000	926430000
WHEEL CYLINDER 11/16″ ADAPTER	**DISC BRAKE CYLINDER PULLER**	**O-RING ADAPTER**	**DISC BRAKE PISTON WRENCH**
Installing cup onto piston of rear drum brake wheel cylinder (size 11/16 in).	Pressing cone spring (front disc brake).	Installing spindle O-ring (front disc brake).	Used with SPACER (926440000) to rotate front disc brake piston.

926440000	926460000
SPACER	**WHEEL CYLINDER 3/4″ ADAPTER**
Used as a set with WRENCH (926430000). Attach this tool to WRENCH using two 6-mm dia. bolts (length: less than 15 mm).	Installing cup onto piston of rear drum brake wheel cylinder (size 3/4 in).

87909C06

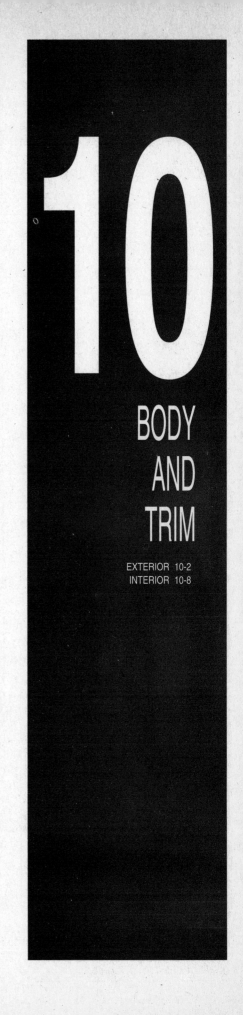

10

BODY
AND
TRIM

EXTERIOR

Doors

REMOVAL & INSTALLATION

▶ **See Figures 1 and 2**

➡ **If the door being removed is to be reinstalled, matchmark the hinge position.**

1. If the door is to be replaced with a new one, remove the trim panels weather sheets and all moldings.
2. If the door is to be replaced with a new one, remove the glass, locks and latches.
3. Support the door with a floor jack. Use a piece of cloth or wood between the jack and the door to prevent damage to the door.
4. Remove the spring pin and the upper and lower hinge-to-body attaching bolts.
5. Lift the door from the car.

To install:
6. Install the door on the jack and position it to the door hinges.
7. Install the upper and lower hinge-to-body attaching bolts.
8. Install the spring pin.
9. Perform the adjustment procedures outlined in this section.

ADJUSTMENT

➡ **The holes for the hinges are oversized to provide for latitude in alignment. Align the door hinges first, then the striker.**

Hinges

1. If a door is being installed, first mount the door and tighten the hinge bolts lightly.

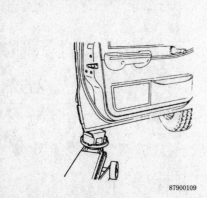

Fig. 1 Support the door with a floor jack. Use a piece of cloth or wood between the jack and the door to prevent damage to the door

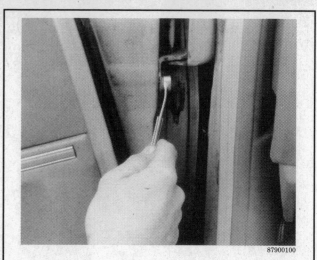

Fig. 2 Remove the upper and lower hinge-to-body attaching bolts

2. If the door has not been removed, determine which hinge bolts must be loosed to effect alignment.
3. Loosen the necessary bolts just enough to allow the door to be moved with a padded prybar.
4. Move the door in small movements and check the fit after each movement. Be sure that there is no binding or interference with adjacent panels. Keep repeating this procedure until the door is properly aligned.
5. Tighten all the bolts. Shims may be either fabricated or purchased to install behind the hinges as an aid in alignment.

Striker Plate

▶ **See Figure 3**

➡ **The striker is attached to the pillar using oversized holes, providing latitude in movement.**

Striker adjustment is made by loosening the bolts and moving the striker plate in the desired direction or adding or deleting shims behind the plate, or both. The striker is properly adjusted when the locking latch enters the striker without rubbing and the door closes fully and solidly, with no play when closed.

Hood

REMOVAL & INSTALLATION

▶ **See Figures 4 and 5**

➡ **You are going to need an assistant for this procedure.**

1. Open the hood and trace the outline of the hinges on the body.
2. While an assistant holds the hood, remove the hinge-to-body bolts and lift the hood off.

To install:
3. While an assistant holds the hood, align the hinges and the outlines previously made.

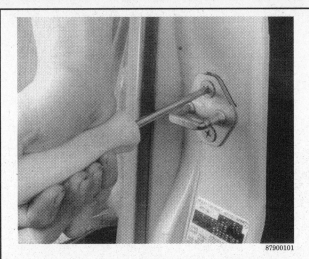

Fig. 3 The striker plate may be adjusted by loosening the screws and moving the plate

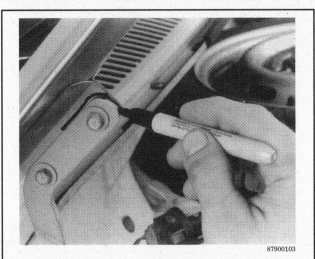

Fig. 4 Open the hood and trace the outline of the hinges on the body

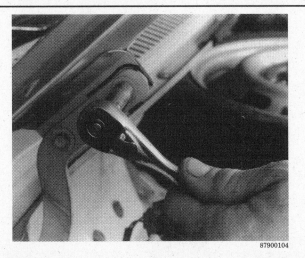

Fig. 5 Remove the hinge-to-body bolts and lift the hood off

4. Fasten the hinge-to-body bolts and check that the hood closes properly.
5. Adjust hood alignment, if necessary.

ALIGNMENT

Hood alignment can be adjusted front-to-rear or side-to-side by loosening the hood-to-hinge or hinge-to-body bolts. The front edge of the hood can be adjusted for closing height by adding or deleting shims under the hinges. The rear edge of the hood can be adjusted for closing height by raising or lowering the hood bumpers.

Tailgate, Hatch or Trunk Lid

REMOVAL & INSTALLATION

➡**You will need an assistant during this procedure. Be careful not to scratch coated surfaces of the body and window glass during removal. Place a cloth over the affected area. Be careful not to damage the trim panels. Have an assistant help you when handling heavy parts. Be careful not to damage or lose small parts.**

Station Wagon

1. Remove the clips from the trim panel using Clip Puller (925580000) or equivalent and detach the trim panel. Be careful not to damage the clips or their holes.
2. Unfasten the connector from the rear gate defogger terminal. Do not pull the lead wire, but unlock the connector and disengage.
3. Disengage the wiper connector and rear washer hose.
4. Unlock the connector and disengage from rear gate door switch. Do not pull the lead wire.
5. Disengage the license lamp connector.
6. Disengage the high mount stop lamp connector, if applicable
7. Disengage the auto door lock actuator connector.
8. If the disengaged harness is re-used, tie connector with a string and place on the upper side of the rear gate for ready use.

✳✳WARNING

Do not forcefully pull cords, lead wires, etc. since damage may result. Carefully extract them in a wavy motion while holding the connectors.

9. Remove the rear wiper arm, the cap and nut.
10. Detach the trim panel, unfasten the bolt from the rear wiper and remove the wiper.
11. Completely open the rear gate.
12. Remove the bolts which secure the gas stay to the rear gate.
13. Remove trim side rail, and unfasten roof trim clips as far as the center pillar.
14. Hang roof trim down to prevent it from bending.

15. Remove the nuts which hold the hinge with a ratchet wrench placed between the roof trim and the car body, and detach the hinge.

✳✳WARNING

Remove the bolts one at a time. Have a helper hold the rear gate while removing the bolts to prevent it from dropping. Be sure to place a folded cloth between the rear gate and body to prevent scratches.

16. Remove the rear gate.

To install:
17. Position the rear gate onto the roof hinge.
18. Install the rear gate retaining nuts and tighten securely.
19. Position the roof trim and secure it using the retaining clips.
20. Install the trim side rails.
21. Install the gas stays to the rear gate and tighten the retaining bolts.
22. Close the rear gate and install the rear wiper, trim panel and wiper arm.
23. Connect the wiring harness to the rear wiper system.
24. Engage the auto door lock actuator connector.
25. Engage the license lamp connector.
26. Engage the high mount stop lamp connector.
27. Connect the rear gate door switch.
28. Engage the wiper connector and rear washer hose.
29. Engage the connector to the rear gate defogger terminal.
30. Position the rear gate trim panel and install the retaining clips.

3-Door Models

▶ See Figure 6

1. Fold the left and right rear backrest forward.
2. Remove the shoulder anchors of the left and right front seat belts.
3. Remove the left and right tonneau cover levers.
4. Remove the left and right rear quarter upper trim.
5. Remove the rear skirt trim.
6. Remove the rear quarter rear trim panel.
7. Using Clip Puller (925580000) or equivalent, remove the clips which secure the rear gate trim panel.
8. Remove the trim panel.

✳✳WARNING

Be careful not to damage clip and clip holes.

9. Disengage the gas stay harness connector from the rear gate.
10. Remove the stud bolts which secure gas stay to rear gate.
11. Remove the rear rail trim panel.

✳✳WARNING

Remove the bolts one at a time. Have a helper hold the rear gate while removing the bolts to prevent it from dropping. Be sure to place a folded cloth between the rear gate and body to prevent scratches.

12. With a wrench inserted into the access hole, loosen the nuts which secure the hinge and remove the rear gate from the roof panel.

To install:
13. Position the rear gate onto the hinges and tighten the retaining nuts.
14. Install the rear trim panel.
15. Install the gas stays to the rear gate and tighten the stud bolts.
16. Connect the gas stay harness to the rear gate.
17. Position the rear gate trim panel onto the rear gate and install the retainer clips.
18. Install the rear quarter, left and right upper and skirt trim.
19. Install the left and right tonneau cover levers.
20. Install the shoulder anchors of the left and right front seat belts.
21. Raise the left and right rear backrest.

Sedan

1. Open the trunk lid and mark the hinge to trunk lid position.
2. Unfasten the trunk lid mounting bolts and remove the trunk lid from the hinges.
3. Installation is the reverse of removal. Make sure to line up the marks on the trunk lid with the hinges during installation.

ALIGNMENT

Tailgate, Hatch and Trunk lid

Remove the glass stay, striker and buffer, and loosen bolts on hinges securing the back door to the body. Then adjust the clearance at the top of the end gate and the roof of the body to 0.31–0.47 in. (8.0–12mm) Side clearance should be 0-0.059 in. (0-1.5mm). Bottom of end gate to body clearance should be 0.27-0.0.15 in. (6.9-3.9mm) . Install the glass stay, striker and buffer and tighten the hinge bolts.

Striker

Loosen the striker mounting bolt, and adjust sideward alignment so that center of latch lines up with the center of striker. Be sure to adjust striker so that it engages latch in full lock position.

To vertically align latch and striker, adjust so that back door latch and striker do not interfere with each other. Move the door up and down to make sure that it opens and closes properly.

Bumpers

REMOVAL & INSTALLATION

Front

▶ See Figure 7

The front bumper can be removed without using a two-post lift. However, use of a two-post lift saves time and facilitates bumper removal. The following procedures apply when remov-

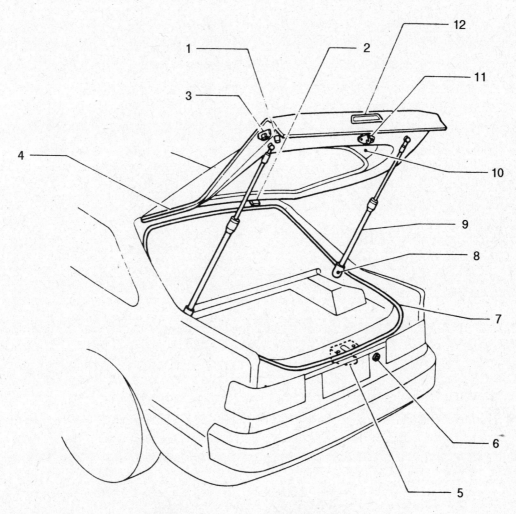

1. Stopper
2. Hinge
3. Buffer
4. Outer weatherstrip
5. Latch
6. Key cylinder
7. Weatherstrip
8. Stay cover
9. Gas stay
10. Rear gate trim panel
11. Striker
12. Height-mount stop lamp

87900111

Fig. 6 Hatchback components

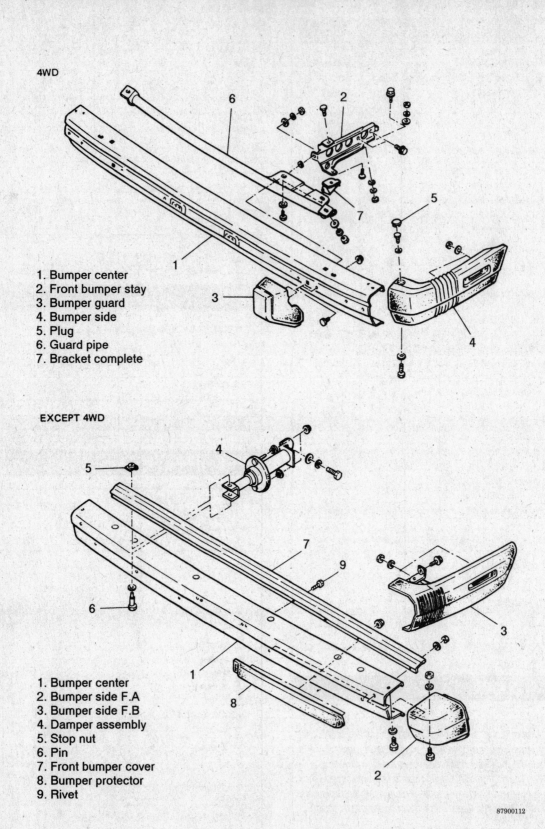

4WD

1. Bumper center
2. Front bumper stay
3. Bumper guard
4. Bumper side
5. Plug
6. Guard pipe
7. Bracket complete

EXCEPT 4WD

1. Bumper center
2. Bumper side F.A
3. Bumper side F.B
4. Damper assembly
5. Stop nut
6. Pin
7. Front bumper cover
8. Bumper protector
9. Rivet

87900112

Fig. 7 Exploded view of the front bumper and components

ing the bumper, with or without the use of a two-post lift, unless otherwise noted.

1. Before lifting the vehicle, remove the negative (-) battery cable.

2. If not using a lift, remove the battery and canister.

3. If a lift is being used, remove the left and right undercovers.

4. Remove the left and right hold down bands from the main harness and move the harness away from the bumper.

5. On models equipped with automatic transaxle, remove the clips that secure the automatic transaxle lines, and move the lines away from the front bumper.

6. On models with air conditioning, move the left transaxle line away from the bumper.

7. Insert rags between the front bumper and the car body to ensure sufficient clearance to insert a service tool to remove the bumper mounting bolts.

8. Disengage the harness connectors from the left and right front turn signal lamps.

9. Place a container under the headlight washer unit to catch the fluid, and disconnect the headlight washer hoses.

10. Remove the bolts that secure the front bumper. With the help of an assistant, remove the bumper.

11. Reverse steps 1 through 10 to install the bumper.

12. Clearance between the bumper and upper skirt is 0.2 in. (6mm) when viewed from the front of the car.

Rear

4 DOOR SEDAN AND 3 DOOR MODELS

1. Open the trunk lid.
2. Remove the trunk trim panel clips and detach the trim.
3. Remove both the side and center trunk covers.
4. Disengage the rear light harness connector.
5. Remove the 2 flange nuts.
6. Extract the rear bumper half way. Unfasten the grommet from the license plate harness, and remove the connector through the hole in the skirt section.
7. Remove the rear bumper horizontally.
8. Installation is the reverse of removal.

STATION WAGON

1. Remove the 2 bolts that secure each lower end of the bumper to the body.
2. Remove the plug from the wall on each side of the center sub trunk and unfasten the rear bumper retaining bolts.
3. Remove the bumper assembly from the vehicle.
4. Installation is the reverse of removal.

Grille

REMOVAL & INSTALLATION

▶ See Figures 8 and 9

To remove the grille on all Subaru models, requires only that the grille retaining screws and clips be unfastened and the grille removed from the vehicle. Use care not to break the grille when pulling it away from the vehicle body.

Fig. 8 Remove the screws securing the front grille . . .

87906135

Fig. 9 . . . then remove the grille

87906136

Outside Mirrors

REMOVAL & INSTALLATION

1. Unfasten the two mirror retaining screws and remove the mirror.
2. Installation is the reverse of removal.

Antenna

REMOVAL & INSTALLATION

1. Disconnect the negative battery cable.
2. Disconnect the antenna wire from the radio.

3. Push the antenna wire through the access hole under the instrument panel.

➡ **To make installation easier, tie a string to the end of the antenna wire before removing it from the vehicle. Pull the string up with the antenna wire and allow one end to stay visible at the inside of the vehicle. When installing the antenna, tie the wire to the other end of the string and pull it through.**

4. On models with the antenna on the side of the windshield:
   a. Remove the A pillar trim.
   b. Loosen the antenna mounting nut located beneath the trim panel.
   c. Move the antenna upward slightly then pull it out of the pillar with the antenna lead.
5. On models with roof mounted antenna, remove the antenna base mounting screw and pull the antenna off of the roof, drawing the wire out of the opening.
To install:
6. Install the antenna in position, guiding the wire into position. Install the antenna base plate, making sure it is flush with the body.
7. Connect the wire to the radio and check the operation.
8. Install any removed trim.

Fenders

REMOVAL & INSTALLATION

1. Raise and support the front of the vehicle with jackstands so that it is just off of the ground.
2. Remove the tire and wheel assembly.
3. Unfasten the inner fender cover assembly bolts and remove it.

INTERIOR

Instrument Panel and Pads

REMOVAL & INSTALLATION

◗ **See Figures 10 and 11**

1. Disconnect the negative (-) battery cable.
2. Remove the trim panel on the drivers side and the luggage shelf on the front passenger side.
3. Remove the radio or console box.
4. Remove the steering column attaching bolts.
5. Disconnect the speedometer cable.
6. Disconnect the electrical wiring harness.
7. Disconnect the cables and vacuum hoses for the heater control.
8. Remove the fasteners on the side pillars.
9. Unfasten the clips and remove the defroster grille.
10. Remove the fasteners at the top of the instrument panel.
11. Remove the defroster and ventilator ducts.

4. On some models it will be necessary to remove the grille and front combination lamp assemblies, before removing the fender.
5. Remove the fender mounting bolts.

➡ **The fender is joined to the body with sealer at some points. When removing the fender, a small putty knife will help to break the seal in these areas.**

6. Remove the fender from the vehicle. Be careful of the painted surfaces.
To install:
7. Install the fender in position, do not tighten the bolts.
8. Check the fender-to-hood-to-door clearance. Once the clearance is correct and even, tighten all of the mounting bolts.
9. Install the grille and combination light assemblies if removed.
10. Install the inner fender assembly and its mounting bolts.
11. Install the wheel and tire assembly. Lower the vehicle.

Sunroof

REMOVAL & INSTALLATION

1. Place the sunroof in the open position.
2. Remove handle from the base plate.
3. Remove the male hinge from the female hinge while lifting out the glass.
To install:
4. Connect the male and female hinges while installing the glass.

➡ **Ensure that the weatherstrip is installed properly. If it is rolled in or caught by the car body, raise the weatherstrip.**

5. Install the handle on the base plate.
6. Ensure the safety lock and handle lock operate properly.

12. Remove the instrument panel.
To install:
13. Install the instrument panel.
14. Install the defroster and ventilator ducts.
15. Install the defroster grille and fasten the clips.
16. Engage any electrical connections, wires, or hoses that were removed.
17. Fasten the steering column attaching bolts.
18. Install the console box or radio.
19. Install the luggage shelf and the trim panel.
20. Connect the negative battery cable.

Console

REMOVAL & INSTALLATION

◗ **See Figures 12, 13, 14, 15 and 16**

1. Disconnect the negative (-) battery cable.

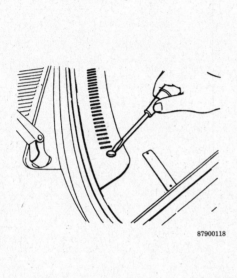

Fig. 10 Unfasten the clips and remove the defroster grille

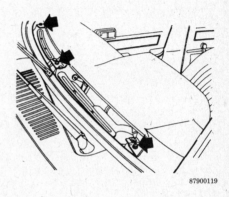

Fig. 11 Remove the fasteners at the top of the instrument panel

2. Remove the tray at the hand brake cover by disengaging the hook at the rear of the tray.

3. Remove the fasteners holding the console box and hand brake cover to the floor.

4. Remove the console box retaining fasteners.

5. Disengage the radio electrical connector.

6. On automatic transaxle equipped vehicles remove the indicator cover

7. Remove the parking brake cover by loosening the fastener in the pocket.

8. Remove the console box.

To install:

9. Install the console box and retaining fasteners.

10. Install the parking brake cover and the fastener in the pocket.

11. On automatic transaxle equipped vehicles install the indicator cover.

12. Engage the radio electrical connector.

13. Install the console box retaining fasteners.

14. Install the fasteners holding the console box and hand brake cover to the floor.

15. Install the tray at the hand brake cover.

16. Connect the negative battery cable.

Door Panels

REMOVAL & INSTALLATION

▶ **See Figures 17, 18, 19, 20 and 21**

1. Remove the screws which hold the gusset cover, and detach the cover.

2. Remove screws which hold pull handle and other screws located further inside.

3. Remove the remote handle cover.

4. Remove the window handle by unfastening the retaining clip.

5. Remove the clip attached to trim panel using Clip Puller (925580000) or equivalent.

6. Remove the trim panel.

7. Installation is the reverse of removal.

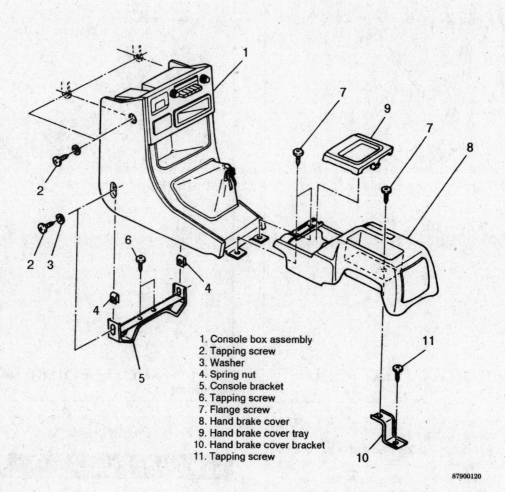

1. Console box assembly
2. Tapping screw
3. Washer
4. Spring nut
5. Console bracket
6. Tapping screw
7. Flange screw
8. Hand brake cover
9. Hand brake cover tray
10. Hand brake cover bracket
11. Tapping screw

87900120

Fig. 12 Exploded view of the console

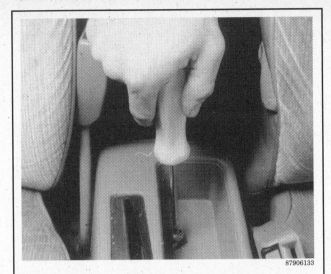

Fig. 13 Remove the screws from the handbrake cover

Fig. 16 Remove the center console

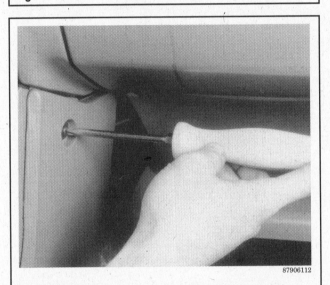

Fig. 14 Remove the screws from the center console

Fig. 17 Loosen the door handle screws and remove the door handle

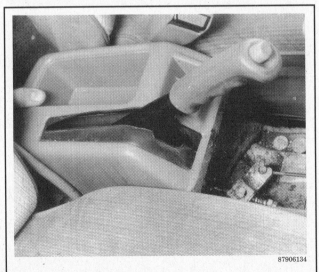

Fig. 15 Remove the handbrake cover

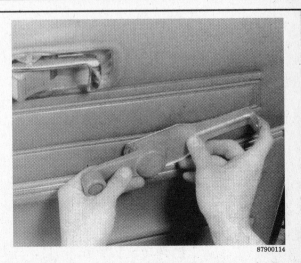

Fig. 18 Special tools are available to remove the window handle

Fig. 19 Loosen the screws retaining the door handle cover and remove the cover

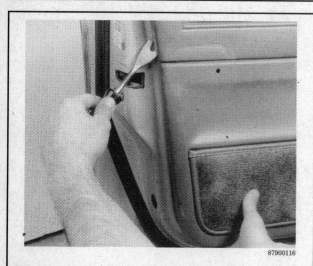

Fig. 20 Use a clip puller to disengage the trim panel clips . . .

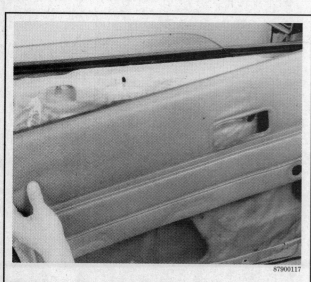

Fig. 21 . . . then remove the trim panel

Interior Trim

REMOVAL & INSTALLATION

Removal of the interior trim panels is very simple if the time is taken to do it carefully. To remove any of the panels all that is needed is a screwdriver and a trim removal tool.

1. Select the panel that you are going to remove and locate all of the retaining screws. Many of the screws are hidden behind plastic covers, so keep this in mind when looking.

2. Remove the mounting screws and carefully pry the panel away from the body.

3. Release any retaining clips as needed. Be careful not to scratch or gouge the panels.

To install:

4. Install the panels making sure that they are aligned properly on all sides before tightening the screws.

5. Tighten the screws use an alternating pattern to tighten the panel evenly and prevent warpage.

Headliner

REMOVAL & INSTALLATION

1. Completely open front and rear doors and lower windows all the way.

2. Remove the seat belt anchor bolts at the upper section of the center pillar.

3. Remove the rear seat cushion and backrest.

4. Remove the front pillar and upper trim panel.

5. Remove the center pillar and upper trim panel (4-door sedan).

6. Remove the rear pillar upper trim panel (station wagons).

7. Remove upper side of rear quarter window garnish.

8. Remove roof side rear trim rail.

9. Remove front roof side trim rail.

10. Remove various assist rails.

11. Remove sun visor, sun visor hook and rearview mirror.

12. Move front seats all the way forward and fully fold left and right backrests.

13. Remove interior lamp and disconnect harness.

14. Remove clips that hold the roof trim, being careful not to scratch the trim. It is advisable to position Clip Puller (925580000) or equivalent on roof trim's surface so that roof trim will not be scratched.

15. Disengage the roof trim, being careful not to break the edges during removal.

To install:

16. Position the roof trim in the vehicle being careful not to break the edges.

17. Install the clips into the roof trim.

18. Install the interior lamp and connect the wiring harness.

19. Raise the front seats and slide them as far to the rear as possible.

20. Install the rearview mirror, sun visor hook and the sun visor.

21. Install the various assist rails.

22. Install the front and rear roof side trim rail.
23. Install upper side of rear quarter window garnish.
24. Install the rear pillar upper trim panel (station wagons).
25. Install the center pillar and upper trim panel (4-door sedan).
26. Install the front pillar and upper trim panel.
27. Install the rear seat cushion and backrest.
28. Install the seat belt anchor bolts at the upper section of the center.
29. Close all doors and windows.

Door Locks

REMOVAL & INSTALLATION

➡**A key code is stamped on the lock cylinder to aid in replacing lost keys.**

1. Remove the door trim panel as outlined in this section.
2. Pull the weather sheet, gently, away from the door lock access holes.
3. Using a screwdriver, push the lock cylinder retaining clip upward, noting the position of the lock cylinder.
4. Remove the lock cylinder from the door.

➡**It's a good idea to open the window before checking the lock operation, just in case it doesn't work properly.**

5. Installation is the reverse of removal.

Door Glass

REMOVAL & INSTALLATION

▶ **See Figures 22 and 23**

1. Remove the trim panel.
2. Remove the remote assembly (if so equipped).
3. Remove the sealing cover.
4. Remove the rear view mirror from the door.
5. Remove the outer weatherstrip.
6. Remove the inner stabilizer.
7. Loosen the upper stopper bolt from the front of door and glass stoppers, then move the door glass.
8. Remove the upper stopper from the rear of the door.
9. Remove the two bolts which hold the glass holder to the regulator slider.

➡**When removing bolts on the regulator slider, move the glass to a position where the bolts can be seen through the service hole. Mark the position and tightening allowance of upper stopper bolts before removal. This will make adjustment after installation easy.**

10. Open the door, hold the door glass with both hands and pull it straight up from the door panel.
11. Installation is the reverse of removal.

Regulator

REMOVAL & INSTALLATION

▶ **See Figures 24 and 25**

1. Remove the door panel and window glass as described in this section.
2. Remove the sealing cover.
3. Remove the wire clip (manual type only).
4. Remove the regulator base plate and rail.
5. Remove the regulator assembly through the service hole in the underside of the door.
6. Replace any worn or broken parts.
7. Lubricate all sliding parts and reinstall.
8. Tighten the base plate mounting bolts 4-7 ft. lbs. (5-9 Nm) and the rail mounting nut 7-13 ft. lbs. (9-17 Nm).

Electric Window Motor

REMOVAL & INSTALLATION

1. Follow the procedures for removing the door panel, window glass and regulator as described in this section.
2. Disengage the electrical connectors to the window motor.
3. Unbolt the motor and remove it through the lower service hole in the underside of the door.
4. Installation is the reverse of removal.

Windshield and Rear Window Glass

➡**Bonded windshields require special tools and procedures. Due to this fact, removal and installation should be left to a qualified technician. The windshield knife cannot be used on the rear window of the sedan without damaging the surrounding grill. If the grill is not to be damaged, the windshield must be removed by using piano wire.**

REMOVAL & INSTALLATION

▶ **See Figures 26 and 27**

1. Carefully remove the wiper arms and windshield molding.
2. Put protective tape on the body to prevent damage.
3. Apply soapy water to the surface of the adhesive agent so the knife blade slides smoothly.
4. Cut off excess adhesive agent.
5. Remove stoppers and spacers from glass.
6. Put the windshield knife into layer of adhesive.
7. Hold windshield knife in one hand and cut adhesive by pulling putty knife parallel to the glass while holding knife edge at a right angle. Make sure that the knife stays along the surface of the glass.

➡**When first putting knife into layer of adhesive, select a point with a wide gap between the body and glass.**

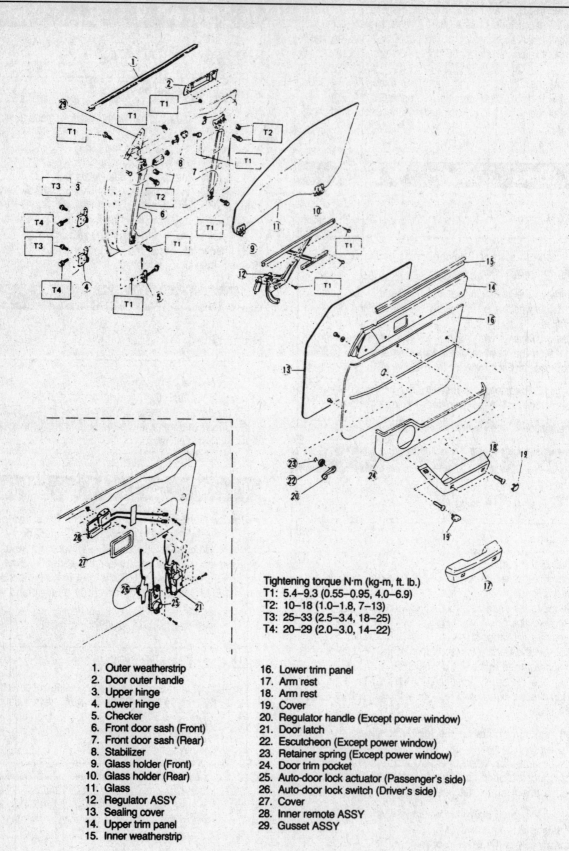

Tightening torque N·m (kg-m, ft. lb.)
T1: 5.4–9.3 (0.55–0.95, 4.0–6.9)
T2: 10–18 (1.0–1.8, 7–13)
T3: 25–33 (2.5–3.4, 18–25)
T4: 20–29 (2.0–3.0, 14–22)

1. Outer weatherstrip
2. Door outer handle
3. Upper hinge
4. Lower hinge
5. Checker
6. Front door sash (Front)
7. Front door sash (Rear)
8. Stabilizer
9. Glass holder (Front)
10. Glass holder (Rear)
11. Glass
12. Regulator ASSY
13. Sealing cover
14. Upper trim panel
15. Inner weatherstrip

16. Lower trim panel
17. Arm rest
18. Arm rest
19. Cover
20. Regulator handle (Except power window)
21. Door latch
22. Escutcheon (Except power window)
23. Retainer spring (Except power window)
24. Door trim pocket
25. Auto-door lock actuator (Passenger's side)
26. Auto-door lock switch (Driver's side)
27. Cover
28. Inner remote ASSY
29. Gusset ASSY

87900123

Fig. 22 Exploded view of front door and glass

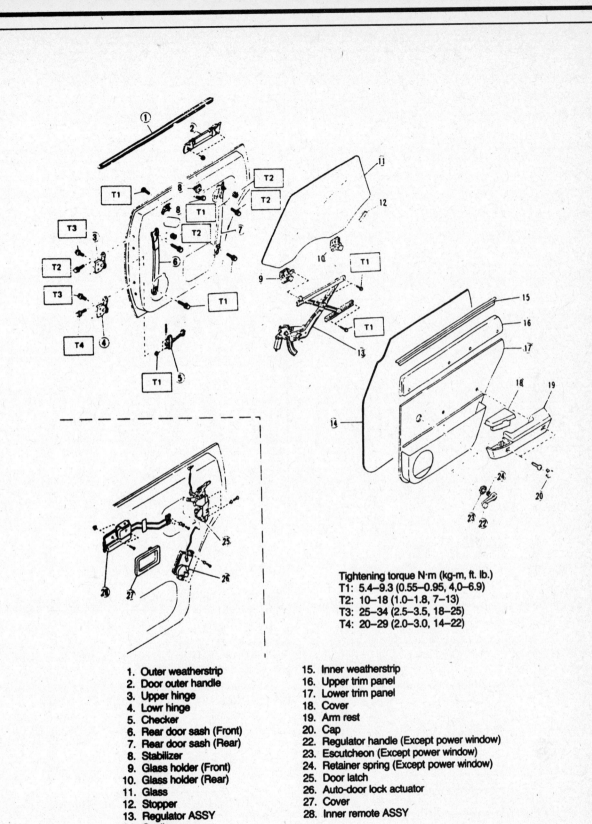

Tightening torque N·m (kg-m, ft. lb.)
T1: 5.4—9.3 (0.55—0.95, 4,0—6.9)
T2: 10—18 (1.0—1.8, 7—13)
T3: 25—34 (2.5—3.5, 18—25)
T4: 20—29 (2.0—3.0, 14—22)

1. Outer weatherstrip
2. Door outer handle
3. Upper hinge
4. Lowr hinge
5. Checker
6. Rear door sash (Front)
7. Rear door sash (Rear)
8. Stabilizer
9. Glass holder (Front)
10. Glass holder (Rear)
11. Glass
12. Stopper
13. Regulator ASSY
14. Sealing cover

15. Inner weatherstrip
16. Upper trim panel
17. Lower trim panel
18. Cover
19. Arm rest
20. Cap
22. Regulator handle (Except power window)
23. Escutcheon (Except power window)
24. Retainer spring (Except power window)
25. Door latch
26. Auto-door lock actuator
27. Cover
28. Inner remote ASSY

87900124

Fig. 23 Exploded view rear door and glass

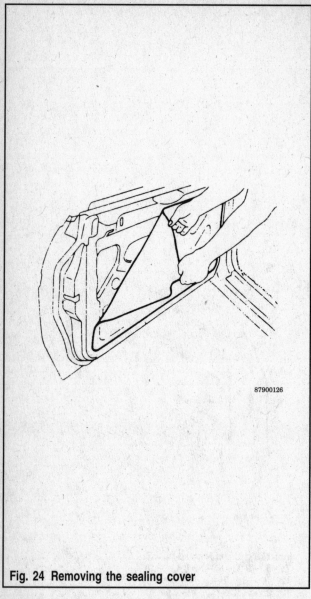

Fig. 24 Removing the sealing cover

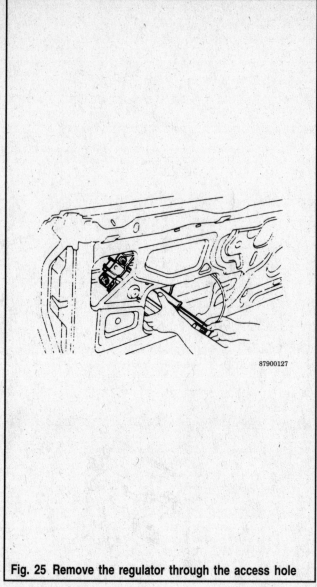

Fig. 25 Remove the regulator through the access hole

8. Working from the inside of the car, apply even pressure to the windshield and push it outward, while an assistant removes it from the car.

To install:

9. After cutting layer of adhesive, remove the dam rubber left on the body.

10. Remove the remaining space stopper. At this time, also remove two-sided tape from spacer the stopper completely.

11. Using a cutting knife, cut layer of adhesive sticking to the body and finish it into a smooth surface of about 0.07 in. (2mm) in thickness.

12. Thoroughly remove chips, dirt and dust from the body surface.

13. Clean the body wall surface and the upper surface of the layer of adhesive with a solvent such as alcohol.

✳✳CAUTION

Never smoke or have any form of an open flame nearby when using alcohol, as it is extremely flammable.

14. Place new spacer stoppers into positions from which the old ones where removed.

15. Remove the tack paper from the back of the spacer stopper and stick it to the body firmly.

16. Place the windshield onto the body then adjust the position of the glass so that the gap between the body and glass is uniform on all sides.

17. Matchmark the body and glass in several places.

18. Remove the glass from the body and clean the surface of glass to be adhered with alcohol.

19. Using a sponge, apply primer to the part of the glass and the part of the body to be adhered.

20. Allow the primer to dry for about 10 minutes before proceeding to the next step.

➡**Cover all surfaces that primer may come into contact with, as it is very hard to remove.**

21. Cut the nozzle tip of the adhesive cartridge to a 45° angle, open the cartridge, attach the nozzle and place it into the gun.

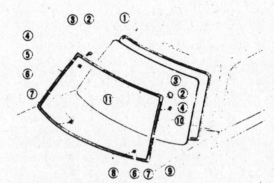

1. Dam rubber
2. Fastener
3. Corner joint (Upper)
4. Spacer
5. Side molding (RH)
6. Stopper
7. Corner joint (Lower)
8. Lower molding
9. Glass
10. Side molding (LH)
11. Upper molding

Rear window glass [4-Door Sedan]

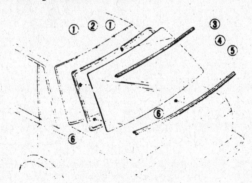

1. Spacer
2. Dam rubber
3. Upper molding
4. Glass
5. Stopper

87900128

Fig. 26 Exploded view of rear window glass

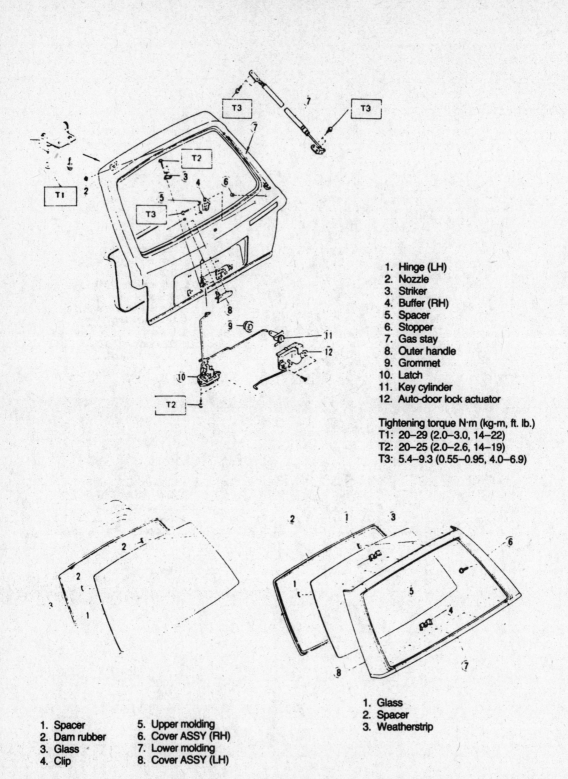

1. Hinge (LH)
2. Nozzle
3. Striker
4. Buffer (RH)
5. Spacer
6. Stopper
7. Gas stay
8. Outer handle
9. Grommet
10. Latch
11. Key cylinder
12. Auto-door lock actuator

Tightening torque N·m (kg-m, ft. lb.)
T1: 20–29 (2.0–3.0, 14–22)
T2: 20–25 (2.0–2.6, 14–19)
T3: 5.4–9.3 (0.55–0.95, 4.0–6.9)

1. Spacer
2. Dam rubber
3. Glass
4. Clip
5. Upper molding
6. Cover ASSY (RH)
7. Lower molding
8. Cover ASSY (LH)

1. Glass
2. Spacer
3. Weatherstrip

87900125

Fig. 27 Exploded view rear gate and glass on station wagons

22. Apply the adhesive uniformly to all sides of adhesion surface while operating gun along the face of the glass edge. Adhesive build up should be 0.47-0.5 in. (12-15mm) from glass surface.

23. With the help of an assistant, place the glass onto the body and align the matchmarks. Press the glass firmly into position, then add adhesive where needed.

24. Install the upper windshield molding and remove the excess adhesive with a spatula. Clean with alcohol or white gasoline.

25. After the molding has been installed, do not open the doors or move the car unless it is absolutely necessary. If the doors must be opened, lower the windows, and open and close the doors very gently. After one hour the car can be tested for water leakage.

26. Install the front lower molding, front pillar cover, wiper wheel assembly and wiper arm assembly.

➡**When testing for water leakage, do not squirt a strong hose stream on the vehicle. If the vehicle must be moved, do so gently, sudden shock could cause the windshield to shift. After completing all operations, leave the vehicle alone for 24 hours. After 24 hours the vehicle may be driven, but should not be subjected to heavy shock for at least three days.**

Stationary Glass

REMOVAL & INSTALLATION

Rear Quarter Window

HATCHBACK

▶ **See Figures 28 and 29**

1. Remove the hinge covers by prying them off with a screwdriver.
2. Open the glass halfway and remove the lock retaining fasteners.
3. Remove the hinge set screws.
4. Remove the glass.
5. Remove the hinge plates and lock assembly from the glass.
6. Remove the weatherstrip.
   To install:
7. Install the weatherstrip.
8. Install the hinge plates and lock assemblies.
9. Install the glass and temporarily fasten the set screws, then make sure the glass is positioned properly.
10. Fasten the set screws and the lock retaining fasteners.
11. Install the hinge covers.

Rear Quarter Window

SEDAN AND NOTCHBACK

▶ **See Figure 30**

1. Remove the inner trim.
2. Remove the rear pillar moulding or opera grille.
3. Remove the rear quarter glass in the same manner as the windshield as outlined in this section.
4. Installation is the reverse of removal.

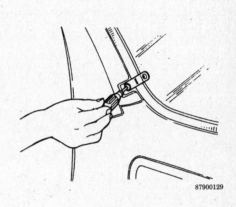

Fig. 28 Remove the hinges . . .

Inside Rear View Mirror

REMOVAL & INSTALLATION

▶ **See Figure 31**

1. Unfasten the retainer from the rear view mirror bracket and remove the mirror.
2. Installation is the reverse of removal.

Seats

REMOVAL & INSTALLATION

Front

1. Slide the front seat all the way back using the slide adjuster lever.

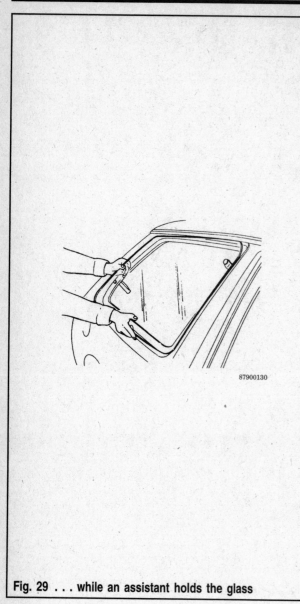

87900130

Fig. 29 . . . while an assistant holds the glass

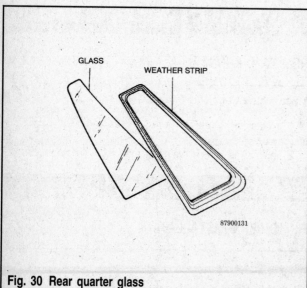

GLASS

WEATHER STRIP

87900131

Fig. 30 Rear quarter glass

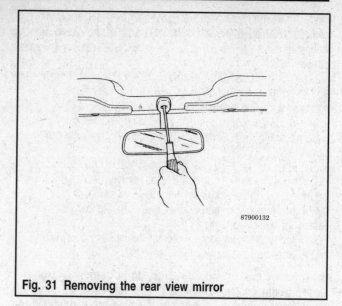

87900132

Fig. 31 Removing the rear view mirror

2. Remove the bolts that secure the front section of the seat.

3. Move the seat all the way forward.

4. Remove the bolt cover on the rear end of the slide rail on the door side.

5. Remove the bolts that secure the rear section of the front seat.

6. Remove the front seat from the vehicle.

To install:

7. Fold the backrest forward.

8. Move the lower slide rails forward so that the front seat is positioned all the way back.

9. Position the front seat and align the mounting holes.

10. Tighten the bolt that holds the front section of the seat on the tunnel side.

11. Tighten the bolt that holds the front section of the seat on the door side.

12. Move the front seat all the way forward.

13. Tighten the bolts that hold the rear section of the seat on the tunnel side, then tighten the bolts on the door side.

14. Install the bolt cover at the rear of the seat on the door side.

15. Move the seats back and forth to make sure that the slide rails function properly without binding.

Rear

1. Remove the bolts that secure the front of the rear cushion to the floor.

2. Slightly raise the front side of the rear seat cushion and push the center of the rear section down. With the seat cushion held in that position, move it forward until it is unhooked.

3. Pass the rear seat belt through the slit in the rear section of the cushion.

4. Fold the rear seat backrest forward and remove the bolts which hold the hinge to the right side of the backrest.

5. Tilt the rear seat backrest approximately 15 in.(400mm) forward and slide it toward the right until it can be detached from the left bracket.

6. Remove the rear seat from the vehicle.

7. Installation is the reverse of removal

Seat Belt Systems

REMOVAL & INSTALLATION

Front

1. Disconnect the negative (-) battery cable.
2. Remove the rear cushion and rear back rest (if necessary).
3. Remove the side sill cover, rear pillar trim and/or the rear quarter trim panel (if necessary).

4. Remove the outer belt as follows.
   a. Lap belt anchor bolt and the shoulder belt anchor bolt.
   b. Felt guide and retractor bolt.
5. Unfasten the inner belt anchor bolt, disconnect the seat belt switch (if equipped) and then remove the inner belt.
6. Installation is the reversal of removal.
7. Torque the anchor bolts to 18-25 ft. lbs. (25-34 Nm).

Rear

1. Remove the rear seat cushion and outer anchor bolt.
2. Unfasten the inner anchor bolt and remove the belt.
3. Installation is the reverse of removal.
4. Tighten the anchor bolts to 18-25 ft. lbs. (25-34 Nm).

Special Tools, Body

925580000	925610000	926661000 *8	*927000000
PULLER	WRENCH	REMOVER	ENGINE SUPPORT ASSY
Trim clip.	Door hinge.	Used to remove and install trunk torsion bar.	For supporting engine.
*927010000	925091000	926110000	499827100
BRACKET (ENGINE SUPPORT)	BAND TIGHTENER	COIL SPRING COMPRESSOR	ADAPTER ASSY
Used together with ENGINE SUPPORT ASSY.	Used to tighten axle boor clip.	Used to remove and install coil spring.	For connection between speedometer and speedometer cable when checking speedometer, with rear wheels on free rollers.

*8 This tool is for 4-Door Sedan and XT.
  Former REMOVER (926660000) is only for 4-Door Sedan.

* Newly adopted tool

87900C02

Special Tools, Body

498477000	921520000	921540000	921550000
REPLACER HANDLE	STEERING GEARBOX SPANNER	ENGINE SUPPORTER	STEERING GEARBOX WRENCH
Used with INSTALLER (922450000, 922460000, 922470000) to install bearing and oil seal into housing.	Used to loose and tighten steering gearbox lock nut.	Used to support engine when installing and removing transmission.	Used to adjust steering gear box backlash.
922111000	**922430000**	**922441000**	**922450000**
INSTALLER	AXLE SHAFT INSTALLER	HOUSING STAND	OIL SEAL INSTALLER
Used to install oil seal and outer races of inner and outer bearing into front hub.	Used to press-fit front and axle shafts into each housing.	Used when installing bearing and oil seal into rear trailing arm or front housing.	Used to install outer oil seal into front housing.
922460000	**922470000**	**922493000**	**921122000**
OIL SEAL INSTALLER	BEARING INSTALLER	BRAKE DRUM REMOVER	BRAKE DRUM REMOVER
Used to install inner oil seal into front housing.	Used to install inner and outer ball bearings into rear trailing arm or front housing.	Used to remove brake drum and axle shaft. Combine this tool with REMOVER (921122000) from which plate 2 is removed.	Used to remove housing.

87900C01

How to Remove Stains from Fabric Interior

For rest results, spots and stains should be removed as soon as possible. Never use gasoline, lacquer thinner, acetone, nail polish remover or bleach. Use a 3' x 3" piece of cheesecloth. Squeeze most of the liquid from the fabric and wipe the stained fabric from the outside of the stain toward the center with a lifting motion. Turn the cheesecloth as soon as one side becomes soiled. When using water to remove a stain, be sure to wash the entire section after the spot has been removed to avoid water stains. Encrusted spots can be broken up with a dull knife and vacuumed before removing the stain.

Type of Stain	How to Remove It
Surface spots	Brush the spots out with a small hand brush or use a commercial preparation such as K2R to lift the stain.
Mildew	Clean around the mildew with warm suds. Rinse in cold water and soak the mildew area in a solution of 1 part table salt and 2 parts water. Wash with upholstery cleaner.
Water stains	Water stains in fabric materials can be removed with a solution made from 1 cup of table salt dissolved in 1 quart of water. Vigorously scrub the solution into the stain and rinse with clear water. Water stains in nylon or other synthetic fabrics should be removed with a commercial type spot remover.
Chewing gum, tar, crayons, shoe polish (greasy stains)	Do not use a cleaner that will soften gum or tar. Harden the deposit with an ice cube and scrape away as much as possible with a dull knife. Moisten the remainder with cleaning fluid and scrub clean.
Ice cream, candy	Most candy has a sugar base and can be removed with a cloth wrung out in warm water. Oily candy, after cleaning with warm water, should be cleaned with upholstery cleaner. Rinse with warm water and clean the remainder with cleaning fluid.
Wine, alcohol, egg, milk, soft drink (non-greasy stains)	Do not use soap. Scrub the stain with a cloth wrung out in warm water. Remove the remainder with cleaning fluid.
Grease, oil, lipstick, butter and related stains	Use a spot remover to avoid leaving a ring. Work from the outisde of the stain to the center and dry with a clean cloth when the spot is gone.
Headliners (cloth)	Mix a solution of warm water and foam upholstery cleaner to give thick suds. Use only foam—liquid may streak or spot. Clean the entire headliner in one operation using a circular motion with a natural sponge.
Headliner (vinyl)	Use a vinyl cleaner with a sponge and wipe clean with a dry cloth.
Seats and door panels	Mix 1 pint upholstery cleaner in 1 gallon of water. Do not soak the fabric around the buttons.
Leather or vinyl fabric	Use a multi-purpose cleaner full strength and a stiff brush. Let stand 2 minutes and scrub thoroughly. Wipe with a clean, soft rag.
Nylon or synthetic fabrics	For normal stains, use the same procedures you would for washing cloth upholstery. If the fabric is extremely dirty, use a multi-purpose cleaner full strength with a stiff scrub brush. Scrub thoroughly in all directions and wipe with a cotton towel or soft rag.

87900C03

GLOSSARY

AIR/FUEL RATIO: The ratio of air-to-gasoline by weight in the fuel mixture drawn into the engine.

AIR INJECTION: One method of reducing harmful exhaust emissions by injecting air into each of the exhaust ports of an engine. The fresh air entering the hot exhaust manifold causes any remaining fuel to be burned before it can exit the tailpipe.

ALTERNATOR: A device used for converting mechanical energy into electrical energy.

AMMETER: An instrument, calibrated in amperes, used to measure the flow of an electrical current in a circuit. Ammeters are always connected in series with the circuit being tested.

AMPERE: The rate of flow of electrical current present when one volt of electrical pressure is applied against one ohm of electrical resistance.

ANALOG COMPUTER: Any microprocessor that uses similar (analogous) electrical signals to make its calculations.

ARMATURE: A laminated, soft iron core wrapped by a wire that converts electrical energy to mechanical energy as in a motor or relay. When rotated in a magnetic field, it changes mechanical energy into electrical energy as in a generator.

ATMOSPHERIC PRESSURE: The pressure on the Earth's surface caused by the weight of the air in the atmosphere. At sea level, this pressure is 14.7 psi at 32°F (101 kPa at 0°C).

ATOMIZATION: The breaking down of a liquid into a fine mist that can be suspended in air.

AXIAL PLAY: Movement parallel to a shaft or bearing bore.

BACKFIRE: The sudden combustion of gases in the intake or exhaust system that results in a loud explosion.

BACKLASH: The clearance or play between two parts, such as meshed gears.

BACKPRESSURE: Restrictions in the exhaust system that slow the exit of exhaust gases from the combustion chamber.

BAKELITE: A heat resistant, plastic insulator material commonly used in printed circuit boards and transistorized components.

BALL BEARING: A bearing made up of hardened inner and outer races between which hardened steel balls roll.

BALLAST RESISTOR: A resistor in the primary ignition circuit that lowers voltage after the engine is started to reduce wear on ignition components.

BEARING: A friction reducing, supportive device usually located between a stationary part and a moving part.

BIMETAL TEMPERATURE SENSOR: Any sensor or switch made of two dissimilar types of metal that bend when heated or cooled due to the different expansion rates of the alloys. These types of sensors usually function as an on/off switch.

BLOWBY: Combustion gases, composed of water vapor and unburned fuel, that leak past the piston rings into the crankcase during normal engine operation. These gases are removed by the PCV system to prevent the buildup of harmful acids in the crankcase.

BRAKE PAD: A brake shoe and lining assembly used with disc brakes.

BRAKE SHOE: The backing for the brake lining. The term is, however, usually applied to the assembly of the brake backing and lining.

BUSHING: A liner, usually removable, for a bearing; an anti-friction liner used in place of a bearing.

CALIPER: A hydraulically activated device in a disc brake system, which is mounted straddling the brake rotor (disc). The caliper contains at least one piston and two brake pads. Hydraulic pressure on the piston(s) forces the pads against the rotor.

CAMSHAFT: A shaft in the engine on which are the lobes (cams) which operate the valves. The camshaft is driven by the crankshaft, via a belt, chain or gears, at one half the crankshaft speed.

CAPACITOR: A device which stores an electrical charge.

CARBON MONOXIDE (CO): A colorless, odorless gas given off as a normal byproduct of combustion. It is poisonous and extremely dangerous in confined areas, building up slowly to toxic levels without warning if adequate ventilation is not available.

CARBURETOR: A device, usually mounted on the intake manifold of an engine, which mixes the air and fuel in the proper proportion to allow even combustion.

CATALYTIC CONVERTER: A device installed in the exhaust system, like a muffler, that converts harmful byproducts of combustion into carbon dioxide and water vapor by means of a heat-producing chemical reaction.

CENTRIFUGAL ADVANCE: A mechanical method of advancing the spark timing by using flyweights in the distributor that react to centrifugal force generated by the distributor shaft rotation.

CHECK VALVE: Any one-way valve installed to permit the flow of air, fuel or vacuum in one direction only.

CHOKE: A device, usually a moveable valve, placed in the intake path of a carburetor to restrict the flow of air.

CIRCUIT: Any unbroken path through which an electrical current can flow. Also used to describe fuel flow in some instances.

CIRCUIT BREAKER: A switch which protects an electrical circuit from overload by opening the circuit when the current flow exceeds a predetermined level. Some circuit breakers must be reset manually, while most reset automatically.

COIL (IGNITION): A transformer in the ignition circuit which steps up the voltage provided to the spark plugs.

COMBINATION MANIFOLD: An assembly which includes both the intake and exhaust manifolds in one casting.

COMBINATION VALVE: A device used in some fuel systems that routes fuel vapors to a charcoal storage canister instead of venting them into the atmosphere. The valve relieves fuel tank pressure and allows fresh air into the tank as the fuel level drops to prevent a vapor lock situation.

COMPRESSION RATIO: The comparison of the total volume of the cylinder and combustion chamber with the piston at BDC and the piston at TDC.

CONDENSER: 1. An electrical device which acts to store an electrical charge, preventing voltage surges. 2. A radiator-like device in the air conditioning system in which refrigerant gas condenses into a liquid, giving off heat.

CONDUCTOR: Any material through which an electrical current can be transmitted easily.

CONTINUITY: Continuous or complete circuit. Can be checked with an ohmmeter.

COUNTERSHAFT: An intermediate shaft which is rotated by a mainshaft and transmits, in turn, that rotation to a working part.

CRANKCASE: The lower part of an engine in which the crankshaft and related parts operate.

CRANKSHAFT: The main driving shaft of an engine which receives reciprocating motion from the pistons and converts it to rotary motion.

CYLINDER: In an engine, the round hole in the engine block in which the piston(s) ride.

CYLINDER BLOCK: The main structural member of an engine in which is found the cylinders, crankshaft and other principal parts.

CYLINDER HEAD: The detachable portion of the engine, usually fastened to the top of the cylinder block and containing all or most of the combustion chambers. On overhead valve engines, it contains the valves and their operating parts. On overhead cam engines, it contains the camshaft as well.

DEAD CENTER: The extreme top or bottom of the piston stroke.

DETONATION: An unwanted explosion of the air/fuel mixture in the combustion chamber caused by excess heat and compression, advanced timing, or an overly lean mixture. Also referred to as "ping".

DIAPHRAGM: A thin, flexible wall separating two cavities, such as in a vacuum advance unit.

DIESELING: A condition in which hot spots in the combustion chamber cause the engine to run on after the key is turned off.

DIFFERENTIAL: A geared assembly which allows the transmission of motion between drive axles, giving one axle the ability to turn faster than the other.

DIODE: An electrical device that will allow current to flow in one direction only.

DISC BRAKE: A hydraulic braking assembly consisting of a brake disc, or rotor, mounted on an axle, and a caliper assembly containing, usually two brake pads which are activated by hydraulic pressure. The pads are forced against the sides of the disc, creating friction which slows the vehicle.

DISTRIBUTOR: A mechanically driven device on an engine which is responsible for electrically firing the spark plug at a predetermined point of the piston stroke.

DOWEL PIN: A pin, inserted in mating holes in two different parts allowing those parts to maintain a fixed relationship.

DRUM BRAKE: A braking system which consists of two brake shoes and one or two wheel cylinders, mounted on a fixed backing plate, and a brake drum, mounted on an axle, which revolves around the assembly.

DWELL: The rate, measured in degrees of shaft rotation, at which an electrical circuit cycles on and off.

ELECTRONIC CONTROL UNIT (ECU): Ignition module, module, amplifier or igniter. See Module for definition.

ELECTRONIC IGNITION: A system in which the timing and firing of the spark plugs is controlled by an electronic control unit, usually called a module. These systems have no points or condenser.

END-PLAY: The measured amount of axial movement in a shaft.

ENGINE: A device that converts heat into mechanical energy.

EXHAUST MANIFOLD: A set of cast passages or pipes which conduct exhaust gases from the engine.

FEELER GAUGE: A blade, usually metal, of precisely predetermined thickness, used to measure the clearance between two parts.

FIRING ORDER: The order in which combustion occurs in the cylinders of an engine. Also the order in which spark is distributed to the plugs by the distributor.

FLOODING: The presence of too much fuel in the intake manifold and combustion chamber which prevents the air/fuel mixture from firing, thereby causing a no-start situation.

FLYWHEEL: A disc shaped part bolted to the rear end of the crankshaft. Around the outer perimeter is affixed the ring gear. The starter drive engages the ring gear, turning the flywheel, which rotates the crankshaft, imparting the initial starting motion to the engine.

FOOT POUND (ft. lbs. or sometimes, ft.lb.): The amount of energy or work needed to raise an item weighing one pound, a distance of one foot.

FUSE: A protective device in a circuit which prevents circuit overload by breaking the circuit when a specific amperage is present. The device is constructed around a strip or wire of a lower amperage rating than the circuit it is designed to protect. When an amperage higher than that stamped on the fuse is present in the circuit, the strip or wire melts, opening the circuit.

GEAR RATIO: The ratio between the number of teeth on meshing gears.

GENERATOR: A device which converts mechanical energy into electrical energy.

HEAT RANGE: The measure of a spark plug's ability to dissipate heat from its firing end. The higher the heat range, the hotter the plug fires.

HUB: The center part of a wheel or gear.

HYDROCARBON (HC): Any chemical compound made up of hydrogen and carbon. A major pollutant formed by the engine as a byproduct of combustion.

HYDROMETER: An instrument used to measure the specific gravity of a solution.

INCH POUND (inch lbs.; sometimes in.lb. or in. lbs.): One twelfth of a foot pound.

INDUCTION: A means of transferring electrical energy in the form of a magnetic field. Principle used in the ignition coil to increase voltage.

INJECTOR: A device which receives metered fuel under relatively low pressure and is activated to inject the fuel into the engine under relatively high pressure at a predetermined time.

INPUT SHAFT: The shaft to which torque is applied, usually carrying the driving gear or gears.

INTAKE MANIFOLD: A casting of passages or pipes used to conduct air or a fuel/air mixture to the cylinders.

JOURNAL: The bearing surface within which a shaft operates.

KEY: A small block usually fitted in a notch between a shaft and a hub to prevent slippage of the two parts.

MANIFOLD: A casting of passages or set of pipes which connect the cylinders to an inlet or outlet source.

MANIFOLD VACUUM: Low pressure in an engine intake manifold formed just below the throttle plates. Manifold vacuum is highest at idle and drops under acceleration.

MASTER CYLINDER: The primary fluid pressurizing device in a hydraulic system. In automotive use, it is found in brake and hydraulic clutch systems and is pedal activated, either directly or, in a power brake system, through the power booster.

MODULE: Electronic control unit, amplifier or igniter of solid state or integrated design which controls the current flow in the ignition primary circuit based on input from the pick-up coil. When the module opens the primary circuit, high secondary voltage is induced in the coil.

NEEDLE BEARING: A bearing which consists of a number (usually a large number) of long, thin rollers.

OHM:(Ω) The unit used to measure the resistance of conductor-to-electrical flow. One ohm is the amount of resistance that limits current flow to one ampere in a circuit with one volt of pressure.

OHMMETER: An instrument used for measuring the resistance, in ohms, in an electrical circuit.

OUTPUT SHAFT: The shaft which transmits torque from a device, such as a transmission.

OVERDRIVE: A gear assembly which produces more shaft revolutions than that transmitted to it.

OVERHEAD CAMSHAFT (OHC): An engine configuration in which the camshaft is mounted on top of the cylinder head and operates the valve either directly or by means of rocker arms.

OVERHEAD VALVE (OHV): An engine configuration in which all of the valves are located in the cylinder head and the camshaft is located in the cylinder block. The camshaft operates the valves via lifters and pushrods.

OXIDES OF NITROGEN (NOx): Chemical compounds of nitrogen produced as a byproduct of combustion. They combine with hydrocarbons to produce smog.

OXYGEN SENSOR: Used with the feedback system to sense the presence of oxygen in the exhaust gas and signal the computer which can reference the voltage signal to an air/fuel ratio.

PINION: The smaller of two meshing gears.

PISTON RING: An open-ended ring which fits into a groove on the outer diameter of the piston. Its chief function is to form a seal between the piston and cylinder wall. Most automotive pistons have three rings: two for compression sealing; one for oil sealing.

PRELOAD: A predetermined load placed on a bearing during assembly or by adjustment.

PRIMARY CIRCUIT: The low voltage side of the ignition system which consists of the ignition switch, ballast resistor or resistance wire, bypass, coil, electronic control unit and pick-up coil as well as the connecting wires and harnesses.

PRESS FIT: The mating of two parts under pressure, due to the inner diameter of one being smaller than the outer diameter of the other, or vice versa; an interference fit.

RACE: The surface on the inner or outer ring of a bearing on which the balls, needles or rollers move.

REGULATOR: A device which maintains the amperage and/or voltage levels of a circuit at predetermined values.

RELAY: A switch which automatically opens and/or closes a circuit.

RESISTANCE: The opposition to the flow of current through a circuit or electrical device, and is measured in ohms. Resistance is equal to the voltage divided by the amperage.

RESISTOR: A device, usually made of wire, which offers a preset amount of resistance in an electrical circuit.

RING GEAR: The name given to a ring-shaped gear attached to a differential case, or affixed to a flywheel or as part of a planetary gear set.

ROLLER BEARING: A bearing made up of hardened inner and outer races between which hardened steel rollers move.

ROTOR: 1. The disc-shaped part of a disc brake assembly, upon which the brake pads bear; also called, brake disc. 2. The device mounted atop the distributor shaft, which passes current to the distributor cap tower contacts.

SECONDARY CIRCUIT: The high voltage side of the ignition system, usually above 20,000 volts. The secondary includes the ignition coil, coil wire, distributor cap and rotor, spark plug wires and spark plugs.

SENDING UNIT: A mechanical, electrical, hydraulic or electromagnetic device which transmits information to a gauge.

SENSOR: Any device designed to measure engine operating conditions or ambient pressures and temperatures. Usually electronic in nature and designed to send a voltage signal to an on-board computer, some sensors may operate as a simple on/off switch or they may provide a variable voltage signal (like a potentiometer) as conditions or measured parameters change.

SHIM: Spacers of precise, predetermined thickness used between parts to establish a proper working relationship.

SLAVE CYLINDER: In automotive use, a device in the hydraulic clutch system which is activated by hydraulic force, disengaging the clutch.

SOLENOID: A coil used to produce a magnetic field, the effect of which is to produce work.

SPARK PLUG: A device screwed into the combustion chamber of a spark ignition engine. The basic construction is a conductive core inside of a ceramic insulator, mounted in an outer conductive base. An electrical charge from the spark plug wire travels along the conductive core and jumps a preset air gap to a grounding point or points at the end of the conductive base. The resultant spark ignites the fuel/air mixture in the combustion chamber.

SPLINES: Ridges machined or cast onto the outer diameter of a shaft or inner diameter of a bore to enable parts to mate without rotation.

TACHOMETER: A device used to measure the rotary speed of an engine, shaft, gear, etc., usually in rotations per minute.

THERMOSTAT: A valve, located in the cooling system of an engine, which is closed when cold and opens gradually in response to engine heating, controlling the temperature of the coolant and rate of coolant flow.

TOP DEAD CENTER (TDC): The point at which the piston reaches the top of its travel on the compression stroke.

TORQUE: The twisting force applied to an object.

TORQUE CONVERTER: A turbine used to transmit power from a driving member to a driven member via hydraulic action, providing changes in drive ratio and torque. In automotive use, it links the driveplate at the rear of the engine to the automatic transmission.

TRANSDUCER: A device used to change a force into an electrical signal.

TRANSISTOR: A semi-conductor component which can be actuated by a small voltage to perform an electrical switching function.

TUNE-UP: A regular maintenance function, usually associated with the replacement and adjustment of parts and components in the electrical and fuel systems of a vehicle for the purpose of attaining optimum performance.

TURBOCHARGER: An exhaust driven pump which compresses intake air and forces it into the combustion chambers at higher than atmospheric pressures. The increased air pressure allows more fuel to be burned and results in increased horsepower being produced.

VACUUM ADVANCE: A device which advances the ignition timing in response to increased engine vacuum.

VACUUM GAUGE: An instrument used to measure the presence of vacuum in a chamber.

VALVE: A device which control the pressure, direction of flow or rate of flow of a liquid or gas.

VALVE CLEARANCE: The measured gap between the end of the valve stem and the rocker arm, cam lobe or follower that activates the valve.

VISCOSITY: The rating of a liquid's internal resistance to flow.

VOLTMETER: An instrument used for measuring electrical force in units called volts. Voltmeters are always connected parallel with the circuit being tested.

WHEEL CYLINDER: Found in the automotive drum brake assembly, it is a device, actuated by hydraulic pressure, which, through internal pistons, pushes the brake shoes outward against the drums.

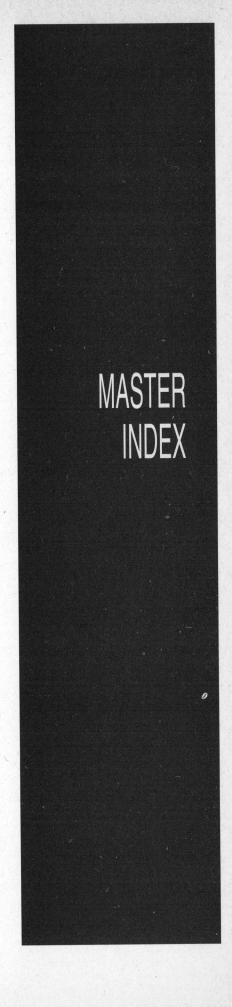

MASTER
INDEX